AVAILABLE NOW

Social Indicators of Development 1994

Data on Diskette

This software edition of **Social Indicators of Development** provides the same social and economic indicators, for more than 190 countries, as the print edition. The 1994 edition focuses on poverty indicators that describe the characteristics of poverty and the effectiveness of efforts to reduce poverty. Unlike the print edition of the Indicators, which presents data for three broad time spans, the software edition presents time series data for 25 years.

The indicators for each country are accessible through ☆STARS☆—the World Bank's Socio-economic Time-series Access and Retrieval System. This convenient and user-friendly system allows the user to view and manipulate the data and to export data selections to other computer programs, such as Lotus 1-2-3, Javelin Plus, and Aremos, and to word-processing programs that read ASCII characters.

The Social Indicators diskette set includes the complete ☆STARS☆ software and data on double-density 3 1/2" diskettes for use on personal computers with a hard disk and at least 512K memory and MS-DOS version 2.1 or higher. A user's manual provides a complete guide to getting started, viewing and extracting data, and using extract files.

For details on how to order this—and other statistical data collections available in ☆STARS☆—please turn the page.

Order Form

☐ **Yes, Please send me Social Indicators of Development 1994 on diskette and other products as indicated below.**

Quantity	Title	Stock Number	Price	Total
	Social Indicators of Development 1994			
_____	Print edition	44788	$24.95	_____
_____	Diskettes	12573	$70.00	_____
	World Tables 1994			
_____	Print edition	44789	$39.95	_____
_____	Diskettes	12575	$95.00	_____
	World Debt Tables 1993-1994			
_____	Print edition vol. 1	12567	$16.95	_____
_____	Print edition, 2 vol. set	12569	$125.00	_____
_____	Diskettes	12431	$95.00	_____
	African Development Indicators			
_____	English print edition	12044	$21.95	_____
_____	Diskettes	12135	$70.00	_____
	World Development Report 1993 - Investing in Health			
_____	English paperback print edition	60890	$19.95	_____
	World Development Indicators 1993			
_____	Diskettes	12432	$70.00	_____

	Subtotal US$	_____
	*Shipping and handling US$	_____
	Airmail surcharge outside USA US$	_____
	Total US$	_____

☐ Enclosed is my check payable to World Bank in U.S. Dollars drawn on a U.S. Bank.
☐ Charge my ☐ VISA ☐ Mastercard ☐ American Express

_____
Credit card account number   Expiration date

_____
Signature

☐ Enclosed is my purchase order; send invoice. (Institutional customers only.)

Please print clearly

Name_____

Address_____

_____

City_____ State_____ Postal Code_____

Country_____ Telephone_____

CUSTOMERS IN THE U.S.
Complete this form and mail to:
World Bank Publications
Box 7247-8619
Philadelphia, PA 19170-8619
U.S.A.

Telephone orders:
(202) 473-1155
Facsimile orders:
(202) 676-0581
Telex orders:
WUI 64145
Customer service:
(202) 473-1155

CUSTOMERS OUTSIDE THE U.S.
Prices and payment terms vary by country. Contact your local distributor (listed at the back of this book) before placing an order. When requesting information about specific prices and payment terms, provide the complete title and stock number of the publications you wish to order. If no distributor is listed for your country, complete this order form and return it to the U.S. address. Orders received in the U.S. from countries with authorized distributors will be returned to the customer.

*Shipping and Handling.
In the U.S. add $5.00. For airmail delivery outside the U.S. add US$8.00 for the first item and US$6.00 for each additional item.

SD94

Social Indicators of Development 1994

Published for the World Bank
The Johns Hopkins University Press
Baltimore and London

ISBN 0-8018-4788-5
ISSN 1012-8026

Contents

Symbols, Abbreviations, and Conventions

..	Data not available or nonexistent
0, 0.0	Zero or less than half the unit shown and not known more precisely
Annual percent	Percentage change between adjacent years (not a multiyear average)
DHS	*Demographic and Health Survey*
DPT	Diphtheria, pertussis, and tetanus
ESCAP	Economic and Social Commission for Asia and Pacific
GDP	Gross domestic product
GNP	Gross national product
IMR	Infant mortality rate
INED	Institute Nationale d'Etude Démographique
KAP	Knowledge, Attitude, and Practice Survey
Kg	Kilogram (2.2 pounds)
Km	Kilometer (0.62 miles)
LE	Life expectancy at birth
Mre	Most recent estimate
Pop.	Population
PVSR	*Population and Vital Statistics Report*
Sq. km	Square kilometer (0.3861 square miles)
Thou.	Thousands
USBOC	United States Bureau of Census
†	According to UNESCO, illiteracy is less than 5%

The cutoff date for all data is March 1994.

Introduction

The 1994 edition of *Social Indicators of Development* continues to address the most pressing issue now facing the Bank and its member countries: how to reduce poverty. Priority Poverty Indicators (PPIs), identified in the Bank's *Poverty Reduction Handbook*, are presented on the first page of each country table; other indicators covering human resources, natural resources, expenditures, and investment in human capital are presented on the second page. PPIs are used for monitoring levels and trends in poverty and, along with related social conditions, provide a framework for assessing human welfare in low- and middle-income countries.

A new feature, "*supplementary poverty indicators*," has been introduced in this edition. These indicators include access to, expenditure on, and coverage of social security for basic public goods such as health care and clean drinking water.

Social Indicators of Development is issued annually, on diskette as well as in book form. In the book, observations are presented for three periods: 1970-1975, 1980-1985, and the most recent estimate (MRE: the latest available estimate between 1987 and 1992). The diskettes contain time series for 1965-1992; however, for many indicators, data are only available for a few benchmark years. The diskettes, which use the ☆STARS☆ retrieval system for easy retrieval of data into Lotus, Javelin, Aremos, or ASCII format, may be obtained by using the order form in the front of the book or by contacting the Distribution Unit, Office of the Publisher, World Bank, 1818 H Street N.W., Washington, D.C. 20433 (202-473-1155).

The 192 economies presented in the country pages include both Bank members and nonmembers, reflecting a wide variety of political, social, economic, and cultural conditions. Recent changes in national boundaries affect the presentation of data in the following ways. Most social data for Germany refer to the unified Germany, but in general, economic information refers to the Federal Republic of Germany before unification (see footnotes). Although data are sparse, this edition shows country pages for several newly independent countries: Bosnia and Herzegovina, Croatia, Czech Republic, Former Yugoslav Republic of Macedonia, Marshall Islands, Federated States of Micronesia, Slovak Republic, Slovenia, and the Federal Republic of Yugoslavia. Country pages for other economies with sparse data are omitted in the book. These economies, along with basic indicators, are listed in Table 1a.

The technical notes and demographic parameters are an integral part of the document; readers are strongly urged to read them before trying to draw conclusions from the data. Country-specific notes present nonstandard features of the data.

Overview of Social and Economic Conditions

While the emphasis is on country data, international comparisons are also provided by a table on social and economic conditions that presents a selected array of indicators for 115 economies. It compares a few important areas of development over 30 years. The left-hand page of the table reports selected social and economic conditions, and the right-hand page shows changes in these conditions. Countries are arranged under regional headings, and income groups are listed at the bottom of the page. Only low- and middle-income economies with populations of more than 2 million are included here; however, the summary measures aggregate all economies in the relevant category.

Country Pages

The country pages identify poverty trends for each country, the social issues and problems accompanying development, and the extent to which public policy may affect poverty and related social conditions. The pages contain poverty measures and underlying economic variables such as wages and prices, as well as related information on health status and access to basic services. The role of the government and the share of output (GDP) dedicated to social expenditures are also included where possible, although this is an area requiring considerably more work before such measures can be reported for most countries.

The country pages also offer international comparisons by presenting aggregated data (mostly weighted by population) for reference groups. The three reference groups for each country are the income category in which the economy is classified, the next higher income category, and the geographic region.

Priority Poverty Indicators

Levels of poverty can be assessed by monitoring changes in a number of key areas. These are known as Priority Poverty Indicators (PPIs).

Two thresholds (upper and lower "poverty lines") have been established to convey more precisely what is meant by "poverty" in each country. These are presented along with "headcount indexes" that report what percentage of the country's population is below each threshold. In general, as countries develop, poverty lines change. At present, poverty lines, of variable quality and reliability, are available for about 25 countries; the coverage is expected to increase as more national household income and budget surveys—important sources of data concerning poverty lines—are processed.

Income indicators track the income-earning opportunities and living standards of the poor. Since unskilled labor is often the only factor of production owned by the poor, unskilled wages can be taken as a barometer of their incomes. Such wage data are generally difficult to come by, as they require special surveys and are rarely available from the official statistical system. Furthermore, where labor remuneration other than cash is involved, estimating such wages poses the additional challenge of placing a cash value on payments-in-kind or on other arrangements. Nonetheless, unskilled wages are included, where available, in this volume. Because the poor typically spend nearly all their incomes on consumption, and nearly half of this consumption is on food, the information available on food prices is also reported, disaggregated by urban-rural residence.

Social indicators track the provision and outcome of social services. Taken together with the income indicators,

they follow progress in reducing poverty in countries where household-based surveys are not available.

Supplementary Poverty Indicators

Supplementary Poverty Indicators trace the vulnerability of a country's population. The poorest households are usually the most vulnerable and the least able to protect themselves from contingencies. If households do not have access to such social cushions as unemployment benefits or health care, sudden emergencies can be catastrophic. The indicators reported here give some indication of the extent to which the population is unprotected by such basic safety nets.

Three charts are included on the PPI page. The first two show changes in population and GNP per capita, with the same scale maintained across countries to make international comparisons easier. Values for the country are shown as bars; averages for the income group in which the country is classified are represented by lines. The third chart is a *development diamond*. It portrays relationships among four socio-economic indicators for a given country and compares them with the average of the country's income group. Life expectancy, gross primary school enrollment, access to safe water, and GNP per capita are presented, one on each axis, and then connected (with a bold line) to form a polygon—the "diamond." The shape of the diamond can thus easily be compared with the income group to which it belongs. The averages for each income group are indexed (equal to 1); this reference diamond is drawn as a fine line. Any point outside the reference diamond represents a value better than the group average, and any point inside the reference diamond represents a value below the group average. Where data are not available, only part of the diamond appears. Since the reference diamond represents different values in different income groups, comparisons should be limited to the same income group.

Resources and Expenditures

The main themes covered in the right-hand page are human resources, natural resources, income, expenditure, and investment in human capital. Other demographic data, such as sex ratios, birth and death rates, and long-term population estimates, are available in the World Development Indicators at the back of the *World Development Report* and are therefore not included in this volume.

Internationally comparable environmental indicators are not available for most countries; however, efforts are underway in the World Bank and elsewhere to develop measures for monitoring and evaluating environmental characteristics. For example, the 1993 U.N. System of National Accounts (SNA) provides for "satellite" accounts on environmental issues. The U.N. Environment Programme and others are collaborating on a Global Environmental Monitoring System that seeks to measure air and water quality. Geographic information systems (including those based on remote sensing) are being harnessed to study environmental issues.

Also lacking are data measuring physical or fabricated capital. Few countries can estimate the stock of income-generating or productive wealth that these assets represent. However, some sectoral flows indicators, say on housing or infrastructure, are available from the United Nations' International Comparison Program (ICP) and are incorporated here. Additional efforts are needed in the international statistical community to develop indicators for repair and maintenance. These indicators are increasingly recognized as a critical factor in assigning worth to physical capital.

Income and outlay indicators suggest how basic resources are used and enhanced. The data also suggest what improvements in human capital are taking place with what inputs and what is being done to raise the quality of labor in particular.

The income section reports the approximate distribution of income among households. These data are gathered through nationwide studies of income distributions, usually based on household surveys, which tend to be infrequent.

Selected elements of expenditure as percentages of GDP are also reported, usually based on information collected for ICP but sometimes taken directly from national accounts. These give a general context for conventional social indicators. For example, cereal imports and other signals of trends in food availability are viewed against the background of food's share in GDP expenditure. Shares in GDP expenditure also shed light on the relative income distribution in a country.

The series may ultimately be reported in "international dollars" per capita, which is the ICP objective. It is given here in original national currency values, partly because ICP results are not available for all countries but also because relative values in the prices actually applying in each country are also useful for poverty analysis. As shown, the indicators represent the relative importance of different outlays in national price structures. Data for 1975 and 1980 are obtained from ICP Phases III and IV. Coverage increased from 34 countries in 1975 to 60 in 1980 and 64 in 1985, although no countries in the Latin American continent participated in 1985. Coverage dropped to only 30 European countries in 1990 but is expected to increase to more than 80 countries in the surveys now being conducted, which will have a base-year of 1993. Data for 1985 are from ICP Phase V reports by Eurostat, for Africa; Economic and Social Commission for Asia and the Pacific (ESCAP), for Asia; and Economic Commission for Europe (ECA) and the Organization for Economic Cooperation and Development (OECD), for Europe and other industrialized countries. The 1990 data come from OECD.

Staple goods as defined here comprise bread, cereals, potatoes, and tubers but exclude pulses. Staples are less expensive than, say, meat and may include items of fairly low nutritional value. To show that they form a significant share of food consumption in most poor developing countries, a separate measure of staples' share in GDP expenditure is given (with a complementary measure for spending on meat, fish, milk, cheese, and eggs).

Tools for Social Monitoring

The country pages form an evolving framework that, as the World Bank continues to expand its indicator range, will aid in evaluating and monitoring social progress. Researchers are invited to seek additional information, or address related questions, by writing to Chief, Socio-Economic Data Division, World Bank, 1818 H Street N.W., Washington, D.C. 20433.

Table 1. Social and Economic Conditions

Current Conditions

	Population (millions) 1992	GNP per capita (US $) 1992	Share of agriculture in GDP(%)		Infant mortality (per 1,000 live births)		Child Malnutrition (%) 1990	Primary school enrollment rate (%)		Percent Illiterate (aged 15+) 1990
			1975	1992	1970	1992		1975	1991	
Sub-Saharan Africa	546.4	520	23	18	138	99	28	56	..	51
Angola	9.7	..	..	..	178	124	20	..	..	58
Benin	5.0	410	31	..	155	110	35	50	66	77
Burkina Faso	9.5	300	38	..	178	132	46	16	37	82
Burundi	5.8	210	61	49	138	106	31	22	70	50
Cameroon	12.2	820	29	22	126	61	14	97	..	46
Central African Rep.	3.2	410	35	41	139	105	..	73	..	62
Chad	6.0	220	43	42	171	122	35	35	65	70
Congo	2.4	1,030	14	13	126	114	24	..	..	43
Cote d'Ivoire	12.9	670	28	32	135	91	12	62	69	46
Ethiopia	54.8	110	44	44	158	122	38	24	25	..
Ghana	15.8	450	48	49	111	81	27	71	..	40
Guinea	6.1	510	..	33	181	133	23	30	37	76
Kenya	25.7	310	30	23	102	66	18	95	..	31
Liberia	2.4	..	25	..	178	142	20	62	..	61
Madagascar	12.4	230	30	31	181	93	33	95	..	20
Malawi	9.1	210	35	26	193	134	60	..	..	..
Mali	9.0	310	61	42	204	130	25	24	25	68
Mauritania	2.1	530	27	26	165	117	31	19	55	66
Mozambique	16.5	60	..	..	156	162	..	..	63	67
Niger	8.2	280	50	37	170	123	49	20	..	72
Nigeria	101.9	320	31	35	139	84	36	51	71	49
Rwanda	7.3	250	49	41	142	117	30	56	..	50
Senegal	7.8	780	30	19	135	68	18	41	..	62
Sierra Leone	4.4	160	32	..	197	143	23	39	..	79
Somalia	8.3	..	49	..	158	132	..	59	..	76
South Africa	39.8	2,670	8	4	79	53	..	..	..	..
Sudan	26.5	..	38	32	149	99	..	47	..	73
Tanzania	25.9	110	37	53	132	92	25	53	69	..
Togo	3.9	390	27	36	134	85	24	99	..	57
Uganda	17.5	170	0	54	109	122	23	44	71	52
Zaire	39.8	..	17	..	128	91	29	88	..	28
Zambia	8.3	..	13	..	106	107	23	97	..	27
Zimbabwe	10.4	570	16	20	96	47	10	73	..	33
Middle East & N. Africa	252.6	1,950	9	14	133	58	21	79	100	45
Algeria	26.3	1,840	10	12	139	55	9	93	..	43
Egypt, Arab Rep.	54.7	640	28	17	158	57	10	71	100 +	52
Iran, Islamic Rep.	59.6	2,200	11	23	131	65	43	93	100 +	46
Iraq	19.2	..	..	..	102	58	..	94	..	40
Jordan	3.9	1,120	..	6	..	28	6	..	..	20
Lebanon	3.8	..	..	..	50	34	..	..	..	20
Libya	4.9	..	2	..	122	68	..	..	..	36
Morocco	26.2	1,030	17	15	128	57	12	62	66	51
Saudi Arabia	16.8	7,510	1	..	119	28	..	58	..	38
Syrian Arab Rep.	13.0	..	18	..	96	36	..	96	100 +	36
Tunisia	8.4	1,720	18	16	121	48	8	97	100 +	35
Yemen, Rep.	13.0	..	..	20	175	106	30	41	..	62
East Asia & Pacific	1,688.9	760	33	21	77	39	25	117	100 +	24
Cambodia	9.1	..	..	..	161	116	..	..	..	65
China	1,162.2	470	32	24	69	31	21	126	100 +	27
Indonesia	184.3	670	30	19	118	66	40	86	..	23
Korea, DR	22.6	..	..	..	51	24	..	..	..	..
Korea, Rep.	43.7	6,790	24	..	51	13	..	107	100 +	4
Lao PDR	4.4	250	..	..	146	97	37	58	98	..
Malaysia	18.6	2,790	28	..	45	14	17	91	93	22
Mongolia	2.3	..	..	30	102	60	..	108	89	..
Myanmar	43.7	..	47	59	121	72	32	83	..	19
Papua New Guinea	4.1	950	30	25	112	54	35	56	..	48
Philippines	64.3	770	30	22	66	40	34	107	100 +	10
Thailand	58.0	1,840	27	12	73	26	13	83	100 +	7
Viet Nam	69.3	..	..	35	104	36	42	119	..	12

+ Ratios exceed 100; for exact magnitude see country pages.

Average Annual Percentage Change, 1975 to Latest Available Year

	Population	GNP per capita	Private consumption per capita	Infant Mortality a/	Primary school enrollment a/
Sub-Saharan Africa	3	-1	-1	-30	1
Angola	2.8	..	..	-30.4	-5.3
Benin	3.1	0.1	-1.0	-28.8	1.8
Burkina Faso	2.6	1.1	0.6	-25.8	5.4
Burundi	2.8	1.4	0.9	-23.3	7.5
Cameroon	2.9	2.1	0.0	-51.5	0.3
Central African Rep.	2.7	-1.9	-0.5	-24.6	-0.5
Chad	2.3	0.6	2.2	-28.7	3.9
Congo	3.1	1.8	0.0	-9.6	..
Cote d'Ivoire	3.9	-3.1	-3.7	-32.4	0.7
Ethiopia	3.0	-1.2	..	-22.7	0.3
Ghana	3.0	-1.0	0.1	-26.8	0.5
Guinea	2.3	..	..	-26.4	1.3
Kenya	3.8	0.6	0.6	-35.3	0.0
Liberia	2.5	-4.2	..	-20.1	-5.1
Madagascar	2.9	-2.7	-3.4	-48.7	-0.2
Malawi	3.3	-0.5	-0.7	-30.6	1.2
Mali	2.5	-1.6	0.0	-36.3	0.3
Mauritania	2.4	-0.5	0.7	-29.1	6.9
Mozambique	2.6	-3.6	-0.9	4.0	-2.3
Niger	3.3	-2.8	0.9	-27.6	2.5
Nigeria	3.1	-1.8	-1.0	-39.7	2.1
Rwanda	2.4	1.2	0.7	-17.8	1.6
Senegal	2.9	-0.5	-0.1	-49.6	2.5
Sierra Leone	2.3	-0.9	-2.3	-27.6	1.4
Somalia	3.1	-1.4	..	-16.3	-12.8
South Africa	2.6	-0.6	-0.6	-32.7	..
Sudan	2.8	-1.8	-1.0	-33.9	0.4
Tanzania	3.1	-0.7	..	-30.6	1.7
Togo	3.2	-1.4	2.0	-36.5	0.8
Uganda	2.5	0.4	..	12.1	2.9
Zaire	3.2	-2.4	-1.9	-29.1	-1.2
Zambia	3.2	-3.0	0.9	0.9	-0.4
Zimbabwe	3.3	-0.4	-2.2	-51.7	3.2
Middle East & N. Africa	3.2	-1.9	..	-57.1	1.5
Algeria	3.0	0.4	0.4	-60.5	0.1
Egypt, Arab Rep.	2.5	3.1	2.7	-63.9	2.2
Iran, Islamic Rep.	3.5	-2.0	-1.7	-50.5	1.2
Iraq	3.3	-9.6	..	-43.1	1.1
Jordan	4.3	-5.4	..	..	-0.1
Lebanon	2.1	..	..	-31.5	0.9
Libya	4.2	-6.5	..	-44.4	..
Morocco	2.5	1.6	1.3	-55.3	0.4
Saudi Arabia	5.3	-2.4	..	-76.5	1.9
Syrian Arab Rep.	3.3	-0.5	0.2	-62.3	0.8
Tunisia	2.5	1.8	2.2	-60.4	1.2
Yemen, Rep.	3.5	..	..	-39.5	4.2
East Asia & Pacific	1.6	5.8	4.9	-53.1	0.2
Cambodia	1.9	..	..	-27.8	..
China	1.4	7.3	6.0	-55.1	-0.2
Indonesia	1.9	4.2	3.8	-44.1	2.2
Korea, DR	1.8	..	..	-53.3	-1.0
Korea, Rep.	1.3	7.1	6.1	-74.9	-0.1
Lao PDR	2.3	..	..	-33.5	3.3
Malaysia	2.5	3.6	3.5	-69.0	0.1
Mongolia	2.8	-0.2	..	-41.2	-1.2
Myanmar	2.1	0.5	..	-40.5	1.4
Papua New Guinea	2.4	-0.5	-0.9	-51.8	1.6
Philippines	2.4	-0.3	0.4	-39.8	0.2
Thailand	2.0	5.2	3.6	-64.2	1.9
Viet Nam	2.1	..	..	-65.4	-1.0

a. These are percent changes, 1970 to 1992.

xi

Table 1. Social and Economic Conditions (continued)

Current Conditions

	Population (millions) 1992	GNP per capita (US $) 1992	Share of agriculture in GDP(%) 1975	Share of agriculture in GDP(%) 1992	Infant mortality (per 1,000 live births) 1975	Infant mortality (per 1,000 live births) 1992	Child Malnutrition (%) 1990	Primary school enrollment rate (%) 1975	Primary school enrollment rate (%) 1991	Percent Illiterate (aged 15+) 1990
South Asia	1,177.9	310	39	29	138	85	61	74	..	54
Afghanistan	21.5	..	..	..	198	162	..	26	..	71
Bangladesh	114.4	220	62	34	140	91	67	73	..	65
India	883.6	310	37	29	137	79	63	79	..	52
Nepal	19.9	170	69	49	157	99	70	51	..	74
Pakistan	119.3	420	30	24	142	95	40	46	..	65
Sri Lanka	17.4	540	29	24	53	18	37	77	100 +	12
Europe & Central Asia	494.6	..	..	..	..	..	30	..	..	..
Albania	3.4	..	..	40	66	32	..	..	..	..
Armenia	3.7	780	..	..	..	21	..	..	..	..
Azerbaijan	7.4	740	..	..	..	32	..	..	..	..
Belarus	10.3	2,930	..	..	..	15	..	..	..	..
Bosnia and Herzegovina	4.4	..	..	..	..	19	..	..	..	..
Bulgaria	8.5	1,330	..	14	27	16	..	99	92	..
Croatia	4.8	..	..	..	..	12	..	..	..	..
Czech Republic	10.3	2,450	..	..	21	10	..	..	..	..
Georgia	5.5	850	..	..	..	19	..	..	..	..
Greece	10.3	7,290	17	..	30	8	..	104	..	7
Hungary	10.3	2,970	18	7	36	15	..	99	89	..
Kazakhstan	17.0	1,680	..	..	..	31	..	..	..	..
Kyrgyz Republic	4.5	820	..	..	..	37	..	..	..	..
Latvia	2.6	1,930	..	24	23	17	..	..	..	..
Lithuania	3.8	1,310	..	..	..	16	..	..	..	..
Macedonia, FYR b/	2.2	..	..	..	..	29	..	..	..	..
Moldova	4.4	1,300	..	..	..	23	..	..	..	..
Poland	38.4	1,910	..	7	33	14	..	100	98	..
Portugal	9.8	..	..	..	56	9	..	113	100 +	15
Romania	22.7	1,100	..	23	49	23	..	107	90	..
Russian Federation	149.0	2,510	..	..	..	20	..	..	..	..
Slovak Republic	5.3	1,930	..	6	25	13	..	..	100	..
Slovenia	2.0	..	..	5	..	8	..	..	..	..
Tajikistan	5.6	490	..	..	..	49	..	..	..	..
Turkey	58.5	1,980	26	13	147	54	..	108	..	19
Turkmenistan	3.9	1,230	..	..	..	54	..	..	..	..
Ukraine	52.1	1,820	..	..	..	18	..	..	..	..
Uzbekistan	21.5	690	..	33	..	42	..	..	..	..
Yugoslavia, Fed. Rep.	10.6	..	14	..	..	28	..	103	..	7
Latin America & Caribbean	453.3	2,690	11	..	82	44	11	99	100 +	15
Argentina	33.1	6,050	6	6	52	29	..	106	100 +	5
Bolivia	7.5	680	20	..	153	82	11	85	..	23
Brazil	153.9	2,770	11	..	95	57	7	88	100 +	19
Chile	13.6	2,730	7	..	78	17	3	118	98	7
Colombia	33.4	1,330	24	16	74	21	10	118	100 +	13
Costa Rica	3.2	1,960	20	18	62	14	6	107	100 +	7
Cuba	10.8	..	..	..	39	10	5	124	100 +	6
Dominican Republic	7.3	1,050	21	18	90	41	10	104	..	17
Ecuador	11.0	1,070	18	13	100	45	17	104	..	14
El Salvador	5.4	1,170	23	9	103	40	16	75	76	27
Guatemala	9.7	980	..	25	100	62	29	61	79	45
Haiti	6.7	..	..	..	141	93	37	60	..	47
Honduras	5.4	580	25	19	110	49	21	88	100 +	27
Jamaica	2.4	1,340	7	..	43	14	7	97	100 +	2
Mexico	85.0	3,470	11	8	72	35	14	109	100 +	13
Nicaragua	3.9	340	22	30	106	56	11	82	100 +	..
Panama	2.5	2,420	11	11	47	21	16	114	..	12
Paraguay	4.5	1,380	37	24	57	36	4	102	100 +	10
Peru	22.4	950	16	..	108	52	11	113	..	15
Puerto Rico	3.6	6,590	3	1	29	13	..	107	..	..
Uruguay	3.1	3,340	15	11	46	20	7	107	100 +	4
Venezuela	20.2	2,910	5	5	53	33	6	97	99	8
Low-income	3,194.6	390	36	30	110	73	38	94	..	39
Middle-income	1,401.0	2,490	..	..	83	35	..	97	..	..
High-income	828.2	21,960	4	..	20	7	..	102	..	..

b. Former Yugoslav Republic of Macedonia

Average Annual Percentage Change, 1975 to Latest Available Year

	Population	GNP per capita	Private consumption per capita	Infant Mortality a/	Primary school enrollment a/
South Asia	**2.3**	**2.6**	**2.4**	**-40.2**	**1.9**
Afghanistan	2.5	..	..	-18.0	-0.6
Bangladesh	2.4	2.0	1.2	-35.0	0.4
India	2.2	2.6	2.5	-42.4	1.6
Nepal	2.6	1.4	..	-37.1	3.7
Pakistan	3.1	3.6	2.0	-33.1	0.0
Sri Lanka	1.5	3.0	3.1	-66.9	2.1
Europe & Central Asia	**0.9**	**..**	**..**	**..**	**..**
Albania	2.0	..	0.7	-51.2	-0.8
Armenia	1.4	..	..	..	..
Azerbaijan	1.5	..	..	..	..
Belarus	0.6	..	..	..	..
Bosnia and Herzegovina	0.7	..	..	..	..
Bulgaria	0.0	1.2	7.7	-42.1	-0.5
Croatia	0.4	..	..	..	..
Czech Republic	0.1	..	..	-52.1	..
Georgia	0.7	..	..	..	..
Greece	0.7	1.1	2.8	-72.3	-0.5
Hungary	-0.1	1.0	0.7	-59.1	-0.7
Kazakhstan	1.2	-0.1	..	..	..
Kyrgyzstan	1.9	..	..	..	..
Latvia	0.4	0.2	..	-24.3	..
Lithuania	0.8	..	..	..	..
Macedonia, FYR b/	1.1	..	..	..	..
Moldova	0.8	..	..	..	..
Poland	0.7	0.1	0.4	-57.2	-0.1
Portugal	0.4	2.5	2.2	-83.2	0.5
Romania	0.5	1.0	..	-52.8	-1.1
Russian Federation	0.6	..	..	..	..
Slovak Republic	0.6	..	..	-49.9	0.5
Slovenia	0.7	..	..	..	..
Tajikistan	2.9	..	..	..	..
Turkey	2.3	1.9	2.0	-63.3	0.1
Turkmenistan	2.5	..	..	..	..
Ukraine	0.4	..	..	..	..
Uzbekistan	2.5	..	..	..	..
Yugoslavia, Fed. Rep.	..	..	..	..	-0.6
Latin America & Caribbean	**2.1**	**..**	**0.6**	**-48.3**	**0.4**
Argentina	1.4	-1.1	..	-44.4	0.1
Bolivia	2.6	-2.3	1.3	-46.5	0.0
Brazil	2.1	0.6	0.7	-39.7	1.2
Chile	1.6	4.1	1.8	-78.2	-1.2
Colombia	2.0	1.5	1.3	-71.5	-0.4
Costa Rica	2.9	-0.1	-0.2	-77.2	-0.2
Cuba	0.9	..	..	-73.6	-1.2
Dominican Republic	2.2	0.0	0.4	-54.4	-0.7
Ecuador	2.7	0.1	0.5	-54.9	0.8
El Salvador	1.5	-1.5	-2.0	-61.3	0.1
Guatemala	2.9	-1.2	-1.3	-38.1	1.6
Haiti	1.9	-1.0	-0.7	-34.0	-0.5
Honduras	3.4	-0.2	-0.2	-55.5	1.1
Jamaica	1.0	-1.4	-0.7	-67.6	0.6
Mexico	2.1	0.7	0.9	-51.7	0.3
Nicaragua	2.8	-5.9	-5.9	-47.2	1.3
Panama	2.2	0.5	0.4	-54.9	-0.5
Paraguay	3.2	1.1	-0.3	-37.3	0.4
Peru	2.3	-2.1	-1.9	-51.9	-2.0
Puerto Rico	1.0	0.4	1.5	-54.5	-2.1
Uruguay	0.6	-0.8	0.6	-56.9	0.2
Venezuela	2.8	-1.8	0.3	-38.2	0.1
Low-income	**2.0**	**3.6**	**3.0**	**-43.3**	**0.6**
Middle-income	**1.8**	**0.3**	**..**	**-57.2**	**0.5**
High-income	**0.7**	**2.1**	**2.2**	**-63.9**	**0.1**

Country Pages

Afghanistan

Priority Poverty Indicators

Indicator	Unit of measure	Latest single year 1970-75	Latest single year 1980-85	Most recent estimate 1987-92	Same region/income group South Asia	Same region/income group Low-income	Next higher income group
POVERTY							
Upper poverty line	local curr.	..	..	..	..	..	..
→ Headcount index	% of pop.	..	..	..	28	19	..
Lower poverty line	local curr.	..	..	..	..	..	..
Headcount index	% of pop.	..	..	..	..	..	..
GNP per capita	US$	..	..	..	310	390	..
SHORT TERM INCOME INDICATORS							
Unskilled urban wages	local curr.	..	..	..	..	..	..
Unskilled rural wages	"	..	..	..	..	..	..
Rural terms of trade	"	..	..	..	..	..	..
→ Consumer price index	1987=100	..	86	467	..	..	..
Lower income	"	..	..	..	..	..	..
Food [a]	"	..	82	368	..	..	..
Urban	"	..	..	..	..	..	..
Rural	"	..	..	..	..	..	..
SOCIAL INDICATORS							
Public expenditure on basic social services	% of GDP	..	..	..	..	..	..
Gross enrollment ratios							
Primary	% school age pop.	26	20	24	103	103	..
Male	"	44	27	32	117	113	..
Female	"	8	13	17	88	96	..
Mortality							
Infant mortality	per thou. live births	194.0	183.0	162.0	85.0	73.0	45.0
Under 5 mortality	"	..	..	242.6	116.0	108.0	59.0
Immunization							
Measles	% age group	..	14.0	19.0	56.6	72.7	..
DPT	"	..	15.0	23.0	75.0	80.6	..
→ Child malnutrition (under-5)	"	..	..	..	60.9	38.3	..
Life expectancy							
Total	years	38	40	43	60	62	68
Female advantage	"	0.0	1.0	1.0	1.0	2.4	6.4
Total fertility rate	births per woman	7.1	6.9	6.9	4.0	3.4	3.1
Maternal mortality rate	per 100,000 live births	..	600	..	..	..	..

Supplementary Poverty Indicators

Indicator	Unit of measure	1970-75	1980-85	1987-92	South Asia	Low-income	Next higher
Expenditures on social security	% of total gov't exp.	..	..	..	..	..	..
Social security coverage	% econ. active pop.	..	..	..	..	..	..
Access to safe water: total	% of pop.	9.0	21.0	21.0	71.9	68.4	..
Urban	"	40.0	39.0	44.0	74.2	78.9	..
Rural	"	5.0	17.0	16.0	70.0	60.3	..
Access to health care	"	..	49.0	..	..	..	..

Population growth rate (annual average, percent)

1970-75, 1980-85, 1987-92 — Afghanistan / Low-income

GNP per capita growth rate (annual average, percent)

1970-75, 1980-85, 1987-92 — Afghanistan / Low-income

Development diamond [b]

Life expectancy — GNP per capita — Gross primary enrollment — Access to safe water — Afghanistan / Low-income

a. See the technical notes, p.389.   b. The development diamond, based on four key indicators, shows the average level of development in the country compared with its income group. See the introduction.

2

Afghanistan

Indicator	Unit of measure	Latest single year 1970-75	Latest single year 1980-85	Most recent estimate 1987-92	Same region/income group South Asia	Same region/income group Low-income	Next higher income group
Resources and Expenditures							
HUMAN RESOURCES							
Population (mre=1992)	thousands	14,038	18,087	21,538	1,177,918	3,194,535	942,547
Age dependency ratio	ratio	0.86	0.91	0.91	0.73	0.67	0.66
Urban	% of pop.	13.3	16.9	18.9	25.4	26.7	57.0
Population growth rate	annual %	2.5	2.5	2.7	2.1	1.8	1.4
Urban	"	6.0	4.0	4.6	3.4	3.4	4.8
Labor force (15-64)	thousands	4,569	4,971	6,509	428,847	1,478,954	..
Agriculture	% of labor force	64	61	..	..	..	..
Industry	"	13	14	..	..	..	..
Female	"	7	8	9	22	33	36
Females per 100 males							
Urban	number	..	..	..	..	..	..
Rural	"	..	..	..	..	..	..
NATURAL RESOURCES							
Area	thou. sq. km	652.09	652.09	652.09	5,133.49	38,401.06	40,697.37
Density	pop. per sq. km	21.5	27.7	32.2	224.8	81.7	22.8
Agricultural land	% of land area	58.4	58.4	58.4	58.9	50.9	..
Change in agricultural land	annual %	0.0	0.0	0.0	-0.2	0.0	..
Agricultural land under irrigation	%	6.4	6.8	7.3	29.0	18.2	..
Forests and woodland	thou. sq. km	19	19	19	..	..	..
Deforestation (net)	annual %	..	..	..	..	..	..
INCOME							
Household income							
Share of top 20% of households	% of income	..	..	..	41	42	..
Share of bottom 40% of households	"	..	..	..	21	19	..
Share of bottom 20% of households	"	..	..	..	9	8	..
EXPENDITURE							
Food	% of GDP	..	..	..	..	..	..
Staples	"	..	..	..	..	..	..
Meat, fish, milk, cheese, eggs	"	..	..	..	..	..	..
Cereal imports	thou. metric tonnes	13	58	156	7,721	46,537	74,924
Food aid in cereals	"	10	50	53	2,558	9,008	4,054
Food production per capita	1987 = 100	101	95	65	116	123	..
Fertilizer consumption	kg/ha	1.0	1.9	1.3	71.5	61.9	..
Share of agriculture in GDP	% of GDP	..	..	..	28.7	29.6	..
Housing	% of GDP	..	..	..	..	..	..
Average household size	persons per household	..	..	..	..	..	..
Urban	"	..	..	..	..	..	..
Fixed investment: housing	% of GDP	..	..	..	..	..	..
Fuel and power	% of GDP	..	..	..	..	..	..
Energy consumption per capita	kg of oil equiv.	56	68	119	209	335	1,882
Households with electricity							
Urban	% of households	..	..	..	..	..	..
Rural	"	..	..	..	..	..	..
Transport and communication	% of GDP	..	..	..	..	..	..
Fixed investment: transport equipment	"	..	..	..	..	..	..
Total road length	thou. km	..	..	..	..	..	..
INVESTMENT IN HUMAN CAPITAL							
Health							
Population per physician	persons	15,417	13,237	8,935	2,459	..	..
Population per nurse	"	15,121	8,955	8,899	..	..	..
Population per hospital bed	"	5,025	3,699	4,003	1,652	1,050	516
Oral rehydration therapy (under-5)	% of cases	..	..	26	18	39	..
Education							
Gross enrollment ratio							
Secondary	% of school-age pop.	8	9	8	40	41	..
Female	"	2	6	6	29	35	..
Pupil-teacher ratio: primary	pupils per teacher	42	37	..	59	37	26
Pupil-teacher ratio: secondary	"	12	18	..	23	19	..
Pupils reaching grade 4	% of cohort	67	..	..	..	..	..
Repeater rate: primary	% of total enroll	27	6	..	..	..	..
Illiteracy	% of pop. (age 15+)	..	76	71	54	39	..
Female	% of fem. (age 15+)	..	91	86	68	52	..
Newspaper circulation	per thou. pop.	7	4	9	..	..	100

World Bank International Economics Department, April 1994

Albania

Indicator	Unit of measure	Latest single year 1970-75	Latest single year 1980-85	Most recent estimate 1987-92	Same region/income group Europe & Central Asia	Same region/income group Lower-middle-income	Next higher income group
Priority Poverty Indicators							
POVERTY							
Upper poverty line	local curr.	..	..	..	..	..	..
Headcount index	% of pop.	..	..	..	..	..	..
Lower poverty line	local curr.	..	..	..	..	..	..
Headcount index	% of pop.	..	..	..	..	..	..
GNP per capita	US$	..	..	..	..	..	3,870
SHORT TERM INCOME INDICATORS							
Unskilled urban wages	local curr.	..	..	..	..	..	..
Unskilled rural wages	"	..	..	..	..	..	..
Rural terms of trade	"	..	..	..	..	..	..
Consumer price index	1987=100	101	100	100	..	..	..
Lower income	"	..	..	..	..	..	..
Food[a]	"	..	..	211	..	..	..
Urban	"	..	..	..	..	..	..
Rural	"	..	..	..	..	..	..
SOCIAL INDICATORS							
Public expenditure on basic social services	% of GDP	..	..	..	..	..	..
Gross enrollment ratios							
Primary	% school age pop.	106	103	101	..	..	107
Male	"	109	104	100	..	..	..
Female	"	102	102	101	..	..	..
Mortality							
Infant mortality	per thou. live births	58.0	45.0	32.0	30.0	45.0	40.0
Under 5 mortality	"	..	..	39.6	38.0	59.0	51.0
Immunization							
Measles	% age group	..	96.0	87.0	..	..	82.0
DPT	"	..	96.0	94.0	..	..	73.8
Child malnutrition (under-5)	"	..	..	..	..	..	..
Life expectancy							
Total	years	68	70	73	70	68	69
Female advantage	"	3.5	5.0	5.1	8.6	6.4	6.3
Total fertility rate	births per woman	4.9	3.5	2.9	2.2	3.1	2.9
Maternal mortality rate	per 100,000 live births	..	..	..	58	..	..
Supplementary Poverty Indicators							
Expenditures on social security	% of total gov't exp.	..	..	..	..	..	..
Social security coverage	% econ. active pop.	..	..	..	..	..	..
Access to safe water: total	% of pop.	..	..	..	..	..	85.6
Urban	"	..	..	..	..	..	94.3
Rural	"	..	..	..	..	..	73.0
Access to health care	"	..	100.0	100.0	..	..	..

Population growth rate
(annual average, percent)

□ Albania
— Lower-middle-income

GNP per capita growth rate
(annual average, percent)

Development diamond[b]

Life expectancy

GNP per capita

Gross primary enrollment

Access to safe water

— Albania
— Lower-middle-income

a. See the technical notes, p.389.   b. The development diamond, based on four key indicators, shows the average level of development in the country compared with its income group. See the introduction.

4

Albania

Indicator	Unit of measure	Latest single year 1970-75	Latest single year 1980-85	Most recent estimate 1987-92	Same region/income group Europe & Central Asia	Same region/income group Lower-middle-income	Next higher income group
Resources and Expenditures							
HUMAN RESOURCES							
Population (mre=1992)	thousands	2,402	2,962	3,363	495,241	942,547	477,960
Age dependency ratio	ratio	0.80	0.66	0.63	0.56	0.66	0.64
Urban	% of pop.	32.8	34.8	36.4	63.3	57.0	71.7
Population growth rate	annual %	2.2	2.1	1.9	0.5	1.4	1.6
Urban	"	2.8	2.7	2.7	..	4.8	2.5
Labor force (15-64)	thousands	1,043	1,398	1,668	..	..	181,414
Agriculture	% of labor force	61	56	..	..	..	..
Industry	"	23	26	..	..	..	..
Female	"	40	41	41	46	36	29
Females per 100 males							
Urban	number	..	..	..	..	..	..
Rural	"	..	..	..	..	..	..
NATURAL RESOURCES							
Area	thou. sq. km	28.75	28.75	28.75	24,165.06	40,697.37	21,836.02
Density	pop. per sq. km	83.6	103.0	114.8	20.4	22.8	21.5
Agricultural land	% of land area	39.4	40.6	40.3	..	..	41.7
Change in agricultural land	annual %	-3.7	-0.1	-0.4	..	..	0.3
Agricultural land under irrigation	%	30.7	35.9	38.4	..	..	9.3
Forests and woodland	thou. sq. km	10	10	10	..	..	..
Deforestation (net)	annual %	..	..	0.0	..	..	..
INCOME							
Household income							
Share of top 20% of households	% of income	..	..	..	..	..	..
Share of bottom 40% of households	"	..	..	..	..	..	..
Share of bottom 20% of households	"	..	..	..	..	..	..
EXPENDITURE							
Food	% of GDP	..	17.9	..	..	..	..
Staples	"	..	3.3	..	..	..	..
Meat, fish, milk, cheese, eggs	"	..	8.0	..	..	..	..
Cereal imports	thou. metric tonnes	92	78	545	45,972	74,924	49,174
Food aid in cereals	"	..	..	451	1,639	4,054	282
Food production per capita	1987 = 100	86	94	67	..	..	109
Fertilizer consumption	kg/ha	57.9	84.6	28.4	..	..	68.8
Share of agriculture in GDP	% of GDP	..	27.9	40.1	..	..	8.1
Housing	% of GDP	..	4.2	..	..	..	..
Average household size	persons per household	..	..	..	..	..	..
Urban	"	..	..	..	..	..	..
Fixed investment: housing	% of GDP	..	5.9	..	..	..	..
Fuel and power	% of GDP	..	0.9	..	..	..	..
Energy consumption per capita	kg of oil equiv.	662	1,169	421	3,190	1,882	1,649
Households with electricity							
Urban	% of households	..	..	..	..	..	..
Rural	"	..	..	..	..	..	..
Transport and communication	% of GDP	..	5.6	..	..	..	..
Fixed investment: transport equipment	"	..	12.3	..	..	..	..
Total road length	thou. km	..	..	..	..	..	..
INVESTMENT IN HUMAN CAPITAL							
Health							
Population per physician	persons	1,068	1,076	..	378	..	..
Population per nurse	"	232	..	..	..	..	..
Population per hospital bed	"	141	..	246	134	516	385
Oral rehydration therapy (under-5)	% of cases	..	..	..	..	..	54
Education							
Gross enrollment ratio							
Secondary	% of school-age pop.	35	72	79	..	..	53
Female	"	27	68	74	..	..	..
Pupil-teacher ratio: primary	pupils per teacher	25	20	19	..	26	25
Pupil-teacher ratio: secondary	"	18	29	20	..	..	..
Pupils reaching grade 4	% of cohort	..	100	..	..	..	71
Repeater rate: primary	% of total enroll	..	..	..	..	..	11
Illiteracy	% of pop. (age 15+)	..	..	..	..	..	14
Female	% of fem. (age 15+)	..	..	..	..	..	17
Newspaper circulation	per thou. pop.	48	51	42	..	100	117

World Bank International Economics Department, April 1994

5

Algeria

Indicator	Unit of measure	Latest single year		Most recent estimate 1987-92	Same region/income group		Next higher income group
		1970-75	1980-85		Mid-East & North Africa	Lower-middle-income	

Priority Poverty Indicators

Indicator	Unit of measure	1970-75	1980-85	1987-92	Mid-East & North Africa	Lower-middle-income	Next higher income group
POVERTY							
Upper poverty line	local curr.	..	..	..	..	..	..
Headcount index	% of pop.	..	..	..	..	..	..
Lower poverty line	local curr.	..	..	..	..	..	..
Headcount index	% of pop.	..	..	..	..	..	..
GNP per capita	US$	860	2,620	1,840	1,950	..	3,870
SHORT TERM INCOME INDICATORS							
Unskilled urban wages	local curr.	..	..	..	..	..	..
Unskilled rural wages	"	..	..	..	..	..	..
Rural terms of trade	"	..	..	..	..	..	..
Consumer price index	1987=100	31	83	223	..	..	..
Lower income	"	..	..	..	..	..	..
Food[a]	"	..	79	161	..	..	..
Urban	"	..	..	..	..	..	..
Rural	"	..	..	..	..	..	..
SOCIAL INDICATORS							
Public expenditure on basic social services	% of GDP	..	..	12.7	..	..	..
Gross enrollment ratios							
Primary	% school age pop.	93	92	95	100	..	107
Male	"	109	102	103	107	..	..
Female	"	75	82	88	88	..	..
Mortality							
Infant mortality	per thou. live births	132.0	88.0	55.0	58.0	45.0	40.0
Under 5 mortality	"	..	..	73.1	78.0	59.0	51.0
Immunization							
Measles	% age group	..	17.0	83.0	81.8	..	82.0
DPT	"	..	33.0	89.0	83.9	..	73.8
Child malnutrition (under-5)	"	..	..	9.2	20.9	..	..
Life expectancy							
Total	years	54	60	67	64	68	69
Female advantage	"	2.0	2.0	1.0	2.4	6.4	6.3
Total fertility rate	births per woman	7.4	6.4	4.3	4.9	3.1	2.9
Maternal mortality rate	per 100,000 live births	..	129	..	..	..	..

Supplementary Poverty Indicators

Indicator	Unit of measure	1970-75	1980-85	1987-92	Mid-East & North Africa	Lower-middle-income	Next higher income group
Expenditures on social security	% of total gov't exp.	..	..	..	..	..	..
Social security coverage	% econ. active pop.	..	..	62.0	..	..	..
Access to safe water: total	% of pop.	..	69.0	78.0	85.0	..	85.6
Urban	"	84.0	85.0	90.0	97.0	..	94.3
Rural	"	..	55.0	65.0	70.1	..	73.0
Access to health care	"	..	..	90.0	84.6	..	..

Population growth rate (annual average, percent)

□ Algeria
— Lower-middle-income

GNP per capita growth rate (annual average, percent)

Development diamond[b]

Life expectancy — GNP per capita — Gross primary enrollment — Access to safe water

— Algeria
— Lower-middle-income

a. See the technical notes, p.389. b. The development diamond, based on four key indicators, shows the average level of development in the country compared with its income group. See the introduction.

Algeria

Indicator	Unit of measure	Latest single year 1970-75	Latest single year 1980-85	Most recent estimate 1987-92	Mid-East & North Africa	Lower-middle-income	Next higher income group
Resources and Expenditures							
HUMAN RESOURCES							
Population (mre=1992)	thousands	16,018	21,879	26,254	252,555	942,547	477,960
Age dependency ratio	ratio	1.07	1.00	0.86	0.87	0.66	0.64
Urban	% of pop.	40.3	47.5	54.3	54.7	57.0	71.7
Population growth rate	annual %	3.1	3.1	2.4	2.8	1.4	1.6
Urban	"	3.5	4.9	4.1	3.8	4.8	2.5
Labor force (15-64)	thousands	3,455	4,834	6,293	69,280	..	181,414
Agriculture	% of labor force	39	0	0			
Industry	"	24	0	0	..	..	..
Female	"	7	9	10	15	36	29
Females per 100 males							
Urban	number	..	..	..	..	..	..
Rural	"	..	..	..	..	..	..
NATURAL RESOURCES							
Area	thou. sq. km	2,381.74	2,381.74	2,381.74	10,487.21	40,697.37	21,836.02
Density	pop. per sq. km	6.7	9.2	10.8	23.4	22.8	21.5
Agricultural land	% of land area	18.4	16.4	16.2	30.2	..	41.7
Change in agricultural land	annual %	-1.3	-1.4	-0.1	0.5	..	0.3
Agricultural land under irrigation	%	0.6	0.9	1.0	31.0	..	9.3
Forests and woodland	thou. sq. km	41	46	41	..	..	..
Deforestation (net)	annual %	..	..	..	..	..	..
INCOME							
Household income							
Share of top 20% of households	% of income	..	..	47	..	..	..
Share of bottom 40% of households	"	..	..	18	..	..	..
Share of bottom 20% of households	"	..	..	7	..	..	..
EXPENDITURE							
Food	% of GDP	..	..	19.9	..	..	..
Staples	"	..	..	6.2	..	..	..
Meat, fish, milk, cheese, eggs	"	..	..	5.9	..	..	..
Cereal imports	thou. metric tonnes	1,669	5,266	4,685	38,007	74,924	49,174
Food aid in cereals	"	54	2	20	2,484	4,054	282
Food production per capita	1987 = 100	131	111	112	116	..	109
Fertilizer consumption	kg/ha	2.8	7.2	2.5	96.7	..	68.8
Share of agriculture in GDP	% of GDP	9.9	8.7	12.0	13.7	..	8.1
Housing	% of GDP	..	..	5.7	..	..	..
Average household size	persons per household	..	..	..	..	..	..
Urban	"	..	..	..	..	..	..
Fixed investment: housing	% of GDP	2.2	..	6.5	..	..	..
Fuel and power	% of GDP	..	..	1.2	..	..	..
Energy consumption per capita	kg of oil equiv.	373	905	988	1,109	1,882	1,649
Households with electricity							
Urban	% of households	..	..	..	..	..	..
Rural	"	..	..	..	..	..	..
Transport and communication	% of GDP	..	..	3.2	..	..	..
Fixed investment: transport equipment	"	5.9	..	2.3	..	..	..
Total road length	thou. km	78	78	75	..	..	..
INVESTMENT IN HUMAN CAPITAL							
Health							
Population per physician	persons	8,095	2,341	2,332	..	..	..
Population per nurse	"	..	331	330	..	..	..
Population per hospital bed	"	352	..	400	636	516	385
Oral rehydration therapy (under-5)	% of cases	..	..	26	56	..	54
Education							
Gross enrollment ratio							
Secondary	% of school-age pop.	20	50	60	59	..	53
Female	"	14	42	53	50	..	..
Pupil-teacher ratio: primary	pupils per teacher	41	28	28	27	26	25
Pupil-teacher ratio: secondary	"	27	22	17	21	..	..
Pupils reaching grade 4	% of cohort	93	96	96	..	..	71
Repeater rate: primary	% of total enroll	13	8	7	..	..	11
Illiteracy	% of pop. (age 15+)	74	51	43	45	..	14
Female	% of fem. (age 15+)	..	65	55	58	..	17
Newspaper circulation	per thou. pop.	18	21	51	39	100	117

World Bank International Economics Department, April 1994

Angola

Indicator	Unit of measure	Latest single year 1970-75	Latest single year 1980-85	Most recent estimate 1987-92	Same region/income group Sub-Saharan Africa	Same region/income group Lower-middle-income	Next higher income group
Priority Poverty Indicators							
POVERTY							
Upper poverty line	local curr.	..	..	..	..	..	..
Headcount index	% of pop.	..	..	..	..	..	..
Lower poverty line	local curr.	..	..	..	..	..	..
Headcount index	% of pop.	..	..	..	..	..	..
GNP per capita	US$	..	700	650	520	..	3,870
SHORT TERM INCOME INDICATORS							
Unskilled urban wages	local curr.	..	..	..	..	..	..
Unskilled rural wages	"	..	..	..	..	..	..
Rural terms of trade	"	..	..	..	..	..	..
Consumer price index	1987=100	..	..	..	..	..	..
Lower income	"	..	..	..	..	..	..
Food[a]	"	..	..	..	..	..	..
Urban	"	..	..	..	..	..	..
Rural	"	..	..	..	..	..	..
SOCIAL INDICATORS							
Public expenditure on basic social services	% of GDP	..	3.3	10.0	..	..	..
Gross enrollment ratios							
Primary	% school age pop.	66	98	91	66	..	107
Male	"	85	147	95	79	..	..
Female	"	48	121	87	62	..	..
Mortality							
Infant mortality	per thou. live births	173.0	149.0	124.0	99.0	45.0	40.0
Under 5 mortality	"	..	..	208.9	169.0	59.0	51.0
Immunization							
Measles	% age group	..	43.0	39.0	54.0	..	82.0
DPT	"	..	7.0	26.0	54.6	..	73.8
Child malnutrition (under-5)	"	..	..	20.0	28.4	..	..
Life expectancy							
Total	years	38	42	46	52	68	69
Female advantage	"	3.1	3.2	3.2	3.4	6.4	6.3
Total fertility rate	births per woman	6.4	6.4	6.6	6.1	3.1	2.9
Maternal mortality rate	per 100,000 live births	..	..	650	..	..	..
Supplementary Poverty Indicators							
Expenditures on social security	% of total gov't exp.	..	..	..	..	..	..
Social security coverage	% econ. active pop.	..	..	..	..	..	..
Access to safe water: total	% of pop.	..	33.0	50.0	41.1	..	85.6
Urban	"	..	87.0	99.0	77.8	..	94.3
Rural	"	..	15.0	30.0	27.3	..	73.0
Access to health care	"	..	70.0	..	..	..	..

Population growth rate
(annual average, percent)

☐ Angola
— Lower-middle-income

GNP per capita growth rate
(annual average, percent)

Development diamond[b]

Life expectancy — GNP per capita — Gross primary enrollment — Access to safe water

— Angola
— Lower-middle-income

a. See the technical notes, p.389.   b. The development diamond, based on four key indicators, shows the average level of development in the country compared with its income group. See the introduction.

Angola

Indicator	Unit of measure	Latest single year 1970-75	Latest single year 1980-85	Most recent estimate 1987-92	Same region/income group Sub-Saharan Africa	Same region/income group Lower-middle-income	Next higher income group
Resources and Expenditures							
HUMAN RESOURCES							
Population (mre=1992)	thousands	6,110	7,976	9,732	546,390	942,547	477,960
Age dependency ratio	ratio	0.87	0.91	0.93	0.95	0.66	0.64
Urban	% of pop.	17.8	24.5	29.9	29.5	57.0	71.7
Population growth rate	annual %	2.5	2.7	2.8	2.9	1.4	1.6
Urban	"	5.7	5.6	5.4	5.1	4.8	2.5
Labor force (15-64)	thousands	2,957	3,719	4,261	224,025	..	181,414
Agriculture	% of labor force	76	74	..	..	..	..
Industry	"	9	10	..	..	..	..
Female	"	41	40	38	37	36	29
Females per 100 males							
Urban	number	..	..	..	..	..	..
Rural	"	..	..	..	..	..	..
NATURAL RESOURCES							
Area	thou. sq. km	1,246.70	1,246.70	1,246.70	24,274.03	40,697.37	21,836.02
Density	pop. per sq. km	4.9	6.4	7.6	21.9	22.8	21.5
Agricultural land	% of land area	26.0	26.0	26.0	52.7	..	41.7
Change in agricultural land	annual %	0.0	0.0	0.2	0.1	..	0.3
Agricultural land under irrigation	%	..	..	..	0.8	..	9.3
Forests and woodland	thou. sq. km	542	533	520	..	..	..
Deforestation (net)	annual %	..	..	0.7	..	..	..
INCOME							
Household income							
Share of top 20% of households	% of income	..	..	..	..	..	..
Share of bottom 40% of households	"	..	..	..	..	..	..
Share of bottom 20% of households	"	..	..	..	..	..	..
EXPENDITURE							
Food	% of GDP	..	..	50.6	..	..	..
Staples	"	..	..	19.9	..	..	..
Meat, fish, milk, cheese, eggs	"	..	..	15.6	..	..	..
Cereal imports	thou. metric tonnes	163	284	307	20,311	74,924	49,174
Food aid in cereals	"	..	84	145	4,303	4,054	282
Food production per capita	1987 = 100	117	89	78	90	..	109
Fertilizer consumption	kg/ha	0.1	0.6	0.2	4.2	..	68.8
Share of agriculture in GDP	% of GDP	..	14.4	12.9	18.6	..	8.1
Housing	% of GDP	..	..	8.1	..	..	..
Average household size	persons per household	..	..	..	..	..	..
Urban	"	..	..	..	..	..	..
Fixed investment: housing	% of GDP	..	..	3.9	..	..	..
Fuel and power	% of GDP	..	..	3.0	..	..	..
Energy consumption per capita	kg of oil equiv.	151	126	96	258	1,882	1,649
Households with electricity							
Urban	% of households	..	..	..	..	..	..
Rural	"	..	..	..	..	..	..
Transport and communication	% of GDP	..	..	3.3	..	..	..
Fixed investment: transport equipment	"	..	..	1.3	..	..	..
Total road length	thou. km	72	72	73	..	..	..
INVESTMENT IN HUMAN CAPITAL							
Health							
Population per physician	persons	8,597	16,141	..	..	..	..
Population per nurse	"	1,715	921	..	..	..	..
Population per hospital bed	"	368	..	771	1,329	516	385
Oral rehydration therapy (under-5)	% of cases	..	..	48	36	..	54
Education							
Gross enrollment ratio							
Secondary	% of school-age pop.	9	12	12	18	..	53
Female	"	8	..	..	14	..	..
Pupil-teacher ratio: primary	pupils per teacher	32	31	32	39	26	25
Pupil-teacher ratio: secondary	"	18	..	..	..	..	..
Pupils reaching grade 4	% of cohort	..	..	26	..	..	71
Repeater rate: primary	% of total enroll	..	36	..	..	..	11
Illiteracy	% of pop. (age 15+)	..	64	58	51	..	14
Female	% of fem. (age 15+)	..	77	72	62	..	17
Newspaper circulation	per thou. pop.	13	14	13	14	100	117

World Bank International Economics Department, April 1994

Antigua and Barbuda

Indicator	Unit of measure	Latest single year		Most recent estimate 1987-92	Same region/income group		Next higher income group
		1970-75	1980-85		Latin America Caribbean	Upper-middle-income	

Priority Poverty Indicators

Indicator	Unit of measure	1970-75	1980-85	1987-92	Latin America Caribbean	Upper-middle-income	Next higher income group
POVERTY							
Upper poverty line	local curr.	..	..	..	..	..	..
Headcount index	% of pop.	..	..	..	..	..	..
Lower poverty line	local curr.	..	..	..	..	..	..
Headcount index	% of pop.	..	..	..	..	..	..
GNP per capita	US$	..	3,520	5,980	2,690	3,870	21,960
SHORT TERM INCOME INDICATORS							
Unskilled urban wages	local curr.	..	..	..	..	..	..
Unskilled rural wages	"	..	..	..	..	..	..
Rural terms of trade	"	..	..	..	..	..	..
Consumer price index	1987=100	..	..	..	..	..	..
Lower income	"	..	..	..	..	..	..
Food[a]	"	..	96	129	..	..	..
Urban	"	..	..	..	..	..	..
Rural	"	..	..	..	..	..	..
SOCIAL INDICATORS							
Public expenditure on basic social services	% of GDP	..	..	..	..	..	..
Gross enrollment ratios							
Primary	% school age pop.	..	..	..	106	107	103
Male	"	..	..	..	..	..	103
Female	"	..	..	..	..	..	103
Mortality							
Infant mortality	per thou. live births	..	24.4	20.0	44.0	40.0	7.0
Under 5 mortality	"	..	..	24.5	56.0	51.0	10.0
Immunization							
Measles	% age group	..	73.0	89.0	78.9	82.0	82.4
DPT	"	..	94.0	99.0	73.8	73.8	90.1
Child malnutrition (under-5)	"	..	9.9	..	10.5	..	..
Life expectancy							
Total	years	67	72	74	68	69	77
Female advantage	"	3.8	3.9	5.6	5.6	6.3	6.4
Total fertility rate	births per woman	2.6	2.0	1.7	3.0	2.9	1.7
Maternal mortality rate	per 100,000 live births	..	..	..	..	..	..

Supplementary Poverty Indicators

Indicator	Unit of measure	1970-75	1980-85	1987-92	Latin America Caribbean	Upper-middle-income	Next higher income group
Expenditures on social security	% of total gov't exp.	..	..	..	..	..	..
Social security coverage	% econ. active pop.	..	..	..	..	..	..
Access to safe water: total	% of pop.	..	..	..	80.3	85.6	..
Urban	"	..	..	..	91.0	94.3	..
Rural	"	..	..	..	64.3	73.0	..
Access to health care	"	..	100.0	100.0	..	..	..

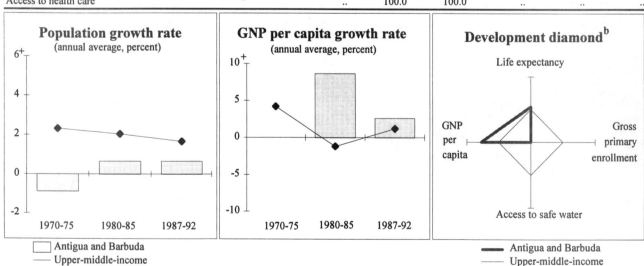

Population growth rate (annual average, percent)

☐ Antigua and Barbuda
— Upper-middle-income

GNP per capita growth rate (annual average, percent)

Development diamond[b]

Life expectancy

GNP per capita — Gross primary enrollment

Access to safe water

━━ Antigua and Barbuda
— Upper-middle-income

a. See the technical notes, p.389.   b. The development diamond, based on four key indicators, shows the average level of development in the country compared with its income group. See the introduction.

Antigua and Barbuda

Indicator	Unit of measure	Latest single year 1970-75	Latest single year 1980-85	Most recent estimate 1987-92	Same region/income group Latin America Caribbean	Same region/income group Upper-middle-income	Next higher income group
Resources and Expenditures							
HUMAN RESOURCES							
Population (mre=1992)	thousands	63	63	66	453,294	477,960	828,221
Age dependency ratio	ratio	..	0.97	0.68	0.67	0.64	0.50
Urban	% of pop.	30.8	30.8	33.0	72.9	71.7	78.1
Population growth rate	annual %	-1.2	0.6	0.8	1.7	1.6	0.7
Urban	"	-3.1	0.6	2.4	2.6	2.5	0.9
Labor force (15-64)	thousands	..	..	..	166,091	181,414	390,033
Agriculture	% of labor force	..	..	..	..	..	..
Industry	"	..	..	..	..	..	..
Female	"	..	..	..	27	29	38
Females per 100 males							
Urban	number	117	..	..	..	..	..
Rural	"	116	..	..	..	..	..
NATURAL RESOURCES							
Area	thou. sq. km	0.44	0.44	0.44	20,507.48	21,836.02	31,709.00
Density	pop. per sq. km	143.2	143.2	148.8	21.7	21.5	24.5
Agricultural land	% of land area	25.0	27.3	27.3	40.2	41.7	42.7
Change in agricultural land	annual %	0.0	0.0	0.0	0.5	0.3	-0.2
Agricultural land under irrigation	%	..	..	..	3.2	9.3	16.1
Forests and woodland	thou. sq. km	0	0	0	..	..	..
Deforestation (net)	annual %	..	..	..	..	..	..
INCOME							
Household income							
Share of top 20% of households	% of income	..	..	..	..	..	..
Share of bottom 40% of households	"	..	..	..	..	..	..
Share of bottom 20% of households	"	..	..	..	..	..	..
EXPENDITURE							
Food	% of GDP	..	..	..	..	..	..
Staples	"	..	..	..	..	..	..
Meat, fish, milk, cheese, eggs	"	..	..	..	..	..	..
Cereal imports	thou. metric tonnes	6	5	5	25,032	49,174	70,626
Food aid in cereals	"	..	0	0	1,779	282	2
Food production per capita	1987 = 100	79	120	101	104	109	101
Fertilizer consumption	kg/ha	..	..	..	15.5	68.8	162.1
Share of agriculture in GDP	% of GDP	..	4.3	3.5	8.9	8.1	2.4
Housing	% of GDP	..	..	..	..	..	..
Average household size	persons per household	4.3	..	..	..	..	..
Urban	"	..	..	..	..	..	..
Fixed investment: housing	% of GDP	..	..	..	..	..	..
Fuel and power	% of GDP	..	..	..	..	..	..
Energy consumption per capita	kg of oil equiv.	4,365	1,746	1,955	912	1,649	5,101
Households with electricity							
Urban	% of households	..	..	..	..	..	..
Rural	"	..	..	..	..	..	..
Transport and communication	% of GDP	..	..	..	..	..	..
Fixed investment: transport equipment	"	..	..	..	..	..	..
Total road length	thou. km	..	..	..	..	..	..
INVESTMENT IN HUMAN CAPITAL							
Health							
Population per physician	persons	2,863	..	..	..	..	..
Population per nurse	"	459	..	..	..	..	..
Population per hospital bed	"	153	..	..	508	385	144
Oral rehydration therapy (under-5)	% of cases	..	..	50	62	54	..
Education							
Gross enrollment ratio							
Secondary	% of school-age pop.	..	..	..	47	53	92
Female	"	..	..	..	..	..	94
Pupil-teacher ratio: primary	pupils per teacher	22	..	..	25	25	18
Pupil-teacher ratio: secondary	"	24	..	15	..	..	..
Pupils reaching grade 4	% of cohort	..	..	..	..	71	..
Repeater rate: primary	% of total enroll	2	..	..	14	11	..
Illiteracy	% of pop. (age 15+)	..	..	..	15	14	..
Female	% of fem. (age 15+)	..	..	..	17	17	..
Newspaper circulation	per thou. pop.	63	..	92	99	117	..

World Bank International Economics Department, April 1994

Argentina

Indicator	Unit of measure	Latest single year		Most recent estimate	Same region/income group		Next higher income group
		1970-75	1980-85	1987-92	Latin America Caribbean	Upper-middle-income	

Priority Poverty Indicators

Indicator	Unit of measure	1970-75	1980-85	1987-92	Latin America Caribbean	Upper-middle-income	Next higher income group
POVERTY							
Upper poverty line	local curr.	..	..	..	..	..	..
Headcount index	% of pop.	..	..	..	..	..	..
Lower poverty line	local curr.	..	..	..	..	..	..
Headcount index	% of pop.	..	..	..	..	..	..
GNP per capita	US$	2,470	3,150	6,050	2,690	3,870	21,960
SHORT TERM INCOME INDICATORS							
Unskilled urban wages	local curr.	..	..	..	..	..	..
Unskilled rural wages	"	..	..	..	..	..	..
Rural terms of trade	"	..	..	..	..	..	..
Consumer price index	1987=100	0	23	1,153,714	..	..	..
Lower income	"	..	..	..	..	..	..
Food[a]	"	..	22	1,045,281	..	..	..
Urban	"	..	..	..	..	..	..
Rural	"	..	..	..	..	..	..
SOCIAL INDICATORS							
Public expenditure on basic social services	% of GDP	..	15.6	16.3	..	..	..
Gross enrollment ratios							
Primary	% school age pop.	106	107	107	106	107	103
Male	"	106	107	107	..	..	103
Female	"	106	108	114	..	..	103
Mortality							
Infant mortality	per thou. live births	49.0	36.0	29.0	44.0	40.0	7.0
Under 5 mortality	"	..	..	35.8	56.0	51.0	10.0
Immunization							
Measles	% age group	..	90.0	99.0	78.9	82.0	82.4
DPT	"	..	66.0	84.0	73.8	73.8	90.1
Child malnutrition (under-5)	"	..	..	..	10.5	..	..
Life expectancy							
Total	years	67	70	71	68	69	77
Female advantage	"	6.6	6.7	6.7	5.6	6.3	6.4
Total fertility rate	births per woman	3.2	3.2	2.8	3.0	2.9	1.7
Maternal mortality rate	per 100,000 live births	..	85	140	..	..	..

Supplementary Poverty Indicators

Indicator	Unit of measure	1970-75	1980-85	1987-92	Latin America Caribbean	Upper-middle-income	Next higher income group
Expenditures on social security	% of total gov't exp.	..	35.6	35.0	..	..	..
Social security coverage	% econ. active pop.	..	79.1	..	..	..	..
Access to safe water: total	% of pop.	66.0	..	..	80.3	85.6	..
Urban	"	76.0	..	..	91.0	94.3	..
Rural	"	26.0	..	..	64.3	73.0	..
Access to health care	"	..	..	..	..	..	..

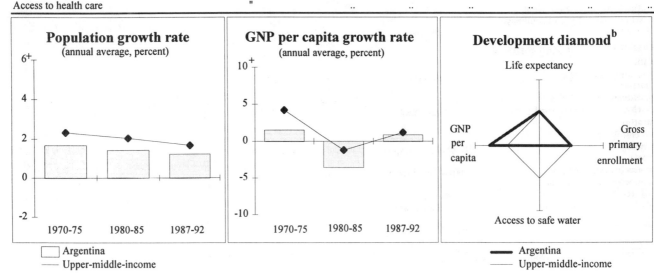

Population growth rate (annual average, percent)

GNP per capita growth rate (annual average, percent)

Development diamond[b]
Life expectancy — GNP per capita — Gross primary enrollment — Access to safe water

☐ Argentina
— Upper-middle-income

▬ Argentina
— Upper-middle-income

a. See the technical notes, p.389. b. The development diamond, based on four key indicators, shows the average level of development in the country compared with its income group. See the introduction.

Argentina

Indicator	Unit of measure	Latest single year 1970-75	Latest single year 1980-85	Most recent estimate 1987-92	Same region/income group Latin America Caribbean	Same region/income group Upper-middle-income	Next higher income group
Resources and Expenditures							
HUMAN RESOURCES							
Population (mre=1992)	thousands	26,052	30,331	33,101	453,294	477,960	828,221
Age dependency ratio	ratio	0.58	0.64	0.63	0.67	0.64	0.50
Urban	% of pop.	80.7	84.6	86.7	72.9	71.7	78.1
Population growth rate	annual %	1.7	1.4	1.2	1.7	1.6	0.7
Urban	"	2.3	1.8	1.5	2.6	2.5	0.9
Labor force (15-64)	thousands	9,891	10,884	11,910	166,091	181,414	390,033
Agriculture	% of labor force	15	13	..	..	..	..
Industry	"	34	34	..	..	..	..
Female	"	26	27	28	27	29	38
Females per 100 males							
Urban	number	..	104	..	..	..	..
Rural	"	..	80	..	..	..	..
NATURAL RESOURCES							
Area	thou. sq. km	2,766.89	2,766.89	2,766.89	20,507.48	21,836.02	31,709.00
Density	pop. per sq. km	9.4	11.0	11.8	21.7	21.5	24.5
Agricultural land	% of land area	62.3	62.1	61.9	40.2	41.7	42.7
Change in agricultural land	annual %	0.0	-0.1	-0.1	0.5	0.3	-0.2
Agricultural land under irrigation	%	0.8	1.0	1.0	3.2	9.3	16.1
Forests and woodland	thou. sq. km	603	597	591	..	..	..
Deforestation (net)	annual %	..	..	..	..	..	..
INCOME							
Household income							
Share of top 20% of households	% of income	50	47	51			
Share of bottom 40% of households	"	14	16	14	..	..	..
Share of bottom 20% of households	"	4	5	5	..	..	..
EXPENDITURE							
Food	% of GDP	..	23.1	..	..	..	..
Staples	"	..	2.6	..	..	..	..
Meat, fish, milk, cheese, eggs	"	..	8.4	..	..	..	..
Cereal imports	thou. metric tonnes	0	1	20	25,032	49,174	70,626
Food aid in cereals	"	..	..	..	1,779	282	2
Food production per capita	1987 = 100	90	100	97	104	109	101
Fertilizer consumption	kg/ha	0.4	1.0	1.0	15.5	68.8	162.1
Share of agriculture in GDP	% of GDP	6.4	7.6	6.0	8.9	8.1	2.4
Housing	% of GDP	..	6.5	..	..	..	..
Average household size	persons per household	3.8	..	..	..	..	..
Urban	"	..	..	..	..	..	..
Fixed investment: housing	% of GDP	..	6.2	..	..	..	..
Fuel and power	% of GDP	..	1.6	..	..	..	..
Energy consumption per capita	kg of oil equiv.	1,304	1,291	1,351	912	1,649	5,101
Households with electricity							
Urban	% of households	..	..	..	..	..	..
Rural	"	..	..	..	..	..	..
Transport and communication	% of GDP	..	8.6	..	..	..	..
Fixed investment: transport equipment	"	..	2.3	..	..	..	..
Total road length	thou. km	207	212	211	..	..	..
INVESTMENT IN HUMAN CAPITAL							
Health							
Population per physician	persons	535	370	..	..	..	..
Population per nurse	"	960	980	..	..	..	..
Population per hospital bed	"	179	..	216	508	385	144
Oral rehydration therapy (under-5)	% of cases	..	..	70	62	54	..
Education							
Gross enrollment ratio							
Secondary	% of school-age pop.	54	71	71	47	53	92
Female	"	57	75	74	..	..	94
Pupil-teacher ratio: primary	pupils per teacher	18	20	18	25	25	18
Pupil-teacher ratio: secondary	"	7	8	7	..	..	..
Pupils reaching grade 4	% of cohort	73	76	..	..	71	..
Repeater rate: primary	% of total enroll	9	..	..	14	11	..
Illiteracy	% of pop. (age 15+)	7	5	5	15	14	..
Female	% of fem. (age 15+)	..	6	5	17	17	..
Newspaper circulation	per thou. pop.	106	112	124	99	117	..

World Bank International Economics Department, April 1994

Armenia

| Indicator | Unit of measure | Latest single year | | Most recent estimate | Same region/income group | | Next higher income group |
		1970-75	1980-85	1987-92	Europe & Central Asia	Lower-middle-income	
Priority Poverty Indicators							
POVERTY							
Upper poverty line	local curr.	..	..	..	..	..	..
Headcount index	% of pop.	..	..	17	..	..	..
Lower poverty line	local curr.	..	..	..	..	..	..
Headcount index	% of pop.	..	..	11	..	..	..
GNP per capita	US$	..	..	780	..	..	3,870
SHORT TERM INCOME INDICATORS							
Unskilled urban wages	local curr.	..	..	..	..	..	..
Unskilled rural wages	"	..	..	..	..	..	..
Rural terms of trade	"	..	..	..	..	..	..
Consumer price index	1987=100	..	..	..	..	..	..
Lower income	"	..	..	..	..	..	..
Food[a]	"	..	..	..	..	..	..
Urban	"	..	..	..	..	..	..
Rural	"	..	..	..	..	..	..
SOCIAL INDICATORS							
Public expenditure on basic social services	% of GDP	..	..	8.0	..	..	..
Gross enrollment ratios							
Primary	% school age pop.	..	..	..	..	..	107
Male	"	..	..	..	..	..	..
Female	"	..	..	..	..	..	..
Mortality							
Infant mortality	per thou. live births	..	31.0	21.0	30.0	45.0	40.0
Under 5 mortality	"	..	..	25.2	38.0	59.0	51.0
Immunization							
Measles	% age group	..	..	..	..	..	82.0
DPT	"	..	..	..	..	..	73.8
Child malnutrition (under-5)	"	..	..	..	..	..	..
Life expectancy							
Total	years	..	73	70	70	68	69
Female advantage	"	..	5.2	5.9	8.6	6.4	6.3
Total fertility rate	births per woman	2.8	2.5	2.8	2.2	3.1	2.9
Maternal mortality rate	per 100,000 live births	..	27	35	58	..	..
Supplementary Poverty Indicators							
Expenditures on social security	% of total gov't exp.	..	..	..	..	..	..
Social security coverage	% econ. active pop.	..	..	..	..	..	..
Access to safe water: total	% of pop.	..	..	..	..	..	85.6
Urban	"	..	..	..	..	..	94.3
Rural	"	..	..	..	..	..	73.0
Access to health care	"	..	..	..	..	..	..

Population growth rate
(annual average, percent)

GNP per capita growth rate
(annual average, percent)

Development diamond[b]

Life expectancy

GNP per capita — Gross primary enrollment

Access to safe water

Armenia
Lower-middle-income

Armenia
Lower-middle-income

a. See the technical notes, p.389. b. The development diamond, based on four key indicators, shows the average level of development in the country compared with its income group. See the introduction.

Armenia

Indicator	Unit of measure	Latest single year 1970-75	Latest single year 1980-85	Most recent estimate 1987-92	Same region/income group Europe & Central Asia	Same region/income group Lower-middle-income	Next higher income group
Resources and Expenditures							
HUMAN RESOURCES							
Population (mre=1992)	thousands	2,826	3,339	3,677	495,241	942,547	477,960
Age dependency ratio	ratio	..	..	0.61	0.56	0.66	0.64
Urban	% of pop.	..	..	68.0	63.3	57.0	71.7
Population growth rate	annual %	..	1.4	1.8	0.5	1.4	1.6
Urban	"	..	..	..	..	4.8	2.5
Labor force (15-64)	thousands	..	..	..	..	..	181,414
Agriculture	% of labor force	..	..	..	..	..	..
Industry	"	..	..	..	..	..	..
Female	"	..	..	..	..	..	..
Females per 100 males		..	..	..	46	36	29
Urban	number	..	..	..	..	..	..
Rural	"	..	..	..	..	..	..
NATURAL RESOURCES							
Area	thou. sq. km	..	..	30.00	24,165.06	40,697.37	21,836.02
Density	pop. per sq. km	..	..	120.3	20.4	22.8	21.5
Agricultural land	% of land area	..	..	..	..	..	41.7
Change in agricultural land	annual %	..	..	..	..	..	0.3
Agricultural land under irrigation	%	..	..	..	..	..	9.3
Forests and woodland	thou. sq. km	..	..	..	..	..	..
Deforestation (net)	annual %	..	..	..	..	..	..
INCOME							
Household income							
Share of top 20% of households	% of income	..	..	..	..	..	..
Share of bottom 40% of households	"	..	..	..	..	..	..
Share of bottom 20% of households	"	..	..	..	..	..	..
EXPENDITURE							
Food	% of GDP	..	..	19.8	..	..	..
Staples	"	..	..	3.6	..	..	..
Meat, fish, milk, cheese, eggs	"	..	..	8.9	..	..	..
Cereal imports	thou. metric tonnes	..	..	400	45,972	74,924	49,174
Food aid in cereals	"	..	..	3	1,639	4,054	282
Food production per capita	1987 = 100	..	..	..	..	..	109
Fertilizer consumption	kg/ha	..	..	..	..	..	68.8
Share of agriculture in GDP	% of GDP	..	14.7	20.0	..	..	8.1
Housing	% of GDP	..	..	4.7	..	..	..
Average household size	persons per household	..	..	4.7	..	..	..
Urban	"	..	..	..	..	..	..
Fixed investment: housing	% of GDP	..	..	4.9	..	..	..
Fuel and power	% of GDP	..	..	1.0	..	..	..
Energy consumption per capita	kg of oil equiv.	..	..	..	3,190	1,882	1,649
Households with electricity							
Urban	% of households	..	..	..	..	..	..
Rural	"	..	..	..	..	..	..
Transport and communication	% of GDP	..	..	6.2	..	..	..
Fixed investment: transport equipment	"	..	..	10.3	..	..	..
Total road length	thou. km	..	9	12	..	..	..
INVESTMENT IN HUMAN CAPITAL							
Health							
Population per physician	persons	..	..	264	378	..	..
Population per nurse	"	..	..	..	..	..	..
Population per hospital bed	"	..	..	120	134	516	385
Oral rehydration therapy (under-5)	% of cases	..	..	..	..	..	54
Education							
Gross enrollment ratio							
Secondary	% of school-age pop.	..	..	..	..	..	53
Female	"	..	..	..	..	..	..
Pupil-teacher ratio: primary	pupils per teacher	..	..	..	..	26	25
Pupil-teacher ratio: secondary	"	..	..	..	..	..	..
Pupils reaching grade 4	% of cohort	..	..	..	..	..	71
Repeater rate: primary	% of total enroll	..	..	..	..	..	11
Illiteracy	% of pop. (age 15+)	..	..	..	..	..	14
Female	% of fem. (age 15+)	..	..	..	..	..	17
Newspaper circulation	per thou. pop.	..	..	..	..	100	117

World Bank International Economics Department, April 1994

15

Australia

Indicator	Unit of measure	Latest single year		Most recent estimate 1987-92	Same region/income group High-income
		1970-75	1980-85		
Priority Poverty Indicators					
POVERTY					
Upper poverty line	local curr.	..	..	..	..
Headcount index	% of pop.	..	..	..	..
Lower poverty line	local curr.	..	..	..	..
Headcount index	% of pop.	..	..	..	..
GNP per capita	US$	7,120	11,760	17,260	21,960
SHORT TERM INCOME INDICATORS					
Unskilled urban wages	local curr.	..	..	..	..
Unskilled rural wages	"	..	..	..	..
Rural terms of trade	"	..	..	..	..
Consumer price index	1987=100	34	85	129	..
Lower income	"	..	..		
Food[a]	"	22	87	129	..
Urban	"	..	..	..	..
Rural	"	..	..	..	..
SOCIAL INDICATORS					
Public expenditure on basic social services	% of GDP	..	..	..	..
Gross enrollment ratios					
Primary	% school age pop.	107	106	107	103
Male	"	107	107	107	103
Female	"	107	105	107	103
Mortality					
Infant mortality	per thou. live births	14.2	9.9	7.0	7.0
Under 5 mortality	"	..	..	9.0	10.0
Immunization					
Measles	% age group	..	68.0	68.0	82.4
DPT	"	..	..	90.0	90.1
Child malnutrition (under-5)	"	..	..	..	..
Life expectancy					
Total	years	72	75	77	77
Female advantage	"	6.8	6.6	6.3	6.4
Total fertility rate	births per woman	2.2	2.0	1.9	1.7
Maternal mortality rate	per 100,000 live births	..	11	..	..
Supplementary Poverty Indicators					
Expenditures on social security	% of total gov't exp.	22.4	25.7	27.5	..
Social security coverage	% econ. active pop.	..	..	..	..
Access to safe water: total	% of pop.	..	..	..	..
Urban	"	..	..	..	..
Rural	"	..	..	..	..
Access to health care	"	..	98.6	100.0	..

Population growth rate
(annual average, percent)

□ Australia
— High-income

GNP per capita growth rate
(annual average, percent)

Development diamond[b]

—— Australia
— High-income

a. See the technical notes, p.389. b. The development diamond, based on four key indicators, shows the average level of development in the country compared with its income group. See the introduction.

Australia

Indicator	Unit of measure	Latest single year		Most recent estimate 1987-92	Same region/income group
		1970-75	1980-85		High-income

Resources and Expenditures

HUMAN RESOURCES

Indicator	Unit of measure	1970-75	1980-85	1987-92	High-income
Population (mre=1992)	thousands	13,893	15,758	17,483	828,221
Age dependency ratio	ratio	0.57	0.51	0.50	0.50
Urban	% of pop.	85.9	85.5	85.5	78.1
Population growth rate	annual %	1.2	1.4	1.1	0.7
Urban	"	1.4	1.3	1.5	0.9
Labor force (15-64)	thousands	5,993	7,364	8,169	390,033
Agriculture	% of labor force	7	7	..	..
Industry	"	34	32	..	..
Female	"	34	38	38	38
Females per 100 males					
Urban	number	99	100	..	..
Rural	"	83	87	..	..

NATURAL RESOURCES

Indicator	Unit of measure	1970-75	1980-85	1987-92	High-income
Area	thou. sq. km	7,713.36	7,713.36	7,713.36	31,709.00
Density	pop. per sq. km	1.8	2.0	2.2	24.5
Agricultural land	% of land area	63.1	61.3	60.0	42.7
Change in agricultural land	annual %	-0.2	0.0	-0.9	-0.2
Agricultural land under irrigation	%	0.3	0.4	0.4	16.1
Forests and woodland	thou. sq. km	1,377	1,060	1,060	..
Deforestation (net)	annual %	..	..	0.0	..

INCOME

Indicator	Unit of measure	1970-75	1980-85	1987-92	High-income
Household income					
Share of top 20% of households	% of income	..	42	..	..
Share of bottom 40% of households	"	..	16	..	..
Share of bottom 20% of households	"	..	4	..	..

EXPENDITURE

Indicator	Unit of measure	1970-75	1980-85	1987-92	High-income
Food	% of GDP	..	8.3	..	..
Staples	"	..	1.2	..	..
Meat, fish, milk, cheese, eggs	"	..	3.6	..	..
Cereal imports	thou. metric tonnes	4	25	33	70,626
Food aid in cereals	"	..	..	..	2
Food production per capita	1987 = 100	97	96	99	101
Fertilizer consumption	kg/ha	1.5	2.4	2.8	162.1
Share of agriculture in GDP	% of GDP	5.0	4.0	3.0	2.4
Housing	% of GDP	..	13.7	..	..
Average household size	persons per household	3.3	3.0	..	..
Urban	"	3.3	2.9	..	..
Fixed investment: housing	% of GDP	24.5	5.3	..	..
Fuel and power	% of GDP	..	1.4	..	..
Energy consumption per capita	kg of oil equiv.	4,393	4,691	5,263	5,101
Households with electricity					
Urban	% of households	98.9	..	..	..
Rural	"	95.1	..	..	..
Transport and communication	% of GDP	..	8.7	..	..
Fixed investment: transport equipment	"	..	4.2	..	..
Total road length	thou. km	845	797	799	..

INVESTMENT IN HUMAN CAPITAL

Indicator	Unit of measure	1970-75	1980-85	1987-92	High-income
Health					
Population per physician	persons	834	524	..	..
Population per nurse	"	..	140	..	..
Population per hospital bed	"	83	..	183	144
Oral rehydration therapy (under-5)	% of cases	..	..	..	..
Education					
Gross enrollment ratio					
Secondary	% of school-age pop.	87	79	82	92
Female	"	87	80	83	94
Pupil-teacher ratio: primary	pupils per teacher	21	16	17	18
Pupil-teacher ratio: secondary	"	15	12	13	..
Pupils reaching grade 4	% of cohort	76	96	100	..
Repeater rate: primary	% of total enroll	..	..	..	..
Illiteracy	% of pop. (age 15+)	..	..	†	..
Female	% of fem. (age 15+)	..	..	†	..
Newspaper circulation	per thou. pop.	383	295	246	..

World Bank International Economics Department, April 1994

17

Austria

Indicator	Unit of measure	Latest single year 1970-75	1980-85	Most recent estimate 1987-92	Same region/income group High-income
Priority Poverty Indicators					
POVERTY					
Upper poverty line	local curr.	..	..	..	..
Headcount index	% of pop.	..	..	..	..
Lower poverty line	local curr.	..	..	..	..
Headcount index	% of pop.	..	..	..	..
GNP per capita	US$	4,730	9,100	22,380	21,960
SHORT TERM INCOME INDICATORS					
Unskilled urban wages	local curr.	..	..	..	..
Unskilled rural wages	"	..	..	..	..
Rural terms of trade	"	..	..	..	..
Consumer price index	1987=100	59	97	116	..
Lower income	"	..	..	..	..
Food[a]	"	47	97	114	..
Urban	"	..	..	..	..
Rural	"	..	..	..	..
SOCIAL INDICATORS					
Public expenditure on basic social services	% of GDP	..	..	..	..
Gross enrollment ratios					
Primary	% school age pop.	102	100	103	103
Male	"	102	101	103	103
Female	"	101	99	102	103
Mortality					
Infant mortality	per thou. live births	20.5	11.2	7.4	7.0
Under 5 mortality	"	..	..	9.6	10.0
Immunization					
Measles	% age group	..	90.0	60.0	82.4
DPT	"	..	90.0	90.0	90.1
Child malnutrition (under-5)	"	..	..	..	..
Life expectancy					
Total	years	71	73	77	77
Female advantage	"	7.3	7.2	7.1	6.4
Total fertility rate	births per woman	1.8	1.5	1.6	1.7
Maternal mortality rate	per 100,000 live births	..	11		..
Supplementary Poverty Indicators					
Expenditures on social security	% of total gov't exp.	..	..	..	..
Social security coverage	% econ. active pop.	..	..	..	..
Access to safe water: total	% of pop.	..	..	..	..
Urban	"	..	..	..	..
Rural	"	..	..	..	..
Access to health care	"	..	..	100.0	..

Population growth rate
(annual average, percent)

GNP per capita growth rate
(annual average, percent)

Development diamond[b]

□ Austria
— High-income

— Austria
High-income

a. See the technical notes, p.389.   b. The development diamond, based on four key indicators, shows the average level of development in the country compared with its income group. See the introduction.

Austria

Indicator	Unit of measure	Latest single year		Most recent estimate 1987-92	Same region/income group
		1970-75	1980-85		High-income

Resources and Expenditures

Indicator	Unit of measure	1970-75	1980-85	1987-92	High-income
HUMAN RESOURCES					
Population (mre=1992)	thousands	7,556	7,555	7,883	828,221
Age dependency ratio	ratio	0.62	0.48	0.50	0.50
Urban	% of pop.	53.2	56.4	59.3	78.1
Population growth rate	annual %	-0.1	0.0	0.8	0.7
Urban	"	0.5	0.6	1.5	0.9
Labor force (15-64)	thousands	3,198	3,504	3,573	390,033
Agriculture	% of labor force	12	9	..	..
Industry	"	42	41	..	..
Female	"	40	40	40	38
Females per 100 males					
Urban	number	116	109	..	..
Rural	"	106	100	..	..
NATURAL RESOURCES					
Area	thou. sq. km	83.85	83.85	83.85	31,709.00
Density	pop. per sq. km	90.1	90.1	93.3	24.5
Agricultural land	% of land area	45.8	42.4	42.5	42.7
Change in agricultural land	annual %	-0.1	0.1	0.5	-0.2
Agricultural land under irrigation	%	0.1	0.1	0.1	16.1
Forests and woodland	thou. sq. km	33	32	32	..
Deforestation (net)	annual %	..	..	-0.5	..
INCOME					
Household income					
Share of top 20% of households	% of income	..	..	..	..
Share of bottom 40% of households	"	..	..	..	..
Share of bottom 20% of households	"	..	..	..	..
EXPENDITURE					
Food	% of GDP	11.4	10.3	..	..
Staples	"	1.8	1.6	..	..
Meat, fish, milk, cheese, eggs	"	5.5	4.8	..	..
Cereal imports	thou. metric tonnes	146	107	100	70,626
Food aid in cereals	"	..	..	..	2
Food production per capita	1987 = 100	94	106	100	101
Fertilizer consumption	kg/ha	82.6	110.6	84.4	162.1
Share of agriculture in GDP	% of GDP	5.0	3.3	2.8	2.4
Housing	% of GDP	7.7	11.1	..	..
Average household size	persons per household	2.9	..	..	..
Urban	"	..	..	..	..
Fixed investment: housing	% of GDP	5.9	2.5	..	..
Fuel and power	% of GDP	2.4	3.3	..	..
Energy consumption per capita	kg of oil equiv.	2,698	3,072	3,266	5,101
Households with electricity					
Urban	% of households	..	..	..	..
Rural	"	..	..	..	..
Transport and communication	% of GDP	8.5	10.0	..	..
Fixed investment: transport equipment	"	1.7	1.9	..	..
Total road length	thou. km	103	107	125	..
INVESTMENT IN HUMAN CAPITAL					
Health					
Population per physician	persons	543	388	231	..
Population per nurse	"	303	184	..	..
Population per hospital bed	"	92	90	94	144
Oral rehydration therapy (under-5)	% of cases	..	..	..	..
Education					
Gross enrollment ratio					
Secondary	% of school-age pop.	74	78	104	92
Female	"	76	80	100	94
Pupil-teacher ratio: primary	pupils per teacher	19	10	11	18
Pupil-teacher ratio: secondary	"	17	10	8	..
Pupils reaching grade 4	% of cohort	94	99	98	..
Repeater rate: primary	% of total enroll	5	..	..	..
Illiteracy	% of pop. (age 15+)	..	..	..	..
Female	% of fem. (age 15+)	..	..	..	..
Newspaper circulation	per thou. pop.	318	351	351	..

World Bank International Economics Department, April 1994

Azerbaijan

| Indicator | Unit of measure | Latest single year | | Most recent estimate 1987-92 | Same region/income group | | Next higher income group |
		1970-75	1980-85		Europe & Central Asia	Lower-middle-income	
Priority Poverty Indicators							
POVERTY							
Upper poverty line	local curr.	..	..	..	..	..	..
Headcount index	% of pop.	..	..	49	..	..	..
Lower poverty line	local curr.	..	..	..	..	..	..
Headcount index	% of pop.	..	..	30	..	..	..
GNP per capita	US$	..	..	740	..	..	3,870
SHORT TERM INCOME INDICATORS							
Unskilled urban wages	local curr.	..	..	..	..	..	..
Unskilled rural wages	"	..	..	..	..	..	..
Rural terms of trade	"	..	..	..	..	..	..
Consumer price index	1987=100	..	..	..	..	..	..
Lower income	"	..	..	..	..	..	..
Food[a]	"	..	..	..	..	..	..
Urban	"	..	..	..	..	..	..
Rural	"	..	..	..	..	..	..
SOCIAL INDICATORS							
Public expenditure on basic social services	% of GDP	..	..	8.0	..	..	..
Gross enrollment ratios							
Primary	% school age pop.	..	..	..	..	..	107
Male	"	..	..	..	..	..	..
Female	"	..	..	..	..	..	..
Mortality							
Infant mortality	per thou. live births	..	43.0	32.0	30.0	45.0	40.0
Under 5 mortality	"	..	..	39.0	38.0	59.0	51.0
Immunization							
Measles	% age group	..	..	..	..	..	82.0
DPT	"	..	..	..	..	..	73.8
Child malnutrition (under-5)	"	..	..	..	..	..	..
Life expectancy							
Total	years	..	69	71	70	68	69
Female advantage	"	..	7.7	8.0	8.6	6.4	6.3
Total fertility rate	births per woman	3.9	2.9	2.7	2.2	3.1	2.9
Maternal mortality rate	per 100,000 live births	..	39	29	58	..	..
Supplementary Poverty Indicators							
Expenditures on social security	% of total gov't exp.	..	..	..	..	..	..
Social security coverage	% econ. active pop.	..	..	..	..	..	..
Access to safe water: total	% of pop.	..	..	..	..	..	85.6
Urban	"	..	..	..	..	..	94.3
Rural	"	..	..	..	..	..	73.0
Access to health care	"	..	..	..	..	..	..

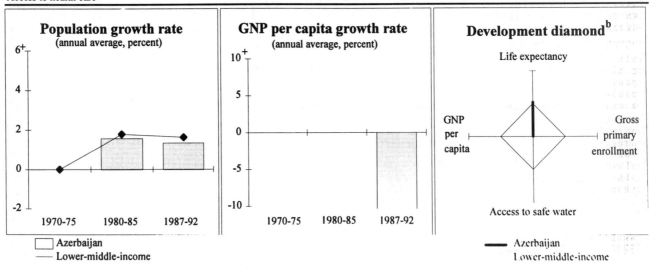

Population growth rate (annual average, percent)

☐ Azerbaijan
— Lower-middle-income

GNP per capita growth rate (annual average, percent)

Development diamond[b]

Life expectancy

GNP per capita — Gross primary enrollment

Access to safe water

— Azerbaijan
— Lower-middle-income

a. See the technical notes, p.389.   b. The development diamond, based on four key indicators, shows the average level of development in the country compared with its income group. See the introduction

Azerbaijan

Indicator	Unit of measure	Latest single year 1970-75	Latest single year 1980-85	Most recent estimate 1987-92	Same region/income group Europe & Central Asia	Same region/income group Lower-middle-income	Next higher income group
Resources and Expenditures							
HUMAN RESOURCES							
Population (mre=1992)	thousands	..	6,669	7,370	495,241	942,547	477,960
Age dependency ratio	ratio	..	..	0.65	0.56	0.66	0.64
Urban	% of pop.	..	..	54.0	63.3	57.0	71.7
Population growth rate	annual %	..	1.6	1.8	0.5	1.4	1.6
Urban	"	..	..	..	..	4.8	2.5
Labor force (15-64)	thousands	..	3,816	3,986	..	..	181,414
Agriculture	% of labor force	..	..	14	..	..	..
Industry	"	..	..	11	..	..	..
Female	"	..	..	..	46	36	29
Females per 100 males							
Urban	number	..	..	..	..	..	..
Rural	"	..	..	..	..	..	..
NATURAL RESOURCES							
Area	thou. sq. km	..	..	86.60	24,165.06	40,697.37	21,836.02
Density	pop. per sq. km	..	..	83.6	20.4	22.8	21.5
Agricultural land	% of land area	..	..	..	..	..	41.7
Change in agricultural land	annual %	..	..	..	..	..	0.3
Agricultural land under irrigation	%	..	..	..	..	..	9.3
Forests and woodland	thou. sq. km	..	..	..	..	..	..
Deforestation (net)	annual %	..	..	..	..	..	..
INCOME							
Household income							
Share of top 20% of households	% of income	..	..	..	..	..	..
Share of bottom 40% of households	"	..	..	..	..	..	..
Share of bottom 20% of households	"	..	..	..	..	..	..
EXPENDITURE							
Food	% of GDP	..	..	19.8	..	..	..
Staples	"	..	..	3.6	..	..	..
Meat, fish, milk, cheese, eggs	"	..	..	8.9	..	..	..
Cereal imports	thou. metric tonnes	..	..	200	45,972	74,924	49,174
Food aid in cereals	"	..	..	..	1,639	4,054	282
Food production per capita	1987 = 100	..	..	..	..	..	109
Fertilizer consumption	kg/ha	..	..	..	..	..	68.8
Share of agriculture in GDP	% of GDP	..	24.3	31.0	..	..	8.1
Housing	% of GDP	..	..	4.7	..	..	..
Average household size	persons per household	..	..	4.8	..	..	..
Urban	"	..	..	..	..	..	..
Fixed investment: housing	% of GDP	..	..	4.9	..	..	..
Fuel and power	% of GDP	..	..	1.0	..	..	..
Energy consumption per capita	kg of oil equiv.	..	..	..	3,190	1,882	1,649
Households with electricity							
Urban	% of households	..	..	..	..	..	..
Rural	"	..	..	..	..	..	..
Transport and communication	% of GDP	..	..	6.2	..	..	..
Fixed investment: transport equipment	"	..	..	10.3	..	..	..
Total road length	thou. km	..	26	30	..	..	..
INVESTMENT IN HUMAN CAPITAL							
Health							
Population per physician	persons	..	..	254	378	..	..
Population per nurse	"	..	..	..	..	..	..
Population per hospital bed	"	..	..	101	134	516	385
Oral rehydration therapy (under-5)	% of cases	..	..	..	..	..	54
Education							
Gross enrollment ratio							
Secondary	% of school-age pop.	..	..	..	..	..	53
Female	"	..	..	..	..	..	..
Pupil-teacher ratio: primary	pupils per teacher	..	..	..	..	26	25
Pupil-teacher ratio: secondary	"	..	..	..	..	..	..
Pupils reaching grade 4	% of cohort	..	..	..	..	..	71
Repeater rate: primary	% of total enroll	..	..	..	..	..	11
Illiteracy	% of pop. (age 15+)	..	..	..	..	..	14
Female	% of fem. (age 15+)	..	..	..	..	..	17
Newspaper circulation	per thou. pop.	..	..	..	..	100	117

World Bank International Economics Department, April 1994

The Bahamas

Indicator	Unit of measure	Latest single year		Most recent estimate 1987-92	Same region/income group High-income
		1970-75	1980-85		

Priority Poverty Indicators section

Priority Poverty Indicators

Indicator	Unit of measure	1970-75	1980-85	1987-92	High-income
POVERTY					
Upper poverty line	local curr.	..	..	..	..
Headcount index	% of pop.	..	..	..	..
Lower poverty line	local curr.	..	..	..	..
Headcount index	% of pop.	..	..	..	..
GNP per capita	US$	2,720	9,010	12,070	21,960
SHORT TERM INCOME INDICATORS					
Unskilled urban wages	local curr.	..	..	..	..
Unskilled rural wages	"	..	..	..	..
Rural terms of trade	"	..	..	..	..
Consumer price index	1987=100	48	90	130	..
Lower income	"	..	..	..	..
Food[a]	"	39	85	134	..
Urban	"	..	..	..	..
Rural	"	..	..	..	..
SOCIAL INDICATORS					
Public expenditure on basic social services	% of GDP	..	..	..	..
Gross enrollment ratios					
Primary	% school age pop.	..	..	99	103
Male	"	..	..	..	103
Female	"	..	..	..	103
Mortality					
Infant mortality	per thou. live births	34.2	26.7	25.0	7.0
Under 5 mortality	"	..	..	30.6	10.0
Immunization					
Measles	% age group	..	62.0	87.0	82.4
DPT	"	..	62.0	86.0	90.1
Child malnutrition (under-5)	"	..	..	..	..
Life expectancy					
Total	years	66	70	72	77
Female advantage	"	6.7	7.5	7.1	6.4
Total fertility rate	births per woman	3.4	3.2	2.1	1.7
Maternal mortality rate	per 100,000 live births	..	38	69	..

Supplementary Poverty Indicators

Indicator	Unit of measure	1970-75	1980-85	1987-92	High-income
Expenditures on social security	% of total gov't exp.	6.4	10.9	..	..
Social security coverage	% econ. active pop.	..	..	85.9	..
Access to safe water: total	% of pop.	65.0	..	90.0	..
Urban	"	100.0	100.0	98.0	..
Rural	"	13.0	..	75.0	..
Access to health care	"	..	100.0	100.0	..

Population growth rate
(annual average, percent)

The Bahamas
High-income

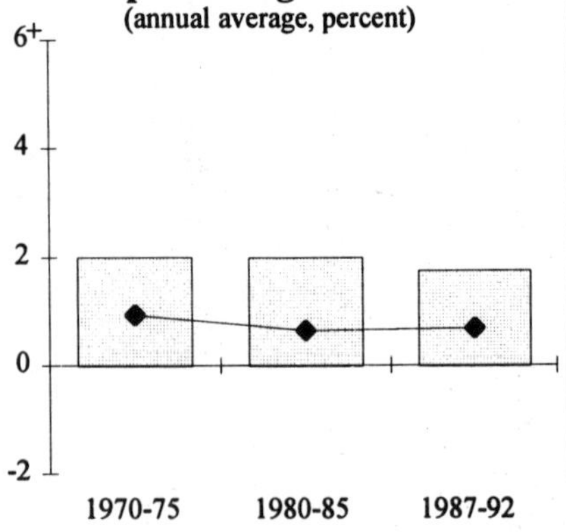

GNP per capita growth rate
(annual average, percent)

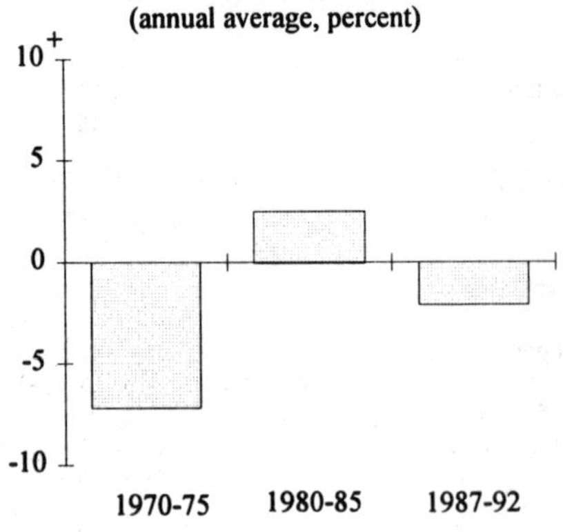

Development diamond[b]

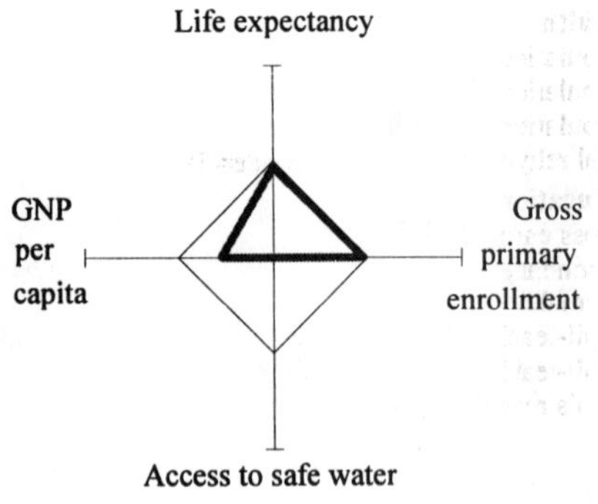

The Bahamas
High-income

a. See the technical notes, p.389.   b. The development diamond, based on four key indicators, shows the average level of development in the country compared with its income group. See the introduction.

22

The Bahamas

Indicator	Unit of measure	Latest single year 1970-75	Latest single year 1980-85	Most recent estimate 1987-92	Same region/income group High-income
Resources and Expenditures					
HUMAN RESOURCES					
Population (mre=1992)	thousands	189	232	262	828,221
Age dependency ratio	ratio	..	0.71	0.53	0.50
Urban	% of pop.	59.3	62.3	65.2	78.1
Population growth rate	annual %	2.1	1.3	1.2	0.7
Urban	"	2.6	1.9	1.9	0.9
Labor force (15-64)	thousands	..	..	..	390,033
Agriculture	% of labor force	..	..	..	..
Industry	"	..	..	..	..
Female	"	..	..	..	38
Females per 100 males					
Urban	number	..	..	..	..
Rural	"	..	..	..	..
NATURAL RESOURCES					
Area	thou. sq. km	13.88	13.88	13.88	31,709.00
Density	pop. per sq. km	13.6	16.7	18.7	24.5
Agricultural land	% of land area	1.0	1.2	1.2	42.7
Change in agricultural land	annual %	0.0	9.1	0.0	-0.2
Agricultural land under irrigation	%	..	..	..	16.1
Forests and woodland	thou. sq. km	3	3	3	..
Deforestation (net)	annual %	..	..	..	..
INCOME					
Household income					
Share of top 20% of households	% of income	51	..	..	..
Share of bottom 40% of households	"	12	..	..	..
Share of bottom 20% of households	"	3	..	..	..
EXPENDITURE					
Food	% of GDP	..	7.4	..	..
Staples	"	..	1.3	..	..
Meat, fish, milk, cheese, eggs	"	..	2.8	..	..
Cereal imports	thou. metric tonnes	14	20	14	70,626
Food aid in cereals	"	..	..	..	2
Food production per capita	1987 = 100	86	94	79	101
Fertilizer consumption	kg/ha	114.1	41.7	25.0	162.1
Share of agriculture in GDP	% of GDP	..	1.9	1.8	2.4
Housing	% of GDP	..	13.8	..	..
Average household size	persons per household	4.1	..	..	..
Urban	"	..	..	..	..
Fixed investment: housing	% of GDP	..	4.8	..	..
Fuel and power	% of GDP	..	2.9	..	..
Energy consumption per capita	kg of oil equiv.	9,233	6,586	6,985	5,101
Households with electricity					
Urban	% of households	..	..	..	..
Rural	"	..	..	..	..
Transport and communication	% of GDP	..	10.2	..	..
Fixed investment: transport equipment	"	..	2.9	..	..
Total road length	thou. km	..	..	..	..
INVESTMENT IN HUMAN CAPITAL					
Health					
Population per physician	persons	1,315	1,060	773	..
Population per nurse	"	263	206	209	..
Population per hospital bed	"	196	227	..	144
Oral rehydration therapy (under-5)	% of cases	..	..	45	..
Education					
Gross enrollment ratio					
Secondary	% of school-age pop.	..	..	93	92
Female	"	..	..	..	94
Pupil-teacher ratio: primary	pupils per teacher	25	19	..	18
Pupil-teacher ratio: secondary	"	37	19	..	..
Pupils reaching grade 4	% of cohort	..	..	84	..
Repeater rate: primary	% of total enroll	..	..	..	..
Illiteracy	% of pop. (age 15+)	..	..	..	..
Female	% of fem. (age 15+)	..	..	..	..
Newspaper circulation	per thou. pop.	164	144	137	..

World Bank International Economics Department, April 1994

Bahrain

Indicator	Unit of measure	Latest single year 1970-75	Latest single year 1980-85	Most recent estimate 1987-92	Same region/income group Mid-East & North Africa	Same region/income group Upper-middle-income	Next higher income group
Priority Poverty Indicators							
POVERTY							
Upper poverty line	local curr.	..	..	..	..	..	..
Headcount index	% of pop.	..	..	..	..	..	..
Lower poverty line	local curr.	..	..	..	..	..	..
Headcount index	% of pop.	..	..	..	..	..	..
GNP per capita	US$	..	8,260	7,150	1,950	3,870	21,960
SHORT TERM INCOME INDICATORS							
Unskilled urban wages	local curr.	..	..	..	..	..	..
Unskilled rural wages	"	..	..	..	..	..	..
Rural terms of trade	"	..	..	..	..	..	..
Consumer price index	1987=100	48	104	103	..	..	..
Lower income	"	..	..	..	..	..	..
Food[a]	"	..	105	102	..	..	..
Urban	"	..	..	..	..	..	..
Rural	"	..	..	..	..	..	..
SOCIAL INDICATORS							
Public expenditure on basic social services	% of GDP	..	..	..	..	..	..
Gross enrollment ratios							
Primary	% school age pop.	96	112	95	100	107	103
Male	"	107	113	95	107	..	103
Female	"	85	110	95	88	..	103
Mortality							
Infant mortality	per thou. live births	55.0	36.0	21.0	58.0	40.0	7.0
Under 5 mortality	"	..	..	36.3	78.0	51.0	10.0
Immunization							
Measles	% age group	..	50.0	85.0	81.8	82.0	82.4
DPT	"	..	64.0	97.0	83.9	73.8	90.1
Child malnutrition (under-5)	"	..	..	..	20.9	..	..
Life expectancy							
Total	years	64	67	70	64	69	77
Female advantage	"	3.7	2.5	2.9	2.4	6.3	6.4
Total fertility rate	births per woman	6.2	4.9	3.7	4.9	2.9	1.7
Maternal mortality rate	per 100,000 live births	..	34		..	..	..
Supplementary Poverty Indicators							
Expenditures on social security	% of total gov't exp.	..	..	..	..	..	..
Social security coverage	% econ. active pop.	..	..	..	..	..	..
Access to safe water: total	% of pop.	100.0	100.0	100.0	85.0	85.6	..
Urban	"	100.0	100.0	100.0	97.0	94.3	..
Rural	"	100.0	100.0	100.0	70.1	73.0	..
Access to health care	"	..	100.0	100.0	84.6	..	..

Population growth rate
(annual average, percent)

Bahrain
Upper-middle-income

GNP per capita growth rate
(annual average, percent)

Development diamond[b]

Bahrain
Upper-middle-income

a. See the technical notes, p.389.   b. The development diamond, based on four key indicators, shows the average level of development in the country compared with its income group. See the introduction.

Bahrain

Indicator	Unit of measure	Latest single year 1970-75	Latest single year 1980-85	Most recent estimate 1987-92	Mid-East & North Africa	Upper-middle-income	Next higher income group
Resources and Expenditures							
HUMAN RESOURCES							
Population (mre=1992)	thousands	262	425	530	252,555	477,960	828,221
Age dependency ratio	ratio	0.83	0.55	0.65	0.87	0.64	0.50
Urban	% of pop.	79.2	81.7	83.5	54.7	71.7	78.1
Population growth rate	annual %	4.7	4.3	2.7	2.8	1.6	0.7
Urban	"	4.8	4.6	3.0	3.8	2.5	0.9
Labor force (15-64)	thousands	81	181	236	69,280	181,414	390,033
Agriculture	% of labor force	5	3	..	..	..	..
Industry	"	36	35	..	..	..	..
Female	"	9	11	10	15	29	38
Females per 100 males							
Urban	number	72	..	..	..	..	..
Rural	"	93	..	..	..	..	..
NATURAL RESOURCES							
Area	thou. sq. km	0.68	0.68	0.68	10,487.21	21,836.02	31,709.00
Density	pop. per sq. km	385.3	625.0	758.8	23.4	21.5	24.5
Agricultural land	% of land area	8.8	8.8	8.8	30.2	41.7	42.7
Change in agricultural land	annual %	0.0	0.0	0.0	0.5	0.3	-0.2
Agricultural land under irrigation	%	16.7	16.7	16.7	31.0	9.3	16.1
Forests and woodland	thou. sq. km	..	..	..	..	..	..
Deforestation (net)	annual %	..	..	..	..	..	..
INCOME							
Household income							
Share of top 20% of households	% of income	..	..	..	..	..	..
Share of bottom 40% of households	"	..	..	..	..	..	..
Share of bottom 20% of households	"	..	..	..	..	..	..
EXPENDITURE							
Food	% of GDP	..	..	..	..	..	..
Staples	"	..	..	..	..	..	..
Meat, fish, milk, cheese, eggs	"	..	..	..	..	..	..
Cereal imports	thou. metric tonnes	30	86	108	38,007	49,174	70,626
Food aid in cereals	"	..	..	..	2,484	282	2
Food production per capita	1987 = 100	..	..	..	116	109	101
Fertilizer consumption	kg/ha	3.8	80.0	116.7	96.7	68.8	162.1
Share of agriculture in GDP	% of GDP	..	1.2	0.9	13.7	8.1	2.4
Housing	% of GDP	..	..	..	..	..	..
Average household size	persons per household	6.4	..	..	..	..	..
Urban	"	..	..	..	..	..	..
Fixed investment: housing	% of GDP	..	..	..	..	..	..
Fuel and power	% of GDP	..	..	..	..	..	..
Energy consumption per capita	kg of oil equiv.	9,267	11,398	10,883	1,109	1,649	5,101
Households with electricity							
Urban	% of households	..	..	..	..	..	..
Rural	"	..	..	..	..	..	..
Transport and communication	% of GDP	..	..	..	..	..	..
Fixed investment: transport equipment	"	..	..	..	..	..	..
Total road length	thou. km	..	..	..	..	..	..
INVESTMENT IN HUMAN CAPITAL							
Health							
Population per physician	persons	2,333	820	..	..	..	..
Population per nurse	"	252	370	..	..	..	..
Population per hospital bed	"	230	302	..	636	385	144
Oral rehydration therapy (under-5)	% of cases	..	..	73	56	54	..
Education							
Gross enrollment ratio							
Secondary	% of school-age pop.	52	84	97	59	53	92
Female	"	55	82	97	50	..	94
Pupil-teacher ratio: primary	pupils per teacher	22	20	22	27	25	18
Pupil-teacher ratio: secondary	"	24	21	20	21	..	..
Pupils reaching grade 4	% of cohort	99	100	94	..	71	..
Repeater rate: primary	% of total enroll	..	9	8	..	11	..
Illiteracy	% of pop. (age 15+)	60	27	23	45	14	..
Female	% of fem. (age 15+)	..	37	31	58	17	..
Newspaper circulation	per thou. pop.	101	61	58	39	117	..

World Bank International Economics Department, April 1994

Bangladesh

Indicator	Unit of measure	Latest single year 1970-75	Latest single year 1980-85	Most recent estimate 1987-92	Same region/income group South Asia	Same region/income group Low-income	Next higher income group
Priority Poverty Indicators							
POVERTY							
Upper poverty line	local curr.	..	..	..	..	..	..
Headcount index	% of pop.	..	79	49	28	19	..
Lower poverty line	local curr.	..	..	..	..	..	..
Headcount index	% of pop.	..	54	29	..	..	..
GNP per capita	US$	130	150	220	310	390	..
SHORT TERM INCOME INDICATORS							
Unskilled urban wages	local curr.	..	..	..	..	..	..
Unskilled rural wages	"	..	..	..	..	..	..
Rural terms of trade	"	..	..	95	..	..	..
Consumer price index	1987=100	32	82	145	..	..	..
Lower income	"	..	..	..	..	..	..
Food[a]	"	5	80	135	..	..	..
Urban	"	..	..	..	..	..	..
Rural	"	..	..	..	..	..	..
SOCIAL INDICATORS							
Public expenditure on basic social services	% of GDP	..	..	2.4	..	..	..
Gross enrollment ratios							
Primary	% school age pop.	73	60	77	103	103	..
Male	"	95	70	83	117	113	..
Female	"	51	50	71	88	96	..
Mortality							
Infant mortality	per thou. live births	140.0	128.0	91.0	85.0	73.0	45.0
Under 5 mortality	"	..	..	129.4	116.0	108.0	59.0
Immunization							
Measles	% age group	..	1.0	83.0	56.6	72.7	..
DPT	"	..	2.0	87.0	75.0	80.6	..
Child malnutrition (under-5)	"	91.3	71.7	66.5	60.9	38.3	..
Life expectancy							
Total	years	45	49	55	60	62	68
Female advantage	"	-1.5	-0.9	1.0	1.0	2.4	6.4
Total fertility rate	births per woman	7.0	6.0	4.0	4.0	3.4	3.1
Maternal mortality rate	per 100,000 live births	..	3000	400	..	..	..
Supplementary Poverty Indicators							
Expenditures on social security	% of total gov't exp.	..	..	..	..	..	..
Social security coverage	% econ. active pop.	..	..	..	..	..	..
Access to safe water: total	% of pop.	56.0	46.0	80.0	71.9	68.4	..
Urban	"	22.0	24.0	37.0	74.2	78.9	..
Rural	"	61.0	49.0	89.0	70.0	60.3	..
Access to health care	"	..	45.0	38.0	..	..	..

Population growth rate
(annual average, percent)

GNP per capita growth rate
(annual average, percent)

Development diamond[b]

Life expectancy

GNP per capita

Gross primary enrollment

Access to safe water

Bangladesh
Low-income

a. See the technical notes, p.389.   b. The development diamond, based on four key indicators, shows the average level of development in the country compared with its income group. See the introduction.

Bangladesh

Indicator	Unit of measure	Latest single year 1970-75	Latest single year 1980-85	Most recent estimate 1987-92	Same region/income group South Asia	Same region/income group Low-income	Next higher income group
Resources and Expenditures							
HUMAN RESOURCES							
Population (mre=1992)	thousands	76,582	98,028	114,440	1,177,918	3,194,535	942,547
Age dependency ratio	ratio	0.98	0.95	0.81	0.73	0.67	0.66
Urban	% of pop.	9.3	13.7	17.6	25.4	26.7	57.0
Population growth rate	annual %	2.8	2.5	2.0	2.1	1.8	1.4
Urban	"	6.5	6.0	5.6	3.4	3.4	4.8
Labor force (15-64)	thousands	22,548	28,845	35,533	428,847	1,478,954	..
Agriculture	% of labor force	78	75	..	..	..	..
Industry	"	5	6	..	..	..	..
Female	"	6	7	8	22	33	36
Females per 100 males							
Urban	number	87	72	..	..	..	..
Rural	"	95	95	..	..	..	..
NATURAL RESOURCES							
Area	thou. sq. km	144.00	144.00	144.00	5,133.49	38,401.06	40,697.37
Density	pop. per sq. km	531.8	680.8	778.8	224.8	81.7	22.8
Agricultural land	% of land area	74.7	74.8	74.8	58.9	50.9	..
Change in agricultural land	annual %	0.0	0.0	-3.0	-0.2	0.0	..
Agricultural land under irrigation	%	14.8	21.3	31.1	29.0	18.2	..
Forests and woodland	thou. sq. km	22	21	19			..
Deforestation (net)	annual %	..	..	3.2	..	..	..
INCOME							
Household income							
Share of top 20% of households	% of income	42	39	39	41	42	..
Share of bottom 40% of households	"	18	22	23	21	19	..
Share of bottom 20% of households	"	7	9	10	9	8	..
EXPENDITURE							
Food	% of GDP	..	49.1	..	..	..	..
Staples	"	..	29.9	..	..	..	..
Meat, fish, milk, cheese, eggs	"	..	9.7	..	..	..	..
Cereal imports	thou. metric tonnes	2,551	2,583	1,339	7,721	46,537	74,924
Food aid in cereals	"	2,076	1,500	1,429	2,558	9,008	4,054
Food production per capita	1987 = 100	108	97	95	116	123	..
Fertilizer consumption	kg/ha	22.1	55.5	103.0	71.5	61.9	..
Share of agriculture in GDP	% of GDP	62.0	41.8	34.5	28.7	29.6	..
Housing	% of GDP	..	14.5	..	..	..	..
Average household size	persons per household	5.6	5.8	..	..	..	..
Urban	"	5.9	6.1	..	..	..	..
Fixed investment: housing	% of GDP	..	5.7	..	..	..	..
Fuel and power	% of GDP	..	5.4	..	..	..	..
Energy consumption per capita	kg of oil equiv.	23	40	59	209	335	1,882
Households with electricity							
Urban	% of households	..	..	..	..	..	..
Rural	"	..	..	..	..	..	..
Transport and communication	% of GDP	..	2.6	..	..	..	..
Fixed investment: transport equipment	"	..	1.3	..	..	..	..
Total road length	thou. km	4	10	11	..	..	..
INVESTMENT IN HUMAN CAPITAL							
Health							
Population per physician	persons	8,447	6,560	5,304	2,459	..	..
Population per nurse	"	65,781	8,755	6,417	..	..	..
Population per hospital bed	"	6,467	3,508	3,158	1,652	1,050	516
Oral rehydration therapy (under-5)	% of cases	..	..	26	18	39	..
Education							
Gross enrollment ratio							
Secondary	% of school-age pop.	26	18	19	40	41	..
Female	"	11	10	12	29	35	..
Pupil-teacher ratio: primary	pupils per teacher	51	47	63	59	37	26
Pupil-teacher ratio: secondary	"	24	28	28	23	19	..
Pupils reaching grade 4	% of cohort	..	28	45	..	..	..
Repeater rate: primary	% of total enroll	..	18	7	..	..	..
Illiteracy	% of pop. (age 15+)	74	68	65	54	39	..
Female	% of fem. (age 15+)	..	81	78	68	52	..
Newspaper circulation	per thou. pop.	5	6	6	..	..	100

World Bank International Economics Department, April 1994

Barbados

Indicator	Unit of measure	Latest single year		Most recent estimate	Same region/income group		Next higher income group
		1970-75	1980-85	1987-92	Latin America Caribbean	Upper-middle-income	

Priority Poverty Indicators

POVERTY
Upper poverty line	local curr.	..	..	..	..	..	..
Headcount index	% of pop.	..	..	..	..	..	..
Lower poverty line	local curr.	..	..	..	..	..	..
Headcount index	% of pop.	..	..	..	..	..	..
GNP per capita	US$	1,520	4,670	6,540	2,690	3,870	21,960

SHORT TERM INCOME INDICATORS
Unskilled urban wages	local curr.	..	..	..	..	..	..
Unskilled rural wages	"	..	..	..	..	..	..
Rural terms of trade	"	..	..	..	..	..	..
Consumer price index	1987=100	41	96	129	..	..	..
Lower income	"	..	..	..	..	..	..
Food[a]	"	17	93	127	..	..	..
Urban	"	..	..	..	..	..	..
Rural	"	..	..	..	..	..	..

SOCIAL INDICATORS
Public expenditure on basic social services	% of GDP	..	..	..	..	..	..
Gross enrollment ratios							
Primary	% school age pop.	103	110	106	106	107	103
Male	"	103	113	103	..	..	103
Female	"	103	108	110	..	..	103
Mortality							
Infant mortality	per thou. live births	33.0	13.1	10.0	44.0	40.0	7.0
Under 5 mortality	"	..	..	12.5	56.0	51.0	10.0
Immunization							
Measles	% age group	..	84.0	87.0	78.9	82.0	82.4
DPT	"	..	83.0	91.0	73.8	73.8	90.1
Child malnutrition (under-5)	"	..	5.3	..	10.5	..	..
Life expectancy							
Total	years	69	73	75	68	69	77
Female advantage	"	5.1	5.0	5.0	5.6	6.3	6.4
Total fertility rate	births per woman	2.7	1.9	1.8	3.0	2.9	1.7
Maternal mortality rate	per 100,000 live births	..	24	27	..	..	..

Supplementary Poverty Indicators

Expenditures on social security	% of total gov't exp.	6.4	16.2	19.8	..	..	..
Social security coverage	% econ. active pop.	..	..	96.9	..	..	..
Access to safe water: total	% of pop.	100.0	100.0	100.0	80.3	85.6	..
Urban	"	100.0	100.0	100.0	91.0	94.3	..
Rural	"	100.0	99.0	100.0	64.3	73.0	..
Access to health care	"	..	100.0	100.0	..	..	..

Population growth rate
(annual average, percent)

□ Barbados
— Upper-middle-income

GNP per capita growth rate
(annual average, percent)

Development diamond[b]

— Barbados
— Upper-middle-income

a. See the technical notes, p.389.   b. The development diamond, based on four key indicators, shows the average level of development in the country compared with its income group. See the introduction.

28

Barbados

Indicator	Unit of measure	Latest single year 1970-75	Latest single year 1980-85	Most recent estimate 1987-92	Same region/income group Latin America Caribbean	Same region/income group Upper-middle-income	Next higher income group
Resources and Expenditures							
HUMAN RESOURCES							
Population (mre=1992)	thousands	246	253	259	453,294	477,960	828,221
Age dependency ratio	ratio	0.70	0.63	0.53	0.67	0.64	0.50
Urban	% of pop.	38.6	42.2	45.9	72.9	71.7	78.1
Population growth rate	annual %	0.5	0.3	0.3	1.7	1.6	0.7
Urban	"	1.1	1.3	1.6	2.6	2.5	0.9
Labor force (15-64)	thousands	107	127	141	166,091	181,414	390,033
Agriculture	% of labor force	14	10	..	..	..	..
Industry	"	23	21	..	..	..	..
Female	"	43	47	47	27	29	38
Females per 100 males							
Urban	number	..	..	..	..	..	..
Rural	"	..	..	..	..	..	..
NATURAL RESOURCES							
Area	thou. sq. km	0.43	0.43	0.43	20,507.48	21,836.02	31,709.00
Density	pop. per sq. km	571.2	589.3	600.2	21.7	21.5	24.5
Agricultural land	% of land area	86.1	86.1	86.1	40.2	41.7	42.7
Change in agricultural land	annual %	0.0	0.0	0.0	0.5	0.3	-0.2
Agricultural land under irrigation	%	..	..	..	3.2	9.3	16.1
Forests and woodland	thou. sq. km	..	..	..	..	..	..
Deforestation (net)	annual %	..	..	..	..	..	..
INCOME							
Household income							
Share of top 20% of households	% of income	44	..	..	..	..	..
Share of bottom 40% of households	"	19	..	..	..	..	..
Share of bottom 20% of households	"	7	..	..	..	..	..
EXPENDITURE							
Food	% of GDP	..	22.4	..	..	..	..
Staples	"	..	4.6	..	..	..	..
Meat, fish, milk, cheese, eggs	"	..	12.0	..	..	..	..
Cereal imports	thou. metric tonnes	38	59	61	25,032	49,174	70,626
Food aid in cereals	"	0	0	..	1,779	282	2
Food production per capita	1987 = 100	83	78	75	104	109	101
Fertilizer consumption	kg/ha	113.5	90.1	73.0	15.5	68.8	162.1
Share of agriculture in GDP	% of GDP	11.5	6.2	5.6	8.9	8.1	2.4
Housing	% of GDP	..	11.7	..	..	..	..
Average household size	persons per household	4.0	..	..	..	..	..
Urban	"	..	..	..	..	..	..
Fixed investment: housing	% of GDP	..	3.7	..	..	..	..
Fuel and power	% of GDP	..	3.7	..	..	..	..
Energy consumption per capita	kg of oil equiv.	1,315	1,646	1,387	912	1,649	5,101
Households with electricity							
Urban	% of households	..	..	..	..	..	..
Rural	"	..	..	..	..	..	..
Transport and communication	% of GDP	..	4.3	..	..	..	..
Fixed investment: transport equipment	"	..	1.7	..	..	..	..
Total road length	thou. km	1	2	2	..	..	..
INVESTMENT IN HUMAN CAPITAL							
Health							
Population per physician	persons	1,914	1,123	..	..	..	..
Population per nurse	"	296	223	..	..	..	..
Population per hospital bed	"	98	117	..	508	385	144
Oral rehydration therapy (under-5)	% of cases	..	..	15	62	54	..
Education							
Gross enrollment ratio							
Secondary	% of school-age pop.	77	93	87	47	53	92
Female	"	81	94	83	..	..	94
Pupil-teacher ratio: primary	pupils per teacher	..	21	17	25	25	18
Pupil-teacher ratio: secondary	"	20	20	20	..	..	..
Pupils reaching grade 4	% of cohort	64	91	..	..	71	..
Repeater rate: primary	% of total enroll	..	..	..	14	11	..
Illiteracy	% of pop. (age 15+)	1	..	..	15	14	..
Female	% of fem. (age 15+)	..	..	..	17	17	..
Newspaper circulation	per thou. pop.	100	158	117	99	117	..

World Bank International Economics Department, April 1994

Belarus

Indicator	Unit of measure	Latest single year 1970-75	Latest single year 1980-85	Most recent estimate 1987-92	Same region/income group Europe & Central Asia	Same region/income group Upper-middle-income	Next higher income group
Priority Poverty Indicators							
POVERTY							
Upper poverty line	local curr.	..	..	..	..	..	..
Headcount index	% of pop.	..	..	7	..	..	..
Lower poverty line	local curr.	..	..	..	..	..	..
Headcount index	% of pop.	..	..	2	..	..	..
GNP per capita	US$	..	..	2,930	..	3,870	21,960
SHORT TERM INCOME INDICATORS							
Unskilled urban wages	local curr.	..	141	3862	..	..	..
Unskilled rural wages	"	..	155	3507	..	..	..
Rural terms of trade	"	..	..	..	..	..	..
Consumer price index	1987=100	..	..	..	..	..	..
Lower income	"	..	..	..	..	..	..
Food[a]	"	..	91	197	..	..	..
Urban	"	..	..	..	..	..	..
Rural	"	..	..	..	..	..	..
SOCIAL INDICATORS							
Public expenditure on basic social services	% of GDP	..	..	8.0	..	..	..
Gross enrollment ratios							
Primary	% school age pop.	..	..	..	..	107	103
Male	"	..	..	..	..	..	103
Female	"	..	..	..	..	..	103
Mortality							
Infant mortality	per thou. live births	16.6	14.7	14.8	30.0	40.0	7.0
Under 5 mortality	"	..	..	18.0	38.0	51.0	10.0
Immunization							
Measles	% age group	..	..	..	..	82.0	82.4
DPT	"	..	..	..	..	73.8	90.1
Child malnutrition (under-5)	"	..	..	..	..	..	..
Life expectancy							
Total	years	72	71	71	70	69	77
Female advantage	"	8.0	8.8	9.5	8.6	6.3	6.4
Total fertility rate	births per woman	2.2	2.1	1.9	2.2	2.9	1.7
Maternal mortality rate	per 100,000 live births	..	29	25	58	..	..
Supplementary Poverty Indicators							
Expenditures on social security	% of total gov't exp.	..	..	..	..	..	..
Social security coverage	% econ. active pop.	..	..	..	..	..	..
Access to safe water: total	% of pop.	..	..	..	..	85.6	..
Urban	"	..	..	..	..	94.3	..
Rural	"	..	..	..	..	73.0	..
Access to health care	"	..	100.0	100.0	..	..	..

Population growth rate
(annual average, percent)

GNP per capita growth rate
(annual average, percent)

Development diamond[b]

Life expectancy

GNP per capita — Gross primary enrollment

Access to safe water

☐ Belarus
— Upper-middle-income

— Belarus
— Upper-middle-income

a. See the technical notes, p.389. b. The development diamond, based on four key indicators, shows the average level of development in the country compared with its income group. See the introduction.

30

Belarus

Indicator	Unit of measure	Latest single year 1970-75	Latest single year 1980-85	Most recent estimate 1987-92	Same region/income group Europe & Central Asia	Same region/income group Upper-middle-income	Next higher income group
Resources and Expenditures							
HUMAN RESOURCES							
Population (mre=1992)	thousands	..	9,975	10,296	495,241	477,960	828,221
Age dependency ratio	ratio	..	..	0.56	0.56	0.64	0.50
Urban	% of pop.	..	62.3	65.5	63.3	71.7	78.1
Population growth rate	annual %	..	0.7	0.2	0.5	1.6	0.7
Urban	"	..	2.0	1.8	..	2.5	0.9
Labor force (15-64)	thousands	..	..	..	..	181,414	390,033
Agriculture	% of labor force	..	..	..	..	..	..
Industry	"	..	..	..	..	..	..
Female	"	..	..	..	46	29	38
Females per 100 males							
Urban	number	..	..	..	..	..	..
Rural	"	..	..	..	..	..	..
NATURAL RESOURCES							
Area	thou. sq. km	..	..	207.60	24,165.06	21,836.02	31,709.00
Density	pop. per sq. km	..	..	49.5	20.4	21.5	24.5
Agricultural land	% of land area	..	..	..	..	41.7	42.7
Change in agricultural land	annual %	..	..	..	..	0.3	-0.2
Agricultural land under irrigation	%	..	..	..	..	9.3	16.1
Forests and woodland	thou. sq. km	..	..	..	..	..	..
Deforestation (net)	annual %	..	..	-0.5	..	..	..
INCOME							
Household income							
Share of top 20% of households	% of income	..	..	..	..	..	..
Share of bottom 40% of households	"	..	..	..	..	..	..
Share of bottom 20% of households	"	..	..	..	..	..	..
EXPENDITURE							
Food	% of GDP	..	..	19.8	..	..	..
Staples	"	..	..	3.6	..	..	..
Meat, fish, milk, cheese, eggs	"	..	..	8.9	..	..	..
Cereal imports	thou. metric tonnes	..	..	3,100	45,972	49,174	70,626
Food aid in cereals	"	..	..	..	1,639	282	2
Food production per capita	1987 = 100	..	..	..	..	109	101
Fertilizer consumption	kg/ha	..	..	..	..	68.8	162.1
Share of agriculture in GDP	% of GDP	..	25.6	21.3	..	8.1	2.4
Housing	% of GDP	..	..	4.7	..	..	..
Average household size	persons per household	..	..	3.2	..	..	..
Urban	"	..	..	..	..	..	..
Fixed investment: housing	% of GDP	..	..	4.9	..	..	..
Fuel and power	% of GDP	..	..	1.0	..	..	..
Energy consumption per capita	kg of oil equiv.	..	..	4,154	3,190	1,649	5,101
Households with electricity							
Urban	% of households	..	..	..	..	..	..
Rural	"	..	..	..	..	..	..
Transport and communication	% of GDP	..	..	6.2	..	..	..
Fixed investment: transport equipment	"	..	..	10.3	..	..	..
Total road length	thou. km	..	46	90	..	..	..
INVESTMENT IN HUMAN CAPITAL							
Health							
Population per physician	persons	..	..	251	378	..	..
Population per nurse	"	..	..	..	..	..	..
Population per hospital bed	"	..	..	8	134	385	144
Oral rehydration therapy (under-5)	% of cases	..	..	..	..	54	..
Education							
Gross enrollment ratio							
Secondary	% of school-age pop.	..	..	..	..	53	92
Female	"	..	..	..	..	..	94
Pupil-teacher ratio: primary	pupils per teacher	..	..	..	..	25	18
Pupil-teacher ratio: secondary	"	..	..	..	..	..	..
Pupils reaching grade 4	% of cohort	..	..	..	..	71	..
Repeater rate: primary	% of total enroll	..	..	..	..	11	..
Illiteracy	% of pop. (age 15+)	..	..	..	..	14	..
Female	% of fem. (age 15+)	..	..	..	..	17	..
Newspaper circulation	per thou. pop.	..	..	286	..	117	..

World Bank International Economics Department, April 1994

Belgium

Priority Poverty Indicators

Indicator	Unit of measure	Latest single year 1970-75	Latest single year 1980-85	Most recent estimate 1987-92	Same region/income group High-income
POVERTY					
Upper poverty line	local curr.	..	..	..	..
Headcount index	% of pop.	..	..	..	..
Lower poverty line	local curr.	..	..	..	..
Headcount index	% of pop.	..	..	..	..
GNP per capita	US$	5,930	8,290	20,880	21,960
SHORT TERM INCOME INDICATORS					
Unskilled urban wages	local curr.	..	..	..	..
Unskilled rural wages	"	..	..	..	..
Rural terms of trade	"	..	..	..	..
Consumer price index	1987=100	51	97	114	..
Lower income	"	..	..	..	..
Food[a]	"	39	99	109	..
Urban	"	..	..	..	..
Rural	"	..	..	..	..
SOCIAL INDICATORS					
Public expenditure on basic social services	% of GDP	..	..	..	..
Gross enrollment ratios					
Primary	% school age pop.	102	99	99	103
Male	"	102	99	98	103
Female	"	102	99	100	103
Mortality					
Infant mortality	per thou. live births	16.1	9.8	8.9	7.0
Under 5 mortality	"	..	..	11.2	10.0
Immunization					
Measles	% age group	..	90.0	75.0	82.4
DPT	"	..	95.0	94.0	90.1
Child malnutrition (under-5)	"	..	..	..	..
Life expectancy					
Total	years	71	74	76	77
Female advantage	"	6.5	6.9	6.9	6.4
Total fertility rate	births per woman	1.7	1.5	1.6	1.7
Maternal mortality rate	per 100,000 live births	..	10	..	..

Supplementary Poverty Indicators

Indicator	Unit of measure	1970-75	1980-85	1987-92	High-income
Expenditures on social security	% of total gov't exp.	43.4	38.2	42.0	..
Social security coverage	% econ. active pop.	..	..	..	..
Access to safe water: total	% of pop.	..	92.0	..	..
Urban	"	..	94.0	..	..
Rural	"	..	91.0	..	..
Access to health care	"	..	100.0	100.0	..

Population growth rate
(annual average, percent)

☐ Belgium
— High-income

GNP per capita growth rate
(annual average, percent)

Development diamond[b]

—— Belgium
— High-income

a. See the technical notes, p.389.   b. The development diamond, based on four key indicators, shows the average level of development in the country compared with its income group. See the introduction.

32

Belgium

Indicator	Unit of measure	Latest single year 1970-75	Latest single year 1980-85	Most recent estimate 1987-92	Same region/income group High-income
Resources and Expenditures					

HUMAN RESOURCES

Indicator	Unit of measure	1970-75	1980-85	1987-92	High-income
Population (mre=1992)	thousands	9,795	9,858	10,040	828,221
Age dependency ratio	ratio	0.57	0.48	0.51	0.50
Urban	% of pop.	94.9	95.9	96.5	78.1
Population growth rate	annual %	0.3	0.1	0.4	0.7
Urban	"	0.4	0.2	0.4	0.9
Labor force (15-64)	thousands	3,767	4,092	4,155	390,033
Agriculture	% of labor force	4	3	..	..
Industry	"	40	36	..	..
Female	"	32	34	34	38
Females per 100 males					
Urban	number	..	..	..	..
Rural	"	..	..	..	..

NATURAL RESOURCES

Indicator	Unit of measure	1970-75	1980-85	1987-92	High-income
Area	thou. sq. km	..	..	..	31,709.00
Density	pop. per sq. km	..	..	..	24.5
Agricultural land	% of land area	..	..	..	42.7
Change in agricultural land	annual %	..	..	..	-0.2
Agricultural land under irrigation	%	..	..	..	16.1
Forests and woodland	thou. sq. km	..	..	..	..
Deforestation (net)	annual %	..	..	0.0	..

INCOME
Household income

Indicator	Unit of measure	1970-75	1980-85	1987-92	High-income
Share of top 20% of households	% of income	..	..	..	..
Share of bottom 40% of households	"	..	..	..	..
Share of bottom 20% of households	"	..	..	..	..

EXPENDITURE

Indicator	Unit of measure	1970-75	1980-85	1987-92	High-income
Food	% of GDP	12.4	11.7	..	..
Staples	"	1.9	1.5	..	..
Meat, fish, milk, cheese, eggs	"	6.7	6.5	..	..
Cereal imports	thou. metric tonnes	..	..	..	70,626
Food aid in cereals	"	..	..	..	2
Food production per capita	1987 = 100	..	..	..	101
Fertilizer consumption	kg/ha	..	..	..	162.1
Share of agriculture in GDP	% of GDP	2.8	2.2	1.8	2.4
Housing	% of GDP	9.6	12.8	..	..
Average household size	persons per household	2.9	2.7	..	..
Urban	"	..	..	..	..
Fixed investment: housing	% of GDP	5.7	1.6	..	..
Fuel and power	% of GDP	3.6	5.0	..	..
Energy consumption per capita	kg of oil equiv.	4,346	4,466	5,101	5,101
Households with electricity					
Urban	% of households	..	..	..	..
Rural	"	..	..	..	..
Transport and communication	% of GDP	6.9	8.3	..	..
Fixed investment: transport equipment	"	1.9	1.7	..	..
Total road length	thou. km	125	128	138	..

INVESTMENT IN HUMAN CAPITAL

Health

Indicator	Unit of measure	1970-75	1980-85	1987-92	High-income
Population per physician	persons	647	331	311	..
Population per nurse	"	..	108	..	..
Population per hospital bed	"	120	107	121	144
Oral rehydration therapy (under-5)	% of cases	..	..	..	..

Education
Gross enrollment ratio

Indicator	Unit of measure	1970-75	1980-85	1987-92	High-income
Secondary	% of school-age pop.	84	98	102	92
Female	"	83	98	103	94
Pupil-teacher ratio: primary	pupils per teacher	19	17	10	18
Pupil-teacher ratio: secondary	"	..	..	..	..
Pupils reaching grade 4	% of cohort	..	79	86	..
Repeater rate: primary	% of total enroll	24	17	16	..
Illiteracy	% of pop. (age 15+)	..	..	†	..
Female	% of fem. (age 15+)	..	..	†	..
Newspaper circulation	per thou. pop.	239	223	301	..

World Bank International Economics Department, April 1994

Belize

Indicator	Unit of measure	Latest single year 1970-75	1980-85	Most recent estimate 1987-92	Same region/income group Latin America Caribbean	Lower-middle-income	Next higher income group
Priority Poverty Indicators							
POVERTY							
Upper poverty line	local curr.	..	..	..	..	..	..
Headcount index	% of pop.	..	..	..	..	..	..
Lower poverty line	local curr.	..	..	..	..	..	..
Headcount index	% of pop.	..	..	..	..	..	..
GNP per capita	US$	790	1,220	2,220	2,690	..	3,870
SHORT TERM INCOME INDICATORS							
Unskilled urban wages	local curr.	..	..	..	..	..	..
Unskilled rural wages	"	..	..	..	..	..	..
Rural terms of trade	"	..	..	..	..	..	..
Consumer price index	1987=100	..	97	118	..	..	..
Lower income	"	..	..	..	..	..	..
Food[a]	"	..	98	120	..	..	..
Urban	"	..	..	..	..	..	..
Rural	"	..	..	..	..	..	..
SOCIAL INDICATORS							
Public expenditure on basic social services	% of GDP	..	..	9.0	..	..	..
Gross enrollment ratios							
Primary	% school age pop.	..	..	..	106	..	107
Male	"	..	..	..	..	..	..
Female	"	..	..	..	..	..	..
Mortality							
Infant mortality	per thou. live births	..	54.0	41.0	44.0	45.0	40.0
Under 5 mortality	"	..	..	51.7	56.0	59.0	51.0
Immunization							
Measles	% age group	..	..	81.0	78.9	..	82.0
DPT	"	..	..	84.0	73.8	..	73.8
Child malnutrition (under-5)	"	..	5.7	..	10.5	..	..
Life expectancy							
Total	years	59	65	69	68	68	69
Female advantage	"	3.9	3.9	5.9	5.6	6.4	6.3
Total fertility rate	births per woman	6.9	5.5	4.5	3.0	3.1	2.9
Maternal mortality rate	per 100,000 live births	..	..	..	..	..	..
Supplementary Poverty Indicators							
Expenditures on social security	% of total gov't exp.	..	4.0	3.0	..	..	..
Social security coverage	% econ. active pop.	..	..	..	..	..	..
Access to safe water: total	% of pop.	..	63.0	73.0	80.3	..	85.6
Urban	"	..	100.0	100.0	91.0	..	94.3
Rural	"	..	26.0	44.0	64.3	..	73.0
Access to health care	"	..	75.0	..	..	..	..

Population growth rate
(annual average, percent)

- Belize
- Lower-middle-income

GNP per capita growth rate
(annual average, percent)

Development diamond[b]

- Belize
- Lower-middle-income

a. See the technical notes, p.389.   b. The development diamond, based on four key indicators, shows the average level of development in the country compared with its income group. See the introduction.

Belize

Resources and Expenditures

Indicator	Unit of measure	Latest single year 1970-75	Latest single year 1980-85	Most recent estimate 1987-92	Same region/income group Latin America Caribbean	Same region/income group Lower-middle-income	Next higher income group
HUMAN RESOURCES							
Population (mre=1992)	thousands	129	166	199	453,294	942,547	477,960
Age dependency ratio	ratio	..	0.98	0.87	0.67	0.66	0.64
Urban	% of pop.	53.0	50.2	48.0	72.9	57.0	71.7
Population growth rate	annual %	1.8	2.6	2.6	1.7	1.4	1.6
Urban	"	1.4	1.9	2.6	2.6	4.8	2.5
Labor force (15-64)	thousands	..	54	..	166,091	..	181,414
Agriculture	% of labor force	..	..	..	..	..	..
Industry	"	..	..	..	..	..	..
Female	"	..	..	..	27	36	29
Females per 100 males							
Urban	number	..	..	..	..	..	..
Rural	"	..	..	..	..	..	..
NATURAL RESOURCES							
Area	thou. sq. km	22.96	22.96	22.96	20,507.48	40,697.37	21,836.02
Density	pop. per sq. km	5.6	7.2	8.5	21.7	22.8	21.5
Agricultural land	% of land area	3.7	4.4	4.6	40.2	..	41.7
Change in agricultural land	annual %	1.2	4.1	1.0	0.5	..	0.3
Agricultural land under irrigation	%	1.2	2.0	1.9	3.2	..	9.3
Forests and woodland	thou. sq. km	10	10	10	..	..	..
Deforestation (net)	annual %	..	..	0.0	..	..	..
INCOME							
Household income							
Share of top 20% of households	% of income	..	..	..	..	..	..
Share of bottom 40% of households	"	..	..	..	..	..	..
Share of bottom 20% of households	"	..	..	..	..	..	..
EXPENDITURE							
Food	% of GDP	..	..	24.2	..	..	..
Staples	"	..	..	9.1	..	..	..
Meat, fish, milk, cheese, eggs	"	..	..	7.6	..	..	..
Cereal imports	thou. metric tonnes	13	10	20	25,032	74,924	49,174
Food aid in cereals	"	1	0	5	1,779	4,054	282
Food production per capita	1987 = 100	87	95	99	104	..	109
Fertilizer consumption	kg/ha	24.7	24.0	49.5	15.5	..	68.8
Share of agriculture in GDP	% of GDP	..	17.8	16.7	8.9	..	8.1
Housing	% of GDP	..	..	9.8	..	..	..
Average household size	persons per household	5.2	..	..	..	..	..
Urban	"	..	..	..	..	..	..
Fixed investment: housing	% of GDP	..	..	6.2	..	..	..
Fuel and power	% of GDP	..	..	3.4	..	..	..
Energy consumption per capita	kg of oil equiv.	505	457	436	912	1,882	1,649
Households with electricity							
Urban	% of households	..	..	..	..	..	..
Rural	"	..	..	..	..	..	..
Transport and communication	% of GDP	..	..	10.7	..	..	..
Fixed investment: transport equipment	"	..	..	5.7	..	..	..
Total road length	thou. km	..	2	..	..	..	..
INVESTMENT IN HUMAN CAPITAL							
Health							
Population per physician	persons	2,926	3,681	1,562	..	..	..
Population per nurse	"	441	497	361	..	..	..
Population per hospital bed	"	185	..	..	508	516	385
Oral rehydration therapy (under-5)	% of cases	..	..	65	62	..	54
Education							
Gross enrollment ratio							
Secondary	% of school-age pop.	..	..	..	47	..	53
Female	"	..	..	..	..	..	..
Pupil-teacher ratio: primary	pupils per teacher	28	25	26	25	26	25
Pupil-teacher ratio: secondary	"	14	13	..	..	..	..
Pupils reaching grade 4	% of cohort	65	..	..	..	..	71
Repeater rate: primary	% of total enroll	..	..	..	14	..	11
Illiteracy	% of pop. (age 15+)	9	..	..	15	..	14
Female	% of fem. (age 15+)	..	..	..	17	..	17
Newspaper circulation	per thou. pop.	31	..	..	99	100	117

World Bank International Economics Department, April 1994

35

Benin

| Indicator | Unit of measure | Latest single year | | Most recent estimate 1987-92 | Same region/income group | | Next higher income group |
		1970-75	1980-85		Sub-Saharan Africa	Low-income	

Priority Poverty Indicators

Indicator	Unit of measure	1970-75	1980-85	1987-92	Sub-Saharan Africa	Low-income	Next higher income group
POVERTY							
Upper poverty line	local curr.	..	..	..	..	..	..
Headcount index	% of pop.	..	..	..	..	19	..
Lower poverty line	local curr.	..	..	..	..	..	..
Headcount index	% of pop.	..	..	..	..	..	..
GNP per capita	US$	200	290	410	520	390	..
SHORT TERM INCOME INDICATORS							
Unskilled urban wages	local curr.	..	..	..	..	..	..
Unskilled rural wages	"	..	..	..	..	..	..
Rural terms of trade	"	..	..	..	..	..	..
Consumer price index	1987=100	..	..	..	..	..	..
Lower income	"	..	..	..	..	..	..
Food[a]	"	..	..	..	..	..	..
Urban	"	..	..	..	..	..	..
Rural	"	..	..	..	..	..	..
SOCIAL INDICATORS							
Public expenditure on basic social services	% of GDP	..	..	..	..	..	..
Gross enrollment ratios							
Primary	% school age pop.	50	67	66	66	103	..
Male	"	70	89	78	79	113	..
Female	"	31	44	39	62	96	..
Mortality							
Infant mortality	per thou. live births	151.0	120.0	110.0	99.0	73.0	45.0
Under 5 mortality	"	..	..	182.8	169.0	108.0	59.0
Immunization							
Measles	% age group	..	23.0	70.0	54.0	72.7	..
DPT	"	..	17.0	67.0	54.6	80.6	..
Child malnutrition (under-5)	"	..	..	35.0	28.4	38.3	..
Life expectancy							
Total	years	45	48	51	52	62	68
Female advantage	"	2.7	3.3	3.3	3.4	2.4	6.4
Total fertility rate	births per woman	6.9	6.5	6.2	6.1	3.4	3.1
Maternal mortality rate	per 100,000 live births	..	1680	161	..	..	..

Supplementary Poverty Indicators

Indicator	Unit of measure	1970-75	1980-85	1987-92	Sub-Saharan Africa	Low-income	Next higher income group
Expenditures on social security	% of total gov't exp.	..	..	..	..	..	..
Social security coverage	% econ. active pop.	..	..	..	..	..	..
Access to safe water: total	% of pop.	34.0	50.0	..	41.1	68.4	..
Urban	"	100.0	80.0	..	77.8	78.9	..
Rural	"	20.0	34.0	..	27.3	60.3	..
Access to health care	"	..	..	99.0	..	..	..

Population growth rate
(annual average, percent)

Benin
Low-income

GNP per capita growth rate
(annual average, percent)

Development diamond[b]

Benin
Low-income

a. See the technical notes, p.389. b. The development diamond, based on four key indicators, shows the average level of development in the country compared with its income group. See the introduction.

Benin

Indicator	Unit of measure	Latest single year 1970-75	Latest single year 1980-85	Most recent estimate 1987-92	Same region/income group Sub-Saharan Africa	Same region/income group Low-income	Next higher income group
Resources and Expenditures							
HUMAN RESOURCES							
Population (mre=1992)	thousands	3,029	4,043	5,047	546,390	3,194,535	942,547
Age dependency ratio	ratio	0.94	0.98	1.00	0.95	0.67	0.66
Urban	% of pop.	24.9	34.8	39.6	29.5	26.7	57.0
Population growth rate	annual %	2.6	3.2	3.2	2.9	1.8	1.4
Urban	"	8.1	5.1	5.1	5.1	3.4	4.8
Labor force (15-64)	thousands	1,592	1,964	2,311	224,025	1,478,954	..
Agriculture	% of labor force	76	70	..	..	..	..
Industry	"	6	7	..	..	..	..
Female	"	48	48	47	37	33	36
Females per 100 males							
Urban	number	121	..	96	..	..	..
Rural	"	117	..	119	..	..	..
NATURAL RESOURCES							
Area	thou. sq. km	112.62	112.62	112.62	24,274.03	38,401.06	40,697.37
Density	pop. per sq. km	26.9	35.9	43.4	21.9	81.7	22.8
Agricultural land	% of land area	20.0	20.6	20.9	52.7	50.9	..
Change in agricultural land	annual %	1.6	0.9	0.4	0.1	0.0	..
Agricultural land under irrigation	%	0.2	0.3	0.3	0.8	18.2	..
Forests and woodland	thou. sq. km	42	37	34	..	..	..
Deforestation (net)	annual %	..	..	1.3	..	..	..
INCOME							
Household income							
Share of top 20% of households	% of income	..	..	..	..	42	..
Share of bottom 40% of households	"	..	..	..	..	19	..
Share of bottom 20% of households	"	..	..	..	..	8	..
EXPENDITURE							
Food	% of GDP	..	30.5	..	..	..	..
Staples	"	..	9.9	..	..	..	..
Meat, fish, milk, cheese, eggs	"	..	11.3	..	..	..	..
Cereal imports	thou. metric tonnes	12	67	2,012	20,311	46,537	74,924
Food aid in cereals	"	9	21	4	4,303	9,008	4,054
Food production per capita	1987 = 100	89	107	110	90	123	..
Fertilizer consumption	kg/ha	1.1	5.0	4.9	4.2	61.9	..
Share of agriculture in GDP	% of GDP	30.5	32.0	37.2	18.6	29.6	..
Housing	% of GDP	..	9.8	..	..	..	..
Average household size	persons per household	..	..	..	..	..	..
Urban	"	..	..	..	..	..	..
Fixed investment: housing	% of GDP	..	4.0	..	..	..	..
Fuel and power	% of GDP	..	2.0	..	..	..	..
Energy consumption per capita	kg of oil equiv.	53	47	19	258	335	1,882
Households with electricity							
Urban	% of households	..	..	..	..	..	..
Rural	"	..	..	..	..	..	..
Transport and communication	% of GDP	..	11.6	..	..	..	..
Fixed investment: transport equipment	"	..	1.0	..	..	..	..
Total road length	thou. km	7	8	8	..	..	..
INVESTMENT IN HUMAN CAPITAL							
Health							
Population per physician	persons	28,570	13,406	..	..	..	..
Population per nurse	"	2,597	1,755	..	..	..	..
Population per hospital bed	"	851	886	..	1,329	1,050	516
Oral rehydration therapy (under-5)	% of cases	..	..	45	36	39	..
Education							
Gross enrollment ratio							
Secondary	% of school-age pop.	9	17	12	18	41	..
Female	"	5	10	7	14	35	..
Pupil-teacher ratio: primary	pupils per teacher	53	33	35	39	37	26
Pupil-teacher ratio: secondary	"	38	37	35	..	19	..
Pupils reaching grade 4	% of cohort	64	63	..	..	..	..
Repeater rate: primary	% of total enroll	21	27	26	..	..	..
Illiteracy	% of pop. (age 15+)	..	81	77	51	39	..
Female	% of fem. (age 15+)	..	88	84	62	52	..
Newspaper circulation	per thou. pop.	1	0	3	14	..	100

World Bank International Economics Department, April 1994

37

Bermuda

Indicator	Unit of measure	Latest single year		Most recent estimate 1987-92	Same region/income group High-income
		1970-75	1980-85		
Priority Poverty Indicators					
POVERTY					
Upper poverty line	local curr.	..	..	..	..
Headcount index	% of pop.	..	..	..	..
Lower poverty line	local curr.	..	..	..	..
Headcount index	% of pop.	..	..	..	..
GNP per capita	US$	6,790	18,500	23,740	21,960
SHORT TERM INCOME INDICATORS					
Unskilled urban wages	local curr.	..	..	..	..
Unskilled rural wages	"	..	..	..	..
Rural terms of trade	"	..	..	..	..
Consumer price index	1987=100	..	..	..	..
Lower income	"	..	..	..	..
Food[a]	"	..	93	122	..
Urban	"	..	..	..	..
Rural	"	..	..	..	..
SOCIAL INDICATORS					
Public expenditure on basic social services	% of GDP	..	..	..	..
Gross enrollment ratios					
Primary	% school age pop.	..	..	..	103
Male	"	..	..	..	103
Female	"	..	..	..	103
Mortality					
Infant mortality	per thou. live births	..	..	7.8	7.0
Under 5 mortality	"	..	..	..	10.0
Immunization					
Measles	% age group	..	..	63.0	82.4
DPT	"	..	..	62.0	90.1
Child malnutrition (under-5)	"	..	..	..	..
Life expectancy					
Total	years	..	..	..	77
Female advantage	"	..	..	..	6.4
Total fertility rate	births per woman	..	..	..	1.7
Maternal mortality rate	per 100,000 live births	..	..	..	..
Supplementary Poverty Indicators					
Expenditures on social security	% of total gov't exp.	..	..	..	..
Social security coverage	% econ. active pop.	..	..	..	..
Access to safe water: total	% of pop.	..	..	..	..
Urban	"	..	..	..	..
Rural	"	..	..	..	..
Access to health care	"	..	..	..	..

Population growth rate
(annual average, percent)

- Bermuda
- High-income

GNP per capita growth rate
(annual average, percent)

Development diamond[b]

- Bermuda
- High-income

a. See the technical notes, p.389.   b. The development diamond, based on four key indicators, shows the average level of development in the country compared with its income group. See the introduction.

Bermuda

Indicator	Unit of measure	Latest single year 1970-75	Latest single year 1980-85	Most recent estimate 1987-92	Same region/income group High-income
Resources and Expenditures					
HUMAN RESOURCES					
Population (mre=1992)	thousands	53	56	62	828,221
Age dependency ratio	ratio	..	..	..	0.50
Urban	% of pop.	99.9	99.9	..	78.1
Population growth rate	annual %	-0.8	0.7	0.8	0.7
Urban	"	-0.8	0.4	..	0.9
Labor force (15-64)	thousands	..	..	..	390,033
Agriculture	% of labor force	..	..	..	..
Industry	"	..	..	..	..
Female	"	..	..	..	38
Females per 100 males					
Urban	number	..	..	..	..
Rural	"	..	..	..	..
NATURAL RESOURCES					
Area	thou. sq. km	0.05	0.05	0.05	31,709.00
Density	pop. per sq. km	1060.0	1120.0	1220.0	24.5
Agricultural land	% of land area	..	..	..	42.7
Change in agricultural land	annual %	..	..	..	-0.2
Agricultural land under irrigation	%	..	..	..	16.1
Forests and woodland	thou. sq. km	0	0	0	..
Deforestation (net)	annual %	..	..	..	..
INCOME					
Household income					
Share of top 20% of households	% of income	..	..	..	..
Share of bottom 40% of households	"	..	..	..	..
Share of bottom 20% of households	"	..	..	..	..
EXPENDITURE					
Food	% of GDP	..	..	..	..
Staples	"	..	..	..	..
Meat, fish, milk, cheese, eggs	"	..	..	..	..
Cereal imports	thou. metric tonnes	3	5	2	70,626
Food aid in cereals	"	..	..	..	2
Food production per capita	1987 = 100	..	..	..	101
Fertilizer consumption	kg/ha	..	..	..	162.1
Share of agriculture in GDP	% of GDP	..	..	..	2.4
Housing	% of GDP	..	..	..	..
Average household size	persons per household	3.4	2.9	..	..
Urban	"	3.1	2.9	..	..
Fixed investment: housing	% of GDP	..	..	..	..
Fuel and power	% of GDP	..	..	..	..
Energy consumption per capita	kg of oil equiv.	3,623	3,143	2,829	5,101
Households with electricity					
Urban	% of households	..	..	..	..
Rural	"	..	..	..	..
Transport and communication	% of GDP	..	..	..	..
Fixed investment: transport equipment	"	..	..	..	..
Total road length	thou. km	..	..	..	..
INVESTMENT IN HUMAN CAPITAL					
Health					
Population per physician	persons	846	1,324	..	..
Population per nurse	"	..	..	..	..
Population per hospital bed	"	107	..	..	144
Oral rehydration therapy (under-5)	% of cases	..	..	..	..
Education					
Gross enrollment ratio					
Secondary	% of school-age pop.	..	..	..	92
Female	"	..	..	..	94
Pupil-teacher ratio: primary	pupils per teacher	21	17	..	18
Pupil-teacher ratio: secondary	"	14	11	..	..
Pupils reaching grade 4	% of cohort	..	97	..	..
Repeater rate: primary	% of total enroll	7	..	..	..
Illiteracy	% of pop. (age 15+)	2	..	..	..
Female	% of fem. (age 15+)	..	..	..	..
Newspaper circulation	per thou. pop.	208	288	298	..

World Bank International Economics Department, April 1994

Bhutan

Indicator	Unit of measure	Latest single year 1970-75	Latest single year 1980-85	Most recent estimate 1987-92	Same region/income group South Asia	Same region/income group Low-income	Next higher income group
Priority Poverty Indicators							
POVERTY							
Upper poverty line	local curr.	..	..	..	..	..	..
Headcount index	% of pop.	..	..	..	28	19	..
Lower poverty line	local curr.	..	..	..	..	..	..
Headcount index	% of pop.	..	..	..	..	..	..
GNP per capita	US$	..	130	180	310	390	..
SHORT TERM INCOME INDICATORS							
Unskilled urban wages	local curr.	..	..	..	..	..	..
Unskilled rural wages	"	..	..	..	..	..	..
Rural terms of trade	"	..	..	..	..	..	..
Consumer price index	1987=100	..	86	167	..	..	..
Lower income	"	..	..	..	..	..	..
Food[a]	"	..	..	..	..	..	..
Urban	"	..	..	..	..	..	..
Rural	"	..	..	..	..	..	..
SOCIAL INDICATORS							
Public expenditure on basic social services	% of GDP	..	..	..	..	..	..
Gross enrollment ratios							
Primary	% school age pop.	6	27	25	103	103	..
Male	"	11	34	31	117	113	..
Female	"	1	19	19	88	96	..
Mortality							
Infant mortality	per thou. live births	178.0	154.0	129.0	85.0	73.0	45.0
Under 5 mortality	"	..	..	191.1	116.0	108.0	59.0
Immunization							
Measles	% age group	..	11.0	36.0	56.6	72.7	..
DPT	"	..	10.0	46.0	75.0	80.6	..
Child malnutrition (under-5)	"	..	..	..	60.9	38.3	..
Life expectancy							
Total	years	41	44	48	60	62	68
Female advantage	"	1.5	1.5	1.2	1.0	2.4	6.4
Total fertility rate	births per woman	6.0	5.9	5.9	4.0	3.4	3.1
Maternal mortality rate	per 100,000 live births	..	..	1305	..	..	..
Supplementary Poverty Indicators							
Expenditures on social security	% of total gov't exp.	..	1.0	0.5	..	..	..
Social security coverage	% econ. active pop.	..	..	..	..	..	..
Access to safe water: total	% of pop.	..	..	32.0	71.9	68.4	..
Urban	"	..	..	60.0	74.2	78.9	..
Rural	"	..	19.0	30.0	70.0	60.3	..
Access to health care	"	..	50.0	65.0	..	..	..

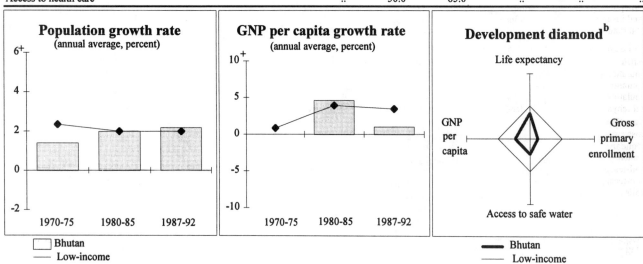

Population growth rate (annual average, percent) — Bhutan / Low-income

GNP per capita growth rate (annual average, percent) — Bhutan / Low-income

Development diamond[b] — Life expectancy, GNP per capita, Gross primary enrollment, Access to safe water — Bhutan / Low-income

a. See the technical notes, p.389.   b. The development diamond, based on four key indicators, shows the average level of development in the country compared with its income group. See the introduction.

40

Bhutan

Indicator	Unit of measure	Latest single year 1970-75	Latest single year 1980-85	Most recent estimate 1987-92	Same region/income group South Asia	Same region/income group Low-income	Next higher income group
Resources and Expenditures							
HUMAN RESOURCES							
Population (mre=1992)	thousands	1,047	1,286	1,497	1,177,918	3,194,535	942,547
Age dependency ratio	ratio	0.77	0.76	0.78	0.73	0.67	0.66
Urban	% of pop.	3.5	4.5	5.7	25.4	26.7	57.0
Population growth rate	annual %	1.5	2.0	2.2	2.1	1.8	1.4
Urban	"	3.9	4.7	6.1	3.4	3.4	4.8
Labor force (15-64)	thousands	525	632	724	428,847	1,478,954	..
Agriculture	% of labor force	93	92	..	..	..	..
Industry	"	2	3	..	..	..	..
Female	"	34	33	32	22	33	36
Females per 100 males							
Urban	number	..	..	..	..	..	..
Rural	"	..	..	..	..	..	..
NATURAL RESOURCES							
Area	thou. sq. km	47.00	47.00	47.00	5,133.49	38,401.06	40,697.37
Density	pop. per sq. km	22.3	27.4	31.2	224.8	81.7	22.8
Agricultural land	% of land area	7.9	8.4	8.6	58.9	50.9	..
Change in agricultural land	annual %	0.5	0.5	0.0	-0.2	0.0	..
Agricultural land under irrigation	%	5.9	7.6	8.4	29.0	18.2	..
Forests and woodland	thou. sq. km	26	26	26	..	..	..
Deforestation (net)	annual %	..	..	0.7	..	..	..
INCOME							
Household income							
Share of top 20% of households	% of income	..	..	..	41	42	..
Share of bottom 40% of households	"	..	..	..	21	19	..
Share of bottom 20% of households	"	..	..	..	9	8	..
EXPENDITURE							
Food	% of GDP	..	..	..	..	..	..
Staples	"	..	..	..	..	..	..
Meat, fish, milk, cheese, eggs	"	..	..	..	..	..	..
Cereal imports	thou. metric tonnes	3	12	37	7,721	46,537	74,924
Food aid in cereals	"	..	5	4	2,558	9,008	4,054
Food production per capita	1987 = 100	97	101	94	116	123	..
Fertilizer consumption	kg/ha	0.3	0.3	0.3	71.5	61.9	..
Share of agriculture in GDP	% of GDP	..	51.7	39.9	28.7	29.6	..
Housing	% of GDP	..	..	..	..	..	..
Average household size	persons per household	..	..	..	..	..	..
Urban	"	..	..	..	..	..	..
Fixed investment: housing	% of GDP	..	..	..	..	..	..
Fuel and power	% of GDP	..	..	..	..	..	..
Energy consumption per capita	kg of oil equiv.	0	11	15	209	335	1,882
Households with electricity							
Urban	% of households	..	..	..	..	..	..
Rural	"	..	..	..	..	..	..
Transport and communication	% of GDP	..	..	..	..	..	..
Fixed investment: transport equipment	"	..	..	..	..	..	..
Total road length	thou. km	..	..	..	..	..	..
INVESTMENT IN HUMAN CAPITAL							
Health							
Population per physician	persons	..	23,308	13,112	2,459	..	..
Population per nurse	"	..	2,985	..	..	..	..
Population per hospital bed	"	..	..	..	1,652	1,050	516
Oral rehydration therapy (under-5)	% of cases	..	..	65	18	39	..
Education							
Gross enrollment ratio							
Secondary	% of school-age pop.	1	4	5	40	41	..
Female	"	0	1	2	29	35	..
Pupil-teacher ratio: primary	pupils per teacher	24	39	37	59	37	26
Pupil-teacher ratio: secondary	"	..	8	5	23	19	..
Pupils reaching grade 4	% of cohort	..	..	..	..	..	..
Repeater rate: primary	% of total enroll	..	..	17	..	..	..
Illiteracy	% of pop. (age 15+)	..	68	62	54	39	..
Female	% of fem. (age 15+)	..	81	75	68	52	..
Newspaper circulation	per thou. pop.	..	..	..	..	..	100

World Bank International Economics Department, April 1994

Bolivia

Indicator	Unit of measure	Latest single year 1970-75	Latest single year 1980-85	Most recent estimate 1987-92	Same region/income group Latin America Caribbean	Same region/income group Lower-middle-income	Next higher income group
Priority Poverty Indicators							
POVERTY							
Upper poverty line	local curr.	..	..	..	..	..	..
Headcount index	% of pop.	..	..	..	..	..	..
Lower poverty line	local curr.	..	..	..	..	..	..
Headcount index	% of pop.	..	..	..	..	..	..
GNP per capita	US$	360	430	680	2,690		3,870
SHORT TERM INCOME INDICATORS							
Unskilled urban wages	local curr.	..	..	..	..	..	..
Unskilled rural wages	"	..	..	..	..	..	..
Rural terms of trade	"	..	..	..	..	..	..
Consumer price index	1987=100	0	23	190	..	..	..
Lower income	"		..		..	..	..
Food[a]	"		24	184		..	..
Urban	"	..	..	..	..	..	..
Rural	"	..	..	..	..	..	..
SOCIAL INDICATORS							
Public expenditure on basic social services	% of GDP	..	..	..	..	..	..
Gross enrollment ratios							
Primary	% school age pop.	85	91	85	106	..	107
Male	"	94	96	89	..	..	..
Female	"	76	85	81	..	..	..
Mortality							
Infant mortality	per thou. live births	151.0	103.0	82.0	44.0	45.0	40.0
Under 5 mortality	"	..	..	110.5	56.0	59.0	51.0
Immunization							
Measles	% age group	..	17.0	73.0	78.9	..	82.0
DPT	"	..	24.0	58.0	73.8	..	73.8
Child malnutrition (under-5)	"	..	14.5	11.4	10.5	..	..
Life expectancy							
Total	years	47	54	60	68	68	69
Female advantage	"	4.4	4.3	4.1	5.6	6.4	6.3
Total fertility rate	births per woman	6.5	6.2	4.7	3.0	3.1	2.9
Maternal mortality rate	per 100,000 live births	..	480	48	..	..	..
Supplementary Poverty Indicators							
Expenditures on social security	% of total gov't exp.	..	2.4	17.9	..	..	..
Social security coverage	% econ. active pop.	..	..	16.9	..	..	..
Access to safe water: total	% of pop.	34.0	53.0	66.0	80.3	..	85.6
Urban	"	81.0	82.0	90.0	91.0	..	94.3
Rural	"	6.0	27.0	40.0	64.3	..	73.0
Access to health care	"	..	..	..	..	..	..

Population growth rate (annual average, percent)

□ Bolivia
— Lower-middle-income

GNP per capita growth rate (annual average, percent)

Development diamond[b]

Life expectancy

GNP per capita — Gross primary enrollment

Access to safe water

— Bolivia
— Lower-middle-income

a. See the technical notes, p.389. b. The development diamond, based on four key indicators, shows the average level of development in the country compared with its income group. See the introduction.

Bolivia

Indicator	Unit of measure	Latest single year 1970-75	1980-85	Most recent estimate 1987-92	Latin America Caribbean	Lower-middle-income	Next higher income group
Resources and Expenditures							
HUMAN RESOURCES							
Population (mre=1992)	thousands	4,894	6,342	7,524	453,294	942,547	477,960
Age dependency ratio	ratio	0.87	0.88	0.83	0.67	0.66	0.64
Urban	% of pop.	41.5	47.6	52.4	72.9	57.0	71.7
Population growth rate	annual %	2.6	2.5	2.4	1.7	1.4	1.6
Urban	"	2.9	4.0	3.7	2.6	4.8	2.5
Labor force (15-64)	thousands	1,565	1,987	2,405	166,091	..	181,414
Agriculture	% of labor force	49	46	..	..	..	..
Industry	"	20	20	..	..	..	..
Female	"	22	24	26	27	36	29
Females per 100 males							
Urban	number	99	108	108	..	..	..
Rural	"	99	100	100	..	..	..
NATURAL RESOURCES							
Area	thou. sq. km	1,098.58	1,098.58	1,098.58	20,507.48	40,697.37	21,836.02
Density	pop. per sq. km	4.5	5.8	6.7	21.7	22.8	21.5
Agricultural land	% of land area	26.8	26.8	26.7	40.2	..	41.7
Change in agricultural land	annual %	0.1	-0.1	0.0	0.5	..	0.3
Agricultural land under irrigation	%	0.4	0.6	0.6	3.2	..	9.3
Forests and woodland	thou. sq. km	568	559	555	..	..	..
Deforestation (net)	annual %	..	..	1.2	..	..	..
INCOME							
Household income							
Share of top 20% of households	% of income	59	..	48	..	..	..
Share of bottom 40% of households	"	13	..	15	..	..	..
Share of bottom 20% of households	"	4	..	6	..	..	..
EXPENDITURE							
Food	% of GDP	..	29.4	..	..	..	..
Staples	"	..	6.9	..	..	..	..
Meat, fish, milk, cheese, eggs	"	..	12.8	..	..	..	..
Cereal imports	thou. metric tonnes	241	400	381	25,032	74,924	49,174
Food aid in cereals	"	22	111	226	1,779	4,054	282
Food production per capita	1987 = 100	101	101	110	104	..	109
Fertilizer consumption	kg/ha	0.1	0.2	0.2	15.5	..	68.8
Share of agriculture in GDP	% of GDP	20.3	36.9	32.6	8.9	..	8.1
Housing	% of GDP	..	9.6	..	..	..	..
Average household size	persons per household	..	..	..	..	..	..
Urban	"	..	..	..	..	..	..
Fixed investment: housing	% of GDP	6.8	1.2	..	..	..	..
Fuel and power	% of GDP	..	1.3	..	..	..	..
Energy consumption per capita	kg of oil equiv.	241	271	255	912	1,882	1,649
Households with electricity							
Urban	% of households	..	..	..	..	..	..
Rural	"	..	..	..	..	..	..
Transport and communication	% of GDP	..	9.0	..	..	..	..
Fixed investment: transport equipment	"	6.7	1.8	..	..	..	..
Total road length	thou. km	37	41	42	..	..	..
INVESTMENT IN HUMAN CAPITAL							
Health							
Population per physician	persons	2,098	1,534	..	..	..	..
Population per nurse	"	3,074	2,466	..	..	..	..
Population per hospital bed	"	499	..	828	508	516	385
Oral rehydration therapy (under-5)	% of cases	..	..	63	62	..	54
Education							
Gross enrollment ratio							
Secondary	% of school-age pop.	31	37	34	47	..	53
Female	"	20	34	31	..	..	..
Pupil-teacher ratio: primary	pupils per teacher	22	25	25	25	26	25
Pupil-teacher ratio: secondary	"	19	..	..	..	..	..
Pupils reaching grade 4	% of cohort	52	59	..	..	..	71
Repeater rate: primary	% of total enroll	..	..	..	14	..	11
Illiteracy	% of pop. (age 15+)	..	28	23	15	..	14
Female	% of fem. (age 15+)	..	36	29	17	..	17
Newspaper circulation	per thou. pop.	41	45	56	99	100	117

World Bank International Economics Department, April 1994

43

Bosnia and Herzegovina

Indicator	Unit of measure	Latest single year 1970-75	Latest single year 1980-85	Most recent estimate 1987-92	Same region/income group Europe & Central Asia	Same region/income group Lower-middle-income	Next higher income group
Priority Poverty Indicators							
POVERTY							
Upper poverty line	local curr.	..	..	..	..	..	..
Headcount index	% of pop.	..	..	..	..	..	..
Lower poverty line	local curr.	..	..	..	..	..	..
Headcount index	% of pop.	..	..	..	..	..	..
GNP per capita	US$	..	..	..	..	..	3,870
SHORT TERM INCOME INDICATORS							
Unskilled urban wages	local curr.	..	..	..	..	..	..
Unskilled rural wages	"	..	..	..	..	..	..
Rural terms of trade	"	..	..	..	..	..	..
Consumer price index	1987=100	..	..	..	..	..	..
Lower income	"	..	..	..	..	..	..
Food[a]	"	..	..	..	..	..	..
Urban	"	..	..	..	..	..	..
Rural	"	..	..	..	..	..	..
SOCIAL INDICATORS							
Public expenditure on basic social services	% of GDP	..	..	..	..	..	..
Gross enrollment ratios							
Primary	% school age pop.	..	..	..	..	..	107
Male	"	..	..	..	..	..	..
Female	"	..	..	..	..	..	..
Mortality							
Infant mortality	per thou. live births	..	..	19.0	30.0	45.0	40.0
Under 5 mortality	"	..	..	22.9	38.0	59.0	51.0
Immunization							
Measles	% age group	..	..	..	..	..	82.0
DPT	"	..	..	..	..	..	73.8
Child malnutrition (under-5)	"	..	..	..	..	..	..
Life expectancy							
Total	years	..	..	71	70	68	69
Female advantage	"	..	..	5.2	8.6	6.4	6.3
Total fertility rate	births per woman	..	..	74.1	2.2	3.1	2.9
Maternal mortality rate	per 100,000 live births	..	..	..	58	..	..
Supplementary Poverty Indicators							
Expenditures on social security	% of total gov't exp.	..	..	..	..	..	..
Social security coverage	% econ. active pop.	..	..	..	..	..	..
Access to safe water: total	% of pop.	..	..	..	..	..	85.6
Urban	"	..	..	..	..	..	94.3
Rural	"	..	..	..	..	..	73.0
Access to health care	"	..	..	..	..	..	..

Population growth rate
(annual average, percent)

□ Bosnia and Herzegovina
— Lower-middle-income

GNP per capita growth rate
(annual average, percent)

Development diamond[b]

— Bosnia and Herzegovina
— Lower-middle-income

a. See the technical notes, p.389.   b. The development diamond, based on four key indicators, shows the average level of development in the country compared with its income group. See the introduction.

Bosnia and Herzegovina

Indicator	Unit of measure	Latest single year		Most recent estimate 1987-92	Same region/income group		Next higher income group
		1970-75	1980-85		Europe & Central Asia	Lower-middle-income	

Resources and Expenditures

Indicator	Unit of measure	1970-75	1980-85	1987-92	Europe & Central Asia	Lower-middle-income	Next higher income group
HUMAN RESOURCES							
Population (mre=1992)	thousands	3,880	4,316	4,383	495,241	942,547	477,960
Age dependency ratio	ratio	..	..	..	0.56	0.66	0.64
Urban	% of pop.	..	..	..	63.3	57.0	71.7
Population growth rate	annual %	1.1	1.2	0.0	0.5	1.4	1.6
Urban	"	..	..	..	..	4.8	2.5
Labor force (15-64)	thousands	..	..	..	..	..	181,414
Agriculture	% of labor force	..	..	..	..	..	..
Industry	"	..	..	..	..	..	..
Female	"	..	..	..	46	36	29
Females per 100 males							
Urban	number	..	..	..	..	..	..
Rural	"	..	..	..	..	..	..
NATURAL RESOURCES							
Area	thou. sq. km	..	..	51.13	24,165.06	40,697.37	21,836.02
Density	pop. per sq. km	..	..	..	20.4	22.8	21.5
Agricultural land	% of land area	..	..	..	..	..	41.7
Change in agricultural land	annual %	..	..	..	..	..	0.3
Agricultural land under irrigation	%	..	..	..	..	..	9.3
Forests and woodland	thou. sq. km	..	..	..	..	..	..
Deforestation (net)	annual %	..	..	..	..	..	..
INCOME							
Household income							
Share of top 20% of households	% of income	..	..	..	..	..	..
Share of bottom 40% of households	"	..	..	..	..	..	..
Share of bottom 20% of households	"	..	..	..	..	..	..
EXPENDITURE							
Food	% of GDP	..	..	..	..	..	..
Staples	"	..	..	..	..	..	..
Meat, fish, milk, cheese, eggs	"	..	..	..	..	..	..
Cereal imports	thou. metric tonnes	..	..	..	45,972	74,924	49,174
Food aid in cereals	"	..	..	..	1,639	4,054	282
Food production per capita	1987 = 100	..	..	..	..	..	109
Fertilizer consumption	kg/ha	..	..	..	..	..	68.8
Share of agriculture in GDP	% of GDP	..	..	..	..	..	8.1
Housing	% of GDP	..	..	..	..	..	..
Average household size	persons per household	..	..	..	..	..	..
Urban	"	..	..	..	..	..	..
Fixed investment: housing	% of GDP	..	..	..	..	..	..
Fuel and power	% of GDP	..	..	..	..	..	..
Energy consumption per capita	kg of oil equiv.	..	..	..	3,190	1,882	1,649
Households with electricity							
Urban	% of households	..	..	..	..	..	..
Rural	"	..	..	..	..	..	..
Transport and communication	% of GDP	..	..	..	..	..	..
Fixed investment: transport equipment	"	..	..	..	..	..	..
Total road length	thou. km	..	..	..	..	..	..
INVESTMENT IN HUMAN CAPITAL							
Health							
Population per physician	persons	..	..	..	378	..	..
Population per nurse	"	..	..	..	..	..	..
Population per hospital bed	"	..	..	..	134	516	385
Oral rehydration therapy (under-5)	% of cases	..	..	..	..	..	54
Education							
Gross enrollment ratio							
Secondary	% of school-age pop.	..	..	..	..	..	53
Female	"	..	..	..	..	..	..
Pupil-teacher ratio: primary	pupils per teacher	..	..	..	..	26	25
Pupil-teacher ratio: secondary	"	..	..	..	..	..	..
Pupils reaching grade 4	% of cohort	..	..	..	..	..	71
Repeater rate: primary	% of total enroll	..	..	..	..	..	11
Illiteracy	% of pop. (age 15+)	..	..	..	..	..	14
Female	% of fem. (age 15+)	..	..	..	..	..	17
Newspaper circulation	per thou. pop.	..	..	..	..	100	117

World Bank International Economics Department, April 1994

Botswana

Indicator	Unit of measure	Latest single year		Most recent estimate	Same region/income group		Next higher income group
		1970-75	1980-85	1987-92	Sub-Saharan Africa	Upper-middle-income	

Priority Poverty Indicators

POVERTY							
Upper poverty line	local curr.	..	..	..	..	..	..
Headcount index	% of pop.	..	..	..	..	..	..
Lower poverty line	local curr.	..	..	..	..	..	..
Headcount index	% of pop.	..	..	..	..	..	..
GNP per capita	US$	360	1,040	2,790	520	3,870	21,960
SHORT TERM INCOME INDICATORS							
Unskilled urban wages	local curr.	..	..	..	..	..	..
Unskilled rural wages	"	..	..	..	..	..	..
Rural terms of trade	"	..	..	..	..	..	..
Consumer price index	1987=100	28	83	175	..	..	..
Lower income	"	..	..	..	..	..	..
Food[a]	"	..	83	176	..	..	..
Urban	"	..	..	..	..	..	..
Rural	"	..	..	..	..	..	..
SOCIAL INDICATORS							
Public expenditure on basic social services	% of GDP	..	..	..	..	..	
Gross enrollment ratios							
Primary	% school age pop.	72	110	119	66	107	103
Male	"	65	105	116	79	..	103
Female	"	79	115	121	62	..	103
Mortality							
Infant mortality	per thou. live births	95.0	50.0	35.0	99.0	40.0	7.0
Under 5 mortality	"	..	..	42.9	169.0	51.0	10.0
Immunization							
Measles	% age group	..	68.0	60.0	54.0	82.0	82.4
DPT	"	..	68.0	63.0	54.6	73.8	90.1
Child malnutrition (under-5)	"	..	..	27.0	28.4	..	..
Life expectancy							
Total	years	51	65	68	52	69	77
Female advantage	"	3.1	3.8	3.9	3.4	6.3	6.4
Total fertility rate	births per woman	6.9	6.8	4.7	6.1	2.9	1.7
Maternal mortality rate	per 100,000 live births	..	90	..	..	..	..

Supplementary Poverty Indicators

Expenditures on social security	% of total gov't exp.	..	..	..	..	..	..
Social security coverage	% econ. active pop.	..	..	..	..	..	..
Access to safe water: total	% of pop.	45.0	54.0	56.0	41.1	85.6	..
Urban	"	95.0	84.0	98.0	77.8	94.3	..
Rural	"	39.0	46.0	46.0	27.3	73.0	..
Access to health care	"	..	..	85.0	..	..	..

Population growth rate
(annual average, percent)

GNP per capita growth rate
(annual average, percent)

Development diamond[b]

☐ Botswana
— Upper-middle-income

━━ Botswana
— Upper-middle-income

a. See the technical notes, p.389.   b. The development diamond, based on four key indicators, shows the average level of development in the country compared with its income group. See the introduction.

Botswana

Indicator	Unit of measure	Latest single year 1970-75	Latest single year 1980-85	Most recent estimate 1987-92	Same region/income group Sub-Saharan Africa	Same region/income group Upper-middle-income	Next higher income group
Resources and Expenditures							
HUMAN RESOURCES							
Population (mre=1992)	thousands	755	1,075	1,361	546,390	477,960	828,221
Age dependency ratio	ratio	1.10	1.08	0.99	0.95	0.64	0.50
Urban	% of pop.	12.0	19.5	27.3	29.5	71.7	78.1
Population growth rate	annual %	3.8	3.5	3.1	2.9	1.6	0.7
Urban	"	10.0	8.1	7.5	5.1	2.5	0.9
Labor force (15-64)	thousands	278	381	478	224,025	181,414	390,033
Agriculture	% of labor force	78	70	..	..	..	..
Industry	"	8	13	..	..	..	..
Female	"	41	36	35	37	29	38
Females per 100 males							
Urban	number	99	86	..	..	..	..
Rural	"	145	137	..	..	..	..
NATURAL RESOURCES							
Area	thou. sq. km	581.73	581.73	581.73	24,274.03	21,836.02	31,709.00
Density	pop. per sq. km	1.3	1.9	2.3	21.9	21.5	24.5
Agricultural land	% of land area	60.6	60.6	60.7	52.7	41.7	42.7
Change in agricultural land	annual %	0.1	0.0	0.1	0.1	0.3	-0.2
Agricultural land under irrigation	%	0.0	0.0	0.0	0.8	9.3	16.1
Forests and woodland	thou. sq. km	111	110	109	..	..	..
Deforestation (net)	annual %	..	..	0.5	..	..	..
INCOME							
Household income							
Share of top 20% of households	% of income	60	..	..	..	..	..
Share of bottom 40% of households	"	8	..	..	..	..	..
Share of bottom 20% of households	"	2	..	..	..	..	..
EXPENDITURE							
Food	% of GDP	..	14.2	..	..	..	..
Staples	"	..	6.6	..	..	..	..
Meat, fish, milk, cheese, eggs	"	..	4.3	..	..	..	..
Cereal imports	thou. metric tonnes	24	155	80	20,311	49,174	70,626
Food aid in cereals	"	5	39	0	4,303	282	2
Food production per capita	1987 = 100	119	78	61	90	109	101
Fertilizer consumption	kg/ha	0.1	0.0	0.0	4.2	68.8	162.1
Share of agriculture in GDP	% of GDP	31.6	6.5	5.1	18.6	8.1	2.4
Housing	% of GDP	..	4.7	..	..	..	..
Average household size	persons per household	..	5.4	..	..	..	..
Urban	"	..	..	..	..	..	..
Fixed investment: housing	% of GDP	4.6	2.3	..	..	..	..
Fuel and power	% of GDP	..	1.2	..	..	..	..
Energy consumption per capita	kg of oil equiv.	306	417	395	258	1,649	5,101
Households with electricity							
Urban	% of households	..	..	..	..	..	..
Rural	"	..	..	..	..	..	..
Transport and communication	% of GDP	..	4.3	..	..	..	..
Fixed investment: transport equipment	"	2.3	4.5	..	..	..	..
Total road length	thou. km	10	8	9	..	..	..
INVESTMENT IN HUMAN CAPITAL							
Health							
Population per physician	persons	7,499	6,910	5,146	..	..	..
Population per nurse	"	1,897	703	..	..	..	..
Population per hospital bed	"	..	421	..	1,329	385	144
Oral rehydration therapy (under-5)	% of cases	..	..	64	36	54	..
Education							
Gross enrollment ratio							
Secondary	% of school-age pop.	16	31	54	18	53	92
Female	"	16	33	57	14	..	94
Pupil-teacher ratio: primary	pupils per teacher	33	32	30	39	25	18
Pupil-teacher ratio: secondary	"	21	25	20	..	..	..
Pupils reaching grade 4	% of cohort	94	96	92	..	..	..
Repeater rate: primary	% of total enroll	3	6	5	..	71	..
Illiteracy	% of pop. (age 15+)	59	30	26	51	11	..
Female	% of fem. (age 15+)	..	40	35	62	14	..
Newspaper circulation	per thou. pop.	19	18	14	14	17	..

World Bank International Economics Department, April 1994

Brazil

Indicator	Unit of measure	Latest single year 1970-75	1980-85	Most recent estimate 1987-92	Same region/income group Latin America Caribbean	Upper-middle-income	Next higher income group
Priority Poverty Indicators							
POVERTY							
Upper poverty line	local curr.	..	..	..	..	..	..
Headcount index	% of pop.	..	..	..	..	..	..
Lower poverty line	local curr.	..	..	..	..	..	..
Headcount index	% of pop.	48	26	..	..	..	..
GNP per capita	US$	1,070	1,640	2,770	2,690	3,870	21,960
SHORT TERM INCOME INDICATORS							
Unskilled urban wages	local curr.	..	..	..	..	..	..
Unskilled rural wages	"	..	..	..	..	..	..
Rural terms of trade	"	..	..	..	..	..	..
Consumer price index	1987=100	0	12	19,767,360	..	..	..
Lower income	"	..	..	..	..	..	..
Food[a]	"	..	15	1,397,383	..	..	..
Urban	"	..	..	..	..	..	..
Rural	"	..	..	..	..	..	..
SOCIAL INDICATORS							
Public expenditure on basic social services	% of GDP	..	..	..	..	..	..
Gross enrollment ratios							
Primary	% school age pop.	88	101	106	106	107	103
Male	"	89	108	..	..	..	103
Female	"	87	99	..	..	..	103
Mortality							
Infant mortality	per thou. live births	91.0	71.0	57.0	44.0	40.0	7.0
Under 5 mortality	"	..	..	73.0	56.0	51.0	10.0
Immunization							
Measles	% age group	..	80.0	83.0	78.9	82.0	82.4
DPT	"	..	67.0	75.0	73.8	73.8	90.1
Child malnutrition (under-5)	"	..	..	7.1	10.5	..	..
Life expectancy							
Total	years	60	63	66	68	69	77
Female advantage	"	4.6	5.1	5.6	5.6	6.3	6.4
Total fertility rate	births per woman	4.7	3.8	2.8	3.0	2.9	1.7
Maternal mortality rate	per 100,000 live births	..	150	140	..	..	..
Supplementary Poverty Indicators							
Expenditures on social security	% of total gov't exp.	50.0	20.7	32.1	..	..	..
Social security coverage	% econ. active pop.	..	..	..	..	..	..
Access to safe water: total	% of pop.	55.0	84.0	87.0	80.3	85.6	..
Urban	"	87.0	89.0	95.0	91.0	94.3	..
Rural	"	28.0	71.0	61.0	64.3	73.0	..
Access to health care	"	..	..	..	..	..	..

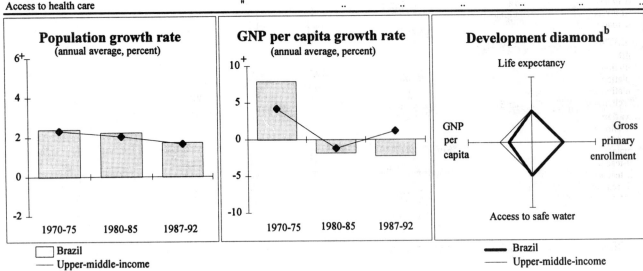

Population growth rate (annual average, percent)

GNP per capita growth rate (annual average, percent)

Development diamond[b] — Life expectancy / GNP per capita / Gross primary enrollment / Access to safe water

□ Brazil
— Upper-middle-income

— Brazil
— Upper-middle-income

a. See the technical notes, p.389.   b. The development diamond, based on four key indicators, shows the average level of development in the country compared with its income group. See the introduction.

Brazil

Indicator	Unit of measure	Latest single year 1970-75	Latest single year 1980-85	Most recent estimate 1987-92	Same region/income group Latin America Caribbean	Same region/income group Upper-middle-income	Next higher income group

Resources and Expenditures

Indicator	Unit of measure	1970-75	1980-85	1987-92	Latin America Caribbean	Upper-middle-income	Next higher income group
HUMAN RESOURCES							
Population (mre=1992)	thousands	108,032	135,564	153,850	453,294	477,960	828,221
Age dependency ratio	ratio	0.78	0.69	0.64	0.67	0.64	0.50
Urban	% of pop.	61.2	70.9	76.6	72.9	71.7	78.1
Population growth rate	annual %	2.4	2.1	1.6	1.7	1.6	0.7
Urban	"	4.1	3.5	2.5	2.6	2.5	0.9
Labor force (15-64)	thousands	37,492	49,642	57,525	166,091	181,414	390,033
Agriculture	% of labor force	38	31	..	..	..	..
Industry	"	24	27	..	..	..	..
Female	"	24	27	28	27	29	38
Females per 100 males							
Urban	number	110	105	..	..	..	..
Rural	"	93	90	..	..	..	..
NATURAL RESOURCES							
Area	thou. sq. km	8,511.97	8,511.97	8,511.97	20,507.48	21,836.02	31,709.00
Density	pop. per sq. km	12.7	15.9	17.8	21.7	21.5	24.5
Agricultural land	% of land area	24.2	27.2	29.2	40.2	41.7	42.7
Change in agricultural land	annual %	1.7	0.8	1.1	0.5	0.3	-0.2
Agricultural land under irrigation	%	0.5	0.9	1.1	3.2	9.3	16.1
Forests and woodland	thou. sq. km	5,306	5,057	4,905	..	..	..
Deforestation (net)	annual %	..	..	0.6	..	..	..
INCOME							
Household income							
Share of top 20% of households	% of income	62	63	68	..	..	..
Share of bottom 40% of households	"	9	8	7	..	..	..
Share of bottom 20% of households	"	3	2	2	..	..	..
EXPENDITURE							
Food	% of GDP	24.2	26.1	..	..	..	..
Staples	"	6.0	6.6	..	..	..	..
Meat, fish, milk, cheese, eggs	"	9.9	10.3	..	..	..	..
Cereal imports	thou. metric tonnes	2,244	4,857	5,854	25,032	49,174	70,626
Food aid in cereals	"	31	10	9	1,779	282	2
Food production per capita	1987 = 100	94	110	117	104	109	101
Fertilizer consumption	kg/ha	9.7	13.9	13.1	15.5	68.8	162.1
Share of agriculture in GDP	% of GDP	10.7	10.5	9.6	8.9	8.1	2.4
Housing	% of GDP	7.6	7.6	..	..	..	..
Average household size	persons per household	4.8	4.2	..	..	..	..
Urban	"	4.6	4.1	..	..	..	..
Fixed investment: housing	% of GDP	2.6	2.6	..	..	..	..
Fuel and power	% of GDP	2.8	1.2	..	..	..	..
Energy consumption per capita	kg of oil equiv.	506	600	681	912	1,649	5,101
Households with electricity							
Urban	% of households	..	88.5	..	..	..	..
Rural	"	..	..	..	..	..	..
Transport and communication	% of GDP	7.7	5.7	..	..	..	..
Fixed investment: transport equipment	"	2.6	1.9	..	..	..	..
Total road length	thou. km	1,489	1,438	1,670	..	..	..
INVESTMENT IN HUMAN CAPITAL							
Health							
Population per physician	persons	1,600	684	..	..	..	..
Population per nurse	"	2,322	1,206	..	..	..	..
Population per hospital bed	"	200	..	301	508	385	144
Oral rehydration therapy (under-5)	% of cases	..	..	62	62	54	..
Education							
Gross enrollment ratio							
Secondary	% of school-age pop.	26	36	39	47	53	92
Female	"	28	41	..	..	..	94
Pupil-teacher ratio: primary	pupils per teacher	22	24	23	25	25	18
Pupil-teacher ratio: secondary	"	15	..	..	..	..	..
Pupils reaching grade 4	% of cohort	54	59	50	..	71	..
Repeater rate: primary	% of total enroll	15	20	19	14	11	..
Illiteracy	% of pop. (age 15+)	34	22	19	15	14	..
Female	% of fem. (age 15+)	..	23	20	17	17	..
Newspaper circulation	per thou. pop.	39	57	54	99	117	..

World Bank International Economics Department, April 1994

Brunei

Indicator	Unit of measure	Latest single year		Most recent estimate 1987-92	Same region/income group High-income	Next
		1970-75	1980-85			
Priority Poverty Indicators						
POVERTY						
Upper poverty line	local curr.	..	..	..	..	
Headcount index	% of pop.	..	..	..	..	
Lower poverty line	local curr.	..	..	..	..	
Headcount index	% of pop.	..	..	..	..	
GNP per capita	US$	..	17,410	11,990	21,960	
SHORT TERM INCOME INDICATORS						
Unskilled urban wages	local curr.	..	..	..	..	
Unskilled rural wages	"	..	..	..	..	
Rural terms of trade	"	..	..	..	..	
Consumer price index	1987=100	..	..	..	..	
Lower income	"	..	..	..	..	
Food[a]	"	..	98	103	..	
Urban	"	..	..	..	..	
Rural	"	..	..	..	..	
SOCIAL INDICATORS						
Public expenditure on basic social services	% of GDP	..	..	..	..	
Gross enrollment ratios						
Primary	% school age pop.	..	..	110	103	
Male	"	..	..	112	103	
Female	"	..	..	107	103	
Mortality						
Infant mortality	per thou. live births	27.2	17.4	7.3	7.0	
Under 5 mortality	"	..	..	9.3	10.0	
Immunization						
Measles	% age group	..	98.0	100.0	82.4	
DPT	"	..	88.0	91.0	90.1	
Child malnutrition (under-5)	"	..	..	..	..	
Life expectancy						
Total	years	..	71	74	77	
Female advantage	"	..	2.0	3.8	6.4	
Total fertility rate	births per woman	5.4	3.8	3.1	1.7	
Maternal mortality rate	per 100,000 live births	..	..	..	..	
Supplementary Poverty Indicators						
Expenditures on social security	% of total gov't exp.	..	..	..	..	
Social security coverage	% econ. active pop.	..	..	..	..	
Access to safe water: total	% of pop.	..	..	..	..	
Urban	"	..	..	..	..	
Rural	"	..	..	..	..	
Access to health care	"	..	96.0	..	..	

Population growth rate
(annual average, percent)

☐ Brunei
— High-income

GNP per capita growth rate
(annual average, percent)

Development diamond[b]

— Brunei
— High-income

a. See the technical notes, p.389.   b. The development diamond, based on four key indicators, shows the average level of development in the country compared with its income group. See the introduction.

50

Brunei

Indicator	Unit of measure	Latest single year 1970-75	Latest single year 1980-85	Most recent estimate 1987-92	Same region/income group High-income
Resources and Expenditures					
HUMAN RESOURCES					
Population (mre=1992)	thousands	161	219	273	828,221
Age dependency ratio	ratio	..	0.65	0.61	0.50
Urban	% of pop.	62.0	57.7	57.7	78.1
Population growth rate	annual %	3.8	4.2	3.0	0.7
Urban	"	3.9	3.4	3.0	0.9
Labor force (15-64)	thousands	..	..	..	390,033
Agriculture	% of labor force	..	..	..	..
Industry	"	..	..	..	..
Female	"	..	..	..	38
Females per 100 males					
Urban	number	..	..	..	..
Rural	"	..	..	..	..
NATURAL RESOURCES					
Area	thou. sq. km	5.77	5.77	5.77	31,709.00
Density	pop. per sq. km	27.9	38.0	45.9	24.5
Agricultural land	% of land area	3.2	2.5	2.5	42.7
Change in agricultural land	annual %	-5.6	0.0	0.0	-0.2
Agricultural land under irrigation	%	..	7.7	7.7	16.1
Forests and woodland	thou. sq. km	4	3	2	..
Deforestation (net)	annual %	..	..	..	..
INCOME					
Household income					
Share of top 20% of households	% of income	..	..	..	..
Share of bottom 40% of households	"	..	..	..	..
Share of bottom 20% of households	"	..	..	..	..
EXPENDITURE					
Food	% of GDP	..	..	..	..
Staples	"	..	..	..	..
Meat, fish, milk, cheese, eggs	"	..	..	..	..
Cereal imports	thou. metric tonnes	14	34	48	70,626
Food aid in cereals	"	..	..	..	2
Food production per capita	1987 = 100	126	125	93	101
Fertilizer consumption	kg/ha	..	68.9	338.5	162.1
Share of agriculture in GDP	% of GDP	1.4	1.2	2.2	2.4
Housing	% of GDP	..	..	..	..
Average household size	persons per household	5.8	..	..	..
Urban	"	5.8	..	..	..
Fixed investment: housing	% of GDP	..	..	..	..
Fuel and power	% of GDP	..	..	..	..
Energy consumption per capita	kg of oil equiv.	1,180	4,872	7,341	5,101
Households with electricity					
Urban	% of households	..	..	..	..
Rural	"	..	..	..	..
Transport and communication	% of GDP	..	..	..	..
Fixed investment: transport equipment	"	..	..	..	..
Total road length	thou. km	1	..	..	..
INVESTMENT IN HUMAN CAPITAL					
Health					
Population per physician	persons	3,333	1,810	..	..
Population per nurse	"	536	262	..	..
Population per hospital bed	"	285	319	..	144
Oral rehydration therapy (under-5)	% of cases	..	..	..	..
Education					
Gross enrollment ratio					
Secondary	% of school-age pop.	..	..	..	92
Female		..	..	..	94
Pupil-teacher ratio: primary	pupils per teacher	19	16	15	18
Pupil-teacher ratio: secondary	"	20	12	13	..
Pupils reaching grade 4	% of cohort	..	94	..	..
Repeater rate: primary	% of total enroll	8	10	..	..
Illiteracy	% of pop. (age 15+)	36	22	..	..
Female	% of fem. (age 15+)	..	..	..	..
Newspaper circulation	per thou. pop.	48	..	39	..

World Bank International Economics Department, April 1994

Bulgaria

| Indicator | Unit of measure | Latest single year | | Most recent estimate 1987-92 | Same region/income group | | Next higher income group |
		1970-75	1980-85		Europe & Central Asia	Lower-middle-income	

Priority Poverty Indicators

Indicator	Unit of measure	1970-75	1980-85	1987-92	Europe & Central Asia	Lower-middle-income	Next higher income group
POVERTY							
Upper poverty line	local curr.	..	..	..	..	..	..
Headcount index	% of pop.	..	..	..	..	..	..
Lower poverty line	local curr.	..	..	..	..	..	..
Headcount index	% of pop.	..	..	..	..	..	..
GNP per capita	US$	..	2,060	1,330	..	..	3,870
SHORT TERM INCOME INDICATORS							
Unskilled urban wages	local curr.	..	..	..	..	..	..
Unskilled rural wages	"	..	..	..	..	..	..
Rural terms of trade	"	..	..	..	..	..	..
Consumer price index	1987=100	..	..	..	..	..	..
Lower income	"	..	..	..	..	..	..
Food[a]	"	..	96	424	..	..	..
Urban	"	..	..	..	..	..	..
Rural	"	..	..	..	..	..	..
SOCIAL INDICATORS							
Public expenditure on basic social services	% of GDP	..	..	6.3	..	..	..
Gross enrollment ratios							
Primary	% school age pop.	99	102	92	..	..	107
Male	"	99	103	93	..	..	..
Female	"	99	102	91	..	..	..
Mortality							
Infant mortality	per thou. live births	23.1	15.4	15.8	30.0	45.0	40.0
Under 5 mortality	"	..	..	19.5	38.0	59.0	51.0
Immunization							
Measles	% age group	..	99.0	97.0	..	..	82.0
DPT	"	..	99.0	99.0	..	..	73.8
Child malnutrition (under-5)	"	..	..	..	..	..	..
Life expectancy							
Total	years	71	71	71	70	68	69
Female advantage	"	5.2	5.9	7.0	8.6	6.4	6.3
Total fertility rate	births per woman	2.2	2.0	1.5	2.2	3.1	2.9
Maternal mortality rate	per 100,000 live births	..	22	..	58	..	..

Supplementary Poverty Indicators

Indicator	Unit of measure	1970-75	1980-85	1987-92	Europe & Central Asia	Lower-middle-income	Next higher income group
Expenditures on social security	% of total gov't exp.	..	..	16.7	..	..	..
Social security coverage	% econ. active pop.	..	..	..	..	..	..
Access to safe water: total	% of pop.	..	..	..	..	..	85.6
Urban	"	..	..	..	..	..	94.3
Rural	"	..	..	..	..	..	73.0
Access to health care	"	..	100.0	100.0	..	..	..

Population growth rate
(annual average, percent)

GNP per capita growth rate
(annual average, percent)

Development diamond[b]

Life expectancy

GNP per capita — Gross primary enrollment

Access to safe water

□ Bulgaria
— Lower-middle-income

▬ Bulgaria
— Lower-middle-income

a. See the technical notes, p.389.   b. The development diamond, based on four key indicators, shows the average level of development in the country compared with its income group. See the introduction.

52

Bulgaria

Indicator	Unit of measure	Latest single year 1970-75	Latest single year 1980-85	Most recent estimate 1987-92	Europe & Central Asia	Lower-middle-income	Next higher income group
Resources and Expenditures							
HUMAN RESOURCES							
Population (mre=1992)	thousands	8,721	8,941	8,505	495,241	942,547	477,960
Age dependency ratio	ratio	0.49	0.48	0.50	0.56	0.66	0.64
Urban	% of pop.	57.5	64.5	68.9	63.3	57.0	71.7
Population growth rate	annual %	0.5	0.2	-0.8	0.5	1.4	1.6
Urban	"	2.5	1.2	0.1	..	4.8	2.5
Labor force (15-64)	thousands	4,496	4,483	4,492		..	181,414
Agriculture	% of labor force	27	18	..	..	..	..
Industry	"	42	45	..	..	..	..
Female	"	46	46	46	46	36	29
Females per 100 males							
Urban	number	96	100	..	..	..	..
Rural	"	105	100	..	..	..	..
NATURAL RESOURCES							
Area	thou. sq. km	110.91	110.91	110.91	24,165.06	40,697.37	21,836.02
Density	pop. per sq. km	78.6	80.6	77.3	20.4	22.8	21.5
Agricultural land	% of land area	53.9	55.8	55.7	..	..	41.7
Change in agricultural land	annual %	-1.4	-0.1	0.0	..	..	0.3
Agricultural land under irrigation	%	18.9	19.9	20.1	..	..	9.3
Forests and woodland	thou. sq. km	38	39	39	..	..	..
Deforestation (net)	annual %	..	..	-0.3	..	..	..
INCOME							
Household income							
Share of top 20% of households	% of income	..	..	..	..	..	..
Share of bottom 40% of households	"	..	..	..	..	..	..
Share of bottom 20% of households	"	..	..	..	..	..	..
EXPENDITURE							
Food	% of GDP	..	..	17.0	..	..	..
Staples	"	..	..	1.8	..	..	..
Meat, fish, milk, cheese, eggs	"	..	..	8.2	..	..	..
Cereal imports	thou. metric tonnes	665	1,792	131	45,972	74,924	49,174
Food aid in cereals	"	..	..	200	1,639	4,054	282
Food production per capita	1987 = 100	88	86	76	..	..	109
Fertilizer consumption	kg/ha	114.0	140.1	68.9	..	..	68.8
Share of agriculture in GDP	% of GDP	..	11.9	13.9	..	..	8.1
Housing	% of GDP	..	..	6.7	..	..	..
Average household size	persons per household	3.1	..	..	..	..	..
Urban	"	3.0	..	..	..	..	..
Fixed investment: housing	% of GDP	..	..	1.1	..	..	..
Fuel and power	% of GDP	..	..	1.8	..	..	..
Energy consumption per capita	kg of oil equiv.	2,662	3,400	2,422	3,190	1,882	1,649
Households with electricity							
Urban	% of households	..	..	..	..	..	..
Rural	"	..	..	..	..	..	..
Transport and communication	% of GDP	..	..	7.0	..	..	..
Fixed investment: transport equipment	"	..	..	2.7	..	..	..
Total road length	thou. km	..	38	37	..	..	..
INVESTMENT IN HUMAN CAPITAL							
Health							
Population per physician	persons	537	276	319	378	..	..
Population per nurse	"	239	155	..	..	..	..
Population per hospital bed	"	129	90	100	134	516	385
Oral rehydration therapy (under-5)	% of cases	..	..	..	..	..	54
Education							
Gross enrollment ratio							
Secondary	% of school-age pop.	89	102	71	..	..	53
Female		..	102	73	..	..	..
Pupil-teacher ratio: primary	pupils per teacher	20	18	15	..	26	25
Pupil-teacher ratio: secondary	"	13	17	14	..	..	..
Pupils reaching grade 4	% of cohort	96	95	37	..	..	71
Repeater rate: primary	% of total enroll	2	2	3	..	..	11
Illiteracy	% of pop. (age 15+)	..	..	..	..	..	14
Female	% of fem. (age 15+)	..	..	..	..	..	17
Newspaper circulation	per thou. pop.	232	234	471	..	100	117

World Bank International Economics Department, April 1994

Burkina Faso

Indicator	Unit of measure	Latest single year 1970-75	Latest single year 1980-85	Most recent estimate 1987-92	Same region/income group Sub-Saharan Africa	Same region/income group Low-income	Next higher income group
Priority Poverty Indicators							
POVERTY							
Upper poverty line	local curr.	..	..	..	..	..	..
Headcount index	% of pop.	..	..	..	..	19	..
Lower poverty line	local curr.	..	..	..	..	..	..
Headcount index	% of pop.	..	..	..	..	..	..
GNP per capita	US$	110	170	300	520	390	..
SHORT TERM INCOME INDICATORS							
Unskilled urban wages	local curr.	..	..	..	..	..	..
Unskilled rural wages	"	..	..	..	..	..	..
Rural terms of trade	"	..	..	..	..	..	..
Consumer price index	1987=100	43	106	103	..	..	..
Lower income	"	..	..	..	..	..	..
Food[a]	"	..	122	105	..	..	..
Urban	"	..	..	..	..	..	..
Rural	"	..	..	..	..	..	..
SOCIAL INDICATORS							
Public expenditure on basic social services	% of GDP	..	..	9.5	..	..	..
Gross enrollment ratios							
Primary	% school age pop.	16	29	31	66	103	..
Male	"	21	36	37	79	113	..
Female	"	12	21	24	62	96	..
Mortality							
Infant mortality	per thou. live births	173.0	149.0	132.0	99.0	73.0	45.0
Under 5 mortality	"	..	..	195.7	169.0	108.0	59.0
Immunization							
Measles	% age group	..	38.0	42.0	54.0	72.7	..
DPT	"	..	2.0	37.0	54.6	80.6	..
Child malnutrition (under-5)	"	..	..	45.5	28.4	38.3	..
Life expectancy							
Total	years	41	45	48	52	62	68
Female advantage	"	3.2	3.1	3.3	3.4	2.4	6.4
Total fertility rate	births per woman	6.4	6.5	6.9	6.1	3.4	3.1
Maternal mortality rate	per 100,000 live births	..	600	..	..	..	..
Supplementary Poverty Indicators							
Expenditures on social security	% of total gov't exp.	6.0	6.7	..	..	..	..
Social security coverage	% econ. active pop.	..	..	..	..	..	..
Access to safe water: total	% of pop.	25.0	67.0	..	41.1	68.4	..
Urban	"	50.0	43.0	..	77.8	78.9	..
Rural	"	23.0	69.0	..	27.3	60.3	..
Access to health care	"	..	70.0	..	..	..	..

Population growth rate (annual average, percent)

Burkina Faso
Low-income

GNP per capita growth rate (annual average, percent)

Development diamond[b]

Life expectancy

GNP per capita

Gross primary enrollment

Access to safe water

Burkina Faso
Low-income

a. See the technical notes, p.389.   b. The development diamond, based on four key indicators, shows the average level of development in the country compared with its income group. See the introduction.

Burkina Faso

Indicator	Unit of measure	Latest single year 1970-75	Latest single year 1980-85	Most recent estimate 1987-92	Same region/income group Sub-Saharan Africa	Same region/income group Low-income	Next higher income group
Resources and Expenditures							
HUMAN RESOURCES							
Population (mre=1992)	thousands	6,202	7,881	9,546	546,390	3,194,535	942,547
Age dependency ratio	ratio	0.88	0.90	0.96	0.95	0.67	0.66
Urban	% of pop.	6.3	11.4	16.9	29.5	26.7	57.0
Population growth rate	annual %	2.1	2.6	2.9	2.9	1.8	1.4
Urban	"	4.0	7.8	8.1	5.1	3.4	4.8
Labor force (15-64)	thousands	3,111	3,765	4,355	224,025	1,478,954	..
Agriculture	% of labor force	87	87	..	..	..	..
Industry	"	4	4	..	..	..	..
Female	"	48	47	46	37	33	36
Females per 100 males							
Urban	number	94	..	..	..	..	..
Rural	"	110	..	..	..	..	..
NATURAL RESOURCES							
Area	thou. sq. km	274.20	274.20	274.20	24,274.03	38,401.06	40,697.37
Density	pop. per sq. km	22.6	28.7	33.8	21.9	81.7	22.8
Agricultural land	% of land area	45.8	47.6	49.5	52.7	50.9	..
Change in agricultural land	annual %	0.7	0.4	0.0	0.1	0.0	..
Agricultural land under irrigation	%	0.1	0.1	0.2	0.8	18.2	..
Forests and woodland	thou. sq. km	75	69	65	..	..	..
Deforestation (net)	annual %	..	..	0.7	..	..	..
INCOME							
Household income							
Share of top 20% of households	% of income	..	..	..	..	42	..
Share of bottom 40% of households	"	..	..	..	..	19	..
Share of bottom 20% of households	"	..	..	..	..	8	..
EXPENDITURE							
Food	% of GDP	..	..	35.7	..	..	..
Staples	"	..	..	13.9	..	..	..
Meat, fish, milk, cheese, eggs	"	..	..	14.6	..	..	..
Cereal imports	thou. metric tonnes	26	205	145	20,311	46,537	74,924
Food aid in cereals	"	28	128	87	4,303	9,008	4,054
Food production per capita	1987 = 100	107	117	128	90	123	..
Fertilizer consumption	kg/ha	0.1	0.9	1.9	4.2	61.9	..
Share of agriculture in GDP	% of GDP	37.5	42.4	41.6	18.6	29.6	..
Housing	% of GDP	..	..	15.2	..	..	..
Average household size	persons per household	..	..	..	..	..	..
Urban	"	..	..	..	..	..	..
Fixed investment: housing	% of GDP	..	..	3.5	..	..	..
Fuel and power	% of GDP	..	..	11.7	..	..	..
Energy consumption per capita	kg of oil equiv.	12	18	16	258	335	1,882
Households with electricity							
Urban	% of households	..	..	..	..	..	..
Rural	"	..	..	..	..	..	..
Transport and communication	% of GDP	..	..	15.0	..	..	..
Fixed investment: transport equipment	"	..	..	2.0	..	..	..
Total road length	thou. km	17	9	11	..	..	..
INVESTMENT IN HUMAN CAPITAL							
Health							
Population per physician	persons	97,121	57,191	57,307	..	..	..
Population per nurse	"	3,999	1,683	1,682	..	..	..
Population per hospital bed	"	1,750	..	3,392	1,329	1,050	516
Oral rehydration therapy (under-5)	% of cases	..	..	15	36	39	..
Education							
Gross enrollment ratio							
Secondary	% of school-age pop.	2	5	8	18	41	..
Female	"	1	3	5	14	35	..
Pupil-teacher ratio: primary	pupils per teacher	47	58	58	39	37	26
Pupil-teacher ratio: secondary	"	23	23	31	..	19	..
Pupils reaching grade 4	% of cohort	72	82	88	..	..	..
Repeater rate: primary	% of total enroll	17	14	17	..	..	..
Illiteracy	% of pop. (age 15+)	91	86	82	51	39	..
Female	% of fem. (age 15+)	..	94	91	62	52	..
Newspaper circulation	per thou. pop.	0	0	0	14	..	100

World Bank International Economics Department, April 1994

Burundi

Indicator	Unit of measure	Latest single year 1970-75	Latest single year 1980-85	Most recent estimate 1987-92	Same region/income group Sub-Saharan Africa	Same region/income group Low-income	Next higher income group
Priority Poverty Indicators							
POVERTY							
Upper poverty line	local curr.	..	..	..	..	..	..
Headcount index	% of pop.	..	..	..	..	19	..
Lower poverty line	local curr.	..	..	..	..	..	..
Headcount index	% of pop.	..	..	..	..	..	..
GNP per capita	US$	100	250	210	520	390	..
SHORT TERM INCOME INDICATORS							
Unskilled urban wages	local curr.	..	..	..	..	..	..
Unskilled rural wages	"	..	..	..	..	..	..
Rural terms of trade	"	..	..	..	..	..	..
Consumer price index	1987=100	30	92	142	..	..	..
Lower income	"	..	..	..	..	..	..
Food[a]	"	22	109	145	..	..	..
Urban	"	..	..	..	..	..	..
Rural	"	..	..	..	..	..	..
SOCIAL INDICATORS							
Public expenditure on basic social services	% of GDP	..	..	7.9	..	..	..
Gross enrollment ratios							
Primary	% school age pop.	22	53	70	66	103	..
Male	"	28	62	77	79	113	..
Female	"	17	44	63	62	96	..
Mortality							
Infant mortality	per thou. live births	137.0	118.0	106.0	99.0	73.0	45.0
Under 5 mortality	"	..	..	175.1	169.0	108.0	59.0
Immunization							
Measles	% age group	..	42.0	75.0	54.0	72.7	..
DPT	"	..	38.0	83.0	54.6	80.6	..
Child malnutrition (under-5)	"	..	..	31.0	28.4	38.3	..
Life expectancy							
Total	years	44	48	48	52	62	68
Female advantage	"	3.2	3.4	3.3	3.4	2.4	6.4
Total fertility rate	births per woman	6.8	6.8	6.8	6.1	3.4	3.1
Maternal mortality rate	per 100,000 live births	..	..	..	..	..	..
Supplementary Poverty Indicators							
Expenditures on social security	% of total gov't exp.	1.5	..	..	..	..	..
Social security coverage	% econ. active pop.	..	..	..	..	..	..
Access to safe water: total	% of pop.	..	26.0	37.0	41.1	68.4	..
Urban	"	77.0	98.0	92.0	77.8	78.9	..
Rural	"	..	21.0	34.0	27.3	60.3	..
Access to health care	"	..	45.3	65.0	..	..	..

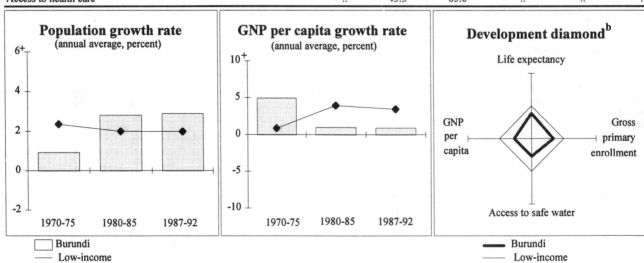

Population growth rate
(annual average, percent)

GNP per capita growth rate
(annual average, percent)

Development diamond[b]

Life expectancy — GNP per capita — Gross primary enrollment — Access to safe water

☐ Burundi
— Low-income

━━ Burundi
— Low-income

a. See the technical notes, p.389.   b. The development diamond, based on four key indicators, shows the average level of development in the country compared with its income group. See the introduction.

Burundi

Indicator	Unit of measure	Latest single year 1970-75	Latest single year 1980-85	Most recent estimate 1987-92	Sub-Saharan Africa	Low-income	Next higher income group
Resources and Expenditures							
HUMAN RESOURCES							
Population (mre=1992)	thousands	3,680	4,750	5,812	546,390	3,194,535	942,547
Age dependency ratio	ratio	0.84	0.91	0.96	0.95	0.67	0.66
Urban	% of pop.	3.2	4.8	5.6	29.5	26.7	57.0
Population growth rate	annual %	1.4	2.9	2.8	2.9	1.8	1.4
Urban	"	6.5	5.0	5.7	5.1	3.4	4.8
Labor force (15-64)	thousands	2,137	2,520	2,966	224,025	1,478,954	..
Agriculture	% of labor force	93	93	..	..	..	..
Industry	"	2	2	..	..	..	..
Female	"	49	48	47	37	33	36
Females per 100 males							
Urban	number	86	74	..	..	..	..
Rural	"	104	116	..	..	..	..
NATURAL RESOURCES							
Area	thou. sq. km	27.83	27.83	27.83	24,274.03	38,401.06	40,697.37
Density	pop. per sq. km	132.2	170.7	203.1	21.9	81.7	22.8
Agricultural land	% of land area	81.3	87.1	88.3	52.7	50.9	..
Change in agricultural land	annual %	1.7	0.8	0.6	0.1	0.0	..
Agricultural land under irrigation	%	2.2	3.0	3.3	0.8	18.2	..
Forests and woodland	thou. sq. km	1	1	1	..	..	..
Deforestation (net)	annual %	..	..	0.0	..	..	..
INCOME							
Household income							
Share of top 20% of households	% of income	..	..	..	..	42	..
Share of bottom 40% of households	"	..	..	..	..	19	..
Share of bottom 20% of households	"	..	..	..	..	8	..
EXPENDITURE							
Food	% of GDP	..	42.5	..	..	..	..
Staples	"	..	17.4	..	..	..	..
Meat, fish, milk, cheese, eggs	"	..	11.8	..	..	..	..
Cereal imports	thou. metric tonnes	9	19	19	20,311	46,537	74,924
Food aid in cereals	"	6	17	2	4,303	9,008	4,054
Food production per capita	1987 = 100	107	100	97	90	123	..
Fertilizer consumption	kg/ha	0.4	1.0	0.2	4.2	61.9	..
Share of agriculture in GDP	% of GDP	61.3	56.0	48.8	18.6	29.6	..
Housing	% of GDP	..	8.6	..	..	..	..
Average household size	persons per household	..	..	..	..	..	..
Urban	"	..	5.5	..	..	..	..
Fixed investment: housing	% of GDP	..	3.3	..	..	..	..
Fuel and power	% of GDP	..	1.8	..	..	..	..
Energy consumption per capita	kg of oil equiv.	7	21	24	258	335	1,882
Households with electricity							
Urban	% of households	..	..	..	..	..	..
Rural	"	..	..	..	..	..	..
Transport and communication	% of GDP	..	1.7	..	..	..	..
Fixed investment: transport equipment	"	..	3.2	..	..	..	..
Total road length	thou. km	10	3	6	..	..	..
INVESTMENT IN HUMAN CAPITAL							
Health							
Population per physician	persons	81,057	21,370	..	..	..	..
Population per nurse	"	5,346	3,071	..	..	..	..
Population per hospital bed	"	890	..	..	1,329	1,050	516
Oral rehydration therapy (under-5)	% of cases	..	..	49	36	39	..
Education							
Gross enrollment ratio							
Secondary	% of school-age pop.	3	4	6	18	41	..
Female	"	2	2	4	14	35	..
Pupil-teacher ratio: primary	pupils per teacher	31	56	66	39	37	26
Pupil-teacher ratio: secondary	"	22	17	18	..	19	..
Pupils reaching grade 4	% of cohort	73	83	84	..	..	..
Repeater rate: primary	% of total enroll	26	18	22	..	..	..
Illiteracy	% of pop. (age 15+)	..	58	50	51	39	..
Female	% of fem. (age 15+)	..	68	60	62	52	..
Newspaper circulation	per thou. pop.	0	..	4	14	..	100

World Bank International Economics Department, April 1994

Cambodia

Indicator	Unit of measure	Latest single year 1970-75	Latest single year 1980-85	Most recent estimate 1987-92	Same region/income group East Asia	Same region/income group Low-income	Next higher income group
Priority Poverty Indicators							
POVERTY							
Upper poverty line	local curr.	..	..	..	..	..	..
Headcount index	% of pop.	..	..	..	12	19	..
Lower poverty line	local curr.	..	..	..	..	..	..
Headcount index	% of pop.	..	..	..	9	..	..
GNP per capita	US$	..	..	200	760	390	..
SHORT TERM INCOME INDICATORS							
Unskilled urban wages	local curr.	..	..	..	..	..	..
Unskilled rural wages	"	..	..	..	..	..	..
Rural terms of trade	"	..	..	..	..	..	..
Consumer price index	1987=100	..	..	..	..	..	..
Lower income	"	..	..	..	..	..	..
Food[a]	"	..	..	..	..	..	..
Urban	"	..	..	..	..	..	..
Rural	"	..	..	..	..	..	..
SOCIAL INDICATORS							
Public expenditure on basic social services	% of GDP	..	..	8.0	..	..	..
Gross enrollment ratios							
Primary	% school age pop.	42	..	..	121	103	..
Male	"	48	..	..	126	113	..
Female	"	35	..	..	117	96	..
Mortality							
Infant mortality	per thou. live births	181.0	160.0	116.0	39.0	73.0	45.0
Under 5 mortality	"	..	..	169.4	49.0	108.0	59.0
Immunization							
Measles	% age group	..	..	38.0	88.4	72.7	..
DPT	"	..	..	38.0	89.5	80.6	..
Child malnutrition (under-5)	"	..	20.0	..	24.7	38.3	..
Life expectancy							
Total	years	40	43	51	68	62	68
Female advantage	"	2.7	2.9	2.9	3.6	2.4	6.4
Total fertility rate	births per woman	5.5	4.8	4.5	2.4	3.4	3.1
Maternal mortality rate	per 100,000 live births	..	500	9000	114	..	..
Supplementary Poverty Indicators							
Expenditures on social security	% of total gov't exp.	..	..	..	..	..	..
Social security coverage	% econ. active pop.	..	..	..	..	..	..
Access to safe water: total	% of pop.	45.0	..	..	72.0	68.4	..
Urban	"	97.0	..	20.0	83.4	78.9	..
Rural	"	38.0	24.0	12.0	60.2	60.3	..
Access to health care	"	..	..	..	..	..	..

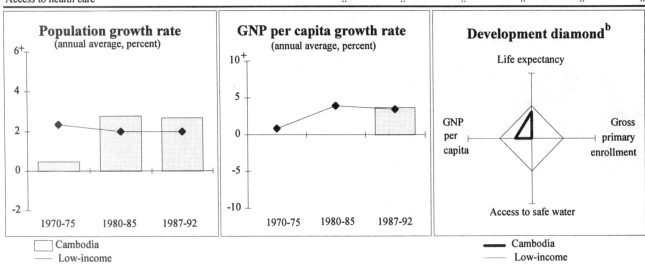

Population growth rate (annual average, percent)

□ Cambodia
— Low-income

GNP per capita growth rate (annual average, percent)

Development diamond[b]

Life expectancy

GNP per capita — Gross primary enrollment

Access to safe water

— Cambodia
— Low-income

a. See the technical notes, p.389.   b. The development diamond, based on four key indicators, shows the average level of development in the country compared with its income group. See the introduction.

Cambodia

Indicator	Unit of measure	Latest single year 1970-75	Latest single year 1980-85	Most recent estimate 1987-92	Same region/income group East Asia	Same region/income group Low-income	Next higher income group
Resources and Expenditures							
HUMAN RESOURCES							
Population (mre=1992)	thousands	7,098	7,462	9,054	1,688,909	3,194,535	942,547
Age dependency ratio	ratio	0.80	0.54	0.69	0.55	0.67	0.66
Urban	% of pop.	10.3	10.8	12.1	29.4	26.7	57.0
Population growth rate	annual %	0.5	3.1	2.5	1.4	1.8	1.4
Urban	"	-2.2	4.1	4.7	2.9	3.4	4.8
Labor force (15-64)	thousands	3,205	3,602	3,800	928,465	1,478,954	..
Agriculture	% of labor force	76	74	..	..	..	..
Industry	"	5	7	..	..	..	..
Female	"	41	41	37	41	33	36
Females per 100 males							
Urban	number	..	..	..	..	..	..
Rural	"	..	..	..	..	..	..
NATURAL RESOURCES							
Area	thou. sq. km	181.04	181.04	181.04	16,367.18	38,401.06	40,697.37
Density	pop. per sq. km	39.2	41.2	48.8	101.8	81.7	22.8
Agricultural land	% of land area	20.5	20.6	20.7	44.5	50.9	..
Change in agricultural land	annual %	0.0	0.3	0.3	0.1	0.0	..
Agricultural land under irrigation	%	2.5	2.5	2.5	14.5	18.2	..
Forests and woodland	thou. sq. km	134	134	134	..	..	..
Deforestation (net)	annual %	..	..	1.0	..	..	..
INCOME							
Household income							
Share of top 20% of households	% of income	..	..	..	42	42	..
Share of bottom 40% of households	"	..	..	..	18	19	..
Share of bottom 20% of households	"	..	..	..	7	8	..
EXPENDITURE							
Food	% of GDP	..	..	19.8	..	..	..
Staples	"	..	..	3.6	..	..	..
Meat, fish, milk, cheese, eggs	"	..	..	8.9	..	..	..
Cereal imports	thou. metric tonnes	112	55	81	33,591	46,537	74,924
Food aid in cereals	"	226	27	62	581	9,008	4,054
Food production per capita	1987 = 100	112	126	134	133	123	..
Fertilizer consumption	kg/ha	0.0	0.5	2.6	75.1	61.9	..
Share of agriculture in GDP	% of GDP	..	..	44.3	21.5	29.6	..
Housing	% of GDP	..	..	4.7	..	..	..
Average household size	persons per household	..	..	..	..	..	..
Urban	"	..	..	..	..	..	..
Fixed investment: housing	% of GDP	..	..	4.9	..	..	..
Fuel and power	% of GDP	..	..	1.0	..	..	..
Energy consumption per capita	kg of oil equiv.	54	57	55	593	335	1,882
Households with electricity							
Urban	% of households	..	..	..	..	..	..
Rural	"	..	..	..	..	..	..
Transport and communication	% of GDP	..	..	6.2	..	..	..
Fixed investment: transport equipment	"	..	..	10.3	..	..	..
Total road length	thou. km	..	..	..	..	..	..
INVESTMENT IN HUMAN CAPITAL							
Health							
Population per physician	persons	16,248	16,365	9,192	..	..	..
Population per nurse	"	1,376	..	264	..	..	..
Population per hospital bed	"	925	..	478	553	1,050	516
Oral rehydration therapy (under-5)	% of cases	..	..	6	51	39	..
Education							
Gross enrollment ratio							
Secondary	% of school-age pop.	10	..	..	53	41	..
Female	"	6	..	..	47	35	..
Pupil-teacher ratio: primary	pupils per teacher	24	..	..	23	37	26
Pupil-teacher ratio: secondary	"	39	..	..	16	19	..
Pupils reaching grade 4	% of cohort	..	..	..	89	..	..
Repeater rate: primary	% of total enroll	..	..	..	6	..	..
Illiteracy	% of pop. (age 15+)	..	71	30	24	39	..
Female	% of fem. (age 15+)	..	83	35	34	52	..
Newspaper circulation	per thou. pop.	10	..	..	..	..	100

World Bank International Economics Department, April 1994

Cameroon

Indicator	Unit of measure	Latest single year		Most recent estimate 1987-92	Same region/income group		Next higher income group
		1970-75	1980-85		Sub-Saharan Africa	Lower-middle-income	
Priority Poverty Indicators							
POVERTY							
Upper poverty line	local curr.	..	..	..	..	..	..
Headcount index	% of pop.	..	..	..	..	..	..
Lower poverty line	local curr.	..	..	..	..	..	..
Headcount index	% of pop.	..	..	..	..	..	..
GNP per capita	US$	310	830	820	520	..	3,870
SHORT TERM INCOME INDICATORS							
Unskilled urban wages	local curr.	..	..	..	..	..	..
Unskilled rural wages	"	..	..	..	..	..	..
Rural terms of trade	"	..	..	..	..	..	..
Consumer price index	1987=100	29	80	106	..	..	..
Lower income	"	..	..	..	..	..	..
Food[a]	"	..	93	93	..	..	..
Urban	"	..	..	..	..	..	..
Rural	"	..	..	..	..	..	..
SOCIAL INDICATORS							
Public expenditure on basic social services	% of GDP	..	..	..	..	..	..
Gross enrollment ratios							
Primary	% school age pop.	97	102	101	66	..	107
Male	"	108	110	109	79	..	..
Female	"	87	93	93	62	..	..
Mortality							
Infant mortality	per thou. live births	119.0	88.0	61.0	99.0	45.0	40.0
Under 5 mortality	"	..	..	116.7	169.0	59.0	51.0
Immunization							
Measles	% age group	..	47.0	56.0	54.0	..	82.0
DPT	"	..	50.0	56.0	54.6	..	73.8
Child malnutrition (under-5)	"	..	..	13.6	28.4	..	..
Life expectancy							
Total	years	46	51	56	52	68	69
Female advantage	"	3.0	3.0	3.4	3.4	6.4	6.3
Total fertility rate	births per woman	6.0	6.5	5.8	6.1	3.1	2.9
Maternal mortality rate	per 100,000 live births	..	430	..	..	..	..
Supplementary Poverty Indicators							
Expenditures on social security	% of total gov't exp.	..	4.2	7.2	..	..	..
Social security coverage	% econ. active pop.	..	..	..	..	..	..
Access to safe water: total	% of pop.	32.0	31.0	34.0	41.1	..	85.6
Urban	"	77.0	43.0	47.0	77.8	..	94.3
Rural	"	21.0	24.0	27.0	27.3	..	73.0
Access to health care	"	..	20.0	15.0	..	..	..

Population growth rate (annual average, percent)

Cameroon
Lower-middle-income

GNP per capita growth rate (annual average, percent)

Development diamond[b]

Life expectancy

GNP per capita — Gross primary enrollment

Access to safe water

Cameroon
Lower-middle-income

a. See the technical notes, p.389.   b. The development diamond, based on four key indicators, shows the average level of development in the country compared with its income group. See the introduction.

Cameroon

Indicator	Unit of measure	Latest single year 1970-75	Latest single year 1980-85	Most recent estimate 1987-92	Same region/income group Sub-Saharan Africa	Same region/income group Lower-middle-income	Next higher income group
Resources and Expenditures							
HUMAN RESOURCES							
Population (mre=1992)	thousands	7,439	9,969	12,242	546,390	942,547	477,960
Age dependency ratio	ratio	0.83	0.98	0.98	0.95	0.66	0.64
Urban	% of pop.	26.9	35.7	42.1	29.5	57.0	71.7
Population growth rate	annual %	3.0	2.6	3.0	2.9	1.4	1.6
Urban	"	8.0	5.1	5.2	5.1	4.8	2.5
Labor force (15-64)	thousands	3,345	3,958	4,568	224,025	..	181,414
Agriculture	% of labor force	77	70	..	..	..	..
Industry	"	7	8	..	..	..	..
Female	"	37	34	33	37	36	29
Females per 100 males							
Urban	number	..	..	..	..	..	..
Rural	"	..	..	..	..	..	..
NATURAL RESOURCES							
Area	thou. sq. km	475.44	475.44	475.44	24,274.03	40,697.37	21,836.02
Density	pop. per sq. km	15.7	21.0	25.0	21.9	22.8	21.5
Agricultural land	% of land area	31.6	32.8	32.9	52.7	..	41.7
Change in agricultural land	annual %	0.8	0.0	0.1	0.1	..	0.3
Agricultural land under irrigation	%	0.1	0.1	0.2	0.8	..	9.3
Forests and woodland	thou. sq. km	262	251	244	..	..	..
Deforestation (net)	annual %	..	..	0.6	..	..	..
INCOME							
Household income							
Share of top 20% of households	% of income	..	..	..	..	..	..
Share of bottom 40% of households	"	..	..	..	..	..	..
Share of bottom 20% of households	"	..	..	..	..	..	..
EXPENDITURE							
Food	% of GDP	..	16.0	..	..	..	..
Staples	"	..	4.9	..	..	..	..
Meat, fish, milk, cheese, eggs	"	..	6.9	..	..	..	..
Cereal imports	thou. metric tonnes	69	141	424	20,311	74,924	49,174
Food aid in cereals	"	4	13	8	4,303	4,054	282
Food production per capita	1987 = 100	117	98	81	90	..	109
Fertilizer consumption	kg/ha	0.9	3.7	1.2	4.2	..	68.8
Share of agriculture in GDP	% of GDP	29.1	20.6	22.0	18.6	..	8.1
Housing	% of GDP	..	10.9	..	..	..	..
Average household size	persons per household	5.2	..	..	..	..	..
Urban	"	..	..	..	..	..	..
Fixed investment: housing	% of GDP	4.1	6.4	..	..	..	..
Fuel and power	% of GDP	..	1.7	..	..	..	..
Energy consumption per capita	kg of oil equiv.	65	110	77	258	1,882	1,649
Households with electricity							
Urban	% of households	..	..	..	..	..	..
Rural	"	..	..	..	..	..	..
Transport and communication	% of GDP	..	7.9	..	..	..	..
Fixed investment: transport equipment	"	3.7	2.1	..	..	..	..
Total road length	thou. km	44	65	70	..	..	..
INVESTMENT IN HUMAN CAPITAL							
Health							
Population per physician	persons	13,700	..	12,195	..	..	..
Population per nurse	"	13,700	..	1,690	..	..	..
Population per hospital bed	"	400	..	393	1,329	516	385
Oral rehydration therapy (under-5)	% of cases	..	..	84	36	..	54
Education							
Gross enrollment ratio							
Secondary	% of school-age pop.	13	23	28	18	..	53
Female	"	8	17	23	14	..	..
Pupil-teacher ratio: primary	pupils per teacher	51	51	51	39	26	25
Pupil-teacher ratio: secondary	"	32	34	32	..	..	..
Pupils reaching grade 4	% of cohort	80	82	85	..	..	71
Repeater rate: primary	% of total enroll	25	29	29	..	..	11
Illiteracy	% of pop. (age 15+)	..	52	46	51	..	14
Female	% of fem. (age 15+)	..	64	57	62	..	17
Newspaper circulation	per thou. pop.	3	4	7	14	100	117

World Bank International Economics Department, April 1994

Canada

Indicator	Unit of measure	Latest single year		Most recent estimate 1987-92	Same region/income group High-income
		1970-75	1980-85		

Priority Poverty Indicators

POVERTY
Indicator	Unit of measure	1970-75	1980-85	1987-92	High-income
Upper poverty line	local curr.	..	..	..	..
Headcount index	% of pop.	..	..	..	..
Lower poverty line	local curr.	..	..	..	..
Headcount index	% of pop.	..	..	..	..
GNP per capita	US$	7,250	14,230	20,710	21,960

SHORT TERM INCOME INDICATORS
Unskilled urban wages	local curr.	..	..	..	..
Unskilled rural wages	"	..	..	..	..
Rural terms of trade	"	..	..	..	..
Consumer price index	1987=100	42	92	123	..
Lower income	"	..	..	..	..
Food[a]	"	26	91	116	..
Urban	"	..	..	..	..
Rural	"	..	..	..	..

SOCIAL INDICATORS
Public expenditure on basic social services	% of GDP	..	..	..	..
Gross enrollment ratios					
Primary	% school age pop.	99	105	107	103
Male	"	99	106	108	103
Female	"	99	104	106	103
Mortality					
Infant mortality	per thou. live births	14.2	7.9	6.8	7.0
Under 5 mortality	"	..	..	8.8	10.0
Immunization					
Measles	% age group	..	..	85.0	82.4
DPT	"	..	80.0	85.0	90.1
Child malnutrition (under-5)	"	..	..	..	..
Life expectancy					
Total	years	73	76	78	77
Female advantage	"	7.1	6.8	6.2	6.4
Total fertility rate	births per woman	1.8	1.7	1.9	1.7
Maternal mortality rate	per 100,000 live births	..	2	..	..

Supplementary Poverty Indicators

Expenditures on social security	% of total gov't exp.	30.1	27.2	28.1	..
Social security coverage	% econ. active pop.	..	..	..	..
Access to safe water: total	% of pop.	..	..	..	..
Urban	"	..	..	..	..
Rural	"	..	..	..	..
Access to health care	"	..	..	..	..

Population growth rate
(annual average, percent)

GNP per capita growth rate
(annual average, percent)

Development diamond[b]

Life expectancy

GNP per capita — Gross primary enrollment

Access to safe water

□ Canada
— High-income

━━ Canada
— High-income

a. See the technical notes, p.389.   b. The development diamond, based on four key indicators, shows the average level of development in the country compared with its income group. See the introduction.

Canada

Indicator	Unit of measure	Latest single year 1970-75	Latest single year 1980-85	Most recent estimate 1987-92	Same region/income group High-income

Resources and Expenditures

HUMAN RESOURCES

Indicator	Unit of measure	1970-75	1980-85	1987-92	High-income
Population (mre=1992)	thousands	22,697	25,165	27,445	828,221
Age dependency ratio	ratio	0.54	0.47	0.49	0.50
Urban	% of pop.	75.6	76.4	77.5	78.1
Population growth rate	annual %	1.5	0.8	1.5	0.7
Urban	"	1.5	0.9	1.8	0.9
Labor force (15-64)	thousands	10,161	12,723	13,583	390,033
Agriculture	% of labor force	6	5	..	..
Industry	"	30	29	..	..
Female	"	36	40	40	38
Females per 100 males					
Urban	number	102	102	..	..
Rural	"	90	93	..	..

NATURAL RESOURCES

Indicator	Unit of measure	1970-75	1980-85	1987-92	High-income
Area	thou. sq. km	9,976.14	9,976.14	9,976.14	31,709.00
Density	pop. per sq. km	2.3	2.5	2.7	24.5
Agricultural land	% of land area	7.3	8.1	8.0	42.7
Change in agricultural land	annual %	0.3	-0.2	-0.2	-0.2
Agricultural land under irrigation	%	0.7	1.0	1.2	16.1
Forests and woodland	thou. sq. km	3,302	3,500	3,600	..
Deforestation (net)	annual %	..	..	..	..

INCOME

Indicator	Unit of measure	1970-75	1980-85	1987-92	High-income
Household income					
Share of top 20% of households	% of income	..	..	40	..
Share of bottom 40% of households	"	..	..	18	..
Share of bottom 20% of households	"	..	..	6	..

EXPENDITURE

Indicator	Unit of measure	1970-75	1980-85	1987-92	High-income
Food	% of GDP	..	7.3	..	..
Staples	"	..	1.1	..	..
Meat, fish, milk, cheese, eggs	"	..	3.6	..	..
Cereal imports	thou. metric tonnes	862	692	1,016	70,626
Food aid in cereals	"	..	..	..	2
Food production per capita	1987 = 100	91	110	107	101
Fertilizer consumption	kg/ha	19.4	31.2	29.1	162.1
Share of agriculture in GDP	% of GDP	4.5	2.8	2.4	2.4
Housing	% of GDP	..	13.5	..	..
Average household size	persons per household	3.5	2.9	..	..
Urban	"	..	2.8	..	..
Fixed investment: housing	% of GDP	6.5	4.5	..	..
Fuel and power	% of GDP	..	2.4	..	..
Energy consumption per capita	kg of oil equiv.	7,097	7,680	7,912	5,101
Households with electricity					
Urban	% of households	..	..	..	..
Rural	"	..	..	..	..
Transport and communication	% of GDP	..	9.3	..	..
Fixed investment: transport equipment	"	2.5	2.3	..	..
Total road length	thou. km	494	279	826	..

INVESTMENT IN HUMAN CAPITAL

Indicator	Unit of measure	1970-75	1980-85	1987-92	High-income
Health					
Population per physician	persons	684	511	450	..
Population per nurse	"	138	121	..	..
Population per hospital bed	"	101	..	64	144
Oral rehydration therapy (under-5)	% of cases	..	..	..	..
Education					
Gross enrollment ratio					
Secondary	% of school-age pop.	91	103	104	92
Female	"	92	103	104	94
Pupil-teacher ratio: primary	pupils per teacher	10	17	15	18
Pupil-teacher ratio: secondary	"	18	15	14	..
Pupils reaching grade 4	% of cohort	96	94	97	..
Repeater rate: primary	% of total enroll	..	..	..	..
Illiteracy	% of pop. (age 15+)	..	..	†	..
Female	% of fem. (age 15+)	..	..	†	..
Newspaper circulation	per thou. pop.	215	224	229	..

World Bank International Economics Department, April 1994

Cape Verde

Indicator	Unit of measure	Latest single year 1970-75	1980-85	Most recent estimate 1987-92	Sub-Saharan Africa	Lower-middle-income	Next higher income group
Priority Poverty Indicators							
POVERTY							
Upper poverty line	local curr.	..	..	..	..	..	..
Headcount index	% of pop.	..	..	..	..	..	..
Lower poverty line	local curr.	..	..	..	..	..	..
Headcount index	% of pop.	..	..	..	..	..	..
GNP per capita	US$	220	340	850	520	..	3,870
SHORT TERM INCOME INDICATORS							
Unskilled urban wages	local curr.	..	..	..	..	..	..
Unskilled rural wages	"	..	..	..	..	..	..
Rural terms of trade	"	..	..	..	..	..	..
Consumer price index	1987=100	..	87	136	..	..	..
Lower income	"	..	..	..	..	..	..
Food[a]	"	..	85	103	..	..	..
Urban	"	..	..	..	..	..	..
Rural	"	..	..	..	..	..	..
SOCIAL INDICATORS							
Public expenditure on basic social services	% of GDP	..	..	16.0	..	..	..
Gross enrollment ratios							
Primary	% school age pop.	145	113	115	66	..	107
Male	"	152	116	117	79	..	..
Female	"	138	111	113	62	..	..
Mortality							
Infant mortality	per thou. live births	82.0	66.0	40.0	99.0	45.0	40.0
Under 5 mortality	"	..	..	50.1	169.0	59.0	51.0
Immunization							
Measles	% age group	..	54.0	78.0	54.0	..	82.0
DPT	"	..	39.0	88.0	54.6	..	73.8
Child malnutrition (under-5)	"	..	..	..	28.4	..	..
Life expectancy							
Total	years	57	64	68	52	68	69
Female advantage	"	3.0	2.0	2.1	3.4	6.4	6.3
Total fertility rate	births per woman	7.0	6.3	4.3	6.1	3.1	2.9
Maternal mortality rate	per 100,000 live births	..	134	..	..	..	..
Supplementary Poverty Indicators							
Expenditures on social security	% of total gov't exp.	..	..	..	..	..	..
Social security coverage	% econ. active pop.	..	..	..	..	..	..
Access to safe water: total	% of pop.	..	60.0	74.0	41.1	..	85.6
Urban	"	..	83.0	87.0	77.8	..	94.3
Rural	"	..	50.0	65.0	27.3	..	73.0
Access to health care	"	..	..	81.0	..	..	..

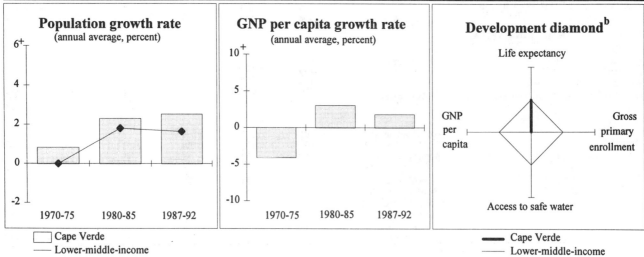

Population growth rate (annual average, percent)

GNP per capita growth rate (annual average, percent)

Development diamond[b]
Life expectancy — GNP per capita — Gross primary enrollment — Access to safe water

Cape Verde
Lower-middle-income

a. See the technical notes, p.389.   b. The development diamond, based on four key indicators, shows the average level of development in the country compared with its income group. See the introduction.

64

Cape Verde

Indicator	Unit of measure	Latest single year 1970-75	Latest single year 1980-85	Most recent estimate 1987-92	Same region/income group Sub-Saharan Africa	Same region/income group Lower-middle-income	Next higher income group
Resources and Expenditures							
HUMAN RESOURCES							
Population (mre=1992)	thousands	278	324	389	546,390	942,547	477,960
Age dependency ratio	ratio	1.09	0.97	0.97	0.95	0.66	0.64
Urban	% of pop.	21.4	25.9	30.0	29.5	57.0	71.7
Population growth rate	annual %	0.4	2.8	2.3	2.9	1.4	1.6
Urban	"	2.1	4.8	4.6	5.1	4.8	2.5
Labor force (15-64)	thousands	97	121	149	224,025	..	181,414
Agriculture	% of labor force	58	52	..	..	..	..
Industry	"	19	23	..	..	..	..
Female	"	26	29	29	37	36	29
Females per 100 males							
Urban	number	..	..	..	..	..	..
Rural	"	..	..	..	..	..	..
NATURAL RESOURCES							
Area	thou. sq. km	4.03	4.03	4.03	24,274.03	40,697.37	21,836.02
Density	pop. per sq. km	69.0	80.4	94.3	21.9	22.8	21.5
Agricultural land	% of land area	16.1	16.1	15.9	52.7	..	41.7
Change in agricultural land	annual %	0.0	0.0	0.0	0.1	..	0.3
Agricultural land under irrigation	%	3.1	3.1	3.1	0.8	..	9.3
Forests and woodland	thou. sq. km	0	0	0	..	..	..
Deforestation (net)	annual %	..	..	..	..	..	..
INCOME							
Household income							
Share of top 20% of households	% of income	..	..	..	..	..	..
Share of bottom 40% of households	"	..	..	..	..	..	..
Share of bottom 20% of households	"	..	..	..	..	..	..
EXPENDITURE							
Food	% of GDP	..	..	24.3	..	..	..
Staples	"	..	..	8.2	..	..	..
Meat, fish, milk, cheese, eggs	"	..	..	8.5	..	..	..
Cereal imports	thou. metric tonnes	40	67	67	20,311	74,924	49,174
Food aid in cereals	"	7	50	57	4,303	4,054	282
Food production per capita	1987 = 100	86	75	87	90	..	109
Fertilizer consumption	kg/ha	1.5	1.5	1.7	4.2	..	68.8
Share of agriculture in GDP	% of GDP	8.5	11.6	12.7	18.6	..	8.1
Housing	% of GDP	..	..	3.7	..	..	..
Average household size	persons per household	..	..	..	..	..	..
Urban	"	..	..	..	..	..	..
Fixed investment: housing	% of GDP	..	..	4.4	..	..	..
Fuel and power	% of GDP	..	..	1.8	..	..	..
Energy consumption per capita	kg of oil equiv.	791	327	290	258	1,882	1,649
Households with electricity							
Urban	% of households	..	..	..	..	..	..
Rural	"	..	..	..	..	..	..
Transport and communication	% of GDP	..	..	9.2	..	..	..
Fixed investment: transport equipment	"	..	..	3.8	..	..	..
Total road length	thou. km	..	..	..	..	..	..
INVESTMENT IN HUMAN CAPITAL							
Health							
Population per physician	persons	12,136	5,117	..	..	..	..
Population per nurse	"	4,091	716	..	..	..	..
Population per hospital bed	"	710	457	..	1,329	516	385
Oral rehydration therapy (under-5)	% of cases	..	..	5	36	..	54
Education							
Gross enrollment ratio							
Secondary	% of school-age pop.	8	13	19	18	..	53
Female	"	8	12	19	14	..	..
Pupil-teacher ratio: primary	pupils per teacher	52	39	33	39	26	25
Pupil-teacher ratio: secondary	"	26	34	30	..	..	..
Pupils reaching grade 4	% of cohort	..	91	92	..	..	71
Repeater rate: primary	% of total enroll	..	28	19	..	..	11
Illiteracy	% of pop. (age 15+)	63	53	..	51	..	14
Female	% of fem. (age 15+)	..	..	..	62	..	17
Newspaper circulation	per thou. pop.	..	..	..	14	100	117

World Bank International Economics Department, April 1994

Central African Republic

Indicator	Unit of measure	Latest single year 1970-75	Latest single year 1980-85	Most recent estimate 1987-92	Same region/income group Sub-Saharan Africa	Same region/income group Low-income	Next higher income group
Priority Poverty Indicators							
POVERTY							
Upper poverty line	local curr.	..	..	..	..	..	..
Headcount index	% of pop.	..	..	..	..	19	..
Lower poverty line	local curr.	..	..	..	..	..	..
Headcount index	% of pop.	..	..	..	..	..	..
GNP per capita	US$	170	270	410	520	390	
SHORT TERM INCOME INDICATORS							
Unskilled urban wages	local curr.	..	..	..	..	..	..
Unskilled rural wages	"	..	..	..	..	..	..
Rural terms of trade	"	..	..	..	..	..	..
Consumer price index	1987=100	..	105	94	..	..	..
Lower income	"	..	..	..	..	..	..
Food[a]	"	..	111	94	..	..	..
Urban	"	..	..	..	..	..	..
Rural	"	..	..	..	..	..	..
SOCIAL INDICATORS							
Public expenditure on basic social services	% of GDP	..	..	7.7	..	..	..
Gross enrollment ratios							
Primary	% school age pop.	73	74	68	66	103	..
Male	"	96	92	85	79	113	..
Female	"	51	57	52	62	96	..
Mortality							
Infant mortality	per thou. live births	132.0	115.0	105.0	99.0	73.0	45.0
Under 5 mortality	"	..	..	173.2	169.0	108.0	59.0
Immunization							
Measles	% age group	..	23.0	82.0	54.0	72.7	..
DPT	"	..	20.0	82.0	54.6	80.6	..
Child malnutrition (under-5)	"	39.4	30.0	..	28.4	38.3	..
Life expectancy							
Total	years	43	46	47	52	62	68
Female advantage	"	5.2	5.2	4.7	3.4	2.4	6.4
Total fertility rate	births per woman	5.0	5.5	5.8	6.1	3.4	3.1
Maternal mortality rate	per 100,000 live births	..	600		..	..	..
Supplementary Poverty Indicators							
Expenditures on social security	% of total gov't exp.	..	..	..	..	..	..
Social security coverage	% econ. active pop.	..	..	..	..	..	..
Access to safe water: total	% of pop.	..	..	12.0	41.1	68.4	..
Urban	"	..	..	14.0	77.8	78.9	..
Rural	"	..	..	11.0	27.3	60.3	..
Access to health care	"	..	..	12.5			

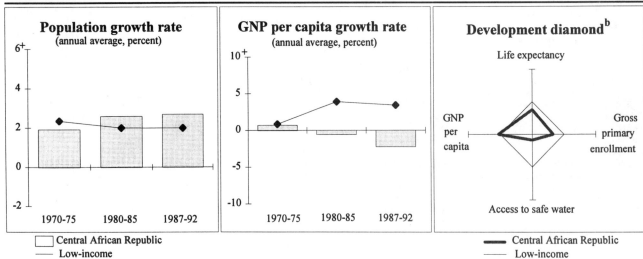

Population growth rate (annual average, percent)

GNP per capita growth rate (annual average, percent)

Development diamond[b]

Life expectancy / GNP per capita / Gross primary enrollment / Access to safe water

— Central African Republic
— Low-income

a. See the technical notes, p.389.   b. The development diamond, based on four key indicators, shows the average level of development in the country compared with its income group. See the introduction.

Central African Republic

Indicator	Unit of measure	Latest single year 1970-75	Latest single year 1980-85	Most recent estimate 1987-92	Same region/income group Sub-Saharan Africa	Same region/income group Low-income	Next higher income group
Resources and Expenditures							
HUMAN RESOURCES							
Population (mre=1992)	thousands	2,034	2,631	3,170	546,390	3,194,535	942,547
Age dependency ratio	ratio	0.80	0.83	0.85	0.95	0.67	0.66
Urban	% of pop.	34.2	42.5	48.3	29.5	26.7	57.0
Population growth rate	annual %	2.2	2.5	2.6	2.9	1.8	1.4
Urban	"	4.4	4.5	4.2	5.1	3.4	4.8
Labor force (15-64)	thousands	1,123	1,282	1,436	224,025	1,478,954	..
Agriculture	% of labor force	78	72	..	..	..	..
Industry	"	5	6	..	..	..	..
Female	"	49	47	45	37	33	36
Females per 100 males							
Urban	number	111	..	..	..	..	..
Rural	"	119	..	..	..	..	..
NATURAL RESOURCES							
Area	thou. sq. km	622.98	622.98	622.98	24,274.03	38,401.06	40,697.37
Density	pop. per sq. km	3.3	4.2	5.0	21.9	81.7	22.8
Agricultural land	% of land area	7.9	8.0	8.0	52.7	50.9	..
Change in agricultural land	annual %	0.4	0.0	0.0	0.1	0.0	..
Agricultural land under irrigation	%	..	..	..	0.8	18.2	..
Forests and woodland	thou. sq. km	359	359	358	..	..	..
Deforestation (net)	annual %	..	..	0.4	..	..	..
INCOME							
Household income							
Share of top 20% of households	% of income	..	..	..	..	42	..
Share of bottom 40% of households	"	..	..	..	..	19	..
Share of bottom 20% of households	"	..	..	..	..	8	..
EXPENDITURE							
Food	% of GDP	..	..	33.0	..	..	..
Staples	"	..	..	10.7	..	..	..
Meat, fish, milk, cheese, eggs	"	..	..	12.3	..	..	..
Cereal imports	thou. metric tonnes	10	22	40	20,311	46,537	74,924
Food aid in cereals	"	1	12	3	4,303	9,008	4,054
Food production per capita	1987 = 100	108	85	86	90	123	..
Fertilizer consumption	kg/ha	0.4	0.6	0.2	4.2	61.9	..
Share of agriculture in GDP	% of GDP	35.4	37.1	41.0	18.6	29.6	..
Housing	% of GDP	..	..	10.6	..	..	..
Average household size	persons per household	5.1	..	..	..	..	..
Urban	"	..	..	..	..	..	..
Fixed investment: housing	% of GDP	..	..	2.8	..	..	..
Fuel and power	% of GDP	..	..	2.1	..	..	..
Energy consumption per capita	kg of oil equiv.	25	33	29	258	335	1,882
Households with electricity							
Urban	% of households	..	..	..	..	..	..
Rural	"	..	..	..	..	..	..
Transport and communication	% of GDP	..	..	12.6	..	..	..
Fixed investment: transport equipment	"	..	..	0.7	..	..	..
Total road length	thou. km	22	20	24	..	..	..
INVESTMENT IN HUMAN CAPITAL							
Health							
Population per physician	persons	44,024	23,433	25,894	..	..	..
Population per nurse	"	2,450	2,205	..	..	..	..
Population per hospital bed	"	533	642	1,171	1,329	1,050	516
Oral rehydration therapy (under-5)	% of cases	..	..	24	36	39	..
Education							
Gross enrollment ratio							
Secondary	% of school-age pop.	8	16	12	18	41	..
Female	"	3	8	7	14	35	..
Pupil-teacher ratio: primary	pupils per teacher	67	66	90	39	37	26
Pupil-teacher ratio: secondary	"	40	74	38	..	19	..
Pupils reaching grade 4	% of cohort	76	74	83	..	..	..
Repeater rate: primary	% of total enroll	35	29	31	..	..	..
Illiteracy	% of pop. (age 15+)	..	69	62	51	39	..
Female	% of fem. (age 15+)	..	81	75	62	52	..
Newspaper circulation	per thou. pop.	0	..	1	14	..	100

World Bank International Economics Department, April 1994

Chad

Indicator	Unit of measure	Latest single year 1970-75	Latest single year 1980-85	Most recent estimate 1987-92	Same region/income group Sub-Saharan Africa	Same region/income group Low-income	Next higher income group

Priority Poverty Indicators

Indicator	Unit of measure	1970-75	1980-85	1987-92	Sub-Saharan Africa	Low-income	Next higher income group
POVERTY							
Upper poverty line	local curr.	..	..	..	..	..	..
Headcount index	% of pop.	..	..	..	..	19	..
Lower poverty line	local curr.	..	..	..	..	..	..
Headcount index	% of pop.	..	..	..	..	..	..
GNP per capita	US$	150	130	220	520	390	..
SHORT TERM INCOME INDICATORS							
Unskilled urban wages	local curr.	..	..	..	..	..	..
Unskilled rural wages	"	..	..	..	..	..	..
Rural terms of trade	"	..	..	..	..	..	..
Consumer price index	1987=100	..	122	110	..	..	..
Lower income	"	..	..	..	..	..	..
Food[a]	"	..	158	100	..	..	..
Urban	"	..	..	..	..	..	..
Rural	"	..	..	..	..	..	..
SOCIAL INDICATORS							
Public expenditure on basic social services	% of GDP	..	..	5.5	..	..	..
Gross enrollment ratios							
Primary	% school age pop.	35	43	65	66	103	..
Male	"	51	63	89	79	113	..
Female	"	18	24	41	62	96	..
Mortality							
Infant mortality	per thou. live births	166.0	143.0	122.0	99.0	73.0	45.0
Under 5 mortality	"	..	..	205.2	169.0	108.0	59.0
Immunization							
Measles	% age group	..	8.0	28.0	54.0	72.7	..
DPT	"	..	1.0	18.0	54.6	80.6	..
Child malnutrition (under-5)	"	..	35.0	..	28.4	38.3	..
Life expectancy							
Total	years	39	43	47	52	62	68
Female advantage	"	3.1	3.2	3.2	3.4	2.4	6.4
Total fertility rate	births per woman	6.0	5.9	5.9	6.1	3.4	3.1
Maternal mortality rate	per 100,000 live births	..	700	..	..	..	..

Supplementary Poverty Indicators

Indicator	Unit of measure	1970-75	1980-85	1987-92	Sub-Saharan Africa	Low-income	Next higher income group
Expenditures on social security	% of total gov't exp.	..	..	..	..	..	..
Social security coverage	% econ. active pop.	..	..	..	..	..	..
Access to safe water: total	% of pop.	26.0	..	..	41.1	68.4	..
Urban	"	43.0	..	..	77.8	78.9	..
Rural	"	23.0	..	..	27.3	60.3	..
Access to health care	"	..	30.0	..	..	..	..

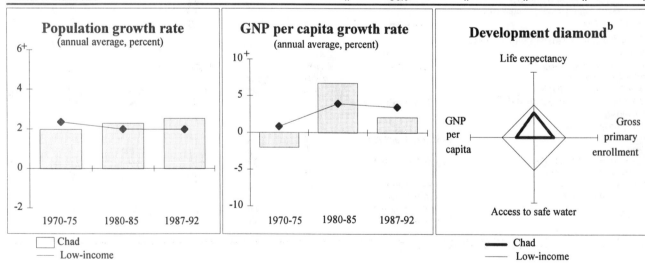

Population growth rate (annual average, percent) — Chad, Low-income, 1970-75, 1980-85, 1987-92

GNP per capita growth rate (annual average, percent) — 1970-75, 1980-85, 1987-92

Development diamond[b] — Life expectancy, GNP per capita, Gross primary enrollment, Access to safe water — Chad, Low-income

a. See the technical notes, p.389.   b. The development diamond, based on four key indicators, shows the average level of development in the country compared with its income group. See the introduction.

Chad

World Bank International Economics Department, April 1994

Indicator	Unit of measure	Latest single year 1970-75	Latest single year 1980-85	Most recent estimate 1987-92	Same region/income group Sub-Saharan Africa	Same region/income group Low-income	Next higher income group
Resources and Expenditures							
HUMAN RESOURCES							
Population (mre=1992)	thousands	4,030	5,018	5,977	546,390	3,194,535	942,547
Age dependency ratio	ratio	0.83	0.80	0.86	0.95	0.67	0.66
Urban	% of pop.	15.6	26.0	33.8	29.5	26.7	57.0
Population growth rate	annual %	2.0	2.4	2.6	2.9	1.8	1.4
Urban	"	7.0	6.7	5.8	5.1	3.4	4.8
Labor force (15-64)	thousands	1,496	1,790	2,056	224,025	1,478,954	..
Agriculture	% of labor force	87	83	..	..	..	..
Industry	"	4	5	..	..	..	..
Female	"	23	22	21	37	33	36
Females per 100 males							
Urban	number	..	..	..	..	..	..
Rural	"	..	..	..	..	..	..
NATURAL RESOURCES							
Area	thou. sq. km	1,284.00	1,284.00	1,284.00	24,274.03	38,401.06	40,697.37
Density	pop. per sq. km	3.1	3.9	4.5	21.9	81.7	22.8
Agricultural land	% of land area	38.1	38.2	38.3	52.7	50.9	..
Change in agricultural land	annual %	0.2	0.0	0.0	0.1	0.0	..
Agricultural land under irrigation	%	0.0	0.0	0.0	0.8	18.2	..
Forests and woodland	thou. sq. km	139	131	127	..	..	..
Deforestation (net)	annual %	..	..	0.8	..	..	..
INCOME							
Household income							
Share of top 20% of households	% of income	..	..	..	..	42	..
Share of bottom 40% of households	"	..	..	..	..	19	..
Share of bottom 20% of households	"	..	..	..	..	8	..
EXPENDITURE							
Food	% of GDP	..	..	55.1	..	..	..
Staples	"	..	..	21.5	..	..	..
Meat, fish, milk, cheese, eggs	"	..	..	22.6	..	..	..
Cereal imports	thou. metric tonnes	10	101	61	20,311	46,537	74,924
Food aid in cereals	"	20	163	61	4,303	9,008	4,054
Food production per capita	1987 = 100	96	90	102	90	123	..
Fertilizer consumption	kg/ha	0.1	0.2	0.2	4.2	61.9	..
Share of agriculture in GDP	% of GDP	43.1	43.2	41.7	18.6	29.6	..
Housing	% of GDP	..	..	7.8	..	..	..
Average household size	persons per household	..	..	..	..	..	..
Urban	"	..	..	..	..	..	..
Fixed investment: housing	% of GDP	..	..	2.1	..	..	..
Fuel and power	% of GDP	..	..	6.0	..	..	..
Energy consumption per capita	kg of oil equiv.	20	19	16	258	335	1,882
Households with electricity							
Urban	% of households	..	..	..	..	..	..
Rural	"	..	..	..	..	..	..
Transport and communication	% of GDP	..	..	9.8	..	..	..
Fixed investment: transport equipment	"	..	..	1.2	..	..	..
Total road length	thou. km	31	27	27	..	..	..
INVESTMENT IN HUMAN CAPITAL							
Health							
Population per physician	persons	61,898	..	30,031	..	..	..
Population per nurse	"	8,014	..	..	..	..	..
Population per hospital bed	"	763	..	1,373	1,329	1,050	516
Oral rehydration therapy (under-5)	% of cases	..	..	15	36	39	..
Education							
Gross enrollment ratio							
Secondary	% of school-age pop.	3	6	7	18	41	..
Female	"	0	2	3	14	35	..
Pupil-teacher ratio: primary	pupils per teacher	85	71	64	39	37	26
Pupil-teacher ratio: secondary	"	35	..	35	..	19	..
Pupils reaching grade 4	% of cohort	..	..	79	..	..	..
Repeater rate: primary	% of total enroll	35	..	33	..	..	..
Illiteracy	% of pop. (age 15+)	..	77	70	51	39	..
Female	% of fem. (age 15+)	..	88	82	62	52	..
Newspaper circulation	per thou. pop.	0	0	0	14	..	100

69

Chile

Indicator	Unit of measure	Latest single year 1970-75	Latest single year 1980-85	Most recent estimate 1987-92	Same region/income group Latin America Caribbean	Same region/income group Lower-middle-income	Next higher income group
Priority Poverty Indicators							
POVERTY							
Upper poverty line	local curr.	..	..	..	..	..	..
Headcount index	% of pop.	..	..	..	..	..	..
Lower poverty line	local curr.	..	..	..	..	..	..
Headcount index	% of pop.	..	..	..	..	..	..
GNP per capita	US$	960	1,430	2,730	2,690	..	3,870
SHORT TERM INCOME INDICATORS							
Unskilled urban wages	local curr.	..	..	..	..	..	..
Unskilled rural wages	"	..	..	..	..	..	..
Rural terms of trade	"	..	..	..	..	..	..
Consumer price index	1987=100	2	70	238	..	..	..
Lower income	"	..	..	..	..	..	..
Food[a]	"	6	65	217	..	..	..
Urban	"	..	..	..	..	..	..
Rural	"	..	..	..	..	..	..
SOCIAL INDICATORS							
Public expenditure on basic social services	% of GDP	..	..	..	..	..	..
Gross enrollment ratios							
Primary	% school age pop.	118	106	98	106	..	107
Male	"	119	107	99	..	..	..
Female	"	118	104	97	..	..	..
Mortality							
Infant mortality	per thou. live births	70.0	24.0	17.0	44.0	45.0	40.0
Under 5 mortality	"	..	..	20.9	56.0	59.0	51.0
Immunization							
Measles	% age group	..	77.0	93.0	78.9	..	82.0
DPT	"	..	84.0	90.0	73.8	..	73.8
Child malnutrition (under-5)	"	..	2.3	2.5	10.5	..	..
Life expectancy							
Total	years	64	71	72	68	68	69
Female advantage	"	6.3	7.0	7.1	5.6	6.4	6.3
Total fertility rate	births per woman	3.6	2.8	2.7	3.0	3.1	2.9
Maternal mortality rate	per 100,000 live births	180	55	40	..	..	..
Supplementary Poverty Indicators							
Expenditures on social security	% of total gov't exp.	23.8	37.1	31.7	..	..	..
Social security coverage	% econ. active pop.	..	..	79.2	..	..	..
Access to safe water: total	% of pop.	70.0	87.0	86.0	80.3	..	85.6
Urban	"	78.0	98.0	100.0	91.0	..	94.3
Rural	"	28.0	29.0	21.0	64.3	..	73.0
Access to health care	"	..	94.7	95.0	..	..	..

Population growth rate
(annual average, percent)

GNP per capita growth rate
(annual average, percent)

Development diamond[b]

☐ Chile
— Lower-middle-income

▬ Chile
— Lower-middle-income

a. See the technical notes, p.389.   b. The development diamond, based on four key indicators, shows the average level of development in the country compared with its income group. See the introduction.

Chile

Indicator	Unit of measure	Latest single year 1970-75	Latest single year 1980-85	Most recent estimate 1987-92	Same region/income group Latin America Caribbean	Same region/income group Lower-middle-income	Next higher income group
Resources and Expenditures							
HUMAN RESOURCES							
Population (mre=1992)	thousands	10,350	12,122	13,599	453,294	942,547	477,960
Age dependency ratio	ratio	0.73	0.59	0.58	0.67	0.66	0.64
Urban	% of pop.	78.4	83.2	85.1	72.9	57.0	71.7
Population growth rate	annual %	1.6	1.7	1.6	1.7	1.4	1.6
Urban	"	2.4	2.2	1.9	2.6	4.8	2.5
Labor force (15-64)	thousands	3,322	4,276	4,922	166,091	..	181,414
Agriculture	% of labor force	20	16	..	..	..	..
Industry	"	27	25	..	..	..	..
Female	"	25	28	29	27	36	29
Females per 100 males							
Urban	number	115	108	..	..	..	..
Rural	"	84	78	..	..	..	..
NATURAL RESOURCES							
Area	thou. sq. km	756.95	756.95	756.95	20,507.48	40,697.37	21,836.02
Density	pop. per sq. km	13.7	16.0	17.7	21.7	22.8	21.5
Agricultural land	% of land area	21.8	23.5	24.0	40.2	..	41.7
Change in agricultural land	annual %	2.0	0.4	0.8	0.5	..	0.3
Agricultural land under irrigation	%	7.6	7.1	7.1	3.2	..	9.3
Forests and woodland	thou. sq. km	87	88	88	..	..	..
Deforestation (net)	annual %	..	..	..	..	..	..
INCOME							
Household income							
Share of top 20% of households	% of income	..	..	52	..	..	..
Share of bottom 40% of households	"	..	..	17	..	..	..
Share of bottom 20% of households	"	..	..	7	..	..	..
EXPENDITURE							
Food	% of GDP	..	21.4	..	..	..	..
Staples	"	..	5.3	..	..	..	..
Meat, fish, milk, cheese, eggs	"	..	8.1	..	..	..	..
Cereal imports	thou. metric tonnes	716	486	1,095	25,032	74,924	49,174
Food aid in cereals	"	323	10	13	1,779	4,054	282
Food production per capita	1987 = 100	94	97	119	104	..	109
Fertilizer consumption	kg/ha	5.6	11.6	17.3	15.5	..	68.8
Share of agriculture in GDP	% of GDP	6.6	7.4	8.5	8.9	..	8.1
Housing	% of GDP	..	10.0	..	..	..	..
Average household size	persons per household	5.0	..	..	..	..	..
Urban	"	5.0	..	..	..	..	..
Fixed investment: housing	% of GDP	4.5	4.2	..	..	..	..
Fuel and power	% of GDP	..	1.6	..	..	..	..
Energy consumption per capita	kg of oil equiv.	567	570	837	912	1,882	1,649
Households with electricity							
Urban	% of households	..	..	..	..	..	..
Rural	"	..	..	..	..	..	..
Transport and communication	% of GDP	..	8.0	..	..	..	..
Fixed investment: transport equipment	"	2.8	2.9	..	..	..	..
Total road length	thou. km	75	79	80	..	..	..
INVESTMENT IN HUMAN CAPITAL							
Health							
Population per physician	persons	2,160	1,231	2,152	..	..	..
Population per nurse	"	459	371	335	..	..	..
Population per hospital bed	"	265	294	320	508	516	385
Oral rehydration therapy (under-5)	% of cases	..	..	1	62	..	54
Education							
Gross enrollment ratio							
Secondary	% of school-age pop.	48	67	72	47	..	53
Female	"	52	70	75	..	..	..
Pupil-teacher ratio: primary	pupils per teacher	35	33	25	25	26	25
Pupil-teacher ratio: secondary	"	16	..	..	..	..	..
Pupils reaching grade 4	% of cohort	84	96	..	..	..	71
Repeater rate: primary	% of total enroll	12	7	..	14	..	11
Illiteracy	% of pop. (age 15+)	11	8	7	15	..	14
Female	% of fem. (age 15+)	..	8	7	17	..	17
Newspaper circulation	per thou. pop.	90	94	455	99	100	117

World Bank International Economics Department, April 1994

China

Indicator	Unit of measure	Latest single year 1970-75	Latest single year 1980-85	Most recent estimate 1987-92	Same region/income group East Asia	Same region/income group Low-income	Next higher income group
Priority Poverty Indicators							
POVERTY							
Upper poverty line	local curr.	..	180	324	..	..	..
Headcount index	% of pop.	..	26	11	12	19	..
Lower poverty line	local curr.	..	161	287	..	..	..
Headcount index	% of pop.	..	20	9	9	..	..
GNP per capita	US$	..	380	470	760	390	
SHORT TERM INCOME INDICATORS							
Unskilled urban wages	local curr.	..	..	..	..	..	..
Unskilled rural wages	"	..	..	..	..	..	..
Rural terms of trade	"	..	..	..	..	..	..
Consumer price index	1987=100	62	86	150	..	..	..
Lower income	"	..	..	..	..	..	..
Food[a]	"	..	85	146	..	..	..
Urban	"	..	..	..	..	..	..
Rural	"	..	..	..	..	..	..
SOCIAL INDICATORS							
Public expenditure on basic social services	% of GDP	..	..	..	..	..	..
Gross enrollment ratios							
Primary	% school age pop.	126	124	123	121	103	..
Male	"	135	132	127	126	113	..
Female	"	115	114	118	117	96	..
Mortality							
Infant mortality	per thou. live births	48.0	37.0	31.0	39.0	73.0	45.0
Under 5 mortality	"	..	..	37.8	49.0	108.0	59.0
Immunization							
Measles	% age group	..	74.0	95.0	88.4	72.7	..
DPT	"	..	78.0	95.0	89.5	80.6	..
Child malnutrition (under-5)	"	..	..	21.3	24.7	38.3	..
Life expectancy							
Total	years	64	68	69	68	62	68
Female advantage	"	1.5	2.9	3.2	3.6	2.4	6.4
Total fertility rate	births per woman	3.4	2.3	2.0	2.4	3.4	3.1
Maternal mortality rate	per 100,000 live births	..	44	115	114	..	..
Supplementary Poverty Indicators							
Expenditures on social security	% of total gov't exp.	..	..	..	..	..	..
Social security coverage	% econ. active pop.	..	..	..	..	..	..
Access to safe water: total	% of pop.	..	..	78.0	72.0	68.4	..
Urban	"	..	81.0	87.0	83.4	78.9	..
Rural	"	..	..	66.0	60.2	60.3	..
Access to health care	"	..	..	..	..	..	..

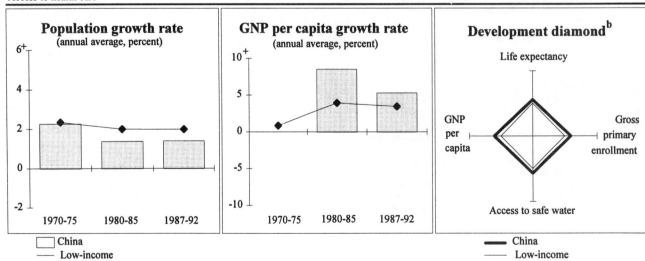

Population growth rate (annual average, percent)

GNP per capita growth rate (annual average, percent)

Development diamond[b]
Life expectancy / GNP per capita / Gross primary enrollment / Access to safe water

China / Low-income

a. See the technical notes, p.389.   b. The development diamond, based on four key indicators, shows the average level of development in the country compared with its income group. See the introduction.

72

China

Indicator	Unit of measure	Latest single year 1970-75	Latest single year 1980-85	Most recent estimate 1987-92	Same region/income group East Asia	Same region/income group Low-income	Next higher income group
Resources and Expenditures							
HUMAN RESOURCES							
Population (mre=1992)	thousands	916,395	1,051,013	1,162,165	1,688,909	3,194,535	942,547
Age dependency ratio	ratio	0.78	0.54	0.50	0.55	0.67	0.66
Urban	% of pop.	17.3	23.7	26.8	29.4	26.7	57.0
Population growth rate	annual %	1.8	1.4	1.2	1.4	1.8	1.4
Urban	"	2.4	4.4	2.6	2.9	3.4	4.8
Labor force (15-64)	thousands	481,759	617,906	698,525	928,465	1,478,954	..
Agriculture	% of labor force	76	74	..	..	..	..
Industry	"	12	14	..	..	..	..
Female	"	42	43	43	41	33	36
Females per 100 males							
Urban	number	..	88	..	..	..	..
Rural	"	..	95	..	..	..	..
NATURAL RESOURCES							
Area	thou. sq. km	9,561.00	9,561.00	9,561.00	16,367.18	38,401.06	40,697.37
Density	pop. per sq. km	95.9	109.9	120.1	101.8	81.7	22.8
Agricultural land	% of land area	43.1	50.3	53.4	44.5	50.9	..
Change in agricultural land	annual %	1.2	1.4	0.0	0.1	0.0	..
Agricultural land under irrigation	%	10.5	9.4	9.6	14.5	18.2	..
Forests and woodland	thou. sq. km	1,389	1,279	1,247	..	..	..
Deforestation (net)	annual %	..	..	..	..	..	..
INCOME							
Household income							
Share of top 20% of households	% of income	..	39	42	42	42	..
Share of bottom 40% of households	"	..	18	17	18	19	..
Share of bottom 20% of households	"	..	7	6	7	8	..
EXPENDITURE							
Food	% of GDP	..	43.1	..	..	..	..
Staples	"	..	..	..	..	..	..
Meat, fish, milk, cheese, eggs	"	..	..	..	..	..	..
Cereal imports	thou. metric tonnes	3,718	5,852	11,661	33,591	46,537	74,924
Food aid in cereals	"	..	262	172	581	9,008	4,054
Food production per capita	1987 = 100	90	119	140	133	123	..
Fertilizer consumption	kg/ha	16.1	35.3	58.7	75.1	61.9	..
Share of agriculture in GDP	% of GDP	..	33.7	27.2	21.5	29.6	..
Housing	% of GDP	..	5.5	..	..	..	..
Average household size	persons per household	..	4.8	..	..	..	..
Urban	"	..	3.8	..	..	..	..
Fixed investment: housing	% of GDP	..	..	..	..	..	..
Fuel and power	% of GDP	..	1.8	..	..	..	..
Energy consumption per capita	kg of oil equiv.	342	491	600	593	335	1,882
Households with electricity							
Urban	% of households	..	..	..	..	..	..
Rural	"	..	..	..	..	..	..
Transport and communication	% of GDP	..	0.9	..	..	..	..
Fixed investment: transport equipment	"	..	..	..	..	..	..
Total road length	thou. km	..	915	..	..	..	..
INVESTMENT IN HUMAN CAPITAL							
Health							
Population per physician	persons	1,400	1,011	..	..	..	..
Population per nurse	"	2,400	1,617	..	..	..	..
Population per hospital bed	"	600	505	388	553	1,050	516
Oral rehydration therapy (under-5)	% of cases	..	..	54	51	39	..
Education							
Gross enrollment ratio							
Secondary	% of school-age pop.	47	39	51	53	41	..
Female	"	38	32	45	47	35	..
Pupil-teacher ratio: primary	pupils per teacher	29	25	22	23	37	26
Pupil-teacher ratio: secondary	"	21	18	15	16	19	..
Pupils reaching grade 4	% of cohort	..	76	89	89	..	..
Repeater rate: primary	% of total enroll	..	..	6	6	..	..
Illiteracy	% of pop. (age 15+)	..	32	27	24	39	..
Female	% of fem. (age 15+)	..	45	38	34	52	..
Newspaper circulation	per thou. pop.	..	52	..	..	..	100

World Bank International Economics Department, April 1994

Colombia

Indicator	Unit of measure	Latest single year 1970-75	Latest single year 1980-85	Most recent estimate 1987-92	Same region/income group Latin America Caribbean	Same region/income group Lower-middle-income	Next higher income group
Priority Poverty Indicators							
POVERTY							
Upper poverty line	local curr.	..	..	..	..	..	..
Headcount index	% of pop.	..	..	..	..	..	..
Lower poverty line	local curr.	..	..	..	..	..	..
Headcount index	% of pop.	..	..	..	..	..	..
GNP per capita	US$	550	1,290	1,330	2,690	..	3,870
SHORT TERM INCOME INDICATORS							
Unskilled urban wages	local curr.	..	..	..	..	..	..
Unskilled rural wages	"	..	..	..	..	..	..
Rural terms of trade	"	..	..	..	..	..	..
Consumer price index	1987=100	8	68	345	..	..	..
Lower income	"	..	..	..	..	..	..
Food[a]	"	3	67	134	..	..	..
Urban	"	..	..	..	..	..	..
Rural	"	..	..	..	..	..	..
SOCIAL INDICATORS							
Public expenditure on basic social services	% of GDP	3.9	4.0	..	..	..	..
Gross enrollment ratios							
Primary	% school age pop.	118	107	111	106	..	107
Male	"	116	105	110	..	..	..
Female	"	120	109	112	..	..	..
Mortality							
Infant mortality	per thou. live births	68.0	40.0	21.0	44.0	45.0	40.0
Under 5 mortality	"	..	..	25.2	56.0	59.0	51.0
Immunization							
Measles	% age group	..	52.0	75.0	78.9	..	82.0
DPT	"	..	60.0	84.0	73.8	..	73.8
Child malnutrition (under-5)	"	..	17.2	10.1	10.5	..	..
Life expectancy							
Total	years	62	67	69	68	68	69
Female advantage	"	3.5	5.3	5.9	5.6	6.4	6.3
Total fertility rate	births per woman	4.7	3.5	2.7	3.0	3.1	2.9
Maternal mortality rate	per 100,000 live births	..	130	110	..	..	..
Supplementary Poverty Indicators							
Expenditures on social security	% of total gov't exp.	..	..	..	..	..	..
Social security coverage	% econ. active pop.	..	..	30.2	..	..	..
Access to safe water: total	% of pop.	64.0	..	92.0	80.3	..	85.6
Urban	"	86.0	89.0	100.0	91.0	..	94.3
Rural	"	33.0	20.0	76.0	64.3	..	73.0
Access to health care	"	..	87.6	97.0	..	..	..

Population growth rate
(annual average, percent)

Colombia
Lower-middle-income

GNP per capita growth rate
(annual average, percent)

Development diamond[b]

Life expectancy

GNP per capita — Gross primary enrollment

Access to safe water

Colombia
Lower-middle-income

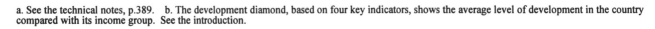

a. See the technical notes, p.389. b. The development diamond, based on four key indicators, shows the average level of development in the country compared with its income group. See the introduction.

Colombia

Indicator	Unit of measure	Latest single year 1970-75	Latest single year 1980-85	Most recent estimate 1987-92	Same region/income group Latin America Caribbean	Same region/income group Lower-middle-income	Next higher income group
Resources and Expenditures							
HUMAN RESOURCES							
Population (mre=1992)	thousands	23,776	29,481	33,399	453,294	942,547	477,960
Age dependency ratio	ratio	0.84	0.71	0.63	0.67	0.66	0.64
Urban	% of pop.	60.7	67.0	71.1	72.9	57.0	71.7
Population growth rate	annual %	2.1	2.0	1.7	1.7	1.4	1.6
Urban	"	3.3	2.9	2.5	2.6	4.8	2.5
Labor force (15-64)	thousands	7,060	9,195	10,897	166,091	..	181,414
Agriculture	% of labor force	37	34	..	..	..	..
Industry	"	23	23	..	..	..	..
Female	"	22	22	22	27	36	29
Females per 100 males							
Urban	number	126	115	..	..	..	..
Rural	"	90	85	..	..	..	..
NATURAL RESOURCES							
Area	thou. sq. km	1,138.91	1,138.91	1,138.91	20,507.48	40,697.37	21,836.02
Density	pop. per sq. km	20.9	25.9	28.8	21.7	22.8	21.5
Agricultural land	% of land area	40.4	43.1	44.2	40.2	..	41.7
Change in agricultural land	annual %	0.7	0.6	0.2	0.5	..	0.3
Agricultural land under irrigation	%	0.7	1.0	1.1	3.2	..	9.3
Forests and woodland	thou. sq. km	548	518	500	..	..	..
Deforestation (net)	annual %	..	..	0.6	..	..	..
INCOME							
Household income							
Share of top 20% of households	% of income	59	..	56	..	..	..
Share of bottom 40% of households	"	11	..	11	..	..	..
Share of bottom 20% of households	"	4	..	4	..	..	..
EXPENDITURE							
Food	% of GDP	26.7	23.1	..	..	..	..
Staples	"	6.0	4.8	..	..	..	..
Meat, fish, milk, cheese, eggs	"	12.7	11.1	..	..	..	..
Cereal imports	thou. metric tonnes	323	858	1,662	25,032	74,924	49,174
Food aid in cereals	"	28	4	8	1,779	4,054	282
Food production per capita	1987 = 100	94	93	103	104	..	109
Fertilizer consumption	kg/ha	5.1	8.1	11.8	15.5	..	68.8
Share of agriculture in GDP	% of GDP	23.9	17.0	15.7	8.9	..	8.1
Housing	% of GDP	6.1	8.9	..	..	..	..
Average household size	persons per household	5.7	5.2	..	..	..	..
Urban	"	5.5	5.1	..	..	..	..
Fixed investment: housing	% of GDP	2.3	2.3	..	..	..	..
Fuel and power	% of GDP	1.3	1.4	..	..	..	..
Energy consumption per capita	kg of oil equiv.	479	568	670	912	1,882	1,649
Households with electricity							
Urban	% of households	..	..	..	..	..	..
Rural	"	..	..	..	..	..	..
Transport and communication	% of GDP	7.3	9.5	..	..	..	..
Fixed investment: transport equipment	"	2.7	2.5	..	..	..	..
Total road length	thou. km	54	100	129	..	..	..
INVESTMENT IN HUMAN CAPITAL							
Health							
Population per physician	persons	2,256	1,229	..	..	..	..
Population per nurse	"	..	649	..	..	..	..
Population per hospital bed	"	451	596	703	508	516	385
Oral rehydration therapy (under-5)	% of cases	..	..	40	62	..	54
Education							
Gross enrollment ratio							
Secondary	% of school-age pop.	39	46	55	47	..	53
Female	"	39	46	60	..	..	..
Pupil-teacher ratio: primary	pupils per teacher	32	30	30	25	26	25
Pupil-teacher ratio: secondary	"	20	21	21	..	..	..
Pupils reaching grade 4	% of cohort	52	68	73	..	..	71
Repeater rate: primary	% of total enroll	15	17	12	14	..	11
Illiteracy	% of pop. (age 15+)	19	15	13	15	..	14
Female	% of fem. (age 15+)	..	16	14	17	..	17
Newspaper circulation	per thou. pop.	52	40	62	99	100	117

World Bank International Economics Department, April 1994

Comoros

| Indicator | Unit of measure | Latest single year | | Most recent estimate 1987-92 | Same region/income group | | Next higher income group |
		1970-75	1980-85		Sub-Saharan Africa	Low-income	
Priority Poverty Indicators							
POVERTY							
Upper poverty line	local curr.	..	..	..	..	..	..
Headcount index	% of pop.	..	..	..	..	19	..
Lower poverty line	local curr.	..	..	..	..	..	..
Headcount index	% of pop.	..	..	..	..	..	..
GNP per capita	US$	170	300	510	520	390	..
SHORT TERM INCOME INDICATORS							
Unskilled urban wages	local curr.	..	..	3500	..	..	..
Unskilled rural wages	"	..	..	..	..	..	..
Rural terms of trade	"	..	..	..	..	..	..
Consumer price index	1987=100	..	..	..	..	..	..
Lower income	"	..	..	..	..	..	..
Food[a]	"	..	..	..	..	..	..
Urban	"	..	..	..	..	..	..
Rural	"	..	..	..	..	..	..
SOCIAL INDICATORS							
Public expenditure on basic social services	% of GDP	..	..	5.2	..	..	..
Gross enrollment ratios							
Primary	% school age pop.	46	82	75	66	103	..
Male	"	64	91	82	79	113	..
Female	"	29	72	68	62	96	..
Mortality							
Infant mortality	per thou. live births	135.0	109.0	89.0	99.0	73.0	45.0
Under 5 mortality	"	..	..	126.4	169.0	108.0	59.0
Immunization							
Measles	% age group	..	18.0	71.0	54.0	72.7	..
DPT	"	..	31.0	71.0	54.6	80.6	..
Child malnutrition (under-5)	"	..	..	..	28.4	38.3	..
Life expectancy							
Total	years	47	52	56	52	62	68
Female advantage	"	1.0	1.0	1.0	3.4	2.4	6.4
Total fertility rate	births per woman	7.0	7.0	6.7	6.1	3.4	3.1
Maternal mortality rate	per 100,000 live births	..	500	..	..	..	..
Supplementary Poverty Indicators							
Expenditures on social security	% of total gov't exp.	..	..	..	..	..	..
Social security coverage	% econ. active pop.	..	..	..	..	..	..
Access to safe water: total	% of pop.	..	..	..	41.1	68.4	..
Urban	"	..	..	..	77.8	78.9	..
Rural	"	..	..	..	27.3	60.3	..
Access to health care	"	..	82.4	..	..	..	..

Population growth rate
(annual average, percent)

Comoros
Low-income

GNP per capita growth rate
(annual average, percent)

Development diamond[b]

Life expectancy

GNP per capita — Gross primary enrollment

Access to safe water

Comoros
Low-income

a. See the technical notes, p.389.   b. The development diamond, based on four key indicators, shows the average level of development in the country compared with its income group. See the introduction.

Comoros

Indicator	Unit of measure	Latest single year 1970-75	Latest single year 1980-85	Most recent estimate 1987-92	Same region/income group Sub-Saharan Africa	Same region/income group Low-income	Next higher income group
Resources and Expenditures							
HUMAN RESOURCES							
Population (mre=1992)	thousands	298	395	510	546,390	3,194,535	942,547
Age dependency ratio	ratio	0.93	0.99	1.03	0.95	0.67	0.66
Urban	% of pop.	21.2	25.3	29.0	29.5	26.7	57.0
Population growth rate	annual %	2.0	3.6	3.6	2.9	1.8	1.4
Urban	"	3.8	5.3	5.6	5.1	3.4	4.8
Labor force (15-64)	thousands	155	204	244	224,025	1,478,954	..
Agriculture	% of labor force	85	83	0	..	..	..
Industry	"	5	6	..	..	..	..
Female	"	43	41	40	37	33	36
Females per 100 males							
Urban	number	..	104	..	..	..	..
Rural	"	..	108	..	..	..	..
NATURAL RESOURCES							
Area	thou. sq. km	2.23	2.23	2.23	24,274.03	38,401.06	40,697.37
Density	pop. per sq. km	133.6	177.1	220.6	21.9	81.7	22.8
Agricultural land	% of land area	47.1	50.2	51.6	52.7	50.9	..
Change in agricultural land	annual %	0.0	2.8	0.0	0.1	0.0	..
Agricultural land under irrigation	%	..	..	..	0.8	18.2	..
Forests and woodland	thou. sq. km	0	0	0	..	..	..
Deforestation (net)	annual %	..	..	..	..	..	..
INCOME							
Household income							
Share of top 20% of households	% of income	..	..	..	..	42	..
Share of bottom 40% of households	"	..	..	..	..	19	..
Share of bottom 20% of households	"	..	..	..	..	8	..
EXPENDITURE							
Food	% of GDP	..	..	45.8	..	..	..
Staples	"	..	..	15.1	..	..	..
Meat, fish, milk, cheese, eggs	"	..	..	14.7	..	..	..
Cereal imports	thou. metric tonnes	12	19	40	20,311	46,537	74,924
Food aid in cereals	"	1	5	5	4,303	9,008	4,054
Food production per capita	1987 = 100	119	88	79	90	123	..
Fertilizer consumption	kg/ha	..	..	0.9	4.2	61.9	..
Share of agriculture in GDP	% of GDP	..	36.1	39.6	18.6	29.6	..
Housing	% of GDP	..	..	4.2	..	..	..
Average household size	persons per household	..	..	..	..	..	..
Urban	"	..	..	..	..	..	..
Fixed investment: housing	% of GDP	..	..	0.4	..	..	..
Fuel and power	% of GDP	..	..	1.7	..	..	..
Energy consumption per capita	kg of oil equiv.	34	41	35	258	335	1,882
Households with electricity							
Urban	% of households	..	..	..	..	..	..
Rural	"	..	..	..	..	..	..
Transport and communication	% of GDP	..	..	1.5	..	..	..
Fixed investment: transport equipment	"	..	..	1.9	..	..	..
Total road length	thou. km	..	1	..	..	..	..
INVESTMENT IN HUMAN CAPITAL							
Health							
Population per physician	persons	14,000	12,290	6,582	..	..	..
Population per nurse	"	1,727	2,268	..	..	..	..
Population per hospital bed	"	476	..	..	1,329	1,050	516
Oral rehydration therapy (under-5)	% of cases	..	..	79	36	39	..
Education							
Gross enrollment ratio							
Secondary	% of school-age pop.	7	28	17	18	41	..
Female	"	2	22	15	14	35	..
Pupil-teacher ratio: primary	pupils per teacher	47	35	36	39	37	26
Pupil-teacher ratio: secondary	"	25	31	26	..	19	..
Pupils reaching grade 4	% of cohort	..	..	..	..	..	..
Repeater rate: primary	% of total enroll	..	33	..	..	..	..
Illiteracy	% of pop. (age 15+)	..	52	..	51	39	..
Female	% of fem. (age 15+)	..	..	..	62	52	..
Newspaper circulation	per thou. pop.	..	..	..	14	..	100

World Bank International Economics Department, April 1994

Congo

Indicator	Unit of measure	Latest single year 1970-75	Latest single year 1980-85	Most recent estimate 1987-92	Same region/income group Sub-Saharan Africa	Same region/income group Lower-middle-income	Next higher income group
Priority Poverty Indicators							
POVERTY							
Upper poverty line	local curr.	..	..	..	..	..	..
Headcount index	% of pop.	..	..	..	..	..	..
Lower poverty line	local curr.	..	..	..	..	..	..
Headcount index	% of pop.	..	..	..	..	..	..
GNP per capita	US$	500	1,050	1,030	520	..	3,870
SHORT TERM INCOME INDICATORS							
Unskilled urban wages	local curr.	..	..	..	..	..	..
Unskilled rural wages	"	..	..	..	..	..	..
Rural terms of trade	"	..	..	..	..	..	..
Consumer price index	1987=100	36	96	115	..	..	..
Lower income	"	..	..	..	..	..	..
Food[a]	"	..	98	113	..	..	..
Urban	"	..	..	..	..	..	..
Rural	"	..	..	..	..	..	..
SOCIAL INDICATORS							
Public expenditure on basic social services	% of GDP	..	..	..	..	..	..
Gross enrollment ratios							
Primary	% school age pop.	133	..	..	66	..	107
Male	"	..	..	..	79	..	..
Female	"	..	..	..	62	..	..
Mortality							
Infant mortality	per thou. live births	125.0	124.0	114.0	99.0	45.0	40.0
Under 5 mortality	"	..	..	166.3	169.0	59.0	51.0
Immunization							
Measles	% age group	..	67.0	69.0	54.0	..	82.0
DPT	"	..	54.0	..	54.6	..	73.8
Child malnutrition (under-5)	"	..	22.0	23.5	28.4	..	..
Life expectancy							
Total	years	47	50	51	52	68	69
Female advantage	"	5.2	5.7	4.9	3.4	6.4	6.3
Total fertility rate	births per woman	6.0	6.0	6.6	6.1	3.1	2.9
Maternal mortality rate	per 100,000 live births	..	..	..	..	..	..
Supplementary Poverty Indicators							
Expenditures on social security	% of total gov't exp.	0.5	4.4	..	..	..	..
Social security coverage	% econ. active pop.	..	..	..	..	..	..
Access to safe water: total	% of pop.	38.0	..	20.0	41.1	..	85.6
Urban	"	81.0	..	42.0	77.8	..	94.3
Rural	"	9.0	..	7.0	27.3	..	73.0
Access to health care	"	..	..	..	..	..	..

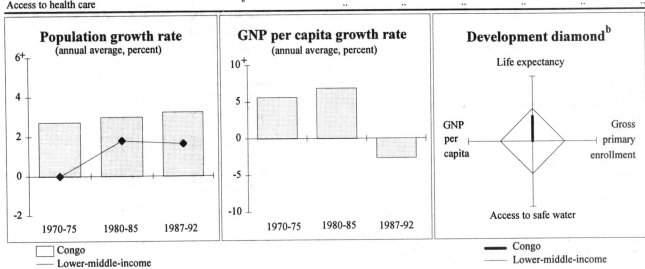

Population growth rate (annual average, percent)

□ Congo
— Lower-middle-income

GNP per capita growth rate (annual average, percent)

Development diamond[b]
Life expectancy
GNP per capita — Gross primary enrollment
Access to safe water

— Congo
— Lower-middle-income

a. See the technical notes, p.389.   b. The development diamond, based on four key indicators, shows the average level of development in the country compared with its income group. See the introduction.

Congo

Indicator	Unit of measure	Latest single year 1970-75	Latest single year 1980-85	Most recent estimate 1987-92	Same region/income group Sub-Saharan Africa	Same region/income group Lower-middle-income	Next higher income group
Resources and Expenditures							
HUMAN RESOURCES							
Population (mre=1992)	thousands	1,447	1,938	2,428	546,390	942,547	477,960
Age dependency ratio	ratio	0.85	0.95	0.98	0.95	0.66	0.64
Urban	% of pop.	33.8	38.0	41.7	29.5	57.0	71.7
Population growth rate	annual %	2.8	3.1	3.2	2.9	1.4	1.6
Urban	"	3.4	4.3	4.6	5.1	4.8	2.5
Labor force (15-64)	thousands	582	710	820	224,025	..	181,414
Agriculture	% of labor force	64	62	..	..	..	..
Industry	"	12	12	..	..	..	..
Female	"	40	39	39	37	36	29
Females per 100 males							
Urban	number	..	..	..	..	..	..
Rural	"	..	..	..	..	..	..
NATURAL RESOURCES							
Area	thou. sq. km	342.00	342.00	342.00	24,274.03	40,697.37	21,836.02
Density	pop. per sq. km	4.2	5.7	6.9	21.9	22.8	21.5
Agricultural land	% of land area	29.7	29.8	29.8	52.7	..	41.7
Change in agricultural land	annual %	0.0	0.0	0.0	0.1	..	0.3
Agricultural land under irrigation	%	0.0	0.0	0.0	0.8	..	9.3
Forests and woodland	thou. sq. km	215	213	211	..	..	..
Deforestation (net)	annual %	..	..	0.2	..	..	..
INCOME							
Household income							
Share of top 20% of households	% of income	..	..	..	..	..	..
Share of bottom 40% of households	"	..	..	..	..	..	..
Share of bottom 20% of households	"	..	..	..	..	..	..
EXPENDITURE							
Food	% of GDP	..	17.4	..	..	..	..
Staples	"	..	7.7	..	..	..	..
Meat, fish, milk, cheese, eggs	"	..	5.9	..	..	..	..
Cereal imports	thou. metric tonnes	36	100	130	20,311	74,924	49,174
Food aid in cereals	"	2	1	4	4,303	4,054	282
Food production per capita	1987 = 100	107	99	95	90	..	109
Fertilizer consumption	kg/ha	0.2	0.5	0.0	4.2	..	68.8
Share of agriculture in GDP	% of GDP	14.5	7.5	13.0	18.6	..	8.1
Housing	% of GDP	..	4.4	..	..	..	..
Average household size	persons per household	..	5.3	..	..	..	..
Urban	"	5.5	6.1	..	..	..	..
Fixed investment: housing	% of GDP	..	6.1	..	..	..	..
Fuel and power	% of GDP	..	1.5	..	..	..	..
Energy consumption per capita	kg of oil equiv.	144	177	131	258	1,882	1,649
Households with electricity							
Urban	% of households	..	..	..	..	..	..
Rural	"	..	..	..	..	..	..
Transport and communication	% of GDP	..	6.9	..	..	..	..
Fixed investment: transport equipment	"	..	2.4	..	..	..	..
Total road length	thou. km	8	9	9	..	..	..
INVESTMENT IN HUMAN CAPITAL							
Health							
Population per physician	persons	9,945	8,429	..	..	..	..
Population per nurse	"	814	595	..	..	..	..
Population per hospital bed	"	228	..	..	1,329	516	385
Oral rehydration therapy (under-5)	% of cases	..	..	26	36	..	54
Education							
Gross enrollment ratio							
Secondary	% of school-age pop.	33	..	..	18	..	53
Female	"	..	..	..	14	..	..
Pupil-teacher ratio: primary	pupils per teacher	59	61	66	39	26	25
Pupil-teacher ratio: secondary	"	46	41	35	..	..	..
Pupils reaching grade 4	% of cohort	92	88	87	..	..	71
Repeater rate: primary	% of total enroll	26	30	36	..	..	11
Illiteracy	% of pop. (age 15+)	..	48	43	51	..	14
Female	% of fem. (age 15+)	..	62	56	62	..	17
Newspaper circulation	per thou. pop.	1	4	7	14	100	117

World Bank International Economics Department, April 1994

Costa Rica

Indicator	Unit of measure	Latest single year 1970-75	Latest single year 1980-85	Most recent estimate 1987-92	Same region/income group Latin America Caribbean	Same region/income group Lower-middle-income	Next higher income group
Priority Poverty Indicators							
POVERTY							
Upper poverty line	local curr.	..	..	..	..	..	..
Headcount index	% of pop.	..	..	..	..	..	..
Lower poverty line	local curr.	..	..	..	..	..	..
Headcount index	% of pop.	..	..	..	..	..	..
GNP per capita	US$	950	1,330	1,960	2,690	..	3,870
SHORT TERM INCOME INDICATORS							
Unskilled urban wages	local curr.	..	..	..	..	..	..
Unskilled rural wages	"	..	..	..	..	..	..
Rural terms of trade	"	..	..	..	..	..	..
Consumer price index	1987=100	12	77	263	..	..	..
Lower income	"	..	..	..	..	..	..
Food[a]	"	5	78	211	..	..	..
Urban	"	..	..	..	..	..	..
Rural	"	..	..	..	..	..	..
SOCIAL INDICATORS							
Public expenditure on basic social services	% of GDP	..	..	..	..	..	..
Gross enrollment ratios							
Primary	% school age pop.	107	97	103	106	..	107
Male	"	108	98	103	..	..	..
Female	"	106	96	102	..	..	..
Mortality							
Infant mortality	per thou. live births	37.8	18.9	14.0	44.0	45.0	40.0
Under 5 mortality	"	..	..	17.2	56.0	59.0	51.0
Immunization							
Measles	% age group	..	83.0	90.0	78.9	..	82.0
DPT	"	..	82.0	95.0	73.8	..	73.8
Child malnutrition (under-5)	"	..	6.0	6.0	10.5	..	..
Life expectancy							
Total	years	68	74	76	68	68	69
Female advantage	"	4.1	4.5	4.6	5.6	6.4	6.3
Total fertility rate	births per woman	4.3	3.5	3.1	3.0	3.1	2.9
Maternal mortality rate	per 100,000 live births	..	26	18	..	..	..
Supplementary Poverty Indicators							
Expenditures on social security	% of total gov't exp.	26.4	14.5	13.8	..	..	..
Social security coverage	% econ. active pop.	..	..	68.7	..	..	..
Access to safe water: total	% of pop.	72.0	90.0	94.0	80.3	..	85.6
Urban	"	100.0	100.0	100.0	91.0	..	94.3
Rural	"	56.0	82.0	84.0	64.3	..	73.0
Access to health care	"	..	94.8	97.0	..	..	..

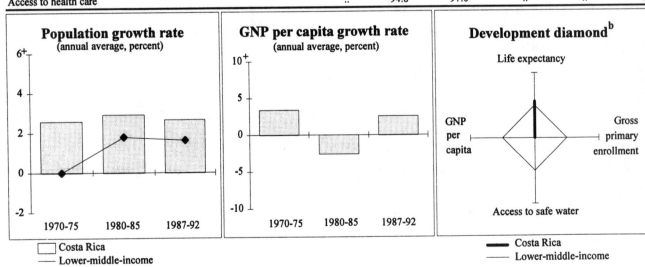

Population growth rate (annual average, percent)

GNP per capita growth rate (annual average, percent)

Development diamond[b]
Life expectancy
GNP per capita — Gross primary enrollment
Access to safe water

Costa Rica
Lower-middle-income

a. See the technical notes, p.389.   b. The development diamond, based on four key indicators, shows the average level of development in the country compared with its income group. See the introduction.

Costa Rica

Indicator	Unit of measure	Latest single year 1970-75	Latest single year 1980-85	Most recent estimate 1987-92	Latin America Caribbean	Lower-middle-income	Next higher income group
Resources and Expenditures							
HUMAN RESOURCES							
Population (mre=1992)	thousands	1,968	2,642	3,193	453,294	942,547	477,960
Age dependency ratio	ratio	0.84	0.69	0.68	0.67	0.66	0.64
Urban	% of pop.	41.3	44.9	48.1	72.9	57.0	71.7
Population growth rate	annual %	2.7	2.9	2.5	1.7	1.4	1.6
Urban	"	3.5	3.7	3.6	2.6	4.8	2.5
Labor force (15-64)	thousands	638	904	1,075	166,091	..	181,414
Agriculture	% of labor force	37	31	..	..	..	..
Industry	"	22	23	..	..	..	..
Female	"	20	22	22	27	36	29
Females per 100 males							
Urban	number	118	114	..	..	..	..
Rural	"	90	93	..	..	..	..
NATURAL RESOURCES							
Area	thou. sq. km	51.10	51.10	51.10	20,507.48	40,697.37	21,836.02
Density	pop. per sq. km	38.5	51.7	60.9	21.7	22.8	21.5
Agricultural land	% of land area	41.6	54.9	56.0	40.2	..	41.7
Change in agricultural land	annual %	3.6	2.0	0.0	0.5	..	0.3
Agricultural land under irrigation	%	1.7	3.9	4.2	3.2	..	9.3
Forests and woodland	thou. sq. km	22	16	16	..	..	..
Deforestation (net)	annual %	..	..	3.1	..	..	..
INCOME							
Household income							
Share of top 20% of households	% of income	55	..	51	..	..	..
Share of bottom 40% of households	"	12	..	13	..	..	..
Share of bottom 20% of households	"	3	..	4	..	..	..
EXPENDITURE							
Food	% of GDP	..	23.6	..	..	..	..
Staples	"	..	6.1	..	..	..	..
Meat, fish, milk, cheese, eggs	"	..	8.0	..	..	..	..
Cereal imports	thou. metric tonnes	113	138	484	25,032	74,924	49,174
Food aid in cereals	"	1	164	90	1,779	4,054	282
Food production per capita	1987 = 100	108	95	93	104	..	109
Fertilizer consumption	kg/ha	31.2	28.8	42.1	15.5	..	68.8
Share of agriculture in GDP	% of GDP	20.3	18.9	18.0	8.9	..	8.1
Housing	% of GDP	..	6.5	..	..	..	..
Average household size	persons per household	6.0	..	..	..	..	..
Urban	"	87.0	..	..	..	..	..
Fixed investment: housing	% of GDP	..	8.1	..	..	..	..
Fuel and power	% of GDP	..	1.0	..	..	..	..
Energy consumption per capita	kg of oil equiv.	504	514	566	912	1,882	1,649
Households with electricity							
Urban	% of households	..	..	..	..	..	..
Rural	"	..	..	..	..	..	..
Transport and communication	% of GDP	..	5.7	..	..	..	..
Fixed investment: transport equipment	"	..	3.9	..	..	..	..
Total road length	thou. km	24	29	36	..	..	..
INVESTMENT IN HUMAN CAPITAL							
Health							
Population per physician	persons	1,622	1,011	1,032	..	..	..
Population per nurse	"	459	475	..	..	..	..
Population per hospital bed	"	253	302	..	508	516	385
Oral rehydration therapy (under-5)	% of cases	..	..	78	62	..	54
Education							
Gross enrollment ratio							
Secondary	% of school-age pop.	42	40	43	47	..	53
Female	"	45	42	45	..	..	..
Pupil-teacher ratio: primary	pupils per teacher	29	31	32	25	26	25
Pupil-teacher ratio: secondary	"	24	18	22	..	..	..
Pupils reaching grade 4	% of cohort	79	93	91	..	..	71
Repeater rate: primary	% of total enroll	6	11	11	14	..	11
Illiteracy	% of pop. (age 15+)	12	8	7	15	..	14
Female	% of fem. (age 15+)	..	8	7	17	..	17
Newspaper circulation	per thou. pop.	88	67	101	99	100	117

World Bank International Economics Department, April 1994

Côte d'Ivoire

Indicator	Unit of measure	Latest single year 1970-75	Latest single year 1980-85	Most recent estimate 1987-92	Same region/income group Sub-Saharan Africa	Same region/income group Lower-middle-income	Next higher income group
Priority Poverty Indicators							
POVERTY							
Upper poverty line	local curr.	..	..	..	..	..	..
Headcount index	% of pop.	..	..	..	..	..	..
Lower poverty line	local curr.	..	..	..	..	..	..
Headcount index	% of pop.	..	..	..	..	..	..
GNP per capita	US$	530	660	670	520	..	3,870
SHORT TERM INCOME INDICATORS							
Unskilled urban wages	local curr.	..	..	..	..	..	..
Unskilled rural wages	"	..	..	..	..	..	..
Rural terms of trade	"	..	..	..	..	..	..
Consumer price index	1987=100	31	88	113	..	..	..
Lower income	"	..	..	..	..	..	..
Food[a]	"	18	78	100	..	..	..
Urban	"	..	..	..	..	..	..
Rural	"	..	..	..	..	..	..
SOCIAL INDICATORS							
Public expenditure on basic social services	% of GDP	..	..	..	..	..	..
Gross enrollment ratios							
Primary	% school age pop.	62	75	69	66	..	107
Male	"	77	88	81	79	..	..
Female	"	47	62	58	62	..	..
Mortality							
Infant mortality	per thou. live births	129.0	106.0	91.0	99.0	45.0	40.0
Under 5 mortality	"	..	..	129.3	169.0	59.0	51.0
Immunization							
Measles	% age group	..	28.0	42.0	54.0	..	82.0
DPT	"	..	25.0	48.0	54.6	..	73.8
Child malnutrition (under-5)	"	30.6	..	12.4	28.4	..	..
Life expectancy							
Total	years	45	53	56	52	68	69
Female advantage	"	3.2	3.0	5.7	3.4	6.4	6.3
Total fertility rate	births per woman	7.4	7.4	6.6	6.1	3.1	2.9
Maternal mortality rate	per 100,000 live births	..	..	..	..	..	..
Supplementary Poverty Indicators							
Expenditures on social security	% of total gov't exp.	..	..	..	..	..	..
Social security coverage	% econ. active pop.	..	..	..	..	..	..
Access to safe water: total	% of pop.	44.0	..	83.0	41.1	..	85.6
Urban	"	98.0	..	100.0	77.8	..	94.3
Rural	"	29.0	..	75.0	27.3	..	73.0
Access to health care	"	..	..	60.0	..	..	..

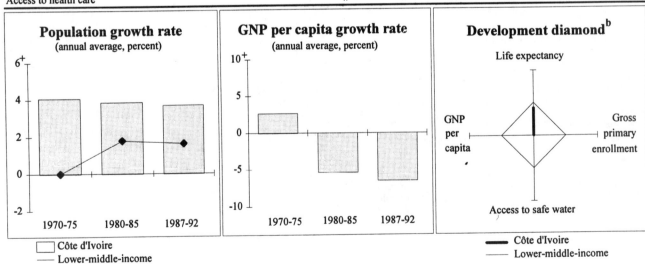

Population growth rate (annual average, percent)

GNP per capita growth rate (annual average, percent)

Development diamond[b]

□ Côte d'Ivoire
— Lower-middle-income

—— Côte d'Ivoire
— Lower-middle-income

a. See the technical notes, p.389.   b. The development diamond, based on four key indicators, shows the average level of development in the country compared with its income group. See the introduction.

Côte d'Ivoire

Indicator	Unit of measure	Latest single year 1970-75	Latest single year 1980-85	Most recent estimate 1987-92	Same region/income group Sub-Saharan Africa	Same region/income group Lower-middle-income	Next higher income group
Resources and Expenditures							
HUMAN RESOURCES							
Population (mre=1992)	thousands	6,755	9,936	12,886	546,390	942,547	477,960
Age dependency ratio	ratio	1.00	1.00	1.01	0.95	0.66	0.64
Urban	% of pop.	32.1	37.6	41.7	29.5	57.0	71.7
Population growth rate	annual %	4.0	3.8	3.6	2.9	1.4	1.6
Urban	"	7.0	3.7	5.2	5.1	4.8	2.5
Labor force (15-64)	thousands	3,153	4,053	4,840	224,025	..	181,414
Agriculture	% of labor force	71	65	..	..	..	..
Industry	"	7	8	..	..	..	..
Female	"	37	35	34	37	36	29
Females per 100 males							
Urban	number	76	..	..	..	..	..
Rural	"	103	..	..	..	..	..
NATURAL RESOURCES							
Area	thou. sq. km	322.46	322.46	322.46	24,274.03	40,697.37	21,836.02
Density	pop. per sq. km	21.0	30.8	38.5	21.9	22.8	21.5
Agricultural land	% of land area	50.1	52.1	52.5	52.7	..	41.7
Change in agricultural land	annual %	0.3	0.6	0.0	0.1	..	0.3
Agricultural land under irrigation	%	0.2	0.3	0.4	0.8	..	9.3
Forests and woodland	thou. sq. km	111	86	71	..	..	..
Deforestation (net)	annual %	..	..	1.0	..	..	..
INCOME							
Household income							
Share of top 20% of households	% of income	50	61	42	..	..	..
Share of bottom 40% of households	"	20	15	19	..	..	..
Share of bottom 20% of households	"	9	5	7	..	..	..
EXPENDITURE							
Food	% of GDP	..	24.4	..	..	..	..
Staples	"	..	8.4	..	..	..	..
Meat, fish, milk, cheese, eggs	"	..	6.5	..	..	..	..
Cereal imports	thou. metric tonnes	82	554	568	20,311	74,924	49,174
Food aid in cereals	"	4	1	37	4,303	4,054	282
Food production per capita	1987 = 100	99	100	89	90	..	109
Fertilizer consumption	kg/ha	2.4	2.5	2.3	4.2	..	68.8
Share of agriculture in GDP	% of GDP	28.2	25.2	32.1	18.6	..	8.1
Housing	% of GDP	..	3.0	..	..	..	..
Average household size	persons per household	..	..	..	..	..	..
Urban	"	..	..	..	..	..	..
Fixed investment: housing	% of GDP	..	2.8	..	..	..	..
Fuel and power	% of GDP	..	0.8	..	..	..	..
Energy consumption per capita	kg of oil equiv.	172	150	125	258	1,882	1,649
Households with electricity							
Urban	% of households	..	..	..	..	..	..
Rural	"	..	..	..	..	..	..
Transport and communication	% of GDP	..	6.1	..	..	..	..
Fixed investment: transport equipment	"	3.2	2.1	..	..	..	..
Total road length	thou. km	45	47	49	..	..	..
INVESTMENT IN HUMAN CAPITAL							
Health							
Population per physician	persons	15,521	14,255	..	..	..	..
Population per nurse	"	2,040	..	..	..	..	..
Population per hospital bed	"	864	..	1,269	1,329	516	385
Oral rehydration therapy (under-5)	% of cases	..	..	16	36	..	54
Education							
Gross enrollment ratio							
Secondary	% of school-age pop.	13	20	24	18	..	53
Female	"	7	12	16	14	..	..
Pupil-teacher ratio: primary	pupils per teacher	44	36	37	39	26	25
Pupil-teacher ratio: secondary	"	32	38	..	..	..	..
Pupils reaching grade 4	% of cohort	88	83	83	..	..	71
Repeater rate: primary	% of total enroll	21	28	..	..	..	11
Illiteracy	% of pop. (age 15+)	..	51	46	51	..	14
Female	% of fem. (age 15+)	..	66	60	62	..	17
Newspaper circulation	per thou. pop.	5	7	8	14	100	117

World Bank International Economics Department, April 1994

Croatia

Indicator	Unit of measure	Latest single year		Most recent estimate	Same region/income group		Next higher income group
		1970-75	1980-85	1987-92	Europe & Central Asia	Lower-middle-income	

Priority Poverty Indicators

Indicator	Unit of measure	1970-75	1980-85	1987-92	Europe & Central Asia	Lower-middle-income	Next higher income group
POVERTY							
Upper poverty line	local curr.	..	..	..	..	..	..
Headcount index	% of pop.	..	..	..	..	..	..
Lower poverty line	local curr.	..	..	..	..	..	..
Headcount index	% of pop.	..	..	..	..	..	..
GNP per capita	US$	..	..	..	..	..	3,870
SHORT TERM INCOME INDICATORS							
Unskilled urban wages	local curr.	..	..	..	..	..	..
Unskilled rural wages	"	..	..	..	..	..	..
Rural terms of trade	"	..	..	..	..	..	..
Consumer price index	1987=100	..	..	..	..	..	..
Lower income	"	..	..	..	..	..	..
Food[a]	"	..	..	..	..	..	..
Urban	"	..	..	..	..	..	..
Rural	"	..	..	..	..	..	..
SOCIAL INDICATORS							
Public expenditure on basic social services	% of GDP	..	..	..	..	..	..
Gross enrollment ratios							
Primary	% school age pop.	..	..	..	..	..	107
Male	"	..	..	..	..	..	..
Female	"	..	..	..	..	..	..
Mortality							
Infant mortality	per thou. live births	..	18.5	11.7	30.0	45.0	40.0
Under 5 mortality	"	..	..	14.4	38.0	59.0	51.0
Immunization							
Measles	% age group	..	..	..	..	..	82.0
DPT	"	..	..	..	..	..	73.8
Child malnutrition (under-5)	"	..	..	..	..	..	..
Life expectancy							
Total	years	..	69	73	70	68	69
Female advantage	"	..	9.0	7.7	8.6	6.4	6.3
Total fertility rate	births per woman	..	..	1.7	2.2	3.1	2.9
Maternal mortality rate	per 100,000 live births	..	..	..	58	..	..

Supplementary Poverty Indicators

Indicator	Unit of measure	1970-75	1980-85	1987-92	Europe & Central Asia	Lower-middle-income	Next higher income group
Expenditures on social security	% of total gov't exp.	..	..	..	..	..	..
Social security coverage	% econ. active pop.	..	..	..	..	..	..
Access to safe water: total	% of pop.	..	..	..	..	..	85.6
Urban	"	..	..	..	..	..	94.3
Rural	"	..	..	..	..	..	73.0
Access to health care	"	..	..	..	..	..	..

Population growth rate
(annual average, percent)

Croatia
Lower-middle-income

GNP per capita growth rate
(annual average, percent)

Development diamond[b]

Life expectancy
GNP per capita
Gross primary enrollment
Access to safe water

Croatia
Lower-middle-income

a. See the technical notes, p.389.   b. The development diamond, based on four key indicators, shows the average level of development in the country compared with its income group. See the introduction.

Croatia

Indicator	Unit of measure	1970-75	1980-85	Most recent estimate 1987-92	Europe & Central Asia	Lower-middle-income	Next higher income group
Resources and Expenditures							
HUMAN RESOURCES							
Population (mre=1992)	thousands	4,514	4,657	4,789	495,241	942,547	477,960
Age dependency ratio	ratio	..	..	0.50	0.56	0.66	0.64
Urban	% of pop.	..	..	..	63.3	57.0	71.7
Population growth rate	annual %	0.4	0.3	0.0	0.5	1.4	1.6
Urban	"	..	..	..	..	4.8	2.5
Labor force (15-64)	thousands	..	..	..	..	..	181,414
Agriculture	% of labor force	..	..	..	..	..	..
Industry	"	..	..	..	..	..	..
Female	"	..	..	..	46	36	29
Females per 100 males							
Urban	number	..	..	..	..	..	..
Rural	"	..	..	..	..	..	..
NATURAL RESOURCES							
Area	thou. sq. km	..	..	56.54	24,165.06	40,697.37	21,836.02
Density	pop. per sq. km	..	..	84.7	20.4	22.8	21.5
Agricultural land	% of land area	..	..	..	..	..	41.7
Change in agricultural land	annual %	..	..	..	..	..	0.3
Agricultural land under irrigation	%	..	..	..	..	..	9.3
Forests and woodland	thou. sq. km	..	..	..	..	..	..
Deforestation (net)	annual %	..	..	..	..	..	..
INCOME							
Household income							
Share of top 20% of households	% of income	..	..	..	..	..	..
Share of bottom 40% of households	"	..	..	..	..	..	..
Share of bottom 20% of households	"	..	..	..	..	..	..
EXPENDITURE							
Food	% of GDP	..	..	..	..	..	..
Staples	"	..	..	..	..	..	..
Meat, fish, milk, cheese, eggs	"	..	..	..	..	..	..
Cereal imports	thou. metric tonnes	..	..	34	45,972	74,924	49,174
Food aid in cereals	"	..	..	..	1,639	4,054	282
Food production per capita	1987 = 100	..	..	..	..	..	109
Fertilizer consumption	kg/ha	..	..	..	..	..	68.8
Share of agriculture in GDP	% of GDP	..	..	..	..	..	8.1
Housing	% of GDP	..	..	..	..	..	..
Average household size	persons per household	..	..	..	..	..	..
Urban	"	..	..	..	..	..	..
Fixed investment: housing	% of GDP	..	..	..	..	..	..
Fuel and power	% of GDP	..	..	..	..	..	..
Energy consumption per capita	kg of oil equiv.	..	..	..	3,190	1,882	1,649
Households with electricity							
Urban	% of households	..	..	..	..	..	..
Rural	"	..	..	..	..	..	..
Transport and communication	% of GDP	..	..	..	..	..	..
Fixed investment: transport equipment	"	..	..	..	..	..	..
Total road length	thou. km	..	..	..	..	..	..
INVESTMENT IN HUMAN CAPITAL							
Health							
Population per physician	persons	..	..	..	378	..	..
Population per nurse	"	..	..	..	..	..	..
Population per hospital bed	"	..	..	..	134	516	385
Oral rehydration therapy (under-5)	% of cases	..	..	..	..	..	54
Education							
Gross enrollment ratio							
Secondary	% of school-age pop.	..	..	..	..	..	53
Female	"	..	..	..	..	..	..
Pupil-teacher ratio: primary	pupils per teacher	..	..	..	..	26	25
Pupil-teacher ratio: secondary	"	..	..	..	..	..	..
Pupils reaching grade 4	% of cohort	..	..	..	..	..	71
Repeater rate: primary	% of total enroll	..	..	..	..	..	11
Illiteracy	% of pop. (age 15+)	..	..	..	..	..	14
Female	% of fem. (age 15+)	..	..	..	..	..	17
Newspaper circulation	per thou. pop.	..	..	..	..	100	117

World Bank International Economics Department, April 1994

Cuba

Indicator	Unit of measure	Latest single year 1970-75	Latest single year 1980-85	Most recent estimate 1987-92	Same region/income group Latin America Caribbean	Same region/income group Lower-middle-income	Next higher income group
Priority Poverty Indicators							
POVERTY							
Upper poverty line	local curr.	..	..	..	..	..	..
Headcount index	% of pop.	..	..	..	..	..	..
Lower poverty line	local curr.	..	..	..	..	..	..
Headcount index	% of pop.	..	..	..	..	..	..
GNP per capita	US$	..	..	..	2,690	..	3,870
SHORT TERM INCOME INDICATORS							
Unskilled urban wages	local curr.	..	..	..	..	..	..
Unskilled rural wages	"	..	..	..	..	..	..
Rural terms of trade	"	..	..	..	..	..	..
Consumer price index	1987=100	..	..	..	..	..	..
Lower income	"	..	..	..	..	..	..
Food[a]	"	..	..	..	..	..	..
Urban	"	..	..	..	..	..	..
Rural	"	..	..	..	..	..	..
SOCIAL INDICATORS							
Public expenditure on basic social services	% of GDP	..	..	..	..	..	..
Gross enrollment ratios							
Primary	% school age pop.	124	104	102	106	..	107
Male	"	126	107	103	..	..	..
Female	"	122	101	102	..	..	..
Mortality							
Infant mortality	per thou. live births	24.9	16.5	10.2	44.0	45.0	40.0
Under 5 mortality	"	..	..	12.7	56.0	59.0	51.0
Immunization							
Measles	% age group	..	80.0	99.0	78.9	..	82.0
DPT	"	..	67.0	99.0	73.8	..	73.8
Child malnutrition (under-5)	"	..	5.0	..	10.5	..	..
Life expectancy							
Total	years	71	74	76	68	68	69
Female advantage	"	3.3	3.4	3.7	5.6	6.4	6.3
Total fertility rate	births per woman	3.6	2.0	1.7	3.0	3.1	2.9
Maternal mortality rate	per 100,000 live births	..	31	39	..	..	..
Supplementary Poverty Indicators							
Expenditures on social security	% of total gov't exp.	..	..	..	..	..	..
Social security coverage	% econ. active pop.	..	..	..	..	..	..
Access to safe water: total	% of pop.	56.0	..	97.7	80.3	..	85.6
Urban	"	96.0	..	91.0	91.0	..	94.3
Rural	"	15.0	..	100.0	64.3	..	73.0
Access to health care	"	..	..	100.0	..	..	..

Population growth rate
(annual average, percent)

Cuba
Lower-middle-income

GNP per capita growth rate
(annual average, percent)

Development diamond[b]

Life expectancy

GNP per capita

Gross primary enrollment

Access to safe water

Cuba
Lower-middle-income

a. See the technical notes, p.389.   b. The development diamond, based on four key indicators, shows the average level of development in the country compared with its income group. See the introduction.

Cuba

Indicator	Unit of measure	Latest single year 1970-75	Latest single year 1980-85	Most recent estimate 1987-92	Same region/income group Latin America Caribbean	Same region/income group Lower-middle-income	Next higher income group
Resources and Expenditures							
HUMAN RESOURCES							
Population (mre=1992)	thousands	9,292	10,098	10,822	453,294	942,547	477,960
Age dependency ratio	ratio	0.77	0.53	0.46	0.67	0.66	0.64
Urban	% of pop.	64.2	71.0	74.6	72.9	57.0	71.7
Population growth rate	annual %	1.5	1.0	0.8	1.7	1.4	1.6
Urban	"	2.8	1.9	1.4	2.6	4.8	2.5
Labor force (15-64)	thousands	3,047	3,987	4,623	166,091	..	181,414
Agriculture	% of labor force	27	24	..	..	..	..
Industry	"	28	29	..	..	..	..
Female	"	25	31	32	27	36	29
Females per 100 males							
Urban	number	103	104	..	..	..	..
Rural	"	85	89	..	..	..	..
NATURAL RESOURCES							
Area	thou. sq. km	110.86	110.86	110.86	20,507.48	40,697.37	21,836.02
Density	pop. per sq. km	83.8	91.1	96.8	21.7	22.8	21.5
Agricultural land	% of land area	52.4	54.0	57.4	40.2	..	41.7
Change in agricultural land	annual %	2.1	0.5	0.0	0.5	..	0.3
Agricultural land under irrigation	%	10.1	14.5	14.4	3.2	..	9.3
Forests and woodland	thou. sq. km	24	27	28	..	..	..
Deforestation (net)	annual %	..	..	1.1	..	..	..
INCOME							
Household income							
Share of top 20% of households	% of income	..	..	..	..	..	..
Share of bottom 40% of households	"	..	..	..	..	..	..
Share of bottom 20% of households	"	..	..	..	..	..	..
EXPENDITURE							
Food	% of GDP	..	..	..	..	..	..
Staples	"	..	..	..	..	..	..
Meat, fish, milk, cheese, eggs	"	..	..	..	..	..	..
Cereal imports	thou. metric tonnes	1,559	2,215	1,673	25,032	74,924	49,174
Food aid in cereals	"	..	2	1	1,779	4,054	282
Food production per capita	1987 = 100	80	102	80	104	..	109
Fertilizer consumption	kg/ha	57.6	98.7	53.2	15.5	..	68.8
Share of agriculture in GDP	% of GDP	..	..	..	8.9	..	8.1
Housing	% of GDP	..	..	..	..	..	..
Average household size	persons per household	4.5	..	..	..	..	..
Urban	"	4.1	..	..	..	..	..
Fixed investment: housing	% of GDP	..	..	..	..	..	..
Fuel and power	% of GDP	..	..	..	..	..	..
Energy consumption per capita	kg of oil equiv.	929	1,043	978	912	1,882	1,649
Households with electricity							
Urban	% of households	..	98.6	..	..	..	..
Rural	"	..	..	..	..	..	..
Transport and communication	% of GDP	..	..	..	..	..	..
Fixed investment: transport equipment	"	..	..	..	..	..	..
Total road length	thou. km	..	..	..	..	..	..
INVESTMENT IN HUMAN CAPITAL							
Health							
Population per physician	persons	1,222	530	275	..	..	..
Population per nurse	"	..	285	82	..	..	..
Population per hospital bed	"	217	..	207	508	516	385
Oral rehydration therapy (under-5)	% of cases	..	..	80	62	..	54
Education							
Gross enrollment ratio							
Secondary	% of school-age pop.	42	82	88	47	..	53
Female	"	42	85	94	..	..	..
Pupil-teacher ratio: primary	pupils per teacher	23	14	12	25	26	25
Pupil-teacher ratio: secondary	"	13	12	10	..	..	..
Pupils reaching grade 4	% of cohort	94	96	93	..	..	71
Repeater rate: primary	% of total enroll	8	3	4	14	..	11
Illiteracy	% of pop. (age 15+)	..	8	6	15	..	14
Female	% of fem. (age 15+)	..	9	7	17	..	17
Newspaper circulation	per thou. pop.	92	117	172	99	100	117

World Bank International Economics Department, April 1994

Cyprus

Indicator	Unit of measure	Latest single year		Most recent estimate 1987-92	Same region/income group High-income
		1970-75	1980-85		

Priority Poverty Indicators

POVERTY

Indicator	Unit of measure	1970-75	1980-85	1987-92	High-income
Upper poverty line	local curr.	..	..	..	..
Headcount index	% of pop.	..	..	..	..
Lower poverty line	local curr.	..	..	..	..
Headcount index	% of pop.	..	..	..	..
GNP per capita	US$	..	..	9,820	21,960
SHORT TERM INCOME INDICATORS					
Unskilled urban wages	local curr.	..	..	..	..
Unskilled rural wages	"	..	..	..	..
Rural terms of trade	"	..	..	..	..
Consumer price index	1987=100	47	96	125	..
Lower income	"	..	..	..	..
Food[a]	"	..	94	122	..
Urban	"	..	..	..	..
Rural	"	..	..	..	..
SOCIAL INDICATORS					
Public expenditure on basic social services	% of GDP	..	8.1	..	..
Gross enrollment ratios					
Primary	% school age pop.	..	103	103	103
Male	"	..	103	103	103
Female	"	..	102	103	103
Mortality					
Infant mortality	per thou. live births	29.0	16.0	11.0	7.0
Under 5 mortality	"	..	..	13.6	10.0
Immunization					
Measles	% age group	..	60.0	74.0	82.4
DPT	"	..	91.0	88.0	90.1
Child malnutrition (under-5)	"	..	..	..	..
Life expectancy					
Total	years	71	75	77	77
Female advantage	"	2.9	4.5	4.4	6.4
Total fertility rate	births per woman	2.5	2.4	2.4	1.7
Maternal mortality rate	per 100,000 live births	..	..	..	..

Supplementary Poverty Indicators

Indicator	Unit of measure	1970-75	1980-85	1987-92	High-income
Expenditures on social security	% of total gov't exp.	14.0	17.6	19.6	..
Social security coverage	% econ. active pop.	..	..	..	..
Access to safe water: total	% of pop.	95.0	100.0	100.0	..
Urban	"	94.0	100.0	100.0	..
Rural	"	96.0	100.0	100.0	..
Access to health care	"	..	100.0	95.0	..

Population growth rate
(annual average, percent)

GNP per capita growth rate
(annual average, percent)

Development diamond[b]

□ Cyprus
— High-income

—— Cyprus
—— High-income

a. See the technical notes, p.389.   b. The development diamond, based on four key indicators, shows the average level of development in the country compared with its income group. See the introduction.

Cyprus

Indicator	Unit of measure	Latest single year 1970-75	Latest single year 1980-85	Most recent estimate 1987-92	Same region/income group High-income
Resources and Expenditures					
HUMAN RESOURCES					
Population (mre=1992)	thousands	609	666	718	828,221
Age dependency ratio	ratio	0.56	0.56	0.58	0.50
Urban	% of pop.	43.4	49.5	54.2	78.1
Population growth rate	annual %	-0.2	0.9	1.1	0.7
Urban	"	1.0	2.2	2.4	0.9
Labor force (15-64)	thousands	275	312	333	390,033
Agriculture	% of labor force	32	26	..	..
Industry	"	31	33	..	..
Female	"	34	35	36	38
Females per 100 males					
Urban	number	..	..	..	..
Rural	"	..	..	..	..
NATURAL RESOURCES					
Area	thou. sq. km	9.25	9.25	9.25	31,709.00
Density	pop. per sq. km	65.8	72.0	76.8	24.5
Agricultural land	% of land area	17.8	17.6	17.4	42.7
Change in agricultural land	annual %	0.0	-0.6	-0.6	-0.2
Agricultural land under irrigation	%	18.3	18.4	22.4	16.1
Forests and woodland	thou. sq. km	1	1	1	..
Deforestation (net)	annual %	..	..	0.0	..
INCOME					
Household income					
Share of top 20% of households	% of income	..	..	..	..
Share of bottom 40% of households	"	..	..	..	..
Share of bottom 20% of households	"	..	..	..	..
EXPENDITURE					
Food	% of GDP	..	19.0	..	..
Staples	"	..	..	..	..
Meat, fish, milk, cheese, eggs	"	..	..	..	..
Cereal imports	thou. metric tonnes	195	412	438	70,626
Food aid in cereals	"	19	2	0	2
Food production per capita	1987 = 100	87	101	92	101
Fertilizer consumption	kg/ha	89.5	111.4	137.9	162.1
Share of agriculture in GDP	% of GDP	15.7	7.5	6.0	2.4
Housing	% of GDP	..	7.2	..	..
Average household size	persons per household	3.9	..	..	..
Urban	"	..	..	..	..
Fixed investment: housing	% of GDP	..	..	..	..
Fuel and power	% of GDP	..	1.6	..	..
Energy consumption per capita	kg of oil equiv.	931	1,604	2,306	5,101
Households with electricity					
Urban	% of households	..	..	..	..
Rural	"	..	..	..	..
Transport and communication	% of GDP	..	12.5	..	..
Fixed investment: transport equipment	"	..	..	..	..
Total road length	thou. km	10	12	10	..
INVESTMENT IN HUMAN CAPITAL					
Health					
Population per physician	persons	1,247	1,060	746	..
Population per nurse	"	367	355	..	..
Population per hospital bed	"	186	180	..	144
Oral rehydration therapy (under-5)	% of cases	..	..	4	..
Education					
Gross enrollment ratio					
Secondary	% of school-age pop.	..	94	90	92
Female	"	..	95	91	94
Pupil-teacher ratio: primary	pupils per teacher	27	23	18	18
Pupil-teacher ratio: secondary	"	21	17	13	..
Pupils reaching grade 4	% of cohort	91	..	..	..
Repeater rate: primary	% of total enroll	1	0	0	..
Illiteracy	% of pop. (age 15+)	..	..	..	..
Female	% of fem. (age 15+)	..	..	..	..
Newspaper circulation	per thou. pop.	128	116	111	..

World Bank International Economics Department, April 1994

Czech Republic

Indicator	Unit of measure	Latest single year 1970-75	Latest single year 1980-85	Most recent estimate 1987-92	Same region/income group Europe & Central Asia	Same region/income group Lower-middle-income	Next higher income group
Priority Poverty Indicators							
POVERTY							
Upper poverty line	local curr.	..	..	..	..	..	..
Headcount index	% of pop.	..	..	..	..	..	..
Lower poverty line	local curr.	..	..	..	..	..	..
Headcount index	% of pop.	..	..	..	..	..	..
GNP per capita	US$	..	..	2,450	..	..	3,870
SHORT TERM INCOME INDICATORS							
Unskilled urban wages	local curr.	..	..	..	..	..	..
Unskilled rural wages	"	..	..	..	..	..	..
Rural terms of trade	"	..	..	..	..	..	..
Consumer price index	1987=100	..	..	..	..	..	..
Lower income	"	..	..	..	..	..	..
Food[a]	"	..	..	..	..	..	..
Urban	"	..	..	..	..	..	..
Rural	"	..	..	..	..	..	..
SOCIAL INDICATORS							
Public expenditure on basic social services	% of GDP	..	..	..	..	..	..
Gross enrollment ratios							
Primary	% school age pop.	..	..	..	..	..	107
Male	"	..	..	..	..	..	..
Female	"	..	..	..	..	..	..
Mortality							
Infant mortality	per thou. live births	..	..	9.9	30.0	45.0	40.0
Under 5 mortality	"	..	..	12.3	38.0	59.0	51.0
Immunization							
Measles	% age group	..	..	..	..	..	82.0
DPT	"	..	..	..	..	..	73.8
Child malnutrition (under-5)	"	..	..	..	..	..	..
Life expectancy							
Total	years	..	..	72	70	68	69
Female advantage	"	..	..	7.6	8.6	6.4	6.3
Total fertility rate	births per woman	..	..	1.9	2.2	3.1	2.9
Maternal mortality rate	per 100,000 live births	..	..	..	58	..	..
Supplementary Poverty Indicators							
Expenditures on social security	% of total gov't exp.	..	..	..	..	..	..
Social security coverage	% econ. active pop.	..	..	..	..	..	..
Access to safe water: total	% of pop.	..	..	..	..	..	85.6
Urban	"	..	..	..	..	..	94.3
Rural	"	..	..	..	..	..	73.0
Access to health care	"	..	..	..	..	..	..

Population growth rate
(annual average, percent)

GNP per capita growth rate
(annual average, percent)

Development diamond[b]

Life expectancy
GNP per capita — Gross primary enrollment
Access to safe water

☐ Czech Republic
— Lower-middle-income

━ Czech Republic
— Lower-middle-income

a. See the technical notes, p.389. b. The development diamond, based on four key indicators, shows the average level of development in the country compared with its income group. See the introduction.

Czech Republic

Indicator	Unit of measure	Latest single year 1970-75	Latest single year 1980-85	Most recent estimate 1987-92	Same region/income group Europe & Central Asia	Same region/income group Lower-middle-income	Next higher income group
Resources and Expenditures							
HUMAN RESOURCES							
Population (mre=1992)	thousands	..	..	10,315	495,241	942,547	477,960
Age dependency ratio	ratio	..	..	..	0.56	0.66	0.64
Urban	% of pop.	..	..	..	63.3	57.0	71.7
Population growth rate	annual %	0.7	0.1	0.1	0.5	1.4	1.6
Urban	"	..	..	..	..	4.8	2.5
Labor force (15-64)	thousands	..	..	..	..	..	181,414
Agriculture	% of labor force	..	..	..	..	..	..
Industry	"	..	..	..	..	..	..
Female	"	..	..	..	46	36	29
Females per 100 males							
Urban	number	..	..	..	..	..	..
Rural	"	..	..	..	..	..	..
NATURAL RESOURCES							
Area	thou. sq. km	..	..	78.86	24,165.06	40,697.37	21,836.02
Density	pop. per sq. km	..	..	..	20.4	22.8	21.5
Agricultural land	% of land area	..	..	..	..	..	41.7
Change in agricultural land	annual %	..	..	..	..	..	0.3
Agricultural land under irrigation	%	..	..	..	..	..	9.3
Forests and woodland	thou. sq. km	..	..	..	..	..	..
Deforestation (net)	annual %	..	..	..	..	..	..
INCOME							
Household income							
Share of top 20% of households	% of income	..	..	..	..	..	..
Share of bottom 40% of households	"	..	..	..	..	..	..
Share of bottom 20% of households	"	..	..	..	..	..	..
EXPENDITURE							
Food	% of GDP	..	..	..	..	..	..
Staples	"	..	..	..	..	..	..
Meat, fish, milk, cheese, eggs	"	..	..	..	..	..	..
Cereal imports	thou. metric tonnes	..	..	..	45,972	74,924	49,174
Food aid in cereals	"	..	..	..	1,639	4,054	282
Food production per capita	1987 = 100	..	..	..	..	..	109
Fertilizer consumption	kg/ha	..	..	..	..	..	68.8
Share of agriculture in GDP	% of GDP	..	..	..	..	..	8.1
Housing	% of GDP	..	..	..	..	..	..
Average household size	persons per household	..	..	..	..	..	..
Urban	"	..	..	..	..	..	..
Fixed investment: housing	% of GDP	..	..	..	..	..	..
Fuel and power	% of GDP	..	..	..	..	..	..
Energy consumption per capita	kg of oil equiv.	..	..	..	3,190	1,882	1,649
Households with electricity							
Urban	% of households	..	..	..	..	..	..
Rural	"	..	..	..	..	..	..
Transport and communication	% of GDP	..	..	..	..	..	..
Fixed investment: transport equipment	"	..	..	..	..	..	..
Total road length	thou. km	..	..	..	..	..	..
INVESTMENT IN HUMAN CAPITAL							
Health							
Population per physician	persons	..	..	..	378	..	..
Population per nurse	"	..	..	..	..	..	..
Population per hospital bed	"	..	..	..	134	516	385
Oral rehydyration therapy (under-5)	% of cases	..	..	..	..	..	54
Education							
Gross enrollment ratio							
Secondary	% of school-age pop.	..	..	..	..	..	53
Female	"	..	..	..	..	..	..
Pupil-teacher ratio: primary	pupils per teacher	..	..	..	..	26	25
Pupil-teacher ratio: secondary	"	..	..	..	..	..	..
Pupils reaching grade 4	% of cohort	..	..	..	..	..	71
Repeater rate: primary	% of total enroll	..	..	..	..	..	11
Illiteracy	% of pop. (age 15+)	..	..	..	..	..	14
Female	% of fem. (age 15+)	..	..	..	..	..	17
Newspaper circulation	per thou. pop.	..	..	..	..	100	117

World Bank International Economics Department, April 1994

Denmark

Indicator	Unit of measure	Latest single year 1970-75	Latest single year 1980-85	Most recent estimate 1987-92	Same region/income group High-income
Priority Poverty Indicators					
POVERTY					
Upper poverty line	local curr.	..	..	..	..
Headcount index	% of pop.	..	..	..	..
Lower poverty line	local curr.	..	..	..	..
Headcount index	% of pop.	..	..	..	..
GNP per capita	US$	6,900	11,380	26,000	21,960
SHORT TERM INCOME INDICATORS					
Unskilled urban wages	local curr.	..	..	..	..
Unskilled rural wages	"	..	..	..	..
Rural terms of trade	"	..	..	..	..
Consumer price index	1987=100	39	93	118	..
Lower income	"	..	..	..	..
Food[a]	"	..	97	109	..
Urban	"	..	..	..	..
Rural	"	..	..	..	..
SOCIAL INDICATORS					
Public expenditure on basic social services	% of GDP	..	..	..	..
Gross enrollment ratios					
Primary	% school age pop.	104	98	96	103
Male	"	95	98	96	103
Female	"	97	98	96	103
Mortality					
Infant mortality	per thou. live births	10.4	7.9	6.5	7.0
Under 5 mortality	"	..	..	8.4	10.0
Immunization					
Measles	% age group	..	20.0	86.0	82.4
DPT	"	..	85.0	95.0	90.1
Child malnutrition (under-5)	"	..	..	..	..
Life expectancy					
Total	years	74	74	75	77
Female advantage	"	5.5	6.0	5.9	6.4
Total fertility rate	births per woman	1.9	1.5	1.8	1.7
Maternal mortality rate	per 100,000 live births	..	4	..	..
Supplementary Poverty Indicators					
Expenditures on social security	% of total gov't exp.	35.9	33.3	37.6	..
Social security coverage	% econ. active pop.	..	..	..	..
Access to safe water: total	% of pop.	..	..	..	..
Urban	"	99.0	..	..	..
Rural	"	95.9	..	..	..
Access to health care	"	..	100.0	100.0	..

Population growth rate
(annual average, percent)

- Denmark
- High-income

GNP per capita growth rate
(annual average, percent)

Development diamond[b]

- Denmark
- High-income

a. See the technical notes, p.389.   b. The development diamond, based on four key indicators, shows the average level of development in the country compared with its income group. See the introduction.

Denmark

Indicator	Unit of measure	Latest single year 1970-75	Latest single year 1980-85	Most recent estimate 1987-92	Same region/income group High-income
Resources and Expenditures					
HUMAN RESOURCES					
Population (mre=1992)	thousands	5,060	5,114	5,170	828,221
Age dependency ratio	ratio	0.56	0.50	0.47	0.50
Urban	% of pop.	81.8	84.4	85.1	78.1
Population growth rate	annual %	0.3	0.0	0.3	0.7
Urban	"	0.8	0.2	0.5	0.9
Labor force (15-64)	thousands	2,534	2,784	2,867	390,033
Agriculture	% of labor force	9	7	..	..
Industry	"	34	32	..	..
Female	"	40	44	45	38
Females per 100 males					
Urban	number	104	101	..	..
Rural	"	90	87	..	..
NATURAL RESOURCES					
Area	thou. sq. km	43.07	43.08	43.09	31,709.00
Density	pop. per sq. km	117.5	118.7	119.6	24.5
Agricultural land	% of land area	69.3	66.9	65.4	42.7
Change in agricultural land	annual %	0.2	-0.7	-0.7	-0.2
Agricultural land under irrigation	%	6.1	14.5	15.7	16.1
Forests and woodland	thou. sq. km	5	5	5	..
Deforestation (net)	annual %	..	..	0.0	..
INCOME					
Household income					
Share of top 20% of households	% of income	..	39	..	..
Share of bottom 40% of households	"	..	17	..	..
Share of bottom 20% of households	"	..	5	..	..
EXPENDITURE					
Food	% of GDP	10.3	9.1	..	..
Staples	"	1.6	1.3	..	..
Meat, fish, milk, cheese, eggs	"	5.0	4.4	..	..
Cereal imports	thou. metric tonnes	262	404	534	70,626
Food aid in cereals	"	..	..	..	2
Food production per capita	1987 = 100	93	122	126	101
Fertilizer consumption	kg/ha	217.6	223.6	209.5	162.1
Share of agriculture in GDP	% of GDP	5.1	4.9	3.5	2.4
Housing	% of GDP	12.8	13.7	..	..
Average household size	persons per household	2.7	..	..	..
Urban	"	2.5	..	..	..
Fixed investment: housing	% of GDP	6.8	3.6	..	..
Fuel and power	% of GDP	3.4	3.4	..	..
Energy consumption per capita	kg of oil equiv.	3,551	3,825	3,729	5,101
Households with electricity					
Urban	% of households	..	..	..	..
Rural	"	..	..	..	..
Transport and communication	% of GDP	7.8	9.4	..	..
Fixed investment: transport equipment	"	2.3	1.9	..	..
Total road length	thou. km	67	70	71	..
INVESTMENT IN HUMAN CAPITAL					
Health					
Population per physician	persons	694	399	390	
Population per nurse	"	..	61	..	..
Population per hospital bed	"	103	..	177	144
Oral rehydration therapy (under-5)	% of cases	..	..	..	..
Education					
Gross enrollment ratio					
Secondary	% of school-age pop.	80	105	108	92
Female	"	75	105	110	94
Pupil-teacher ratio: primary	pupils per teacher	8	12	11	18
Pupil-teacher ratio: secondary	"	..	9	..	..
Pupils reaching grade 4	% of cohort	100	99	100	..
Repeater rate: primary	% of total enroll	0	0	0	..
Illiteracy	% of pop. (age 15+)	..	..	†	..
Female	% of fem. (age 15+)	..	..	†	..
Newspaper circulation	per thou. pop.	341	355	352	..

World Bank International Economics Department, April 1994

Djibouti

Indicator	Unit of measure	Latest single year 1970-75	Latest single year 1980-85	Most recent estimate 1987-92	Same region/income group Sub-Saharan Africa	Same region/income group Lower-middle-income	Next higher income group
Priority Poverty Indicators							
POVERTY							
Upper poverty line	local curr.	..	..	..	..	..	..
Headcount index	% of pop.	..	..	..	..	..	..
Lower poverty line	local curr.	..	..	..	..	..	..
Headcount index	% of pop.	..	..	..	..	..	..
GNP per capita	US$	..	..	..	520	..	3,870
SHORT TERM INCOME INDICATORS							
Unskilled urban wages	local curr.	..	..	..	..	..	..
Unskilled rural wages	"	..	..	..	..	..	..
Rural terms of trade	"	..	..	..	..	..	..
Consumer price index	1987=100	..	81	100	..	..	..
Lower income	"	..	..	..	..	..	..
Food[a]	"	..	..	..	..	..	..
Urban	"	..	..	..	..	..	..
Rural	"	..	..	..	..	..	..
SOCIAL INDICATORS							
Public expenditure on basic social services	% of GDP	..	..	4.9	..	..	..
Gross enrollment ratios							
Primary	% school age pop.	..	43	39	66	..	107
Male	"	..	50	44	79	..	..
Female	"	..	36	35	62	..	..
Mortality							
Infant mortality	per thou. live births	154.0	132.0	115.0	99.0	45.0	40.0
Under 5 mortality	"	..	..	192.3	169.0	59.0	51.0
Immunization							
Measles	% age group	..	27.0	61.0	54.0	..	82.0
DPT	"	..	30.0	60.0	54.6	..	73.8
Child malnutrition (under-5)	"	..	40.0	..	28.4	..	..
Life expectancy							
Total	years	41	45	49	52	68	69
Female advantage	"	3.2	3.2	3.2	3.4	6.4	6.3
Total fertility rate	births per woman	6.6	6.6	5.8	6.1	3.1	2.9
Maternal mortality rate	per 100,000 live births	..	..	..	..	..	..
Supplementary Poverty Indicators							
Expenditures on social security	% of total gov't exp.	..	..	..	..	..	..
Social security coverage	% econ. active pop.	..	..	..	..	..	..
Access to safe water: total	% of pop.	..	43.0	..	41.1	..	85.6
Urban	"	..	50.0	..	77.8	..	94.3
Rural	"	..	20.0	..	27.3	..	73.0
Access to health care	"	..	37.0	..	..	..	..

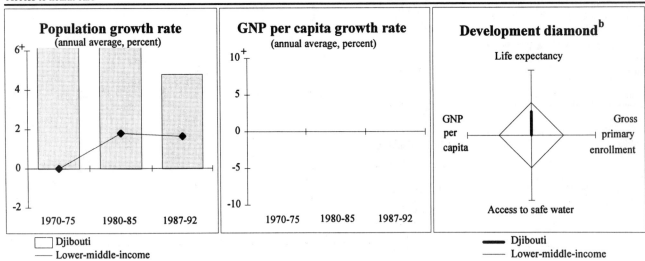

Population growth rate (annual average, percent)

GNP per capita growth rate (annual average, percent)

Development diamond[b]

Life expectancy — GNP per capita — Gross primary enrollment — Access to safe water

☐ Djibouti
— Lower-middle-income

— Djibouti
— Lower-middle-income

a. See the technical notes, p.389. b. The development diamond, based on four key indicators, shows the average level of development in the country compared with its income group. See the introduction.

Djibouti

Indicator	Unit of measure	Latest single year 1970-75	Latest single year 1980-85	Most recent estimate 1987-92	Same region/income group Sub-Saharan Africa	Same region/income group Lower-middle-income	Next higher income group
Resources and Expenditures							
HUMAN RESOURCES							
Population (mre=1992)	thousands	205	391	546	546,390	942,547	477,960
Age dependency ratio	ratio	0.88	0.90	0.89	0.95	0.66	0.64
Urban	% of pop.	68.5	77.7	79.1	29.5	57.0	71.7
Population growth rate	annual %	6.6	6.6	4.7	2.9	1.4	1.6
Urban	"	8.5	7.6	6.3	5.1	4.8	2.5
Labor force (15-64)	thousands	..	..	..	224,025	..	181,414
Agriculture	% of labor force	..	..	..	..	..	..
Industry	"	..	..	..	..	..	..
Female	"	..	..	..	37	36	29
Females per 100 males							
Urban	number	..	..	..	..	..	..
Rural	"	..	..	..	..	..	..
NATURAL RESOURCES							
Area	thou. sq. km	23.20	23.20	23.20	24,274.03	40,697.37	21,836.02
Density	pop. per sq. km	8.8	16.9	22.5	21.9	22.8	21.5
Agricultural land	% of land area	8.6	8.6	8.6	52.7	..	41.7
Change in agricultural land	annual %	0.0	0.0	0.0	0.1	..	0.3
Agricultural land under irrigation	%	..	..	..	0.8	..	9.3
Forests and woodland	thou. sq. km	0	0	0	..	..	..
Deforestation (net)	annual %	..	..	..	..	..	..
INCOME							
Household income							
Share of top 20% of households	% of income	..	..	..	..	..	..
Share of bottom 40% of households	"	..	..	..	..	..	..
Share of bottom 20% of households	"	..	..	..	..	..	..
EXPENDITURE							
Food	% of GDP	..	..	42.4	..	..	..
Staples	"	..	..	16.5	..	..	..
Meat, fish, milk, cheese, eggs	"	..	..	17.4	..	..	..
Cereal imports	thou. metric tonnes	12	64	101	20,311	74,924	49,174
Food aid in cereals	"	..	15	7	4,303	4,054	282
Food production per capita	1987 = 100	..	..	..	90	..	109
Fertilizer consumption	kg/ha	..	0.1	0.5	4.2	..	68.8
Share of agriculture in GDP	% of GDP	..	2.2	2.4	18.6	..	8.1
Housing	% of GDP	..	..	6.0	..	..	..
Average household size	persons per household	..	..	..	..	..	..
Urban	"	..	..	..	..	..	..
Fixed investment: housing	% of GDP	..	..	3.5	..	..	..
Fuel and power	% of GDP	..	..	4.6	..	..	..
Energy consumption per capita	kg of oil equiv.	2,171	1,261	995	258	1,882	1,649
Households with electricity							
Urban	% of households	..	..	..	..	..	..
Rural	"	..	..	..	..	..	..
Transport and communication	% of GDP	..	..	7.5	..	..	..
Fixed investment: transport equipment	"	..	..	2.0	..	..	..
Total road length	thou. km	..	3	..	..	..	..
INVESTMENT IN HUMAN CAPITAL							
Health							
Population per physician	persons	3,364	4,463	5,917	..	..	..
Population per nurse	"	989	540	724	..	..	..
Population per hospital bed	"	157	265	..	1,329	516	385
Oral rehydration therapy (under-5)	% of cases	..	..	56	36	..	54
Education							
Gross enrollment ratio							
Secondary	% of school-age pop.	..	14	14	18	..	53
Female	"	..	11	12	14	..	..
Pupil-teacher ratio: primary	pupils per teacher	36	49	47	39	26	25
Pupil-teacher ratio: secondary	"	16	23	31	..	..	..
Pupils reaching grade 4	% of cohort	..	98	89	..	..	71
Repeater rate: primary	% of total enroll	19	12	13	..	..	11
Illiteracy	% of pop. (age 15+)	..	..	..	51	..	14
Female	% of fem. (age 15+)	..	..	..	62	..	17
Newspaper circulation	per thou. pop.	..	..	..	14	100	117

World Bank International Economics Department, April 1994

Dominica

Indicator	Unit of measure	Latest single year 1970-75	Latest single year 1980-85	Most recent estimate 1987-92	Same region/income group Latin America Caribbean	Same region/income group Lower-middle-income	Next higher income group
Priority Poverty Indicators							
POVERTY							
Upper poverty line	local curr.	..	..	..	..	..	..
Headcount index	% of pop.	..	..	..	..	..	..
Lower poverty line	local curr.	..	..	..	..	..	..
Headcount index	% of pop.	..	..	..	..	..	..
GNP per capita	US$	380	1,230	2,520	2,690	..	3,870
SHORT TERM INCOME INDICATORS							
Unskilled urban wages	local curr.	..	..	..	..	..	..
Unskilled rural wages	"	..	..	..	..	..	..
Rural terms of trade	"	..	..	..	..	..	..
Consumer price index	1987=100	35	94	126	..	..	..
Lower income	"		..	..	..	..	..
Food[a]	"	..	90	109	..	..	..
Urban	"	..	..	..	..	..	..
Rural	"	..	..	..	..	..	..
SOCIAL INDICATORS							
Public expenditure on basic social services	% of GDP	..	..	..	..	..	..
Gross enrollment ratios							
Primary	% school age pop.	..	..	95	106	..	107
Male	"	..	..	94	..	..	..
Female	"	..	..	96	..	..	..
Mortality							
Infant mortality	per thou. live births	26.9	13.9	18.0	44.0	45.0	40.0
Under 5 mortality	"	..	..	21.9	56.0	59.0	51.0
Immunization							
Measles	% age group	..	85.0	88.0	78.9	..	82.0
DPT	"	..	84.0	94.0	73.8	..	73.8
Child malnutrition (under-5)	"	..	4.8	..	10.5	..	..
Life expectancy							
Total	years	..	71	72	68	68	69
Female advantage	"	..	3.0	3.0	5.6	6.4	6.3
Total fertility rate	births per woman	5.5	3.5	2.5	3.0	3.1	2.9
Maternal mortality rate	per 100,000 live births	..	..	..	..	..	..
Supplementary Poverty Indicators							
Expenditures on social security	% of total gov't exp.	..	..	..	..	..	..
Social security coverage	% econ. active pop.	..	..	..	..	..	..
Access to safe water: total	% of pop.	..	..	..	80.3	..	85.6
Urban	"	..	..	..	91.0	..	94.3
Rural	"	..	..	..	64.3	..	73.0
Access to health care	"	..	100.0	100.0	..	..	..

Population growth rate
(annual average, percent)

Dominica

Lower-middle-income

GNP per capita growth rate
(annual average, percent)

Development diamond[b]

Life expectancy — GNP per capita — Gross primary enrollment — Access to safe water

Dominica

Lower-middle-income

a. See the technical notes, p.389.   b. The development diamond, based on four key indicators, shows the average level of development in the country compared with its income group. See the introduction.

Dominica

Indicator	Unit of measure	Latest single year 1970-75	Latest single year 1980-85	Most recent estimate 1987-92	Same region/income group Latin America Caribbean	Same region/income group Lower-middle-income	Next higher income group
Resources and Expenditures							
HUMAN RESOURCES							
Population (mre=1992)	thousands	71	74	72	453,294	942,547	477,960
Age dependency ratio	ratio	..	0.89	0.68	0.67	0.66	0.64
Urban	% of pop.	..	..	..	72.9	57.0	71.7
Population growth rate	annual %	0.6	-0.3	-0.1	1.7	1.4	1.6
Urban	"	..	..	..	2.6	4.8	2.5
Labor force (15-64)	thousands	..	..	..	166,091	..	181,414
Agriculture	% of labor force	..	..	..	..	..	..
Industry	"	..	..	..	..	..	..
Female	"	..	..	..	27	36	29
Females per 100 males							
Urban	number	..	..	..	..	..	..
Rural	"	..	..	..	..	..	..
NATURAL RESOURCES							
Area	thou. sq. km	0.75	0.75	0.75	20,507.48	40,697.37	21,836.02
Density	pop. per sq. km	94.5	98.1	96.0	21.7	22.8	21.5
Agricultural land	% of land area	25.3	25.3	25.3	40.2	..	41.7
Change in agricultural land	annual %	0.0	0.0	0.0	0.5	..	0.3
Agricultural land under irrigation	%	..	..	..	3.2	..	9.3
Forests and woodland	thou. sq. km	0	0	0	..	..	..
Deforestation (net)	annual %	..	..	..	..	..	..
INCOME							
Household income							
Share of top 20% of households	% of income	..	..	..	..	..	..
Share of bottom 40% of households	"	..	..	..	..	..	..
Share of bottom 20% of households	"	..	..	..	..	..	..
EXPENDITURE							
Food	% of GDP	..	..	..	..	..	..
Staples	"	..	..	..	..	..	..
Meat, fish, milk, cheese, eggs	"	..	..	..	..	..	..
Cereal imports	thou. metric tonnes	6	7	8	25,032	74,924	49,174
Food aid in cereals	"	0	0	10	1,779	4,054	282
Food production per capita	1987 = 100	111	131	162	104	..	109
Fertilizer consumption	kg/ha	..	142.1	179.0	15.5	..	68.8
Share of agriculture in GDP	% of GDP	..	23.3	20.5	8.9	..	8.1
Housing	% of GDP	..	..	..	..	..	..
Average household size	persons per household	..	..	..	..	..	..
Urban	"	..	..	..	..	..	..
Fixed investment: housing	% of GDP	..	..	..	..	..	..
Fuel and power	% of GDP	..	..	..	..	..	..
Energy consumption per capita	kg of oil equiv.	169	231	292	912	1,882	1,649
Households with electricity							
Urban	% of households	..	..	..	..	..	..
Rural	"	..	..	..	..	..	..
Transport and communication	% of GDP	..	..	..	..	..	..
Fixed investment: transport equipment	"	..	..	..	..	..	..
Total road length	thou. km	..	..	..	..	..	..
INVESTMENT IN HUMAN CAPITAL							
Health							
Population per physician	persons	6,218	2,952	..	..	..	..
Population per nurse	"	486	..	..	..	..	..
Population per hospital bed	"	225	..	..	508	516	385
Oral rehydration therapy (under-5)	% of cases	..	..	50	62	..	54
Education							
Gross enrollment ratio							
Secondary	% of school-age pop.	..	..	..	47	..	53
Female	"	..	..	..	..	..	..
Pupil-teacher ratio: primary	pupils per teacher	25	15	20	25	26	25
Pupil-teacher ratio: secondary	"	26	..	..	..	..	..
Pupils reaching grade 4	% of cohort	74	79	..	..	..	71
Repeater rate: primary	% of total enroll	..	..	5	14	..	11
Illiteracy	% of pop. (age 15+)	6	..	..	15	..	14
Female	% of fem. (age 15+)	..	..	..	17	..	17
Newspaper circulation	per thou. pop.	..	..	..	99	100	117

World Bank International Economics Department, April 1994

Dominican Republic

Indicator	Unit of measure	Latest single year 1970-75	Latest single year 1980-85	Most recent estimate 1987-92	Same region/income group Latin America Caribbean	Same region/income group Lower-middle-income	Next higher income group
Priority Poverty Indicators							
POVERTY							
Upper poverty line	local curr.	..	..	..	..	..	..
Headcount index	% of pop.	..	..	..	..	..	..
Lower poverty line	local curr.	..	..	..	..	..	..
Headcount index	% of pop.	..	..	..	..	..	..
GNP per capita	US$	660	780	1,050	2,690	..	3,870
SHORT TERM INCOME INDICATORS							
Unskilled urban wages	local curr.	..	..	..	..	..	..
Unskilled rural wages	"	..	..	..	..	..	..
Rural terms of trade	"	..	..	..	..	..	..
Consumer price index	1987=100	23	79	539	..	..	..
Lower income	"	..	..	..	..	..	..
Food[a]	"	..	74	227	..	..	..
Urban	"	..	..	..	..	..	..
Rural	"	..	..	..	..	..	..
SOCIAL INDICATORS							
Public expenditure on basic social services	% of GDP	..	..	..	..	..	..
Gross enrollment ratios							
Primary	% school age pop.	104	126	95	106	..	107
Male	"	100	124	95	..	..	..
Female	"	100	129	96	..	..	..
Mortality							
Infant mortality	per thou. live births	80.0	50.0	41.0	44.0	45.0	40.0
Under 5 mortality	"		..	51.3	56.0	59.0	51.0
Immunization							
Measles	% age group	..	19.0	69.0	78.9	..	82.0
DPT	"	..	20.0	47.0	73.8	..	73.8
Child malnutrition (under-5)	"	..	..	10.4	10.5	..	..
Life expectancy							
Total	years	60	64	68	68	68	69
Female advantage	"	3.6	3.9	4.4	5.6	6.4	6.3
Total fertility rate	births per woman	5.8	4.0	3.0	3.0	3.1	2.9
Maternal mortality rate	per 100,000 live births	..	300	..	..	..	..
Supplementary Poverty Indicators							
Expenditures on social security	% of total gov't exp.	6.0	7.0	0.5	..	..	..
Social security coverage	% econ. active pop.	..	..	11.3	..	..	..
Access to safe water: total	% of pop.	55.0	51.0	67.0	80.3	..	85.6
Urban	"	88.0	73.0	82.0	91.0	..	94.3
Rural	"	27.0	24.0	45.0	64.3	..	73.0
Access to health care	"	..	..	..	..	..	..

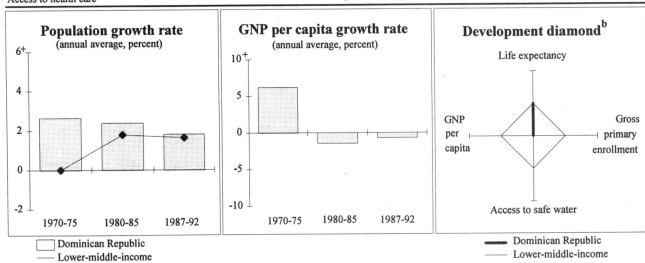

Population growth rate (annual average, percent)

GNP per capita growth rate (annual average, percent)

Development diamond[b]

Life expectancy

GNP per capita — Gross primary enrollment

Access to safe water

- Dominican Republic
- Lower-middle-income

a. See the technical notes, p.389.   b. The development diamond, based on four key indicators, shows the average level of development in the country compared with its income group. See the introduction.

98

Dominican Republic

Indicator	Unit of measure	Latest single year 1970-75	Latest single year 1980-85	Most recent estimate 1987-92	Same region/income group Latin America Caribbean	Same region/income group Lower-middle-income	Next higher income group
Resources and Expenditures							
HUMAN RESOURCES							
Population (mre=1992)	thousands	5,048	6,416	7,321	453,294	942,547	477,960
Age dependency ratio	ratio	0.94	0.75	0.68	0.67	0.66	0.64
Urban	% of pop.	45.3	55.7	62.1	72.9	57.0	71.7
Population growth rate	annual %	2.5	2.2	1.7	1.7	1.4	1.6
Urban	"	4.8	4.1	3.1	2.6	4.8	2.5
Labor force (15-64)	thousands	1,340	1,862	2,322	166,091	..	181,414
Agriculture	% of labor force	50	46	..	..	..	..
Industry	"	15	15	..	..	..	..
Female	"	12	14	16	27	36	29
Females per 100 males							
Urban	number	118	106	..	..	..	..
Rural	"	92	99	..	..	..	..
NATURAL RESOURCES							
Area	thou. sq. km	48.73	48.73	48.73	20,507.48	40,697.37	21,836.02
Density	pop. per sq. km	103.6	131.7	147.7	21.7	22.8	21.5
Agricultural land	% of land area	69.2	72.8	73.1	40.2	..	41.7
Change in agricultural land	annual %	0.9	0.0	0.0	0.5	..	0.3
Agricultural land under irrigation	%	4.2	5.6	6.4	3.2	..	9.3
Forests and woodland	thou. sq. km	6	6	6	..	..	..
Deforestation (net)	annual %	..	..	2.4	..	..	..
INCOME							
Household income							
Share of top 20% of households	% of income	..	..	56	..	..	..
Share of bottom 40% of households	"	..	..	12	..	..	..
Share of bottom 20% of households	"	..	..	4	..	..	..
EXPENDITURE							
Food	% of GDP	..	37.6	..	..	..	..
Staples	"	..	10.3	..	..	..	..
Meat, fish, milk, cheese, eggs	"	..	11.4	..	..	..	..
Cereal imports	thou. metric tonnes	226	426	715	25,032	74,924	49,174
Food aid in cereals	"	16	107	14	1,779	4,054	282
Food production per capita	1987 = 100	102	95	80	104	..	109
Fertilizer consumption	kg/ha	21.8	17.3	27.4	15.5	..	68.8
Share of agriculture in GDP	% of GDP	21.5	19.7	17.6	8.9	..	8.1
Housing	% of GDP	..	12.4	..	..	..	..
Average household size	persons per household	5.0	..	..	..	..	..
Urban	"	5.0	..	..	..	..	..
Fixed investment: housing	% of GDP	..	7.6	..	..	..	..
Fuel and power	% of GDP	..	3.8	..	..	..	..
Energy consumption per capita	kg of oil equiv.	390	386	347	912	1,882	1,649
Households with electricity							
Urban	% of households	..	..	..	..	..	..
Rural	"	..	..	..	..	..	..
Transport and communication	% of GDP	..	3.3	..	..	..	..
Fixed investment: transport equipment	"	..	1.9	..	..	..	..
Total road length	thou. km	12	18	..	..	..	..
INVESTMENT IN HUMAN CAPITAL							
Health							
Population per physician	persons	2,299	1,765	..	..	..	..
Population per nurse	"	2,240	1,210	..	..	..	..
Population per hospital bed	"	400	..	529	508	516	385
Oral rehydration therapy (under-5)	% of cases	..	..	31	62	..	54
Education							
Gross enrollment ratio							
Secondary	% of school-age pop.	36	51	..	47	..	53
Female	"	..	57	..	..	..	..
Pupil-teacher ratio: primary	pupils per teacher	51	44	47	25	26	25
Pupil-teacher ratio: secondary	"	26	37	..	..	..	..
Pupils reaching grade 4	% of cohort	34	62	62	..	..	71
Repeater rate: primary	% of total enroll	22	13	17	14	..	11
Illiteracy	% of pop. (age 15+)	33	20	17	15	..	14
Female	% of fem. (age 15+)	..	22	18	17	..	17
Newspaper circulation	per thou. pop.	39	39	33	99	100	117

World Bank International Economics Department, April 1994

Ecuador

Indicator	Unit of measure	Latest single year 1970-75	1980-85	Most recent estimate 1987-92	Same region/income group Latin America Caribbean	Lower-middle-income	Next higher income group
Priority Poverty Indicators							
POVERTY							
Upper poverty line	local curr.	..	..	..	..	..	..
Headcount index	% of pop.	..	..	..	..	..	..
Lower poverty line	local curr.	..	..	..	..	..	..
Headcount index	% of pop.	..	..	..	..	..	..
GNP per capita	US$	540	1,180	1,070	2,690		3,870
SHORT TERM INCOME INDICATORS							
Unskilled urban wages	local curr.	..	..	..	..	..	..
Unskilled rural wages	"	..	..	..	..	..	..
Rural terms of trade	"	..	..	..	..	..	..
Consumer price index	1987=100	11	63	949	..	..	..
Lower income	"	..	..	..	..	..	..
Food[a]	"	..	63	677	..	..	..
Urban	"	..	..	..	..	..	..
Rural	"	..	..	..	..	..	..
SOCIAL INDICATORS							
Public expenditure on basic social services	% of GDP	..	7.1	3.9	..	..	..
Gross enrollment ratios							
Primary	% school age pop.	104	116	116	106	..	107
Male	"	106	117	119	..	..	..
Female	"	102	116	117	..	..	..
Mortality							
Infant mortality	per thou. live births	95.0	62.0	45.0	44.0	45.0	40.0
Under 5 mortality	"	..	..	57.6	56.0	59.0	51.0
Immunization							
Measles	% age group	..	40.0	54.0	78.9	..	82.0
DPT	"	..	36.0	89.0	73.8	..	73.8
Child malnutrition (under-5)	"	..	..	16.5	10.5	..	..
Life expectancy							
Total	years	59	64	67	68	68	69
Female advantage	"	3.1	4.1	4.3	5.6	6.4	6.3
Total fertility rate	births per woman	6.1	4.7	3.5	3.0	3.1	2.9
Maternal mortality rate	per 100,000 live births	..	220	170	..	..	..
Supplementary Poverty Indicators							
Expenditures on social security	% of total gov't exp.	..	..	..	..	..	..
Social security coverage	% econ. active pop.	21.0	27.0	28.0	..	..	..
Access to safe water: total	% of pop.	36.0	57.0	70.0	80.3	..	85.6
Urban	"	67.0	81.0	87.0	91.0	..	94.3
Rural	"	8.0	31.0	49.0	64.3	..	73.0
Access to health care	"	..	..	80.0	..	..	..

Population growth rate
(annual average, percent)

- Ecuador
- Lower-middle-income

GNP per capita growth rate
(annual average, percent)

Development diamond[b]

- Ecuador
- Lower-middle-income

a. See the technical notes, p.389.   b. The development diamond, based on four key indicators, shows the average level of development in the country compared with its income group. See the introduction.

Ecuador

Indicator	Unit of measure	Latest single year 1970-75	Latest single year 1980-85	Most recent estimate 1987-92	Same region/income group Latin America Caribbean	Same region/income group Lower-middle-income	Next higher income group
Resources and Expenditures							
HUMAN RESOURCES							
Population (mre=1992)	thousands	7,035	9,309	11,023	453,294	942,547	477,960
Age dependency ratio	ratio	0.93	0.82	0.74	0.67	0.66	0.64
Urban	% of pop.	42.4	51.6	58.0	72.9	57.0	71.7
Population growth rate	annual %	3.0	2.6	2.2	1.7	1.4	1.6
Urban	"	4.3	4.4	3.7	2.6	4.8	2.5
Labor force (15-64)	thousands	2,136	2,839	3,489	166,091	..	181,414
Agriculture	% of labor force	45	39	..	..	..	..
Industry	"	20	20	..	..	..	..
Female	"	18	19	19	27	36	29
Females per 100 males							
Urban	number	113	109	..	..	..	..
Rural	"	94	95	..	..	..	..
NATURAL RESOURCES							
Area	thou. sq. km	283.56	283.56	283.56	20,507.48	40,697.37	21,836.02
Density	pop. per sq. km	24.8	32.8	38.0	21.7	22.8	21.5
Agricultural land	% of land area	19.5	26.2	28.6	40.2	..	41.7
Change in agricultural land	annual %	4.2	1.8	0.6	0.5	..	0.3
Agricultural land under irrigation	%	9.5	7.5	7.0	3.2	..	9.3
Forests and woodland	thou. sq. km	153	124	106	..	..	..
Deforestation (net)	annual %	..	..	1.8	..	..	..
INCOME							
Household income							
Share of top 20% of households	% of income	72	..	50	..	..	..
Share of bottom 40% of households	"	5	..	13	..	..	..
Share of bottom 20% of households	"	2	..	4	..	..	..
EXPENDITURE							
Food	% of GDP	23.1	21.4	..	..	..	..
Staples	"	..	5.3	..	..	..	..
Meat, fish, milk, cheese, eggs	"	..	6.0	..	..	..	..
Cereal imports	thou. metric tonnes	203	279	446	25,032	74,924	49,174
Food aid in cereals	"	13	18	45	1,779	4,054	282
Food production per capita	1987 = 100	109	94	104	104	..	109
Fertilizer consumption	kg/ha	6.1	10.0	10.7	15.5	..	68.8
Share of agriculture in GDP	% of GDP	17.9	13.3	13.2	8.9	..	8.1
Housing	% of GDP	6.6	4.4	..	..	..	..
Average household size	persons per household	5.3	5.1	4.7	..	..	..
Urban	"	..	..	..	..	..	..
Fixed investment: housing	% of GDP	3.6	2.2	..	..	..	..
Fuel and power	% of GDP	..	0.9	..	..	..	..
Energy consumption per capita	kg of oil equiv.	330	518	524	912	1,882	1,649
Households with electricity							
Urban	% of households	..	..	..	..	..	..
Rural	"	..	..	..	..	..	..
Transport and communication	% of GDP	5.2	7.9	..	..	..	..
Fixed investment: transport equipment	"	..	4.3	..	..	..	..
Total road length	thou. km	33	38	38	..	..	..
INVESTMENT IN HUMAN CAPITAL							
Health							
Population per physician	persons	2,900	822	984	..	..	..
Population per nurse	"	2,684	613	616	..	..	..
Population per hospital bed	"	400	535	625	508	516	385
Oral rehydration therapy (under-5)	% of cases	..	..	70	62	..	54
Education							
Gross enrollment ratio							
Secondary	% of school-age pop.	40	55	56	47	..	53
Female	"	38	56	57	..	..	..
Pupil-teacher ratio: primary	pupils per teacher	38	32	29	25	26	25
Pupil-teacher ratio: secondary	"	19	15	14	..	..	..
Pupils reaching grade 4	% of cohort	71	74	..	..	..	71
Repeater rate: primary	% of total enroll	11	8	6	14	..	11
Illiteracy	% of pop. (age 15+)	26	17	14	15	..	14
Female	% of fem. (age 15+)	..	20	16	17	..	17
Newspaper circulation	per thou. pop.	47	63	87	99	100	117

World Bank International Economics Department, April 1994

Arab Republic of Egypt

Indicator	Unit of measure	Latest single year 1970-75	Latest single year 1980-85	Most recent estimate 1987-92	Same region/income group Mid-East & North Africa	Same region/income group Low-income	Next higher income group
Priority Poverty Indicators							
POVERTY							
Upper poverty line	local curr.	..	..	..	..	..	..
Headcount index	% of pop.	..	..	..	..	19	..
Lower poverty line	local curr.	..	..	..	..	..	..
Headcount index	% of pop.	..	..	..	..	..	..
GNP per capita	US$	320	670	640	1,950	390	..
SHORT TERM INCOME INDICATORS							
Unskilled urban wages	local curr.	..	..	..	..	..	..
Unskilled rural wages	"	..	..	..	..	..	..
Rural terms of trade	"	..	..	..	..	..	..
Consumer price index	1987=100	19	67	227			
Lower income	"	..	..	..	..	..	..
Food[a]	"	11	65	211	..	..	..
Urban	"	..	..	179	..	..	..
Rural	"	..	..	182	..	..	..
SOCIAL INDICATORS							
Public expenditure on basic social services	% of GDP	..	5.3	4.9	..	..	..
Gross enrollment ratios							
Primary	% school age pop.	71	91	101	100	103	..
Male	"	85	101	109	107	113	..
Female	"	57	82	93	88	96	..
Mortality							
Infant mortality	per thou. live births	150.0	112.0	57.0	58.0	73.0	45.0
Under 5 mortality	"	..	..	86.6	78.0	108.0	59.0
Immunization							
Measles	% age group	..	74.0	89.0	81.8	72.7	..
DPT	"	..	95.0	86.0	83.9	80.6	..
Child malnutrition (under-5)	"	..	21.2	10.4	20.9	38.3	..
Life expectancy							
Total	years	52	57	62	64	62	68
Female advantage	"	2.6	2.5	2.4	2.4	2.4	6.4
Total fertility rate	births per woman	5.5	5.1	3.8	4.9	3.4	3.1
Maternal mortality rate	per 100,000 live births	..	266	..	..	..	..
Supplementary Poverty Indicators							
Expenditures on social security	% of total gov't exp.	8.4	11.6	12.0	..	..	..
Social security coverage	% econ. active pop.	..	..	..	..	..	..
Access to safe water: total	% of pop.	93.0	..	90.0	85.0	68.4	..
Urban	"	94.0	..	95.0	97.0	78.9	..
Rural	"	93.0	..	86.0	70.1	60.3	..
Access to health care	"	..	99.0	99.0	84.6	..	..

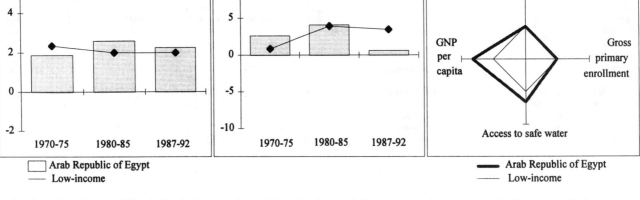

Population growth rate (annual average, percent)

GNP per capita growth rate (annual average, percent)

Development diamond[b]

Life expectancy — GNP per capita — Gross primary enrollment — Access to safe water

☐ Arab Republic of Egypt
— Low-income

— Arab Republic of Egypt
— Low-income

a. See the technical notes, p.389.   b. The development diamond, based on four key indicators, shows the average level of development in the country compared with its income group. See the introduction.

Arab Republic of Egypt

Indicator	Unit of measure	Latest single year 1970-75	Latest single year 1980-85	Most recent estimate 1987-92	Same region/income group Mid-East & North Africa	Same region/income group Low-income	Next higher income group
Resources and Expenditures							
HUMAN RESOURCES							
Population (mre=1992)	thousands	36,289	46,511	54,679	252,555	3,194,535	942,547
Age dependency ratio	ratio	0.79	0.77	0.76	0.87	0.67	0.66
Urban	% of pop.	43.5	43.9	44.3	54.7	26.7	57.0
Population growth rate	annual %	2.0	2.6	2.1	2.8	1.8	1.4
Urban	"	2.6	2.6	2.5	3.8	3.4	4.8
Labor force (15-64)	thousands	10,037	12,837	15,405	69,280	1,478,954	..
Agriculture	% of labor force	49	46	..	..	..	..
Industry	"	18	20	..	..	..	..
Female	"	8	9	10	15	33	36
Females per 100 males							
Urban	number	..	..	..	..	..	..
Rural	"	..	..	..	..	..	..
NATURAL RESOURCES							
Area	thou. sq. km	1,001.45	1,001.45	1,001.45	10,487.21	38,401.06	40,697.37
Density	pop. per sq. km	36.2	46.4	53.5	23.4	81.7	22.8
Agricultural land	% of land area	2.8	2.5	2.7	30.2	50.9	..
Change in agricultural land	annual %	-0.6	0.2	-0.2	0.5	0.0	..
Agricultural land under irrigation	%	100.0	100.0	100.0	31.0	18.2	..
Forests and woodland	thou. sq. km	0	0	0	..	..	..
Deforestation (net)	annual %	..	..	..	..	..	..
INCOME							
Household income							
Share of top 20% of households	% of income	49	..	..	..	42	..
Share of bottom 40% of households	"	15	..	..	..	19	..
Share of bottom 20% of households	"	5	..	..	..	8	..
EXPENDITURE							
Food	% of GDP	..	33.9	..	..	..	..
Staples	"	..	6.8	..	..	..	..
Meat, fish, milk, cheese, eggs	"	..	13.5	..	..	..	..
Cereal imports	thou. metric tonnes	4,214	8,903	7,330	38,007	46,537	74,924
Food aid in cereals	"	610	1,951	1,611	2,484	9,008	4,054
Food production per capita	1987 = 100	107	103	115	116	123	..
Fertilizer consumption	kg/ha	177.4	345.8	343.7	96.7	61.9	..
Share of agriculture in GDP	% of GDP	28.1	19.3	17.1	13.7	29.6	..
Housing	% of GDP	..	6.2	..	..	..	..
Average household size	persons per household	..	..	..	..	..	..
Urban	"	..	..	..	..	..	..
Fixed investment: housing	% of GDP	10.5	2.7	..	..	..	..
Fuel and power	% of GDP	..	1.7	..	..	..	..
Energy consumption per capita	kg of oil equiv.	254	535	586	1,109	335	1,882
Households with electricity							
Urban	% of households	..	..	..	..	..	..
Rural	"	..	..	..	..	..	..
Transport and communication	% of GDP	..	2.5	..	..	..	..
Fixed investment: transport equipment	"	8.2	4.3	..	..	..	..
Total road length	thou. km	26	31	31	..	..	..
INVESTMENT IN HUMAN CAPITAL							
Health							
Population per physician	persons	1,866	732	1,316	..	..	..
Population per nurse	"	2,315	782	489	..	..	..
Population per hospital bed	"	491	483	536	636	1,050	516
Oral rehydration therapy (under-5)	% of cases	..	..	58	56	39	..
Education							
Gross enrollment ratio							
Secondary	% of school-age pop.	43	66	80	59	41	..
Female	"	31	54	73	50	35	..
Pupil-teacher ratio: primary	pupils per teacher	35	32	24	27	37	26
Pupil-teacher ratio: secondary	"	34	22	21	21	19	..
Pupils reaching grade 4	% of cohort	95	82	..	..	..	..
Repeater rate: primary	% of total enroll	7	2	..	..	..	..
Illiteracy	% of pop. (age 15+)	..	55	52	45	39	..
Female	% of fem. (age 15+)	..	71	66	58	52	..
Newspaper circulation	per thou. pop.	25	79	57	39	..	100

World Bank International Economics Department, April 1994

El Salvador

Indicator	Unit of measure	Latest single year 1970-75	Latest single year 1980-85	Most recent estimate 1987-92	Same region/income group Latin America Caribbean	Same region/income group Lower-middle-income	Next higher income group
Priority Poverty Indicators							
POVERTY							
Upper poverty line	local curr.	..	..	..	..	..	..
Headcount index	% of pop.	..	..	..	..	..	..
Lower poverty line	local curr.	..	..	..	..	..	..
Headcount index	% of pop.	..	..	..	..	..	..
GNP per capita	US$	430	840	1,170	2,690	..	3,870
SHORT TERM INCOME INDICATORS							
Unskilled urban wages	local curr.	..	..	..	..	..	..
Unskilled rural wages	"	..	..	..	..	..	..
Rural terms of trade	"	..	..	..	..	..	..
Consumer price index	1987=100	..	61	222	..	..	..
Lower income	"	..	..	..	..	..	..
Food[a]	"	..	61	244	..	..	..
Urban	"	..	..	..	..	..	..
Rural	"	..	..	..	..	..	..
SOCIAL INDICATORS							
Public expenditure on basic social services	% of GDP	..	..	..	..	..	..
Gross enrollment ratios							
Primary	% school age pop.	75	74	76	106	..	107
Male	"	76	73	76	..	..	..
Female	"	74	75	77	..	..	..
Mortality							
Infant mortality	per thou. live births	99.0	71.0	40.0	44.0	45.0	40.0
Under 5 mortality	"	..	..	50.0	56.0	59.0	51.0
Immunization							
Measles	% age group	..	41.0	53.0	78.9	..	82.0
DPT	"	..	44.0	60.0	73.8	..	73.8
Child malnutrition (under-5)	"	..	..	15.5	10.5	..	..
Life expectancy							
Total	years	59	57	66	68	68	69
Female advantage	"	4.5	13.2	4.9	5.6	6.4	6.3
Total fertility rate	births per woman	6.1	5.0	3.8	3.0	3.1	2.9
Maternal mortality rate	per 100,000 live births	..	148	..	..	..	..
Supplementary Poverty Indicators							
Expenditures on social security	% of total gov't exp.	3.4	2.4	2.2	..	..	..
Social security coverage	% econ. active pop.	..	..	..	..	..	..
Access to safe water: total	% of pop.	53.0	52.0	43.0	80.3	..	85.6
Urban	"	89.0	68.0	78.0	91.0	..	94.3
Rural	"	28.0	40.0	15.0	64.3	..	73.0
Access to health care	"	..	..	..	..	..	..

Population growth rate
(annual average, percent)

GNP per capita growth rate
(annual average, percent)

Development diamond[b]

- El Salvador
- Lower-middle-income

a. See the technical notes, p.389.   b. The development diamond, based on four key indicators, shows the average level of development in the country compared with its income group. See the introduction.

104

El Salvador

Indicator	Unit of measure	Latest single year 1970-75	Latest single year 1980-85	Most recent estimate 1987-92	Same region/income group Latin America Caribbean	Same region/income group Lower-middle-income	Next higher income group
Resources and Expenditures							
HUMAN RESOURCES							
Population (mre=1992)	thousands	4,085	4,739	5,380	453,294	942,547	477,960
Age dependency ratio	ratio	0.95	0.98	0.86	0.67	0.66	0.64
Urban	% of pop.	40.4	42.7	45.3	72.9	57.0	71.7
Population growth rate	annual %	2.4	1.1	1.9	1.7	1.4	1.6
Urban	"	2.9	1.7	2.9	2.6	4.8	2.5
Labor force (15-64)	thousands	1,367	1,832	2,306	166,091	..	181,414
Agriculture	% of labor force	49	43	..	..	..	..
Industry	"	17	19	..	..	..	..
Female	"	23	25	25	27	36	29
Females per 100 males							
Urban	number	119	..	..	..	..	..
Rural	"	96	..	..	..	..	..
NATURAL RESOURCES							
Area	thou. sq. km	21.04	21.04	21.04	20,507.48	40,697.37	21,836.02
Density	pop. per sq. km	194.2	225.2	250.9	21.7	22.8	21.5
Agricultural land	% of land area	60.5	64.8	64.8	40.2	..	41.7
Change in agricultural land	annual %	0.0	0.5	0.0	0.5	..	0.3
Agricultural land under irrigation	%	2.6	8.2	8.9	3.2	..	9.3
Forests and woodland	thou. sq. km	2	1	1	..	..	..
Deforestation (net)	annual %	..	..	6.9	..	..	..
INCOME							
Household income							
Share of top 20% of households	% of income	..	..	..	..	..	..
Share of bottom 40% of households	"	..	..	..	..	..	..
Share of bottom 20% of households	"	..	..	..	..	..	..
EXPENDITURE							
Food	% of GDP	..	25.7	..	..	..	..
Staples	"	..	9.1	..	..	..	..
Meat, fish, milk, cheese, eggs	"	..	10.1	..	..	..	..
Cereal imports	thou. metric tonnes	108	224	242	25,032	74,924	49,174
Food aid in cereals	"	4	194	96	1,779	4,054	282
Food production per capita	1987 = 100	102	98	113	104	..	109
Fertilizer consumption	kg/ha	74.5	63.1	57.8	15.5	..	68.8
Share of agriculture in GDP	% of GDP	23.0	18.2	9.3	8.9	..	8.1
Housing	% of GDP	..	5.5	..	..	..	..
Average household size	persons per household	4.6	..	..	..	..	..
Urban	"	..	..	..	..	..	..
Fixed investment: housing	% of GDP	1.9	3.4	..	..	..	..
Fuel and power	% of GDP	..	1.4	..	..	..	..
Energy consumption per capita	kg of oil equiv.	188	..	..	912	1,882	1,649
Households with electricity							
Urban	% of households	..	..	..	..	..	..
Rural	"	..	..	..	..	..	..
Transport and communication	% of GDP	..	8.1	..	..	..	..
Fixed investment: transport equipment	"	3.3	2.4	..	..	..	..
Total road length	thou. km	11	12	12	..	..	..
INVESTMENT IN HUMAN CAPITAL							
Health							
Population per physician	persons	4,096	2,816	..	..	..	..
Population per nurse	"	889	930	..	..	..	..
Population per hospital bed	"	500	..	699	508	516	385
Oral rehydration therapy (under-5)	% of cases	..	..	45	62	..	54
Education							
Gross enrollment ratio							
Secondary	% of school-age pop.	19	27	25	47	..	53
Female	"	17	28	27	..	..	..
Pupil-teacher ratio: primary	pupils per teacher	53	42	44	25	26	25
Pupil-teacher ratio: secondary	"	25	12	..	..	..	..
Pupils reaching grade 4	% of cohort	58	66	..	..	..	71
Repeater rate: primary	% of total enroll	7	8	8	14	..	11
Illiteracy	% of pop. (age 15+)	43	31	27	15	..	14
Female	% of fem. (age 15+)	..	35	30	17	..	17
Newspaper circulation	per thou. pop.	57	50	88	99	100	117

World Bank International Economics Department, April 1994

Equatorial Guinea

Indicator	Unit of measure	Latest single year 1970-75	Latest single year 1980-85	Most recent estimate 1987-92	Same region/income group Sub-Saharan Africa	Same region/income group Low-income	Next higher income group
Priority Poverty Indicators							
POVERTY							
Upper poverty line	local curr.	..	..	..	..	..	..
Headcount index	% of pop.	..	..	..	..	19	..
Lower poverty line	local curr.	..	..	..	..	..	..
Headcount index	% of pop.	..	..	..	..	..	..
GNP per capita	US$	..	..	330	520	390	..
SHORT TERM INCOME INDICATORS							
Unskilled urban wages	local curr.	..	..	..	..	..	..
Unskilled rural wages	"	..	..	..	..	..	..
Rural terms of trade		..	..	..	..	..	..
Consumer price index	1987=100	..	140	98	..	..	..
Lower income	"	..	..	..	..	..	..
Food[a]	"	..	..	..	..	..	..
Urban	"	..	..	..	..	..	..
Rural	"	..	..	..	..	..	..
SOCIAL INDICATORS							
Public expenditure on basic social services	% of GDP	..	..	7.1	..	..	..
Gross enrollment ratios							
Primary	% school age pop.	78	147	..	66	103	..
Male	"	87	..	..	79	113	..
Female	"	69	..	..	62	96	..
Mortality							
Infant mortality	per thou. live births	160.0	137.0	117.0	99.0	73.0	45.0
Under 5 mortality	"	..	..	195.9	169.0	108.0	59.0
Immunization							
Measles	% age group	..	11.0	..	54.0	72.7	..
DPT	"	..	3.0	..	54.6	80.6	..
Child malnutrition (under-5)	"	..	..	..	28.4	38.3	..
Life expectancy							
Total	years	40	44	48	52	62	68
Female advantage	"	2.4	2.1	3.9	3.4	2.4	6.4
Total fertility rate	births per woman	5.0	5.0	5.5	6.1	3.4	3.1
Maternal mortality rate	per 100,000 live births	..	..	430	..	..	..
Supplementary Poverty Indicators							
Expenditures on social security	% of total gov't exp.	..	..	..	..	..	..
Social security coverage	% econ. active pop.	..	..	..	..	..	..
Access to safe water: total	% of pop.	..	..	..	41.1	68.4	..
Urban	"	..	..	..	77.8	78.9	..
Rural	"	..	..	..	27.3	60.3	..
Access to health care	"	..	..	..	..	..	..

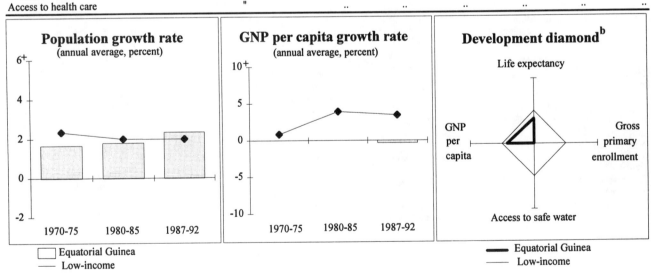

a. See the technical notes, p.389.   b. The development diamond, based on four key indicators, shows the average level of development in the country compared with its income group. See the introduction.

Equatorial Guinea

Indicator	Unit of measure	Latest single year 1970-75	Latest single year 1980-85	Most recent estimate 1987-92	Same region/income group Sub-Saharan Africa	Same region/income group Low-income	Next higher income group
Resources and Expenditures							
HUMAN RESOURCES							
Population (mre=1992)	thousands	313	373	437	546,390	3,194,535	942,547
Age dependency ratio	ratio	0.79	0.73	0.81	0.95	0.67	0.66
Urban	% of pop.	27.1	27.7	29.4	29.5	26.7	57.0
Population growth rate	annual %	1.6	1.9	2.3	2.9	1.8	1.4
Urban	"	1.9	2.1	3.6	5.1	3.4	4.8
Labor force (15-64)	thousands	149	169	189	224,025	1,478,954	..
Agriculture	% of labor force	70	66	..	..	..	..
Industry	"	10	11	..	..	..	..
Female	"	42	41	40	37	33	36
Females per 100 males							
Urban	number	..	..	..	..	..	..
Rural	"	..	..	..	..	..	..
NATURAL RESOURCES							
Area	thou. sq. km	28.05	28.05	28.05	24,274.03	38,401.06	40,697.37
Density	pop. per sq. km	11.2	13.3	15.2	21.9	81.7	22.8
Agricultural land	% of land area	11.9	11.9	11.9	52.7	50.9	..
Change in agricultural land	annual %	0.0	0.0	0.0	0.1	0.0	..
Agricultural land under irrigation	%	..	..	..	0.8	18.2	..
Forests and woodland	thou. sq. km	13	13	13	..	..	..
Deforestation (net)	annual %	..	..	0.5	..	..	..
INCOME							
Household income							
Share of top 20% of households	% of income	..	..	..	..	42	..
Share of bottom 40% of households	"	..	..	..	..	19	..
Share of bottom 20% of households	"	..	..	..	..	8	..
EXPENDITURE							
Food	% of GDP	..	..	28.1	..	..	..
Staples	"	..	..	11.9	..	..	..
Meat, fish, milk, cheese, eggs	"	..	..	11.2	..	..	..
Cereal imports	thou. metric tonnes	2	11	9	20,311	46,537	74,924
Food aid in cereals	"	..	7	4	4,303	9,008	4,054
Food production per capita	1987 = 100	..	..	..	90	123	..
Fertilizer consumption	kg/ha	0.3	0.3	..	4.2	61.9	..
Share of agriculture in GDP	% of GDP	..	64.4	47.6	18.6	29.6	..
Housing	% of GDP	..	..	11.6	..	..	..
Average household size	persons per household	..	..	..	..	..	..
Urban	"	..	..	..	..	..	..
Fixed investment: housing	% of GDP	..	..	5.6	..	..	..
Fuel and power	% of GDP	..	..	4.7	..	..	..
Energy consumption per capita	kg of oil equiv.	64	78	69	258	335	1,882
Households with electricity							
Urban	% of households	..	..	..	..	..	..
Rural	"	..	..	..	..	..	..
Transport and communication	% of GDP	..	..	5.3	..	..	..
Fixed investment: transport equipment	"	..	..	5.5	..	..	..
Total road length	thou. km	..	2	..	..	..	..
INVESTMENT IN HUMAN CAPITAL							
Health							
Population per physician	persons	11,520	..	4,212	..	..	..
Population per nurse	"	1,252	..	557	..	..	..
Population per hospital bed	"	..	..	..	1,329	1,050	516
Oral rehydration therapy (under-5)	% of cases	..	..	40	36	39	..
Education							
Gross enrollment ratio							
Secondary	% of school-age pop.	11	14	..	18	41	..
Female	"	4	..	..	14	35	..
Pupil-teacher ratio: primary	pupils per teacher	57	68	..	39	37	26
Pupil-teacher ratio: secondary	"	35	..	..	..	19	..
Pupils reaching grade 4	% of cohort	..	..	..	..	..	..
Repeater rate: primary	% of total enroll	..	..	..	..	..	..
Illiteracy	% of pop. (age 15+)	..	55	50	51	39	..
Female	% of fem. (age 15+)	..	69	63	62	52	..
Newspaper circulation	per thou. pop.	..	3	5	14	..	100

World Bank International Economics Department, April 1994

Estonia

Indicator	Unit of measure	Latest single year 1970-75	Latest single year 1980-85	Most recent estimate 1987-92	Same region/income group Europe & Central Asia	Same region/income group Upper-middle-income	Next higher income group
Priority Poverty Indicators							
POVERTY							
Upper poverty line	local curr.	..	..	..	..	..	..
Headcount index	% of pop.	..	..	3	..	..	..
Lower poverty line	local curr.	..	..	..	..	..	..
Headcount index	% of pop.	..	..	1	..	..	..
GNP per capita	US$	..	..	2,760	..	3,870	21,960
SHORT TERM INCOME INDICATORS							
Unskilled urban wages	local curr.	..	..	..	..	..	..
Unskilled rural wages	"	..	..	..	..	..	..
Rural terms of trade	"	..	..	..	..	..	..
Consumer price index	1987=100	..	..	..	..	..	..
Lower income	"	..	..	..	..	..	..
Food[a]	"	..	..	..	..	..	..
Urban	"	..	..	..	..	..	..
Rural	"	..	..	..	..	..	..
SOCIAL INDICATORS							
Public expenditure on basic social services	% of GDP	..	..	7.5	..	..	..
Gross enrollment ratios						107	103
Primary	% school age pop.	..	..	..	..	..	103
Male	"	..	..	..	..	..	103
Female	"	..	..	..	..	..	
Mortality							
Infant mortality	per thou. live births	18.5	17.4	13.0	30.0	40.0	7.0
Under 5 mortality	"	..	..	15.9	38.0	51.0	10.0
Immunization						82.0	82.4
Measles	% age group	..	..	..	..	73.8	90.1
DPT	"	..	..	..	..	..	..
Child malnutrition (under-5)	"	..	..	..	..		
Life expectancy							
Total	years	70	70	70	70	69	77
Female advantage	"	8.9	9.3	10.0	8.6	6.3	6.4
Total fertility rate	births per woman	2.1	2.1	1.8	2.2	2.9	1.7
Maternal mortality rate	per 100,000 live births	..	27	41	58	..	..
Supplementary Poverty Indicators							
Expenditures on social security	% of total gov't exp.	..	..	..	..	..	..
Social security coverage	% econ. active pop.	..	..	..	..	85.6	..
Access to safe water: total	% of pop.	..	..	..	..	94.3	..
Urban	"	..	..	..	..	73.0	..
Rural	"	..	..	..	..		..
Access to health care	"	..	..	..	..		..

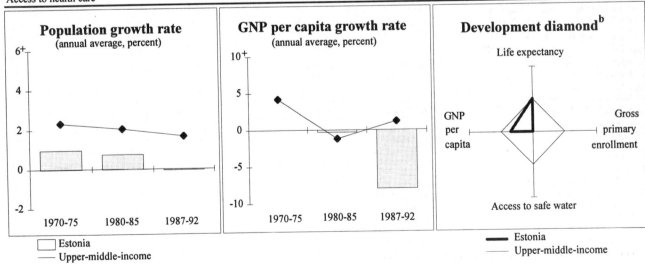

Population growth rate (annual average, percent)

GNP per capita growth rate (annual average, percent)

Development diamond[b]

Estonia
Upper-middle-income

Estonia
Upper-middle-income

a. See the technical notes, p.389.   b. The development diamond, based on four key indicators, shows the average level of development in the country compared with its income group. See the introduction.

Estonia

Indicator	Unit of measure	Latest single year 1970-75	Latest single year 1980-85	Most recent estimate 1987-92	Europe & Central Asia	Upper-middle-income	Next higher income group
Resources and Expenditures							
HUMAN RESOURCES							
Population (mre=1992)	thousands	1,432	1,536	1,554	495,241	477,960	828,221
Age dependency ratio	ratio	..	..	0.54	0.56	0.64	0.50
Urban	% of pop.	..	..	72.0	63.3	71.7	78.1
Population growth rate	annual %	0.8	0.7	-0.8	0.5	1.6	0.7
Urban	"	..	..	..	..	2.5	0.9
Labor force (15-64)	thousands	..	811	743	..	181,414	390,033
Agriculture	% of labor force	..	..	19	..	..	..
Industry	"	..	..	39	..	..	..
Female	"	..	54	53	46	29	38
Females per 100 males							
Urban	number	..	..	..	..	..	..
Rural	"	..	..	..	..	..	..
NATURAL RESOURCES							
Area	thou. sq. km	..	..	45.10	24,165.06	21,836.02	31,709.00
Density	pop. per sq. km	..	..	34.7	20.4	21.5	24.5
Agricultural land	% of land area	..	..	..	..	41.7	42.7
Change in agricultural land	annual %	..	..	..	..	0.3	-0.2
Agricultural land under irrigation	%	..	..	..	..	9.3	16.1
Forests and woodland	thou. sq. km	..	..	..	..	..	..
Deforestation (net)	annual %	..	..	..	..	..	..
INCOME							
Household income							
Share of top 20% of households	% of income	..	..	..	..	..	..
Share of bottom 40% of households	"	..	..	..	..	..	..
Share of bottom 20% of households	"	..	..	..	..	..	..
EXPENDITURE							
Food	% of GDP	..	..	18.6	..	..	..
Staples	"	..	..	3.4	..	..	..
Meat, fish, milk, cheese, eggs	"	..	..	8.4	..	..	..
Cereal imports	thou. metric tonnes	..	..	276	45,972	49,174	70,626
Food aid in cereals	"	..	..	195	1,639	282	2
Food production per capita	1987 = 100	..	..	..	..	109	101
Fertilizer consumption	kg/ha	..	..	..	..	68.8	162.1
Share of agriculture in GDP	% of GDP	..	20.7	17.1	..	8.1	2.4
Housing	% of GDP	..	..	4.4	..	..	..
Average household size	persons per household	..	..	3.1	..	..	..
Urban	"	..	..	..	..	..	..
Fixed investment: housing	% of GDP	..	..	4.4	..	..	..
Fuel and power	% of GDP	..	..	0.9	..	..	..
Energy consumption per capita	kg of oil equiv.	..	..	..	3,190	1,649	5,101
Households with electricity							
Urban	% of households	..	..	..	..	..	..
Rural	"	..	..	..	..	..	..
Transport and communication	% of GDP	..	..	5.9	..	..	..
Fixed investment: transport equipment	"	..	..	9.3	..	..	..
Total road length	thou. km	..	27	30	..	..	..
INVESTMENT IN HUMAN CAPITAL							
Health							
Population per physician	persons	..	..	208	378	..	..
Population per nurse	"	..	..	..	..	..	..
Population per hospital bed	"	..	..	82	134	385	144
Oral rehydyration therapy (under-5)	% of cases	..	..	..	..	54	..
Education							
Gross enrollment ratio							
Secondary	% of school-age pop.	..	..	..	..	53	92
Female	"	..	..	..	..	..	94
Pupil-teacher ratio: primary	pupils per teacher	..	..	..	..	25	18
Pupil-teacher ratio: secondary	"	..	..	..	..	..	..
Pupils reaching grade 4	% of cohort	..	..	..	..	71	..
Repeater rate: primary	% of total enroll	..	..	..	..	11	..
Illiteracy	% of pop. (age 15+)	..	..	..	..	14	..
Female	% of fem. (age 15+)	..	..	..	..	17	..
Newspaper circulation	per thou. pop.	..	..	..	..	117	..

World Bank International Economics Department, April 1994

109

Ethiopia

Indicator	Unit of measure	Latest single year 1970-75	Latest single year 1980-85	Most recent estimate 1987-92	Same region/income group Sub-Saharan Africa	Same region/income group Low-income	Next higher income group
Priority Poverty Indicators							
POVERTY							
Upper poverty line	local curr.	..	..	..	..	19	..
Headcount index	% of pop.	..	..	..	..		..
Lower poverty line	local curr.	..	..	..	..	..	..
Headcount index	% of pop.	..	..	..	..	..	..
GNP per capita	US$	80	110	110	520	390	..
SHORT TERM INCOME INDICATORS							
Unskilled urban wages	local curr.	..	..	..	..	..	..
Unskilled rural wages	"	..	..	..	..	..	..
Rural terms of trade	"	..	..	..	..	..	..
Consumer price index	1987=100	38	114	182	..	..	..
Lower income	"	..	..	..	..	..	..
Food[a]	"	30	126	191	..	..	..
Urban	"	..	..	..	..	..	..
Rural	"	..	..	..	..	..	..
SOCIAL INDICATORS							
Public expenditure on basic social services	% of GDP	..	..	..	..	..	..
Gross enrollment ratios							
Primary	% school age pop.	24	36	25	66	103	..
Male	"	32	43	29	79	113	..
Female	"	15	28	21	62	96	..
Mortality							
Infant mortality	per thou. live births	155.0	159.0	122.0	99.0	73.0	45.0
Under 5 mortality	"	..	..	205.2	169.0	108.0	59.0
Immunization							
Measles	% age group	..	12.0	37.0	54.0	72.7	..
DPT	"	..	6.0	44.0	54.6	80.6	..
Child malnutrition (under-5)	"	..	38.1	38.1	28.4	38.3	..
Life expectancy							
Total	years	43	43	49	52	62	68
Female advantage	"	1.0	3.2	3.6	3.4	2.4	6.4
Total fertility rate	births per woman	5.8	7.0	7.5	6.1	3.4	3.1
Maternal mortality rate	per 100,000 live births	..	452	..	..	..	..
Supplementary Poverty Indicators							
Expenditures on social security	% of total gov't exp.	4.7	5.7	3.9	..	..	..
Social security coverage	% econ. active pop.	..	..	..	..	..	..
Access to safe water: total	% of pop.	8.0	16.0	18.0	41.1	68.4	..
Urban	"	58.0	69.0	70.0	77.8	78.9	..
Rural	"	1.0	9.0	11.0	27.3	60.3	..
Access to health care	"	..	44.0	45.0	..	..	..

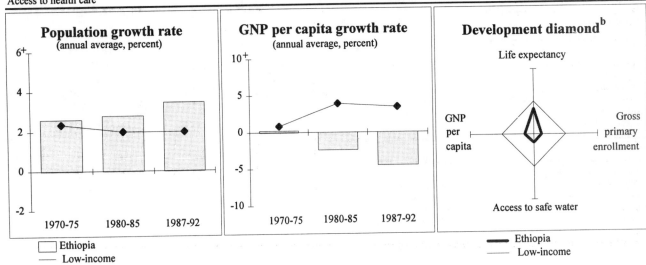

a. See the technical notes, p.389.   b. The development diamond, based on four key indicators, shows the average level of development in the country compared with its income group. See the introduction.

Ethiopia

Indicator	Unit of measure	Latest single year 1970-75	Latest single year 1980-85	Most recent estimate 1987-92	Same region/income group Sub-Saharan Africa	Same region/income group Low-income	Next higher income group
		Resources and Expenditures					
HUMAN RESOURCES							
Population (mre=1992)	thousands	32,954	43,350	54,790	546,390	3,194,535	942,547
Age dependency ratio	ratio	0.89	0.92	1.01	0.95	0.67	0.66
Urban	% of pop.	9.5	11.5	12.7	29.5	26.7	57.0
Population growth rate	annual %	2.6	2.8	3.4	2.9	1.8	1.4
Urban	"	4.5	4.6	5.2	5.1	3.4	4.8
Labor force (15-64)	thousands	15,912	19,182	22,192	224,025	1,478,954	..
Agriculture	% of labor force	82	80	..	..	..	..
Industry	"	7	8	..	..	..	..
Female	"	40	38	37	37	33	36
Females per 100 males							
Urban	number	102	123	123	..	..	..
Rural	"	96	102	102	..	..	..
NATURAL RESOURCES							
Area	thou. sq. km	1,221.90	1,221.90	1,221.90	24,274.03	38,401.06	40,697.37
Density	pop. per sq. km	27.0	35.5	43.3	21.9	81.7	22.8
Agricultural land	% of land area	53.9	53.7	53.4	52.7	50.9	..
Change in agricultural land	annual %	-0.1	-0.1	-0.1	0.1	0.0	..
Agricultural land under irrigation	%	0.3	0.3	0.3	0.8	18.2	..
Forests and woodland	thou. sq. km	286	276	270	..	..	..
Deforestation (net)	annual %	..	..	0.3	..	..	..
INCOME							
Household income							
Share of top 20% of households	% of income	..	41	..	..	42	..
Share of bottom 40% of households	"	..	21	..	..	19	..
Share of bottom 20% of households	"	..	9	..	..	8	..
EXPENDITURE							
Food	% of GDP	..	43.3	..	..	..	..
Staples	"	..	21.1	..	..	..	..
Meat, fish, milk, cheese, eggs	"	..	9.4	..	..	..	..
Cereal imports	thou. metric tonnes	67	741	1,045	20,311	46,537	74,924
Food aid in cereals	"	54	869	963	4,303	9,008	4,054
Food production per capita	1987 = 100	98	87	84	90	123	..
Fertilizer consumption	kg/ha	0.5	1.1	1.7	4.2	61.9	..
Share of agriculture in GDP	% of GDP	44.1	39.6	44.4	18.6	29.6	..
Housing	% of GDP	..	12.1	..	..	..	..
Average household size	persons per household	5.0	..	..	..	..	..
Urban	"	4.0	..	..	..	..	..
Fixed investment: housing	% of GDP	3.9	3.0	..	..	..	..
Fuel and power	% of GDP	..	6.3	..	..	..	..
Energy consumption per capita	kg of oil equiv.	15	16	21	258	335	1,882
Households with electricity							
Urban	% of households	..	..	..	..	..	..
Rural	"	..	..	..	..	..	..
Transport and communication	% of GDP	..	7.3	..	..	..	..
Fixed investment: transport equipment	"	1.2	1.6	..	..	..	..
Total road length	thou. km	23	38	38	..	..	..
INVESTMENT IN HUMAN CAPITAL							
Health							
Population per physician	persons	86,100	78,936	32,499	..	..	..
Population per nurse	"	..	5,402	..	..	..	..
Population per hospital bed	"	3,500	3,384	4,141	1,329	1,050	516
Oral rehydration therapy (under-5)	% of cases	..	..	32	36	39	..
Education							
Gross enrollment ratio							
Secondary	% of school-age pop.	6	12	12	18	41	..
Female	"	4	9	11	14	35	..
Pupil-teacher ratio: primary	pupils per teacher	44	48	30	39	37	26
Pupil-teacher ratio: secondary	"	34	43	34	..	19	..
Pupils reaching grade 4	% of cohort	59	39	56	..	..	..
Repeater rate: primary	% of total enroll	..	12	11	..	..	..
Illiteracy	% of pop. (age 15+)	96	38	..	51	39	..
Female	% of fem. (age 15+)	..	..	..	62	52	..
Newspaper circulation	per thou. pop.	2	1	1	14	..	100

World Bank International Economics Department, April 1994
Data for Eritrea, not yet disaggregated, are included in Ethiopia.

Fiji

Indicator	Unit of measure	Latest single year 1970-75	Latest single year 1980-85	Most recent estimate 1987-92	Same region/income group East Asia	Same region/income group Lower-middle-income	Next higher income group
Priority Poverty Indicators							
POVERTY							
Upper poverty line	local curr.	..	..	..		..	..
Headcount index	% of pop.	..	..	..	12	..	..
Lower poverty line	local curr.	..	..	..		..	..
Headcount index	% of pop.	..	..	..	9	..	..
GNP per capita	US$	1,030	1,650	2,010	760	..	3,870
SHORT TERM INCOME INDICATORS							
Unskilled urban wages	local curr.	..	..	..	..	..	..
Unskilled rural wages	"	..	..	..	..	..	..
Rural terms of trade	"	..	..	..	..	..	..
Consumer price index	1987=100	43	93	143	..	..	..
Lower income	"	..	..	..	..	..	..
Food[a]	"	24	142	143	..	..	..
Urban	"	..	..	..	..	..	..
Rural	"	..	..	..	..	..	..
SOCIAL INDICATORS							
Public expenditure on basic social services	% of GDP	..	10.6	..	..	..	..
Gross enrollment ratios							
Primary	% school age pop.	115	122	126	121	..	107
Male	"	115	122	124	126	..	..
Female	"	115	122	127	117	..	..
Mortality							
Infant mortality	per thou. live births	45.0	31.0	23.0	39.0	45.0	40.0
Under 5 mortality	"	..	..	27.5	49.0	59.0	51.0
Immunization							
Measles	% age group	..	57.0	69.0	88.4	..	82.0
DPT	"	..	69.0	98.0	89.5	..	73.8
Child malnutrition (under-5)	"	..	..	..	24.7	..	..
Life expectancy							
Total	years	65	69	72	68	68	69
Female advantage	"	3.1	4.0	4.2	3.6	6.4	6.3
Total fertility rate	births per woman	3.7	3.5	3.0	2.4	3.1	2.9
Maternal mortality rate	per 100,000 live births	..	47	90	114	..	..
Supplementary Poverty Indicators							
Expenditures on social security	% of total gov't exp.	2.5	7.6	4.0	..	..	..
Social security coverage	% econ. active pop.	..	..	..	..	..	..
Access to safe water: total	% of pop.	69.0	..	80.0	72.0	..	85.6
Urban	"	89.0	..	95.0	83.4	..	94.3
Rural	"	56.0	..	68.0	60.2	..	73.0
Access to health care	"	..	100.0	99.9	..	..	..

Population growth rate (annual average, percent)

Fiji
— Lower-middle-income

GNP per capita growth rate (annual average, percent)

Development diamond[b]

Life expectancy — GNP per capita — Gross primary enrollment — Access to safe water

Fiji
— Lower-middle-income

a. See the technical notes, p.389.   b. The development diamond, based on four key indicators, shows the average level of development in the country compared with its income group. See the introduction.

Fiji

Indicator	Unit of measure	Latest single year 1970-75	Latest single year 1980-85	Most recent estimate 1987-92	Same region/income group East Asia	Same region/income group Lower-middle-income	Next higher income group
Resources and Expenditures							
HUMAN RESOURCES							
Population (mre=1992)	thousands	576	697	750	1,688,909	942,547	477,960
Age dependency ratio	ratio	0.74	0.71	0.67	0.55	0.66	0.64
Urban	% of pop.	36.7	41.2	44.0	29.4	57.0	71.7
Population growth rate	annual %	1.9	1.6	1.2	1.4	1.4	1.6
Urban	"	3.0	2.8	2.1	2.9	4.8	2.5
Labor force (15-64)	thousands	181	231	264	928,465	..	181,414
Agriculture	% of labor force	49	46	..	..	..	..
Industry	"	17	17	..	..	..	..
Female	"	15	19	21	41	36	29
Females per 100 males							
Urban	number	..	..	..	..	..	..
Rural	"	..	..	..	..	..	..
NATURAL RESOURCES							
Area	thou. sq. km	18.27	18.27	18.27	16,367.18	40,697.37	21,836.02
Density	pop. per sq. km	31.5	38.2	40.6	101.8	22.8	21.5
Agricultural land	% of land area	16.2	16.4	16.5	44.5	..	41.7
Change in agricultural land	annual %	0.0	0.7	0.7	0.1	..	0.3
Agricultural land under irrigation	%	0.3	0.3	0.3	14.5	..	9.3
Forests and woodland	thou. sq. km	12	12	12	..	..	..
Deforestation (net)	annual %	..	..	..	..	..	..
INCOME							
Household income							
Share of top 20% of households	% of income	48	..	..	42	..	..
Share of bottom 40% of households	"	15	..	..	18	..	..
Share of bottom 20% of households	"	5	..	..	7	..	..
EXPENDITURE							
Food	% of GDP	..	19.5	..	..	..	..
Staples	"	..	..	..	..	..	..
Meat, fish, milk, cheese, eggs	"	..	..	..	..	..	..
Cereal imports	thou. metric tonnes	57	86	106	33,591	74,924	49,174
Food aid in cereals	"	14	2	5	581	4,054	282
Food production per capita	1987 = 100	85	88	96	133	..	109
Fertilizer consumption	kg/ha	39.7	45.5	46.4	75.1	..	68.8
Share of agriculture in GDP	% of GDP	23.5	16.4	16.3	21.5	..	8.1
Housing	% of GDP	..	9.2	..	..	..	..
Average household size	persons per household	..	..	..	..	..	..
Urban	"	..	..	..	..	..	..
Fixed investment: housing	% of GDP	..	..	..	..	..	..
Fuel and power	% of GDP	..	..	..	..	..	..
Energy consumption per capita	kg of oil equiv.	516	..	..	593	1,882	1,649
Households with electricity							
Urban	% of households	..	..	..	..	..	..
Rural	"	..	..	..	..	..	..
Transport and communication	% of GDP	..	8.5	..	..	..	..
Fixed investment: transport equipment	"	..	..	..	..	..	..
Total road length	thou. km	3	4	..	..	..	..
INVESTMENT IN HUMAN CAPITAL							
Health							
Population per physician	persons	2,100	2,025	2,792	..	..	..
Population per nurse	"	600	490	..	..	..	..
Population per hospital bed	"	300	364	..	553	516	385
Oral rehydration therapy (under-5)	% of cases	..	..	16	51	..	54
Education							
Gross enrollment ratio							
Secondary	% of school-age pop.	66	51	61	53	..	53
Female	"	66	51	62	47	..	..
Pupil-teacher ratio: primary	pupils per teacher	32	29	31	23	26	25
Pupil-teacher ratio: secondary	"	24	16	18	16	..	..
Pupils reaching grade 4	% of cohort	94	95	..	89	..	71
Repeater rate: primary	% of total enroll	7	3	..	6	..	11
Illiteracy	% of pop. (age 15+)	..	15	..	24	..	14
Female	% of fem. (age 15+)	..	19	..	34	..	17
Newspaper circulation	per thou. pop.	35	98	37	..	100	117

World Bank International Economics Department, April 1994

Finland

Indicator	Unit of measure	Latest single year 1970-75	Latest single year 1980-85	Most recent estimate 1987-92	Same region/income group High-income
Priority Poverty Indicators					
POVERTY					
Upper poverty line	local curr.	..	..	..	..
Headcount index	% of pop.	..	..	..	..
Lower poverty line	local curr.	..	..	..	..
Headcount index	% of pop.	..	..	..	..
GNP per capita	US$	5,390	11,000	21,970	21,960
SHORT TERM INCOME INDICATORS					
Unskilled urban wages	local curr.	..	..	..	..
Unskilled rural wages	"	..	..	..	..
Rural terms of trade	"	..	..	..	..
Consumer price index	1987=100	37	93	127	..
Lower income	"	..	..	..	..
Food[a]	"	20	95	113	..
Urban	"	..	..	..	..
Rural	"	..	..	..	..
SOCIAL INDICATORS					
Public expenditure on basic social services	% of GDP	..	..	..	..
Gross enrollment ratios					
Primary	% school age pop.	102	102	99	103
Male	"	103	103	99	103
Female	"	101	102	99	103
Mortality					
Infant mortality	per thou. live births	9.5	6.3	5.8	7.0
Under 5 mortality	"	..	..	7.6	10.0
Immunization					
Measles	% age group	..	81.0	97.0	82.4
DPT	"	..	92.0	95.0	90.1
Child malnutrition (under-5)	"	..	..	..	..
Life expectancy					
Total	years	71	74	75	77
Female advantage	"	8.4	7.9	8.0	6.4
Total fertility rate	births per woman	1.7	1.8	1.9	1.7
Maternal mortality rate	per 100,000 live births	..	5	..	..
Supplementary Poverty Indicators					
Expenditures on social security	% of total gov't exp.	..	..	..	..
Social security coverage	% econ. active pop.	..	..	..	..
Access to safe water: total	% of pop.	..	100.0	..	..
Urban	"	86.6	100.0	..	..
Rural	"	54.2	99.0	..	..
Access to health care	"	..	100.0	100.0	..

Population growth rate
(annual average, percent)

GNP per capita growth rate
(annual average, percent)

Development diamond[b]

Finland
High-income

a. See the technical notes, p.389.   b. The development diamond, based on four key indicators, shows the average level of development in the country compared with its income group. See the introduction.

Finland

Indicator	Unit of measure	Latest single year 1970-75	Latest single year 1980-85	Most recent estimate 1987-92	Same region/income group High-income
Resources and Expenditures					
HUMAN RESOURCES					
Population (mre=1992)	thousands	4,711	4,902	5,047	828,221
Age dependency ratio	ratio	0.48	0.47	0.50	0.50
Urban	% of pop.	58.3	59.8	59.9	78.1
Population growth rate	annual %	0.4	0.4	0.7	0.7
Urban	"	3.2	0.4	0.9	0.9
Labor force (15-64)	thousands	2,313	2,488	2,566	390,033
Agriculture	% of labor force	16	12	..	..
Industry	"	35	35	..	..
Female	"	45	47	47	38
Females per 100 males					
Urban	number	109	105	..	..
Rural	"	95	92	..	..
NATURAL RESOURCES					
Area	thou. sq. km	338.13	338.13	338.13	31,709.00
Density	pop. per sq. km	13.9	14.5	14.8	24.5
Agricultural land	% of land area	9.2	8.4	8.7	42.7
Change in agricultural land	annual %	-0.4	-1.2	3.5	-0.2
Agricultural land under irrigation	%	1.4	2.4	2.4	16.1
Forests and woodland	thou. sq. km	232	232	232	..
Deforestation (net)	annual %	..	..	0.0	..
INCOME					
Household income					
Share of top 20% of households	% of income	..	38	..	..
Share of bottom 40% of households	"	..	18	..	..
Share of bottom 20% of households	"	..	6	..	..
EXPENDITURE					
Food	% of GDP	..	10.7	..	..
Staples	"	..	2.0	..	..
Meat, fish, milk, cheese, eggs	"	..	4.8	..	..
Cereal imports	thou. metric tonnes	267	130	82	70,626
Food aid in cereals	"	..	..	..	2
Food production per capita	1987 = 100	100	108	91	101
Fertilizer consumption	kg/ha	184.5	199.4	125.2	162.1
Share of agriculture in GDP	% of GDP	9.7	7.2	4.8	2.4
Housing	% of GDP	..	9.8	..	..
Average household size	persons per household	2.7	2.6	..	..
Urban	"	2.5	2.5	..	..
Fixed investment: housing	% of GDP	8.1	3.8	..	..
Fuel and power	% of GDP	..	2.5	..	..
Energy consumption per capita	kg of oil equiv.	4,253	5,336	5,560	5,101
Households with electricity					
Urban	% of households	..	..	..	..
Rural	"	..	..	..	..
Transport and communication	% of GDP	..	9.3	..	..
Fixed investment: transport equipment	"	2.6	1.6	..	..
Total road length	thou. km	74	76	76	..
INVESTMENT IN HUMAN CAPITAL					
Health					
Population per physician	persons	961	443	406	..
Population per nurse	"	128	59	..	..
Population per hospital bed	"	77	64	93	144
Oral rehydration therapy (under-5)	% of cases	..	..	..	..
Education					
Gross enrollment ratio					
Secondary	% of school-age pop.	89	104	121	92
Female	"	94	112	133	94
Pupil-teacher ratio: primary	pupils per teacher	19	15	18	18
Pupil-teacher ratio: secondary	"	15	14	..	..
Pupils reaching grade 4	% of cohort	98	100	98	..
Repeater rate: primary	% of total enroll	..	..	0	..
Illiteracy	% of pop. (age 15+)	..	..	†	..
Female	% of fem. (age 15+)	..	..	†	..
Newspaper circulation	per thou. pop.	439	512	558	..

World Bank International Economics Department, April 1994

115

France

Indicator	Unit of measure	Latest single year 1970-75	Latest single year 1980-85	Most recent estimate 1987-92	Same region/income group High-income
Priority Poverty Indicators					
POVERTY					
Upper poverty line	local curr.	..	..	..	..
Headcount index	% of pop.	..	..	..	..
Lower poverty line	local curr.	..	..	..	..
Headcount index	% of pop.	..	..	..	..
GNP per capita	US$	5,980	9,810	22,260	21,960
SHORT TERM INCOME INDICATORS					
Unskilled urban wages	local curr.	..	..	..	..
Unskilled rural wages	"	..	..	..	..
Rural terms of trade	"	..	..	..	..
Consumer price index	1987=100	36	94	116	..
Lower income	"	..	..	..	..
Food[a]	"	24	95	114	..
Urban	"	..	..	..	..
Rural	"	..	..	..	..
SOCIAL INDICATORS					
Public expenditure on basic social services	% of GDP	..	..	..	..
Gross enrollment ratios					
Primary	% school age pop.	109	109	107	103
Male	"	118	110	108	103
Female	"	117	107	106	103
Mortality					
Infant mortality	per thou. live births	13.8	8.3	7.3	7.0
Under 5 mortality	"	..	..	9.3	10.0
Immunization					
Measles	% age group	..	37.0	69.0	82.4
DPT	"	..	79.0	95.0	90.1
Child malnutrition (under-5)	"	..	..	..	..
Life expectancy					
Total	years	72	75	77	77
Female advantage	"	7.6	8.1	8.3	6.4
Total fertility rate	births per woman	1.9	1.8	1.8	1.7
Maternal mortality rate	per 100,000 live births	..	13	..	..
Supplementary Poverty Indicators					
Expenditures on social security	% of total gov't exp.	..	8.7	43.2	..
Social security coverage	% econ. active pop.	..	..	..	..
Access to safe water: total	% of pop.	..	100.0	..	..
Urban	"	..	100.0	..	..
Rural	"	93.7	100.0	..	..
Access to health care	"	..	..	..	..

Population growth rate
(annual average, percent)

GNP per capita growth rate
(annual average, percent)

Development diamond[b]

France
High-income

France
High-income

a. See the technical notes, p.389.   b. The development diamond, based on four key indicators, shows the average level of development in the country compared with its income group. See the introduction.

France

Indicator	Unit of measure	Latest single year 1970-75	Latest single year 1980-85	Most recent estimate 1987-92	Same region/income group High-income
Resources and Expenditures					
HUMAN RESOURCES					
Population (mre=1992)	thousands	52,699	55,170	57,372	828,221
Age dependency ratio	ratio	0.60	0.52	0.53	0.50
Urban	% of pop.	73.0	73.1	72.7	78.1
Population growth rate	annual %	0.5	0.4	0.6	0.7
Urban	"	1.0	0.4	0.6	0.9
Labor force (15-64)	thousands	22,617	24,639	25,645	390,033
Agriculture	% of labor force	11	9	..	..
Industry	"	37	35	..	..
Female	"	38	40	40	38
Females per 100 males					
Urban	number	101	102	..	..
Rural	"	93	93	..	..
NATURAL RESOURCES					
Area	thou. sq. km	551.50	551.50	551.50	31,709.00
Density	pop. per sq. km	95.6	100.0	103.5	24.5
Agricultural land	% of land area	58.8	57.2	55.3	42.7
Change in agricultural land	annual %	-0.3	-0.2	-0.5	-0.2
Agricultural land under irrigation	%	2.1	3.3	3.9	16.1
Forests and woodland	thou. sq. km	146	146	149	..
Deforestation (net)	annual %	..	..	-0.1	..
INCOME					
Household income					
Share of top 20% of households	% of income	46	..	..	..
Share of bottom 40% of households	"	16	..	..	..
Share of bottom 20% of households	"	5	..	..	..
EXPENDITURE					
Food	% of GDP	12.3	11.3	..	..
Staples	"	1.8	1.6	..	..
Meat, fish, milk, cheese, eggs	"	6.5	6.0	..	..
Cereal imports	thou. metric tonnes	1,295	1,216	968	70,626
Food aid in cereals	"	..	..	..	2
Food production per capita	1987 = 100	90	106	104	101
Fertilizer consumption	kg/ha	144.8	181.1	182.8	162.1
Share of agriculture in GDP	% of GDP	..	3.9	3.1	2.4
Housing	% of GDP	9.4	11.9	..	..
Average household size	persons per household	2.9	..	..	..
Urban	"	2.8	..	..	..
Fixed investment: housing	% of GDP	7.6	2.6	..	..
Fuel and power	% of GDP	2.3	3.4	..	..
Energy consumption per capita	kg of oil equiv.	3,078	3,637	4,034	5,101
Households with electricity					
Urban	% of households	..	..	..	..
Rural	"	..	..	..	..
Transport and communication	% of GDP	7.5	9.0	..	..
Fixed investment: transport equipment	"	2.0	2.7	..	..
Total road length	thou. km	801	805	806	..
INVESTMENT IN HUMAN CAPITAL					
Health					
Population per physician	persons	747	462	346	..
Population per nurse	"	273	111	..	..
Population per hospital bed	"	139	..	109	144
Oral rehydration therapy (under-5)	% of cases	..	..	..	..
Education					
Gross enrollment ratio					
Secondary	% of school-age pop.	82	90	101	92
Female	"	77	94	104	94
Pupil-teacher ratio: primary	pupils per teacher	23	15	12	18
Pupil-teacher ratio: secondary	"	13	15	..	..
Pupils reaching grade 4	% of cohort	87	94	98	..
Repeater rate: primary	% of total enroll	9	8	5	..
Illiteracy	% of pop. (age 15+)	..	..	†	..
Female	% of fem. (age 15+)	..	..	†	..
Newspaper circulation	per thou. pop.	201	188	208	..

World Bank International Economics Department, April 1994

French Guiana

Indicator	Unit of measure	Latest single year 1970-75	Latest single year 1980-85	Most recent estimate 1987-92	Same region/income group Latin America Caribbean	Same region/income group Upper-middle-income	Next higher income group
Priority Poverty Indicators							
POVERTY							
Upper poverty line	local curr.	..	..	..	..	..	..
Headcount index	% of pop.	..	..	..	..	..	..
Lower poverty line	local curr.	..	..	..	..	..	..
Headcount index	% of pop.	..	..	..	..	..	..
GNP per capita	US$	..	..	..	2,690	3,870	21,960
SHORT TERM INCOME INDICATORS							
Unskilled urban wages	local curr.	..	..	..	..	..	..
Unskilled rural wages	"	..	..	..	..	..	..
Rural terms of trade	"	..	..	..	..	..	..
Consumer price index	1987=100	34	94	116	..	..	..
Lower income	"	..	..	..	..	..	..
Food[a]	"	22	94	111	..	..	..
Urban	"	..	..	..	..	..	..
Rural	"	..	..	..	..	..	..
SOCIAL INDICATORS							
Public expenditure on basic social services	% of GDP	..	..	..	..	..	..
Gross enrollment ratios							
Primary	% school age pop.	..	..	..	106	107	103
Male	"	..	..	..	..	..	103
Female	"	..	..	..	..	..	103
Mortality							
Infant mortality	per thou. live births	..	..	..	44.0	40.0	7.0
Under 5 mortality	"	..	..	..	56.0	51.0	10.0
Immunization							
Measles	% age group	..	..	..	78.9	82.0	82.4
DPT	"	..	..	..	73.8	73.8	90.1
Child malnutrition (under-5)	"	..	..	..	10.5	..	..
Life expectancy							
Total	years	..	..	..	68	69	77
Female advantage	"	..	..	..	5.6	6.3	6.4
Total fertility rate	births per woman	..	..	..	3.0	2.9	1.7
Maternal mortality rate	per 100,000 live births	..	..	..	..	..	..
Supplementary Poverty Indicators							
Expenditures on social security	% of total gov't exp.	..	..	..	..	..	..
Social security coverage	% econ. active pop.	..	..	..	..	..	..
Access to safe water: total	% of pop.	..	..	..	80.3	85.6	..
Urban	"	..	..	..	91.0	94.3	..
Rural	"	..	..	..	64.3	73.0	..
Access to health care	"	..	..	..	..	..	..

Population growth rate
(annual average, percent)

GNP per capita growth rate
(annual average, percent)

Development diamond[b]

☐ French Guiana
— Upper-middle-income

— French Guiana
— Upper-middle-income

a. See the technical notes, p.389. b. The development diamond, based on four key indicators, shows the average level of development in the country compared with its income group. See the introduction.

French Guiana

Indicator	Unit of measure	Latest single year 1970-75	Latest single year 1980-85	Most recent estimate 1987-92	Same region/income group Latin America Caribbean	Same region/income group Upper-middle-income	Next higher income group
Resources and Expenditures							
HUMAN RESOURCES							
Population (mre=1992)	thousands	..	..	..	453,294	477,960	828,221
Age dependency ratio	ratio	..	..	..	0.67	0.64	0.50
Urban	% of pop.	..	..	..	72.9	71.7	78.1
Population growth rate	annual %	..	..	..	1.7	1.6	0.7
Urban	"	..	..	..	2.6	2.5	0.9
Labor force (15-64)	thousands	..	..	..	166,091	181,414	390,033
Agriculture	% of labor force	..	..	..	..	..	..
Industry	"	..	..	..	..	..	..
Female	"	..	..	..	27	29	38
Females per 100 males							
Urban	number	..	..	..	..	..	..
Rural	"	..	..	..	..	..	..
NATURAL RESOURCES							
Area	thou. sq. km	90.00	90.00	90.00	20,507.48	21,836.02	31,709.00
Density	pop. per sq. km	..	..	..	21.7	21.5	24.5
Agricultural land	% of land area	0.1	0.1	0.2	40.2	41.7	42.7
Change in agricultural land	annual %	14.3	0.0	0.0	0.5	0.3	-0.2
Agricultural land under irrigation	%	12.5	16.7	9.5	3.2	9.3	16.1
Forests and woodland	thou. sq. km	73	73	73	..	..	..
Deforestation (net)	annual %	..	..	..	..	..	..
INCOME							
Household income							
Share of top 20% of households	% of income	..	..	..	..	..	..
Share of bottom 40% of households	"	..	..	..	..	..	..
Share of bottom 20% of households	"	..	..	..	..	..	..
EXPENDITURE							
Food	% of GDP	..	..	..	..	..	..
Staples	"	..	..	..	..	..	..
Meat, fish, milk, cheese, eggs	"	..	..	..	..	..	..
Cereal imports	thou. metric tonnes	5	12	9	25,032	49,174	70,626
Food aid in cereals	"	..	..	..	1,779	282	2
Food production per capita	1987 = 100	..	..	..	104	109	101
Fertilizer consumption	kg/ha	..	83.7	61.9	15.5	68.8	162.1
Share of agriculture in GDP	% of GDP	..	..	..	8.9	8.1	2.4
Housing	% of GDP	..	..	..	..	..	..
Average household size	persons per household	..	..	..	..	..	..
Urban	"	..	..	..	..	..	..
Fixed investment: housing	% of GDP	..	..	..	..	..	..
Fuel and power	% of GDP	..	..	..	..	..	..
Energy consumption per capita	kg of oil equiv.	..	..	..	912	1,649	5,101
Households with electricity							
Urban	% of households	..	..	..	..	..	..
Rural	"	..	..	..	..	..	..
Transport and communication	% of GDP	..	..	..	..	..	..
Fixed investment: transport equipment	"	..	..	..	..	..	..
Total road length	thou. km	..	..	1	..	..	..
INVESTMENT IN HUMAN CAPITAL							
Health							
Population per physician	persons	..	..	..	..	..	..
Population per nurse	"	..	..	..	..	..	..
Population per hospital bed	"	..	..	..	508	385	144
Oral rehydration therapy (under-5)	% of cases	..	..	..	62	54	..
Education							
Gross enrollment ratio							
Secondary	% of school-age pop.	..	..	..	47	53	92
Female	"	..	..	..	..	..	94
Pupil-teacher ratio: primary	pupils per teacher	29	23	..	25	25	18
Pupil-teacher ratio: secondary	"	18	14	..	..	..	..
Pupils reaching grade 4	% of cohort	..	..	..	..	71	..
Repeater rate: primary	% of total enroll	17	..	..	14	11	..
Illiteracy	% of pop. (age 15+)	..	17	..	15	14	..
Female	% of fem. (age 15+)	..	..	..	17	17	..
Newspaper circulation	per thou. pop.	..	..	..	99	117	..

World Bank International Economics Department, April 1994

French Polynesia

Indicator	Unit of measure	Latest single year 1970-75	Latest single year 1980-85	Most recent estimate 1987-92	Same region/income group High-income
Priority Poverty Indicators					
POVERTY					
Upper poverty line	local curr.	..	..	..	..
Headcount index	% of pop.	..	..	..	..
Lower poverty line	local curr.	..	..	..	..
Headcount index	% of pop.	..	..	..	..
GNP per capita	US$	..	..	..	21,960
SHORT TERM INCOME INDICATORS					
Unskilled urban wages	local curr.	..	..	..	..
Unskilled rural wages	"	..	..	..	..
Rural terms of trade	"	..	..	..	..
Consumer price index	1987=100	..	..	..	..
Lower income	"	..	..	..	..
Food[a]	"	..	106	108	..
Urban	"	..	..	..	..
Rural	"	..	..	..	..
SOCIAL INDICATORS					
Public expenditure on basic social services	% of GDP	..	..	..	..
Gross enrollment ratios					
Primary	% school age pop.	..	..	..	103
Male	"	..	..	..	103
Female	"	..	..	..	103
Mortality					
Infant mortality	per thou. live births	..	..	22.0	7.0
Under 5 mortality	"	..	..	26.4	10.0
Immunization					
Measles	% age group	..	79.0	81.0	82.4
DPT	"	..	76.0	89.0	90.1
Child malnutrition (under-5)	"	..	..	..	..
Life expectancy					
Total	years	..	..	68	77
Female advantage	"	..	..	5.0	6.4
Total fertility rate	births per woman	5.6	..	3.2	1.7
Maternal mortality rate	per 100,000 live births	..	..	..	..
Supplementary Poverty Indicators					
Expenditures on social security	% of total gov't exp.	..	..	..	..
Social security coverage	% econ. active pop.	..	..	..	..
Access to safe water: total	% of pop.	..	..	71.0	..
Urban	"	..	..	100.0	..
Rural	"	..	..	18.0	..
Access to health care	"	..	..	..	..

Population growth rate
(annual average, percent)

GNP per capita growth rate
(annual average, percent)

Development diamond[b]

Life expectancy

GNP per capita — Gross primary enrollment

Access to safe water

☐ French Polynesia
— High-income

━ French Polynesia
— High-income

a. See the technical notes, p.389.   b. The development diamond, based on four key indicators, shows the average level of development in the country compared with its income group. See the introduction.

120

French Polynesia

Indicator	Unit of measure	Latest single year 1970-75	Latest single year 1980-85	Most recent estimate 1987-92	Same region/income group High-income
Resources and Expenditures					
HUMAN RESOURCES					
Population (mre=1992)	thousands	135	171	207	828,221
Age dependency ratio	ratio	..	0.80	0.65	0.50
Urban	% of pop.	58.3	62.2	64.5	78.1
Population growth rate	annual %	3.8	1.8	2.5	0.7
Urban	"	4.7	2.5	3.3	0.9
Labor force (15-64)	thousands	..	..	..	390,033
Agriculture	% of labor force	..	..	..	..
Industry	"	..	..	..	..
Female	"	..	..	..	38
Females per 100 males					
Urban	number	..	..	..	..
Rural	"	..	..	..	..
NATURAL RESOURCES					
Area	thou. sq. km	4.00	4.00	4.00	31,709.00
Density	pop. per sq. km	33.8	42.8	50.5	24.5
Agricultural land	% of land area	12.8	12.8	12.8	42.7
Change in agricultural land	annual %	0.0	0.0	0.0	-0.2
Agricultural land under irrigation	%	..	..	..	16.1
Forests and woodland	thou. sq. km	1	1	1	..
Deforestation (net)	annual %	..	..	..	..
INCOME					
Household income					
Share of top 20% of households	% of income	..	..	..	..
Share of bottom 40% of households	"	..	..	..	..
Share of bottom 20% of households	"	..	..	..	..
EXPENDITURE					
Food	% of GDP	..	..	..	..
Staples	"	..	..	..	..
Meat, fish, milk, cheese, eggs	"	..	..	..	..
Cereal imports	thou. metric tonnes	20	31	33	70,626
Food aid in cereals	"	..	..	..	2
Food production per capita	1987 = 100	137	76	64	101
Fertilizer consumption	kg/ha	6.4	23.4	17.0	162.1
Share of agriculture in GDP	% of GDP	..	..	..	2.4
Housing	% of GDP	..	..	..	..
Average household size	persons per household	..	..	..	..
Urban	"	..	..	..	..
Fixed investment: housing	% of GDP	..	..	..	..
Fuel and power	% of GDP	..	..	..	..
Energy consumption per capita	kg of oil equiv.	1,030	1,637	1,449	5,101
Households with electricity					
Urban	% of households	..	93.0	..	..
Rural	"	..	..	..	..
Transport and communication	% of GDP	..	..	..	..
Fixed investment: transport equipment	"	..	..	..	..
Total road length	thou. km	..	1	..	..
INVESTMENT IN HUMAN CAPITAL					
Health					
Population per physician	persons	..	799	..	..
Population per nurse	"	..	434	..	..
Population per hospital bed	"	..	..	..	144
Oral rehydration therapy (under-5)	% of cases	..	..	..	..
Education					
Gross enrollment ratio					
Secondary	% of school-age pop.	..	..	..	92
Female	"	..	..	..	94
Pupil-teacher ratio: primary	pupils per teacher	24	20	14	18
Pupil-teacher ratio: secondary	"	17	17	14	..
Pupils reaching grade 4	% of cohort	86	93	91	..
Repeater rate: primary	% of total enroll	19	10	..	..
Illiteracy	% of pop. (age 15+)	..	..	..	..
Female	% of fem. (age 15+)	..	..	..	..
Newspaper circulation	per thou. pop.	81	..	106	..

World Bank International Economics Department, April 1994

Gabon

Priority Poverty Indicators

Indicator	Unit of measure	Latest single year 1970-75	Latest single year 1980-85	Most recent estimate 1987-92	Same region/income group Sub-Saharan Africa	Same region/income group Upper-middle-income	Next higher income group
POVERTY							
Upper poverty line	local curr.	..	..	..	..	..	..
Headcount index	% of pop.	..	..	..	..	..	..
Lower poverty line	local curr.	..	..	..	..	..	..
Headcount index	% of pop.	..	..	..	..	..	..
GNP per capita	US$	2,620	3,430	4,450	520	3,870	21,960
SHORT TERM INCOME INDICATORS							
Unskilled urban wages	local curr.	..	..	..	..	..	..
Unskilled rural wages	"	..	..	..	..	..	..
Rural terms of trade	"	..	..	..	..	..	..
Consumer price index	1987=100	32	77	95	..	..	..
Lower income	"	..	..	..	..	..	..
Food[a]	"	..	95	87	..	..	..
Urban	"	..	..	..	..	..	..
Rural	"	..	..	..	..	..	..
SOCIAL INDICATORS							
Public expenditure on basic social services	% of GDP	..	..	7.4	..	..	..
Gross enrollment ratios							
Primary	% school age pop.	102	..	..	66	107	103
Male	"	105	..	..	79	..	103
Female	"	100	..	..	62	..	103
Mortality							
Infant mortality	per thou. live births	132.0	112.0	94.0	99.0	40.0	7.0
Under 5 mortality	"	..	..	152.6	169.0	51.0	10.0
Immunization							
Measles	% age group	..	58.0	66.0	54.0	82.0	82.4
DPT	"	..	14.0	59.0	54.6	73.8	90.1
Child malnutrition (under-5)	"	..	12.8	25.0	28.4	..	..
Life expectancy							
Total	years	45	49	54	52	69	77
Female advantage	"	3.2	4.0	3.0	3.4	6.3	6.4
Total fertility rate	births per woman	4.3	4.5	5.9	6.1	2.9	1.7
Maternal mortality rate	per 100,000 live births	..	190	..	..	..	..

Supplementary Poverty Indicators

Indicator	Unit of measure	1970-75	1980-85	1987-92	Sub-Saharan Africa	Upper-middle-income	Next higher income group
Expenditures on social security	% of total gov't exp.	..	..	..	..	..	..
Social security coverage	% econ. active pop.	..	..	..	41.1	85.6	..
Access to safe water: total	% of pop.	1.0	..	72.0	41.1	85.6	..
Urban	"	6.0	..	90.0	77.8	94.3	..
Rural	"	..	..	50.0	27.3	73.0	..
Access to health care	"	..	80.0	87.0	..	..	..

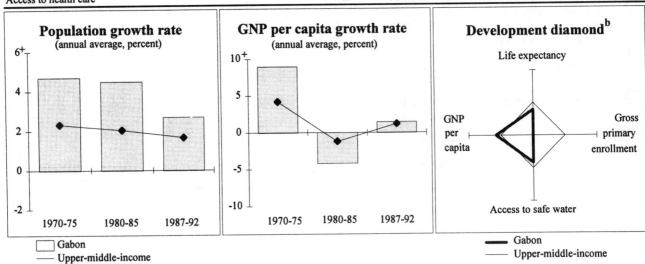

Population growth rate (annual average, percent) — Gabon / Upper-middle-income

GNP per capita growth rate (annual average, percent)

Development diamond[b] — Life expectancy, GNP per capita, Gross primary enrollment, Access to safe water — Gabon / Upper-middle-income

a. See the technical notes, p.389.   b. The development diamond, based on four key indicators, shows the average level of development in the country compared with its income group. See the introduction.

Gabon

Indicator	Unit of measure	Latest single year 1970-75	Latest single year 1980-85	Most recent estimate 1987-92	Same region/income group Sub-Saharan Africa	Same region/income group Upper-middle-income	Next higher income group
Resources and Expenditures							
HUMAN RESOURCES							
Population (mre=1992)	thousands	637	997	1,201	546,390	477,960	828,221
Age dependency ratio	ratio	0.62	0.72	0.83	0.95	0.64	0.50
Urban	% of pop.	30.6	40.9	47.4	29.5	71.7	78.1
Population growth rate	annual %	4.8	4.1	2.8	2.9	1.6	0.7
Urban	"	8.2	6.6	4.6	5.1	2.5	0.9
Labor force (15-64)	thousands	481	518	546	224,025	181,414	390,033
Agriculture	% of labor force	78	75	..	..	..	..
Industry	"	10	11	..	..	..	..
Female	"	40	38	37	37	29	38
Females per 100 males							
Urban	number	..	..	..	..	..	..
Rural	"	..	..	..	..	..	..
NATURAL RESOURCES							
Area	thou. sq. km	267.67	267.67	267.67	24,274.03	21,836.02	31,709.00
Density	pop. per sq. km	2.4	3.7	4.4	21.9	21.5	24.5
Agricultural land	% of land area	20.1	20.0	20.0	52.7	41.7	42.7
Change in agricultural land	annual %	0.4	0.0	0.0	0.1	0.3	-0.2
Agricultural land under irrigation	%	..	..	..	0.8	9.3	16.1
Forests and woodland	thou. sq. km	201	200	199	..	..	..
Deforestation (net)	annual %	..	..	0.6	..	..	..
INCOME							
Household income							
Share of top 20% of households	% of income	..	..	..	..	..	..
Share of bottom 40% of households	"	..	12	..	..	..	..
Share of bottom 20% of households	"	..	5	..	..	..	..
EXPENDITURE							
Food	% of GDP	..	..	20.8	..	..	..
Staples	"	..	..	9.7	..	..	..
Meat, fish, milk, cheese, eggs	"	..	..	6.3	..	..	..
Cereal imports	thou. metric tonnes	63	64	71	20,311	49,174	70,626
Food aid in cereals	"	1	0	..	4,303	282	2
Food production per capita	1987 = 100	104	85	84	90	109	101
Fertilizer consumption	kg/ha	0.1	0.5	0.1	4.2	68.8	162.1
Share of agriculture in GDP	% of GDP	6.4	6.2	8.9	18.6	8.1	2.4
Housing	% of GDP	..	..	1.4	..	..	..
Average household size	persons per household	..	..	..	..	..	..
Urban	"	..	..	..	..	..	..
Fixed investment: housing	% of GDP	..	..	2.1	..	..	..
Fuel and power	% of GDP	..	..	0.3	..	..	..
Energy consumption per capita	kg of oil equiv.	799	723	784	258	1,649	5,101
Households with electricity							
Urban	% of households	..	..	..	..	..	..
Rural	"	..	..	..	..	..	..
Transport and communication	% of GDP	..	..	2.4	..	..	..
Fixed investment: transport equipment	"	..	..	4.3	..	..	..
Total road length	thou. km	7	8	8	..	..	..
INVESTMENT IN HUMAN CAPITAL							
Health							
Population per physician	persons	5,250	2,397	..	..	..	..
Population per nurse	"	569	272	..	..	..	..
Population per hospital bed	"	101	800	..	1,329	385	144
Oral rehydration therapy (under-5)	% of cases	..	..	10	36	54	..
Education							
Gross enrollment ratio							
Secondary	% of school-age pop.	17	..	..	18	53	92
Female	"	12	..	..	14	..	94
Pupil-teacher ratio: primary	pupils per teacher	48	46	44	39	25	18
Pupil-teacher ratio: secondary	"	24	21	32	..	..	..
Pupils reaching grade 4	% of cohort	49	79	79	..	71	..
Repeater rate: primary	% of total enroll	34	32	31	..	11	..
Illiteracy	% of pop. (age 15+)	..	44	39	51	14	..
Female	% of fem. (age 15+)	..	57	52	62	17	..
Newspaper circulation	per thou. pop.	..	18	18	14	117	..

World Bank International Economics Department, April 1994

123

The Gambia

Indicator	Unit of measure	Latest single year 1970-75	Latest single year 1980-85	Most recent estimate 1987-92	Same region/income group Sub-Saharan Africa	Same region/income group Low-income	Next higher income group
Priority Poverty Indicators							
POVERTY							
Upper poverty line	local curr.	..	..	..	..	..	..
Headcount index	% of pop.	..	..	..	..	19	..
Lower poverty line	local curr.	..	..	..	..	..	..
Headcount index	% of pop.	..	..	..	..	..	..
GNP per capita	US$	210	240	370	520	390	..
SHORT TERM INCOME INDICATORS							
Unskilled urban wages	local curr.	..	..	..	..	..	..
Unskilled rural wages	"	..	..	..	..	..	..
Rural terms of trade	"	..	..	..	..	..	..
Consumer price index	1987=100	17	52	161	..	..	..
Lower income	"	..	..	..	..	..	..
Food[a]	"	9	51	138	..	..	..
Urban	"	..	..	..	..	..	..
Rural	"	..	..	..	..	..	..
SOCIAL INDICATORS							
Public expenditure on basic social services	% of GDP	..	..	15.0	..	..	..
Gross enrollment ratios							
Primary	% school age pop.	33	68	68	66	103	..
Male	"	44	84	81	79	113	..
Female	"	21	52	56	62	96	..
Mortality							
Infant mortality	per thou. live births	179.0	154.0	132.0	99.0	73.0	45.0
Under 5 mortality	"	..	..	222.9	169.0	108.0	59.0
Immunization							
Measles	% age group	..	75.0	..	54.0	72.7	..
DPT	"	..	77.0	77.0	54.6	80.6	..
Child malnutrition (under-5)	"	..	20.0	..	28.4	38.3	..
Life expectancy							
Total	years	37	41	45	52	62	68
Female advantage	"	3.1	3.2	1.1	3.4	2.4	6.4
Total fertility rate	births per woman	6.5	6.5	6.5	6.1	3.4	3.1
Maternal mortality rate	per 100,000 live births	..	1500	..	..	..	..
Supplementary Poverty Indicators							
Expenditures on social security	% of total gov't exp.	3.8	3.2	2.7	..	..	..
Social security coverage	% econ. active pop.	..	..	..	..	..	..
Access to safe water: total	% of pop.	12.0	60.0	77.0	41.1	68.4	..
Urban	"	97.0	97.0	..	77.8	78.9	..
Rural	"	3.0	50.0	73.0	27.3	60.3	..
Access to health care	"	..	90.0	..	..	..	..

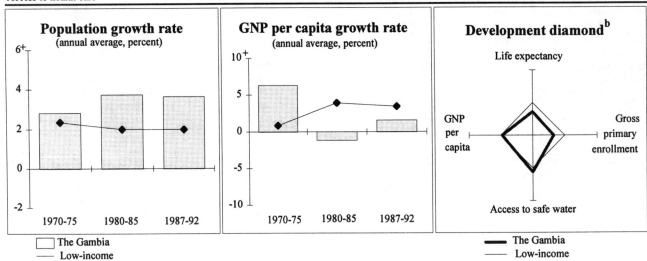

Population growth rate (annual average, percent)

GNP per capita growth rate (annual average, percent)

Development diamond[b]
Life expectancy — GNP per capita — Gross primary enrollment — Access to safe water

The Gambia
Low-income

a. See the technical notes, p.389.   b. The development diamond, based on four key indicators, shows the average level of development in the country compared with its income group. See the introduction.

The Gambia

Indicator	Unit of measure	Latest single year 1970-75	Latest single year 1980-85	Most recent estimate 1987-92	Same region/income group Sub-Saharan Africa	Same region/income group Low-income	Next higher income group
Resources and Expenditures							
HUMAN RESOURCES							
Population (mre=1992)	thousands	533	764	989	546,390	3,194,535	942,547
Age dependency ratio	ratio	0.82	0.82	0.89	0.95	0.67	0.66
Urban	% of pop.	16.6	20.2	23.8	29.5	26.7	57.0
Population growth rate	annual %	3.1	3.9	3.2	2.9	1.8	1.4
Urban	"	5.0	5.9	5.7	5.1	3.4	4.8
Labor force (15-64)	thousands	263	307	340	224,025	1,478,954	..
Agriculture	% of labor force	85	84	..	..	..	..
Industry	"	6	7	..	..	..	..
Female	"	43	41	40	37	33	36
Females per 100 males							
Urban	number	..	..	..	..	..	..
Rural	"	..	..	..	..	..	..
NATURAL RESOURCES							
Area	thou. sq. km	11.30	11.30	11.30	24,274.03	38,401.06	40,697.37
Density	pop. per sq. km	47.2	67.6	84.8	21.9	81.7	22.8
Agricultural land	% of land area	24.2	25.5	27.0	52.7	50.9	..
Change in agricultural land	annual %	1.7	0.0	0.8	0.1	0.0	..
Agricultural land under irrigation	%	4.1	4.7	4.4	0.8	18.2	..
Forests and woodland	thou. sq. km	2	2	2	..	..	..
Deforestation (net)	annual %	..	..	0.0	..	..	..
INCOME							
Household income							
Share of top 20% of households	% of income	..	..	..	..	42	..
Share of bottom 40% of households	"	..	..	..	..	19	..
Share of bottom 20% of households	"	..	..	..	..	8	..
EXPENDITURE							
Food	% of GDP	..	..	43.3	..	..	..
Staples	"	..	..	16.7	..	..	..
Meat, fish, milk, cheese, eggs	"	..	..	17.3	..	..	..
Cereal imports	thou. metric tonnes	15	73	103	20,311	46,537	74,924
Food aid in cereals	"	9	21	11	4,303	9,008	4,054
Food production per capita	1987 = 100	185	89	79	90	123	..
Fertilizer consumption	kg/ha	3.1	15.3	3.3	4.2	61.9	..
Share of agriculture in GDP	% of GDP	31.9	25.4	22.5	18.6	29.6	..
Housing	% of GDP	..	..	7.8	..	..	..
Average household size	persons per household	8.3	..	..	..	..	..
Urban	"	6.1	..	..	..	..	..
Fixed investment: housing	% of GDP	..	..	2.2	..	..	..
Fuel and power	% of GDP	..	..	3.0	..	..	..
Energy consumption per capita	kg of oil equiv.	58	75	60	258	335	1,882
Households with electricity							
Urban	% of households	..	..	..	..	..	..
Rural	"	..	..	..	..	..	..
Transport and communication	% of GDP	..	..	5.2	..	..	..
Fixed investment: transport equipment	"	..	..	2.1	..	..	..
Total road length	thou. km	1	3	3	..	..	..
INVESTMENT IN HUMAN CAPITAL							
Health							
Population per physician	persons	24,500	12,525	..	..	..	..
Population per nurse	"	..	..	..	..	..	..
Population per hospital bed	"	..	613	..	1,329	1,050	516
Oral rehydration therapy (under-5)	% of cases	..	..	48	36	39	..
Education							
Gross enrollment ratio							
Secondary	% of school-age pop.	10	17	18	18	41	..
Female	"	5	10	12	14	35	..
Pupil-teacher ratio: primary	pupils per teacher	26	23	32	39	37	26
Pupil-teacher ratio: secondary	"	20	20	..	..	19	..
Pupils reaching grade 4	% of cohort	96	89	88	..	..	..
Repeater rate: primary	% of total enroll	10	17	18	..	..	..
Illiteracy	% of pop. (age 15+)	..	80	73	51	39	..
Female	% of fem. (age 15+)	..	90	84	62	52	..
Newspaper circulation	per thou. pop.	..	3	2	14	..	100

World Bank International Economics Department, April 1994

125

Georgia

Priority Poverty Indicators

Indicator	Unit of measure	Latest single year 1970-75	Latest single year 1980-85	Most recent estimate 1987-92	Europe & Central Asia	Lower-middle-income	Next higher income group
POVERTY							
Upper poverty line	local curr.	..	..	1,500	..	..	..
Headcount index	% of pop.	..	..	30	..	..	..
Lower poverty line	local curr.	..	..	..	..	..	..
Headcount index	% of pop.	..	..	..	..	..	..
GNP per capita	US$	..	..	850	..	..	3,870
SHORT TERM INCOME INDICATORS							
Unskilled urban wages	local curr.	..	..	..	..	..	..
Unskilled rural wages	"	..	..	..	..	..	..
Rural terms of trade	"	..	..	..	..	..	..
Consumer price index	1987=100	..	..	..	..	..	..
Lower income	"	..	..	..	..	..	..
Food[a]	"	..	..	..	..	..	..
Urban	"	..	..	..	..	..	..
Rural	"	..	..	..	..	..	..
SOCIAL INDICATORS							
Public expenditure on basic social services	% of GDP	..	..	6.2	..	..	..
Gross enrollment ratios							
Primary	% school age pop.	..	..	..	..	..	107
Male	"	..	..	..	..	..	..
Female	"	..	..	..	..	..	..
Mortality							
Infant mortality	per thou. live births	..	26.2	19.0	30.0	45.0	40.0
Under 5 mortality	"	..	..	22.8	38.0	59.0	51.0
Immunization							
Measles	% age group	..	..	..	..	..	82.0
DPT	"	..	..	..	..	..	73.8
Child malnutrition (under-5)	"	..	..	..	..	..	..
Life expectancy							
Total	years	..	71	72	70	68	69
Female advantage	"	..	7.7	7.4	8.6	6.4	6.3
Total fertility rate	births per woman	2.5	2.4	2.2	2.2	3.1	2.9
Maternal mortality rate	per 100,000 live births	..	26	55	58	..	..

Supplementary Poverty Indicators

Indicator	Unit of measure	1970-75	1980-85	1987-92	Europe & Central Asia	Lower-middle-income	Next higher income group
Expenditures on social security	% of total gov't exp.	..	..	..	..	..	..
Social security coverage	% econ. active pop.	..	..	..	..	..	..
Access to safe water: total	% of pop.	..	..	..	..	..	85.6
Urban	"	..	..	..	..	..	94.3
Rural	"	..	..	..	..	..	73.0
Access to health care	"	..	..	..	..	..	..

Population growth rate
(annual average, percent)

GNP per capita growth rate
(annual average, percent)

Development diamond[b]

- Georgia
- Lower-middle-income

a. See the technical notes, p.389. b. The development diamond, based on four key indicators, shows the average level of development in the country compared with its income group. See the introduction.

126

Georgia

Indicator	Unit of measure	Latest single year 1970-75	Latest single year 1980-85	Most recent estimate 1987-92	Same region/income group Europe & Central Asia	Same region/income group Lower-middle-income	Next higher income group

Resources and Expenditures

HUMAN RESOURCES

Indicator	Unit	1970-75	1980-85	1987-92	Europe & Central Asia	Lower-middle-income	Next higher income group
Population (mre=1992)	thousands	..	5,299	5,466	495,241	942,547	477,960
Age dependency ratio	ratio	..	..	0.56	0.56	0.66	0.64
Urban	% of pop.	..	..	56.0	63.3	57.0	71.7
Population growth rate	annual %	..	0.8	-0.2	0.5	1.4	1.6
Urban	"	..	..	..	..	4.8	2.5
Labor force (15-64)	thousands	..	..	2,834	..	..	181,414
Agriculture	% of labor force	..	..	..	..	..	..
Industry	"	..	..	..	..	..	..
Female	"	..	..	47	46	36	29
Females per 100 males							
Urban	number	..	..	..	..	..	..
Rural	"	..	..	..	..	..	..

NATURAL RESOURCES

Indicator	Unit	1970-75	1980-85	1987-92	Europe & Central Asia	Lower-middle-income	Next higher income group
Area	thou. sq. km	..	..	69.70	24,165.06	40,697.37	21,836.02
Density	pop. per sq. km	..	..	78.6	20.4	22.8	21.5
Agricultural land	% of land area	..	..	..	..	..	41.7
Change in agricultural land	annual %	..	..	..	..	..	0.3
Agricultural land under irrigation	%	..	..	..	..	..	9.3
Forests and woodland	thou. sq. km	..	..	..	..	..	..
Deforestation (net)	annual %	..	..	..	..	..	..

INCOME
Household income

Indicator	Unit	1970-75	1980-85	1987-92	Europe & Central Asia	Lower-middle-income	Next higher income group
Share of top 20% of households	% of income	..	..	..	..	..	..
Share of bottom 40% of households	"	..	..	..	..	..	..
Share of bottom 20% of households	"	..	..	..	..	..	..

EXPENDITURE

Indicator	Unit	1970-75	1980-85	1987-92	Europe & Central Asia	Lower-middle-income	Next higher income group
Food	% of GDP	..	..	19.8	..	..	..
Staples	"	..	..	3.6	..	..	..
Meat, fish, milk, cheese, eggs	"	..	..	8.9	..	..	..
Cereal imports	thou. metric tonnes	..	..	500	45,972	74,924	49,174
Food aid in cereals	"	..	..	..	1,639	4,054	282
Food production per capita	1987 = 100	..	..	..	..	..	109
Fertilizer consumption	kg/ha	..	..	..	..	..	68.8
Share of agriculture in GDP	% of GDP	..	24.6	26.8	..	..	8.1
Housing	% of GDP	..	..	4.7	..	..	..
Average household size	persons per household	..	..	4.1	..	..	..
Urban	"	..	..	..	..	..	..
Fixed investment: housing	% of GDP	..	..	4.9	..	..	..
Fuel and power	% of GDP	..	..	1.0	..	..	..
Energy consumption per capita	kg of oil equiv.	..	..	..	3,190	1,882	1,649
Households with electricity							
Urban	% of households	..	..	..	..	..	..
Rural	"	..	..	..	..	..	..
Transport and communication	% of GDP	..	..	6.2	..	..	..
Fixed investment: transport equipment	"	..	..	10.3	..	..	..
Total road length	thou. km	..	32	43	..	..	..

INVESTMENT IN HUMAN CAPITAL

Health

Indicator	Unit	1970-75	1980-85	1987-92	Europe & Central Asia	Lower-middle-income	Next higher income group
Population per physician	persons	..	..	169	378	..	..
Population per nurse	"	..	..	..	..	..	..
Population per hospital bed	"	..	..	90	134	516	385
Oral rehydration therapy (under-5)	% of cases	..	..	..	..	..	54

Education

Gross enrollment ratio

Indicator	Unit	1970-75	1980-85	1987-92	Europe & Central Asia	Lower-middle-income	Next higher income group
Secondary	% of school-age pop.	..	..	..	..	..	53
Female	"	..	..	..	..	..	..
Pupil-teacher ratio: primary	pupils per teacher	..	..	..	..	26	25
Pupil-teacher ratio: secondary	"	..	..	..	..	..	..
Pupils reaching grade 4	% of cohort	..	..	..	..	..	71
Repeater rate: primary	% of total enroll	..	..	..	..	..	11
Illiteracy	% of pop. (age 15+)	..	..	..	..	..	14
Female	% of fem. (age 15+)	..	..	..	..	..	17
Newspaper circulation	per thou. pop.	..	..	..	..	100	117

World Bank International Economics Department, April 1994

Germany

Priority Poverty Indicators

Indicator	Unit of measure	Latest single year 1970-75	Latest single year 1980-85	Most recent estimate 1987-92	Same region/income group High-income
POVERTY					
Upper poverty line	local curr.	..	..	..	..
Headcount index	% of pop.	..	..	..	..
Lower poverty line	local curr.	..	..	..	..
Headcount index	% of pop.	..	..	..	..
GNP per capita*	US$	6,650	10,980	26,180	21,960
SHORT TERM INCOME INDICATORS					
Unskilled urban wages	local curr.	..	..	..	..
Unskilled rural wages	"	..	..	..	..
Rural terms of trade	"	..	..	..	..
Consumer price index	1987=100	68	100	115	..
Lower income	"	..	..	..	..
Food[a]	"	56	100	..	..
Urban	"	..	..	..	..
Rural	"	..	..	..	..
SOCIAL INDICATORS					
Public expenditure on basic social services	% of GDP	..	..	..	..
Gross enrollment ratios*					
Primary	% school age pop.	101	99	107	103
Male	"	101	99	106	103
Female	"	101	99	107	103
Mortality					
Infant mortality	per thou. live births	18.9	9.1	6.2	7.0
Under 5 mortality	"	..	..	8.1	10.0
Immunization					
Measles	% age group	..	40.6	90.0	82.4
DPT	"	..	42.9	80.0	90.1
Child malnutrition (under-5)	"	..	..	..	..
Life expectancy					
Total	years	71	73	76	77
Female advantage	"	6.3	6.6	6.3	6.4
Total fertility rate	births per woman	1.5	1.4	1.3	1.7
Maternal mortality rate	per 100,000 live births	..	11	..	..

Supplementary Poverty Indicators

Indicator	Unit of measure	1970-75	1980-85	1987-92	High-income
Expenditures on social security	% of total gov't exp.	..	..	..	..
Social security coverage	% econ. active pop.	..	..	..	..
Access to safe water: total	% of pop.	..	..	..	..
Urban	"	..	..	..	..
Rural	"	..	..	..	..
Access to health care	"	..	100.0	100.0	..

Population growth rate
(annual average, percent)

GNP per capita growth rate
(annual average, percent)

Development diamond[b]

□ Germany
— High-income

— Germany
— High-income

a. See the technical notes, p.389.   b. The development diamond, based on four key indicators, shows the average level of development in the country compared with its income group. See the introduction.

128

Germany

Indicator	Unit of measure	Latest single year 1970-75	Latest single year 1980-85	Most recent estimate 1987-92	Same region/income group High-income
Resources and Expenditures					
HUMAN RESOURCES					
Population (mre=1992)	thousands	78,679	77,698	80,569	828,221
Age dependency ratio	ratio	0.56	0.44	0.48	0.50
Urban	% of pop.	81.2	84.0	85.7	78.1
Population growth rate	annual %	-0.4	-0.2	0.8	0.7
Urban	"	0.0	0.1	1.0	0.9
Labor force (15-64)	thousands	44,912	48,439	38,674	390,033
Agriculture	% of labor force	9	8	..	..
Industry	"	48	46	..	..
Female	"	41	41	39	38
Females per 100 males					
Urban	number	..	..	..	..
Rural	"	..	..	..	..
NATURAL RESOURCES					
Area	thou. sq. km	356.91	356.91	356.91	31,709.00
Density	pop. per sq. km	220.4	217.7	224.1	24.5
Agricultural land	% of land area	90.1	90.5	90.5	42.7
Change in agricultural land	annual %	0.0	0.5	0.0	-0.2
Agricultural land under irrigation	%	1.4	1.5	1.5	16.1
Forests and woodland	thou. sq. km	73	74	74	..
Deforestation (net)	annual %	..	..	-0.4	..
INCOME					
Household income*					
Share of top 20% of households	% of income	45	7	..	..
Share of bottom 40% of households	"	18	65	..	..
Share of bottom 20% of households	"	7	43	..	..
EXPENDITURE					
Food*	% of GDP	9.9	8.3	..	..
Staples	"	2.0	1.3	..	..
Meat, fish, milk, cheese, eggs	"	3.9	3.9	..	..
Cereal imports	thou. metric tonnes	6,606	6,482	3,313	70,626
Food aid in cereals	"	..	..	..	2
Food production per capita*	1987 = 100	92	109	115	101
Fertilizer consumption	kg/ha	141.2	144.1	130.0	162.1
Share of agriculture in GDP*	% of GDP	2.8	1.8	1.3	2.4
Housing*	% of GDP	9.5	12.7	..	..
Average household size	persons per household	..	..	..	..
Urban	"	..	..	..	..
Fixed investment: housing*	% of GDP	5.2	3.2	..	..
Fuel and power*	% of GDP	2.4	3.7	..	..
Energy consumption per capita*	kg of oil equiv.	4,017	4,631	4,358	5,101
Households with electricity*					
Urban	% of households	..	..	..	..
Rural	"	..	..	..	..
Transport and communication*	% of GDP	7.9	9.1	..	..
Fixed investment: transport equipment*	"	1.7	1.9	..	..
Total road length	thou. km	470	487	501	..
INVESTMENT IN HUMAN CAPITAL					
Health					
Population per physician*	persons	583	433	367	..
Population per nurse	"	..	..	..	..
Population per hospital bed*	"	73	..	118	144
Oral rehydration therapy (under-5)	% of cases	..	..	..	..
Education*					
Gross enrollment ratio					
Secondary	% of school-age pop.	87	94	97	92
Female	"	85	93	103	94
Pupil-teacher ratio: primary	pupils per teacher	24	17	17	18
Pupil-teacher ratio: secondary	"	15	13	12	..
Pupils reaching grade 4	% of cohort	91	94	99	..
Repeater rate: primary	% of total enroll	..	..	..	..
Illiteracy	% of pop. (age 15+)	..	..	..	..
Female	% of fem. (age 15+)	..	..	..	..
Newspaper circulation	per thou. pop.	423	552	..	..

World Bank International Economics Department, April 1994

* Data refer to Federal Republic of Germany before unification.

Ghana

Indicator	Unit of measure	Latest single year 1970-75	Latest single year 1980-85	Most recent estimate 1987-92	Same region/income group Sub-Saharan Africa	Same region/income group Low-income	Next higher income group
Priority Poverty Indicators							
POVERTY							
Upper poverty line	local curr.	..	..	32,981	..	..	..
Headcount index	% of pop.	..	..	36	..	19	..
Lower poverty line	local curr.	..	..	16,491	..	..	..
Headcount index	% of pop.	..	..	7	..	..	..
GNP per capita	US$	280	370	450	520	390	..
SHORT TERM INCOME INDICATORS							
Unskilled urban wages	local curr.	..	..	..	..	..	..
Unskilled rural wages	"	..	..	..	..	..	..
Rural terms of trade	"	..	..	..	..	..	..
Consumer price index	1987=100	0	57	293	..	..	..
Lower income	"	..	..	..	..	..	..
Food[a]	"	..	60	283	..	..	..
Urban	"	..	..	..	..	..	..
Rural	"	..	..	..	..	..	..
SOCIAL INDICATORS							
Public expenditure on basic social services	% of GDP	6.3	3.2	7.4	..	..	..
Gross enrollment ratios							
Primary	% school age pop.	71	76	77	66	103	..
Male	"	80	85	84	79	113	..
Female	"	62	66	69	62	96	..
Mortality							
Infant mortality	per thou. live births	107.0	98.0	81.0	99.0	73.0	45.0
Under 5 mortality	"	..	..	129.1	169.0	108.0	59.0
Immunization							
Measles	% age group	..	..	39.0	54.0	72.7	..
DPT	"	..	22.0	43.0	54.6	80.6	..
Child malnutrition (under-5)	"	..	..	27.1	28.4	38.3	..
Life expectancy							
Total	years	50	52	56	52	62	68
Female advantage	"	3.4	3.5	3.6	3.4	2.4	6.4
Total fertility rate	births per woman	6.6	6.5	6.1	6.1	3.4	3.1
Maternal mortality rate	per 100,000 live births	..	413	1000	..	..	..
Supplementary Poverty Indicators							
Expenditures on social security	% of total gov't exp.	6.9	4.0	6.4	..	..	..
Social security coverage	% econ. active pop.	..	..	..	..	..	..
Access to safe water: total	% of pop.	35.0	56.0	..	41.1	68.4	..
Urban	"	86.0	93.0	..	77.8	78.9	..
Rural	"	14.0	39.0	..	27.3	60.3	..
Access to health care	"	..	64.0	25.0	..	..	..

Population growth rate
(annual average, percent)

GNP per capita growth rate
(annual average, percent)

Development diamond[b]

Life expectancy

GNP per capita — Gross primary enrollment

Access to safe water

— Ghana
— Low-income

a. See the technical notes, p.389.   b. The development diamond, based on four key indicators, shows the average level of development in the country compared with its income group. See the introduction.

130

Ghana

Indicator	Unit of measure	Latest single year 1970-75	Latest single year 1980-85	Most recent estimate 1987-92	Same region/income group Sub-Saharan Africa	Same region/income group Low-income	Next higher income group
Resources and Expenditures							
HUMAN RESOURCES							
Population (mre=1992)	thousands	9,835	12,620	15,788	546,390	3,194,535	942,547
Age dependency ratio	ratio	0.93	0.98	0.98	0.95	0.67	0.66
Urban	% of pop.	30.1	32.3	34.9	29.5	26.7	57.0
Population growth rate	annual %	2.2	3.7	3.0	2.9	1.8	1.4
Urban	"	2.9	4.3	4.3	5.1	3.4	4.8
Labor force (15-64)	thousands	3,813	4,963	6,048	224,025	1,478,954	..
Agriculture	% of labor force	57	56	..	..	..	..
Industry	"	17	18	..	..	..	..
Female	"	42	41	40	37	33	36
Females per 100 males							
Urban	number	..	..	..	..	..	..
Rural	"	..	..	..	..	..	..
NATURAL RESOURCES							
Area	thou. sq. km	238.54	238.54	238.54	24,274.03	38,401.06	40,697.37
Density	pop. per sq. km	41.2	52.9	64.2	21.9	81.7	22.8
Agricultural land	% of land area	34.8	33.8	34.0	52.7	50.9	..
Change in agricultural land	annual %	-0.4	0.0	0.1	0.1	0.0	..
Agricultural land under irrigation	%	0.1	0.1	0.1	0.8	18.2	..
Forests and woodland	thou. sq. km	91	84	80	..	..	..
Deforestation (net)	annual %	..	..	1.3	..	..	..
INCOME							
Household income							
Share of top 20% of households	% of income	..	..	44	..	42	..
Share of bottom 40% of households	"	..	..	18	..	19	..
Share of bottom 20% of households	"	..	..	7	..	8	..
EXPENDITURE							
Food	% of GDP	39.3	..	40.2	..	..	..
Staples	"	..	..	8.6	..	..	..
Meat, fish, milk, cheese, eggs	"	..	..	20.0	..	..	..
Cereal imports	thou. metric tonnes	85	137	319	20,311	46,537	74,924
Food aid in cereals	"	33	96	184	4,303	9,008	4,054
Food production per capita	1987 = 100	133	97	97	90	123	..
Fertilizer consumption	kg/ha	3.1	1.6	1.0	4.2	61.9	..
Share of agriculture in GDP	% of GDP	47.7	44.9	48.6	18.6	29.6	..
Housing	% of GDP	8.4	..	5.6	..	..	..
Average household size	persons per household	4.7	..	..	..	..	..
Urban	"	..	..	..	..	..	..
Fixed investment: housing	% of GDP	..	..	0.4	..	..	..
Fuel and power	% of GDP	..	..	2.3	..	..	..
Energy consumption per capita	kg of oil equiv.	125	78	96	258	335	1,882
Households with electricity							
Urban	% of households	..	..	..	..	..	..
Rural	"	..	..	..	..	..	..
Transport and communication	% of GDP	2.4	..	3.5	..	..	..
Fixed investment: transport equipment	"	1.8	1.2	2.1	..	..	..
Total road length	thou. km	31	35	36	..	..	..
INVESTMENT IN HUMAN CAPITAL							
Health							
Population per physician	persons	12,900	14,894	22,970	..	..	..
Population per nurse	"	693	640	1,669	..	..	..
Population per hospital bed	"	800	638	685	1,329	1,050	516
Oral rehydration therapy (under-5)	% of cases	..	..	21	36	39	..
Education							
Gross enrollment ratio							
Secondary	% of school-age pop.	37	40	38	18	41	..
Female	"	28	31	29	14	35	..
Pupil-teacher ratio: primary	pupils per teacher	30	23	29	39	37	26
Pupil-teacher ratio: secondary	"	23	20	19	..	19	..
Pupils reaching grade 4	% of cohort	82	75	..	..	..	..
Repeater rate: primary	% of total enroll	2	2	..	..	..	..
Illiteracy	% of pop. (age 15+)	70	47	40	51	39	..
Female	% of fem. (age 15+)	..	58	49	62	52	..
Newspaper circulation	per thou. pop.	51	38	13	14	..	100

World Bank International Economics Department, April 1994

Greece

Indicator	Unit of measure	Latest single year 1970-75	Latest single year 1980-85	Most recent estimate 1987-92	Same region/income group Europe & Central Asia	Same region/income group Upper-middle-income	Next higher income group
Priority Poverty Indicators							
POVERTY							
Upper poverty line	local curr.	..	..	..	..	..	..
Headcount index	% of pop.	..	..	..	..	..	..
Lower poverty line	local curr.	..	..	..	..	..	..
Headcount index	% of pop.	..	..	..	..	..	..
GNP per capita	US$	2,370	3,650	7,290	..	3,870	21,960
SHORT TERM INCOME INDICATORS							
Unskilled urban wages	local curr.	..	..	..	..	..	..
Unskilled rural wages	"	..	..	..	..	..	..
Rural terms of trade	"	..	..	..	..	..	..
Consumer price index	1987=100	13	70	215	..	..	..
Lower income	"	..	..	..	..	..	..
Food[a]	"	5	74	187	..	..	..
Urban	"	..	..	..	..	..	..
Rural	"	..	..	..	..	..	..
SOCIAL INDICATORS							
Public expenditure on basic social services	% of GDP	..	..	..	..	..	..
Gross enrollment ratios							
Primary	% school age pop.	104	104	97	..	107	103
Male	"	105	104	97	..	..	103
Female	"	104	104	98	..	..	103
Mortality							
Infant mortality	per thou. live births	24.0	14.1	8.2	30.0	40.0	7.0
Under 5 mortality	"	..	..	10.4	38.0	51.0	10.0
Immunization							
Measles	% age group	..	77.0	76.0	..	82.0	82.4
DPT	"	..	54.0	54.0	..	73.8	90.1
Child malnutrition (under-5)	"	..	..	..	..	..	..
Life expectancy							
Total	years	72	75	77	70	69	77
Female advantage	"	3.6	5.0	5.5	8.6	6.3	6.4
Total fertility rate	births per woman	2.4	1.7	1.4	2.2	2.9	1.7
Maternal mortality rate	per 100,000 live births	..	12	..	58	..	..
Supplementary Poverty Indicators							
Expenditures on social security	% of total gov't exp.	..	..	..	..	..	..
Social security coverage	% econ. active pop.	..	..	..	..	..	..
Access to safe water: total	% of pop.	65.0	..	..	..	85.6	..
Urban	"	88.0	..	..	..	94.3	..
Rural	"	37.0	..	..	..	73.0	..
Access to health care	"	..	..	..	..	..	..

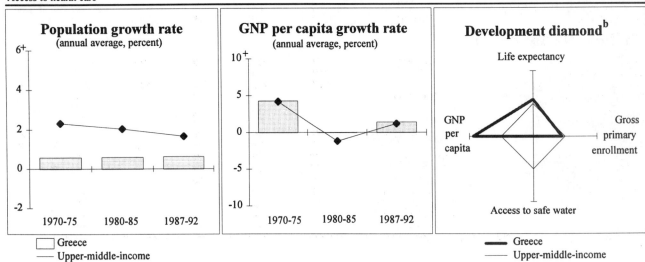

a. See the technical notes, p.389.   b. The development diamond, based on four key indicators, shows the average level of development in the country compared with its income group. See the introduction.

Greece

Indicator	Unit of measure	Latest single year 1970-75	Latest single year 1980-85	Most recent estimate 1987-92	Same region/income group Europe & Central Asia	Same region/income group Upper-middle-income	Next higher income group
Resources and Expenditures							
HUMAN RESOURCES							
Population (mre=1992)	thousands	9,047	9,934	10,300	495,241	477,960	828,221
Age dependency ratio	ratio	0.57	0.52	0.51	0.56	0.64	0.50
Urban	% of pop.	55.3	60.0	63.5	63.3	71.7	78.1
Population growth rate	annual %	0.9	0.4	1.0	0.5	1.6	0.7
Urban	"	2.0	1.2	1.8	..	2.5	0.9
Labor force (15-64)	thousands	3,460	3,780	3,871	..	181,414	390,033
Agriculture	% of labor force	37	31	..	..	..	..
Industry	"	28	29	..	..	..	..
Female	"	26	26	27	46	29	38
Females per 100 males							
Urban	number	105	107	..	..	..	..
Rural	"	108	99	..	..	..	..
NATURAL RESOURCES							
Area	thou. sq. km	131.99	131.99	131.99	24,165.06	21,836.02	31,709.00
Density	pop. per sq. km	68.5	75.3	77.3	20.4	21.5	24.5
Agricultural land	% of land area	70.7	71.3	71.1	..	41.7	42.7
Change in agricultural land	annual %	-0.3	-0.1	0.1	..	0.3	-0.2
Agricultural land under irrigation	%	9.6	12.0	13.1	..	9.3	16.1
Forests and woodland	thou. sq. km	26	26	26	..	..	..
Deforestation (net)	annual %	..	..	0.0	..	..	..
INCOME							
Household income							
Share of top 20% of households	% of income	..	..	..	..	..	..
Share of bottom 40% of households	"	..	..	..	..	..	..
Share of bottom 20% of households	"	..	..	..	..	..	..
EXPENDITURE							
Food	% of GDP	..	20.2	..	..	..	..
Staples	"	..	2.2	..	..	..	..
Meat, fish, milk, cheese, eggs	"	..	9.8	..	..	..	..
Cereal imports	thou. metric tonnes	1,013	453	517	45,972	49,174	70,626
Food aid in cereals	"	..	..	..	1,639	282	2
Food production per capita	1987 = 100	99	106	103	..	109	101
Fertilizer consumption	kg/ha	50.8	74.5	70.4	..	68.8	162.1
Share of agriculture in GDP	% of GDP	16.5	15.5	15.2	..	8.1	2.4
Housing	% of GDP	..	7.9	..	..	..	..
Average household size	persons per household	3.0	..	..	..	..	..
Urban	"	3.0	..	..	..	..	..
Fixed investment: housing	% of GDP	5.6	0.9	..	..	..	..
Fuel and power	% of GDP	..	2.2	..	..	..	..
Energy consumption per capita	kg of oil equiv.	1,344	1,870	2,173	3,190	1,649	5,101
Households with electricity							
Urban	% of households	..	..	..	..	..	..
Rural	"	..	..	..	..	..	..
Transport and communication	% of GDP	..	8.4	..	..	..	..
Fixed investment: transport equipment	"	1.6	2.2	..	..	..	..
Total road length	thou. km	37	38	38	..	..	..
INVESTMENT IN HUMAN CAPITAL							
Health							
Population per physician	persons	600	351	579	378	..	..
Population per nurse	"	990	454	..	..	..	..
Population per hospital bed	"	200	162	196	134	385	144
Oral rehydration therapy (under-5)	% of cases	..	..	..	..	54	..
Education							
Gross enrollment ratio							
Secondary	% of school-age pop.	78	90	98	..	53	92
Female	"	69	89	94	..	..	94
Pupil-teacher ratio: primary	pupils per teacher	30	23	20	..	25	18
Pupil-teacher ratio: secondary	"	28	17	15	..	..	..
Pupils reaching grade 4	% of cohort	96	100	100	..	71	..
Repeater rate: primary	% of total enroll	3	0	0	..	11	..
Illiteracy	% of pop. (age 15+)	16	9	7	..	14	..
Female	% of fem. (age 15+)	..	14	11	..	17	..
Newspaper circulation	per thou. pop.	103	119	140	..	117	..

World Bank International Economics Department, April 1994

Grenada

Indicator	Unit of measure	Latest single year		Most recent estimate 1987-92	Same region/income group		Next higher income group
		1970-75	1980-85		Latin America Caribbean	Lower-middle-income	

Priority Poverty Indicators

POVERTY
Indicator	Unit of measure	1970-75	1980-85	1987-92	Latin America Caribbean	Lower-middle-income	Next higher
Upper poverty line	local curr.	..	..	..	..	..	..
Headcount index	% of pop.	..	..	..	..	..	..
Lower poverty line	local curr.	..	..	..	..	..	..
Headcount index	% of pop.	..	..	..	..	..	..
GNP per capita	US$	..	..	2,310	2,690	..	3,870

SHORT TERM INCOME INDICATORS
Unskilled urban wages	local curr.	..	..	..	..	..	..
Unskilled rural wages	"	..	..	..	..	..	..
Rural terms of trade	"	..	..	..	..	..	..
Consumer price index	1987=100	..	100	120	..	..	..
Lower income	"	..	..	..	..	..	..
Food[a]	"	..	98	84	..	..	..
Urban	"	..	..	..	..	..	..
Rural	"	..	..	..	..	..	..

SOCIAL INDICATORS
Public expenditure on basic social services	% of GDP	..	..	..	..	..	..
Gross enrollment ratios							
Primary	% school age pop.	..	..	..	106	..	107
Male	"	..	..	..	..	..	..
Female	"	..	..	..	..	..	..
Mortality							
Infant mortality	per thou. live births	41.0	39.0	28.6	44.0	45.0	40.0
Under 5 mortality	"	..	..	35.2	56.0	59.0	51.0
Immunization							
Measles	% age group	..	31.0	85.0	78.9	..	82.0
DPT	"	..	76.0	80.0	73.8	..	73.8
Child malnutrition (under-5)	"	..	..	..	10.5	..	..
Life expectancy							
Total	years	65	67	71	68	68	69
Female advantage	"	4.7	4.0	6.0	5.6	6.4	6.3
Total fertility rate	births per woman	4.5	3.6	2.9	3.0	3.1	2.9
Maternal mortality rate	per 100,000 live births	..	..	..	..	..	..

Supplementary Poverty Indicators

Expenditures on social security	% of total gov't exp.	..	..	..	..	..	..
Social security coverage	% econ. active pop.	..	..	..	..	..	..
Access to safe water: total	% of pop.	83.0	..	..	80.3	..	85.6
Urban	"	100.0	..	..	91.0	..	94.3
Rural	"	77.0	..	..	64.3	..	73.0
Access to health care	"	..	..	..	..	..	..

Population growth rate
(annual average, percent)

GNP per capita growth rate
(annual average, percent)

Development diamond[b]

Life expectancy

GNP per capita — Gross primary enrollment

Access to safe water

□ Grenada
— Lower-middle-income

■ Grenada
— Lower-middle-income

a. See the technical notes, p.389. b. The development diamond, based on four key indicators, shows the average level of development in the country compared with its income group. See the introduction.

Grenada

Indicator	Unit of measure	Latest single year 1970-75	Latest single year 1980-85	Most recent estimate 1987-92	Same region/income group Latin America Caribbean	Same region/income group Lower-middle-income	Next higher income group
Resources and Expenditures							
HUMAN RESOURCES							
Population (mre=1992)	thousands	97	94	91	453,294	942,547	477,960
Age dependency ratio	ratio	..	0.71	0.76	0.67	0.66	0.64
Urban	% of pop.	..	..	..	72.9	57.0	71.7
Population growth rate	annual %	..	0.9	0.0	1.7	1.4	1.6
Urban	"	..	..	..	2.6	4.8	2.5
Labor force (15-64)	thousands	..	..	..	166,091	..	181,414
Agriculture	% of labor force	..	..	..	..	..	..
Industry	"	..	..	..	..	..	..
Female	"	..	..	..	27	36	29
Females per 100 males							
Urban	number	..	..	..	..	..	..
Rural	"	..	..	..	..	..	..
NATURAL RESOURCES							
Area	thou. sq. km	0.34	0.34	0.34	20,507.48	40,697.37	21,836.02
Density	pop. per sq. km	283.8	276.2	267.7	21.7	22.8	21.5
Agricultural land	% of land area	50.0	44.1	38.2	40.2	..	41.7
Change in agricultural land	annual %	0.0	0.0	-7.1	0.5	..	0.3
Agricultural land under irrigation	%	..	..	..	3.2	..	9.3
Forests and woodland	thou. sq. km	0	0	0	..	..	..
Deforestation (net)	annual %	..	..	..	..	..	..
INCOME							
Household income							
Share of top 20% of households	% of income	..	..	..	..	..	..
Share of bottom 40% of households	"	..	..	..	..	..	..
Share of bottom 20% of households	"	..	..	..	..	..	..
EXPENDITURE							
Food	% of GDP	..	28.6	..	..	..	..
Staples	"	..	5.9	..	..	..	..
Meat, fish, milk, cheese, eggs	"	..	11.7	..	..	..	..
Cereal imports	thou. metric tonnes	8	9	17	25,032	74,924	49,174
Food aid in cereals	"	0	0	5	1,779	4,054	282
Food production per capita	1987 = 100	85	83	75	104	..	109
Fertilizer consumption	kg/ha	..	..	..	15.5	..	68.8
Share of agriculture in GDP	% of GDP	..	14.2	11.9	8.9	..	8.1
Housing	% of GDP	..	15.1	..	..	..	..
Average household size	persons per household	..	..	..	..	..	..
Urban	"	..	..	..	..	..	..
Fixed investment: housing	% of GDP	..	3.8	..	..	..	..
Fuel and power	% of GDP	..	3.0	..	..	..	..
Energy consumption per capita	kg of oil equiv.	..	224	286	912	1,882	1,649
Households with electricity							
Urban	% of households	..	..	..	..	..	..
Rural	"	..	..	..	..	..	..
Transport and communication	% of GDP	..	8.1	..	..	..	..
Fixed investment: transport equipment	"	..	7.2	..	..	..	..
Total road length	thou. km	..	..	..	..	..	..
INVESTMENT IN HUMAN CAPITAL							
Health							
Population per physician	persons	2,924	2,116	..	..	..	..
Population per nurse	"	..	..	..	..	..	..
Population per hospital bed	"	139	168	..	508	516	385
Oral rehydration therapy (under-5)	% of cases	..	..	70	62	..	54
Education							
Gross enrollment ratio							
Secondary	% of school-age pop.	..	..	..	47	..	53
Female	"	..	..	..	..	..	..
Pupil-teacher ratio: primary	pupils per teacher	37	27	28	25	26	25
Pupil-teacher ratio: secondary	"	21	21	21	..	..	..
Pupils reaching grade 4	% of cohort	..	91	..	..	..	71
Repeater rate: primary	% of total enroll	6	12	..	14	..	11
Illiteracy	% of pop. (age 15+)	2	..	..	15	..	14
Female	% of fem. (age 15+)	..	..	..	17	..	17
Newspaper circulation	per thou. pop.	27	..	..	99	100	117

World Bank International Economics Department, April 1994

135

Guadeloupe

Indicator	Unit of measure	Latest single year		Most recent estimate	Same region/income group		Next higher income group
		1970-75	1980-85	1987-92	Latin America Caribbean	Upper-middle-income	
Priority Poverty Indicators							
POVERTY							
Upper poverty line	local curr.	..	..	..	..	..	..
Headcount index	% of pop.	..	..	..	..	..	..
Lower poverty line	local curr.	..	..	..	..	..	..
Headcount index	% of pop.	..	..	..	..	..	..
GNP per capita	US$	..	..	..	2,690	3,870	21,960
SHORT TERM INCOME INDICATORS							
Unskilled urban wages	local curr.	..	..	..	..	..	..
Unskilled rural wages	"	..	..	..	..	..	..
Rural terms of trade	"	..	..	..	..	..	..
Consumer price index	1987=100	..	..	..	..	..	..
Lower income	"	..	..	..	..	..	..
Food[a]	"	20	94	107	..	..	..
Urban	"	..	..	..	..	..	..
Rural	"	..	..	..	..	..	..
SOCIAL INDICATORS							
Public expenditure on basic social services	% of GDP	..	..	..	..	..	..
Gross enrollment ratios							
Primary	% school age pop.	..	..	..	106	107	103
Male	"	..	..	..	..	..	103
Female	"	..	..	..	..	..	103
Mortality							
Infant mortality	per thou. live births	42.0	15.0	12.0	44.0	40.0	7.0
Under 5 mortality	"	..	..	14.8	56.0	51.0	10.0
Immunization							
Measles	% age group	..	..	..	78.9	82.0	82.4
DPT	"	..	..	..	73.8	73.8	90.1
Child malnutrition (under-5)	"	..	..	..	10.5	..	..
Life expectancy							
Total	years	68	72	74	68	69	77
Female advantage	"	6.2	7.3	6.9	5.6	6.3	6.4
Total fertility rate	births per woman	4.5	2.6	2.2	3.0	2.9	1.7
Maternal mortality rate	per 100,000 live births	..	..	..	..	..	..
Supplementary Poverty Indicators							
Expenditures on social security	% of total gov't exp.	..	..	..	..	..	..
Social security coverage	% econ. active pop.	..	..	..	..	..	..
Access to safe water: total	% of pop.	..	..	..	80.3	85.6	..
Urban	"	..	..	..	91.0	94.3	..
Rural	"	..	..	..	64.3	73.0	..
Access to health care	"	..	..	..	..	..	..

Population growth rate
(annual average, percent)

Legend: Guadeloupe; Upper-middle-income

GNP per capita growth rate
(annual average, percent)

Development diamond[b]

Life expectancy — GNP per capita — Gross primary enrollment — Access to safe water

Legend: Guadeloupe; Upper-middle-income

a. See the technical notes, p.389. b. The development diamond, based on four key indicators, shows the average level of development in the country compared with its income group. See the introduction.

Guadeloupe

Indicator	Unit of measure	Latest single year 1970-75	Latest single year 1980-85	Most recent estimate 1987-92	Same region/income group Latin America Caribbean	Same region/income group Upper-middle-income	Next higher income group

Resources and Expenditures

HUMAN RESOURCES

Indicator	Unit	1970-75	1980-85	1987-92	Latin America Caribbean	Upper-middle-income	Next higher income group
Population (mre=1992)	thousands	329	355	400	453,294	477,960	828,221
Age dependency ratio	ratio	0.92	0.56	0.55	0.67	0.64	0.50
Urban	% of pop.	41.8	45.7	49.6	72.9	71.7	78.1
Population growth rate	annual %	0.1	2.0	1.3	1.7	1.6	0.7
Urban	"	0.7	2.9	2.4	2.6	2.5	0.9
Labor force (15-64)	thousands	113	148	160	166,091	181,414	390,033
Agriculture	% of labor force	22	15	..	..	..	..
Industry	"	22	20	..	..	..	..
Female	"	40	43	44	27	29	38
Females per 100 males							
Urban	number	..	..	..	..	..	..
Rural	"	..	..	..	..	..	..

NATURAL RESOURCES

Indicator	Unit	1970-75	1980-85	1987-92	Latin America Caribbean	Upper-middle-income	Next higher income group
Area	thou. sq. km	1.71	1.71	1.71	20,507.48	21,836.02	31,709.00
Density	pop. per sq. km	192.4	207.6	231.0	21.7	21.5	24.5
Agricultural land	% of land area	34.9	34.3	32.0	40.2	41.7	42.7
Change in agricultural land	annual %	7.3	0.0	0.0	0.5	0.3	-0.2
Agricultural land under irrigation	%	1.7	5.2	5.6	3.2	9.3	16.1
Forests and woodland	thou. sq. km	1	1	1	..	..	..
Deforestation (net)	annual %	..	..	..	..	..	..

INCOME

Indicator	Unit	1970-75	1980-85	1987-92	Latin America Caribbean	Upper-middle-income	Next higher income group
Household income							
Share of top 20% of households	% of income	..	..	..	..	..	..
Share of bottom 40% of households	"	..	..	..	..	..	..
Share of bottom 20% of households	"	..	..	..	..	..	..

EXPENDITURE

Indicator	Unit	1970-75	1980-85	1987-92	Latin America Caribbean	Upper-middle-income	Next higher income group
Food	% of GDP	..	..	..	..	..	..
Staples	"	..	..	..	..	..	..
Meat, fish, milk, cheese, eggs	"	..	..	..	..	..	..
Cereal imports	thou. metric tonnes	79	97	86	25,032	49,174	70,626
Food aid in cereals	"	..	..	..	1,779	282	2
Food production per capita	1987 = 100	114	95	80	104	109	101
Fertilizer consumption	kg/ha	166.7	163.2	163.0	15.5	68.8	162.1
Share of agriculture in GDP	% of GDP	..	..	..	8.9	8.1	2.4
Housing	% of GDP	..	..	..	..	..	..
Average household size	persons per household	..	..	..	..	..	..
Urban	"	..	..	..	..	..	..
Fixed investment: housing	% of GDP	..	..	..	..	..	..
Fuel and power	% of GDP	..	..	..	..	..	..
Energy consumption per capita	kg of oil equiv.	413	665	643	912	1,649	5,101
Households with electricity							
Urban	% of households	..	..	..	..	..	..
Rural	"	..	..	..	..	..	..
Transport and communication	% of GDP	..	..	..	..	..	..
Fixed investment: transport equipment	"	..	..	..	..	..	..
Total road length	thou. km	..	..	..	..	..	..

INVESTMENT IN HUMAN CAPITAL

Indicator	Unit	1970-75	1980-85	1987-92	Latin America Caribbean	Upper-middle-income	Next higher income group
Health							
Population per physician	persons	1,839	758	..	..	..	..
Population per nurse	"	87	..	..	..	..	..
Population per hospital bed	"	90	..	..	508	385	144
Oral rehydration therapy (under-5)	% of cases	..	..	..	62	54	..
Education							
Gross enrollment ratio							
Secondary	% of school-age pop.	..	..	..	47	53	92
Female	"	..	..	..	..	..	94
Pupil-teacher ratio: primary	pupils per teacher	31	22	19	25	25	18
Pupil-teacher ratio: secondary	"	19	14	..	..	..	..
Pupils reaching grade 4	% of cohort	..	96	..	..	71	..
Repeater rate: primary	% of total enroll	20	..	9	14	11	..
Illiteracy	% of pop. (age 15+)	..	10	..	15	14	..
Female	% of fem. (age 15+)	..	..	..	17	17	..
Newspaper circulation	per thou. pop.	73	92	51	99	117	..

World Bank International Economics Department, April 1994

Guatemala

Indicator	Unit of measure	Latest single year 1970-75	Latest single year 1980-85	Most recent estimate 1987-92	Same region/income group Latin America Caribbean	Same region/income group Lower-middle-income	Next higher income group
Priority Poverty Indicators							
POVERTY							
Upper poverty line	local curr.	..	..	..	..	..	..
Headcount index	% of pop.	..	..	..	..	..	..
Lower poverty line	local curr.	..	..	..	..	..	..
Headcount index	% of pop.	..	..	..	..	..	..
GNP per capita	US$	570	1,200	980	2,690	..	3,870
SHORT TERM INCOME INDICATORS							
Unskilled urban wages	local curr.	..	..	..	..	..	..
Unskilled rural wages	"	..	..	..	..	..	..
Rural terms of trade	"	..	..	..	..	..	..
Consumer price index	1987=100	27	65	255	..	..	..
Lower income	"	..	..	..	..	..	..
Food[a]	"	..	62	249	..	..	..
Urban	"	..	..	..	..	..	..
Rural	"	..	..	..	..	..	..
SOCIAL INDICATORS							
Public expenditure on basic social services	% of GDP	..	..	..	..	..	..
Gross enrollment ratios							
Primary	% school age pop.	61	76	79	106	..	107
Male	"	67	83	84	..	..	..
Female	"	56	70	73	..	..	..
Mortality							
Infant mortality	per thou. live births	95.0	73.0	62.0	44.0	45.0	40.0
Under 5 mortality	"	..	..	80.1	56.0	59.0	51.0
Immunization							
Measles	% age group	..	27.0	48.0	78.9	..	82.0
DPT	"	..	54.0	63.0	73.8	..	73.8
Child malnutrition (under-5)	"	..	..	28.5	10.5	..	..
Life expectancy							
Total	years	54	59	65	68	68	69
Female advantage	"	2.9	4.5	4.9	5.6	6.4	6.3
Total fertility rate	births per woman	6.7	5.6	5.1	3.0	3.1	2.9
Maternal mortality rate	per 100,000 live births	..	300	..	..	..	..
Supplementary Poverty Indicators							
Expenditures on social security	% of total gov't exp.	..	..	..	..	..	..
Social security coverage	% econ. active pop.	..	..	27.0	..	..	..
Access to safe water: total	% of pop.	39.0	58.0	61.0	80.3	..	85.6
Urban	"	85.0	89.0	91.0	91.0	..	94.3
Rural	"	14.0	..	41.0	64.3	..	73.0
Access to health care	"	..	59.0	60.0	..	..	..

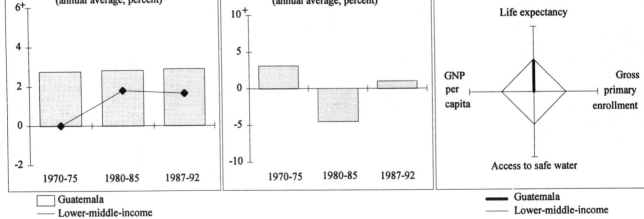

Population growth rate
(annual average, percent)

GNP per capita growth rate
(annual average, percent)

Development diamond[b]

Life expectancy — GNP per capita — Gross primary enrollment — Access to safe water

□ Guatemala
— Lower-middle-income

━ Guatemala
— Lower-middle-income

a. See the technical notes, p.389.   b. The development diamond, based on four key indicators, shows the average level of development in the country compared with its income group. See the introduction.

138

Guatemala

<table>
<tr><td rowspan="3">Indicator</td><td rowspan="3">Unit of measure</td><td colspan="2">Latest single year</td><td rowspan="3">Most recent estimate 1987-92</td><td colspan="2">Same region/income group</td><td rowspan="3">Next higher income group</td></tr>
<tr><td rowspan="2">1970-75</td><td rowspan="2">1980-85</td><td>Latin America Caribbean</td><td>Lower-middle-income</td></tr>
<tr></tr>
<tr><td colspan="8" align="center">Resources and Expenditures</td></tr>
<tr><td colspan="8">HUMAN RESOURCES</td></tr>
<tr><td>Population (mre=1992)</td><td>thousands</td><td>6,023</td><td>7,963</td><td>9,742</td><td>453,294</td><td>942,547</td><td>477,960</td></tr>
<tr><td>Age dependency ratio</td><td>ratio</td><td>0.94</td><td>0.95</td><td>0.93</td><td>0.67</td><td>0.66</td><td>0.64</td></tr>
<tr><td>Urban</td><td>% of pop.</td><td>36.7</td><td>38.1</td><td>40.2</td><td>72.9</td><td>57.0</td><td>71.7</td></tr>
<tr><td>Population growth rate</td><td>annual %</td><td>2.8</td><td>2.9</td><td>2.9</td><td>1.7</td><td>1.4</td><td>1.6</td></tr>
<tr><td>Urban</td><td>"</td><td>3.4</td><td>3.2</td><td>3.9</td><td>2.6</td><td>4.8</td><td>2.5</td></tr>
<tr><td>Labor force (15-64)</td><td>thousands</td><td>1,775</td><td>2,261</td><td>2,816</td><td>166,091</td><td>..</td><td>181,414</td></tr>
<tr><td>Agriculture</td><td>% of labor force</td><td>59</td><td>57</td><td>..</td><td>..</td><td>..</td><td>..</td></tr>
<tr><td>Industry</td><td>"</td><td>17</td><td>17</td><td>..</td><td>..</td><td>..</td><td>..</td></tr>
<tr><td>Female</td><td>"</td><td>13</td><td>15</td><td>17</td><td>27</td><td>36</td><td>29</td></tr>
<tr><td>Females per 100 males</td><td></td><td></td><td></td><td></td><td></td><td></td><td></td></tr>
<tr><td>Urban</td><td>number</td><td>108</td><td>115</td><td>..</td><td>..</td><td>..</td><td>..</td></tr>
<tr><td>Rural</td><td>"</td><td>92</td><td>98</td><td>..</td><td>..</td><td>..</td><td>..</td></tr>
<tr><td colspan="8">NATURAL RESOURCES</td></tr>
<tr><td>Area</td><td>thou. sq. km</td><td>108.89</td><td>108.89</td><td>108.89</td><td>20,507.48</td><td>40,697.37</td><td>21,836.02</td></tr>
<tr><td>Density</td><td>pop. per sq. km</td><td>55.3</td><td>73.1</td><td>86.9</td><td>21.7</td><td>22.8</td><td>21.5</td></tr>
<tr><td>Agricultural land</td><td>% of land area</td><td>26.6</td><td>29.4</td><td>30.4</td><td>40.2</td><td>..</td><td>41.7</td></tr>
<tr><td>Change in agricultural land</td><td>annual %</td><td>0.5</td><td>1.0</td><td>0.3</td><td>0.5</td><td>..</td><td>0.3</td></tr>
<tr><td>Agricultural land under irrigation</td><td>%</td><td>2.1</td><td>2.4</td><td>2.4</td><td>3.2</td><td>..</td><td>9.3</td></tr>
<tr><td>Forests and woodland</td><td>thou. sq. km</td><td>50</td><td>42</td><td>37</td><td>..</td><td>..</td><td>..</td></tr>
<tr><td>Deforestation (net)</td><td>annual %</td><td>..</td><td>..</td><td>1.7</td><td>..</td><td>..</td><td>..</td></tr>
<tr><td colspan="8">INCOME</td></tr>
<tr><td>Household income</td><td></td><td></td><td></td><td></td><td></td><td></td><td></td></tr>
<tr><td>Share of top 20% of households</td><td>% of income</td><td>60</td><td>55</td><td>63</td><td>..</td><td>..</td><td>..</td></tr>
<tr><td>Share of bottom 40% of households</td><td>"</td><td>13</td><td>14</td><td>8</td><td>..</td><td>..</td><td>..</td></tr>
<tr><td>Share of bottom 20% of households</td><td>"</td><td>5</td><td>6</td><td>2</td><td>..</td><td>..</td><td>..</td></tr>
<tr><td colspan="8">EXPENDITURE</td></tr>
<tr><td>Food</td><td>% of GDP</td><td>..</td><td>29.2</td><td>..</td><td>..</td><td>..</td><td>..</td></tr>
<tr><td>Staples</td><td>"</td><td>..</td><td>8.4</td><td>..</td><td>..</td><td>..</td><td>..</td></tr>
<tr><td>Meat, fish, milk, cheese, eggs</td><td>"</td><td>..</td><td>12.3</td><td>..</td><td>..</td><td>..</td><td>..</td></tr>
<tr><td>Cereal imports</td><td>thou. metric tonnes</td><td>151</td><td>140</td><td>329</td><td>25,032</td><td>74,924</td><td>49,174</td></tr>
<tr><td>Food aid in cereals</td><td>"</td><td>9</td><td>23</td><td>251</td><td>1,779</td><td>4,054</td><td>282</td></tr>
<tr><td>Food production per capita</td><td>1987 = 100</td><td>107</td><td>99</td><td>89</td><td>104</td><td>..</td><td>109</td></tr>
<tr><td>Fertilizer consumption</td><td>kg/ha</td><td>19.0</td><td>29.9</td><td>43.4</td><td>15.5</td><td>..</td><td>68.8</td></tr>
<tr><td>Share of agriculture in GDP</td><td>% of GDP</td><td>..</td><td>..</td><td>25.3</td><td>8.9</td><td>..</td><td>8.1</td></tr>
<tr><td>Housing</td><td>% of GDP</td><td>..</td><td>10.8</td><td>..</td><td>..</td><td>..</td><td>..</td></tr>
<tr><td>Average household size</td><td>persons per household</td><td>5.0</td><td>5.3</td><td>..</td><td>..</td><td>..</td><td>..</td></tr>
<tr><td>Urban</td><td>"</td><td>5.0</td><td>..</td><td>..</td><td>..</td><td>..</td><td>..</td></tr>
<tr><td>Fixed investment: housing</td><td>% of GDP</td><td>1.5</td><td>1.3</td><td>..</td><td>..</td><td>..</td><td>..</td></tr>
<tr><td>Fuel and power</td><td>% of GDP</td><td>..</td><td>3.7</td><td>..</td><td>..</td><td>..</td><td>..</td></tr>
<tr><td>Energy consumption per capita</td><td>kg of oil equiv.</td><td>195</td><td>151</td><td>161</td><td>912</td><td>1,882</td><td>1,649</td></tr>
<tr><td>Households with electricity</td><td></td><td></td><td></td><td></td><td></td><td></td><td></td></tr>
<tr><td>Urban</td><td>% of households</td><td>..</td><td>..</td><td>..</td><td>..</td><td>..</td><td>..</td></tr>
<tr><td>Rural</td><td>"</td><td>..</td><td>..</td><td>..</td><td>..</td><td>..</td><td>..</td></tr>
<tr><td>Transport and communication</td><td>% of GDP</td><td>..</td><td>2.7</td><td>..</td><td>..</td><td>..</td><td>..</td></tr>
<tr><td>Fixed investment: transport equipment</td><td>"</td><td>2.4</td><td>1.0</td><td>..</td><td>..</td><td>..</td><td>..</td></tr>
<tr><td>Total road length</td><td>thou. km</td><td>17</td><td>17</td><td>13</td><td>..</td><td>..</td><td>..</td></tr>
<tr><td colspan="8">INVESTMENT IN HUMAN CAPITAL</td></tr>
<tr><td>Health</td><td></td><td></td><td></td><td></td><td></td><td></td><td></td></tr>
<tr><td>Population per physician</td><td>persons</td><td>3,656</td><td>2,184</td><td>..</td><td>..</td><td>..</td><td>..</td></tr>
<tr><td>Population per nurse</td><td>"</td><td>..</td><td>851</td><td>..</td><td>..</td><td>..</td><td>..</td></tr>
<tr><td>Population per hospital bed</td><td>"</td><td>500</td><td>..</td><td>673</td><td>508</td><td>516</td><td>385</td></tr>
<tr><td>Oral rehydration therapy (under-5)</td><td>% of cases</td><td>..</td><td>..</td><td>24</td><td>62</td><td>..</td><td>54</td></tr>
<tr><td>Education</td><td></td><td></td><td></td><td></td><td></td><td></td><td></td></tr>
<tr><td>Gross enrollment ratio</td><td></td><td></td><td></td><td></td><td></td><td></td><td></td></tr>
<tr><td>Secondary</td><td>% of school-age pop.</td><td>12</td><td>19</td><td>28</td><td>47</td><td>..</td><td>53</td></tr>
<tr><td>Female</td><td>"</td><td>11</td><td>16</td><td>..</td><td>..</td><td>..</td><td>..</td></tr>
<tr><td>Pupil-teacher ratio: primary</td><td>pupils per teacher</td><td>35</td><td>37</td><td>34</td><td>25</td><td>26</td><td>25</td></tr>
<tr><td>Pupil-teacher ratio: secondary</td><td>"</td><td>..</td><td>..</td><td>..</td><td>..</td><td>..</td><td>..</td></tr>
<tr><td>Pupils reaching grade 4</td><td>% of cohort</td><td>37</td><td>68</td><td>59</td><td>..</td><td>..</td><td>71</td></tr>
<tr><td>Repeater rate: primary</td><td>% of total enroll</td><td>15</td><td>13</td><td>..</td><td>14</td><td>..</td><td>11</td></tr>
<tr><td>Illiteracy</td><td>% of pop. (age 15+)</td><td>54</td><td>48</td><td>45</td><td>15</td><td>..</td><td>14</td></tr>
<tr><td>Female</td><td>% of fem. (age 15+)</td><td>..</td><td>56</td><td>53</td><td>17</td><td>..</td><td>17</td></tr>
<tr><td>Newspaper circulation</td><td>per thou. pop.</td><td>41</td><td>23</td><td>21</td><td>99</td><td>100</td><td>117</td></tr>
</table>

World Bank International Economics Department, April 1994

Guinea

Indicator	Unit of measure	Latest single year 1970-75	Latest single year 1980-85	Most recent estimate 1987-92	Same region/income group Sub-Saharan Africa	Same region/income group Low-income	Next higher income group
Priority Poverty Indicators							
POVERTY							
Upper poverty line	local curr.	..	..	..	..	..	..
Headcount index	% of pop.	..	..	..	..	19	..
Lower poverty line	local curr.	..	..	..	..	..	..
Headcount index	% of pop.	..	..	..	..	..	..
GNP per capita	US$	..	..	510	520	390	..
SHORT TERM INCOME INDICATORS							
Unskilled urban wages	local curr.	..	..	..	..	..	..
Unskilled rural wages	"	..	..	..	..	..	..
Rural terms of trade	"	..	..	..	..	..	..
Consumer price index	1987=100	..	..	..	..	..	..
Lower income	"	..	..	..	..	..	..
Food[a]	"	..	..	231	..	..	..
Urban	"	..	..	..	..	..	..
Rural	"	..	..	..	..	..	..
SOCIAL INDICATORS							
Public expenditure on basic social services	% of GDP	..	..	6.2	..	..	..
Gross enrollment ratios							
Primary	% school age pop.	30	34	37	66	103	..
Male	"	40	47	50	79	113	..
Female	"	20	22	24	62	96	..
Mortality							
Infant mortality	per thou. live births	177.0	157.0	133.2	99.0	73.0	45.0
Under 5 mortality	"	..	..	225.0	169.0	108.0	59.0
Immunization							
Measles	% age group	..	44.0	39.0	54.0	72.7	..
DPT	"	..	4.0	41.0	54.6	80.6	..
Child malnutrition (under-5)	"	..	..	23.4	28.4	38.3	..
Life expectancy							
Total	years	37	40	44	52	62	68
Female advantage	"	1.0	1.0	-0.1	3.4	2.4	6.4
Total fertility rate	births per woman	6.0	6.2	6.5	6.1	3.4	3.1
Maternal mortality rate	per 100,000 live births	..	..	..	..	..	..
Supplementary Poverty Indicators							
Expenditures on social security	% of total gov't exp.	..	..	..	..	..	..
Social security coverage	% econ. active pop.	..	..	..	..	..	..
Access to safe water: total	% of pop.	14.0	18.0	33.0	41.1	68.4	..
Urban	"	68.0	41.0	56.0	77.8	78.9	..
Rural	"	..	12.0	25.0	27.3	60.3	..
Access to health care	"	..	13.0	32.0	..	..	..

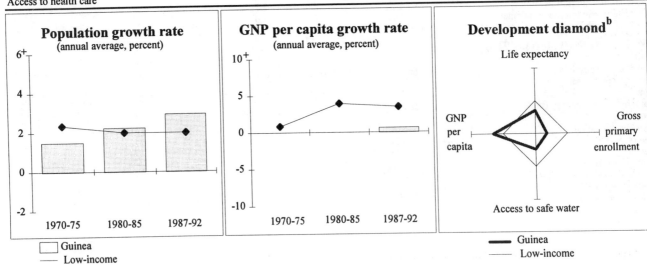

Population growth rate (annual average, percent) — Guinea, Low-income.
GNP per capita growth rate (annual average, percent) — 1970-75, 1980-85, 1987-92.
Development diamond[b]: Life expectancy, GNP per capita, Gross primary enrollment, Access to safe water — Guinea, Low-income.

a. See the technical notes, p.389.   b. The development diamond, based on four key indicators, shows the average level of development in the country compared with its income group. See the introduction.

Guinea

Indicator	Unit of measure	Latest single year 1970-75	Latest single year 1980-85	Most recent estimate 1987-92	Same region/income group Sub-Saharan Africa	Same region/income group Low-income	Next higher income group
Resources and Expenditures							
HUMAN RESOURCES							
Population (mre=1992)	thousands	4,149	4,987	6,097	546,390	3,194,535	942,547
Age dependency ratio	ratio	0.83	0.96	0.96	0.95	0.67	0.66
Urban	% of pop.	16.3	22.3	27.3	29.5	26.7	57.0
Population growth rate	annual %	1.4	2.6	2.9	2.9	1.8	1.4
Urban	"	4.5	5.5	5.7	5.1	3.4	4.8
Labor force (15-64)	thousands	2,393	2,846	3,216	224,025	1,478,954	..
Agriculture	% of labor force	83	81	..	..	..	..
Industry	"	8	9	..	..	..	..
Female	"	42	41	39	37	33	36
Females per 100 males							
Urban	number	..	..	..	..	..	..
Rural	"	..	..	..	..	..	..
NATURAL RESOURCES							
Area	thou. sq. km	245.86	245.86	245.86	24,274.03	38,401.06	40,697.37
Density	pop. per sq. km	16.9	20.3	24.1	21.9	81.7	22.8
Agricultural land	% of land area	27.8	28.0	28.0	52.7	50.9	..
Change in agricultural land	annual %	0.0	0.2	0.0	0.1	0.0	..
Agricultural land under irrigation	%	0.1	0.3	0.4	0.8	18.2	..
Forests and woodland	thou. sq. km	155	149	145	..	..	..
Deforestation (net)	annual %	..	..	1.3	..	..	..
INCOME							
Household income							
Share of top 20% of households	% of income	..	..	..	..	42	..
Share of bottom 40% of households	"	..	..	..	..	19	..
Share of bottom 20% of households	"	..	..	..	..	8	..
EXPENDITURE							
Food	% of GDP	..	..	26.5	..	..	..
Staples	"	..	..	8.6	..	..	..
Meat, fish, milk, cheese, eggs	"	..	..	9.9	..	..	..
Cereal imports	thou. metric tonnes	67	140	338	20,311	46,537	74,924
Food aid in cereals	"	49	52	31	4,303	9,008	4,054
Food production per capita	1987 = 100	98	94	97	90	123	..
Fertilizer consumption	kg/ha	0.2	0.1	0.3	4.2	61.9	..
Share of agriculture in GDP	% of GDP	..	..	32.7	18.6	29.6	..
Housing	% of GDP	..	..	8.5	..	..	..
Average household size	persons per household	..	6.7	..	..	..	..
Urban	"	..	..	..	..	..	..
Fixed investment: housing	% of GDP	..	..	4.8	..	..	..
Fuel and power	% of GDP	..	..	1.7	..	..	..
Energy consumption per capita	kg of oil equiv.	68	74	67	258	335	1,882
Households with electricity							
Urban	% of households	..	..	..	..	..	..
Rural	"	..	..	..	..	..	..
Transport and communication	% of GDP	..	..	10.1	..	..	..
Fixed investment: transport equipment	"	..	..	1.1	..	..	..
Total road length	thou. km	28	29	30	..	..	..
INVESTMENT IN HUMAN CAPITAL							
Health							
Population per physician	persons	50,013	38,961	..	..	..	..
Population per nurse	"	3,715	5,161	..	..	..	..
Population per hospital bed	"	562	..	1,816	1,329	1,050	516
Oral rehydration therapy (under-5)	% of cases	..	..	65	36	39	..
Education							
Gross enrollment ratio							
Secondary	% of school-age pop.	14	13	10	18	41	..
Female	"	7	7	5	14	35	..
Pupil-teacher ratio: primary	pupils per teacher	40	36	49	39	37	26
Pupil-teacher ratio: secondary	"	26	23	19	..	19	..
Pupils reaching grade 4	% of cohort	..	75	80	..	..	..
Repeater rate: primary	% of total enroll	..	27	18	..	..	..
Illiteracy	% of pop. (age 15+)	..	83	76	51	39	..
Female	% of fem. (age 15+)	..	92	87	62	52	..
Newspaper circulation	per thou. pop.	1	3	..	14	..	100

World Bank International Economics Department, April 1994

Guinea-Bissau

Indicator	Unit of measure	Latest single year 1970-75	Latest single year 1980-85	Most recent estimate 1987-92	Same region/income group Sub-Saharan Africa	Same region/income group Low-income	Next higher income group
Priority Poverty Indicators							
POVERTY							
Upper poverty line	local curr.	..	..	..	..	..	..
Headcount index	% of pop.	..	..	..	..	19	..
Lower poverty line	local curr.	..	..	..	..	..	..
Headcount index	% of pop.	..	..	..	..	..	..
GNP per capita	US$	190	190	220	520	390	..
SHORT TERM INCOME INDICATORS							
Unskilled urban wages	local curr.	..	..	..	..	..	..
Unskilled rural wages	"	..	..	..	..	..	..
Rural terms of trade	"	..	..	..	..	..	..
Consumer price index	1987=100	..	..	1,030	..	..	..
Lower income	"	..	..	..	..	..	..
Food[a]	"	..	..	608	..	..	..
Urban	"	..	..	..	..	..	..
Rural	"	..	..	..	..	..	..
SOCIAL INDICATORS							
Public expenditure on basic social services	% of GDP	..	..	8.7	..	..	..
Gross enrollment ratios							
Primary	% school age pop.	64	64	60	66	103	..
Male	"	90	84	77	79	113	..
Female	"	39	43	42	62	96	..
Mortality							
Infant mortality	per thou. live births	183.0	163.0	140.0	99.0	73.0	45.0
Under 5 mortality	"	..	..	236.4	169.0	108.0	59.0
Immunization							
Measles	% age group	..	35.0	60.0	54.0	72.7	..
DPT	"	..	18.0	56.0	54.6	80.6	..
Child malnutrition (under-5)	"	..	24.1	..	28.4	38.3	..
Life expectancy							
Total	years	36	38	39	52	62	68
Female advantage	"	1.7	1.4	1.3	3.4	2.4	6.4
Total fertility rate	births per woman	5.9	6.0	6.0	6.1	3.4	3.1
Maternal mortality rate	per 100,000 live births	..	760	..	..	..	..
Supplementary Poverty Indicators							
Expenditures on social security	% of total gov't exp.	..	..	..	..	..	..
Social security coverage	% econ. active pop.	..	..	..	..	..	..
Access to safe water: total	% of pop.	..	21.0	25.0	41.1	68.4	..
Urban	"	..	..	..	77.8	78.9	..
Rural	"	..	22.0	..	27.3	60.3	..
Access to health care	"	..	64.0	80.0	..	..	..

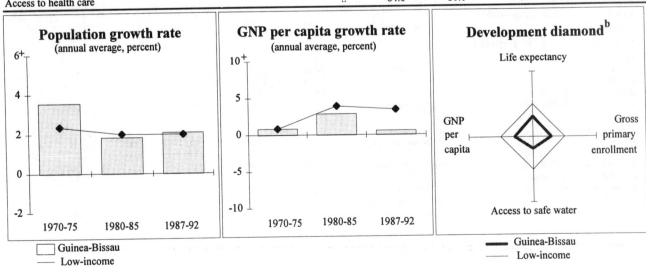

Population growth rate (annual average, percent) — 1970-75, 1980-85, 1987-92; Guinea-Bissau, Low-income

GNP per capita growth rate (annual average, percent) — 1970-75, 1980-85, 1987-92

Development diamond[b] — Life expectancy, GNP per capita, Gross primary enrollment, Access to safe water; Guinea-Bissau, Low-income

a. See the technical notes, p.389.   b. The development diamond, based on four key indicators, shows the average level of development in the country compared with its income group. See the introduction.

Guinea-Bissau

| Indicator | Unit of measure | Latest single year | | Most recent estimate 1987-92 | Same region/income group | | Next higher income group |
		1970-75	1980-85		Sub-Saharan Africa	Low-income	
Resources and Expenditures							
HUMAN RESOURCES							
Population (mre=1992)	thousands	627	886	1,022	546,390	3,194,535	942,547
Age dependency ratio	ratio	0.75	0.87	0.87	0.95	0.67	0.66
Urban	% of pop.	15.9	18.1	20.8	29.5	26.7	57.0
Population growth rate	annual %	4.9	1.8	2.1	2.9	1.8	1.4
Urban	"	5.9	3.3	4.3	5.1	3.4	4.8
Labor force (15-64)	thousands	323	427	473	224,025	1,478,954	..
Agriculture	% of labor force	83	82	..	..	..	..
Industry	"	3	4	..	..	..	..
Female	"	43	42	40	37	33	36
Females per 100 males							
Urban	number	..	..	..	..	..	..
Rural	"	..	..	..	..	..	..
NATURAL RESOURCES							
Area	thou. sq. km	36.12	36.12	36.12	24,274.03	38,401.06	40,697.37
Density	pop. per sq. km	17.4	24.5	27.7	21.9	81.7	22.8
Agricultural land	% of land area	48.5	49.8	50.5	52.7	50.9	..
Change in agricultural land	annual %	0.0	0.4	0.4	0.1	0.0	..
Agricultural land under irrigation	%	..	..	..	0.8	18.2	..
Forests and woodland	thou. sq. km	11	11	11	..	..	..
Deforestation (net)	annual %	..	..	1.0	..	..	..
INCOME							
Household income							
Share of top 20% of households	% of income	..	..	59	..	42	..
Share of bottom 40% of households	"	..	..	9	..	19	..
Share of bottom 20% of households	"	..	..	2	..	8	..
EXPENDITURE							
Food	% of GDP	..	..	36.9	..	..	..
Staples	"	..	..	12.0	..	..	..
Meat, fish, milk, cheese, eggs	"	..	..	13.7	..	..	..
Cereal imports	thou. metric tonnes	22	30	82	20,311	46,537	74,924
Food aid in cereals	"	11	31	16	4,303	9,008	4,054
Food production per capita	1987 = 100	118	110	111	90	123	..
Fertilizer consumption	kg/ha	0.2	0.4	0.4	4.2	61.9	..
Share of agriculture in GDP	% of GDP	47.8	42.5	44.1	18.6	29.6	..
Housing	% of GDP	..	..	11.9	..	..	..
Average household size	persons per household	..	..	..	..	..	..
Urban	"	..	..	..	..	..	..
Fixed investment: housing	% of GDP	..	..	5.8	..	..	..
Fuel and power	% of GDP	..	..	2.4	..	..	..
Energy consumption per capita	kg of oil equiv.	46	37	37	258	335	1,882
Households with electricity							
Urban	% of households	..	..	..	..	..	..
Rural	"	..	..	..	..	..	..
Transport and communication	% of GDP	..	..	14.1	..	..	..
Fixed investment: transport equipment	"	..	..	1.4	..	..	..
Total road length	thou. km	..	4	..	..	..	..
INVESTMENT IN HUMAN CAPITAL							
Health							
Population per physician	persons	17,500	7,262	..	..	..	..
Population per nurse	"	2,821	1,129	..	..	..	..
Population per hospital bed	"	572	538	..	1,329	1,050	516
Oral rehydration therapy (under-5)	% of cases	..	..	5	36	39	..
Education							
Gross enrollment ratio							
Secondary	% of school-age pop.	3	11	7	18	41	..
Female	"	2	5	4	14	35	..
Pupil-teacher ratio: primary	pupils per teacher	38	25	25	39	37	26
Pupil-teacher ratio: secondary	"	11	13	..	..	19	..
Pupils reaching grade 4	% of cohort	..	64	..	..	..	..
Repeater rate: primary	% of total enroll	14	50	42	..	..	..
Illiteracy	% of pop. (age 15+)	..	70	64	51	39	..
Female	% of fem. (age 15+)	..	82	76	62	52	..
Newspaper circulation	per thou. pop.	10	7	6	14	..	100

World Bank International Economics Department, April 1994

Guyana

Indicator	Unit of measure	Latest single year 1970-75	Latest single year 1980-85	Most recent estimate 1987-92	Same region/income group Latin America Caribbean	Same region/income group Low-income	Next higher income group
Priority Poverty Indicators							
POVERTY							
Upper poverty line	local curr.	..	..	..	..		..
Headcount index	% of pop.	..	..	..	..	19	..
Lower poverty line	local curr.	..	..	..	..	..	..
Headcount index	% of pop.	..	..	..	..	..	..
GNP per capita	US$	630	510	330	2,690	390	..
SHORT TERM INCOME INDICATORS							
Unskilled urban wages	local curr.	..	..	..	..	..	..
Unskilled rural wages	"	..	..	..	..	..	..
Rural terms of trade	"	..	..	..	..	..	..
Consumer price index	1987=100	16	72	158	..	..	..
Lower income	"	..	..	..	..	..	..
Food[a]	"	..	71	..	..	..	..
Urban	"	..	..	..	..	..	..
Rural	"	..	..	..	..	..	..
SOCIAL INDICATORS							
Public expenditure on basic social services	% of GDP	..	..	..	..	..	..
Gross enrollment ratios							
Primary	% school age pop.	95	103	112	106	103	..
Male	"	96	104	113	..	113	..
Female	"	95	101	111	..	96	..
Mortality							
Infant mortality	per thou. live births	79.0	63.0	48.0	44.0	73.0	45.0
Under 5 mortality	"	..	..	62.0	56.0	108.0	59.0
Immunization							
Measles	% age group	..	33.0	73.0	78.9	72.7	..
DPT	"	..	43.0	83.0	73.8	80.6	..
Child malnutrition (under-5)	"	32.1	22.1	22.1	10.5	38.3	..
Life expectancy							
Total	years	60	61	65	68	62	68
Female advantage	"	4.1	5.8	5.6	5.6	2.4	6.4
Total fertility rate	births per woman	4.9	3.3	2.6	3.0	3.4	3.1
Maternal mortality rate	per 100,000 live births	..	200	..	..	..	..
Supplementary Poverty Indicators							
Expenditures on social security	% of total gov't exp.	2.5	3.2	..	..	..	..
Social security coverage	% econ. active pop.	..	..	..	..	..	..
Access to safe water: total	% of pop.	84.0	76.0	83.0	80.3	68.4	..
Urban	"	100.0	100.0	100.0	91.0	78.9	..
Rural	"	75.0	65.0	74.0	64.3	60.3	..
Access to health care	"	..	88.8	96.0	..	..	..

Population growth rate
(annual average, percent)

☐ Guyana
— Low-income

GNP per capita growth rate
(annual average, percent)

Development diamond[b]

Life expectancy — GNP per capita — Gross primary enrollment — Access to safe water

— Guyana
— Low-income

a. See the technical notes, p.389. b. The development diamond, based on four key indicators, shows the average level of development in the country compared with its income group. See the introduction.

144

Guyana

Indicator	Unit of measure	Latest single year 1970-75	Latest single year 1980-85	Most recent estimate 1987-92	Same region/income group Latin America Caribbean	Low-income	Next higher income group
Resources and Expenditures							
HUMAN RESOURCES							
Population (mre=1992)	thousands	730	790	806	453,294	3,194,535	942,547
Age dependency ratio	ratio	0.89	0.68	0.62	0.67	0.67	0.66
Urban	% of pop.	29.7	31.1	33.8	72.9	26.7	57.0
Population growth rate	annual %	1.5	0.5	0.6	1.7	1.8	1.4
Urban	"	1.7	1.2	2.0	2.6	3.4	4.8
Labor force (15-64)	thousands	239	337	403	166,091	1,478,954	..
Agriculture	% of labor force	29	27	..	..	..	..
Industry	"	27	26	..	..	..	..
Female	"	23	25	25	27	33	36
Females per 100 males							
Urban	number	103	..	..	..	..	..
Rural	"	103	..	..	..	..	..
NATURAL RESOURCES							
Area	thou. sq. km	214.97	214.97	214.97	20,507.48	38,401.06	40,697.37
Density	pop. per sq. km	3.4	3.7	3.7	21.7	81.7	22.8
Agricultural land	% of land area	7.0	8.8	8.8	40.2	50.9	..
Change in agricultural land	annual %	0.2	0.0	0.1	0.5	0.0	..
Agricultural land under irrigation	%	8.7	7.4	7.5	3.2	18.2	..
Forests and woodland	thou. sq. km	182	164	164	..	..	..
Deforestation (net)	annual %	..	..	0.1	..	..	..
INCOME							
Household income							
Share of top 20% of households	% of income	..	..	..	..	42	..
Share of bottom 40% of households	"	..	..	..	..	19	..
Share of bottom 20% of households	"	..	..	..	..	8	..
EXPENDITURE							
Food	% of GDP	..	..	..	..	..	..
Staples	"	..	..	..	..	..	..
Meat, fish, milk, cheese, eggs	"	..	..	..	..	..	..
Cereal imports	thou. metric tonnes	62	1	55	25,032	46,537	74,924
Food aid in cereals	"	1	0	15	1,779	9,008	4,054
Food production per capita	1987 = 100	110	95	93	104	123	..
Fertilizer consumption	kg/ha	9.3	7.2	9.3	15.5	61.9	..
Share of agriculture in GDP	% of GDP	28.8	22.5	35.0	8.9	29.6	..
Housing	% of GDP	..	..	..	..	..	..
Average household size	persons per household	5.0	..	..	..	..	..
Urban	"	..	..	..	..	..	..
Fixed investment: housing	% of GDP	..	..	..	..	..	..
Fuel and power	% of GDP	..	..	..	..	..	..
Energy consumption per capita	kg of oil equiv.	821	601	350	912	335	1,882
Households with electricity							
Urban	% of households	..	..	..	..	..	..
Rural	"	..	..	..	..	..	..
Transport and communication	% of GDP	..	..	..	..	..	..
Fixed investment: transport equipment	"	..	..	..	..	..	..
Total road length	thou. km	4	9	..	..	..	..
INVESTMENT IN HUMAN CAPITAL							
Health							
Population per physician	persons	4,000	6,220	..	..	..	..
Population per nurse	"	1,128	886	..	..	..	..
Population per hospital bed	"	200	300	..	508	1,050	516
Oral rehydration therapy (under-5)	% of cases	..	..	15	62	39	..
Education							
Gross enrollment ratio							
Secondary	% of school-age pop.	54	63	57	47	41	..
Female	"	55	65	59	..	35	..
Pupil-teacher ratio: primary	pupils per teacher	32	29	29	25	37	26
Pupil-teacher ratio: secondary	"	21	35	..	..	19	..
Pupils reaching grade 4	% of cohort	100	94	..	..	..	..
Repeater rate: primary	% of total enroll	8	4	..	14	..	..
Illiteracy	% of pop. (age 15+)	8	5	4	15	39	..
Female	% of fem. (age 15+)	..	6	5	17	52	..
Newspaper circulation	per thou. pop.	167	89	100	99	..	100

World Bank International Economics Department, April 1994

Haiti

Indicator	Unit of measure	Latest single year 1970-75	Latest single year 1980-85	Most recent estimate 1987-92	Same region/income group Latin America Caribbean	Low-income	Next higher income group
Priority Poverty Indicators							
POVERTY							
Upper poverty line	local curr.	..	..	..	..	..	..
Headcount index	% of pop.	..	..	..	..	19	..
Lower poverty line	local curr.	..	..	..	..	..	..
Headcount index	% of pop.	..	..	..	..	..	..
GNP per capita	US$	150	320	380	2,690	390	..
SHORT TERM INCOME INDICATORS							
Unskilled urban wages	local curr.	..	..	..	..	..	..
Unskilled rural wages	"	..	..	..	..	..	..
Rural terms of trade	"	..	..	..	..	..	..
Consumer price index	1987=100	48	109	135	..	..	..
Lower income	"	..	..	..	..	..	..
Food[a]	"	25	119	141	..	..	..
Urban	"	..	..	..	..	..	..
Rural	"	..	..	..	..	..	..
SOCIAL INDICATORS							
Public expenditure on basic social services	% of GDP	..	..	..	..	..	..
Gross enrollment ratios							
Primary	% school age pop.	60	96	56	106	103	..
Male	"	..	102	58	..	113	..
Female	"	..	90	54	..	96	..
Mortality							
Infant mortality	per thou. live births	135.0	108.0	93.0	44.0	73.0	45.0
Under 5 mortality	"	..	..	151.0	56.0	108.0	59.0
Immunization							
Measles	% age group	..	13.0	31.0	78.9	72.7	..
DPT	"	..	12.0	41.0	73.8	80.6	..
Child malnutrition (under-5)	"	..	..	37.4	10.5	38.3	..
Life expectancy							
Total	years	48	53	55	68	62	68
Female advantage	"	2.9	3.2	3.0	5.6	2.4	6.4
Total fertility rate	births per woman	5.8	5.2	4.7	3.0	3.4	3.1
Maternal mortality rate	per 100,000 live births	..	340	600	..	..	..
Supplementary Poverty Indicators							
Expenditures on social security	% of total gov't exp.	..	..	..	..	..	..
Social security coverage	% econ. active pop.	..	..	..	..	..	..
Access to safe water: total	% of pop.	12.0	38.0	41.0	80.3	68.4	..
Urban	"	46.0	59.0	55.0	91.0	78.9	..
Rural	"	3.0	30.0	36.0	64.3	60.3	..
Access to health care	"	..	..	45.0	..	..	..

Population growth rate
(annual average, percent)

Haiti
— Low-income

GNP per capita growth rate
(annual average, percent)

Development diamond[b]

Life expectancy — GNP per capita — Gross primary enrollment — Access to safe water

—— Haiti
— Low-income

a. See the technical notes, p.389.   b. The development diamond, based on four key indicators, shows the average level of development in the country compared with its income group. See the introduction.

Haiti

Indicator	Unit of measure	Latest single year 1970-75	Latest single year 1980-85	Most recent estimate 1987-92	Same region/income group Latin America Caribbean	Low-income	Next higher income group
Resources and Expenditures							
HUMAN RESOURCES							
Population (mre=1992)	thousands	4,920	5,865	6,715	453,294	3,194,535	942,547
Age dependency ratio	ratio	0.84	0.81	0.79	0.67	0.67	0.66
Urban	% of pop.	21.7	26.0	29.8	72.9	26.7	57.0
Population growth rate	annual %	1.7	1.9	1.8	1.7	1.8	1.4
Urban	"	3.5	3.7	3.9	2.6	3.4	4.8
Labor force (15-64)	thousands	2,441	2,822	3,276	166,091	1,478,954	..
Agriculture	% of labor force	72	70	..	..	..	..
Industry	"	8	8	..	..	..	..
Female	"	45	43	41	27	33	36
Females per 100 males							
Urban	number	144	134	..	..	..	..
Rural	"	103	103	..	..	..	..
NATURAL RESOURCES							
Area	thou. sq. km	27.75	27.75	27.75	20,507.48	38,401.06	40,697.37
Density	pop. per sq. km	177.3	211.4	237.6	21.7	81.7	22.8
Agricultural land	% of land area	51.5	51.1	50.8	40.2	50.9	..
Change in agricultural land	annual %	-1.4	0.0	-0.1	0.5	0.0	..
Agricultural land under irrigation	%	4.9	5.0	5.4	3.2	18.2	..
Forests and woodland	thou. sq. km	1	0	0	..	..	..
Deforestation (net)	annual %	..	..	..	..	..	..
INCOME							
Household income							
Share of top 20% of households	% of income	..	..	..	..	42	..
Share of bottom 40% of households	"	..	..	..	..	19	..
Share of bottom 20% of households	"	..	..	..	..	8	..
EXPENDITURE							
Food	% of GDP	..	..	..	..	..	..
Staples	"	..	..	..	..	..	..
Meat, fish, milk, cheese, eggs	"	..	..	..	..	..	..
Cereal imports	thou. metric tonnes	88	220	456	25,032	46,537	74,924
Food aid in cereals	"	25	101	48	1,779	9,008	4,054
Food production per capita	1987 = 100	101	101	67	104	123	..
Fertilizer consumption	kg/ha	1.5	2.3	1.6	15.5	61.9	..
Share of agriculture in GDP	% of GDP	..	..	..	8.9	29.6	..
Housing	% of GDP	..	..	..	..	..	..
Average household size	persons per household	3.6	..	..	..	..	..
Urban	"	2.2	..	..	..	..	..
Fixed investment: housing	% of GDP	..	..	..	..	..	..
Fuel and power	% of GDP	..	..	..	..	..	..
Energy consumption per capita	kg of oil equiv.	34	51	48	912	335	1,882
Households with electricity							
Urban	% of households	..	..	..	..	..	..
Rural	"	..	..	..	..	..	..
Transport and communication	% of GDP	..	..	..	..	..	..
Fixed investment: transport equipment	"	..	..	..	..	..	..
Total road length	thou. km	3	4	4	..	..	..
INVESTMENT IN HUMAN CAPITAL							
Health							
Population per physician	persons	12,392	7,304	..	..	..	..
Population per nurse	"	7,410	2,268	..	..	..	..
Population per hospital bed	"	1,289	1,384	1,323	508	1,050	516
Oral rehydration therapy (under-5)	% of cases	..	..	20	62	39	..
Education							
Gross enrollment ratio							
Secondary	% of school-age pop.	8	18	22	47	41	..
Female	"	7	17	21	..	35	..
Pupil-teacher ratio: primary	pupils per teacher	41	38	21	25	37	26
Pupil-teacher ratio: secondary	"	16	20	20	..	19	..
Pupils reaching grade 4	% of cohort	..	41	60	..	..	..
Repeater rate: primary	% of total enroll	..	9	15	14	..	..
Illiteracy	% of pop. (age 15+)	79	52	47	15	39	..
Female	% of fem. (age 15+)	..	58	53	17	52	..
Newspaper circulation	per thou. pop.	19	4	7	99	..	100

World Bank International Economics Department, April 1994

Honduras

Indicator	Unit of measure	Latest single year 1970-75	Latest single year 1980-85	Most recent estimate 1987-92	Same region/income group Latin America Caribbean	Same region/income group Low-income	Next higher income group
Priority Poverty Indicators							
POVERTY							
Upper poverty line	local curr.	..	..	..	..	..	..
Headcount index	% of pop.	..	..	..	..	19	..
Lower poverty line	local curr.	..	..	..	..	..	..
Headcount index	% of pop.	..	..	..	..	..	..
GNP per capita	US$	360	790	580	2,690	390	..
SHORT TERM INCOME INDICATORS							
Unskilled urban wages	local curr.	..	..	..	..	..	..
Unskilled rural wages	"	..	..	19	..	..	..
Rural terms of trade	"	..	..	..	..	..	..
Consumer price index	1987=100	42	94	206	..	..	..
Lower income	"	..	..	..	..	..	..
Food[a]	"	34	97	222	..	..	..
Urban	"	..	..	..	..	..	..
Rural	"	..	..	..	..	..	..
SOCIAL INDICATORS							
Public expenditure on basic social services	% of GDP	..	10.3	5.3	..	..	..
Gross enrollment ratios							
Primary	% school age pop.	88	102	105	106	103	..
Male	"	89	101	102	..	113	..
Female	"	86	103	107	..	96	..
Mortality							
Infant mortality	per thou. live births	101.0	62.0	49.0	44.0	73.0	45.0
Under 5 mortality	"	..	..	63.7	56.0	108.0	59.0
Immunization							
Measles	% age group	..	51.0	86.0	78.9	72.7	..
DPT	"	..	48.0	94.0	73.8	80.6	..
Child malnutrition (under-5)	"	..	20.8	20.6	10.5	38.3	..
Life expectancy							
Total	years	54	62	66	68	62	68
Female advantage	"	3.6	4.0	4.3	5.6	2.4	6.4
Total fertility rate	births per woman	7.4	6.2	4.9	3.0	3.4	3.1
Maternal mortality rate	per 100,000 live births	..	82	221	..	..	..
Supplementary Poverty Indicators							
Expenditures on social security	% of total gov't exp.	7.2	..	..	..	..	..
Social security coverage	% econ. active pop.	..	12.8	..	..	..	..
Access to safe water: total	% of pop.	41.0	45.0	70.0	80.3	68.4	..
Urban	"	99.0	46.0	82.0	91.0	78.9	..
Rural	"	10.0	45.0	60.0	64.3	60.3	..
Access to health care	"	..	..	..	..	..	..

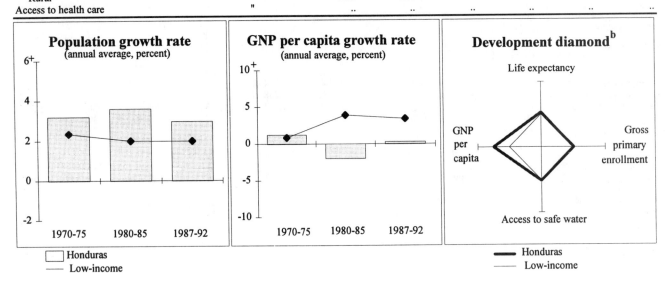

Population growth rate (annual average, percent) — Honduras / Low-income (1970-75, 1980-85, 1987-92)

GNP per capita growth rate (annual average, percent) — (1970-75, 1980-85, 1987-92)

Development diamond[b] — Life expectancy, GNP per capita, Gross primary enrollment, Access to safe water — Honduras / Low-income

a. See the technical notes, p.389.   b. The development diamond, based on four key indicators, shows the average level of development in the country compared with its income group. See the introduction.

Honduras

Indicator	Unit of measure	Latest single year 1970-75	Latest single year 1980-85	Most recent estimate 1987-92	Same region/income group Latin America Caribbean	Same region/income group Low-income	Next higher income group
Resources and Expenditures							
HUMAN RESOURCES							
Population (mre=1992)	thousands	3,081	4,383	5,418	453,294	3,194,535	942,547
Age dependency ratio	ratio	1.04	0.98	0.91	0.67	0.67	0.66
Urban	% of pop.	32.3	39.7	45.3	72.9	26.7	57.0
Population growth rate	annual %	3.3	3.4	3.0	1.7	1.8	1.4
Urban	"	5.5	5.3	4.8	2.6	3.4	4.8
Labor force (15-64)	thousands	909	1,303	1,709	166,091	1,478,954	..
Agriculture	% of labor force	63	60	..	..	..	..
Industry	"	15	16	..	..	..	..
Female	"	15	17	20	27	33	36
Females per 100 males							
Urban	number	120	110	..	..	..	..
Rural	"	100	92	..	..	..	..
NATURAL RESOURCES							
Area	thou. sq. km	112.09	112.09	112.09	20,507.48	38,401.06	40,697.37
Density	pop. per sq. km	27.5	39.1	46.9	21.7	81.7	22.8
Agricultural land	% of land area	35.2	38.3	39.4	40.2	50.9	..
Change in agricultural land	annual %	1.5	0.5	0.7	0.5	0.0	..
Agricultural land under irrigation	%	2.0	2.0	2.0	3.2	18.2	..
Forests and woodland	thou. sq. km	45	37	32	..	..	..
Deforestation (net)	annual %	..	..	2.1	..	..	..
INCOME							
Household income							
Share of top 20% of households	% of income	..	..	64	..	42	..
Share of bottom 40% of households	"	..	..	9	..	19	..
Share of bottom 20% of households	"	..	..	3	..	8	..
EXPENDITURE							
Food	% of GDP	32.6	29.8	..	..	..	..
Staples	"	..	6.1	..	..	..	..
Meat, fish, milk, cheese, eggs	"	..	10.4	..	..	..	..
Cereal imports	thou. metric tonnes	113	112	128	25,032	46,537	74,924
Food aid in cereals	"	31	118	122	1,779	9,008	4,054
Food production per capita	1987 = 100	85	83	84	104	123	..
Fertilizer consumption	kg/ha	5.1	5.3	6.9	15.5	61.9	..
Share of agriculture in GDP	% of GDP	24.6	19.3	18.9	8.9	29.6	..
Housing	% of GDP	17.6	16.2	..	..	..	..
Average household size	persons per household	..	..	..	..	..	..
Urban	"	..	..	..	..	..	..
Fixed investment: housing	% of GDP	3.3	2.3	..	..	..	..
Fuel and power	% of GDP	..	5.1	..	..	..	..
Energy consumption per capita	kg of oil equiv.	204	191	175	912	335	1,882
Households with electricity							
Urban	% of households	..	..	..	..	..	..
Rural	"	..	..	..	..	..	..
Transport and communication	% of GDP	2.4	2.2	..	..	..	..
Fixed investment: transport equipment	"	3.3	1.3	..	..	..	..
Total road length	thou. km	7	12	11	..	..	..
INVESTMENT IN HUMAN CAPITAL							
Health							
Population per physician	persons	3,799	1,513	2,435	..	..	..
Population per nurse	"	1,469	673	..	..	..	..
Population per hospital bed	"	600	800	993	508	1,050	516
Oral rehydration therapy (under-5)	% of cases	..	..	70	62	39	..
Education							
Gross enrollment ratio							
Secondary	% of school-age pop.	16	35	19	47	41	..
Female	"	17	35	34	..	35	..
Pupil-teacher ratio: primary	pupils per teacher	35	38	38	25	37	26
Pupil-teacher ratio: secondary	"	..	..	..	..	19	..
Pupils reaching grade 4	% of cohort	36	46	..	..	..	..
Repeater rate: primary	% of total enroll	..	15	..	14	..	..
Illiteracy	% of pop. (age 15+)	43	32	27	15	39	..
Female	% of fem. (age 15+)	..	35	29	17	52	..
Newspaper circulation	per thou. pop.	32	57	39	99	..	100

World Bank International Economics Department, April 1994

Hong Kong

Indicator	Unit of measure	Latest single year 1970-75	Latest single year 1980-85	Most recent estimate 1987-92	Same region/income group High-income
Priority Poverty Indicators					
POVERTY					
Upper poverty line	local curr.	..	..	..	..
Headcount index	% of pop.	..	..	..	..
Lower poverty line	local curr.	..	..	..	..
Headcount index	% of pop.	..	..	..	..
GNP per capita	US$	2,210	6,120	15,360	21,960
SHORT TERM INCOME INDICATORS					
Unskilled urban wages	local curr.	..	..	..	..
Unskilled rural wages	"	..	..	..	..
Rural terms of trade	"	..	..	..	..
Consumer price index	1987=100	40	92	157	..
Lower income	"	..	..	..	..
Food[a]	"	..	94	151	..
Urban	"	..	..	..	..
Rural	"	..	..	..	..
SOCIAL INDICATORS					
Public expenditure on basic social services	% of GDP	..	..	..	..
Gross enrollment ratios					
Primary	% school age pop.	119	104	108	103
Male	"	122	105	105	103
Female	"	117	103	105	103
Mortality					
Infant mortality	per thou. live births	14.9	8.8	5.8	7.0
Under 5 mortality	"	..	..	7.6	10.0
Immunization					
Measles	% age group	..	..	42.0	82.4
DPT	"	..	87.0	83.0	90.1
Child malnutrition (under-5)	"	..	..	..	..
Life expectancy					
Total	years	71	76	78	77
Female advantage	"	6.4	5.6	5.5	6.4
Total fertility rate	births per woman	2.9	1.8	1.4	1.7
Maternal mortality rate	per 100,000 live births	..	4	4	..
Supplementary Poverty Indicators					
Expenditures on social security	% of total gov't exp.	..	..	..	..
Social security coverage	% econ. active pop.	..	..	..	..
Access to safe water: total	% of pop.	89.0	..	99.0	..
Urban	"	93.0	..	99.0	..
Rural	"	49.0	..	99.0	..
Access to health care	"	..	..	..	..

Population growth rate
(annual average, percent)

1970-75 1980-85 1987-92

☐ Hong Kong
— High-income

GNP per capita growth rate
(annual average, percent)

1970-75 1980-85 1987-92

Development diamond[b]

Life expectancy

GNP per capita — Gross primary enrollment

Access to safe water

— Hong Kong
— High-income

a. See the technical notes, p.389. b. The development diamond, based on four key indicators, shows the average level of development in the country compared with its income group. See the introduction.

Hong Kong

Indicator	Unit of measure	Latest single year 1970-75	Latest single year 1980-85	Most recent estimate 1987-92	Same region/income group High-income

Resources and Expenditures

HUMAN RESOURCES

Indicator	Unit	1970-75	1980-85	1987-92	High-income
Population (mre=1992)	thousands	4,360	5,456	5,812	828,221
Age dependency ratio	ratio	0.56	0.44	0.44	0.50
Urban	% of pop.	90.6	92.9	94.5	78.1
Population growth rate	annual %	2.3	1.6	1.0	0.7
Urban	"	2.5	1.9	1.2	0.9
Labor force (15-64)	thousands	2,034	2,867	3,201	390,033
Agriculture	% of labor force	0	0	..	..
Industry	"	0	0	..	..
Female	"	..	..	..	38
Females per 100 males					
Urban	number	..	87	..	..
Rural	"	..	83	..	..

NATURAL RESOURCES

Indicator	Unit	1970-75	1980-85	1987-92	High-income
Area	thou. sq. km	1.04	1.04	1.04	31,709.00
Density	pop. per sq. km	4192.3	5246.2	5533.7	24.5
Agricultural land	% of land area	9.9	9.1	8.1	42.7
Change in agricultural land	annual %	-16.7	0.0	0.0	-0.2
Agricultural land under irrigation	%	60.0	33.3	25.0	16.1
Forests and woodland	thou. sq. km	0	0	0	..
Deforestation (net)	annual %	..	..	..	..

INCOME

Household income

Indicator	Unit	1970-75	1980-85	1987-92	High-income
Share of top 20% of households	% of income	49	47	..	..
Share of bottom 40% of households	"	15	16	..	..
Share of bottom 20% of households	"	6	5	..	..

EXPENDITURE

Indicator	Unit	1970-75	1980-85	1987-92	High-income
Food	% of GDP	..	8.0	..	..
Staples	"	..	0.9	..	..
Meat, fish, milk, cheese, eggs	"	..	4.3	..	..
Cereal imports	thou. metric tonnes	681	861	786	70,626
Food aid in cereals	"	2	..	..	2
Food production per capita	1987 = 100	98	111	118	101
Fertilizer consumption	kg/ha	..	..	..	162.1
Share of agriculture in GDP	% of GDP	1.1	0.5	0.2	2.4
Housing	% of GDP	..	9.8	..	..
Average household size	persons per household	4.0	3.9	..	..
Urban	"	..	..	..	..
Fixed investment: housing	% of GDP	3.2	6.2	..	..
Fuel and power	% of GDP	..	1.2	..	..
Energy consumption per capita	kg of oil equiv.	966	1,373	1,946	5,101
Households with electricity					
Urban	% of households	..	..	..	..
Rural	"	..	..	..	..
Transport and communication	% of GDP	..	5.8	..	..
Fixed investment: transport equipment	"	1.8	1.3	..	..
Total road length	thou. km	1	1	1	..

INVESTMENT IN HUMAN CAPITAL

Health

Indicator	Unit	1970-75	1980-85	1987-92	High-income
Population per physician	persons	1,488	1,211	..	..
Population per nurse	"	561	795	..	..
Population per hospital bed	"	198	204	234	144
Oral rehydration therapy (under-5)	% of cases	..	..	..	..

Education

Gross enrollment ratio

Indicator	Unit	1970-75	1980-85	1987-92	High-income
Secondary	% of school-age pop.	49	72	75	92
Female	"	47	75	77	94
Pupil-teacher ratio: primary	pupils per teacher	31	28	27	18
Pupil-teacher ratio: secondary	"	..	..	23	
Pupils reaching grade 4	% of cohort	97	..	..	..
Repeater rate: primary	% of total enroll	..	2	..	..
Illiteracy	% of pop. (age 15+)	23	12	..	..
Female	% of fem. (age 15+)	..	19	..	..
Newspaper circulation	per thou. pop.	..	550	649	..

World Bank International Economics Department, April 1994

Hungary

Indicator	Unit of measure	Latest single year 1970-75	Latest single year 1980-85	Most recent estimate 1987-92	Same region/income group Europe & Central Asia	Same region/income group Upper-middle-income	Next higher income group
Priority Poverty Indicators							
POVERTY							
Upper poverty line	local curr.	..	..	..	..	..	..
Headcount index	% of pop.	..	..	..	..	..	..
Lower poverty line	local curr.	..	..	..	..	..	..
Headcount index	% of pop.	..	..	..	..	..	..
GNP per capita	US$	..	1,940	2,970	..	3,870	21,960
SHORT TERM INCOME INDICATORS							
Unskilled urban wages	local curr.	..	..	..	..	..	..
Unskilled rural wages	"	..	..	..	..	..	..
Rural terms of trade	"	..	..	..	..	..	..
Consumer price index	1987=100	46	87	288	..	..	..
Lower income	"	..	..	..	..	..	..
Food[a]	"	40	90	225	..	..	..
Urban	"	..	..	..	..	..	..
Rural	"	..	..	..	..	..	..
SOCIAL INDICATORS							
Public expenditure on basic social services	% of GDP	..	..	..	..	..	..
Gross enrollment ratios							
Primary	% school age pop.	99	98	89	..	107	103
Male	"	99	98	89	..	..	103
Female	"	99	99	89	..	..	103
Mortality							
Infant mortality	per thou. live births	32.8	20.4	14.7	30.0	40.0	7.0
Under 5 mortality	"	..	..	17.9	38.0	51.0	10.0
Immunization							
Measles	% age group	..	99.0	100.0	..	82.0	82.4
DPT	"	..	99.0	100.0	..	73.8	90.1
Child malnutrition (under-5)	"	..	..	..	..	..	..
Life expectancy							
Total	years	70	70	69	70	69	77
Female advantage	"	6.2	8.0	8.8	8.6	6.3	6.4
Total fertility rate	births per woman	2.4	1.9	1.8	2.2	2.9	1.7
Maternal mortality rate	per 100,000 live births	..	28	..	58	..	..
Supplementary Poverty Indicators							
Expenditures on social security	% of total gov't exp.	..	23.9	27.7	..	..	..
Social security coverage	% econ. active pop.	..	..	..	..	..	..
Access to safe water: total	% of pop.	..	99.0	..	..	85.6	..
Urban	"	65.0	100.0	..	..	94.3	..
Rural	"	10.6	98.0	..	..	73.0	..
Access to health care	"	..	100.0	62.0	..	..	..

Population growth rate (annual average, percent)

□ Hungary
— Upper-middle-income

GNP per capita growth rate (annual average, percent)

Development diamond[b]

— Hungary
— Upper-middle-income

a. See the technical notes, p.389.   b. The development diamond, based on four key indicators, shows the average level of development in the country compared with its income group. See the introduction.

Hungary

Indicator	Unit of measure	Latest single year 1970-75	Latest single year 1980-85	Most recent estimate 1987-92	Same region/income group Europe & Central Asia	Same region/income group Upper-middle-income	Next higher income group
Resources and Expenditures							
HUMAN RESOURCES							
Population (mre=1992)	thousands	10,532	10,657	10,313	495,241	477,960	828,221
Age dependency ratio	ratio	0.49	0.50	0.48	0.56	0.64	0.50
Urban	% of pop.	52.8	60.7	65.7	63.3	71.7	78.1
Population growth rate	annual %	0.6	-0.2	-0.3	0.5	1.6	0.7
Urban	"	2.2	1.0	0.7	..	2.5	0.9
Labor force (15-64)	thousands	5,445	5,215	5,328	..	181,414	390,033
Agriculture	% of labor force	22	18	..	..	..	..
Industry	"	44	44	..	..	..	..
Female	"	42	44	45	46	29	38
Females per 100 males							
Urban	number	104	106	..	..	..	..
Rural	"	105	100	..	..	..	..
NATURAL RESOURCES							
Area	thou. sq. km	93.03	93.03	93.03	24,165.06	21,836.02	31,709.00
Density	pop. per sq. km	113.2	114.6	111.2	20.4	21.5	24.5
Agricultural land	% of land area	73.3	70.8	70.0	..	41.7	42.7
Change in agricultural land	annual %	-0.2	-0.2	-0.2	..	0.3	-0.2
Agricultural land under irrigation	%	2.3	2.1	2.2	..	9.3	16.1
Forests and woodland	thou. sq. km	15	16	17	..	..	..
Deforestation (net)	annual %	..	..	-0.6	..	..	..
INCOME							
Household income							
Share of top 20% of households	% of income	34	32	34	..	..	..
Share of bottom 40% of households	"	25	26	26	..	..	..
Share of bottom 20% of households	"	10	11	11	..	..	..
EXPENDITURE							
Food	% of GDP	16.1	16.0	..	..	..	..
Staples	"	2.2	1.9	..	..	..	..
Meat, fish, milk, cheese, eggs	"	6.9	7.6	..	..	..	..
Cereal imports	thou. metric tonnes	191	134	156	45,972	49,174	70,626
Food aid in cereals	"	4	..	..	1,639	282	2
Food production per capita	1987 = 100	93	110	94	..	109	101
Fertilizer consumption	kg/ha	224.3	204.6	54.9	..	68.8	162.1
Share of agriculture in GDP	% of GDP	17.9	16.1	7.1	..	8.1	2.4
Housing	% of GDP	4.5	5.9	..	..	..	..
Average household size	persons per household	3.0	2.8	..	..	..	..
Urban	"	2.8	2.7	..	..	..	..
Fixed investment: housing	% of GDP	5.9	5.6	..	..	..	..
Fuel and power	% of GDP	2.0	2.9	..	..	..	..
Energy consumption per capita	kg of oil equiv.	2,225	2,837	2,392	3,190	1,649	5,101
Households with electricity							
Urban	% of households	..	99.1	..	..	..	..
Rural	"	..	..	..	..	..	..
Transport and communication	% of GDP	4.5	5.8	..	..	..	..
Fixed investment: transport equipment	"	2.9	1.2	..	..	..	..
Total road length	thou. km	..	91	105	..	..	..
INVESTMENT IN HUMAN CAPITAL							
Health							
Population per physician	persons	507	307	335	378	..	..
Population per nurse	"	214	174	..	..	..	..
Population per hospital bed	"	123	109	99	134	385	144
Oral rehydration therapy (under-5)	% of cases	..	..	..	..	54	..
Education							
Gross enrollment ratio							
Secondary	% of school-age pop.	63	72	81	..	53	92
Female	"	58	72	81	..	..	94
Pupil-teacher ratio: primary	pupils per teacher	16	15	12	..	25	18
Pupil-teacher ratio: secondary	"	15	13	12	..	..	..
Pupils reaching grade 4	% of cohort	95	97	98	..	71	..
Repeater rate: primary	% of total enroll	3	3	3	..	11	..
Illiteracy	% of pop. (age 15+)	2	1	..	..	14	..
Female	% of fem. (age 15+)	..	..	..	..	17	..
Newspaper circulation	per thou. pop.	233	250	233	..	117	..

World Bank International Economics Department, April 1994

Iceland

Indicator	Unit of measure	Latest single year		Most recent estimate 1987-92	Same region/income group High-income
		1970-75	1980-85		
Priority Poverty Indicators					
POVERTY					
Upper poverty line	local curr.	..	..	..	..
Headcount index	% of pop.	..	..	..	..
Lower poverty line	local curr.	..	..	..	..
Headcount index	% of pop.	..	..	..	..
GNP per capita	US$	6,350	11,840	23,880	21,960
SHORT TERM INCOME INDICATORS					
Unskilled urban wages	local curr.	..	..	..	..
Unskilled rural wages	"	..	..	..	..
Rural terms of trade	"	..	..	..	..
Consumer price index	1987=100	2	70	195	..
Lower income	"	..	..	..	..
Food[a]	"	..	70	184	..
Urban	"	..	..	..	..
Rural	"	..	..	..	..
SOCIAL INDICATORS					
Public expenditure on basic social services	% of GDP	..	..	..	..
Gross enrollment ratios					
Primary	% school age pop.	100	99	101	103
Male	"	98	99	97	103
Female	"	102	99	102	103
Mortality					
Infant mortality	per thou. live births	12.5	5.7	5.5	7.0
Under 5 mortality	"	..	..	7.3	10.0
Immunization					
Measles	% age group	..	90.0	99.0	82.4
DPT	"	..	92.0	99.0	90.1
Child malnutrition (under-5)	"	..	..	..	..
Life expectancy					
Total	years	74	77	78	77
Female advantage	"	6.0	5.5	5.0	6.4
Total fertility rate	births per woman	2.6	1.9	2.2	1.7
Maternal mortality rate	per 100,000 live births	..	23	..	..
Supplementary Poverty Indicators					
Expenditures on social security	% of total gov't exp.	12.5	14.0	18.5	..
Social security coverage	% econ. active pop.	..	..	..	..
Access to safe water: total	% of pop.	..	..	..	..
Urban	"	..	..	..	..
Rural	"	..	..	..	..
Access to health care	"	..	100.0	..	..

Population growth rate
(annual average, percent)

GNP per capita growth rate
(annual average, percent)

Development diamond[b]

☐ Iceland
— High-income

━ Iceland
— High-income

a. See the technical notes, p.389. b. The development diamond, based on four key indicators, shows the average level of development in the country compared with its income group. See the introduction.

154

Iceland

Indicator	Unit of measure	Latest single year 1970-75	Latest single year 1980-85	Most recent estimate 1987-92	Same region/income group High-income

Resources and Expenditures

HUMAN RESOURCES

Indicator	Unit of measure	1970-75	1980-85	1987-92	High-income
Population (mre=1992)	thousands	218	241	261	828,221
Age dependency ratio	ratio	0.65	0.58	0.56	0.50
Urban	% of pop.	86.6	89.5	91.0	78.1
Population growth rate	annual %	1.4	0.8	1.2	0.7
Urban	"	1.8	1.1	1.4	0.9
Labor force (15-64)	thousands	103	127	140	390,033
Agriculture	% of labor force	14	10	..	..
Industry	"	38	37	..	..
Female	"	38	42	43	38
Females per 100 males					
Urban	number	..	..	..	..
Rural	"	..	..	..	..

NATURAL RESOURCES

Indicator	Unit of measure	1970-75	1980-85	1987-92	High-income
Area	thou. sq. km	103.00	103.00	103.00	31,709.00
Density	pop. per sq. km	2.1	2.3	2.5	24.5
Agricultural land	% of land area	22.8	22.8	22.8	42.7
Change in agricultural land	annual %	0.0	0.0	0.0	-0.2
Agricultural land under irrigation	%	..	..	..	16.1
Forests and woodland	thou. sq. km	1	1	1	..
Deforestation (net)	annual %	..	..	..	..

INCOME

Indicator	Unit of measure	1970-75	1980-85	1987-92	High-income
Household income					
Share of top 20% of households	% of income	..	..	..	..
Share of bottom 40% of households	"	..	..	..	..
Share of bottom 20% of households	"	..	..	..	..

EXPENDITURE

Indicator	Unit of measure	1970-75	1980-85	1987-92	High-income
Food	% of GDP	..	..	..	..
Staples	"	..	..	..	..
Meat, fish, milk, cheese, eggs	"	..	..	..	..
Cereal imports	thou. metric tonnes	30	23	22	70,626
Food aid in cereals	"	3	..	..	2
Food production per capita	1987 = 100	105	96	75	101
Fertilizer consumption	kg/ha	12.3	11.0	10.0	162.1
Share of agriculture in GDP	% of GDP	9.3	9.6	10.2	2.4
Housing	% of GDP	..	..	..	..
Average household size	persons per household	..	..	..	..
Urban	"	..	..	..	..
Fixed investment: housing	% of GDP	..	..	..	..
Fuel and power	% of GDP	..	..	..	..
Energy consumption per capita	kg of oil equiv.	3,615	4,473	4,977	5,101
Households with electricity					
Urban	% of households	..	..	..	..
Rural	"	..	..	..	..
Transport and communication	% of GDP	..	..	..	..
Fixed investment: transport equipment	"	..	..	..	..
Total road length	thou. km	12	12	11	..

INVESTMENT IN HUMAN CAPITAL

Indicator	Unit of measure	1970-75	1980-85	1987-92	High-income
Health					
Population per physician	persons	..	435	..	..
Population per nurse	"	..	87	..	..
Population per hospital bed	"	..	..	..	144
Oral rehydration therapy (under-5)	% of cases	..	..	..	..
Education					
Gross enrollment ratio					
Secondary	% of school-age pop.	80	91	99	92
Female	"	75	87	89	94
Pupil-teacher ratio: primary	pupils per teacher	19	..	..	18
Pupil-teacher ratio: secondary	"	13	..	..	..
Pupils reaching grade 4	% of cohort	100	..	..	..
Repeater rate: primary	% of total enroll	..	..	..	..
Illiteracy	% of pop. (age 15+)	..	..	†	..
Female	% of fem. (age 15+)	..	..	†	..
Newspaper circulation	per thou. pop.	431	402	..	..

World Bank International Economics Department, April 1994

India

Indicator	Unit of measure	Latest single year		Most recent estimate 1987-92	Same region/income group		Next higher income group
		1970-75	1980-85		South Asia	Low-income	

Priority Poverty Indicators

POVERTY

Indicator	Unit of measure	1970-75	1980-85	1987-92	South Asia	Low-income	Next higher
Upper poverty line	local curr.	..	..	1,296	..	..	..
Headcount index	% of pop.	43	..	25	28	19	..
Lower poverty line	local curr.	..	..	..	..	..	..
Headcount index	% of pop.	..	..	..	..	..	..
GNP per capita	US$	160	290	310	310	390	..

SHORT TERM INCOME INDICATORS

Indicator	Unit of measure	1970-75	1980-85	1987-92	South Asia	Low-income	Next higher
Unskilled urban wages	local curr.	..	..	..	..	..	..
Unskilled rural wages	"	..	..	..	..	..	..
Rural terms of trade	"	..	84	94	..	..	..
Consumer price index	1987=100	45	85	161	..	..	..
Lower income	"	..	..	..	..	..	..
Food[a]	"	27	83	147	..	..	..
Urban	"	..	..	..	..	..	..
Rural	"	..	..	..	..	..	..

SOCIAL INDICATORS

Indicator	Unit of measure	1970-75	1980-85	1987-92	South Asia	Low-income	Next higher
Public expenditure on basic social services	% of GDP	..	..	..	..	..	..
Gross enrollment ratios							
Primary	% school age pop.	79	96	103	103	103	..
Male	"	94	111	117	117	113	..
Female	"	62	80	88	88	96	..
Mortality							
Infant mortality	per thou. live births	132.0	108.0	79.0	85.0	73.0	45.0
Under 5 mortality	"	..	..	105.8	116.0	108.0	59.0
Immunization							
Measles	% age group	..	..	56.0	56.6	72.7	..
DPT	"	..	41.0	79.0	75.0	80.6	..
Child malnutrition (under-5)	"	..	49.3	63.0	60.9	38.3	..
Life expectancy							
Total	years	50	55	61	60	62	68
Female advantage	"	-1.9	-0.4	1.1	1.0	2.4	6.4
Total fertility rate	births per woman	5.6	4.8	3.7	4.0	3.4	3.1
Maternal mortality rate	per 100,000 live births	..	460	..	..	..	..

Supplementary Poverty Indicators

Indicator	Unit of measure	1970-75	1980-85	1987-92	South Asia	Low-income	Next higher
Expenditures on social security	% of total gov't exp.	..	..	..	..	..	..
Social security coverage	% econ. active pop.	..	..	..	..	..	..
Access to safe water: total	% of pop.	31.0	57.0	75.0	71.9	68.4	..
Urban	"	80.0	76.0	79.0	74.2	78.9	..
Rural	"	18.0	50.0	73.0	70.0	60.3	..
Access to health care	"	..	75.0	..	..	..	..

Population growth rate
(annual average, percent)

India / Low-income

GNP per capita growth rate
(annual average, percent)

Development diamond[b]

Life expectancy / GNP per capita / Gross primary enrollment / Access to safe water

India / Low-income

a. See the technical notes, p.389.   b. The development diamond, based on four key indicators, shows the average level of development in the country compared with its income group. See the introduction.

156

India

Indicator	Unit of measure	Latest single year 1970-75	Latest single year 1980-85	Most recent estimate 1987-92	Same region/income group South Asia	Same region/income group Low-income	Next higher income group
Resources and Expenditures							
HUMAN RESOURCES							
Population (mre=1992)	thousands	613,459	765,147	883,570	1,177,918	3,194,535	942,547
Age dependency ratio	ratio	0.77	0.72	0.70	0.73	0.67	0.66
Urban	% of pop.	21.3	24.3	26.0	25.4	26.7	57.0
Population growth rate	annual %	2.3	2.0	2.0	2.1	1.8	1.4
Urban	"	3.7	3.0	3.0	3.4	3.4	4.8
Labor force (15-64)	thousands	243,481	293,193	335,523	428,847	1,478,954	..
Agriculture	% of labor force	71	70	..	..	..	..
Industry	"	13	13	..	..	..	..
Female	"	28	26	25	22	33	36
Females per 100 males							
Urban	number	81	88	..	..	..	..
Rural	"	96	94	..	..	..	..
NATURAL RESOURCES							
Area	thou. sq. km	3,287.59	3,287.59	3,287.59	5,133.49	38,401.06	40,697.37
Density	pop. per sq. km	186.6	232.7	263.6	224.8	81.7	22.8
Agricultural land	% of land area	60.8	60.9	61.0	58.9	50.9	..
Change in agricultural land	annual %	0.5	-0.1	0.1	-0.2	0.0	..
Agricultural land under irrigation	%	18.7	23.1	25.2	29.0	18.2	..
Forests and woodland	thou. sq. km	656	672	670	..	..	..
Deforestation (net)	annual %	..	..	0.6	..	..	..
INCOME							
Household income							
Share of top 20% of households	% of income	49	41	41	41	42	..
Share of bottom 40% of households	"	16	20	21	21	19	..
Share of bottom 20% of households	"	6	8	9	9	8	..
EXPENDITURE							
Food	% of GDP	43.6	35.3	..	..	..	..
Staples	"	20.6	12.4	..	..	..	..
Meat, fish, milk, cheese, eggs	"	6.5	7.4	..	..	..	..
Cereal imports	thou. metric tonnes	7,669	205	3,044	7,721	46,537	74,924
Food aid in cereals	"	1,582	304	299	2,558	9,008	4,054
Food production per capita	1987 = 100	100	111	121	116	123	..
Fertilizer consumption	kg/ha	19.3	47.0	70.3	71.5	61.9	..
Share of agriculture in GDP	% of GDP	36.6	29.5	28.8	28.7	29.6	..
Housing	% of GDP	4.4	7.1	..	..	..	..
Average household size	persons per household	5.2	..	..	..	..	..
Urban	"	4.8	..	..	..	..	..
Fixed investment: housing	% of GDP	2.3	2.8	..	..	..	..
Fuel and power	% of GDP	2.4	2.3	..	..	..	..
Energy consumption per capita	kg of oil equiv.	124	170	235	209	335	1,882
Households with electricity							
Urban	% of households	..	..	..	..	..	..
Rural	"	..	..	..	..	..	..
Transport and communication	% of GDP	4.7	5.1	..	..	..	..
Fixed investment: transport equipment	"	1.4	2.3	..	..	..	..
Total road length	thou. km	1,375	1,546	1,636	..	..	..
INVESTMENT IN HUMAN CAPITAL							
Health							
Population per physician	persons	4,900	2,522	2,459	2,459	..	..
Population per nurse	"	3,710	1,701	..	..	..	..
Population per hospital bed	"	1,700	1,300	1,371	1,652	1,050	516
Oral rehydration therapy (under-5)	% of cases	..	..	14	18	39	..
Education							
Gross enrollment ratio							
Secondary	% of school-age pop.	26	38	44	40	41	..
Female	"	16	26	32	29	35	..
Pupil-teacher ratio: primary	pupils per teacher	42	58	60	59	37	26
Pupil-teacher ratio: secondary	"	21	21	23	23	19	..
Pupils reaching grade 4	% of cohort	51	58	..	..	..	..
Repeater rate: primary	% of total enroll	17	..	..	..	..	..
Illiteracy	% of pop. (age 15+)	66	56	52	54	39	..
Female	% of fem. (age 15+)	..	71	66	68	52	..
Newspaper circulation	per thou. pop.	15	20	..	..	..	100

World Bank International Economics Department, April 1994

Indonesia

Indicator	Unit of measure	Latest single year 1970-75	Latest single year 1980-85	Most recent estimate 1987-92	Same region/income group East Asia	Same region/income group Low-income	Next higher income group
Priority Poverty Indicators							
POVERTY							
Upper poverty line	local curr.	..	..	..	..	..	..
Headcount index	% of pop.	..	45	17	12	19	..
Lower poverty line	local curr.	..	..	..	..	..	..
Headcount index	% of pop.	..	29	15	9	..	..
GNP per capita	US$	210	550	670	760	390	..
SHORT TERM INCOME INDICATORS							
Unskilled urban wages	local curr.	..	315	1176	..	..	..
Unskilled rural wages	"	..	..	..	..	..	..
Rural terms of trade	"	..	..	..	..	..	..
Consumer price index	1987=100	28	86	145	..	..	..
Lower income	"	..	..	..	..	..	..
Food[a]	"	..	83	66	..	..	..
Urban	"	..	..	..	..	..	..
Rural	"	..	..	..	..	..	..
SOCIAL INDICATORS							
Public expenditure on basic social services	% of GDP	..	3.8	..	..	..	..
Gross enrollment ratios							
Primary	% school age pop.	86	117	116	121	103	..
Male	"	94	120	119	126	113	..
Female	"	78	114	114	117	96	..
Mortality							
Infant mortality	per thou. live births	114.0	95.0	66.0	39.0	73.0	45.0
Under 5 mortality	"	..	..	90.2	49.0	108.0	59.0
Immunization							
Measles	% age group	..	15.0	80.0	88.4	72.7	..
DPT	"	..	15.0	86.0	89.5	80.6	..
Child malnutrition (under-5)	"	..	..	39.9	24.7	38.3	..
Life expectancy							
Total	years	49	56	60	68	62	68
Female advantage	"	2.9	3.8	3.5	3.6	2.4	6.4
Total fertility rate	births per woman	5.4	4.1	2.9	2.4	3.4	3.1
Maternal mortality rate	per 100,000 live births	..	450	..	114	..	..
Supplementary Poverty Indicators							
Expenditures on social security	% of total gov't exp.	..	..	..	..	..	..
Social security coverage	% econ. active pop.	..	..	..	..	..	..
Access to safe water: total	% of pop.	11.0	38.0	42.0	72.0	68.4	..
Urban	"	41.0	43.0	65.0	83.4	78.9	..
Rural	"	4.0	36.0	32.0	60.2	60.3	..
Access to health care	"	..	..	64.0	..	..	..

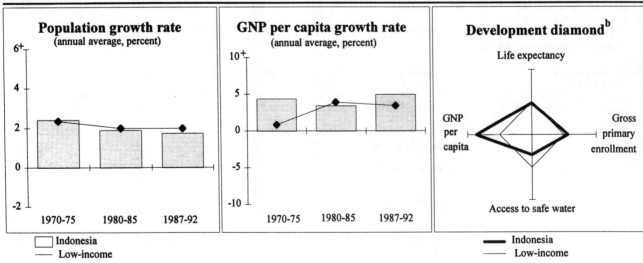

Population growth rate (annual average, percent)

☐ Indonesia
— Low-income

GNP per capita growth rate (annual average, percent)

Development diamond[b]

Life expectancy
GNP per capita
Gross primary enrollment
Access to safe water

—— Indonesia
— Low-income

a. See the technical notes, p.389.　b. The development diamond, based on four key indicators, shows the average level of development in the country compared with its income group. See the introduction.

Indonesia

Indicator	Unit of measure	Latest single year 1970-75	Latest single year 1980-85	Most recent estimate 1987-92	Same region/income group East Asia	Same region/income group Low-income	Next higher income group

Resources and Expenditures

HUMAN RESOURCES

Population (mre=1992)

Indicator	Unit of measure	1970-75	1980-85	1987-92	East Asia	Low-income	Next higher income group
Population (mre=1992)	thousands	132,589	163,036	184,283	1,688,909	3,194,535	942,547
Age dependency ratio	ratio	0.82	0.73	0.64	0.55	0.67	0.66
Urban	% of pop.	19.4	26.2	32.3	29.4	26.7	57.0
Population growth rate	annual %	2.4	1.8	1.6	1.4	1.8	1.4
Urban	"	4.8	4.9	3.8	2.9	3.4	4.8
Labor force (15-64)	thousands	50,526	63,430	74,593	928,465	1,478,954	..
Agriculture	% of labor force	62	57	..	..	..	..
Industry	"	12	13	..	..	..	..
Female	"	31	31	31	41	33	36
Females per 100 males							
Urban	number	102	102	..	..	..	..
Rural	"	110	106	..	..	..	..

NATURAL RESOURCES

Indicator	Unit of measure	1970-75	1980-85	1987-92	East Asia	Low-income	Next higher income group
Area	thou. sq. km	1,904.57	1,904.57	1,904.57	16,367.18	38,401.06	40,697.37
Density	pop. per sq. km	69.6	85.6	95.2	101.8	81.7	22.8
Agricultural land	% of land area	17.7	18.2	18.8	44.5	50.9	..
Change in agricultural land	annual %	1.0	0.2	0.6	0.1	0.0	..
Agricultural land under irrigation	%	15.1	21.4	24.2	14.5	18.2	..
Forests and woodland	thou. sq. km	1,222	1,128	1,092	..	..	..
Deforestation (net)	annual %	..	..	1.1	..	..	..

INCOME

Household income

Indicator	Unit of measure	1970-75	1980-85	1987-92	East Asia	Low-income	Next higher income group
Share of top 20% of households	% of income	52	..	42	42	42	..
Share of bottom 40% of households	"	17	..	21	18	19	..
Share of bottom 20% of households	"	7	..	9	7	8	..

EXPENDITURE

Indicator	Unit of measure	1970-75	1980-85	1987-92	East Asia	Low-income	Next higher income group
Food	% of GDP	..	30.2	..	..	..	..
Staples	"	..	13.1	..	..	..	..
Meat, fish, milk, cheese, eggs	"	..	6.4	..	..	..	..
Cereal imports	thou. metric tonnes	1,424	1,447	3,178	33,591	46,537	74,924
Food aid in cereals	"	301	270	82	581	9,008	4,054
Food production per capita	1987 = 100	90	113	129	133	123	..
Fertilizer consumption	kg/ha	15.3	59.8	71.3	75.1	61.9	..
Share of agriculture in GDP	% of GDP	30.2	23.2	19.2	21.5	29.6	..
Housing	% of GDP	..	8.2	..	..	..	..
Average household size	persons per household	5.0	4.8	..	..	..	..
Urban	"	5.0	5.3	..	..	..	..
Fixed investment: housing	% of GDP	..	3.5	..	..	..	..
Fuel and power	% of GDP	..	4.2	..	..	..	..
Energy consumption per capita	kg of oil equiv.	102	190	303	593	335	1,882
Households with electricity							
Urban	% of households	..	46.7	..	..	..	..
Rural	"	..	..	..	..	..	..
Transport and communication	% of GDP	..	2.6	..	..	..	..
Fixed investment: transport equipment	"	..	1.9	..	..	..	..
Total road length	thou. km	105	207	266	..	..	..

INVESTMENT IN HUMAN CAPITAL

Health

Indicator	Unit of measure	1970-75	1980-85	1987-92	East Asia	Low-income	Next higher income group
Population per physician	persons	26,988	9,412	7,028	..	..	..
Population per nurse	"	4,805	1,255	..	..	..	..
Population per hospital bed	"	1,222	1,796	1,503	553	1,050	516
Oral rehydration therapy (under-5)	% of cases	..	..	45	51	39	..

Education

Gross enrollment ratio

Indicator	Unit of measure	1970-75	1980-85	1987-92	East Asia	Low-income	Next higher income group
Secondary	% of school-age pop.	20	41	45	53	41	..
Female	"	15	33	41	47	35	..
Pupil-teacher ratio: primary	pupils per teacher	29	25	23	23	37	26
Pupil-teacher ratio: secondary	"	16	17	14	16	19	..
Pupils reaching grade 4	% of cohort	78	89	90	89	..	..
Repeater rate: primary	% of total enroll	11	11	10	6	..	..
Illiteracy	% of pop. (age 15+)	43	28	23	24	39	..
Female	% of fem. (age 15+)	..	37	32	34	52	..
Newspaper circulation	per thou. pop.	17	14	29	..	..	100

World Bank International Economics Department, April 1994

Islamic Republic of Iran

Indicator	Unit of measure	Latest single year 1970-75	Latest single year 1980-85	Most recent estimate 1987-92	Same region/income group Mid-East & North Africa	Same region/income group Lower-middle-income	Next higher income group
Priority Poverty Indicators							
POVERTY							
Upper poverty line	local curr.	..	..	..	..	..	..
Headcount index	% of pop.	..	..	..	..	..	..
Lower poverty line	local curr.	..	..	..	..	..	..
Headcount index	% of pop.	..	..	..	..	..	..
GNP per capita	US$	..	3,770	2,200	1,950	..	3,870
SHORT TERM INCOME INDICATORS							
Unskilled urban wages	local curr.	..	..	..	..	..	..
Unskilled rural wages	"	..	..	..	..	..	..
Rural terms of trade	"	..	..	..	..	..	..
Consumer price index	1987=100	15	66	244			
Lower income	"	..	..	..			
Food[a]	"	..	64	172	..	..	..
Urban	"	..	..	..	..	..	..
Rural	"	..	..	..	..	..	..
SOCIAL INDICATORS							
Public expenditure on basic social services	% of GDP	..	11.6	7.0	..	..	..
Gross enrollment ratios							
Primary	% school age pop.	93	98	112	100	..	107
Male	"	114	108	118	107	..	..
Female	"	71	88	105	88	..	..
Mortality							
Infant mortality	per thou. live births	122.0	103.0	65.0	58.0	45.0	40.0
Under 5 mortality	"	..	..	84.4	78.0	59.0	51.0
Immunization							
Measles	% age group	..	51.0	84.0	81.8	..	82.0
DPT	"	..	51.0	88.0	83.9	..	73.8
Child malnutrition (under-5)	"	..	..	43.1	20.9	..	..
Life expectancy							
Total	years	56	60	65	64	68	69
Female advantage	"	-0.7	1.1	1.0	2.4	6.4	6.3
Total fertility rate	births per woman	6.5	6.2	5.5	4.9	3.1	2.9
Maternal mortality rate	per 100,000 live births	..	..	..	..	..	..
Supplementary Poverty Indicators							
Expenditures on social security	% of total gov't exp.	2.4	11.3	13.7	..	..	..
Social security coverage	% econ. active pop.	..	..	..	..	..	..
Access to safe water: total	% of pop.	51.0	72.0	89.0	85.0	..	85.6
Urban	"	76.0	90.0	100.0	97.0	..	94.3
Rural	"	30.0	52.0	75.0	70.1	..	73.0
Access to health care	"	..	67.0	73.0	84.6	..	..

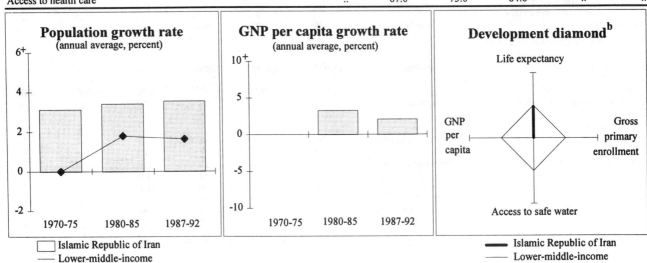

Population growth rate (annual average, percent)

GNP per capita growth rate (annual average, percent)

Development diamond[b]

Life expectancy — GNP per capita — Gross primary enrollment — Access to safe water

☐ Islamic Republic of Iran
— Lower-middle-income

▬ Islamic Republic of Iran
— Lower-middle-income

a. See the technical notes, p.389.   b. The development diamond, based on four key indicators, shows the average level of development in the country compared with its income group. See the introduction.

Islamic Republic of Iran

Indicator	Unit of measure	Latest single year 1970-75	Latest single year 1980-85	Most recent estimate 1987-92	Same region/income group Mid-East & North Africa	Same region/income group Lower-middle-income	Next higher income group
Resources and Expenditures							
HUMAN RESOURCES							
Population (mre=1992)	thousands	33,206	46,374	59,607	252,555	942,547	477,960
Age dependency ratio	ratio	0.95	0.88	0.93	0.87	0.66	0.64
Urban	% of pop.	45.8	53.2	58.3	54.7	57.0	71.7
Population growth rate	annual %	3.2	3.6	3.2	2.8	1.4	1.6
Urban	"	4.9	5.0	4.4	3.8	4.8	2.5
Labor force (15-64)	thousands	9,493	13,023	16,332	69,280	..	181,414
Agriculture	% of labor force	40	36	..	..	..	..
Industry	"	31	33	..	..	..	..
Female	"	14	17	19	15	36	29
Females per 100 males							
Urban	number	98	88	..	..	..	..
Rural	"	102	102	..	..	..	..
NATURAL RESOURCES							
Area	thou. sq. km	1,648.00	1,648.00	1,648.00	10,487.21	40,697.37	21,836.02
Density	pop. per sq. km	20.2	28.1	35.0	23.4	22.8	21.5
Agricultural land	% of land area	36.9	36.0	36.1	30.2	..	41.7
Change in agricultural land	annual %	-0.9	0.0	0.0	0.5	..	0.3
Agricultural land under irrigation	%	9.8	9.7	9.7	31.0	..	9.3
Forests and woodland	thou. sq. km	180	180	180	..	..	..
Deforestation (net)	annual %	..	..	..	..	..	..
INCOME							
Household income							
Share of top 20% of households	% of income	58	..	..	..	..	..
Share of bottom 40% of households	"	11	..	..	..	..	..
Share of bottom 20% of households	"	4	..	..	..	..	..
EXPENDITURE							
Food	% of GDP	14.7	24.8	..	..	..	..
Staples	"	4.5	6.4	..	..	..	..
Meat, fish, milk, cheese, eggs	"	5.0	10.8	..	..	..	..
Cereal imports	thou. metric tonnes	2,109	4,216	4,350	38,007	74,924	49,174
Food aid in cereals	"	51	..	104	2,484	4,054	282
Food production per capita	1987 = 100	101	112	118	116	..	109
Fertilizer consumption	kg/ha	5.6	15.3	19.1	96.7	..	68.8
Share of agriculture in GDP	% of GDP	11.1	19.7	22.7	13.7	..	8.1
Housing	% of GDP	7.7	15.3	..	..	..	..
Average household size	persons per household	..	..	..	..	..	..
Urban	"	..	..	..	..	..	..
Fixed investment: housing	% of GDP	6.7	7.9	..	..	..	..
Fuel and power	% of GDP	1.5	1.6	..	..	..	..
Energy consumption per capita	kg of oil equiv.	960	1,159	1,256	1,109	1,882	1,649
Households with electricity							
Urban	% of households	..	..	..	..	..	..
Rural	"	..	..	..	..	..	..
Transport and communication	% of GDP	3.1	3.9	..	..	..	..
Fixed investment: transport equipment	"	4.6	2.1	..	..	..	..
Total road length	thou. km	50	139	..	..	..	..
INVESTMENT IN HUMAN CAPITAL							
Health							
Population per physician	persons	3,270	2,949	3,141	..	..	..
Population per nurse	"	1,775	1,180	1,154	..	..	..
Population per hospital bed	"	725	658	724	636	516	385
Oral rehydration therapy (under-5)	% of cases	..	..	71	56	..	54
Education							
Gross enrollment ratio							
Secondary	% of school-age pop.	45	45	57	59	..	53
Female	"	33	37	49	50	..	..
Pupil-teacher ratio: primary	pupils per teacher	29	22	31	27	26	25
Pupil-teacher ratio: secondary	"	27	16	27	21	..	..
Pupils reaching grade 4	% of cohort	79	90	94	..	..	71
Repeater rate: primary	% of total enroll	9	10	9	..	..	11
Illiteracy	% of pop. (age 15+)	..	52	46	45	..	14
Female	% of fem. (age 15+)	..	64	57	58	..	17
Newspaper circulation	per thou. pop.	15	21	27	39	100	117

World Bank International Economics Department, April 1994

161

Iraq

Indicator	Unit of measure	Latest single year 1970-75	Latest single year 1980-85	Most recent estimate 1987-92	Same region/income group Mid-East & North Africa	Same region/income group Lower-middle-income	Next higher income group
Priority Poverty Indicators							
POVERTY							
Upper poverty line	local curr.	..	..	..	..	..	..
Headcount index	% of pop.	..	..	..	..	..	..
Lower poverty line	local curr.	..	..	..	..	..	..
Headcount index	% of pop.	..	..	..	..	..	..
GNP per capita	US$	1,140	2,520	2,140	1,950	..	3,870
SHORT TERM INCOME INDICATORS							
Unskilled urban wages	local curr.	..	..	..	..	..	..
Unskilled rural wages	"	..	..	..	..	..	..
Rural terms of trade	"	..	..	..	..	..	..
Consumer price index	1987=100	..	..	..	..	..	..
Lower income	"	..	..	..	..	..	..
Food[a]	"	..	81	256	..	..	..
Urban	"	..	..	..	..	..	..
Rural	"	..	..	..	..	..	..
SOCIAL INDICATORS							
Public expenditure on basic social services	% of GDP	..	..	..	..	..	..
Gross enrollment ratios							
Primary	% school age pop.	94	100	111	100	..	107
Male	"	122	108	120	107	..	..
Female	"	64	92	102	88	..	..
Mortality							
Infant mortality	per thou. live births	96.0	78.0	58.0	58.0	45.0	40.0
Under 5 mortality	"	..	..	69.2	78.0	59.0	51.0
Immunization							
Measles	% age group	..	25.0	73.0	81.8	..	82.0
DPT	"	..	13.0	69.0	83.9	..	73.8
Child malnutrition (under-5)	"	..	..	..	20.9	..	..
Life expectancy							
Total	years	57	62	64	64	68	69
Female advantage	"	1.8	1.8	6.0	2.4	6.4	6.3
Total fertility rate	births per woman	7.1	6.4	5.7	4.9	3.1	2.9
Maternal mortality rate	per 100,000 live births	..	117	..	..	..	..
Supplementary Poverty Indicators							
Expenditures on social security	% of total gov't exp.	..	..	..	..	..	..
Social security coverage	% econ. active pop.	..	..	..	..	..	..
Access to safe water: total	% of pop.	66.0	86.0	93.0	85.0	..	85.6
Urban	"	100.0	100.0	100.0	97.0	..	94.3
Rural	"	11.0	54.0	72.0	70.1	..	73.0
Access to health care	"	..	94.0	93.0	84.6	..	..

Population growth rate
(annual average, percent)

- □ Iraq
- — Lower-middle-income

GNP per capita growth rate
(annual average, percent)

Development diamond[b]

- ▬ Iraq
- — Lower-middle-income

a. See the technical notes, p.389. b. The development diamond, based on four key indicators, shows the average level of development in the country compared with its income group. See the introduction.

Iraq

Indicator	Unit of measure	Latest single year 1970-75	Latest single year 1980-85	Most recent estimate 1987-92	Same region/income group Mid-East & North Africa	Same region/income group Lower-middle-income	Next higher income group
Resources and Expenditures							
HUMAN RESOURCES							
Population (mre=1992)	thousands	11,020	15,319	19,165	252,555	942,547	477,960
Age dependency ratio	ratio	0.96	0.98	0.95	0.87	0.66	0.64
Urban	% of pop.	61.4	68.8	72.9	54.7	57.0	71.7
Population growth rate	annual %	3.3	3.3	3.1	2.8	1.4	1.6
Urban	"	5.0	4.3	3.9	3.8	4.8	2.5
Labor force (15-64)	thousands	2,890	4,259	5,571	69,280	..	181,414
Agriculture	% of labor force	37	30	..	..	..	..
Industry	"	22	22	..	..	..	..
Female	"	13	20	22	15	36	29
Females per 100 males							
Urban	number	94	..	..	..	..	..
Rural	"	108	..	..	..	..	..
NATURAL RESOURCES							
Area	thou. sq. km	438.32	438.32	438.32	10,487.21	40,697.37	21,836.02
Density	pop. per sq. km	25.1	35.0	42.4	23.4	22.8	21.5
Agricultural land	% of land area	21.2	21.6	21.6	30.2	..	41.7
Change in agricultural land	annual %	0.1	0.0	0.0	0.5	..	0.3
Agricultural land under irrigation	%	16.9	18.5	27.0	31.0	..	9.3
Forests and woodland	thou. sq. km	19	19	19	..	..	..
Deforestation (net)	annual %	..	..	..	..	..	..
INCOME							
Household income							
Share of top 20% of households	% of income	..	..	..	..	..	..
Share of bottom 40% of households	"	..	..	..	..	..	..
Share of bottom 20% of households	"	..	..	..	..	..	..
EXPENDITURE							
Food	% of GDP	..	..	..	..	..	..
Staples	"	..	..	..	..	..	..
Meat, fish, milk, cheese, eggs	"	..	..	..	..	..	..
Cereal imports	thou. metric tonnes	745	3,463	2,189	38,007	74,924	49,174
Food aid in cereals	"	0	0	116	2,484	4,054	282
Food production per capita	1987 = 100	108	120	75	116	..	109
Fertilizer consumption	kg/ha	3.5	18.7	14.3	96.7	..	68.8
Share of agriculture in GDP	% of GDP	..	..	..	13.7	..	8.1
Housing	% of GDP	..	..	..	..	..	..
Average household size	persons per household	..	..	..	..	..	..
Urban	"	..	..	..	..	..	..
Fixed investment: housing	% of GDP	..	..	..	..	..	..
Fuel and power	% of GDP	..	..	..	..	..	..
Energy consumption per capita	kg of oil equiv.	513	1,044	979	1,109	1,882	1,649
Households with electricity							
Urban	% of households	..	..	..	..	..	..
Rural	"	..	..	..	..	..	..
Transport and communication	% of GDP	..	..	..	..	..	..
Fixed investment: transport equipment	"	..	..	..	..	..	..
Total road length	thou. km	12	30	40	..	..	..
INVESTMENT IN HUMAN CAPITAL							
Health							
Population per physician	persons	3,237	1,761	1,659	..	..	..
Population per nurse	"	2,297	2,195	99	..	..	..
Population per hospital bed	"	513	528	603	636	516	385
Oral rehydration therapy (under-5)	% of cases	..	..	70	56	..	54
Education							
Gross enrollment ratio							
Secondary	% of school-age pop.	35	55	48	59	..	53
Female	"	21	39	37	50	..	..
Pupil-teacher ratio: primary	pupils per teacher	25	24	25	27	26	25
Pupil-teacher ratio: secondary	"	25	30	23	21	..	..
Pupils reaching grade 4	% of cohort	93	91	90	..	..	71
Repeater rate: primary	% of total enroll	16	21	19	..	..	11
Illiteracy	% of pop. (age 15+)	..	48	40	45	..	14
Female	% of fem. (age 15+)	..	59	51	58	..	17
Newspaper circulation	per thou. pop.	17	18	36	39	100	117

World Bank International Economics Department, April 1994

Ireland

Indicator	Unit of measure	Latest single year 1970-75	Latest single year 1980-85	Most recent estimate 1987-92	Same region/income group High-income
Priority Poverty Indicators					
POVERTY					
Upper poverty line	local curr.	..	..	..	..
Headcount index	% of pop.	..	..	..	..
Lower poverty line	local curr.	..	..	..	..
Headcount index	% of pop.	..	..	..	..
GNP per capita	US$	2,640	4,940	12,210	21,960
SHORT TERM INCOME INDICATORS					
Unskilled urban wages	local curr.	..	..	..	..
Unskilled rural wages	"	..	..	..	..
Rural terms of trade	"	..	..	..	..
Consumer price index	1987=100	27	93	117	..
Lower income	"	..	..	..	..
Food[a]	"	16	93	273	..
Urban	"	..	..	..	..
Rural	"	..	..	..	..
SOCIAL INDICATORS					
Public expenditure on basic social services	% of GDP	..	..	..	..
Gross enrollment ratios					
Primary	% school age pop.	103	100	103	103
Male	"	103	100	103	103
Female	"	103	100	103	103
Mortality					
Infant mortality	per thou. live births	17.5	8.8	5.0	7.0
Under 5 mortality	"	..	..	6.7	10.0
Immunization					
Measles	% age group	..	63.0	78.0	82.4
DPT	"	..	45.0	65.0	90.1
Child malnutrition (under-5)	"	..	..	..	..
Life expectancy					
Total	years	71	73	75	77
Female advantage	"	4.9	5.5	5.5	6.4
Total fertility rate	births per woman	3.4	2.5	2.0	1.7
Maternal mortality rate	per 100,000 live births	..	7	..	..
Supplementary Poverty Indicators					
Expenditures on social security	% of total gov't exp.	..	24.4	26.2	..
Social security coverage	% econ. active pop.	..	..	..	..
Access to safe water: total	% of pop.	..	..	..	..
Urban	"	..	..	..	..
Rural	"	..	..	..	..
Access to health care	"	..	100.0	..	..

Population growth rate
(annual average, percent)

GNP per capita growth rate
(annual average, percent)

Development diamond[b]

Ireland
High-income

a. See the technical notes, p.389. b. The development diamond, based on four key indicators, shows the average level of development in the country compared with its income group. See the introduction.

164

Ireland

Indicator	Unit of measure	Latest single year 1970-75	Latest single year 1980-85	Most recent estimate 1987-92	Same region/income group High-income
Resources and Expenditures					

HUMAN RESOURCES

Indicator	Unit of measure	1970-75	1980-85	1987-92	High-income
Population (mre=1992)	thousands	3,177	3,540	3,547	828,221
Age dependency ratio	ratio	0.73	0.67	0.59	0.50
Urban	% of pop.	53.6	56.3	57.6	78.1
Population growth rate	annual %	1.7	0.3	0.7	0.7
Urban	"	2.4	0.7	1.1	0.9
Labor force (15-64)	thousands	1,192	1,367	1,530	390,033
Agriculture	% of labor force	22	19	..	..
Industry	"	32	34	..	..
Female	"	27	29	29	38
Females per 100 males					
Urban	number	110	106	..	..
Rural	"	85	87	..	..

NATURAL RESOURCES

Indicator	Unit of measure	1970-75	1980-85	1987-92	High-income
Area	thou. sq. km	70.28	70.28	70.28	31,709.00
Density	pop. per sq. km	45.2	50.4	50.1	24.5
Agricultural land	% of land area	83.0	82.8	81.7	42.7
Change in agricultural land	annual %	0.4	0.2	-0.1	-0.2
Agricultural land under irrigation	%	..	..	..	16.1
Forests and woodland	thou. sq. km	3	3	3	..
Deforestation (net)	annual %	..	..	0.0	..

INCOME
Household income

Indicator	Unit of measure	1970-75	1980-85	1987-92	High-income
Share of top 20% of households	% of income	39	..	..	..
Share of bottom 40% of households	"	20	..	..	..
Share of bottom 20% of households	"	7	..	..	..

EXPENDITURE

Indicator	Unit of measure	1970-75	1980-85	1987-92	High-income
Food	% of GDP	17.1	15.2	..	..
Staples	"	3.2	2.5	..	..
Meat, fish, milk, cheese, eggs	"	8.7	7.5	..	..
Cereal imports	thou. metric tonnes	658	500	274	70,626
Food aid in cereals	"	..	..	..	2
Food production per capita	1987 = 100	106	111	124	101
Fertilizer consumption	kg/ha	75.5	108.7	115.9	162.1
Share of agriculture in GDP	% of GDP	15.5	9.6	9.0	2.4
Housing	% of GDP	7.5	6.2	..	..
Average household size	persons per household	3.9	3.7	..	..
Urban	"	4.0	..	..	..
Fixed investment: housing	% of GDP	6.1	6.6	..	..
Fuel and power	% of GDP	3.3	3.3	..	..
Energy consumption per capita	kg of oil equiv.	2,180	2,522	2,881	5,101
Households with electricity					
Urban	% of households	..	99.6	..	..
Rural	"	..	..	..	..
Transport and communication	% of GDP	6.4	8.6	..	..
Fixed investment: transport equipment	"	2.1	3.9	..	..
Total road length	thou. km	89	92	92	..

INVESTMENT IN HUMAN CAPITAL

Health

Indicator	Unit of measure	1970-75	1980-85	1987-92	High-income
Population per physician	persons	983	681	633	..
Population per nurse	"	157	140	..	..
Population per hospital bed	"	79	103	101	144
Oral rehydration therapy (under-5)	% of cases	..	..	..	..

Education

Gross enrollment ratio

Indicator	Unit of measure	1970-75	1980-85	1987-92	High-income
Secondary	% of school-age pop.	86	98	101	92
Female	"	91	103	105	94
Pupil-teacher ratio: primary	pupils per teacher	31	27	27	18
Pupil-teacher ratio: secondary	"	14	15	15	
Pupils reaching grade 4	% of cohort	..	99	99	..
Repeater rate: primary	% of total enroll	..	..	..	..
Illiteracy	% of pop. (age 15+)	..	..	..	..
Female	% of fem. (age 15+)	..	..	..	..
Newspaper circulation	per thou. pop.	218	188	169	..

World Bank International Economics Department, April 1994

Israel

Indicator	Unit of measure	Latest single year 1970-75	Latest single year 1980-85	Most recent estimate 1987-92	Same region/income group High-income
Priority Poverty Indicators					
POVERTY					
Upper poverty line	local curr.	..	..	..	..
Headcount index	% of pop.	..	..	..	..
Lower poverty line	local curr.	..	..	..	..
Headcount index	% of pop.	..	..	..	..
GNP per capita	US$	3,880	6,630	13,220	21,960
SHORT TERM INCOME INDICATORS					
Unskilled urban wages	local curr.	..	..	..	..
Unskilled rural wages	"	..	..	..	..
Rural terms of trade	"	..	..	..	..
Consumer price index	1987=100	0	56	218	..
Lower income	"	..	..	..	..
Food[a]	"	..	56	176	..
Urban	"	..	..	..	..
Rural	"	..	..	..	..
SOCIAL INDICATORS					
Public expenditure on basic social services	% of GDP	..	10.2	..	..
Gross enrollment ratios					
Primary	% school age pop.	97	97	95	103
Male	"	96	95	93	103
Female	"	97	98	96	103
Mortality					
Infant mortality	per thou. live births	22.9	11.9	9.3	7.0
Under 5 mortality	"	..	..	11.7	10.0
Immunization					
Measles	% age group	..	85.0	88.0	82.4
DPT	"	..	92.0	88.0	90.1
Child malnutrition (under-5)	"	..	..	..	..
Life expectancy					
Total	years	72	74	76	77
Female advantage	"	3.7	3.4	3.8	6.4
Total fertility rate	births per woman	3.8	3.1	2.7	1.7
Maternal mortality rate	per 100,000 live births	..	5	..	..
Supplementary Poverty Indicators					
Expenditures on social security	% of total gov't exp.	15.1	14.9	21.0	..
Social security coverage	% econ. active pop.	..	..	..	..
Access to safe water: total	% of pop.	..	..	..	..
Urban	"	..	..	..	..
Rural	"	..	..	..	..
Access to health care	"	..	100.0	100.0	..

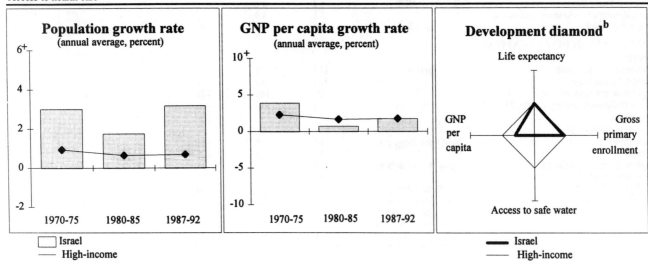

a. See the technical notes, p.389.   b. The development diamond, based on four key indicators, shows the average level of development in the country compared with its income group. See the introduction.

Israel

Indicator	Unit of measure	Latest single year 1970-75	Latest single year 1980-85	Most recent estimate 1987-92	Same region/income group High-income
Resources and Expenditures					
HUMAN RESOURCES					
Population (mre=1992)	thousands	3,455	4,233	5,118	828,221
Age dependency ratio	ratio	0.68	0.70	0.64	0.50
Urban	% of pop.	86.6	90.3	91.6	78.1
Population growth rate	annual %	2.3	1.8	3.1	0.7
Urban	"	2.8	2.1	3.1	0.9
Labor force (15-64)	thousands	1,279	1,610	1,886	390,033
Agriculture	% of labor force	8	6	..	..
Industry	"	34	32	..	..
Female	"	32	34	34	38
Females per 100 males					
Urban	number	102	103	..	..
Rural	"	95	92	..	..
NATURAL RESOURCES					
Area	thou. sq. km	20.77	20.77	20.77	31,709.00
Density	pop. per sq. km	166.4	203.8	238.9	24.5
Agricultural land	% of land area	26.6	28.3	28.5	42.7
Change in agricultural land	annual %	-0.9	2.0	-0.7	-0.2
Agricultural land under irrigation	%	33.3	40.5	30.7	16.1
Forests and woodland	thou. sq. km	1	1	1	..
Deforestation (net)	annual %	..	..	..	..
INCOME					
Household income					
Share of top 20% of households	% of income	39	40	..	..
Share of bottom 40% of households	"	21	18	..	..
Share of bottom 20% of households	"	8	6	..	..
EXPENDITURE					
Food	% of GDP	..	14.9	..	..
Staples	"	..	2.0	..	..
Meat, fish, milk, cheese, eggs	"	..	5.9	..	..
Cereal imports	thou. metric tonnes	1,644	1,714	1,871	70,626
Food aid in cereals	"	53	8	2	2
Food production per capita	1987 = 100	106	105	88	101
Fertilizer consumption	kg/ha	138.1	160.2	177.6	162.1
Share of agriculture in GDP	% of GDP	4.7	3.5	2.3	2.4
Housing	% of GDP	..	13.4	..	..
Average household size	persons per household	3.8	..	..	..
Urban	"	3.7	..	..	..
Fixed investment: housing	% of GDP	13.7	4.5	..	..
Fuel and power	% of GDP	..	1.6	..	..
Energy consumption per capita	kg of oil equiv.	2,218	1,886	2,367	5,101
Households with electricity					
Urban	% of households	..	..	..	..
Rural	"	..	..	..	..
Transport and communication	% of GDP	..	6.7	..	..
Fixed investment: transport equipment	"	0.0	1.4	..	..
Total road length	thou. km	4	5	..	..
INVESTMENT IN HUMAN CAPITAL					
Health					
Population per physician	persons	400	345	..	..
Population per nurse	"	..	107	..	..
Population per hospital bed	"	200	200	219	144
Oral rehydration therapy (under-5)	% of cases	..	..	..	..
Education					
Gross enrollment ratio					
Secondary	% of school-age pop.	66	80	85	92
Female	"	71	85	89	94
Pupil-teacher ratio: primary	pupils per teacher	16	17	17	18
Pupil-teacher ratio: secondary	"	..	..	..	..
Pupils reaching grade 4	% of cohort	96	100	98	..
Repeater rate: primary	% of total enroll	..	..	..	..
Illiteracy	% of pop. (age 15+)	12	5	..	..
Female	% of fem. (age 15+)	..	7	..	..
Newspaper circulation	per thou. pop.	387	196	258	..

World Bank International Economics Department, April 1994

Italy

Indicator	Unit of measure	Latest single year		Most recent estimate	Same region/income group
		1970-75	1980-85	1987-92	High-income

Priority Poverty Indicators

Indicator	Unit of measure	1970-75	1980-85	1987-92	High-income
POVERTY					
Upper poverty line	local curr.	..	..	..	..
Headcount index	% of pop.	..	..	..	..
Lower poverty line	local curr.	..	..	..	..
Headcount index	% of pop.	..	..	..	..
GNP per capita	US$	3,690	7,750	20,460	21,960
SHORT TERM INCOME INDICATORS					
Unskilled urban wages	local curr.	..	..	..	..
Unskilled rural wages	"	..	..	..	..
Rural terms of trade	"	..	..	..	..
Consumer price index	1987=100	22	90	133	..
Lower income	"	..	..	..	..
Food[a]	"	14	91	125	..
Urban	"	..	..	..	..
Rural	"	..	..	..	..
SOCIAL INDICATORS					
Public expenditure on basic social services	% of GDP	..	..	..	..
Gross enrollment ratios					
Primary	% school age pop.	106	96	94	103
Male	"	107	96	94	103
Female	"	106	96	94	103
Mortality					
Infant mortality	per thou. live births	21.2	10.5	8.3	7.0
Under 5 mortality	"	..	..	10.5	10.0
Immunization					
Measles	% age group	..	12.0	50.0	82.4
DPT	"	..	12.0	95.0	90.1
Child malnutrition (under-5)	"	..	..	..	..
Life expectancy					
Total	years	72	75	77	77
Female advantage	"	6.0	6.9	6.6	6.4
Total fertility rate	births per woman	2.2	1.4	1.3	1.7
Maternal mortality rate	per 100,000 live births	..	13	..	..

Supplementary Poverty Indicators

Indicator	Unit of measure	1970-75	1980-85	1987-92	High-income
Expenditures on social security	% of total gov't exp.	..	30.1	28.5	..
Social security coverage	% econ. active pop.	..	..	..	..
Access to safe water: total	% of pop.	..	..	..	..
Urban	"	..	..	..	..
Rural	"	..	..	..	..
Access to health care	"	..	100.0	..	..

Population growth rate
(annual average, percent)

GNP per capita growth rate
(annual average, percent)

Development diamond[b]

- Life expectancy
- GNP per capita
- Gross primary enrollment
- Access to safe water

Legend:
- Italy
- High-income

a. See the technical notes, p.389.   b. The development diamond, based on four key indicators, shows the average level of development in the country compared with its income group. See the introduction.

Italy

Indicator	Unit of measure	Latest single year		Most recent estimate 1987-92	Same region/income group
		1970-75	1980-85		High-income

Resources and Expenditures

HUMAN RESOURCES

Indicator	Unit of measure	1970-75	1980-85	1987-92	High-income
Population (mre=1992)	thousands	55,441	57,141	57,809	828,221
Age dependency ratio	ratio	0.57	0.47	0.47	0.50
Urban	% of pop.	65.6	67.6	69.5	78.1
Population growth rate	annual %	0.6	0.2	0.1	0.7
Urban	"	1.0	0.5	0.5	0.9
Labor force (15-64)	thousands	21,332	22,763	23,419	390,033
Agriculture	% of labor force	15	12	..	..
Industry	"	42	40	..	..
Female	"	30	32	32	38
Females per 100 males					
Urban	number	..	..	..	..
Rural	"	..	..	..	..

NATURAL RESOURCES

Indicator	Unit of measure	1970-75	1980-85	1987-92	High-income
Area	thou. sq. km	301.27	301.27	301.27	31,709.00
Density	pop. per sq. km	184.0	189.7	191.7	24.5
Agricultural land	% of land area	59.6	58.1	57.3	42.7
Change in agricultural land	annual %	0.1	-0.9	0.0	-0.2
Agricultural land under irrigation	%	15.5	17.6	18.6	16.1
Forests and woodland	thou. sq. km	63	64	68	..
Deforestation (net)	annual %	..	..	..	..

INCOME

Indicator	Unit of measure	1970-75	1980-85	1987-92	High-income
Household income					
Share of top 20% of households	% of income	..	..	..	..
Share of bottom 40% of households	"	..	..	..	..
Share of bottom 20% of households	"	..	..	..	..

EXPENDITURE

Indicator	Unit of measure	1970-75	1980-85	1987-92	High-income
Food	% of GDP	20.1	13.6	..	..
Staples	"	3.0	1.8	..	..
Meat, fish, milk, cheese, eggs	"	10.0	7.1	..	..
Cereal imports	thou. metric tonnes	7,059	7,052	7,836	70,626
Food aid in cereals	"	..	..	..	2
Food production per capita	1987 = 100	93	98	97	101
Fertilizer consumption	kg/ha	85.0	123.0	117.8	162.1
Share of agriculture in GDP	% of GDP	7.2	4.5	3.3	2.4
Housing	% of GDP	8.6	9.6	..	..
Average household size	persons per household	3.3	3.0	..	..
Urban	"	..	..	..	..
Fixed investment: housing	% of GDP	6.2	3.6	..	..
Fuel and power	% of GDP	2.0	2.8	..	..
Energy consumption per capita	kg of oil equiv.	2,243	2,391	2,755	5,101
Households with electricity					
Urban	% of households	..	..	..	..
Rural	"	..	..	..	..
Transport and communication	% of GDP	7.1	7.8	..	..
Fixed investment: transport equipment	"	2.1	2.0	..	..
Total road length	thou. km	292	298	304	..

INVESTMENT IN HUMAN CAPITAL

Health

Indicator	Unit of measure	1970-75	1980-85	1987-92	High-income
Population per physician	persons	555	750	213	..
Population per nurse	"	..	250	..	..
Population per hospital bed	"	95	..	133	144
Oral rehydration therapy (under-5)	% of cases	..	..	..	..

Education

Indicator	Unit of measure	1970-75	1980-85	1987-92	High-income
Gross enrollment ratio					
Secondary	% of school-age pop.	70	73	76	92
Female	"	66	72	76	94
Pupil-teacher ratio: primary	pupils per teacher	19	14	12	18
Pupil-teacher ratio: secondary	"	11	10	9	..
Pupils reaching grade 4	% of cohort	..	..	..	..
Repeater rate: primary	% of total enroll	3	1	1	..
Illiteracy	% of pop. (age 15+)	6	4	†	..
Female	% of fem. (age 15+)	..	5	†	..
Newspaper circulation	per thou. pop.	114	81	106	..

World Bank International Economics Department, April 1994

Jamaica

Indicator	Unit of measure	Latest single year 1970-75	Latest single year 1980-85	Most recent estimate 1987-92	Same region/income group Latin America Caribbean	Same region/income group Lower-middle-income	Next higher income group
Priority Poverty Indicators							
POVERTY							
Upper poverty line	local curr.	..	..	..	..	..	..
Headcount index	% of pop.	..	..	..	..	..	..
Lower poverty line	local curr.	..	..	..	..	..	..
Headcount index	% of pop.	..	..	..	..	..	..
GNP per capita	US$	1,250	920	1,340	2,690	..	3,870
SHORT TERM INCOME INDICATORS							
Unskilled urban wages	local curr.	..	..	..	..	..	..
Unskilled rural wages	"	..	..	..	..	..	..
Rural terms of trade	"	..	..	..	..	..	..
Consumer price index	1987=100	14	81	404	..	..	..
Lower income	"	..	..	..	..	..	..
Food[a]	"	6	79	85	..	..	..
Urban	"	..	..	..	..	..	..
Rural	"	..	..	..	..	..	..
SOCIAL INDICATORS							
Public expenditure on basic social services	% of GDP	..	..	..	..	..	..
Gross enrollment ratios							
Primary	% school age pop.	97	100	106	106	..	107
Male	"	97	99	105	..	..	..
Female	"	98	101	108	..	..	..
Mortality							
Infant mortality	per thou. live births	42.0	18.0	14.0	44.0	45.0	40.0
Under 5 mortality	"	..	..	17.1	56.0	59.0	51.0
Immunization							
Measles	% age group	..	60.0	74.0	78.9	..	82.0
DPT	"	..	57.0	86.0	73.8	..	73.8
Child malnutrition (under-5)	"	..	8.0	7.2	10.5	..	..
Life expectancy							
Total	years	69	71	74	68	68	69
Female advantage	"	4.2	4.4	4.5	5.6	6.4	6.3
Total fertility rate	births per woman	5.0	3.6	2.7	3.0	3.1	2.9
Maternal mortality rate	per 100,000 live births	..	100	..	..	..	..
Supplementary Poverty Indicators							
Expenditures on social security	% of total gov't exp.	..	..	..	..	..	..
Social security coverage	% econ. active pop.	..	..	93.2	..	..	..
Access to safe water: total	% of pop.	86.0	..	72.0	80.3	..	85.6
Urban	"	100.0	..	95.0	91.0	..	94.3
Rural	"	79.0	..	46.0	64.3	..	73.0
Access to health care	"	..	..	..	..	..	..

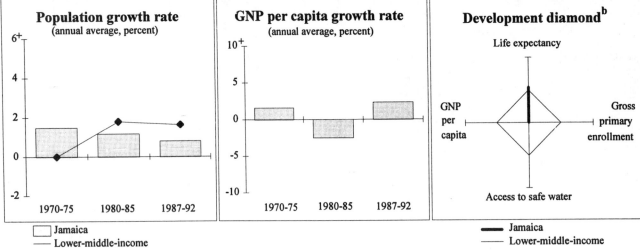

Population growth rate (annual average, percent)

GNP per capita growth rate (annual average, percent)

Development diamond[b]

Life expectancy — GNP per capita — Gross primary enrollment — Access to safe water

☐ Jamaica
— Lower-middle-income

— Jamaica
— Lower-middle-income

a. See the technical notes, p.389.   b. The development diamond, based on four key indicators, shows the average level of development in the country compared with its income group. See the introduction.

Jamaica

Indicator	Unit of measure	Latest single year 1970-75	Latest single year 1980-85	Most recent estimate 1987-92	Latin America Caribbean	Lower-middle-income	Next higher income group
Resources and Expenditures							
HUMAN RESOURCES							
Population (mre=1992)	thousands	2,013	2,260	2,396	453,294	942,547	477,960
Age dependency ratio	ratio	1.04	0.77	0.66	0.67	0.66	0.64
Urban	% of pop.	44.1	49.4	53.5	72.9	57.0	71.7
Population growth rate	annual %	1.4	1.0	0.8	1.7	1.4	1.6
Urban	"	2.6	2.1	2.0	2.6	4.8	2.5
Labor force (15-64)	thousands	803	1,095	1,306	166,091	..	181,414
Agriculture	% of labor force	32	31	..	..	..	..
Industry	"	17	16	..	..	..	..
Female	"	45	46	46	27	36	29
Females per 100 males							
Urban	number	..	..	..	..	..	..
Rural	"	..	..	..	..	..	..
NATURAL RESOURCES							
Area	thou. sq. km	10.99	10.99	10.99	20,507.48	40,697.37	21,836.02
Density	pop. per sq. km	183.2	205.6	216.2	21.7	22.8	21.5
Agricultural land	% of land area	43.9	42.8	42.6	40.2	..	41.7
Change in agricultural land	annual %	-1.0	-1.1	0.4	0.5	..	0.3
Agricultural land under irrigation	%	6.7	7.3	7.6	3.2	..	9.3
Forests and woodland	thou. sq. km	2	2	2	..	..	..
Deforestation (net)	annual %	..	..	9.2	..	..	..
INCOME							
Household income							
Share of top 20% of households	% of income	..	..	49	..	..	..
Share of bottom 40% of households	"	..	..	16	..	..	..
Share of bottom 20% of households	"	..	..	6	..	..	..
EXPENDITURE							
Food	% of GDP	22.4	27.2	..	..	..	..
Staples	"	9.8	10.2	..	..	..	..
Meat, fish, milk, cheese, eggs	"	7.6	8.5	..	..	..	..
Cereal imports	thou. metric tonnes	343	380	459	25,032	74,924	49,174
Food aid in cereals	"	1	225	181	1,779	4,054	282
Food production per capita	1987 = 100	105	95	109	104	..	109
Fertilizer consumption	kg/ha	38.5	25.4	55.8	15.5	..	68.8
Share of agriculture in GDP	% of GDP	7.4	6.0	5.1	8.9	..	8.1
Housing	% of GDP	7.9	11.0	..	..	..	..
Average household size	persons per household	4.0	..	..	..	..	..
Urban	"	..	..	..	..	..	..
Fixed investment: housing	% of GDP	7.0	5.2	..	..	..	..
Fuel and power	% of GDP	1.9	3.8	..	..	..	..
Energy consumption per capita	kg of oil equiv.	1,178	635	1,075	912	1,882	1,649
Households with electricity							
Urban	% of households	..	..	..	..	..	..
Rural	"	..	..	..	..	..	..
Transport and communication	% of GDP	8.5	12.0	..	..	..	..
Fixed investment: transport equipment	"	3.7	4.9	..	..	..	..
Total road length	thou. km	13	17	..	..	..	..
INVESTMENT IN HUMAN CAPITAL							
Health							
Population per physician	persons	2,632	2,006	..	..	..	..
Population per nurse	"	530	479	..	..	..	..
Population per hospital bed	"	200	293	..	508	516	385
Oral rehydration therapy (under-5)	% of cases	..	..	10	62	..	54
Education							
Gross enrollment ratio							
Secondary	% of school-age pop.	58	59	62	47	..	53
Female	"	63	62	66	..	..	..
Pupil-teacher ratio: primary	pupils per teacher	32	35	37	25	26	25
Pupil-teacher ratio: secondary	"	34	31	..	..	..	..
Pupils reaching grade 4	% of cohort	..	97	99	..	..	71
Repeater rate: primary	% of total enroll	4	3	4	14	..	11
Illiteracy	% of pop. (age 15+)	4	2	†	15	..	14
Female	% of fem. (age 15+)	..	2	†	17	..	17
Newspaper circulation	per thou. pop.	65	48	66	99	100	117

World Bank International Economics Department, April 1994

Japan

Indicator	Unit of measure	Latest single year		Most recent estimate 1987-92	Same region/income group High-income
		1970-75	1980-85		
Priority Poverty Indicators					
POVERTY					
Upper poverty line	local curr.	..	..	..	..
Headcount index	% of pop.	..	..	..	..
Lower poverty line	local curr.	..	..	..	..
Headcount index	% of pop.	..	..	..	..
GNP per capita	US$	4,520	11,430	28,190	21,960
SHORT TERM INCOME INDICATORS					
Unskilled urban wages	local curr.	..	..	..	..
Unskilled rural wages	"	..	..	..	..
Rural terms of trade	"	..	..	..	..
Consumer price index	1987=100	63	99	111	..
Lower income	"	..	..	..	..
Food[a]	"	38	101	112	..
Urban	"	..	..	..	..
Rural	"	..	..	..	..
SOCIAL INDICATORS					
Public expenditure on basic social services	% of GDP	..	..	..	..
Gross enrollment ratios					
Primary	% school age pop.	99	102	102	103
Male	"	99	102	102	103
Female	"	99	102	102	103
Mortality					
Infant mortality	per thou. live births	10.0	5.5	4.5	7.0
Under 5 mortality	"	..	..	6.1	10.0
Immunization					
Measles	% age group	..	73.0	66.0	82.4
DPT	"	..	83.0	87.0	90.1
Child malnutrition (under-5)	"	..	..	2.5	..
Life expectancy					
Total	years	74	77	79	77
Female advantage	"	5.2	5.5	6.1	6.4
Total fertility rate	births per woman	1.9	1.8	1.5	1.7
Maternal mortality rate	per 100,000 live births	..	15	..	..
Supplementary Poverty Indicators					
Expenditures on social security	% of total gov't exp.	..	..	..	..
Social security coverage	% econ. active pop.	..	..	..	..
Access to safe water: total	% of pop.	..	..	..	..
Urban	"	..	..	..	..
Rural	"	..	..	..	..
Access to health care	"	..	100.0	..	..

Population growth rate
(annual average, percent)

Japan
High-income

GNP per capita growth rate
(annual average, percent)

Development diamond[b]

Japan
High-income

a. See the technical notes, p.389.   b. The development diamond, based on four key indicators, shows the average level of development in the country compared with its income group. See the introduction.

172

Japan

Indicator	Unit of measure	Latest single year		Most recent estimate 1987-92	Same region/income group
		1970-75	1980-85		High-income
Resources and Expenditures					
HUMAN RESOURCES					
Population (mre=1992)	thousands	111,940	120,754	124,452	828,221
Age dependency ratio	ratio	0.47	0.47	0.47	0.50
Urban	% of pop.	75.7	76.7	77.5	78.1
Population growth rate	annual %	1.6	0.6	0.4	0.7
Urban	"	2.8	0.7	0.6	0.9
Labor force (15-64)	thousands	55,678	59,772	62,950	390,033
Agriculture	% of labor force	15	11	..	
Industry	"	34	34	..	..
Female	"	38	38	38	38
Females per 100 males					
Urban	number	102	101	..	..
Rural	"	107	102	..	..
NATURAL RESOURCES					
Area	thou. sq. km	377.80	377.80	377.80	31,709.00
Density	pop. per sq. km	296.3	319.6	328.0	24.5
Agricultural land	% of land area	14.8	14.3	13.8	42.7
Change in agricultural land	annual %	-0.8	-0.3	-0.7	-0.2
Agricultural land under irrigation	%	56.9	54.9	54.3	16.1
Forests and woodland	thou. sq. km	250	251	251	..
Deforestation (net)	annual %	..	..	0.0	..
INCOME					
Household income					
Share of top 20% of households	% of income	..	..	..	..
Share of bottom 40% of households	"	..	..	..	..
Share of bottom 20% of households	"	..	..	..	..
EXPENDITURE					
Food	% of GDP	13.8	10.8	..	..
Staples	"	2.7	2.3	..	..
Meat, fish, milk, cheese, eggs	"	5.6	4.4	..	..
Cereal imports	thou. metric tonnes	18,846	26,720	27,683	70,626
Food aid in cereals	"	..	..	..	2
Food production per capita	1987 = 100	104	104	95	101
Fertilizer consumption	kg/ha	323.2	378.1	338.8	162.1
Share of agriculture in GDP	% of GDP	5.5	3.2	2.3	2.4
Housing	% of GDP	8.9	11.3	..	..
Average household size	persons per household	3.4	3.2	..	..
Urban	"	3.3	3.1	..	..
Fixed investment: housing	% of GDP	7.6	3.4	..	..
Fuel and power	% of GDP	1.1	1.9	..	..
Energy consumption per capita	kg of oil equiv.	2,746	2,978	3,586	5,101
Households with electricity					
Urban	% of households	..	..	..	..
Rural	"	..	..	..	..
Transport and communication	% of GDP	5.4	5.7	..	..
Fixed investment: transport equipment	"	2.5	3.0	..	..
Total road length	thou. km	1,079	1,125	1,116	..
INVESTMENT IN HUMAN CAPITAL					
Health					
Population per physician	persons	890	663	608	..
Population per nurse	"	306	184	..	..
Population per hospital bed	"	80	86	64	144
Oral rehydration therapy (under-5)	% of cases	..	..	..	..
Education					
Gross enrollment ratio					
Secondary	% of school-age pop.	91	95	97	92
Female	"	92	96	98	94
Pupil-teacher ratio: primary	pupils per teacher	26	24	21	18
Pupil-teacher ratio: secondary	"	..	..	..	..
Pupils reaching grade 4	% of cohort	100	100	100	..
Repeater rate: primary	% of total enroll	0	0	0	..
Illiteracy	% of pop. (age 15+)	..	..	†	..
Female	% of fem. (age 15+)	..	..	†	..
Newspaper circulation	per thou. pop.	525	568	587	..

World Bank International Economics Department, April 1994

Jordan

Indicator	Unit of measure	Latest single year 1970-75	Latest single year 1980-85	Most recent estimate 1987-92	Same region/income group Mid-East & North Africa	Same region/income group Lower-middle-income	Next higher income group
Priority Poverty Indicators							
POVERTY							
Upper poverty line	local curr.	..	..	..	..	..	..
Headcount index	% of pop.	..	..	..	..	..	..
Lower poverty line	local curr.	..	..	..	..	..	..
Headcount index	% of pop.	..	..	..	..	..	..
GNP per capita	US$	..	1,970	1,120	1,950	..	3,870
SHORT TERM INCOME INDICATORS							
Unskilled urban wages	local curr.	..	..	..	..	..	..
Unskilled rural wages	"	..	..	..	..	..	..
Rural terms of trade	"	..	..	..	..	..	..
Consumer price index	1987=100	44	100	175	..	..	..
Lower income	"	..	..	..	..	..	..
Food[a]	"	..	100	171	..	..	..
Urban	"	..	..	..	..	..	..
Rural	"	..	..	..	..	..	..
SOCIAL INDICATORS							
Public expenditure on basic social services	% of GDP	..	12.1	..	..	..	..
Gross enrollment ratios							
Primary	% school age pop.	..	99	97	100	..	107
Male	"	..	98	96	107	..	..
Female	"	..	99	98	88	..	..
Mortality							
Infant mortality	per thou. live births	..	40.0	28.1	58.0	45.0	40.0
Under 5 mortality	"	..	..	36.6	78.0	59.0	51.0
Immunization							
Measles	% age group	..	39.0	85.0	81.8	..	82.0
DPT	"	..	53.0	92.0	83.9	..	73.8
Child malnutrition (under-5)	"	..	..	6.4	20.9	..	..
Life expectancy							
Total	years	..	64	70	64	68	69
Female advantage	"	..	3.1	4.0	2.4	6.4	6.3
Total fertility rate	births per woman	7.7	6.5	5.2	4.9	3.1	2.9
Maternal mortality rate	per 100,000 live births	..	..	..	..	..	..
Supplementary Poverty Indicators							
Expenditures on social security	% of total gov't exp.	8.9	7.3	6.9	..	..	..
Social security coverage	% econ. active pop.	..	..	..	..	..	..
Access to safe water: total	% of pop.	77.0	..	99.0	85.0	..	85.6
Urban	"	98.0	..	100.0	97.0	..	94.3
Rural	"	59.0	..	98.0	70.1	..	73.0
Access to health care	"	..	80.0	..	84.6	..	..

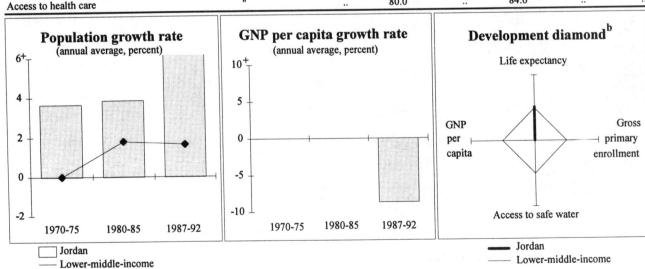

Population growth rate (annual average, percent) — Jordan / Lower-middle-income

GNP per capita growth rate (annual average, percent)

Development diamond[b] — Life expectancy, GNP per capita, Gross primary enrollment, Access to safe water — Jordan / Lower-middle-income

a. See the technical notes, p.389. b. The development diamond, based on four key indicators, shows the average level of development in the country compared with its income group. See the introduction.

Jordan

Indicator	Unit of measure	Latest single year 1970-75	Latest single year 1980-85	Most recent estimate 1987-92	Same region/income group Mid-East & North Africa	Same region/income group Lower-middle-income	Next higher income group
Resources and Expenditures							
HUMAN RESOURCES							
Population (mre=1992)	thousands	1,810	2,644	3,949	252,555	942,547	477,960
Age dependency ratio	ratio	1.00	0.97	0.90	0.87	0.66	0.64
Urban	% of pop.	55.3	64.1	69.4	54.7	57.0	71.7
Population growth rate	annual %	3.5	3.9	7.5	2.8	1.4	1.6
Urban	"	5.2	5.2	8.5	3.8	4.8	2.5
Labor force (15-64)	thousands	634	799	1,084	69,280	..	181,414
Agriculture	% of labor force	19	10	..	..	..	..
Industry	"	26	26	..	..	..	..
Female	"	7	9	11	15	36	29
Females per 100 males							
Urban	number	..	..	..	..	..	..
Rural	"	..	..	..	..	..	..
NATURAL RESOURCES							
Area	thou. sq. km	89.21	89.21	89.21	10,487.21	40,697.37	21,836.02
Density	pop. per sq. km	20.3	29.6	41.1	23.4	22.8	21.5
Agricultural land	% of land area	12.5	12.9	13.4	30.2	..	41.7
Change in agricultural land	annual %	0.1	0.3	0.2	0.5	..	0.3
Agricultural land under irrigation	%	3.2	4.2	5.3	31.0	..	9.3
Forests and woodland	thou. sq. km	1	1	1	..	..	..
Deforestation (net)	annual %	..	..	..	..	..	..
INCOME							
Household income							
Share of top 20% of households	% of income	..	..	48	..	..	..
Share of bottom 40% of households	"	..	..	17	..	..	..
Share of bottom 20% of households	"	..	..	7	..	..	..
EXPENDITURE							
Food	% of GDP	43.6	32.8	..	..	..	..
Staples	"	..	..	..	..	..	..
Meat, fish, milk, cheese, eggs	"	..	..	..	..	..	..
Cereal imports	thou. metric tonnes	176	721	1,578	38,007	74,924	49,174
Food aid in cereals	"	79	28	257	2,484	4,054	282
Food production per capita	1987 = 100	91	125	121	116	..	109
Fertilizer consumption	kg/ha	5.2	13.5	17.2	96.7	..	68.8
Share of agriculture in GDP	% of GDP	..	4.3	6.3	13.7	..	8.1
Housing	% of GDP	5.7	5.7	..	..	..	..
Average household size	persons per household	6.0	..	..	..	..	..
Urban	"	..	..	..	..	..	..
Fixed investment: housing	% of GDP	7.8	9.6	..	..	..	..
Fuel and power	% of GDP	..	..	..	..	..	..
Energy consumption per capita	kg of oil equiv.	453	1,072	813	1,109	1,882	1,649
Households with electricity							
Urban	% of households	..	..	..	..	..	..
Rural	"	..	..	..	..	..	..
Transport and communication	% of GDP	6.3	5.2	..	..	..	..
Fixed investment: transport equipment	"	4.8	3.3	..	..	..	..
Total road length	thou. km	4	5	6	..	..	..
INVESTMENT IN HUMAN CAPITAL							
Health							
Population per physician	persons	2,645	860	767	..	..	..
Population per nurse	"	874	980	497	..	..	..
Population per hospital bed	"	975	830	519	636	516	385
Oral rehydration therapy (under-5)	% of cases	..	..	77	56	..	54
Education							
Gross enrollment ratio							
Secondary	% of school-age pop.	..	79	91	59	..	53
Female	"	..	78	62	50	..	..
Pupil-teacher ratio: primary	pupils per teacher	35	31	24	27	26	25
Pupil-teacher ratio: secondary	"	21	18	16	21	..	..
Pupils reaching grade 4	% of cohort	94	96	97	..	..	71
Repeater rate: primary	% of total enroll	4	5	3	..	..	11
Illiteracy	% of pop. (age 15+)	..	26	20	45	..	14
Female	% of fem. (age 15+)	..	38	30	58	..	17
Newspaper circulation	per thou. pop.	32	68	69	39	100	117

World Bank International Economics Department, April 1994

175

Kazakhstan

Indicator	Unit of measure	Latest single year 1970-75	Latest single year 1980-85	Most recent estimate 1987-92	Same region/income group Europe & Central Asia	Same region/income group Lower-middle-income	Next higher income group
Priority Poverty Indicators							
POVERTY							
Upper poverty line	local curr.	..	..	..	..	..	..
Headcount index	% of pop.	..	..	24	..	..	..
Lower poverty line	local curr.	..	..	..	..	..	..
Headcount index	% of pop.	..	..	10	..	..	..
GNP per capita	US$	..	..	1,680	..	..	3,870
SHORT TERM INCOME INDICATORS							
Unskilled urban wages	local curr.	..	..	..	..	..	..
Unskilled rural wages	"	..	..	..	..	..	..
Rural terms of trade	"	..	..	..	..	..	..
Consumer price index	1987=100	..	..	..	..	..	..
Lower income	"	..	..	..	..	..	..
Food[a]	"	..	..	..	..	..	..
Urban	"	..	..	..	..	..	..
Rural	"	..	..	..	..	..	..
SOCIAL INDICATORS							
Public expenditure on basic social services	% of GDP	..	..	8.0	..	..	..
Gross enrollment ratios							107
Primary	% school age pop.	..	..	..	..	..	
Male	"	..	..	..	..	..	
Female	"	..	..	..	..	..	
Mortality							
Infant mortality	per thou. live births	..	35.8	31.0	30.0	45.0	40.0
Under 5 mortality	"	..	..	37.7	38.0	59.0	51.0
Immunization							82.0
Measles	% age group	..	..	..	..	..	73.8
DPT	"	..	..	..	..	..	
Child malnutrition (under-5)	"	..	..	..	..	..	..
Life expectancy							
Total	years	..	69	68	70	68	69
Female advantage	"	..	9.3	9.3	8.6	6.4	6.3
Total fertility rate	births per woman	3.3	3.1	2.7	2.2	3.1	2.9
Maternal mortality rate	per 100,000 live births	..	56	53	58	..	..
Supplementary Poverty Indicators							
Expenditures on social security	% of total gov't exp.	..	..	..	..	..	..
Social security coverage	% econ. active pop.	..	..	..	..	..	85.6
Access to safe water: total	% of pop.	..	..	..	..	..	94.3
Urban	"	..	..	..	..	..	73.0
Rural	"	..	..	..	..	..	
Access to health care	"	..	..	..	..	..	

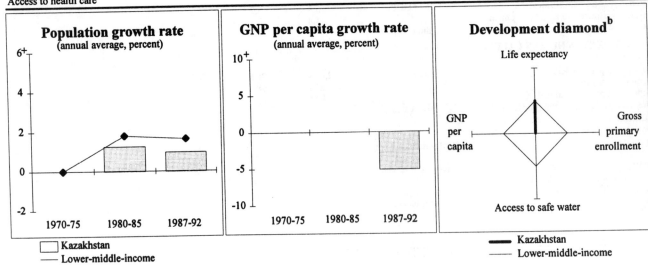

Population growth rate (annual average, percent)

GNP per capita growth rate (annual average, percent)

Development diamond[b]
Life expectancy — GNP per capita — Gross primary enrollment — Access to safe water

☐ Kazakhstan
— Lower-middle-income

— Kazakhstan
— Lower-middle-income

a. See the technical notes, p.389.   b. The development diamond, based on four key indicators, shows the average level of development in the country compared with its income group. See the introduction.

Kazakhstan

Indicator	Unit of measure	Latest single year 1970-75	Latest single year 1980-85	Most recent estimate 1987-92	Same region/income group Europe & Central Asia	Same region/income group Lower-middle-income	Next higher income group
Resources and Expenditures							
HUMAN RESOURCES							
Population (mre=1992)	thousands	..	15,852	17,038	495,241	942,547	477,960
Age dependency ratio	ratio	..	..	0.63	0.56	0.66	0.64
Urban	% of pop.	..	..	57.0	63.3	57.0	71.7
Population growth rate	annual %	..	1.4	0.9	0.5	1.4	1.6
Urban	"	..	..	..	..	4.8	2.5
Labor force (15-64)	thousands	..	8,954	9,262	..	..	181,414
Agriculture	% of labor force	..	..	..	..	..	..
Industry	"	..	..	..	..	..	..
Female	"	..	..	..	..	..	..
Females per 100 males		..	..	..	46	36	29
Urban	number	..	..	..	..	..	..
Rural	"	..	..	..	..	..	..
NATURAL RESOURCES							
Area	thou. sq. km	..	..	2,717.30	24,165.06	40,697.37	21,836.02
Density	pop. per sq. km	..	..	6.2	20.4	22.8	21.5
Agricultural land	% of land area	..	..	..	..	..	41.7
Change in agricultural land	annual %	..	..	..	..	..	0.3
Agricultural land under irrigation	%	..	..	..	..	..	9.3
Forests and woodland	thou. sq. km	..	..	..	..	..	..
Deforestation (net)	annual %	..	..	..	..	..	..
INCOME							
Household income							
Share of top 20% of households	% of income	..	..	..	..	..	..
Share of bottom 40% of households	"	..	..	..	..	..	..
Share of bottom 20% of households	"	..	..	..	..	..	..
EXPENDITURE							
Food	% of GDP	..	..	19.8	..	..	..
Staples	"	..	..	3.6	..	..	..
Meat, fish, milk, cheese, eggs	"	..	..	8.9	..	..	..
Cereal imports	thou. metric tonnes	..	..	..	45,972	74,924	49,174
Food aid in cereals	"	..	..	..	1,639	4,054	282
Food production per capita	1987 = 100	..	..	..	..	..	109
Fertilizer consumption	kg/ha	..	..	..	..	..	68.8
Share of agriculture in GDP	% of GDP	..	24.1	28.5	..	..	8.1
Housing	% of GDP	..	..	4.7	..	..	..
Average household size	persons per household	..	..	4.0	..	..	..
Urban	"	..	..	..	..	..	..
Fixed investment: housing	% of GDP	..	..	4.9	..	..	..
Fuel and power	% of GDP	..	..	1.0	..	..	..
Energy consumption per capita	kg of oil equiv.	..	..	4,722	3,190	1,882	1,649
Households with electricity							
Urban	% of households	..	..	..	..	..	..
Rural	"	..	..	..	..	..	..
Transport and communication	% of GDP	..	..	6.2	..	..	..
Fixed investment: transport equipment	"	..	..	10.3	..	..	..
Total road length	thou. km	..	105	153	..	..	..
INVESTMENT IN HUMAN CAPITAL							
Health							
Population per physician	persons	..	..	253	378	..	..
Population per nurse	"	..	..	..	..	..	..
Population per hospital bed	"	..	..	75	134	516	385
Oral rehydration therapy (under-5)	% of cases	..	..	..	..	..	54
Education							
Gross enrollment ratio							
Secondary	% of school-age pop.	..	..	..	..	..	53
Female	"	..	..	..	..	..	..
Pupil-teacher ratio: primary	pupils per teacher	..	..	..	..	26	25
Pupil-teacher ratio: secondary	"	..	..	..	..	..	..
Pupils reaching grade 4	% of cohort	..	..	..	..	..	71
Repeater rate: primary	% of total enroll	..	..	..	..	..	11
Illiteracy	% of pop. (age 15+)	..	..	..	..	..	14
Female	% of fem. (age 15+)	..	..	..	..	..	17
Newspaper circulation	per thou. pop.	..	..	..	..	100	117

World Bank International Economics Department, April 1994

Kenya

Indicator	Unit of measure	Latest single year 1970-75	Latest single year 1980-85	Most recent estimate 1987-92	Same region/income group Sub-Saharan Africa	Same region/income group Low-income	Next higher income group
Priority Poverty Indicators							
POVERTY							
Upper poverty line	local curr.	..	..	..	..	..	..
Headcount index	% of pop.	..	..	..	..	19	..
Lower poverty line	local curr.	..	..	..	..	..	..
Headcount index	% of pop.	..	..	..	..	..	..
GNP per capita	US$	230	310	310	520	390	..
SHORT TERM INCOME INDICATORS							
Unskilled urban wages	local curr.	..	..	..	..	..	..
Unskilled rural wages	"	..	..	136	..	..	..
Rural terms of trade	"	..	..	..	..	..	..
Consumer price index	1987=100	26	89	225	..	..	..
Lower income	"	..	..	..	..	..	..
Food[a]	"	..	93	59	..	..	..
Urban	"	..	..	..	..	..	..
Rural	"	..	..	..	..	..	..
SOCIAL INDICATORS							
Public expenditure on basic social services	% of GDP	..	7.1	..	..	..	..
Gross enrollment ratios							
Primary	% school age pop.	95	98	95	66	103	..
Male	"	103	101	97	79	113	..
Female	"	87	95	93	62	96	..
Mortality							
Infant mortality	per thou. live births	98.0	81.0	66.0	99.0	73.0	45.0
Under 5 mortality	"	..	..	102.4	169.0	108.0	59.0
Immunization							
Measles	% age group	..	63.0	36.0	54.0	72.7	..
DPT	"	..	70.0	36.0	54.6	80.6	..
Child malnutrition (under-5)	"	..	28.0	18.0	28.4	38.3	..
Life expectancy							
Total	years	51	56	59	52	62	68
Female advantage	"	4.0	4.2	3.7	3.4	2.4	6.4
Total fertility rate	births per woman	8.0	7.9	5.4	6.1	3.4	3.1
Maternal mortality rate	per 100,000 live births	..	510	..	..	..	..
Supplementary Poverty Indicators							
Expenditures on social security	% of total gov't exp.	0.2	0.1	0.1	..	..	..
Social security coverage	% econ. active pop.	..	..	..	..	..	..
Access to safe water: total	% of pop.	17.0	..	28.0	41.1	68.4	..
Urban	"	100.0	..	61.0	77.8	78.9	..
Rural	"	4.0	..	21.0	27.3	60.3	..
Access to health care	"	..	19.3	..	..	..	..

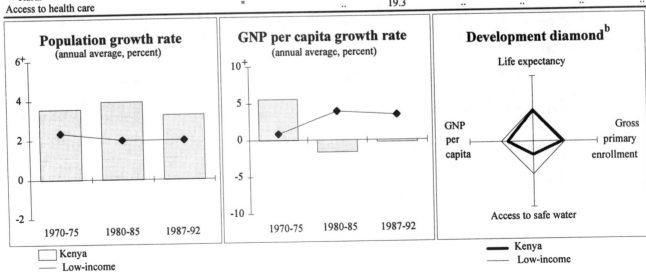

Population growth rate (annual average, percent) — 1970-75, 1980-85, 1987-92 — ☐ Kenya — Low-income

GNP per capita growth rate (annual average, percent) — 1970-75, 1980-85, 1987-92

Development diamond[b] — Life expectancy, GNP per capita, Gross primary enrollment, Access to safe water — ▬ Kenya — ― Low-income

a. See the technical notes, p.389. b. The development diamond, based on four key indicators, shows the average level of development in the country compared with its income group. See the introduction.

Kenya

Indicator	Unit of measure	Latest single year 1970-75	Latest single year 1980-85	Most recent estimate 1987-92	Same region/income group Sub-Saharan Africa	Same region/income group Low-income	Next higher income group
Resources and Expenditures							
HUMAN RESOURCES							
Population (mre=1992)	thousands	13,741	20,241	25,669	546,390	3,194,535	942,547
Age dependency ratio	ratio	1.12	1.16	1.07	0.95	0.67	0.66
Urban	% of pop.	12.9	19.7	25.2	29.5	26.7	57.0
Population growth rate	annual %	3.7	3.8	2.9	2.9	1.8	1.4
Urban	"	7.8	7.6	6.2	5.1	3.4	4.8
Labor force (15-64)	thousands	5,890	8,389	10,807	224,025	1,478,954	..
Agriculture	% of labor force	83	81	..	..	..	..
Industry	"	6	7	..	..	..	..
Female	"	42	41	39	37	33	36
Females per 100 males							
Urban	number	..	..	..	..	..	..
Rural	"	..	..	..	..	..	..
NATURAL RESOURCES							
Area	thou. sq. km	580.37	580.37	580.37	24,274.03	38,401.06	40,697.37
Density	pop. per sq. km	23.7	34.9	43.0	21.9	81.7	22.8
Agricultural land	% of land area	70.8	71.0	71.2	52.7	50.9	..
Change in agricultural land	annual %	0.1	0.1	0.0	0.1	0.0	..
Agricultural land under irrigation	%	0.1	0.1	0.1	0.8	18.2	..
Forests and woodland	thou. sq. km	26	24	23	..	..	..
Deforestation (net)	annual %	..	..	0.8	..	..	..
INCOME							
Household income							
Share of top 20% of households	% of income	60	..	62	..	42	..
Share of bottom 40% of households	"	9	..	10	..	19	..
Share of bottom 20% of households	"	3	..	3	..	8	..
EXPENDITURE							
Food	% of GDP	28.3	23.4	..	..	..	..
Staples	"	12.2	11.3	..	..	..	..
Meat, fish, milk, cheese, eggs	"	7.3	6.7	..	..	..	..
Cereal imports	thou. metric tonnes	86	279	669	20,311	46,537	74,924
Food aid in cereals	"	2	340	162	4,303	9,008	4,054
Food production per capita	1987 = 100	107	99	91	90	123	..
Fertilizer consumption	kg/ha	1.1	2.7	2.4	4.2	61.9	..
Share of agriculture in GDP	% of GDP	30.2	28.5	23.0	18.6	29.6	..
Housing	% of GDP	8.7	8.3	..	..	..	..
Average household size	persons per household	5.0	..	..	..	..	..
Urban	"	5.0	..	..	..	..	..
Fixed investment: housing	% of GDP	3.5	3.1	..	..	..	..
Fuel and power	% of GDP	1.7	1.7	..	..	..	..
Energy consumption per capita	kg of oil equiv.	114	99	92	258	335	1,882
Households with electricity							
Urban	% of households	..	..	..	..	..	..
Rural	"	..	..	..	..	..	..
Transport and communication	% of GDP	5.6	5.6	..	..	..	..
Fixed investment: transport equipment	"	2.7	1.7	..	..	..	..
Total road length	thou. km	50	65	67	..	..	..
INVESTMENT IN HUMAN CAPITAL							
Health							
Population per physician	persons	7,900	6,591	10,147	..	..	..
Population per nurse	"	2,524	948	..	..	..	..
Population per hospital bed	"	800	597	623	1,329	1,050	516
Oral rehydration therapy (under-5)	% of cases	..	..	69	36	39	..
Education							
Gross enrollment ratio							
Secondary	% of school-age pop.	13	21	29	18	41	..
Female	"	9	16	25	14	35	..
Pupil-teacher ratio: primary	pupils per teacher	33	34	31	39	37	26
Pupil-teacher ratio: secondary	"	25	20	18	..	19	..
Pupils reaching grade 4	% of cohort	97	68	77	..	..	..
Repeater rate: primary	% of total enroll	5	13	..	..	..	..
Illiteracy	% of pop. (age 15+)	..	35	31	51	39	..
Female	% of fem. (age 15+)	..	47	42	62	52	..
Newspaper circulation	per thou. pop.	10	11	14	14	..	100

World Bank International Economics Department, April 1994

Kiribati

Indicator	Unit of measure	Latest single year 1970-75	1980-85	Most recent estimate 1987-92	Same region/income group East Asia	Lower-middle-income	Next higher income group
Priority Poverty Indicators							
POVERTY							
Upper poverty line	local curr.	..	..	..	..	..	..
Headcount index	% of pop.	..	..	..	12	..	..
Lower poverty line	local curr.	..	..	..	..	..	..
Headcount index	% of pop.	..	..	..	9	..	..
GNP per capita	US$	..	560	700	760	..	3,870
SHORT TERM INCOME INDICATORS							
Unskilled urban wages	local curr.	..	..	..	..	..	..
Unskilled rural wages	"	..	..	..	..	..	..
Rural terms of trade	"	..	..	..	..	..	..
Consumer price index	1987=100	..	..	..	..	..	..
Lower income	"	..	..	..	..	..	..
Food[a]	"	..	88	110	..	..	..
Urban	"	..	..	..	..	..	..
Rural	"	..	..	..	..	..	..
SOCIAL INDICATORS							
Public expenditure on basic social services	% of GDP	..	..	..	..	..	..
Gross enrollment ratios							
Primary	% school age pop.	..	84	..	121	..	107
Male	"	..	..	..	126	..	..
Female	"	..	..	..	117	..	..
Mortality							
Infant mortality	per thou. live births	98.0	69.0	60.0	39.0	45.0	40.0
Under 5 mortality	"	..	..	80.9	49.0	59.0	51.0
Immunization							
Measles	% age group	..	4.0	63.0	88.4	..	82.0
DPT	"	..	37.0	79.0	89.5	..	73.8
Child malnutrition (under-5)	"	..	..	..	24.7	..	..
Life expectancy							
Total	years	..	52	58	68	68	69
Female advantage	"	..	3.7	4.5	3.6	6.4	6.3
Total fertility rate	births per woman	4.4	4.5	3.8	2.4	3.1	2.9
Maternal mortality rate	per 100,000 live births	..	..	..	114	..	..
Supplementary Poverty Indicators							
Expenditures on social security	% of total gov't exp.	..	..	..	..	..	..
Social security coverage	% econ. active pop.	..	..	..	..	..	..
Access to safe water: total	% of pop.	..	..	73.0	72.0	..	85.6
Urban	"	..	..	91.0	83.4	..	94.3
Rural	"	..	..	63.0	60.2	..	73.0
Access to health care	"	..	100.0	..	..	..	..

Population growth rate
(annual average, percent)

GNP per capita growth rate
(annual average, percent)

Development diamond[b]

Legend: Kiribati / Lower-middle-income

a. See the technical notes, p.389.   b. The development diamond, based on four key indicators, shows the average level of development in the country compared with its income group. See the introduction.

Kiribati

Indicator	Unit of measure	Latest single year 1970-75	Latest single year 1980-85	Most recent estimate 1987-92	Same region/income group East Asia	Same region/income group Lower-middle-income	Next higher income group
Resources and Expenditures							
HUMAN RESOURCES							
Population (mre=1992)	thousands	53	65	75	1,688,909	942,547	477,960
Age dependency ratio	ratio	..	0.73	0.76	0.55	0.66	0.64
Urban	% of pop.	30.1	33.5	36.0	29.4	57.0	71.7
Population growth rate	annual %	1.9	1.6	2.7	1.4	1.4	1.6
Urban	"	4.9	2.7	2.8	2.9	4.8	2.5
Labor force (15-64)	thousands	..	44	..	928,465	..	181,414
Agriculture	% of labor force	..	0	..	..	..	..
Industry	"	..	0	..	..	..	..
Female	"	..	..	..	41	36	29
Females per 100 males							
Urban	number	99	..	..	..	..	..
Rural	"	115	..	..	..	..	..
NATURAL RESOURCES							
Area	thou. sq. km	0.73	0.73	0.73	16,367.18	40,697.37	21,836.02
Density	pop. per sq. km	72.6	89.0	100.0	101.8	22.8	21.5
Agricultural land	% of land area	49.3	50.7	50.7	44.5	..	41.7
Change in agricultural land	annual %	0.0	0.0	0.0	0.1	..	0.3
Agricultural land under irrigation	%	..	..	..	14.5	..	9.3
Forests and woodland	thou. sq. km	0	0	0	..	..	..
Deforestation (net)	annual %	..	..	..	..	..	..
INCOME							
Household income							
Share of top 20% of households	% of income	..	..	..	42	..	..
Share of bottom 40% of households	"	..	..	..	18	..	..
Share of bottom 20% of households	"	..	..	..	7	..	..
EXPENDITURE							
Food	% of GDP	..	..	..	..	..	..
Staples	"	..	..	..	..	..	..
Meat, fish, milk, cheese, eggs	"	..	..	..	..	..	..
Cereal imports	thou. metric tonnes	5	6	9	33,591	74,924	49,174
Food aid in cereals	"	..	1	0	581	4,054	282
Food production per capita	1987 = 100	..	..	..	133	..	109
Fertilizer consumption	kg/ha	..	..	..	75.1	..	68.8
Share of agriculture in GDP	% of GDP	..	27.3	21.3	21.5	..	8.1
Housing	% of GDP	..	..	..	..	..	..
Average household size	persons per household	6.1	..	..	..	..	..
Urban	"	..	..	..	..	..	..
Fixed investment: housing	% of GDP	..	..	..	..	..	..
Fuel and power	% of GDP	..	..	..	..	..	..
Energy consumption per capita	kg of oil equiv.	208	..	..	593	1,882	1,649
Households with electricity							
Urban	% of households	..	..	..	..	..	..
Rural	"	..	..	..	..	..	..
Transport and communication	% of GDP	..	..	..	..	..	..
Fixed investment: transport equipment	"	..	..	..	..	..	..
Total road length	thou. km	..	..	..	..	..	..
INVESTMENT IN HUMAN CAPITAL							
Health							
Population per physician	persons	1,633	1,933	5,143	..	..	..
Population per nurse	"	..	231	190	..	..	..
Population per hospital bed	"	81	208	..	553	516	385
Oral rehydration therapy (under-5)	% of cases	..	..	84	51	..	54
Education							
Gross enrollment ratio							
Secondary	% of school-age pop.	..	..	..	53	..	53
Female	"	..	..	..	47	..	..
Pupil-teacher ratio: primary	pupils per teacher	33	29	29	23	26	25
Pupil-teacher ratio: secondary	"	13	16	15	16	..	..
Pupils reaching grade 4	% of cohort	..	92	93	89	..	71
Repeater rate: primary	% of total enroll	..	3	1	6	..	11
Illiteracy	% of pop. (age 15+)	..	..	..	24	..	14
Female	% of fem. (age 15+)	..	..	..	34	..	17
Newspaper circulation	per thou. pop.	..	..	..	..	100	117

World Bank International Economics Department, April 1994

Democratic People's Republic of Korea

Indicator	Unit of measure	Latest single year 1970-75	Latest single year 1980-85	Most recent estimate 1987-92	Same region/income group East Asia	Same region/income group Lower-middle-income	Next higher income group
Priority Poverty Indicators							
POVERTY							
Upper poverty line	local curr.	..	..	..	..	..	..
Headcount index	% of pop.	..	..	..	12	..	..
Lower poverty line	local curr.	..	..	..	..	..	..
Headcount index	% of pop.	..	..	..	9	..	..
GNP per capita	US$	..	..	..	760	..	3,870
SHORT TERM INCOME INDICATORS							
Unskilled urban wages	local curr.	..	..	..	..	..	..
Unskilled rural wages	"	..	..	..	..	..	..
Rural terms of trade	"	..	..	..	..	..	..
Consumer price index	1987=100	..	..	..	..	..	..
Lower income	"	..	..	..	..	..	..
Food[a]	"	..	..	..	..	..	..
Urban	"	..	..	..	..	..	..
Rural	"	..	..	..	..	..	..
SOCIAL INDICATORS							
Public expenditure on basic social services	% of GDP	..	..	..	..	..	..
Gross enrollment ratios							
Primary	% school age pop.	..	..	104	121	..	107
Male	"	..	..	108	126	..	..
Female	"	..	..	100	117	..	..
Mortality							
Infant mortality	per thou. live births	47.0	30.0	24.0	39.0	45.0	40.0
Under 5 mortality	"	..	..	28.9	49.0	59.0	51.0
Immunization							
Measles	% age group	..	91.0	96.0	88.4	..	82.0
DPT	"	..	52.0	90.0	89.5	..	73.8
Child malnutrition (under-5)	"	..	..	..	24.7	..	..
Life expectancy							
Total	years	62	68	71	68	68	69
Female advantage	"	4.8	6.4	6.2	3.6	6.4	6.3
Total fertility rate	births per woman	5.7	2.8	2.4	2.4	3.1	2.9
Maternal mortality rate	per 100,000 live births	..	41	..	114	..	..
Supplementary Poverty Indicators							
Expenditures on social security	% of total gov't exp.	..	..	..	..	..	..
Social security coverage	% econ. active pop.	..	..	..	..	..	..
Access to safe water: total	% of pop.	..	..	..	72.0	..	85.6
Urban	"	..	..	..	83.4	..	94.3
Rural	"	..	..	..	60.2	..	73.0
Access to health care	"	..	100.0	100.0	..	..	..

Population growth rate
(annual average, percent)

Legend: □ Democratic People's Republic of Korea — Lower-middle-income

GNP per capita growth rate
(annual average, percent)

Development diamond[b]

Legend: ▬ Democratic People's Republic of ---- Lower-middle-income

a. See the technical notes, p.389. b. The development diamond, based on four key indicators, shows the average level of development in the country compared with its income group. See the introduction.

Democratic People's Republic of Korea

Indicator	Unit of measure	Latest single year 1970-75	Latest single year 1980-85	Most recent estimate 1987-92	Same region/income group East Asia	Same region/income group Lower-middle-income	Next higher income group
Resources and Expenditures							
HUMAN RESOURCES							
Population (mre=1992)	thousands	16,562	19,888	22,620	1,688,909	942,547	477,960
Age dependency ratio	ratio	0.82	0.58	0.49	0.55	0.66	0.64
Urban	% of pop.	56.5	58.8	60.4	29.4	57.0	71.7
Population growth rate	annual %	2.2	1.7	1.9	1.4	1.4	1.6
Urban	"	3.4	2.3	2.4	2.9	4.8	2.5
Labor force (15-64)	thousands	6,812	9,084	11,107	928,465	..	181,414
Agriculture	% of labor force	48	43	..	..	..	..
Industry	"	28	30	..	..	..	..
Female	"	45	46	46	41	36	29
Females per 100 males							
Urban	number	..	..	..	..	..	..
Rural	"	..	..	..	..	..	..
NATURAL RESOURCES							
Area	thou. sq. km	120.54	120.54	120.54	16,367.18	40,697.37	21,836.02
Density	pop. per sq. km	137.4	165.0	184.1	101.8	22.8	21.5
Agricultural land	% of land area	15.7	16.7	17.1	44.5	..	41.7
Change in agricultural land	annual %	0.5	0.5	0.5	0.1	..	0.3
Agricultural land under irrigation	%	47.5	63.3	69.9	14.5	..	9.3
Forests and woodland	thou. sq. km	90	90	90	..	..	..
Deforestation (net)	annual %	..	..	..	..	..	..
INCOME							
Household income							
Share of top 20% of households	% of income	..	..	..	42	..	..
Share of bottom 40% of households	"	..	..	..	18	..	..
Share of bottom 20% of households	"	..	..	..	7	..	..
EXPENDITURE							
Food	% of GDP						
Staples	"	..	..	..	..	..	..
Meat, fish, milk, cheese, eggs	"	..	..	..	..	..	..
Cereal imports	thou. metric tonnes	621	200	986	33,591	74,924	49,174
Food aid in cereals	"	..	..	..	581	4,054	282
Food production per capita	1987 = 100	88	109	105	133	..	109
Fertilizer consumption	kg/ha	228.9	421.2	393.7	75.1	..	68.8
Share of agriculture in GDP	% of GDP	..	..	..	21.5	..	8.1
Housing	% of GDP						
Average household size	persons per household	..	..	..	..	..	..
Urban	"	..	..	..	..	..	..
Fixed investment: housing	% of GDP	..	..	..	..	..	..
Fuel and power	% of GDP	..	..	..	..	..	..
Energy consumption per capita	kg of oil equiv.	1,587	1,823	1,737	593	1,882	1,649
Households with electricity							
Urban	% of households	..	..	..	..	..	..
Rural	"	..	..	..	..	..	..
Transport and communication	% of GDP						
Fixed investment: transport equipment	"	..	..	..	..	..	..
Total road length	thou. km	..	..	..	..	..	..
INVESTMENT IN HUMAN CAPITAL							
Health							
Population per physician	persons	..	426	..	..	..	..
Population per nurse	"	..	..	..	..	..	..
Population per hospital bed	"	..	..	..	553	516	385
Oral rehydration therapy (under-5)	% of cases	..	..	72	51	..	54
Education							
Gross enrollment ratio							
Secondary	% of school-age pop.	..	..	..	53	..	53
Female	"	..	..	..	47	..	..
Pupil-teacher ratio: primary	pupils per teacher	..	..	26	23	26	25
Pupil-teacher ratio: secondary	"	..	..	22	16	..	..
Pupils reaching grade 4	% of cohort	..	..	..	89	..	71
Repeater rate: primary	% of total enroll	..	..	..	6	..	11
Illiteracy	% of pop. (age 15+)	..	..	..	24	..	14
Female	% of fem. (age 15+)	..	..	..	34	..	17
Newspaper circulation	per thou. pop.	63	52	230	..	100	117

World Bank International Economics Department, April 1994

Republic of Korea

Indicator	Unit of measure	Latest single year 1970-75	Latest single year 1980-85	Most recent estimate 1987-92	Same region/income group East Asia	Same region/income group Upper-middle-income	Next higher income group
Priority Poverty Indicators							
POVERTY							
Upper poverty line	local curr.	..	..	..	..	..	..
Headcount index	% of pop.	5	13	..	12	..	..
Lower poverty line	local curr.	84	363	..	..	..	..
Headcount index	% of pop.	..	5	..	9	..	..
GNP per capita	US$	580	2,340	6,790	760	3,870	21,960
SHORT TERM INCOME INDICATORS							
Unskilled urban wages	local curr.	..	..	..	..	..	..
Unskilled rural wages	"	..	..	..	..	..	..
Rural terms of trade	"	..	84	130	..	..	..
Consumer price index	1987=100	30	94	143	..	..	..
Lower income	"	..	..	..	..	..	..
Food[a]	"	14	95	144	..	..	..
Urban	"	..	..	..	..	..	..
Rural	"	..	..	..	..	..	..
SOCIAL INDICATORS							
Public expenditure on basic social services	% of GDP	..	7.0	..	..	..	..
Gross enrollment ratios							
Primary	% school age pop.	107	97	105	121	107	103
Male	"	107	96	103	126	..	103
Female	"	107	98	106	117	..	103
Mortality							
Infant mortality	per thou. live births	47.0	30.0	12.8	39.0	40.0	7.0
Under 5 mortality	"	..	..	15.7	49.0	51.0	10.0
Immunization							
Measles	% age group	..	89.0	93.0	88.4	82.0	82.4
DPT	"	..	76.0	74.0	89.5	73.8	90.1
Child malnutrition (under-5)	"	..	..	..	24.7	..	..
Life expectancy							
Total	years	61	68	71	68	69	77
Female advantage	"	5.0	6.4	8.0	3.6	6.3	6.4
Total fertility rate	births per woman	4.1	2.4	1.8	2.4	2.9	1.7
Maternal mortality rate	per 100,000 live births	..	34	30	114	..	..
Supplementary Poverty Indicators							
Expenditures on social security	% of total gov't exp.	5.3	5.4	7.8	..	..	..
Social security coverage	% econ. active pop.	..	..	..	..	..	..
Access to safe water: total	% of pop.	66.0	73.0	93.0	72.0	85.6	..
Urban	"	95.0	90.0	100.0	83.4	94.3	..
Rural	"	38.0	48.0	76.0	60.2	73.0	..
Access to health care	"	..	100.0	100.0	..	..	..

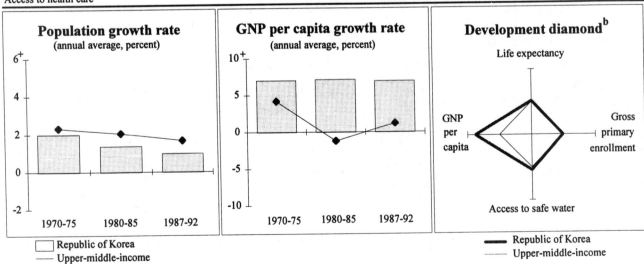

Population growth rate
(annual average, percent)

GNP per capita growth rate
(annual average, percent)

Development diamond[b]

Life expectancy — GNP per capita — Gross primary enrollment — Access to safe water

□ Republic of Korea
— Upper-middle-income

— Republic of Korea
---- Upper-middle-income

a. See the technical notes, p.389.   b. The development diamond, based on four key indicators, shows the average level of development in the country compared with its income group. See the introduction.

Republic of Korea

Indicator	Unit of measure	Latest single year 1970-75	Latest single year 1980-85	Most recent estimate 1987-92	Same region/income group East Asia	Same region/income group Upper-middle-income	Next higher income group
Resources and Expenditures							
HUMAN RESOURCES							
Population (mre=1992)	thousands	35,281	40,806	43,663	1,688,909	477,960	828,221
Age dependency ratio	ratio	0.71	0.52	0.44	0.55	0.64	0.50
Urban	% of pop.	48.0	64.9	74.3	29.4	71.7	78.1
Population growth rate	annual %	1.9	1.0	0.9	1.4	1.6	0.7
Urban	"	5.0	3.5	2.4	2.9	2.5	0.9
Labor force (15-64)	thousands	13,054	16,790	19,423	928,465	181,414	390,033
Agriculture	% of labor force	43	36	..	..	..	..
Industry	"	23	27	..	..	..	..
Female	"	33	34	34	41	29	38
Females per 100 males							
Urban	number	103	102	..	..	..	..
Rural	"	97	94	..	..	..	..
NATURAL RESOURCES							
Area	thou. sq. km	99.02	99.02	99.02	16,367.18	21,836.02	31,709.00
Density	pop. per sq. km	356.3	412.1	437.0	101.8	21.5	24.5
Agricultural land	% of land area	23.0	22.5	22.0	44.5	41.7	42.7
Change in agricultural land	annual %	0.2	-0.2	-0.8	0.1	0.3	-0.2
Agricultural land under irrigation	%	56.2	59.6	61.5	14.5	9.3	16.1
Forests and woodland	thou. sq. km	66	65	65	..	..	..
Deforestation (net)	annual %	..	..	..	..	..	..
INCOME							
Household income							
Share of top 20% of households	% of income	45	..	..	42	..	..
Share of bottom 40% of households	"	18	..	..	18	..	..
Share of bottom 20% of households	"	7	..	..	7	..	..
EXPENDITURE							
Food	% of GDP	32.1	21.7	..	..	..	..
Staples	"	18.1	8.8	..	..	..	..
Meat, fish, milk, cheese, eggs	"	5.6	6.6	..	..	..	..
Cereal imports	thou. metric tonnes	3,124	6,825	10,489	33,591	49,174	70,626
Food aid in cereals	"	234	53	..	581	282	2
Food production per capita	1987 = 100	91	105	109	133	109	101
Fertilizer consumption	kg/ha	380.9	362.9	435.1	75.1	68.8	162.1
Share of agriculture in GDP	% of GDP	24.5	12.8	8.1	21.5	8.1	2.4
Housing	% of GDP	5.6	6.5	..	..	..	..
Average household size	persons per household	5.0	4.5	..	..	..	..
Urban	"	5.0	4.4	..	..	..	..
Fixed investment: housing	% of GDP	4.5	4.6	..	..	..	..
Fuel and power	% of GDP	3.3	2.8	..	..	..	..
Energy consumption per capita	kg of oil equiv.	689	1,314	2,569	593	1,649	5,101
Households with electricity							
Urban	% of households	..	..	..	..	..	..
Rural	"	..	..	..	..	..	..
Transport and communication	% of GDP	4.9	5.6	..	..	..	..
Fixed investment: transport equipment	"	5.4	3.2	..	..	..	..
Total road length	thou. km	46	51	56	..	..	..
INVESTMENT IN HUMAN CAPITAL							
Health							
Population per physician	persons	2,200	1,386	951	..	..	..
Population per nurse	"	1,190	..	454	..	..	..
Population per hospital bed	"	1,900	596	300	553	385	144
Oral rehydration therapy (under-5)	% of cases	..	..	..	51	54	..
Education							
Gross enrollment ratio							
Secondary	% of school-age pop.	56	90	90	53	53	92
Female	"	48	88	91	47	..	94
Pupil-teacher ratio: primary	pupils per teacher	52	38	34	23	25	18
Pupil-teacher ratio: secondary	"	40	37	24	16	..	..
Pupils reaching grade 4	% of cohort	96	98	100	89	71	..
Repeater rate: primary	% of total enroll	0	0	0	6	11	..
Illiteracy	% of pop. (age 15+)	12	5	4	24	14	..
Female	% of fem. (age 15+)	..	9	7	34	17	..
Newspaper circulation	per thou. pop.	170	146	280	..	117	..

World Bank International Economics Department, April 1994

Kuwait

Indicator	Unit of measure	Latest single year 1970-75	Latest single year 1980-85	Most recent estimate 1987-92	Same region/income group High-income
Priority Poverty Indicators					
POVERTY					
Upper poverty line	local curr.	..	..	..	..
Headcount index	% of pop.	..	..	..	..
Lower poverty line	local curr.	..	..	..	..
Headcount index	% of pop.	..	..	..	..
GNP per capita	US$	9,040	15,620	13,920	21,960
SHORT TERM INCOME INDICATORS					
Unskilled urban wages	local curr.	..	..	..	..
Unskilled rural wages	"	..	..	..	..
Rural terms of trade	"	..	..	..	..
Consumer price index	1987=100	55	98	105	..
Lower income	"	..	..	..	..
Food[a]	"	..	102	104	..
Urban	"	..	..	..	..
Rural	"	..	..	..	..
SOCIAL INDICATORS					
Public expenditure on basic social services	% of GDP	..	..	..	..
Gross enrollment ratios					
Primary	% school age pop.	92	103	55	103
Male	"	99	104	56	103
Female	"	85	102	55	103
Mortality					
Infant mortality	per thou. live births	43.0	18.4	14.0	7.0
Under 5 mortality	"	..	..	17.1	10.0
Immunization					
Measles	% age group	..	91.0	98.0	82.4
DPT	"	..	98.0	94.0	90.1
Child malnutrition (under-5)	"	..	6.4	..	..
Life expectancy					
Total	years	67	72	75	77
Female advantage	"	4.0	4.1	4.7	6.4
Total fertility rate	births per woman	6.9	4.9	3.7	1.7
Maternal mortality rate	per 100,000 live births	..	18	..	..
Supplementary Poverty Indicators					
Expenditures on social security	% of total gov't exp.	0.0	6.6	1.8	..
Social security coverage	% econ. active pop.	..	..	..	..
Access to safe water: total	% of pop.	89.0	..	100.0	..
Urban	"	100.0	..	100.0	..
Rural	"	..	..	100.0	..
Access to health care	"	..	100.0	100.0	..

Population growth rate
(annual average, percent)

□ Kuwait
— High-income

GNP per capita growth rate
(annual average, percent)

Development diamond[b]

Life expectancy
GNP per capita — Gross primary enrollment
Access to safe water

— Kuwait
— High-income

a. See the technical notes, p.389.   b. The development diamond, based on four key indicators, shows the average level of development in the country compared with its income group. See the introduction.

Kuwait

Indicator	Unit of measure	Latest single year		Most recent estimate 1987-92	Same region/income group High-income
		1970-75	1980-85		
Resources and Expenditures					
HUMAN RESOURCES					
Population (mre=1992)	thousands	1,007	1,712	1,410	828,221
Age dependency ratio	ratio	0.85	0.62	0.63	0.50
Urban	% of pop.	83.8	93.8	96.3	78.1
Population growth rate	annual %	6.1	3.4	-3.1	0.7
Urban	"	7.6	4.2	-2.8	0.9
Labor force (15-64)	thousands	318	677	894	390,033
Agriculture	% of labor force	2	2	..	..
Industry	"	32	32	..	..
Female	"	12	13	16	38
Females per 100 males					
Urban	number	..	..	..	..
Rural	"	..	..	..	..
NATURAL RESOURCES					
Area	thou. sq. km	17.82	17.82	17.82	31,709.00
Density	pop. per sq. km	56.5	96.1	81.6	24.5
Agricultural land	% of land area	7.6	7.7	7.9	42.7
Change in agricultural land	annual %	0.0	0.0	0.0	-0.2
Agricultural land under irrigation	%	0.7	1.5	1.4	16.1
Forests and woodland	thou. sq. km	0	0	0	..
Deforestation (net)	annual %	..	..	..	..
INCOME					
Household income					
Share of top 20% of households	% of income	..	..	..	..
Share of bottom 40% of households	"	..	..	..	..
Share of bottom 20% of households	"	..	..	..	..
EXPENDITURE					
Food	% of GDP	..	..	..	..
Staples	"	..	..	..	..
Meat, fish, milk, cheese, eggs	"	..	..	..	..
Cereal imports	thou. metric tonnes	216	576	352	70,626
Food aid in cereals	"	..	..	..	2
Food production per capita	1987 = 100	..	..	..	101
Fertilizer consumption	kg/ha	..	5.1	7.1	162.1
Share of agriculture in GDP	% of GDP	0.3	0.6	0.4	2.4
Housing	% of GDP	..	..	..	..
Average household size	persons per household	6.5	..	..	..
Urban	"	..	..	..	..
Fixed investment: housing	% of GDP	..	..	..	..
Fuel and power	% of GDP	..	..	..	..
Energy consumption per capita	kg of oil equiv.	5,764	6,870	7,122	5,101
Households with electricity					
Urban	% of households	..	..	..	..
Rural	"	..	..	..	..
Transport and communication	% of GDP	..	..	..	..
Fixed investment: transport equipment	"	..	..	..	..
Total road length	thou. km	2	4	4	..
INVESTMENT IN HUMAN CAPITAL					
Health					
Population per physician	persons	1,048	617	..	..
Population per nurse	"	259	178	..	..
Population per hospital bed	"	207	241	..	144
Oral rehydration therapy (under-5)	% of cases	..	..	10	..
Education					
Gross enrollment ratio					
Secondary	% of school-age pop.	66	91	51	92
Female	"	61	87	51	94
Pupil-teacher ratio: primary	pupils per teacher	18	18	16	18
Pupil-teacher ratio: secondary	"	12	13	11	..
Pupils reaching grade 4	% of cohort	97	93	..	..
Repeater rate: primary	% of total enroll	11	5	..	..
Illiteracy	% of pop. (age 15+)	40	29	27	..
Female	% of fem. (age 15+)	..	37	33	..
Newspaper circulation	per thou. pop.	84	237	210	..

World Bank International Economics Department, April 1994

Kyrgyz Republic

Indicator	Unit of measure	Latest single year 1970-75	Latest single year 1980-85	Most recent estimate 1987-92	Same region/income group Europe & Central Asia	Same region/income group Lower-middle-income	Next higher income group
Priority Poverty Indicators							
POVERTY							
Upper poverty line	local curr.	..	..	..	..	..	..
Headcount index	% of pop.	..	..	47	..	..	..
Lower poverty line	local curr.	..	..	..	..	..	..
Headcount index	% of pop.	..	..	22	..	..	..
GNP per capita	US$	..	..	820	..	..	3,870
SHORT TERM INCOME INDICATORS							
Unskilled urban wages	local curr.	..	..	..	..	..	..
Unskilled rural wages	"	..	..	..	..	..	..
Rural terms of trade	"	..	..	..	..	..	..
Consumer price index	1987=100	..	..	..	..	..	..
Lower income	"	..	..	..	..	..	..
Food[a]	"	..	..	..	..	..	..
Urban	"	..	..	..	..	..	..
Rural	"	..	..	..	..	..	..
SOCIAL INDICATORS							
Public expenditure on basic social services	% of GDP	..	..	7.1	..	..	..
Gross enrollment ratios							
Primary	% school age pop.	..	..	..	..	..	107
Male	"	..	..	..	..	..	..
Female	"	..	..	..	..	..	..
Mortality							
Infant mortality	per thou. live births	..	..	37.0	30.0	45.0	40.0
Under 5 mortality	"	..	..	45.7	38.0	59.0	51.0
Immunization							
Measles	% age group	..	..	..	..	..	82.0
DPT	"	..	..	..	..	..	73.8
Child malnutrition (under-5)	"	..	..	..	..	..	..
Life expectancy							
Total	years	..	65	66	70	68	69
Female advantage	"	..	8.0	8.0	8.6	6.4	6.3
Total fertility rate	births per woman	4.9	4.2	3.7	2.2	3.1	2.9
Maternal mortality rate	per 100,000 live births	..	49	43	58	..	..
Supplementary Poverty Indicators							
Expenditures on social security	% of total gov't exp.	..	..	..	..	..	..
Social security coverage	% econ. active pop.	..	..	..	..	..	..
Access to safe water: total	% of pop.	..	..	..	..	..	85.6
Urban	"	..	..	..	..	..	94.3
Rural	"	..	..	..	..	..	73.0
Access to health care	"	..	..	..	..	..	..

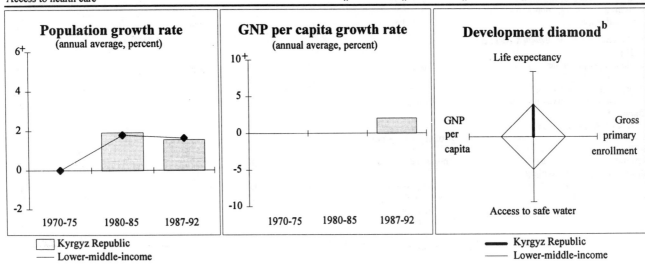

Population growth rate (annual average, percent)

GNP per capita growth rate (annual average, percent)

Development diamond[b]

Kyrgyz Republic
Lower-middle-income

a. See the technical notes, p.389. b. The development diamond, based on four key indicators, shows the average level of development in the country compared with its income group. See the introduction.

188

Kyrgyz Republic

Indicator	Unit of measure	Latest single year 1970-75	Latest single year 1980-85	Most recent estimate 1987-92	Same region/income group Europe & Central Asia	Same region/income group Lower-middle-income	Next higher income group
Resources and Expenditures							
HUMAN RESOURCES							
Population (mre=1992)	thousands	..	3,996	4,493	495,241	942,547	477,960
Age dependency ratio	ratio	..	..	0.79	0.56	0.66	0.64
Urban	% of pop.	..	..	38.0	63.3	57.0	71.7
Population growth rate	annual %	..	2.0	0.9	0.5	1.4	1.6
Urban	"	..	..	..	..	4.8	2.5
Labor force (15-64)	thousands	..	..	1,894	..	..	181,414
Agriculture	% of labor force	..	..	..	..	..	..
Industry	"	..	..	..	..	..	..
Female	"	..	..	49	46	36	29
Females per 100 males							
Urban	number	..	..	..	..	..	..
Rural	"	..	..	..	..	..	..
NATURAL RESOURCES							
Area	thou. sq. km	..	..	198.50	24,165.06	40,697.37	21,836.02
Density	pop. per sq. km	..	..	22.4	20.4	22.8	21.5
Agricultural land	% of land area	..	..	..	..	..	41.7
Change in agricultural land	annual %	..	..	..	..	..	0.3
Agricultural land under irrigation	%	..	..	..	..	..	9.3
Forests and woodland	thou. sq. km	..	..	..	..	..	..
Deforestation (net)	annual %	..	..	..	..	..	..
INCOME							
Household income							
Share of top 20% of households	% of income	..	..	..	..	..	..
Share of bottom 40% of households	"	..	..	..	..	..	..
Share of bottom 20% of households	"	..	..	..	..	..	..
EXPENDITURE							
Food	% of GDP	..	..	17.7	..	..	..
Staples	"	..	..	3.2	..	..	..
Meat, fish, milk, cheese, eggs	"	..	..	7.9	..	..	..
Cereal imports	thou. metric tonnes	..	..	..	45,972	74,924	49,174
Food aid in cereals	"	..	..	..	1,639	4,054	282
Food production per capita	1987 = 100	..	..	..	..	..	109
Fertilizer consumption	kg/ha	..	..	..	..	..	68.8
Share of agriculture in GDP	% of GDP	..	29.9	28.4	..	..	8.1
Housing	% of GDP	..	..	4.2	..	..	..
Average household size	persons per household	..	..	4.7	..	..	..
Urban	"	..	..	..	..	..	..
Fixed investment: housing	% of GDP	..	..	5.4	..	..	..
Fuel and power	% of GDP	..	..	0.9	..	..	..
Energy consumption per capita	kg of oil equiv.	..	..	..	3,190	1,882	1,649
Households with electricity							
Urban	% of households	..	..	..	..	..	..
Rural	"	..	..	..	..	..	..
Transport and communication	% of GDP	..	..	5.6	..	..	..
Fixed investment: transport equipment	"	..	..	11.4	..	..	..
Total road length	thou. km	..	25	29	..	..	..
INVESTMENT IN HUMAN CAPITAL							
Health							
Population per physician	persons	..	..	281	378	..	..
Population per nurse	"	..	..	..	..	..	..
Population per hospital bed	"	..	..	85	134	516	385
Oral rehydration therapy (under-5)	% of cases	..	..	..	..	..	54
Education							
Gross enrollment ratio							
Secondary	% of school-age pop.	..	..	..	..	..	53
Female	"	..	..	..	..	..	..
Pupil-teacher ratio: primary	pupils per teacher	..	..	..	..	26	25
Pupil-teacher ratio: secondary	"	..	..	..	..	..	..
Pupils reaching grade 4	% of cohort	..	..	..	..	..	71
Repeater rate: primary	% of total enroll	..	..	..	..	..	11
Illiteracy	% of pop. (age 15+)	..	..	..	..	..	14
Female	% of fem. (age 15+)	..	..	..	..	..	17
Newspaper circulation	per thou. pop.	..	..	..	..	100	117

World Bank International Economics Department, April 1994

Lao People's Democratic Republic

Indicator	Unit of measure	Latest single year 1970-75	Latest single year 1980-85	Most recent estimate 1987-92	Same region/income group East Asia	Same region/income group Low-income	Next higher income group
Priority Poverty Indicators							
POVERTY							
Upper poverty line	local curr.	..	..	..	..	..	..
Headcount index	% of pop.	..	..	..	12	19	..
Lower poverty line	local curr.	..	..	..	..	..	..
Headcount index	% of pop.	..	..	..	9	..	..
GNP per capita	US$	..	..	250	760	390	..
SHORT TERM INCOME INDICATORS							
Unskilled urban wages	local curr.	..	..	..	..	..	..
Unskilled rural wages	"	..	..	..	..	..	..
Rural terms of trade	"	..	..	..	..	..	..
Consumer price index	1987=100	..	..	..	..	..	..
Lower income	"	..	..	..	..	..	..
Food[a]	"	..	..	..	..	..	..
Urban	"	..	..	..	..	..	..
Rural	"	..	..	..	..	..	..
SOCIAL INDICATORS							
Public expenditure on basic social services	% of GDP	..	..	2.7	..	..	..
Gross enrollment ratios							
Primary	% school age pop.	58	111	98	121	103	..
Male	"	66	121	112	126	113	..
Female	"	40	100	84	117	96	..
Mortality							
Infant mortality	per thou. live births	145.0	122.0	97.0	39.0	73.0	45.0
Under 5 mortality	"	..	..	158.4	49.0	108.0	59.0
Immunization							
Measles	% age group	..	33.0	47.0	88.4	72.7	..
DPT	"	..	4.0	22.0	89.5	80.6	..
Child malnutrition (under-5)	"	..	36.7	36.5	24.7	38.3	..
Life expectancy							
Total	years	40	46	51	68	62	68
Female advantage	"	2.7	3.0	3.0	3.6	2.4	6.4
Total fertility rate	births per woman	6.2	6.7	6.7	2.4	3.4	3.1
Maternal mortality rate	per 100,000 live births	..	..	561	114	..	..
Supplementary Poverty Indicators							
Expenditures on social security	% of total gov't exp.	..	..	..	..	..	..
Social security coverage	% econ. active pop.	..	..	..	..	..	..
Access to safe water: total	% of pop.	41.0	..	29.0	72.0	68.4	..
Urban	"	100.0	..	47.0	83.4	78.9	..
Rural	"	32.0	..	25.0	60.2	60.3	..
Access to health care	"	..	66.7	..	..	..	..

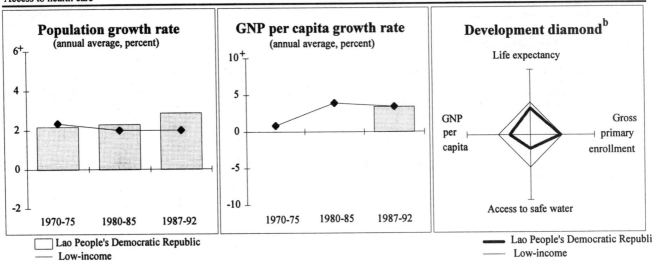

Population growth rate (annual average, percent)

☐ Lao People's Democratic Republic
— Low-income

GNP per capita growth rate (annual average, percent)

Development diamond[b]

Life expectancy

GNP per capita — Gross primary enrollment

Access to safe water

━ Lao People's Democratic Republi
— Low-income

a. See the technical notes, p.389. b. The development diamond, based on four key indicators, shows the average level of development in the country compared with its income group. See the introduction.

Lao People's Democratic Republic

Indicator	Unit of measure	Latest single year 1970-75	Latest single year 1980-85	Most recent estimate 1987-92	Same region/income group East Asia	Same region/income group Low-income	Next higher income group
Resources and Expenditures							
HUMAN RESOURCES							
Population (mre=1992)	thousands	3,024	3,594	4,384	1,688,909	3,194,535	942,547
Age dependency ratio	ratio	0.81	0.84	0.92	0.55	0.67	0.66
Urban	% of pop.	11.4	15.9	19.8	29.4	26.7	57.0
Population growth rate	annual %	1.7	2.8	2.9	1.4	1.8	1.4
Urban	"	4.9	6.0	6.0	2.9	3.4	4.8
Labor force (15-64)	thousands	1,760	2,014	2,340	928,465	1,478,954	..
Agriculture	% of labor force	77	76	..	..	..	..
Industry	"	6	7	..	..	..	..
Female	"	46	45	44	41	33	36
Females per 100 males							
Urban	number	97	..	..	..	..	..
Rural	"	97	..	..	..	..	..
NATURAL RESOURCES							
Area	thou. sq. km	236.80	236.80	236.80	16,367.18	38,401.06	40,697.37
Density	pop. per sq. km	12.8	15.2	18.0	101.8	81.7	22.8
Agricultural land	% of land area	7.1	7.4	7.4	44.5	50.9	..
Change in agricultural land	annual %	0.0	0.6	0.1	0.1	0.0	..
Agricultural land under irrigation	%	2.4	7.0	7.1	14.5	18.2	..
Forests and woodland	thou. sq. km	142	132	126	..	..	..
Deforestation (net)	annual %	..	..	0.9	..	..	..
INCOME							
Household income							
Share of top 20% of households	% of income	..	..	..	42	42	..
Share of bottom 40% of households	"	..	..	..	18	19	..
Share of bottom 20% of households	"	..	..	..	7	8	..
EXPENDITURE							
Food	% of GDP	..	..	52.6	..	..	..
Staples	"	..	..	32.0	..	..	..
Meat, fish, milk, cheese, eggs	"	..	..	10.4	..	..	..
Cereal imports	thou. metric tonnes	24	23	44	33,591	46,537	74,924
Food aid in cereals	"	8	7	10	581	9,008	4,054
Food production per capita	1987 = 100	78	121	110	133	123	..
Fertilizer consumption	kg/ha	0.1	1.2	1.5	75.1	61.9	..
Share of agriculture in GDP	% of GDP	..	..	..	21.5	29.6	..
Housing	% of GDP	..	..	15.6	..	..	..
Average household size	persons per household	..	..	..	..	..	..
Urban	"	..	..	..	..	..	..
Fixed investment: housing	% of GDP	..	..	4.2	..	..	..
Fuel and power	% of GDP	..	..	5.8	..	..	..
Energy consumption per capita	kg of oil equiv.	44	40	41	593	335	1,882
Households with electricity							
Urban	% of households	..	..	..	..	..	..
Rural	"	..	..	..	..	..	..
Transport and communication	% of GDP	..	..	2.8	..	..	..
Fixed investment: transport equipment	"	..	..	0.9	..	..	..
Total road length	thou. km	..	..	..	..	..	..
INVESTMENT IN HUMAN CAPITAL							
Health							
Population per physician	persons	15,156	1,362	4,381	..	..	..
Population per nurse	"	1,386	532	486	..	..	..
Population per hospital bed	"	1,078	..	399	553	1,050	516
Oral rehydration therapy (under-5)	% of cases	..	..	30	51	39	..
Education							
Gross enrollment ratio							
Secondary	% of school-age pop.	7	23	22	53	41	..
Female	"	2	19	17	47	35	..
Pupil-teacher ratio: primary	pupils per teacher	27	25	28	23	37	26
Pupil-teacher ratio: secondary	"	24	12	13	16	19	..
Pupils reaching grade 4	% of cohort	..	31	..	89	..	..
Repeater rate: primary	% of total enroll	..	..	30	6	..	..
Illiteracy	% of pop. (age 15+)	65	56	..	24	39	..
Female	% of fem. (age 15+)	..	24	..	34	52	..
Newspaper circulation	per thou. pop.	2	..	3	..	..	100

World Bank International Economics Department, April 1994

Latvia

Indicator	Unit of measure	Latest single year 1970-75	Latest single year 1980-85	Most recent estimate 1987-92	Same region/income group Europe & Central Asia	Same region/income group Lower-middle-income	Next higher income group
Priority Poverty Indicators							
POVERTY							
Upper poverty line	local curr.	..	..	..	..	..	..
Headcount index	% of pop.	..	..	5	..	..	..
Lower poverty line	local curr.	..	..	..	..	..	..
Headcount index	% of pop.	..	..	1	..	..	..
GNP per capita	US$	..	..	1,930	..	..	3,870
SHORT TERM INCOME INDICATORS							
Unskilled urban wages	local curr.	..	..	..	..	..	..
Unskilled rural wages	"	..	..	..	..	..	..
Rural terms of trade	"	..	..	..	..	..	..
Consumer price index	1987=100	..	..	..	..	..	..
Lower income	"	..	..	..	..	..	..
Food[a]	"	..	..	..	..	..	..
Urban	"	..	..	..	..	..	..
Rural	"	..	..	..	..	..	..
SOCIAL INDICATORS							
Public expenditure on basic social services	% of GDP	..	..	8.0	..	..	..
Gross enrollment ratios							
Primary	% school age pop.	..	..	..	..	..	107
Male	"	..	..	..	..	..	..
Female	"	..	..	..	..	..	..
Mortality							
Infant mortality	per thou. live births	24.0	19.0	17.4	30.0	45.0	40.0
Under 5 mortality	"	..	..	21.0	38.0	59.0	51.0
Immunization							
Measles	% age group	..	..	..	..	..	82.0
DPT	"	..	..	..	..	..	73.8
Child malnutrition (under-5)	"	..	..	..	..	..	..
Life expectancy							
Total	years	..	70	69	70	68	69
Female advantage	"	..	9.0	11.0	8.6	6.4	6.3
Total fertility rate	births per woman	2.0	2.1	1.8	2.2	3.1	2.9
Maternal mortality rate	per 100,000 live births	..	25	57	58	..	..
Supplementary Poverty Indicators							
Expenditures on social security	% of total gov't exp.	..	..	..	..	..	..
Social security coverage	% econ. active pop.	..	..	..	..	..	..
Access to safe water: total	% of pop.	..	..	..	..	..	85.6
Urban	"	..	..	..	..	..	94.3
Rural	"	..	..	..	..	..	73.0
Access to health care	"	..	..	..	..	..	..

Population growth rate
(annual average, percent)

□ Latvia
— Lower-middle-income

GNP per capita growth rate
(annual average, percent)

Development diamond[b]

Life expectancy

GNP per capita — Gross primary enrollment

Access to safe water

— Latvia
— Lower-middle-income

a. See the technical notes, p.389. b. The development diamond, based on four key indicators, shows the average level of development in the country compared with its income group. See the introduction.

Latvia

Indicator	Unit of measure	Latest single year 1970-75	Latest single year 1980-85	Most recent estimate 1987-92	Same region/income group Europe & Central Asia	Same region/income group Lower-middle-income	Next higher income group
				Resources and Expenditures			
HUMAN RESOURCES							
Population (mre=1992)	thousands	..	2,621	2,640	495,241	942,547	477,960
Age dependency ratio	ratio	..	..	0.53	0.56	0.66	0.64
Urban	% of pop.	..	..	71.0	63.3	57.0	71.7
Population growth rate	annual %	..	0.6	-0.8	0.5	1.4	1.6
Urban	"	..	..	..	..	4.8	2.5
Labor force (15-64)	thousands	..	1,395	1,350	..	..	181,414
Agriculture	% of labor force	..	18	16	..	..	..
Industry	"	..	38	31	..	..	..
Female	"	..	..	58	46	36	29
Females per 100 males							
Urban	number	..	..	..	..	..	..
Rural	"	..	..	..	..	..	..
NATURAL RESOURCES							
Area	thou. sq. km	..	..	64.50	24,165.06	40,697.37	21,836.02
Density	pop. per sq. km	..	..	41.3	20.4	22.8	21.5
Agricultural land	% of land area	..	..	..	..	..	41.7
Change in agricultural land	annual %	..	..	..	..	..	0.3
Agricultural land under irrigation	%	..	..	..	..	..	9.3
Forests and woodland	thou. sq. km	..	..	..	..	..	..
Deforestation (net)	annual %	..	..	..	..	..	..
INCOME							
Household income							
Share of top 20% of households	% of income	..	..	..	..	..	..
Share of bottom 40% of households	"	..	..	..	..	..	..
Share of bottom 20% of households	"	..	..	..	..	..	..
EXPENDITURE							
Food	% of GDP	..	..	19.8	..	..	..
Staples	"	..	..	3.6	..	..	..
Meat, fish, milk, cheese, eggs	"	..	..	8.9	..	..	..
Cereal imports	thou. metric tonnes	..	..	..	45,972	74,924	49,174
Food aid in cereals	"	..	..	195	1,639	4,054	282
Food production per capita	1987 = 100	..	..	..	..	..	109
Fertilizer consumption	kg/ha	..	..	..	..	..	68.8
Share of agriculture in GDP	% of GDP	..	20.8	24.0	..	..	8.1
Housing	% of GDP	..	..	4.7	..	..	..
Average household size	persons per household	..	..	3.1	..	..	..
Urban	"	..	..	..	..	..	..
Fixed investment: housing	% of GDP	..	..	4.9	..	..	..
Fuel and power	% of GDP	..	..	1.0	..	..	..
Energy consumption per capita	kg of oil equiv.	..	..	..	3,190	1,882	1,649
Households with electricity							
Urban	% of households	..	..	..	..	..	..
Rural	"	..	..	..	..	..	..
Transport and communication	% of GDP	..	..	6.2	..	..	..
Fixed investment: transport equipment	"	..	..	10.3	..	..	..
Total road length	thou. km	..	27	58	..	..	..
INVESTMENT IN HUMAN CAPITAL							
Health							
Population per physician	persons	..	..	200	378	..	..
Population per nurse	"	..	..	..	..	..	..
Population per hospital bed	"	..	..	72	134	516	385
Oral rehydration therapy (under-5)	% of cases	..	..	..	..	..	54
Education							
Gross enrollment ratio							
Secondary	% of school-age pop.	..	..	..	..	..	53
Female	"	..	..	..	..	..	..
Pupil-teacher ratio: primary	pupils per teacher	..	..	..	..	26	25
Pupil-teacher ratio: secondary	"	..	..	..	..	..	..
Pupils reaching grade 4	% of cohort	..	..	..	..	..	71
Repeater rate: primary	% of total enroll	..	..	..	..	..	11
Illiteracy	% of pop. (age 15+)	..	..	..	..	..	14
Female	% of fem. (age 15+)	..	..	..	..	..	17
Newspaper circulation	per thou. pop.	..	..	..	..	100	117

World Bank International Economics Department, April 1994

Lebanon

Indicator	Unit of measure	Latest single year 1970-75	Latest single year 1980-85	Most recent estimate 1987-92	Same region/income group Mid-East & North Africa	Same region/income group Lower-middle-income	Next higher income group
Priority Poverty Indicators							
POVERTY							
Upper poverty line	local curr.	..	..	..	..	..	..
Headcount index	% of pop.	..	..	..	..	..	..
Lower poverty line	local curr.	..	..	..	..	..	..
Headcount index	% of pop.	..	..	..	..	..	..
GNP per capita	US$	..	..	..	1,950	..	3,870
SHORT TERM INCOME INDICATORS							
Unskilled urban wages	local curr.	..	..	..	..	..	..
Unskilled rural wages	"	..	..	..	..	..	..
Rural terms of trade	"	..	..	..	..	..	..
Consumer price index	1987=100	..	..	..	..	..	..
Lower income	"	..	..	..	..	..	..
Food[a]	"	..	..	..	..	..	..
Urban	"	..	..	..	..	..	..
Rural	"	..	..	..	..	..	..
SOCIAL INDICATORS							
Public expenditure on basic social services	% of GDP	..	..	..	..	..	..
Gross enrollment ratios							
Primary	% school age pop.	121	99	112	100	..	107
Male	"	130	104	115	107	..	..
Female	"	112	94	110	88	..	..
Mortality							
Infant mortality	per thou. live births	48.0	48.0	34.0	58.0	45.0	40.0
Under 5 mortality	"	..	..	41.7	78.0	59.0	51.0
Immunization							
Measles	% age group	..	23.0	15.0	81.8	..	82.0
DPT	"	..	60.0	33.0	83.9	..	73.8
Child malnutrition (under-5)	"	..	..	..	20.9	..	..
Life expectancy							
Total	years	65	65	66	64	68	69
Female advantage	"	3.9	3.9	4.0	2.4	6.4	6.3
Total fertility rate	births per woman	4.9	3.8	3.1	4.9	3.1	2.9
Maternal mortality rate	per 100,000 live births	..	..	..	..	..	..
Supplementary Poverty Indicators							
Expenditures on social security	% of total gov't exp.	..	..	..	..	..	..
Social security coverage	% econ. active pop.	..	..	..	..	..	..
Access to safe water: total	% of pop.	92.0	..	98.0	85.0	..	85.6
Urban	"	95.0	..	100.0	97.0	..	94.3
Rural	"	85.0	77.0	..	70.1	..	73.0
Access to health care	"	..	95.0	..	84.6	..	..

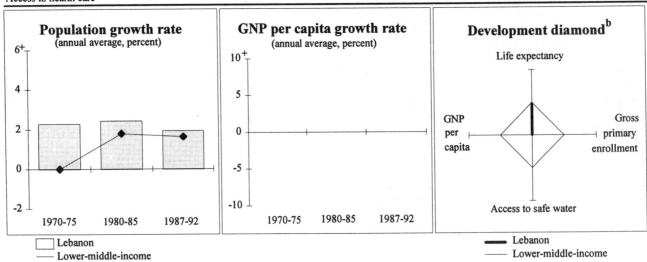

Population growth rate
(annual average, percent)

GNP per capita growth rate
(annual average, percent)

Development diamond[b]

Life expectancy — GNP per capita — Gross primary enrollment — Access to safe water

Lebanon
Lower-middle-income

a. See the technical notes, p.389.   b. The development diamond, based on four key indicators, shows the average level of development in the country compared with its income group. See the introduction.

Lebanon

Indicator	Unit of measure	Latest single year 1970-75	Latest single year 1980-85	Most recent estimate 1987-92	Same region/income group Mid-East & North Africa	Same region/income group Lower-middle-income	Next higher income group
Resources and Expenditures							
HUMAN RESOURCES							
Population (mre=1992)	thousands	2,767	3,195	3,781	252,555	942,547	477,960
Age dependency ratio	ratio	0.86	0.74	0.73	0.87	0.66	0.64
Urban	% of pop.	66.8	79.1	85.2	54.7	57.0	71.7
Population growth rate	annual %	1.2	4.2	2.0	2.8	1.4	1.6
Urban	"	3.4	5.7	2.8	3.8	4.8	2.5
Labor force (15-64)	thousands	771	769	968	69,280	..	181,414
Agriculture	% of labor force	17	14	..	..	..	..
Industry	"	26	27	..	..	..	..
Female	"	20	26	28	15	36	29
Females per 100 males							
Urban	number	97	..	..	..	..	..
Rural	"	99	..	..	..	..	..
NATURAL RESOURCES							
Area	thou. sq. km	10.40	10.40	10.40	10,487.21	40,697.37	21,836.02
Density	pop. per sq. km	266.1	307.2	356.5	23.4	22.8	21.5
Agricultural land	% of land area	33.7	30.1	30.9	30.2	..	41.7
Change in agricultural land	annual %	-1.4	0.0	2.6	0.5	..	0.3
Agricultural land under irrigation	%	24.9	27.9	27.2	31.0	..	9.3
Forests and woodland	thou. sq. km	1	1	1	..	..	..
Deforestation (net)	annual %	..	..	..	..	..	..
INCOME							
Household income							
Share of top 20% of households	% of income	55	..	..	..	..	..
Share of bottom 40% of households	"	11	..	..	..	..	..
Share of bottom 20% of households	"	4	..	..	..	..	..
EXPENDITURE							
Food	% of GDP	..	..	..	..	..	..
Staples	"	..	..	..	..	..	..
Meat, fish, milk, cheese, eggs	"	..	..	..	..	..	..
Cereal imports	thou. metric tonnes	585	579	656	38,007	74,924	49,174
Food aid in cereals	"	26	14	18	2,484	4,054	282
Food production per capita	1987 = 100	84	122	176	116	..	109
Fertilizer consumption	kg/ha	37.7	115.9	99.4	96.7	..	68.8
Share of agriculture in GDP	% of GDP	..	..	..	13.7	..	8.1
Housing	% of GDP	..	..	..	..	..	..
Average household size	persons per household	..	..	..	..	..	..
Urban	"	..	..	..	..	..	..
Fixed investment: housing	% of GDP	..	..	..	..	..	..
Fuel and power	% of GDP	..	..	..	..	..	..
Energy consumption per capita	kg of oil equiv.	774	..	..	1,109	1,882	1,649
Households with electricity							
Urban	% of households	..	..	..	..	..	..
Rural	"	..	..	..	..	..	..
Transport and communication	% of GDP	..	..	..	..	..	..
Fixed investment: transport equipment	"	..	..	..	..	..	..
Total road length	thou. km	..	..	..	..	..	..
INVESTMENT IN HUMAN CAPITAL							
Health							
Population per physician	persons	1,299	752	537	..	..	..
Population per nurse	"	971	..	..	..	..	..
Population per hospital bed	"	230	..	..	636	516	385
Oral rehydyration therapy (under-5)	% of cases	..	..	10	56	..	54
Education							
Gross enrollment ratio							
Secondary	% of school-age pop.	50	56	63	59	..	53
Female	"	33	56	64	50	..	..
Pupil-teacher ratio: primary	pupils per teacher	10	6	7	27	26	25
Pupil-teacher ratio: secondary	"	..	12	..	21	..	..
Pupils reaching grade 4	% of cohort	..	..	..	..	..	71
Repeater rate: primary	% of total enroll	..	..	..	..	..	11
Illiteracy	% of pop. (age 15+)	..	23	20	45	..	14
Female	% of fem. (age 15+)	..	31	27	58	..	17
Newspaper circulation	per thou. pop.	102	76	88	39	100	117

World Bank International Economics Department, April 1994

195

Lesotho

Indicator	Unit of measure	Latest single year 1970-75	Latest single year 1980-85	Most recent estimate 1987-92	Same region/income group Sub-Saharan Africa	Same region/income group Low-income	Next higher income group
Priority Poverty Indicators							
POVERTY							
Upper poverty line	local curr.	..	..	..	..	..	..
Headcount index	% of pop.	..	..	..	..	19	..
Lower poverty line	local curr.	..	..	..	..	..	..
Headcount index	% of pop.	..	..	..	..	..	..
GNP per capita	US$	230	390	590	520	390	..
SHORT TERM INCOME INDICATORS							
Unskilled urban wages	local curr.	..	..	..	..	..	..
Unskilled rural wages	"	..	..	..	..	..	..
Rural terms of trade	"	..	..	..	..	..	..
Consumer price index	1987=100	21	76	197	..	..	..
Lower income	"	..	..	..	..	..	..
Food[a]	"	13	72	45	..	..	..
Urban	"	..	..	..	..	..	..
Rural	"	..	..	..	..	..	..
SOCIAL INDICATORS							
Public expenditure on basic social services	% of GDP	..	..	11.5	..	..	..
Gross enrollment ratios							
Primary	% school age pop.	105	113	107	66	103	..
Male	"	87	101	97	79	113	..
Female	"	123	125	116	62	96	..
Mortality							
Infant mortality	per thou. live births	130.0	60.0	46.0	99.0	73.0	45.0
Under 5 mortality	"	..	..	67.3	169.0	108.0	59.0
Immunization							
Measles	% age group	..	63.0	70.0	54.0	72.7	..
DPT	"	..	69.0	75.0	54.6	80.6	..
Child malnutrition (under-5)	"	..	15.6	13.3	28.4	38.3	..
Life expectancy							
Total	years	51	56	60	52	62	68
Female advantage	"	4.0	6.0	5.0	3.4	2.4	6.4
Total fertility rate	births per woman	5.7	5.5	4.8	6.1	3.4	3.1
Maternal mortality rate	per 100,000 live births	..	..	220	..	..	..
Supplementary Poverty Indicators							
Expenditures on social security	% of total gov't exp.	..	..	..	..	..	..
Social security coverage	% econ. active pop.	..	..	..	..	..	..
Access to safe water: total	% of pop.	17.0	36.0	46.0	41.1	68.4	..
Urban	"	65.0	65.0	59.0	77.8	78.9	..
Rural	"	14.0	30.0	45.0	27.3	60.3	..
Access to health care	"	..	50.0	80.0	..	..	..

Population growth rate
(annual average, percent)

Legend: □ Lesotho; — Low-income

GNP per capita growth rate
(annual average, percent)

Development diamond[b]

Legend: ▬ Lesotho; — Low-income

a. See the technical notes, p.389.   b. The development diamond, based on four key indicators, shows the average level of development in the country compared with its income group. See the introduction.

196

Lesotho

Indicator	Unit of measure	Latest single year 1970-75	Latest single year 1980-85	Most recent estimate 1987-92	Sub-Saharan Africa	Low-income	Next higher income group
Resources and Expenditures							
HUMAN RESOURCES							
Population (mre=1992)	thousands	1,187	1,545	1,856	546,390	3,194,535	942,547
Age dependency ratio	ratio	0.83	0.86	0.88	0.95	0.67	0.66
Urban	% of pop.	10.8	16.1	20.9	29.5	26.7	57.0
Population growth rate	annual %	2.2	2.9	2.4	2.9	1.8	1.4
Urban	"	6.4	6.4	6.0	5.1	3.4	4.8
Labor force (15-64)	thousands	597	730	844	224,025	1,478,954	..
Agriculture	% of labor force	88	86	..	..	..	..
Industry	"	4	4	..	..	..	..
Female	"	47	45	43	37	33	36
Females per 100 males							
Urban	number	128	..	..	..	..	..
Rural	"	100	..	..	..	..	..
NATURAL RESOURCES							
Area	thou. sq. km	30.35	30.35	30.35	24,274.03	38,401.06	40,697.37
Density	pop. per sq. km	39.1	50.9	59.7	21.9	81.7	22.8
Agricultural land	% of land area	78.2	75.9	77.1	52.7	50.9	..
Change in agricultural land	annual %	0.7	0.3	0.0	0.1	0.0	..
Agricultural land under irrigation	%	..	..	..	0.8	18.2	..
Forests and woodland	thou. sq. km	..	..	..	..	..	..
Deforestation (net)	annual %	..	..	..	..	..	..
INCOME							
Household income							
Share of top 20% of households	% of income	..	..	60	..	42	..
Share of bottom 40% of households	"	..	..	9	..	19	..
Share of bottom 20% of households	"	..	..	3	..	8	..
EXPENDITURE							
Food	% of GDP	..	..	..	..	..	..
Staples	"	..	..	..	..	..	..
Meat, fish, milk, cheese, eggs	"	..	..	..	..	..	..
Cereal imports	thou. metric tonnes	56	78	140	20,311	46,537	74,924
Food aid in cereals	"	14	71	29	4,303	9,008	4,054
Food production per capita	1987 = 100	106	87	67	90	123	..
Fertilizer consumption	kg/ha	0.6	1.5	2.5	4.2	61.9	..
Share of agriculture in GDP	% of GDP	28.7	17.6	8.4	18.6	29.6	..
Housing	% of GDP	..	..	..	..	..	..
Average household size	persons per household	..	5.4	..	..	..	..
Urban	"	..	..	..	..	..	..
Fixed investment: housing	% of GDP	2.5	1.8	..	..	..	..
Fuel and power	% of GDP	..	..	..	..	..	..
Energy consumption per capita	kg of oil equiv.	..	..	..	258	335	1,882
Households with electricity							
Urban	% of households	..	..	..	..	..	..
Rural	"	..	..	..	..	..	..
Transport and communication	% of GDP	..	..	..	..	..	..
Fixed investment: transport equipment	"	3.9	7.3	..	..	..	..
Total road length	thou. km	3	4	5	..	..	..
INVESTMENT IN HUMAN CAPITAL							
Health							
Population per physician	persons	30,247	14,306	..	..	..	..
Population per nurse	"	3,857	..	..	..	..	..
Population per hospital bed	"	597	..	..	1,329	1,050	516
Oral rehydration therapy (under-5)	% of cases	..	..	68	36	39	..
Education							
Gross enrollment ratio							
Secondary	% of school-age pop.	13	23	25	18	41	..
Female	"	14	27	30	14	35	..
Pupil-teacher ratio: primary	pupils per teacher	53	55	54	39	37	26
Pupil-teacher ratio: secondary	"	26	21	19	..	19	..
Pupils reaching grade 4	% of cohort	79	78	64	..	..	..
Repeater rate: primary	% of total enroll	6	23	22	..	..	..
Illiteracy	% of pop. (age 15+)	..	26	..	51	39	..
Female	% of fem. (age 15+)	..	16	..	62	52	..
Newspaper circulation	per thou. pop.	1	32	11	14	..	100

World Bank International Economics Department, April 1994

Liberia

Indicator	Unit of measure	Latest single year 1970-75	Latest single year 1980-85	Most recent estimate 1987-92	Same region/income group Sub-Saharan Africa	Same region/income group Low-income	Next higher income group
Priority Poverty Indicators							
POVERTY							
Upper poverty line	local curr.	..	..	..	..	..	..
Headcount index	% of pop.	..	..	..	..	19	..
Lower poverty line	local curr.	..	..	..	..	..	..
Headcount index	% of pop.	..	..	..	..	..	..
GNP per capita	US$	410	480	460	520	390	..
SHORT TERM INCOME INDICATORS							
Unskilled urban wages	local curr.	..	..	..	..	..	..
Unskilled rural wages	"	..	..	..	..	..	..
Rural terms of trade	"	..	..	..	..	..	..
Consumer price index	1987=100	51	92	120	..	..	..
Lower income	"	..	..	..	..	..	..
Food[a]	"	36	101	149	..	..	..
Urban	"	..	..	..	..	..	..
Rural	"	..	..	..	..	..	..
SOCIAL INDICATORS							
Public expenditure on basic social services	% of GDP	..	..	1.0	..	..	..
Gross enrollment ratios							
Primary	% school age pop.	62	40	..	66	103	..
Male	"	80	51	..	79	113	..
Female	"	45	28	..	62	96	..
Mortality							
Infant mortality	per thou. live births	181.0	153.0	142.0	99.0	73.0	45.0
Under 5 mortality	"	..	..	212.0	169.0	108.0	59.0
Immunization							
Measles	% age group	..	83.0	..	54.0	72.7	..
DPT	"	..	45.0	19.0	54.6	80.6	..
Child malnutrition (under-5)	"	..	..	20.3	28.4	38.3	..
Life expectancy							
Total	years	47	51	53	52	62	68
Female advantage	"	3.0	3.0	2.0	3.4	2.4	6.4
Total fertility rate	births per woman	6.5	6.5	6.2	6.1	3.4	3.1
Maternal mortality rate	per 100,000 live births	173	173	..	..	..	..
Supplementary Poverty Indicators							
Expenditures on social security	% of total gov't exp.	0.0	0.6	0.8	..	..	..
Social security coverage	% econ. active pop.	..	..	..	..	..	..
Access to safe water: total	% of pop.	15.0	54.0	..	41.1	68.4	..
Urban	"	100.0	..	..	77.8	78.9	..
Rural	"	6.0	23.0	..	27.3	60.3	..
Access to health care	"	..	35.0	34.0	..	..	..

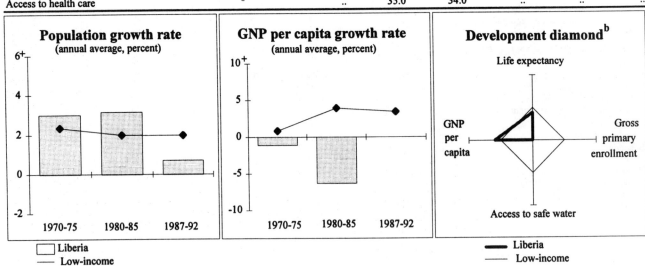

Population growth rate (annual average, percent)

GNP per capita growth rate (annual average, percent)

Development diamond[b]
Life expectancy — Gross primary enrollment — Access to safe water — GNP per capita

— Liberia
— Low-income

a. See the technical notes, p.389.   b. The development diamond, based on four key indicators, shows the average level of development in the country compared with its income group. See the introduction.

Liberia

Indicator	Unit of measure	Latest single year 1970-75	Latest single year 1980-85	Most recent estimate 1987-92	Same region/income group Sub-Saharan Africa	Same region/income group Low-income	Next higher income group
Resources and Expenditures							
HUMAN RESOURCES							
Population (mre=1992)	thousands	1,609	2,199	2,371	546,390	3,194,535	942,547
Age dependency ratio	ratio	0.89	0.93	0.94	0.95	0.67	0.66
Urban	% of pop.	30.3	40.0	47.5	29.5	26.7	57.0
Population growth rate	annual %	3.0	2.6	0.1	2.9	1.8	1.4
Urban	"	5.9	5.1	2.3	5.1	3.4	4.8
Labor force (15-64)	thousands	636	808	964	224,025	1,478,954	..
Agriculture	% of labor force	76	74	..	..	..	..
Industry	"	9	9	..	..	..	..
Female	"	32	31	30	37	33	36
Females per 100 males							
Urban	number	84	..	..	..	..	..
Rural	"	113	..	..	..	..	..
NATURAL RESOURCES							
Area	thou. sq. km	97.75	97.75	97.75	24,274.03	38,401.06	40,697.37
Density	pop. per sq. km	16.5	22.5	24.2	21.9	81.7	22.8
Agricultural land	% of land area	62.7	62.8	62.8	52.7	50.9	..
Change in agricultural land	annual %	0.0	0.0	0.0	0.1	0.0	..
Agricultural land under irrigation	%	0.0	0.0	0.0	0.8	18.2	..
Forests and woodland	thou. sq. km	21	18	17	..	..	..
Deforestation (net)	annual %	..	..	0.6	..	..	..
INCOME							
Household income							
Share of top 20% of households	% of income	73	..	..	..	42	..
Share of bottom 40% of households	"	11	..	..	..	19	..
Share of bottom 20% of households	"	5	..	..	..	8	..
EXPENDITURE							
Food	% of GDP	..	..	..	..	..	..
Staples	"	..	..	..	..	..	..
Meat, fish, milk, cheese, eggs	"	..	..	..	..	..	..
Cereal imports	thou. metric tonnes	41	103	148	20,311	46,537	74,924
Food aid in cereals	"	3	20	157	4,303	9,008	4,054
Food production per capita	1987 = 100	103	96	58	90	123	..
Fertilizer consumption	kg/ha	0.8	0.2	0.1	4.2	61.9	..
Share of agriculture in GDP	% of GDP	24.8	33.3	..	18.6	29.6	..
Housing	% of GDP	..	..	..	..	..	..
Average household size	persons per household	..	..	..	..	..	..
Urban	"	..	..	..	..	..	..
Fixed investment: housing	% of GDP	..	..	..	..	..	..
Fuel and power	% of GDP	..	..	..	..	..	..
Energy consumption per capita	kg of oil equiv.	391	162	45	258	335	1,882
Households with electricity							
Urban	% of households	..	..	..	..	..	..
Rural	"	..	..	..	..	..	..
Transport and communication	% of GDP	..	..	..	..	..	..
Fixed investment: transport equipment	"	..	..	..	..	..	..
Total road length	thou. km	8	5	6	..	..	..
INVESTMENT IN HUMAN CAPITAL							
Health							
Population per physician	persons	12,548	9,407	..	..	..	..
Population per nurse	"	937	1,384	..	..	..	..
Population per hospital bed	"	607	..	..	1,329	1,050	516
Oral rehydration therapy (under-5)	% of cases	..	..	9	36	39	..
Education							
Gross enrollment ratio							
Secondary	% of school-age pop.	17	17	..	18	41	..
Female	"	8	12	..	14	35	..
Pupil-teacher ratio: primary	pupils per teacher	27	16	..	39	37	26
Pupil-teacher ratio: secondary	"	20	46	..	..	19	..
Pupils reaching grade 4	% of cohort	..	..	..	..	..	..
Repeater rate: primary	% of total enroll	..	..	..	..	..	..
Illiteracy	% of pop. (age 15+)	80	68	61	51	39	..
Female	% of fem. (age 15+)	..	79	71	62	52	..
Newspaper circulation	per thou. pop.	8	6	15	14	..	100

World Bank International Economics Department, April 1994

Libya

Indicator	Unit of measure	Latest single year 1970-75	Latest single year 1980-85	Most recent estimate 1987-92	Same region/income group Mid-East & North Africa	Same region/income group Upper-middle-income	Next higher income group
Priority Poverty Indicators							
POVERTY							
Upper poverty line	local curr.	..	..	..	..	..	..
Headcount index	% of pop.	..	..	..	..	..	..
Lower poverty line	local curr.	..	..	..	..	..	..
Headcount index	% of pop.	..	..	..	..	..	..
GNP per capita	US$	4,630	6,810	5,330	1,950	3,870	21,960
SHORT TERM INCOME INDICATORS							
Unskilled urban wages	local curr.	..	..	..	..	..	..
Unskilled rural wages	"	..	..	..	..	..	..
Rural terms of trade	"	..	..	..	..	..	..
Consumer price index	1987=100	..	..	..	..	..	..
Lower income	"	..	..	..	..	..	..
Food[a]	"	..	..	..	..	..	..
Urban	"	..	..	..	..	..	..
Rural	"	..	..	..	..	..	..
SOCIAL INDICATORS							
Public expenditure on basic social services	% of GDP	..	..	6.7	..	..	..
Gross enrollment ratios							
Primary	% school age pop.	..	..	..	100	107	103
Male	"	..	..	..	107	..	103
Female	"	..	..	..	88	..	103
Mortality							
Infant mortality	per thou. live births	117.0	97.0	68.0	58.0	40.0	7.0
Under 5 mortality	"	..	..	83.4	78.0	51.0	10.0
Immunization							
Measles	% age group	..	50.0	59.0	81.8	82.0	82.4
DPT	"	..	51.0	62.0	83.9	73.8	90.1
Child malnutrition (under-5)	"	14.5	..	..	20.9	..	..
Life expectancy							
Total	years	53	58	63	64	69	77
Female advantage	"	3.1	3.4	3.4	2.4	6.3	6.4
Total fertility rate	births per woman	7.6	7.2	6.4	4.9	2.9	1.7
Maternal mortality rate	per 100,000 live births	..	..	..	..	..	..
Supplementary Poverty Indicators							
Expenditures on social security	% of total gov't exp.	..	..	..	..	..	..
Social security coverage	% econ. active pop.	..	..	..	..	..	..
Access to safe water: total	% of pop.	87.0	..	97.0	85.0	85.6	..
Urban	"	100.0	..	100.0	97.0	94.3	..
Rural	"	82.0	..	80.0	70.1	73.0	..
Access to health care	"	..	100.0	100.0	84.6	..	..

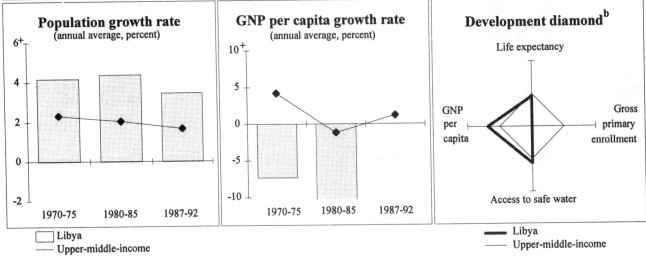

Population growth rate
(annual average, percent)

GNP per capita growth rate
(annual average, percent)

Development diamond[b]

Life expectancy

GNP per capita — Gross primary enrollment

Access to safe water

☐ Libya
— Upper-middle-income

—— Libya
— Upper-middle-income

a. See the technical notes, p.389.   b. The development diamond, based on four key indicators, shows the average level of development in the country compared with its income group. See the introduction.

Libya

Indicator	Unit of measure	Latest single year 1970-75	Latest single year 1980-85	Most recent estimate 1987-92	Same region/income group Mid-East & North Africa	Same region/income group Upper-middle-income	Next higher income group
Resources and Expenditures							
HUMAN RESOURCES							
Population (mre=1992)	thousands	2,446	3,786	4,867	252,555	477,960	828,221
Age dependency ratio	ratio	0.93	0.95	0.95	0.87	0.64	0.50
Urban	% of pop.	61.0	77.1	83.8	54.7	71.7	78.1
Population growth rate	annual %	4.3	4.2	3.5	2.8	1.6	0.7
Urban	"	9.5	6.2	4.3	3.8	2.5	0.9
Labor force (15-64)	thousands	628	904	1,157	69,280	181,414	390,033
Agriculture	% of labor force	23	18	..	..	..	..
Industry	"	27	29	..	..	..	..
Female	"	7	8	10	15	29	38
Females per 100 males							
Urban	number	78	..	..	..	..	..
Rural	"	89	..	..	..	..	..
NATURAL RESOURCES							
Area	thou. sq. km	1,759.54	1,759.54	1,759.54	10,487.21	21,836.02	31,709.00
Density	pop. per sq. km	1.4	2.2	2.7	23.4	21.5	24.5
Agricultural land	% of land area	8.0	8.8	8.8	30.2	41.7	42.7
Change in agricultural land	annual %	1.5	0.1	0.0	0.5	0.3	-0.2
Agricultural land under irrigation	%	1.4	1.5	1.6	31.0	9.3	16.1
Forests and woodland	thou. sq. km	6	7	7	..	..	..
Deforestation (net)	annual %	..	..	..	..	..	..
INCOME							
Household income							
Share of top 20% of households	% of income	..	..	..	..	..	..
Share of bottom 40% of households	"	..	..	..	..	..	..
Share of bottom 20% of households	"	..	..	..	..	..	..
EXPENDITURE							
Food	% of GDP	..	..	17.5	..	..	..
Staples	"	..	..	4.3	..	..	..
Meat, fish, milk, cheese, eggs	"	..	..	10.2	..	..	..
Cereal imports	thou. metric tonnes	601	1,114	2,032	38,007	49,174	70,626
Food aid in cereals	"	..	..	..	2,484	282	2
Food production per capita	1987 = 100	112	86	85	116	109	101
Fertilizer consumption	kg/ha	2.6	3.9	5.5	96.7	68.8	162.1
Share of agriculture in GDP	% of GDP	2.2	3.5	5.0	13.7	8.1	2.4
Housing	% of GDP	..	..	14.2	..	..	..
Average household size	persons per household	5.8	..	..	..	..	..
Urban	"	5.9	..	..	..	..	..
Fixed investment: housing	% of GDP	6.2	2.2	2.7	..	..	..
Fuel and power	% of GDP	..	..	1.7	..	..	..
Energy consumption per capita	kg of oil equiv.	1,525	2,344	2,164	1,109	1,649	5,101
Households with electricity							
Urban	% of households	..	..	..	..	..	..
Rural	"	..	..	..	..	..	..
Transport and communication	% of GDP	..	..	6.3	..	..	..
Fixed investment: transport equipment	"	2.2	0.7	4.3	..	..	..
Total road length	thou. km	..	..	..	..	..	..
INVESTMENT IN HUMAN CAPITAL							
Health							
Population per physician	persons	2,717	693	957	..	..	..
Population per nurse	"	376	350	221	..	..	..
Population per hospital bed	"	262	207	246	636	385	144
Oral rehydration therapy (under-5)	% of cases	..	..	60	56	54	..
Education							
Gross enrollment ratio							
Secondary	% of school-age pop.	..	..	..	59	53	92
Female	"	..	..	..	50	..	94
Pupil-teacher ratio: primary	pupils per teacher	23	16	12	27	25	18
Pupil-teacher ratio: secondary	"	15	14	12	21	..	..
Pupils reaching grade 4	% of cohort	95	..	..	..	71	..
Repeater rate: primary	% of total enroll	16	10	..	..	11	..
Illiteracy	% of pop. (age 15+)	61	44	36	45	14	..
Female	% of fem. (age 15+)	..	60	50	58	17	..
Newspaper circulation	per thou. pop.	17	..	15	39	117	..

World Bank International Economics Department, April 1994

201

Lithuania

Indicator	Unit of measure	Latest single year 1970-75	Latest single year 1980-85	Most recent estimate 1987-92	Same region/income group Europe & Central Asia	Same region/income group Lower-middle-income	Next higher income group
Priority Poverty Indicators							
POVERTY							
Upper poverty line	local curr.	..	..	..	..	..	..
Headcount index	% of pop.	..	..	6	..	..	..
Lower poverty line	local curr.	..	..	..	..	..	..
Headcount index	% of pop.	..	..	1	..	..	..
GNP per capita	US$	..	..	1,310	..	..	3,870
SHORT TERM INCOME INDICATORS							
Unskilled urban wages	local curr.	..	..	..	..	..	..
Unskilled rural wages	"	..	..	..	..	..	..
Rural terms of trade	"	..	..	..	..	..	..
Consumer price index	1987=100	..	..	..	..	..	..
Lower income	"	..	..	..	..	..	..
Food[a]	"	..	..	..	..	..	..
Urban	"	..	..	..	..	..	..
Rural	"	..	..	..	..	..	..
SOCIAL INDICATORS							
Public expenditure on basic social services	% of GDP	..	..	7.3	..	..	..
Gross enrollment ratios							
Primary	% school age pop.	..	..	..	..	..	107
Male	"	..	..	..	..	..	..
Female	"	..	..	..	..	..	..
Mortality							
Infant mortality	per thou. live births	..	15.0	16.4	30.0	45.0	40.0
Under 5 mortality	"	..	..	19.8	38.0	59.0	51.0
Immunization							
Measles	% age group	..	..	..	..	..	82.0
DPT	"	..	..	..	..	..	73.8
Child malnutrition (under-5)	"	..	..	..	..	..	..
Life expectancy							
Total	years	71	69	71	70	68	69
Female advantage	"	7.9	10.0	9.8	8.6	6.4	6.3
Total fertility rate	births per woman	2.2	2.1	2.0	2.2	3.1	2.9
Maternal mortality rate	per 100,000 live births	..	27	29	58	..	..
Supplementary Poverty Indicators							
Expenditures on social security	% of total gov't exp.	..	..	..	..	..	..
Social security coverage	% econ. active pop.	..	..	..	..	..	..
Access to safe water: total	% of pop.	..	..	..	..	..	85.6
Urban	"	..	..	..	..	..	94.3
Rural	"	..	..	..	..	..	73.0
Access to health care	"	..	..	..	..	..	..

Population growth rate
(annual average, percent)

☐ Lithuania
— Lower-middle-income

GNP per capita growth rate
(annual average, percent)

Development diamond[b]

— Lithuania
— Lower-middle-income

a. See the technical notes, p.389.   b. The development diamond, based on four key indicators, shows the average level of development in the country compared with its income group. See the introduction.

Lithuania

Indicator	Unit of measure	Latest single year 1970-75	Latest single year 1980-85	Most recent estimate 1987-92	Europe & Central Asia	Lower-middle-income	Next higher income group
Resources and Expenditures							
HUMAN RESOURCES							
Population (mre=1992)	thousands	..	3,578	3,756	495,241	942,547	477,960
Age dependency ratio	ratio	..	..	0.53	0.56	0.66	0.64
Urban	% of pop.	..	..	68.0	63.3	57.0	71.7
Population growth rate	annual %	..	0.8	0.0	0.5	1.4	1.6
Urban	"	..	..	..	..	4.8	2.5
Labor force (15-64)	thousands	..	1,860	1,828	..	..	181,414
Agriculture	% of labor force	..	20	14	..	..	..
Industry	"	..	40	28	..	..	..
Female	"	..	..	..	46	36	29
Females per 100 males							
Urban	number	..	..	..	..	..	..
Rural	"	..	..	..	..	..	..
NATURAL RESOURCES							
Area	thou. sq. km	..	..	65.20	24,165.06	40,697.37	21,836.02
Density	pop. per sq. km	..	..	57.6	20.4	22.8	21.5
Agricultural land	% of land area	..	..	..	..	..	41.7
Change in agricultural land	annual %	..	..	..	..	..	0.3
Agricultural land under irrigation	%	..	..	..	..	..	9.3
Forests and woodland	thou. sq. km	..	..	..	..	..	..
Deforestation (net)	annual %	..	..	..	..	..	..
INCOME							
Household income							
Share of top 20% of households	% of income	..	..	..	..	..	..
Share of bottom 40% of households	"	..	..	..	..	..	..
Share of bottom 20% of households	"	..	..	..	..	..	..
EXPENDITURE							
Food	% of GDP	..	..	18.0	..	..	..
Staples	"	..	..	3.3	..	..	..
Meat, fish, milk, cheese, eggs	"	..	..	8.1	..	..	..
Cereal imports	thou. metric tonnes	..	..	415	45,972	74,924	49,174
Food aid in cereals	"	..	..	185	1,639	4,054	282
Food production per capita	1987 = 100	..	..	..	..	..	109
Fertilizer consumption	kg/ha	..	..	..	..	..	68.8
Share of agriculture in GDP	% of GDP	..	27.7	21.2	..	..	8.1
Housing	% of GDP	..	..	4.2	..	..	..
Average household size	persons per household	..	..	3.2	..	..	..
Urban	"	..	..	..	..	..	..
Fixed investment: housing	% of GDP	..	..	5.3	..	..	..
Fuel and power	% of GDP	..	..	0.9	..	..	..
Energy consumption per capita	kg of oil equiv.	..	..	..	3,190	1,882	1,649
Households with electricity							
Urban	% of households	..	..	..	..	..	..
Rural	"	..	..	..	..	..	..
Transport and communication	% of GDP	..	..	5.7	..	..	..
Fixed investment: transport equipment	"	..	..	11.0	..	..	..
Total road length	thou. km	..	32	43	..	..	..
INVESTMENT IN HUMAN CAPITAL							
Health							
Population per physician	persons	..	..	223	378	..	..
Population per nurse	"	..	..	..	..	..	..
Population per hospital bed	"	..	..	79	134	516	385
Oral rehydration therapy (under-5)	% of cases	..	..	..	..	..	54
Education							
Gross enrollment ratio							
Secondary	% of school-age pop.	..	..	..	..	..	53
Female	"	..	..	..	..	..	..
Pupil-teacher ratio: primary	pupils per teacher	..	..	..	..	26	25
Pupil-teacher ratio: secondary	"	..	..	..	..	..	..
Pupils reaching grade 4	% of cohort	..	..	..	..	..	71
Repeater rate: primary	% of total enroll	..	..	..	..	..	11
Illiteracy	% of pop. (age 15+)	..	..	..	..	..	14
Female	% of fem. (age 15+)	..	..	..	..	..	17
Newspaper circulation	per thou. pop.	..	..	..	..	100	117

World Bank International Economics Department, April 1994

Luxembourg

Indicator	Unit of measure	Latest single year 1970-75	Latest single year 1980-85	Most recent estimate 1987-92	Same region/income group High-income
Priority Poverty Indicators					
POVERTY					
Upper poverty line	local curr.	..	..	..	..
Headcount index	% of pop.	..	..	..	..
Lower poverty line	local curr.	..	..	..	
Headcount index	% of pop.	..	..	..	..
GNP per capita	US$	7,460	14,070	35,160	21,960
SHORT TERM INCOME INDICATORS					
Unskilled urban wages	local curr.	..	..	..	..
Unskilled rural wages	"	..	..	..	..
Rural terms of trade	"	..	..	..	..
Consumer price index	1987=100	53	100	116	..
Lower income	"	..	..	..	..
Food[a]	"	38	99	98	..
Urban	"	..	..	..	..
Rural	"	..	..	..	..
SOCIAL INDICATORS					
Public expenditure on basic social services	% of GDP	..	..	..	..
Gross enrollment ratios					
Primary	% school age pop.	112	..	90	103
Male	"	112	..	88	103
Female	"	112	..	93	103
Mortality					
Infant mortality	per thou. live births	14.8	9.0	29.0	7.0
Under 5 mortality	"	..	..	35.1	10.0
Immunization					
Measles	% age group	..	..	71.0	82.4
DPT	"	..	..	90.0	90.1
Child malnutrition (under-5)	"	..	..	..	..
Life expectancy					
Total	years	71	73	72	77
Female advantage	"	7.0	6.7	3.1	6.4
Total fertility rate	births per woman	1.6	1.4	2.2	1.7
Maternal mortality rate	per 100,000 live births	..	25	..	..
Supplementary Poverty Indicators					
Expenditures on social security	% of total gov't exp.	46.0	49.2	47.6	..
Social security coverage	% econ. active pop.	..	..	..	..
Access to safe water: total	% of pop.	..	..	..	..
Urban	"	98.8	..	..	..
Rural	"	97.3	..	..	..
Access to health care	"	..	100.0	100.0	..

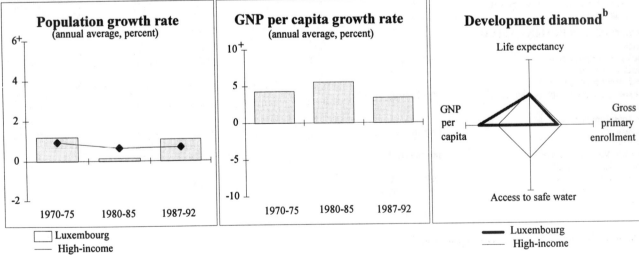

Population growth rate (annual average, percent)

GNP per capita growth rate (annual average, percent)

Development diamond[b]

Luxembourg
High-income

a. See the technical notes, p.389.   b. The development diamond, based on four key indicators, shows the average level of development in the country compared with its income group. See the introduction.

Luxembourg

Indicator	Unit of measure	Latest single year 1970-75	Latest single year 1980-85	Most recent estimate 1987-92	Same region/income group High-income
Resources and Expenditures					
HUMAN RESOURCES					
Population (mre=1992)	thousands	361	367	392	828,221
Age dependency ratio	ratio	0.53	0.44	0.47	0.50
Urban	% of pop.	73.7	81.8	85.0	78.1
Population growth rate	annual %	0.9	0.3	1.3	0.7
Urban	"	2.5	1.1	1.7	0.9
Labor force (15-64)	thousands	144	155	154	390,033
Agriculture	% of labor force	7	5	..	..
Industry	"	39	35	..	..
Female	"	29	32	32	38
Females per 100 males					
Urban	number	103	..	..	..
Rural	"	98	..	..	..
NATURAL RESOURCES					
Area	thou. sq. km	..	..	..	31,709.00
Density	pop. per sq. km	..	..	..	24.5
Agricultural land	% of land area	..	..	..	42.7
Change in agricultural land	annual %	..	..	..	-0.2
Agricultural land under irrigation	%	..	..	..	16.1
Forests and woodland	thou. sq. km	..	..	..	..
Deforestation (net)	annual %	..	..	0.0	..
INCOME					
Household income					
Share of top 20% of households	% of income	..	..	..	..
Share of bottom 40% of households	"	..	..	..	..
Share of bottom 20% of households	"	..	..	..	..
EXPENDITURE					
Food	% of GDP	11.9	9.9	..	..
Staples	"	2.0	1.6	..	..
Meat, fish, milk, cheese, eggs	"	5.9	4.8	..	..
Cereal imports	thou. metric tonnes	..	..	..	70,626
Food aid in cereals	"	..	..	..	2
Food production per capita	1987 = 100	..	..	..	101
Fertilizer consumption	kg/ha	..	..	..	162.1
Share of agriculture in GDP	% of GDP	3.3	2.6	1.4	2.4
Housing	% of GDP	10.7	13.0	..	..
Average household size	persons per household	3.1	..	..	..
Urban	"	2.9	..	..	..
Fixed investment: housing	% of GDP	7.8	2.0	..	..
Fuel and power	% of GDP	3.1	5.5	..	..
Energy consumption per capita	kg of oil equiv.	10,649	8,587	9,722	5,101
Households with electricity					
Urban	% of households	..	..	..	..
Rural	"	..	..	..	..
Transport and communication	% of GDP	7.7	11.0	..	..
Fixed investment: transport equipment	"	1.9	2.5	..	..
Total road length	thou. km	5	5	5	..
INVESTMENT IN HUMAN CAPITAL					
Health					
Population per physician	persons	941	554	508	..
Population per nurse	"	310	242	..	..
Population per hospital bed	"	86	84	..	144
Oral rehydration therapy (under-5)	% of cases	..	..	..	..
Education					
Gross enrollment ratio					
Secondary	% of school-age pop.	59	75	75	92
Female	"	59	74	71	94
Pupil-teacher ratio: primary	pupils per teacher	19	13	13	18
Pupil-teacher ratio: secondary	"	16	..	11	..
Pupils reaching grade 4	% of cohort	90	86	..	..
Repeater rate: primary	% of total enroll	6	6	..	..
Illiteracy	% of pop. (age 15+)	..	..	†	..
Female	% of fem. (age 15+)	..	..	†	..
Newspaper circulation	per thou. pop.	447	365	374	..

World Bank International Economics Department, April 1994

Macao

Indicator	Unit of measure	Latest single year 1970-75	Latest single year 1980-85	Most recent estimate 1987-92	Same region/income group East Asia	Same region/income group Upper-middle-income	Next higher income group
Priority Poverty Indicators							
POVERTY							
Upper poverty line	local curr.	..	..	..	..	..	..
Headcount index	% of pop.	..	..	..	12	..	..
Lower poverty line	local curr.	..	..	..	..	..	..
Headcount index	% of pop.	..	..	..	9	..	..
GNP per capita	US$	..	..	..	760	3,870	21,960
SHORT TERM INCOME INDICATORS							
Unskilled urban wages	local curr.	..	..	..	..	..	..
Unskilled rural wages	"	..	..	..	..	..	..
Rural terms of trade	"	..	..	..	..	..	..
Consumer price index	1987=100	..	..	..	..	..	..
Lower income	"	..	..	..	..	..	..
Food[a]	"	..	95	142	..	..	..
Urban	"	..	..	..	..	..	..
Rural	"	..	..	..	..	..	..
SOCIAL INDICATORS							
Public expenditure on basic social services	% of GDP	..	..	..	..	..	..
Gross enrollment ratios							
Primary	% school age pop.	..	..	..	121	107	103
Male	"	..	..	..	126	..	103
Female	"	..	..	..	117	..	103
Mortality							
Infant mortality	per thou. live births	..	..	8.0	39.0	40.0	7.0
Under 5 mortality	"	..	..	10.2	49.0	51.0	10.0
Immunization							
Measles	% age group	..	3.0	91.0	88.4	82.0	82.4
DPT	"	..	21.0	93.0	89.5	73.8	90.1
Child malnutrition (under-5)	"	..	..	..	24.7	..	..
Life expectancy							
Total	years	61	68	73	68	69	77
Female advantage	"	3.7	3.9	5.6	3.6	6.3	6.4
Total fertility rate	births per woman	4.3	3.8	2.1	2.4	2.9	1.7
Maternal mortality rate	per 100,000 live births	..	..	..	114	..	..
Supplementary Poverty Indicators							
Expenditures on social security	% of total gov't exp.	..	..	..	..	..	..
Social security coverage	% econ. active pop.	..	..	..	..	..	..
Access to safe water: total	% of pop.	..	..	..	72.0	85.6	..
Urban	"	..	..	..	83.4	94.3	..
Rural	"	..	..	100.0	60.2	73.0	..
Access to health care	"	..	..	..	..	..	..

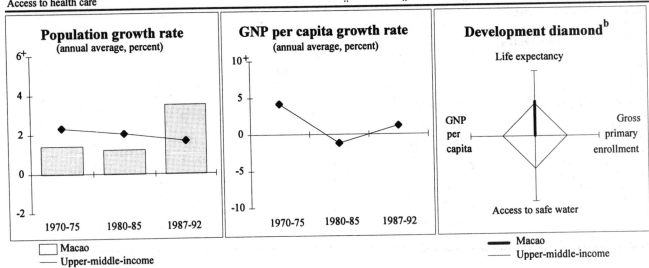

Population growth rate
(annual average, percent)

☐ Macao
— Upper-middle-income

GNP per capita growth rate
(annual average, percent)

Development diamond[b]

Life expectancy

GNP per capita — Gross primary enrollment

Access to safe water

— Macao
— Upper-middle-income

a. See the technical notes, p.389.   b. The development diamond, based on four key indicators, shows the average level of development in the country compared with its income group. See the introduction.

Macao

Indicator	Unit of measure	Latest single year 1970-75	Latest single year 1980-85	Most recent estimate 1987-92	East Asia	Upper-middle-income	Next higher income group
Resources and Expenditures							
HUMAN RESOURCES							
Population (mre=1992)	thousands	267	305	374	1,688,909	477,960	828,221
Age dependency ratio	ratio	..	0.45	0.46	0.55	0.64	0.50
Urban	% of pop.	97.7	98.5	98.7	29.4	71.7	78.1
Population growth rate	annual %	0.0	0.7	5.2	1.4	1.6	0.7
Urban	"	0.1	0.7	5.2	2.9	2.5	0.9
Labor force (15-64)	thousands	..	..	..	928,465	181,414	390,033
Agriculture	% of labor force	..	..	..	..	..	..
Industry	"	..	..	..	..	..	..
Female	"	..	..	..	41	29	38
Females per 100 males							
Urban	number	..	..	..	..	..	..
Rural	"	..	..	..	..	..	..
NATURAL RESOURCES							
Area	thou. sq. km	0.02	0.02	0.02	16,367.18	21,836.02	31,709.00
Density	pop. per sq. km	13350.0	15250.0	17750.0	101.8	21.5	24.5
Agricultural land	% of land area	..	..	..	44.5	41.7	42.7
Change in agricultural land	annual %	..	..	..	0.1	0.3	-0.2
Agricultural land under irrigation	%	..	..	..	14.5	9.3	16.1
Forests and woodland	thou. sq. km	..	..	..	..	..	..
Deforestation (net)	annual %	..	..	..	..	..	..
INCOME							
Household income							
Share of top 20% of households	% of income	..	..	..	42	..	..
Share of bottom 40% of households	"	..	..	..	18	..	..
Share of bottom 20% of households	"	..	..	..	7	..	..
EXPENDITURE							
Food	% of GDP	..	..	..	..	..	..
Staples	"	..	..	..	..	..	..
Meat, fish, milk, cheese, eggs	"	..	..	..	..	..	..
Cereal imports	thou. metric tonnes	27	31	39	33,591	49,174	70,626
Food aid in cereals	"	1	..	..	581	282	2
Food production per capita	1987 = 100	105	76	79	133	109	101
Fertilizer consumption	kg/ha	..	..	..	75.1	68.8	162.1
Share of agriculture in GDP	% of GDP	..	..	..	21.5	8.1	2.4
Housing	% of GDP	..	..	..	..	..	..
Average household size	persons per household	5.0	..	..	..	..	..
Urban	"	..	..	..	..	..	..
Fixed investment: housing	% of GDP	..	..	..	..	..	..
Fuel and power	% of GDP	..	4.2	..	..	..	..
Energy consumption per capita	kg of oil equiv.	371	836	987	593	1,649	5,101
Households with electricity							
Urban	% of households	..	..	..	..	..	..
Rural	"	..	..	..	..	..	..
Transport and communication	% of GDP	..	..	..	..	..	..
Fixed investment: transport equipment	"	..	..	..	..	..	..
Total road length	thou. km	..	..	..	..	..	..
INVESTMENT IN HUMAN CAPITAL							
Health							
Population per physician	persons	1,547	1,000	606	..	..	..
Population per nurse	"	1,015	..	317	..	..	..
Population per hospital bed	"	185	..	..	553	385	144
Oral rehydration therapy (under-5)	% of cases	..	..	..	51	54	..
Education							
Gross enrollment ratio							
Secondary	% of school-age pop.	..	..	..	53	53	92
Female	"	..	..	..	47	..	94
Pupil-teacher ratio: primary	pupils per teacher	28	..	..	23	25	18
Pupil-teacher ratio: secondary	"	21	..	..	16	..	..
Pupils reaching grade 4	% of cohort	..	..	..	89	71	..
Repeater rate: primary	% of total enroll	..	..	..	6	11	..
Literacy	% of pop. (age 15+)	21	..	..	24	14	..
Female	% of fem. (age 15+)	..	..	..	34	17	..
Newspaper circulation	per thou. pop.	..	..	698	..	117	..

World Bank International Economics Department, April 1994

Former Yugoslav Republic of Macedonia

Indicator	Unit of measure	Latest single year 1970-75	Latest single year 1980-85	Most recent estimate 1987-92	Same region/income group Europe & Central Asia	Same region/income group Lower-middle-income	Next higher income group
Priority Poverty Indicators							
POVERTY							
Upper poverty line	local curr.	..	..	..	..	..	..
Headcount index	% of pop.	..	..	..	..	..	..
Lower poverty line	local curr.	..	..	..	..	..	..
Headcount index	% of pop.	..	..	..	..	..	..
GNP per capita	US$	..	..	..	..	..	3,870
SHORT TERM INCOME INDICATORS							
Unskilled urban wages	local curr.	..	..	..	..	..	..
Unskilled rural wages	"	..	..	..	..	..	..
Rural terms of trade	"	..	..	..	..	..	..
Consumer price index	1987=100	..	..	..	..	..	..
Lower income	"	..	..	..	..	..	..
Food[a]	"	..	..	..	..	..	..
Urban	"	..	..	..	..	..	..
Rural	"	..	..	..	..	..	..
SOCIAL INDICATORS							
Public expenditure on basic social services	% of GDP	..	..	..	..	..	..
Gross enrollment ratios							107
Primary	% school age pop.	..	..	..	..	..	..
Male	"	..	..	..	..	..	..
Female	"	..	..	..	..	..	..
Mortality							40.0
Infant mortality	per thou. live births	..	..	29.0	30.0	45.0	40.0
Under 5 mortality	"	..	..	35.1	38.0	59.0	51.0
Immunization							82.0
Measles	% age group	..	..	..	..	..	73.8
DPT	"	..	..	..	..	..	..
Child malnutrition (under-5)	"	..	..	..	..	..	
Life expectancy							69
Total	years	..	..	72	70	68	69
Female advantage	"	..	..	3.1	8.6	6.4	6.3
Total fertility rate	births per woman	..	..	2.2	2.2	3.1	2.9
Maternal mortality rate	per 100,000 live births	..	..	..	58	..	..
Supplementary Poverty Indicators							
Expenditures on social security	% of total gov't exp.	..	..	..	..	..	..
Social security coverage	% econ. active pop.	..	..	..	..	..	85.6
Access to safe water: total	% of pop.	..	..	..	..	..	94.3
Urban	"	..	..	..	..	..	73.0
Rural	"	..	..	..	..	..	
Access to health care	"	..	..	..	..	..	

Population growth rate (annual average, percent)

GNP per capita growth rate (annual average, percent)

Development diamond[b]

☐ Former Yugoslav Republic of Macedonia
— Lower-middle-income

━━ Former Yugoslav Republic of M
— Lower-middle-income

a. See the technical notes, p.389.   b. The development diamond, based on four key indicators, shows the average level of development in the country compared with its income group. See the introduction.

Former Yugoslav Republic of Macedonia

Indicator	Unit of measure	Latest single year 1970-75	1980-85	Most recent estimate 1987-92	Same region/income group Europe & Central Asia	Lower-middle-income	Next higher income group
Resources and Expenditures							
HUMAN RESOURCES							
Population (mre=1992)	thousands	1,778	2,017	2,172	495,241	942,547	477,960
Age dependency ratio	ratio	..	..	..	0.56	0.66	0.64
Urban	% of pop.	..	..	..	63.3	57.0	71.7
Population growth rate	annual %	1.8	0.6	0.9	0.5	1.4	1.6
Urban	"	..	..	..	..	4.8	2.5
Labor force (15-64)	thousands	..	..	..	..	..	181,414
Agriculture	% of labor force	..	..	..	..	..	..
Industry	"	..	..	..	..	..	..
Female	"	..	..	..	46	36	29
Females per 100 males							
Urban	number	..	..	..	..	..	..
Rural	"	..	..	..	..	..	..
NATURAL RESOURCES							
Area	thou. sq. km	..	..	25.70	24,165.06	40,697.37	21,836.02
Density	pop. per sq. km	..	..	..	20.4	22.8	21.5
Agricultural land	% of land area	..	..	..	..	..	41.7
Change in agricultural land	annual %	..	..	..	..	..	0.3
Agricultural land under irrigation	%	..	..	..	..	..	9.3
Forests and woodland	thou. sq. km	..	..	..	..	..	..
Deforestation (net)	annual %	..	..	..	..	..	..
INCOME							
Household income							
Share of top 20% of households	% of income	..	..	..	..	..	..
Share of bottom 40% of households	"	..	..	..	..	..	..
Share of bottom 20% of households	"	..	..	..	..	..	..
EXPENDITURE							
Food	% of GDP	..	..	..	..	..	..
Staples	"	..	..	..	..	..	..
Meat, fish, milk, cheese, eggs	"	..	..	..	..	..	..
Cereal imports	thou. metric tonnes	..	..	..	45,972	74,924	49,174
Food aid in cereals	"	..	..	..	1,639	4,054	282
Food production per capita	1987 = 100	..	..	..	..	..	109
Fertilizer consumption	kg/ha	..	..	..	..	..	68.8
Share of agriculture in GDP	% of GDP	..	..	..	..	..	8.1
Housing	% of GDP	..	..	..	..	..	..
Average household size	persons per household	..	..	..	..	..	..
Urban	"	..	..	..	..	..	..
Fixed investment: housing	% of GDP	..	..	..	..	..	..
Fuel and power	% of GDP	..	..	..	..	..	..
Energy consumption per capita	kg of oil equiv.	..	..	..	3,190	1,882	1,649
Households with electricity							
Urban	% of households	..	..	..	..	..	..
Rural	"	..	..	..	..	..	..
Transport and communication	% of GDP	..	..	..	..	..	..
Fixed investment: transport equipment	"	..	..	..	..	..	..
Total road length	thou. km	..	..	..	..	..	..
INVESTMENT IN HUMAN CAPITAL							
Health							
Population per physician	persons	..	..	..	378	..	..
Population per nurse	"	..	..	..	..	..	..
Population per hospital bed	"	..	..	..	134	516	385
Oral rehydration therapy (under-5)	% of cases	..	..	..	..	..	54
Education							
Gross enrollment ratio							
Secondary	% of school-age pop.	..	..	..	..	..	53
Female	"	..	..	..	..	..	..
Pupil-teacher ratio: primary	pupils per teacher	..	..	..	..	26	25
Pupil-teacher ratio: secondary	"	..	..	..	..	..	..
Pupils reaching grade 4	% of cohort	..	..	..	..	..	71
Repeater rate: primary	% of total enroll	..	..	..	..	..	11
Illiteracy	% of pop. (age 15+)	..	..	..	..	..	14
Female	% of fem. (age 15+)	..	..	..	..	..	17
Newspaper circulation	per thou. pop.	..	..	..	..	100	117

World Bank International Economics Department, April 1994

Madagascar

Indicator	Unit of measure	Latest single year 1970-75	Latest single year 1980-85	Most recent estimate 1987-92	Same region/income group Sub-Saharan Africa	Same region/income group Low-income	Next higher income group
Priority Poverty Indicators							
POVERTY							
Upper poverty line	local curr.	..	..	..	..	..	..
Headcount index	% of pop.	..	..	..	..	19	..
Lower poverty line	local curr.	..	..	..	..	..	..
Headcount index	% of pop.	..	..	..	..	..	..
GNP per capita	US$	280	310	230	520	390	..
SHORT TERM INCOME INDICATORS							
Unskilled urban wages	local curr.	..	..	..	..	..	..
Unskilled rural wages	"	..	..	..	..	..	..
Rural terms of trade	"	..	..	..	..	..	..
Consumer price index	1987=100	20	76	192	..	..	..
Lower income	"	..	..	..	..	..	..
Food[a]	"	12	78	190	..	..	..
Urban	"	..	..	..	..	..	..
Rural	"	..	..	..	..	..	..
SOCIAL INDICATORS							
Public expenditure on basic social services	% of GDP	..	..	..	..	..	..
Gross enrollment ratios							
Primary	% school age pop.	95	118	92	66	103	..
Male	"	103	122	93	79	113	..
Female	"	88	114	91	62	96	..
Mortality							
Infant mortality	per thou. live births	172.0	130.0	93.0	99.0	73.0	45.0
Under 5 mortality	"	..	..	151.0	169.0	108.0	59.0
Immunization							
Measles	% age group	..	28.0	33.0	54.0	72.7	..
DPT	"	..	23.0	46.0	54.6	80.6	..
Child malnutrition (under-5)	"	..	30.0	32.8	28.4	38.3	..
Life expectancy							
Total	years	46	50	51	52	62	68
Female advantage	"	3.0	2.2	2.3	3.4	2.4	6.4
Total fertility rate	births per woman	6.6	6.5	6.1	6.1	3.4	3.1
Maternal mortality rate	per 100,000 live births	..	300	350	..	..	..
Supplementary Poverty Indicators							
Expenditures on social security	% of total gov't exp.	..	..	..	..	..	..
Social security coverage	% econ. active pop.	..	..	..	..	..	..
Access to safe water: total	% of pop.	25.0	30.0	..	41.1	68.4	..
Urban	"	76.0	81.0	..	77.8	78.9	..
Rural	"	14.0	17.0	..	27.3	60.3	..
Access to health care	"	..	65.0	65.0	..	..	..

Population growth rate (annual average, percent)

☐ Madagascar
— Low-income

GNP per capita growth rate (annual average, percent)

Development diamond[b]

Life expectancy — GNP per capita — Gross primary enrollment — Access to safe water

— Madagascar
— Low-income

a. See the technical notes, p.389.   b. The development diamond, based on four key indicators, shows the average level of development in the country compared with its income group. See the introduction.

Madagascar

Indicator	Unit of measure	Latest single year 1970-75	Latest single year 1980-85	Most recent estimate 1987-92	Same region/income group Sub-Saharan Africa	Same region/income group Low-income	Next higher income group
Resources and Expenditures							
HUMAN RESOURCES							
Population (mre=1992)	thousands	7,599	9,985	12,366	546,390	3,194,535	942,547
Age dependency ratio	ratio	0.89	0.91	0.95	0.95	0.67	0.66
Urban	% of pop.	16.1	20.9	25.1	29.5	26.7	57.0
Population growth rate	annual %	2.5	2.9	2.9	2.9	1.8	1.4
Urban	"	5.1	5.4	5.6	5.1	3.4	4.8
Labor force (15-64)	thousands	3,668	4,510	5,243	224,025	1,478,954	..
Agriculture	% of labor force	82	81	..	..	..	..
Industry	"	5	6	..	..	..	..
Female	"	41	40	39	37	33	36
Females per 100 males							
Urban	number	106	..	..	..	..	..
Rural	"	103	..	..	..	..	..
NATURAL RESOURCES							
Area	thou. sq. km	587.04	587.04	587.04	24,274.03	38,401.06	40,697.37
Density	pop. per sq. km	12.9	17.0	20.5	21.9	81.7	22.8
Agricultural land	% of land area	63.2	63.7	63.8	52.7	50.9	..
Change in agricultural land	annual %	0.8	0.1	0.0	0.1	0.0	..
Agricultural land under irrigation	%	1.3	2.2	2.5	0.8	18.2	..
Forests and woodland	thou. sq. km	178	163	154	..	..	..
Deforestation (net)	annual %	..	..	0.8	..	..	..
INCOME							
Household income							
Share of top 20% of households	% of income	..	..	..	..	42	..
Share of bottom 40% of households	"	..	14	..	..	19	..
Share of bottom 20% of households	"	..	5	..	..	8	..
EXPENDITURE							
Food	% of GDP	..	50.6	..	..	..	..
Staples	"	..	22.0	..	..	..	..
Meat, fish, milk, cheese, eggs	"	..	16.4	..	..	..	..
Cereal imports	thou. metric tonnes	72	195	147	20,311	46,537	74,924
Food aid in cereals	"	7	98	41	4,303	9,008	4,054
Food production per capita	1987 = 100	107	95	82	90	123	..
Fertilizer consumption	kg/ha	0.2	0.3	0.3	4.2	61.9	..
Share of agriculture in GDP	% of GDP	30.4	31.3	31.0	18.6	29.6	..
Housing	% of GDP	..	10.0	..	..	..	..
Average household size	persons per household	4.5	..	..	..	..	..
Urban	"	5.0	..	..	..	..	..
Fixed investment: housing	% of GDP	..	1.1	..	..	..	..
Fuel and power	% of GDP	..	5.5	..	..	..	..
Energy consumption per capita	kg of oil equiv.	78	40	38	258	335	1,882
Households with electricity							
Urban	% of households	..	..	..	..	..	..
Rural	"	..	..	..	..	..	..
Transport and communication	% of GDP	..	3.2	..	..	..	..
Fixed investment: transport equipment	"	..	1.0	..	..	..	..
Total road length	thou. km	28	50	50	..	..	..
INVESTMENT IN HUMAN CAPITAL							
Health							
Population per physician	persons	10,093	9,780	8,123	..	..	..
Population per nurse	"	240	1,721	..	..	..	..
Population per hospital bed	"	400	..	1,140	1,329	1,050	516
Oral rehydration therapy (under-5)	% of cases	..	..	11	36	39	..
Education							
Gross enrollment ratio							
Secondary	% of school-age pop.	12	34	19	18	41	..
Female	"	10	28	18	14	35	..
Pupil-teacher ratio: primary	pupils per teacher	60	38	40	39	37	26
Pupil-teacher ratio: secondary	"	26	28	22	..	19	..
Pupils reaching grade 4	% of cohort	69	..	54	..	..	..
Repeater rate: primary	% of total enroll	24	..	35	..	..	..
Illiteracy	% of pop. (age 15+)	..	23	20	51	39	..
Female	% of fem. (age 15+)	..	32	27	62	52	..
Newspaper circulation	per thou. pop.	8	6	4	14	..	100

World Bank International Economics Department, April 1994

211

Malawi

Indicator	Unit of measure	Latest single year 1970-75	Latest single year 1980-85	Most recent estimate 1987-92	Same region/income group Sub-Saharan Africa	Same region/income group Low-income	Next higher income group
Priority Poverty Indicators							
POVERTY							
Upper poverty line	local curr.	..	..	..	..	..	..
Headcount index	% of pop.	..	..	..	..	19	..
Lower poverty line	local curr.	..	..	..	..	..	..
Headcount index	% of pop.	..	..	..	..	..	..
GNP per capita	US$	120	170	210	520	390	..
SHORT TERM INCOME INDICATORS							
Unskilled urban wages	local curr.	..	..	..	..	..	..
Unskilled rural wages	"	..	..	..	..	..	..
Rural terms of trade	"	..	..	..	..	..	..
Consumer price index	1987=100	..	70	233	..	..	..
Lower income	"	..	..	..	..	..	..
Food[a]	"	15	68	250	..	..	..
Urban	"	..	..	..	..	..	..
Rural	"	..	..	..	..	..	..
SOCIAL INDICATORS							
Public expenditure on basic social services	% of GDP	..	..	2.0	..	..	..
Gross enrollment ratios							
Primary	% school age pop.	..	59	66	66	103	..
Male	"	..	67	72	79	113	..
Female	"	..	51	60	62	96	..
Mortality							
Infant mortality	per thou. live births	191.0	163.0	134.3	99.0	73.0	45.0
Under 5 mortality	"	..	..	226.8	169.0	108.0	59.0
Immunization							
Measles	% age group	..	49.0	78.0	54.0	72.7	..
DPT	"	..	52.0	81.0	54.6	80.6	..
Child malnutrition (under-5)	"	..	22.6	60.0	28.4	38.3	..
Life expectancy							
Total	years	41	45	44	52	62	68
Female advantage	"	1.4	1.3	1.4	3.4	2.4	6.4
Total fertility rate	births per woman	7.8	7.6	6.7	6.1	3.4	3.1
Maternal mortality rate	per 100,000 live births	..	250	380	..	..	..
Supplementary Poverty Indicators							
Expenditures on social security	% of total gov't exp.	2.2	0.8	0.0	..	..	..
Social security coverage	% econ. active pop.	..	..	..	..	..	..
Access to safe water: total	% of pop.	..	55.0	53.0	41.1	68.4	..
Urban	"	..	97.0	82.0	77.8	78.9	..
Rural	"	..	50.0	50.0	27.3	60.3	..
Access to health care	"	..	54.0	80.0	..	..	..

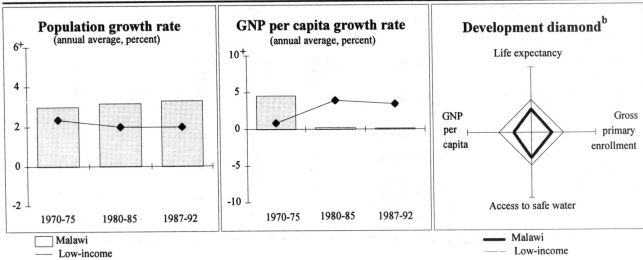

Population growth rate (annual average, percent)

GNP per capita growth rate (annual average, percent)

Development diamond[b]
- Life expectancy
- GNP per capita
- Gross primary enrollment
- Access to safe water

□ Malawi
— Low-income

— Malawi
-- Low-income

a. See the technical notes, p.389.   b. The development diamond, based on four key indicators, shows the average level of development in the country compared with its income group. See the introduction.

Malawi

Indicator	Unit of measure	Latest single year 1970-75	Latest single year 1980-85	Most recent estimate 1987-92	Same region/income group Sub-Saharan Africa	Same region/income group Low-income	Next higher income group
Resources and Expenditures							
HUMAN RESOURCES							
Population (mre=1992)	thousands	5,244	7,188	9,057	546,390	3,194,535	942,547
Age dependency ratio	ratio	0.98	0.94	0.98	0.95	0.67	0.66
Urban	% of pop.	7.7	10.4	12.5	29.5	26.7	57.0
Population growth rate	annual %	3.0	3.3	2.9	2.9	1.8	1.4
Urban	"	7.6	5.9	5.7	5.1	3.4	4.8
Labor force (15-64)	thousands	2,382	3,074	3,689	224,025	1,478,954	..
Agriculture	% of labor force	87	83	..	..	..	..
Industry	"	6	7	..	..	..	..
Female	"	45	43	41	37	33	36
Females per 100 males							
Urban	number	..	..	..	..	..	..
Rural	"	..	..	..	..	..	..
NATURAL RESOURCES							
Area	thou. sq. km	118.48	118.48	118.48	24,274.03	38,401.06	40,697.37
Density	pop. per sq. km	44.3	60.7	74.2	21.9	81.7	22.8
Agricultural land	% of land area	33.1	35.2	37.5	52.7	50.9	..
Change in agricultural land	annual %	0.3	0.8	0.6	0.1	0.0	..
Agricultural land under irrigation	%	0.4	0.5	0.6	0.8	18.2	..
Forests and woodland	thou. sq. km	48	42	35	..	..	..
Deforestation (net)	annual %	..	..	1.3	..	..	..
INCOME							
Household income							
Share of top 20% of households	% of income	..	..	..	..	42	..
Share of bottom 40% of households	"	..	..	..	..	19	..
Share of bottom 20% of households	"	..	..	..	..	8	..
EXPENDITURE							
Food	% of GDP	42.2	22.9	..	..	..	..
Staples	"	20.1	6.8	..	..	..	..
Meat, fish, milk, cheese, eggs	"	6.8	8.5	..	..	..	..
Cereal imports	thou. metric tonnes	41	29	412	20,311	46,537	74,924
Food aid in cereals	"	0	5	321	4,303	9,008	4,054
Food production per capita	1987 = 100	101	83	47	90	123	..
Fertilizer consumption	kg/ha	4.8	10.3	21.4	4.2	61.9	..
Share of agriculture in GDP	% of GDP	34.8	32.5	25.5	18.6	29.6	..
Housing	% of GDP	4.9	6.8	..	..	..	..
Average household size	persons per household	3.1	..	..	..	..	..
Urban	"	3.5	..	..	..	..	..
Fixed investment: housing	% of GDP	3.6	1.1	..	..	..	..
Fuel and power	% of GDP	2.1	3.6	..	..	..	..
Energy consumption per capita	kg of oil equiv.	46	42	40	258	335	1,882
Households with electricity							
Urban	% of households	..	..	..	..	..	..
Rural	"	..	..	..	..	..	..
Transport and communication	% of GDP	6.0	7.8	..	..	..	..
Fixed investment: transport equipment	"	6.7	2.2	..	..	..	..
Total road length	thou. km	11	11	13	..	..	..
INVESTMENT IN HUMAN CAPITAL							
Health							
Population per physician	persons	76,576	11,343	45,737	..	..	..
Population per nurse	"	5,328	3,118	1,800	..	..	..
Population per hospital bed	"	650	..	645	1,329	1,050	516
Oral rehydration therapy (under-5)	% of cases	..	..	14	36	39	..
Education							
Gross enrollment ratio							
Secondary	% of school-age pop.	..	4	4	18	41	..
Female	"	..	2	3	14	35	..
Pupil-teacher ratio: primary	pupils per teacher	61	61	64	39	37	26
Pupil-teacher ratio: secondary	"	19	22	27	..	19	..
Pupils reaching grade 4	% of cohort	67	53	69	..	..	..
Repeater rate: primary	% of total enroll	16	18	21	..	..	..
Illiteracy	% of pop. (age 15+)	..	59	..	51	39	..
Female	% of fem. (age 15+)	..	69	..	62	52	..
Newspaper circulation	per thou. pop.	..	5	3	14	..	100

World Bank International Economics Department, April 1994

Malaysia

Indicator	Unit of measure	Latest single year 1970-75	Latest single year 1980-85	Most recent estimate 1987-92	Same region/income group East Asia	Same region/income group Upper-middle-income	Next higher income group
Priority Poverty Indicators							
POVERTY							
Upper poverty line	local curr.	..	..	..	..	..	..
Headcount index	% of pop.	38	20	16	12	..	..
Lower poverty line	local curr.	..	..	..	..	..	..
Headcount index	% of pop.	14	..	2	9	..	..
GNP per capita	US$	820	1,980	2,790	760	3,870	21,960
SHORT TERM INCOME INDICATORS							
Unskilled urban wages	local curr.	..	..	..	..	..	..
Unskilled rural wages	"	47	58	94	..	..	..
Rural terms of trade	"	..	..	..	..	..	..
Consumer price index	1987=100	63	99	118	..	..	..
Lower income	"	..	..	..	..	..	..
Food[a]	"	43	100	117	..	..	..
Urban	"	..	..	..	..	..	..
Rural	"	..	..	..	..	..	..
SOCIAL INDICATORS							
Public expenditure on basic social services	% of GDP	6.0	6.7	6.8	..	..	..
Gross enrollment ratios							
Primary	% school age pop.	91	101	93	121	107	103
Male	"	92	101	93	126	..	103
Female	"	89	100	93	117	..	103
Mortality							
Infant mortality	per thou. live births	42.0	28.0	14.0	39.0	40.0	7.0
Under 5 mortality	"	..	..	17.1	49.0	51.0	10.0
Immunization							
Measles	% age group	..	20.0	79.0	88.4	82.0	82.4
DPT	"	..	59.0	90.0	89.5	73.8	90.1
Child malnutrition (under-5)	"	..	23.2	17.1	24.7	..	..
Life expectancy							
Total	years	63	68	71	68	69	77
Female advantage	"	3.3	4.0	4.3	3.6	6.3	6.4
Total fertility rate	births per woman	5.2	4.2	3.5	2.4	2.9	1.7
Maternal mortality rate	per 100,000 live births	..	59	20	114	..	..
Supplementary Poverty Indicators							
Expenditures on social security	% of total gov't exp.	..	..	..	..	..	..
Social security coverage	% econ. active pop.	..	..	..	..	..	..
Access to safe water: total	% of pop.	34.0	84.0	79.0	72.0	85.6	..
Urban	"	100.0	96.0	96.0	83.4	94.3	..
Rural	"	6.0	76.0	66.0	60.2	73.0	..
Access to health care	"	..	..	..	..	..	..

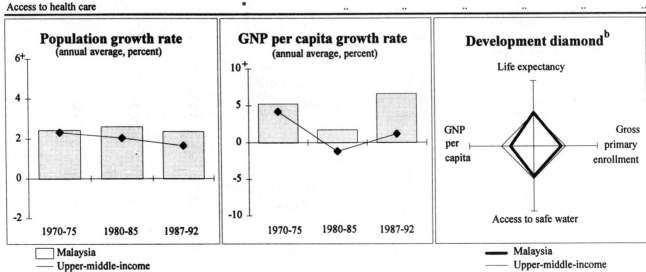

a. See the technical notes, p.389.   b. The development diamond, based on four key indicators, shows the average level of development in the country compared with its income group. See the introduction.

Malaysia

Indicator	Unit of measure	Latest single year 1970-75	1980-85	Most recent estimate 1987-92	Same region/income group East Asia	Upper-middle-income	Next higher income group

Resources and Expenditures

HUMAN RESOURCES

Population (mre=1992)

Indicator	Unit	1970-75	1980-85	1987-92	East Asia	Upper-mid	Next higher
Population (mre=1992)	thousands	12,258	15,682	18,606	1,688,909	477,960	828,221
Age dependency ratio	ratio	0.85	0.74	0.73	0.55	0.64	0.50
Urban	% of pop.	30.7	38.8	44.7	29.4	71.7	78.1
Population growth rate	annual %	2.3	2.7	2.3	1.4	1.6	0.7
Urban	"	4.8	4.8	4.2	2.9	2.5	0.9
Labor force (15-64)	thousands	4,451	6,171	7,469	928,465	181,414	390,033
Agriculture	% of labor force	48	42	..	..	..	..
Industry	"	17	19	..	..	..	..
Female	"	33	35	35	41	29	38
Females per 100 males							
Urban	number	..	..	..	..	..	..
Rural	"	..	..	..	..	..	..

NATURAL RESOURCES

Indicator	Unit	1970-75	1980-85	1987-92	East Asia	Upper-mid	Next higher
Area	thou. sq. km	329.75	329.75	329.75	16,367.18	21,836.02	31,709.00
Density	pop. per sq. km	37.2	47.6	55.1	101.8	21.5	24.5
Agricultural land	% of land area	14.3	14.9	14.9	44.5	41.7	42.7
Change in agricultural land	annual %	1.1	0.4	0.0	0.1	0.3	-0.2
Agricultural land under irrigation	%	6.6	6.8	7.0	14.5	9.3	16.1
Forests and woodland	thou. sq. km	225	206	190	..	..	..
Deforestation (net)	annual %	..	..	2.0	..	..	..

INCOME

Household income

Indicator	Unit	1970-75	1980-85	1987-92	East Asia	Upper-mid	Next higher
Share of top 20% of households	% of income	56	..	54	42	..	..
Share of bottom 40% of households	"	11	..	13	18	..	..
Share of bottom 20% of households	"	4	..	5	7	..	..

EXPENDITURE

Indicator	Unit	1970-75	1980-85	1987-92	East Asia	Upper-mid	Next higher
Food	% of GDP	21.7	..	..	..	..	..
Staples	"	6.4	..	..	..	..	..
Meat, fish, milk, cheese, eggs	"	9.0	..	..	..	..	..
Cereal imports	thou. metric tonnes	765	2,225	3,198	33,591	49,174	70,626
Food aid in cereals	"	1	..	1	581	282	2
Food production per capita	1987 = 100	81	124	152	133	109	101
Fertilizer consumption	kg/ha	52.7	124.6	196.7	75.1	68.8	162.1
Share of agriculture in GDP	% of GDP	28.0	19.4	..	21.5	8.1	2.4
Housing	% of GDP	6.6	..	..	..	..	..
Average household size	persons per household	6.0	5.2	..	..	..	..
Urban	"	6.0	..	..	..	..	..
Fixed investment: housing	% of GDP	3.7	..	..	..	..	..
Fuel and power	% of GDP	1.3	..	..	..	..	..
Energy consumption per capita	kg of oil equiv.	490	950	1,445	593	1,649	5,101
Households with electricity							
Urban	% of households	..	85.0	..	..	..	..
Rural	"	..	30.0	..	..	..	..
Transport and communication	% of GDP	8.4	..	..	..	..	..
Fixed investment: transport equipment	"	2.8	..	..	..	..	..
Total road length	thou. km	20	29	40	..	..	..

INVESTMENT IN HUMAN CAPITAL

Health

Indicator	Unit	1970-75	1980-85	1987-92	East Asia	Upper-mid	Next higher
Population per physician	persons	4,283	3,175	2,440	..	..	..
Population per nurse	"	1,269	1,392	376	..	..	..
Population per hospital bed	"	299	400	430	553	385	144
Oral rehydration therapy (under-5)	% of cases	..	..	47	51	54	..

Education

Gross enrollment ratio

Indicator	Unit	1970-75	1980-85	1987-92	East Asia	Upper-mid	Next higher
Secondary	% of school-age pop.	42	53	58	53	53	92
Female	"	38	53	59	47	..	94
Pupil-teacher ratio: primary	pupils per teacher	32	24	20	23	25	18
Pupil-teacher ratio: secondary	"	28	22	19	16	..	..
Pupils reaching grade 4	% of cohort	..	99	98	89	71	..
Repeater rate: primary	% of total enroll	..	0	0	6	11	..
Illiteracy	% of pop. (age 15+)	42	26	22	24	14	..
Female	% of fem. (age 15+)	..	35	30	34	17	..
Newspaper circulation	per thou. pop.	85	173	141	..	117	..

World Bank International Economics Department, April 1994

Maldives

Indicator	Unit of measure	Latest single year 1970-75	Latest single year 1980-85	Most recent estimate 1987-92	Same region/income group South Asia	Same region/income group Low-income	Next higher income group
Priority Poverty Indicators							
POVERTY							
Upper poverty line	local curr.	..	..	..	..	..	..
Headcount index	% of pop.	..	..	..	28	19	..
Lower poverty line	local curr.	..	..	..	..	..	..
Headcount index	% of pop.	..	..	..	..	..	..
GNP per capita	US$	120	290	500	310	390	..
SHORT TERM INCOME INDICATORS							
Unskilled urban wages	local curr.	..	..	..	..	..	..
Unskilled rural wages	"	..	..	..	..	..	..
Rural terms of trade	"	..	..	..	..	..	..
Consumer price index	1987=100	..	..	..	..	..	..
Lower income	"	..	..	..	..	..	..
Food[a]	"	..	..	..	..	..	..
Urban	"	..	..	..	..	..	..
Rural	"	..	..	..	..	..	..
SOCIAL INDICATORS							
Public expenditure on basic social services	% of GDP	..	..	..	..	..	..
Gross enrollment ratios							
Primary	% school age pop.	..	..	..	103	103	..
Male	"	..	..	..	117	113	..
Female	"	..	..	..	88	96	..
Mortality							
Infant mortality	per thou. live births	112.0	80.0	55.0	85.0	73.0	45.0
Under 5 mortality	"	..	..	73.1	116.0	108.0	59.0
Immunization							
Measles	% age group	..	30.0	88.0	56.6	72.7	..
DPT	"	..	5.0	91.0	75.0	80.6	..
Child malnutrition (under-5)	"	..	56.1	..	60.9	38.3	..
Life expectancy							
Total	years	52	58	62	60	62	68
Female advantage	"	0.0	1.5	3.0	1.0	2.4	6.4
Total fertility rate	births per woman	7.0	6.8	6.0	4.0	3.4	3.1
Maternal mortality rate	per 100,000 live births	..	..	480	..	..	..
Supplementary Poverty Indicators							
Expenditures on social security	% of total gov't exp.	..	1.3	1.0	..	..	..
Social security coverage	% econ. active pop.	..	..	..	..	..	..
Access to safe water: total	% of pop.	..	24.0	70.0	71.9	68.4	..
Urban	"	..	58.0	77.0	74.2	78.9	..
Rural	"	..	12.0	68.0	70.0	60.3	..
Access to health care	"	..	25.0	75.0	..	..	..

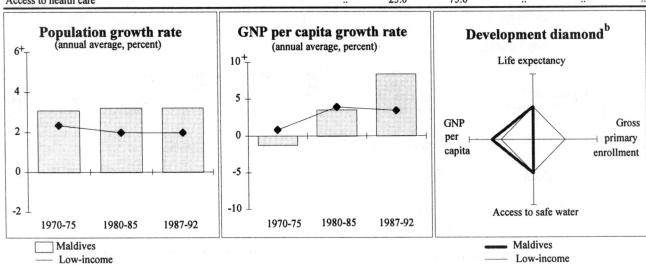

Population growth rate (annual average, percent) — Maldives / Low-income

GNP per capita growth rate (annual average, percent) — Maldives / Low-income

Development diamond[b] — Life expectancy, GNP per capita, Gross primary enrollment, Access to safe water — Maldives / Low-income

a. See the technical notes, p.389. b. The development diamond, based on four key indicators, shows the average level of development in the country compared with its income group. See the introduction.

216

Maldives

Indicator	Unit of measure	Latest single year 1970-75	Latest single year 1980-85	Most recent estimate 1987-92	Same region/income group South Asia	Same region/income group Low-income	Next higher income group
Resources and Expenditures							
HUMAN RESOURCES							
Population (mre=1992)	thousands	133	182	229	1,177,918	3,194,535	942,547
Age dependency ratio	ratio	..	0.88	0.93	0.73	0.67	0.66
Urban	% of pop.	18.0	25.7	31.0	25.4	26.7	57.0
Population growth rate	annual %	3.1	3.4	3.1	2.1	1.8	1.4
Urban	"	8.2	6.0	5.7	3.4	3.4	4.8
Labor force (15-64)	thousands	..	0	0	428,847	1,478,954	..
Agriculture	% of labor force	..	..	..	..	..	..
Industry	"	..	..	..	..	..	..
Female	"	..	..	..	22	33	36
Females per 100 males							
Urban	number	..	..	..	..	..	..
Rural	"	..	..	..	..	..	..
NATURAL RESOURCES							
Area	thou. sq. km	0.30	0.30	0.30	5,133.49	38,401.06	40,697.37
Density	pop. per sq. km	443.3	606.7	740.0	224.8	81.7	22.8
Agricultural land	% of land area	13.3	13.3	13.3	58.9	50.9	..
Change in agricultural land	annual %	0.0	0.0	0.0	-0.2	0.0	..
Agricultural land under irrigation	%	..	..	..	29.0	18.2	..
Forests and woodland	thou. sq. km	0	0	0	..	..	..
Deforestation (net)	annual %	..	..	..	..	..	..
INCOME							
Household income							
Share of top 20% of households	% of income	..	..	..	41	42	..
Share of bottom 40% of households	"	..	..	..	21	19	..
Share of bottom 20% of households	"	..	..	..	9	8	..
EXPENDITURE							
Food	% of GDP	..	..	..	..	..	..
Staples	"	..	..	..	..	..	..
Meat, fish, milk, cheese, eggs	"	..	..	..	..	..	..
Cereal imports	thou. metric tonnes	7	15	31	7,721	46,537	74,924
Food aid in cereals	"	1	2	3	2,558	9,008	4,054
Food production per capita	1987 = 100	110	104	93	116	123	..
Fertilizer consumption	kg/ha	..	..	..	71.5	61.9	..
Share of agriculture in GDP	% of GDP	..	..	..	28.7	29.6	..
Housing	% of GDP	..	..	..	..	..	..
Average household size	persons per household	..	..	..	..	..	..
Urban	"	..	..	..	..	..	..
Fixed investment: housing	% of GDP	..	..	..	..	..	..
Fuel and power	% of GDP	..	..	..	..	..	..
Energy consumption per capita	kg of oil equiv.	15	115	144	209	335	1,882
Households with electricity							
Urban	% of households	..	..	..	..	..	..
Rural	"	..	..	..	..	..	..
Transport and communication	% of GDP	..	..	..	..	..	..
Fixed investment: transport equipment	"	..	..	..	..	..	..
Total road length	thou. km	..	..	..	..	..	..
INVESTMENT IN HUMAN CAPITAL							
Health							
Population per physician	persons	28,500	15,000	14,333	2,459	..	..
Population per nurse	"	548	613	158	..	..	..
Population per hospital bed	"	..	..	..	1,652	1,050	516
Oral rehydration therapy (under-5)	% of cases	..	..	27	18	39	..
Education							
Gross enrollment ratio							
Secondary	% of school-age pop.	..	..	..	40	41	..
Female	"	..	..	..	29	35	..
Pupil-teacher ratio: primary	pupils per teacher	26	..	..	59	37	26
Pupil-teacher ratio: secondary	"	13	..	..	23	19	..
Pupils reaching grade 4	% of cohort	..	..	..	..	..	..
Repeater rate: primary	% of total enroll	..	..	..	..	..	..
Illiteracy	% of pop. (age 15+)	..	..	..	54	39	..
Female	% of fem. (age 15+)	..	..	..	68	52	..
Newspaper circulation	per thou. pop.	..	6	9	..	..	100

World Bank International Economics Department, April 1994

Mali

Indicator	Unit of measure	Latest single year 1970-75	Latest single year 1980-85	Most recent estimate 1987-92	Same region/income group Sub-Saharan Africa	Same region/income group Low-income	Next higher income group
Priority Poverty Indicators							
POVERTY							
Upper poverty line	local curr.	..	..	..	..	..	..
Headcount index	% of pop.	..	..	..	..	19	..
Lower poverty line	local curr.	..	..	..	..	..	..
Headcount index	% of pop.	..	..	..	..	..	..
GNP per capita	US$	120	160	310	520	390	..
SHORT TERM INCOME INDICATORS							
Unskilled urban wages	local curr.	..	..	..	..	..	..
Unskilled rural wages	"	..	..	..	..	..	..
Rural terms of trade	"	..	..	..	..	..	..
Consumer price index	1987=100	..	..	..	..	..	..
Lower income	"	..	..	..	..	..	..
Food[a]	"	..	..	..	..	..	..
Urban	"	..	..	..	..	..	..
Rural	"	..	..	..	..	..	..
SOCIAL INDICATORS							
Public expenditure on basic social services	% of GDP	..	..	..	..	..	..
Gross enrollment ratios							
Primary	% school age pop.	24	23	25	66	103	..
Male	"	32	30	32	79	113	..
Female	"	17	17	19	62	96	..
Mortality							
Infant mortality	per thou. live births	203.0	180.0	130.0	99.0	73.0	45.0
Under 5 mortality	"	..	..	201.1	169.0	108.0	59.0
Immunization							
Measles	% age group	..	11.0	40.0	54.0	72.7	..
DPT	"	..	18.0	35.0	54.6	80.6	..
Child malnutrition (under-5)	"	..	..	25.1	28.4	38.3	..
Life expectancy							
Total	years	39	44	48	52	62	68
Female advantage	"	4.0	0.2	3.5	3.4	2.4	6.4
Total fertility rate	births per woman	6.5	6.7	7.1	6.1	3.4	3.1
Maternal mortality rate	per 100,000 live births	..	..	2325	..	..	..
Supplementary Poverty Indicators							
Expenditures on social security	% of total gov't exp.	..	..	3.0	..	..	..
Social security coverage	% econ. active pop.	..	..	..	..	..	..
Access to safe water: total	% of pop.	..	17.0	49.0	41.1	68.4	..
Urban	"	29.0	46.0	100.0	77.8	78.9	..
Rural	"	..	10.0	36.0	27.3	60.3	..
Access to health care	"	..	20.0	..	..	..	..

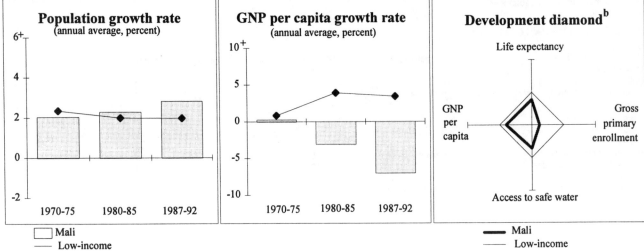

Population growth rate (annual average, percent)

GNP per capita growth rate (annual average, percent)

Development diamond[b]

☐ Mali
— Low-income

— Mali
— Low-income

a. See the technical notes, p.389.   b. The development diamond, based on four key indicators, shows the average level of development in the country compared with its income group. See the introduction.

218

Mali

Indicator	Unit of measure	Latest single year 1970-75	Latest single year 1980-85	Most recent estimate 1987-92	Same region/income group Sub-Saharan Africa	Same region/income group Low-income	Next higher income group
Resources and Expenditures							
HUMAN RESOURCES							
Population (mre=1992)	thousands	5,905	7,389	8,962	546,390	3,194,535	942,547
Age dependency ratio	ratio	0.93	0.98	1.00	0.95	0.67	0.66
Urban	% of pop.	16.2	21.0	25.1	29.5	26.7	57.0
Population growth rate	annual %	2.0	2.4	2.9	2.9	1.8	1.4
Urban	"	4.3	4.9	5.5	5.1	3.4	4.8
Labor force (15-64)	thousands	2,089	2,598	3,130	224,025	1,478,954	..
Agriculture	% of labor force	87	86	..	..	..	..
Industry	"	2	2	..	..	..	..
Female	"	17	17	16	37	33	36
Females per 100 males							
Urban	number	..	..	..	..	..	..
Rural	"	..	..	..	..	..	..
NATURAL RESOURCES							
Area	thou. sq. km	1,240.19	1,240.19	1,240.19	24,274.03	38,401.06	40,697.37
Density	pop. per sq. km	4.8	6.0	7.0	21.9	81.7	22.8
Agricultural land	% of land area	26.1	26.3	26.3	52.7	50.9	..
Change in agricultural land	annual %	0.2	0.1	0.0	0.1	0.0	..
Agricultural land under irrigation	%	0.4	0.6	0.6	0.8	18.2	..
Forests and woodland	thou. sq. km	74	71	69	..	..	..
Deforestation (net)	annual %	..	..	0.9	..	..	..
INCOME							
Household income							
Share of top 20% of households	% of income	..	..	..	..	42	..
Share of bottom 40% of households	"	..	..	..	..	19	..
Share of bottom 20% of households	"	..	..	..	..	8	..
EXPENDITURE							
Food	% of GDP	..	46.2	..	..	..	..
Staples	"	..	18.0	..	..	..	..
Meat, fish, milk, cheese, eggs	"	..	18.9	..	..	..	..
Cereal imports	thou. metric tonnes	120	273	97	20,311	46,537	74,924
Food aid in cereals	"	107	266	36	4,303	9,008	4,054
Food production per capita	1987 = 100	96	89	91	90	123	..
Fertilizer consumption	kg/ha	0.1	0.6	0.5	4.2	61.9	..
Share of agriculture in GDP	% of GDP	61.0	37.2	42.4	18.6	29.6	..
Housing	% of GDP	..	6.5	..	..	..	..
Average household size	persons per household	..	..	..	..	..	..
Urban	"	..	..	..	..	..	..
Fixed investment: housing	% of GDP	..	3.9	..	..	..	..
Fuel and power	% of GDP	..	5.0	..	..	..	..
Energy consumption per capita	kg of oil equiv.	20	25	22	258	335	1,882
Households with electricity							
Urban	% of households	..	..	..	..	..	..
Rural	"	..	..	..	..	..	..
Transport and communication	% of GDP	..	8.2	..	..	..	..
Fixed investment: transport equipment	"	..	2.2	..	..	..	..
Total road length	thou. km	15	13	15	..	..	..
INVESTMENT IN HUMAN CAPITAL							
Health							
Population per physician	persons	42,700	25,392	19,448	..	..	..
Population per nurse	"	2,587	1,348	1,885	..	..	..
Population per hospital bed	"	1,400	..	..	1,329	1,050	516
Oral rehydration therapy (under-5)	% of cases	..	..	41	36	39	..
Education							
Gross enrollment ratio							
Secondary	% of school-age pop.	7	7	7	18	41	..
Female	"	3	4	5	14	35	..
Pupil-teacher ratio: primary	pupils per teacher	41	34	47	39	37	26
Pupil-teacher ratio: secondary	"	19	12	16	..	19	..
Pupils reaching grade 4	% of cohort	69	72	73	..	..	..
Repeater rate: primary	% of total enroll	23	30	27	..	..	..
Illiteracy	% of pop. (age 15+)	..	77	68	51	39	..
Female	% of fem. (age 15+)	..	85	76	62	52	..
Newspaper circulation	per thou. pop.	1	1	1	14	..	100

World Bank International Economics Department, April 1994

219

Malta

Indicator	Unit of measure	Latest single year 1970-75	Latest single year 1980-85	Most recent estimate 1987-92	Same region/income group Europe & Central Asia	Same region/income group Upper-middle-income	Next higher income group
Priority Poverty Indicators							
POVERTY							
Upper poverty line	local curr.	..	..	..	..	..	..
Headcount index	% of pop.	..	..	..	..	..	..
Lower poverty line	local curr.	..	..	..	..	..	..
Headcount index	% of pop.	..	..	..	..	..	..
GNP per capita	US$	1,540	3,410	7,300	..	3,870	21,960
SHORT TERM INCOME INDICATORS							
Unskilled urban wages	local curr.	..	..	..	..	..	..
Unskilled rural wages	"	..	..	..	..	..	..
Rural terms of trade	"	..	..	..	..	..	..
Consumer price index	1987=100	58	98	109	..	..	..
Lower income	"	..	..	..	..	..	..
Food[a]	"	37	97	100	..	..	..
Urban	"	..	..	..	..	..	..
Rural	"	..	..	..	..	..	..
SOCIAL INDICATORS							
Public expenditure on basic social services	% of GDP	..	11.5	..	..	..	..
Gross enrollment ratios							
Primary	% school age pop.	94	107	110	..	107	103
Male	"	96	109	114	..	..	103
Female	"	92	104	105	..	..	103
Mortality							
Infant mortality	per thou. live births	17.5	13.6	8.9	30.0	40.0	7.0
Under 5 mortality	"	..	..	11.2	38.0	51.0	10.0
Immunization							
Measles	% age group	..	10.0	86.0	..	82.0	82.4
DPT	"	..	37.0	85.0	..	73.8	90.1
Child malnutrition (under-5)	"	..	..	..	..	..	..
Life expectancy							
Total	years	71	74	76	70	69	77
Female advantage	"	4.3	4.5	4.6	8.6	6.3	6.4
Total fertility rate	births per woman	2.3	2.0	2.1	2.2	2.9	1.7
Maternal mortality rate	per 100,000 live births	..	33	..	58	..	..
Supplementary Poverty Indicators							
Expenditures on social security	% of total gov't exp.	31.6	35.8	29.9	..	..	..
Social security coverage	% econ. active pop.	..	..	..	..	..	..
Access to safe water: total	% of pop.	..	..	..	..	85.6	..
Urban	"	..	..	..	..	94.3	..
Rural	"	..	..	..	..	73.0	..
Access to health care	"	..	100.0	..	..	..	..

Population growth rate
(annual average, percent)

Malta
Upper-middle-income

GNP per capita growth rate
(annual average, percent)

Development diamond[b]

Malta
Upper-middle-income

a. See the technical notes, p.389.   b. The development diamond, based on four key indicators, shows the average level of development in the country compared with its income group. See the introduction.

Malta

Indicator	Unit of measure	Latest single year 1970-75	Latest single year 1980-85	Most recent estimate 1987-92	Same region/income group Europe & Central Asia	Same region/income group Upper-middle-income	Next higher income group
Resources and Expenditures							
HUMAN RESOURCES							
Population (mre=1992)	thousands	328	344	360	495,241	477,960	828,221
Age dependency ratio	ratio	0.52	0.51	0.52	0.56	0.64	0.50
Urban	% of pop.	80.9	85.6	87.8	63.3	71.7	78.1
Population growth rate	annual %	1.2	-2.0	0.8	0.5	1.6	0.7
Urban	"	2.1	-1.5	1.1	..	2.5	0.9
Labor force (15-64)	thousands	120	139	150	..	181,414	390,033
Agriculture	% of labor force	6	5	..	..	..	..
Industry	"	42	42	..	..	..	..
Female	"	22	22	24	46	29	38
Females per 100 males							
Urban	number	..	..	..	..	..	..
Rural	"	..	..	..	..	..	..
NATURAL RESOURCES							
Area	thou. sq. km	0.32	0.32	0.32	24,165.06	21,836.02	31,709.00
Density	pop. per sq. km	1025.0	1075.0	1115.6	20.4	21.5	24.5
Agricultural land	% of land area	40.6	40.6	40.6	..	41.7	42.7
Change in agricultural land	annual %	-7.1	0.0	0.0	..	0.3	-0.2
Agricultural land under irrigation	%	7.7	7.7	7.7	..	9.3	16.1
Forests and woodland	thou. sq. km	..	..	..	..	..	..
Deforestation (net)	annual %	..	..	..	..	..	..
INCOME							
Household income							
Share of top 20% of households	% of income	..	..	..	..	..	..
Share of bottom 40% of households	"	..	..	..	..	..	..
Share of bottom 20% of households	"	..	..	..	..	..	..
EXPENDITURE							
Food	% of GDP	..	21.3	..	..	..	..
Staples	"	..	..	..	..	..	..
Meat, fish, milk, cheese, eggs	"	..	..	..	..	..	..
Cereal imports	thou. metric tonnes	149	132	155	45,972	49,174	70,626
Food aid in cereals	"	6	9	..	1,639	282	2
Food production per capita	1987 = 100	96	110	107	..	109	101
Fertilizer consumption	kg/ha	21.7	55.7	53.9	..	68.8	162.1
Share of agriculture in GDP	% of GDP	5.6	4.1	3.3	..	8.1	2.4
Housing	% of GDP	..	4.8	..	..	..	..
Average household size	persons per household	..	..	..	..	..	..
Urban	"	..	..	..	..	..	..
Fixed investment: housing	% of GDP	..	..	..	..	..	..
Fuel and power	% of GDP	..	1.7	..	..	..	..
Energy consumption per capita	kg of oil equiv.	841	1,151	1,556	3,190	1,649	5,101
Households with electricity							
Urban	% of households	..	..	..	..	..	..
Rural	"	..	..	..	..	..	..
Transport and communication	% of GDP	..	12.2	..	..	..	..
Fixed investment: transport equipment	"	..	..	..	..	..	..
Total road length	thou. km	1	1	..	..	..	..
INVESTMENT IN HUMAN CAPITAL							
Health							
Population per physician	persons	900	864	..	378	..	..
Population per nurse	"	200	114	..	..	..	..
Population per hospital bed	"	100	..	..	134	385	144
Oral rehydration therapy (under-5)	% of cases	..	..	..	..	54	..
Education							
Gross enrollment ratio							
Secondary	% of school-age pop.	75	78	85	..	53	92
Female	"	69	77	82	..	..	94
Pupil-teacher ratio: primary	pupils per teacher	21	22	21	..	25	18
Pupil-teacher ratio: secondary	"	13	12	13	..	..	..
Pupils reaching grade 4	% of cohort	82	99	99	..	71	..
Repeater rate: primary	% of total enroll	1	3	1	..	11	..
Illiteracy	% of pop. (age 15+)	..	16	..	..	14	..
Female	% of fem. (age 15+)	..	18	..	..	17	..
Newspaper circulation	per thou. pop.	..	157	153	..	117	..

World Bank International Economics Department, April 1994

221

Marshall Islands

Indicator	Unit of measure	Latest single year 1970-75	Latest single year 1980-85	Most recent estimate 1987-92	Same region/income group East Asia	Same region/income group Lower-middle-income	Next higher income group
Priority Poverty Indicators							
POVERTY							
Upper poverty line	local curr.	..	..	..	..	..	..
Headcount index	% of pop.	..	..	..	12	..	..
Lower poverty line	local curr.	..	..	..	..	..	..
Headcount index	% of pop.	..	..	..	9	..	..
GNP per capita	US$	..	..	..	760	..	3,870
SHORT TERM INCOME INDICATORS							
Unskilled urban wages	local curr.	..	..	..	..	..	..
Unskilled rural wages	"	..	..	..	..	..	..
Rural terms of trade	"	..	..	..	..	..	..
Consumer price index	1987=100	..	..	..	..	..	..
Lower income	"	..	..	..	..	..	..
Food[a]	"	..	..	..	..	..	..
Urban	"	..	..	..	..	..	..
Rural	"	..	..	..	..	..	..
SOCIAL INDICATORS							
Public expenditure on basic social services	% of GDP	..	..	..	..	..	..
Gross enrollment ratios							
Primary	% school age pop.	..	..	..	121	..	107
Male	"	..	..	..	126	..	..
Female	"	..	..	..	117	..	..
Mortality							
Infant mortality	per thou. live births	..	..	43.0	39.0	45.0	40.0
Under 5 mortality	"	..	..	..	49.0	59.0	51.0
Immunization							
Measles	% age group	..	..	..	88.4	..	82.0
DPT	"	..	..	..	89.5	..	73.8
Child malnutrition (under-5)	"	..	..	..	24.7	..	..
Life expectancy							
Total	years	..	..	72	68	68	69
Female advantage	"	..	..	4.8	3.6	6.4	6.3
Total fertility rate	births per woman	..	..	5.9	2.4	3.1	2.9
Maternal mortality rate	per 100,000 live births	..	..	..	114	..	..
Supplementary Poverty Indicators							
Expenditures on social security	% of total gov't exp.	..	..	..	..	..	..
Social security coverage	% econ. active pop.	..	..	..	..	..	..
Access to safe water: total	% of pop.	..	..	..	72.0	..	85.6
Urban	"	..	..	..	83.4	..	94.3
Rural	"	..	..	..	60.2	..	73.0
Access to health care	"	..	..	..	..	..	..

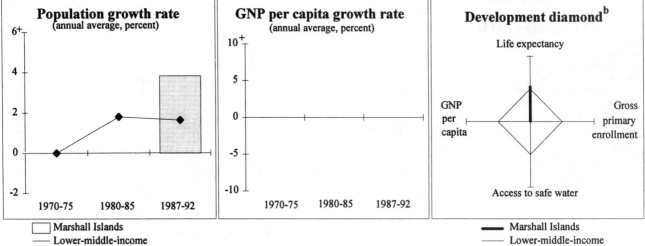

Population growth rate (annual average, percent)

GNP per capita growth rate (annual average, percent)

Development diamond[b]
Life expectancy — GNP per capita — Gross primary enrollment — Access to safe water

— Marshall Islands
— Lower-middle-income

a. See the technical notes, p.389.   b. The development diamond, based on four key indicators, shows the average level of development in the country compared with its income group. See the introduction.

Marshall Islands

Indicator	Unit of measure	Latest single year 1970-75	Latest single year 1980-85	Most recent estimate 1987-92	Same region/income group East Asia	Same region/income group Lower-middle-income	Next higher income group
Resources and Expenditures							
HUMAN RESOURCES							
Population (mre=1992)	thousands	..	38	50	1,688,909	942,547	477,960
Age dependency ratio	ratio	..	..	..	0.55	0.66	0.64
Urban	% of pop.	..	..	..	29.4	57.0	71.7
Population growth rate	annual %	..	..	4.1	1.4	1.4	1.6
Urban	"	..	..	..	2.9	4.8	2.5
Labor force (15-64)	thousands	..	..	..	928,465	..	181,414
Agriculture	% of labor force	..	..	..	..	..	..
Industry	"	..	..	..	..	..	..
Female	"	..	..	..	41	36	29
Females per 100 males							
Urban	number	..	..	..	..	..	..
Rural	"	..	..	..	..	..	..
NATURAL RESOURCES							
Area	thou. sq. km	..	0.18	0.18	16,367.18	40,697.37	21,836.02
Density	pop. per sq. km	..	..	..	101.8	22.8	21.5
Agricultural land	% of land area	..	..	..	44.5	..	41.7
Change in agricultural land	annual %	..	..	..	0.1	..	0.3
Agricultural land under irrigation	%	..	..	..	14.5	..	9.3
Forests and woodland	thou. sq. km	..	..	..	..	..	..
Deforestation (net)	annual %	..	..	..	..	..	..
INCOME							
Household income							
Share of top 20% of households	% of income	..	..	..	42	..	..
Share of bottom 40% of households	"	..	..	..	18	..	..
Share of bottom 20% of households	"	..	..	..	7	..	..
EXPENDITURE							
Food	% of GDP	..	..	..	..	..	..
Staples	"	..	..	..	..	..	..
Meat, fish, milk, cheese, eggs	"	..	..	..	..	..	..
Cereal imports	thou. metric tonnes	..	..	..	33,591	74,924	49,174
Food aid in cereals	"	..	..	..	581	4,054	282
Food production per capita	1987 = 100	..	..	..	133	..	109
Fertilizer consumption	kg/ha	..	..	..	75.1	..	68.8
Share of agriculture in GDP	% of GDP	..	..	..	21.5	..	8.1
Housing	% of GDP	..	..	..	..	..	..
Average household size	persons per household	..	..	..	..	..	..
Urban	"	..	..	..	..	..	..
Fixed investment: housing	% of GDP	..	..	..	..	..	..
Fuel and power	% of GDP	..	..	..	..	..	..
Energy consumption per capita	kg of oil equiv.	..	..	..	593	1,882	1,649
Households with electricity							
Urban	% of households	..	..	..	..	..	..
Rural	"	..	..	..	..	..	..
Transport and communication	% of GDP	..	..	..	..	..	..
Fixed investment: transport equipment	"	..	..	..	..	..	..
Total road length	thou. km	..	..	..	..	..	..
INVESTMENT IN HUMAN CAPITAL							
Health							
Population per physician	persons	..	..	..	..	..	..
Population per nurse	"	..	..	..	..	..	..
Population per hospital bed	"	..	..	..	553	516	385
Oral rehydration therapy (under-5)	% of cases	..	..	..	51	..	54
Education							
Gross enrollment ratio							
Secondary	% of school-age pop.	..	..	..	53	..	53
Female	"	..	..	..	47	..	..
Pupil-teacher ratio: primary	pupils per teacher	..	..	..	23	26	25
Pupil-teacher ratio: secondary	"	..	..	..	16	..	..
Pupils reaching grade 4	% of cohort	..	..	..	89	..	71
Repeater rate: primary	% of total enroll	..	..	..	6	..	11
Illiteracy	% of pop. (age 15+)	..	..	..	24	..	14
Female	% of fem. (age 15+)	..	..	..	34	..	17
Newspaper circulation	per thou. pop.	..	..	..	..	100	117

World Bank International Economics Department, April 1994

Martinique

Indicator	Unit of measure	Latest single year 1970-75	Latest single year 1980-85	Most recent estimate 1987-92	Same region/income group Latin America Caribbean	Same region/income group Upper-middle-income	Next higher income group
Priority Poverty Indicators							
POVERTY							
Upper poverty line	local curr.	..	..	..	..	..	..
Headcount index	% of pop.	..	..	..	..	..	..
Lower poverty line	local curr.	..	..	..	..	..	..
Headcount index	% of pop.	..	..	..	..	..	..
GNP per capita	US$	..	..	..	2,690	3,870	21,960
SHORT TERM INCOME INDICATORS							
Unskilled urban wages	local curr.	..	..	..	..	..	..
Unskilled rural wages	"	..	..	..	..	..	..
Rural terms of trade	"	..	..	..	..	..	..
Consumer price index	1987=100	33	93	117	..	..	..
Lower income	"	..	..	..	..	..	..
Food[a]	"	..	93	110	..	..	..
Urban	"	..	..	..	..	..	..
Rural	"	..	..	..	..	..	..
SOCIAL INDICATORS							
Public expenditure on basic social services	% of GDP	..	..	..	..	..	..
Gross enrollment ratios							
Primary	% school age pop.	..	..	..	106	107	103
Male	"	..	..	..	..	..	103
Female	"	..	..	..	..	..	103
Mortality							
Infant mortality	per thou. live births	35.0	14.0	10.0	44.0	40.0	7.0
Under 5 mortality	"	..	..	12.5	56.0	51.0	10.0
Immunization							
Measles	% age group	..	..	..	78.9	82.0	82.4
DPT	"	..	..	..	73.8	73.8	90.1
Child malnutrition (under-5)	"	..	..	..	10.5	..	..
Life expectancy							
Total	years	69	74	76	68	69	77
Female advantage	"	5.7	7.0	6.5	5.6	6.3	6.4
Total fertility rate	births per woman	4.1	2.1	2.0	3.0	2.9	1.7
Maternal mortality rate	per 100,000 live births	..	..	..	..	..	..
Supplementary Poverty Indicators							
Expenditures on social security	% of total gov't exp.	..	..	..	..	..	..
Social security coverage	% econ. active pop.	..	..	..	..	..	..
Access to safe water: total	% of pop.	..	..	..	80.3	85.6	..
Urban	"	..	..	..	91.0	94.3	..
Rural	"	..	..	..	64.3	73.0	..
Access to health care	"	..	..	..	..	..	..

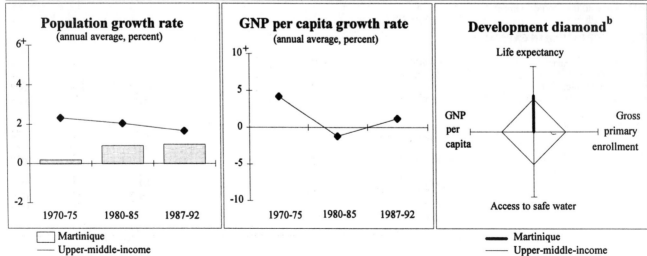

Population growth rate (annual average, percent)

□ Martinique
— Upper-middle-income

GNP per capita growth rate (annual average, percent)

Development diamond[b]

Life expectancy

GNP per capita — Gross primary enrollment

Access to safe water

▬ Martinique
— Upper-middle-income

a. See the technical notes, p.389. b. The development diamond, based on four key indicators, shows the average level of development in the country compared with its income group. See the introduction.

Martinique

Indicator	Unit of measure	Latest single year 1970-75	Latest single year 1980-85	Most recent estimate 1987-92	Same region/income group Latin America Caribbean	Same region/income group Upper-middle-income	Next higher income group
Resources and Expenditures							
HUMAN RESOURCES							
Population (mre=1992)	thousands	329	341	366	453,294	477,960	828,221
Age dependency ratio	ratio	0.87	0.51	0.52	0.67	0.64	0.50
Urban	% of pop.	60.0	70.8	76.0	72.9	71.7	78.1
Population growth rate	annual %	-0.1	1.1	0.9	1.7	1.6	0.7
Urban	"	2.1	2.4	1.7	2.6	2.5	0.9
Labor force (15-64)	thousands	111	149	157	166,091	181,414	390,033
Agriculture	% of labor force	19	13	..	..	..	..
Industry	"	20	18	..	..	..	..
Female	"	39	43	44	27	29	38
Females per 100 males							
Urban	number	..	..	..	..	..	..
Rural	"	..	..	..	..	..	..
NATURAL RESOURCES							
Area	thou. sq. km	1.10	1.10	1.10	20,507.48	21,836.02	31,709.00
Density	pop. per sq. km	299.1	310.0	330.0	21.7	21.5	24.5
Agricultural land	% of land area	34.0	39.6	36.8	40.2	41.7	42.7
Change in agricultural land	annual %	0.0	5.0	0.0	0.5	0.3	-0.2
Agricultural land under irrigation	%	5.6	9.5	10.3	3.2	9.3	16.1
Forests and woodland	thou. sq. km	0	0	0	..	..	..
Deforestation (net)	annual %	..	..	..	..	..	..
INCOME							
Household income							
Share of top 20% of households	% of income	..	..	..	..	..	..
Share of bottom 40% of households	"	..	..	..	..	..	..
Share of bottom 20% of households	"	..	..	..	..	..	..
EXPENDITURE							
Food	% of GDP	..	..	..	..	..	..
Staples	"	..	..	..	..	..	..
Meat, fish, milk, cheese, eggs	"	..	..	..	..	..	..
Cereal imports	thou. metric tonnes	44	56	63	25,032	49,174	70,626
Food aid in cereals	"	..	2	..	1,779	282	2
Food production per capita	1987 = 100	119	114	112	104	109	101
Fertilizer consumption	kg/ha	256.1	359.5	443.6	15.5	68.8	162.1
Share of agriculture in GDP	% of GDP	..	..	..	8.9	8.1	2.4
Housing	% of GDP	..	..	..	..	..	..
Average household size	persons per household	..	..	..	..	..	..
Urban	"	..	..	..	..	..	..
Fixed investment: housing	% of GDP	..	..	..	..	..	..
Fuel and power	% of GDP	..	..	..	..	..	..
Energy consumption per capita	kg of oil equiv.	997	666	653	912	1,649	5,101
Households with electricity							
Urban	% of households	..	..	..	..	..	..
Rural	"	..	..	..	..	..	..
Transport and communication	% of GDP	..	..	..	..	..	..
Fixed investment: transport equipment	"	..	..	..	..	..	..
Total road length	thou. km	..	..	..	..	..	..
INVESTMENT IN HUMAN CAPITAL							
Health							
Population per physician	persons	1,552	722	..	..	..	..
Population per nurse	"	..	..	..	..	..	..
Population per hospital bed	"	99	..	..	508	385	144
Oral rehydration therapy (under-5)	% of cases	..	..	..	62	54	..
Education							
Gross enrollment ratio							
Secondary	% of school-age pop.	..	..	..	47	53	92
Female	"	..	..	..	..	..	94
Pupil-teacher ratio: primary	pupils per teacher	26	19	11	25	25	18
Pupil-teacher ratio: secondary	"	18	13	..	..	..	..
Pupils reaching grade 4	% of cohort	..	..	..	..	71	..
Repeater rate: primary	% of total enroll	18	..	..	14	11	..
Illiteracy	% of pop. (age 15+)	..	7	..	15	14	..
Female	% of fem. (age 15+)	..	..	..	17	17	..
Newspaper circulation	per thou. pop.	82	95	89	99	117	..

World Bank International Economics Department, April 1994

Mauritania

Indicator	Unit of measure	Latest single year 1970-75	Latest single year 1980-85	Most recent estimate 1987-92	Same region/income group Sub-Saharan Africa	Same region/income group Low-income	Next higher income group
Priority Poverty Indicators							
POVERTY							
Upper poverty line	local curr.	..	..	..	..	..	..
Headcount index	% of pop.	..	..	..	..	19	..
Lower poverty line	local curr.	..	..	..	..	..	..
Headcount index	% of pop.	..	..	..	..	..	..
GNP per capita	US$	300	400	530	520	390	..
SHORT TERM INCOME INDICATORS							
Unskilled urban wages	local curr.	..	..	..	..	..	..
Unskilled rural wages	"	..	..	..	..	..	..
Rural terms of trade	"	..	..	..	..	..	..
Consumer price index	1987=100	..	86	142	..	..	..
Lower income	"	..	..	..	..	..	..
Food[a]	"	..	..	..	..	..	..
Urban	"	..	..	..	..	..	..
Rural	"	..	..	..	..	..	..
SOCIAL INDICATORS							
Public expenditure on basic social services	% of GDP	..	..	4.0	..	..	..
Gross enrollment ratios							
Primary	% school age pop.	19	49	55	66	103	..
Male	"	24	60	63	79	113	..
Female	"	13	39	48	62	96	..
Mortality							
Infant mortality	per thou. live births	160.0	137.0	117.2	99.0	73.0	45.0
Under 5 mortality	"	..	..	196.3	169.0	108.0	59.0
Immunization							
Measles	% age group	..	55.0	33.0	54.0	72.7	..
DPT	"	..	21.0	28.0	54.6	80.6	..
Child malnutrition (under-5)	"	..	31.0	31.0	28.4	38.3	..
Life expectancy							
Total	years	40	44	48	52	62	68
Female advantage	"	3.1	3.2	3.4	3.4	2.4	6.4
Total fertility rate	births per woman	6.5	6.5	6.8	6.1	3.4	3.1
Maternal mortality rate	per 100,000 live births	..	..	800	..	..	..
Supplementary Poverty Indicators							
Expenditures on social security	% of total gov't exp.	..	..	..	..	..	..
Social security coverage	% econ. active pop.	..	..	..	..	..	..
Access to safe water: total	% of pop.	17.0	..	66.0	41.1	68.4	..
Urban	"	98.0	73.0	67.0	77.8	78.9	..
Rural	"	10.0	..	65.0	27.3	60.3	..
Access to health care	"	..	30.0	..	..	..	..

Population growth rate
(annual average, percent)

GNP per capita growth rate
(annual average, percent)

Development diamond[b]

- Mauritania
- Low-income

a. See the technical notes, p.389.   b. The development diamond, based on four key indicators, shows the average level of development in the country compared with its income group. See the introduction.

Mauritania

Indicator	Unit of measure	Latest single year 1970-75	Latest single year 1980-85	Most recent estimate 1987-92	Same region/income group Sub-Saharan Africa	Same region/income group Low-income	Next higher income group

Resources and Expenditures

HUMAN RESOURCES

Indicator	Unit of measure	1970-75	1980-85	1987-92	Sub-Saharan Africa	Low-income	Next higher income group
Population (mre=1992)	thousands	1,371	1,729	2,079	546,390	3,194,535	942,547
Age dependency ratio	ratio	0.86	0.88	0.94	0.95	0.67	0.66
Urban	% of pop.	20.3	38.2	49.6	29.5	26.7	57.0
Population growth rate	annual %	2.4	2.3	2.7	2.9	1.8	1.4
Urban	"	9.2	7.2	5.5	5.1	3.4	4.8
Labor force (15-64)	thousands	472	590	724	224,025	1,478,954	..
Agriculture	% of labor force	77	69	..	..	..	..
Industry	"	7	9	..	..	..	..
Female	"	21	21	23	37	33	36
Females per 100 males							
Urban	number	83	..	..	..	..	..
Rural	"	101	..	..	..	..	..

NATURAL RESOURCES

Indicator	Unit of measure	1970-75	1980-85	1987-92	Sub-Saharan Africa	Low-income	Next higher income group
Area	thou. sq. km	1,025.52	1,025.52	1,025.52	24,274.03	38,401.06	40,697.37
Density	pop. per sq. km	1.3	1.7	2.0	21.9	81.7	22.8
Agricultural land	% of land area	38.5	38.5	38.5	52.7	50.9	..
Change in agricultural land	annual %	0.1	0.0	0.0	0.1	0.0	..
Agricultural land under irrigation	%	0.0	0.0	0.0	0.8	18.2	..
Forests and woodland	thou. sq. km	46	45	44	..	..	..
Deforestation (net)	annual %	..	..	0.0	..	..	..

INCOME

Household income

Indicator	Unit of measure	1970-75	1980-85	1987-92	Sub-Saharan Africa	Low-income	Next higher income group
Share of top 20% of households	% of income	..	..	20	..	42	..
Share of bottom 40% of households	"	..	..	40	..	19	..
Share of bottom 20% of households	"	..	..	20	..	8	..

EXPENDITURE

Indicator	Unit of measure	1970-75	1980-85	1987-92	Sub-Saharan Africa	Low-income	Next higher income group
Food	% of GDP	..	..	..	..	..	..
Staples	"	..	..	..	..	..	..
Meat, fish, milk, cheese, eggs	"	..	..	..	..	..	..
Cereal imports	thou. metric tonnes	113	304	290	20,311	46,537	74,924
Food aid in cereals	"	48	135	41	4,303	9,008	4,054
Food production per capita	1987 = 100	86	89	80	90	123	..
Fertilizer consumption	kg/ha	0.0	0.1	0.0	4.2	61.9	..
Share of agriculture in GDP	% of GDP	26.7	20.0	25.9	18.6	29.6	..
Housing	% of GDP	..	..	..	..	..	..
Average household size	persons per household	..	..	5.3	..	..	..
Urban	"	..	..	5.4	..	..	..
Fixed investment: housing	% of GDP	..	..	..	..	..	..
Fuel and power	% of GDP	..	..	..	..	..	..
Energy consumption per capita	kg of oil equiv.	120	124	108	258	335	1,882
Households with electricity							
Urban	% of households	..	..	14.0	..	..	..
Rural	"	..	..	6.0	..	..	..
Transport and communication	% of GDP	..	..	..	..	..	..
Fixed investment: transport equipment	"	..	..	..	..	..	..
Total road length	thou. km	7	7	7	..	..	..

INVESTMENT IN HUMAN CAPITAL

Health

Indicator	Unit of measure	1970-75	1980-85	1987-92	Sub-Saharan Africa	Low-income	Next higher income group
Population per physician	persons	18,126	8,645	..	..	..	..
Population per nurse	"	3,745	1,182	..	..	..	..
Population per hospital bed	"	2,904	1,278	..	1,329	1,050	516
Oral rehydration therapy (under-5)	% of cases	..	..	54	36	39	..

Education

Gross enrollment ratio

Indicator	Unit of measure	1970-75	1980-85	1987-92	Sub-Saharan Africa	Low-income	Next higher income group
Secondary	% of school-age pop.	4	15	14	18	41	..
Female	"	0	8	10	14	35	..
Pupil-teacher ratio: primary	pupils per teacher	35	51	47	39	37	26
Pupil-teacher ratio: secondary	"	24	24	19	..	19	..
Pupils reaching grade 4	% of cohort	97	92	83	..	..	..
Repeater rate: primary	% of total enroll	15	18	20	..	..	..
Illiteracy	% of pop. (age 15+)	..	73	66	51	39	..
Female	% of fem. (age 15+)	..	84	79	62	52	..
Newspaper circulation	per thou. pop.	2	..	1	14	..	100

World Bank International Economics Department, April 1994

227

Mauritius

Indicator	Unit of measure	Latest single year 1970-75	Latest single year 1980-85	Most recent estimate 1987-92	Same region/income group Sub-Saharan Africa	Same region/income group Upper-middle-income	Next higher income group
Priority Poverty Indicators							
POVERTY							
Upper poverty line	local curr.	..	749	1,626	..	..	..
Headcount index	% of pop.	..	20	5	..	..	..
Lower poverty line	local curr.	..	..	..	..	..	..
Headcount index	% of pop.	..	..	..	..	..	..
GNP per capita	US$	710	1,110	2,700	520	3,870	21,960
SHORT TERM INCOME INDICATORS							
Unskilled urban wages	local curr.	..	..	..	..	..	..
Unskilled rural wages	"	..	..	..	..	..	..
Rural terms of trade	"	..	..	..	..	..	..
Consumer price index	1987=100	29	98	156	..	..	..
Lower income	"	..	..	..	..	..	..
Food[a]	"	..	125	147	..	..	..
Urban	"	..	..	..	..	..	..
Rural	"	..	..	..	..	..	..
SOCIAL INDICATORS							
Public expenditure on basic social services	% of GDP	..	..	..	..	..	..
Gross enrollment ratios							
Primary	% school age pop.	107	103	106	66	107	103
Male	"	108	102	104	79	..	103
Female	"	106	104	108	62	..	103
Mortality							
Infant mortality	per thou. live births	55.0	28.0	18.0	99.0	40.0	7.0
Under 5 mortality	"	..	..	22.2	169.0	51.0	10.0
Immunization							
Measles	% age group	..	61.0	75.0	54.0	82.0	82.4
DPT	"	..	85.0	90.0	54.6	73.8	90.1
Child malnutrition (under-5)	"	..	23.8	23.9	28.4	..	..
Life expectancy							
Total	years	63	67	70	52	69	77
Female advantage	"	4.6	5.5	6.5	3.4	6.3	6.4
Total fertility rate	births per woman	3.3	2.5	2.0	6.1	2.9	1.7
Maternal mortality rate	per 100,000 live births	..	99	99	..	..	..
Supplementary Poverty Indicators							
Expenditures on social security	% of total gov't exp.	..	..	..	..	..	..
Social security coverage	% econ. active pop.	..	..	..	..	..	..
Access to safe water: total	% of pop.	60.0	100.0	100.0	41.1	85.6	..
Urban	"	100.0	100.0	100.0	77.8	94.3	..
Rural	"	22.0	100.0	100.0	27.3	73.0	..
Access to health care	"	..	100.0	100.0	..	..	..

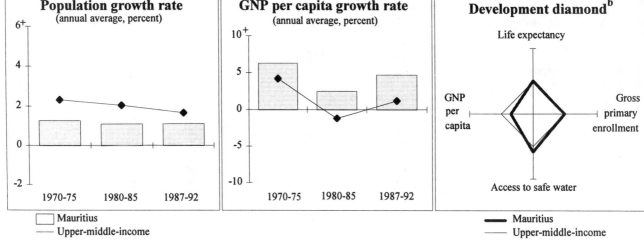

Population growth rate (annual average, percent)

GNP per capita growth rate (annual average, percent)

Development diagram[b]

Life expectancy / GNP per capita / Gross primary enrollment / Access to safe water

☐ Mauritius
— Upper-middle-income

— Mauritius
— Upper-middle-income

a. See the technical notes, p.389.   b. The development diamond, based on four key indicators, shows the average level of development in the country compared with its income group. See the introduction.

228

Mauritius

Indicator	Unit of measure	Latest single year 1970-75	Latest single year 1980-85	Most recent estimate 1987-92	Same region/income group Sub-Saharan Africa	Same region/income group Upper-middle-income	Next higher income group
Resources and Expenditures							
HUMAN RESOURCES							
Population (mre=1992)	thousands	883	1,020	1,099	546,390	477,960	828,221
Age dependency ratio	ratio	0.74	0.57	0.51	0.95	0.64	0.50
Urban	% of pop.	43.4	41.4	40.6	29.5	71.7	78.1
Population growth rate	annual %	1.5	0.6	1.1	2.9	1.6	0.7
Urban	"	2.1	0.1	1.2	5.1	2.5	0.9
Labor force (15-64)	thousands	280	390	457	224,025	181,414	390,033
Agriculture	% of labor force	31	28	..	..	..	..
Industry	"	25	24	..	..	..	..
Female	"	22	25	27	37	29	38
Females per 100 males							
Urban	number	..	..	..	..	..	..
Rural	"	..	..	..	..	..	..
NATURAL RESOURCES							
Area	thou. sq. km	2.04	2.04	2.04	24,274.03	21,836.02	31,709.00
Density	pop. per sq. km	432.8	500.0	532.8	21.9	21.5	24.5
Agricultural land	% of land area	55.7	56.2	55.7	52.7	41.7	42.7
Change in agricultural land	annual %	0.0	0.0	0.0	0.1	0.3	-0.2
Agricultural land under irrigation	%	13.3	14.9	15.0	0.8	9.3	16.1
Forests and woodland	thou. sq. km	1	1	1	..	..	..
Deforestation (net)	annual %	..	..	..	..	..	..
INCOME							
Household income							
Share of top 20% of households	% of income	55	..	..	..	..	..
Share of bottom 40% of households	"	14	..	..	..	..	..
Share of bottom 20% of households	"	5	..	..	..	..	..
EXPENDITURE							
Food	% of GDP	..	17.0	..	..	..	..
Staples	"	..	4.7	..	..	..	..
Meat, fish, milk, cheese, eggs	"	..	6.6	..	..	..	..
Cereal imports	thou. metric tonnes	149	179	207	20,311	49,174	70,626
Food aid in cereals	"	22	9	9	4,303	282	2
Food production per capita	1987 = 100	89	102	112	90	109	101
Fertilizer consumption	kg/ha	213.7	245.4	243.8	4.2	68.8	162.1
Share of agriculture in GDP	% of GDP	19.2	12.8	9.3	18.6	8.1	2.4
Housing	% of GDP	..	13.7	..	..	..	..
Average household size	persons per household	5.3	4.8	..	..	..	..
Urban	"	..	..	..	..	..	..
Fixed investment: housing	% of GDP	6.6	4.5	..	..	..	..
Fuel and power	% of GDP	..	2.2	..	..	..	..
Energy consumption per capita	kg of oil equiv.	348	344	385	258	1,649	5,101
Households with electricity							
Urban	% of households	..	..	..	..	..	..
Rural	"	..	..	..	..	..	..
Transport and communication	% of GDP	..	7.6	..	..	..	..
Fixed investment: transport equipment	"	2.6	1.7	..	..	..	..
Total road length	thou. km	2	2	2	..	..	..
INVESTMENT IN HUMAN CAPITAL							
Health							
Population per physician	persons	4,200	1,899	1,181	..	..	..
Population per nurse	"	608	584	..	..	..	..
Population per hospital bed	"	300	300	..	1,329	385	144
Oral rehydration therapy (under-5)	% of cases	..	..	7	36	54	..
Education							
Gross enrollment ratio							
Secondary	% of school-age pop.	39	51	54	18	53	92
Female	"	35	48	56	14	..	94
Pupil-teacher ratio: primary	pupils per teacher	26	22	21	39	25	18
Pupil-teacher ratio: secondary	"	31	20	21	..	..	..
Pupils reaching grade 4	% of cohort	96	98	99	..	71	..
Repeater rate: primary	% of total enroll	..	6	8	..	11	..
Illiteracy	% of pop. (age 15+)	..	17	..	51	14	..
Female	% of fem. (age 15+)	..	23	..	62	17	..
Newspaper circulation	per thou. pop.	93	66	74	14	117	..

World Bank International Economics Department, April 1994

Mexico

Indicator	Unit of measure	Latest single year 1970-75	Latest single year 1980-85	Most recent estimate 1987-92	Same region/income group Latin America Caribbean	Same region/income group Upper-middle-income	Next higher income group
Priority Poverty Indicators							
POVERTY							
Upper poverty line	local curr.	..	32,424	..	..	..	..
Headcount index	% of pop.	..	20	10	..	..	..
Lower poverty line	local curr.	..	7,742	..	..	..	..
Headcount index	% of pop.	..	10	..	..	..	..
GNP per capita	US$	1,460	2,300	3,470	2,690	3,870	21,960
SHORT TERM INCOME INDICATORS							
Unskilled urban wages	local curr.	..	..	..	..	..	..
Unskilled rural wages	"	..	..	..	..	..	..
Rural terms of trade	"	..	..	..	..	..	..
Consumer price index	1987=100	1	23	461	..	..	..
Lower income	"		..	..	..	..	..
Food[a]	"	..	23	380	..	..	..
Urban	"	..	..	..	..	..	..
Rural	"	..	..	..	..	..	..
SOCIAL INDICATORS							
Public expenditure on basic social services	% of GDP	..	..	..	..	..	..
Gross enrollment ratios							
Primary	% school age pop.	109	119	114	106	107	103
Male	"	112	120	115	..	..	103
Female	"	106	117	112	..	..	103
Mortality							
Infant mortality	per thou. live births	68.0	49.0	35.0	44.0	40.0	7.0
Under 5 mortality	"	..	..	43.0	56.0	51.0	10.0
Immunization							
Measles	% age group	..	30.0	78.0	78.9	82.0	82.4
DPT	"	..	26.0	64.0	73.8	73.8	90.1
Child malnutrition (under-5)	"	..	..	13.9	10.5	..	..
Life expectancy							
Total	years	63	67	70	68	69	77
Female advantage	"	4.7	6.2	6.5	5.6	6.3	6.4
Total fertility rate	births per woman	6.4	4.2	3.2	3.0	2.9	1.7
Maternal mortality rate	per 100,000 live births	..	92	..	..	..	..
Supplementary Poverty Indicators							
Expenditures on social security	% of total gov't exp.	23.5	9.6	12.4	..	..	..
Social security coverage	% econ. active pop.	..	..	40.2	..	..	..
Access to safe water: total	% of pop.	62.0	70.0	78.0	80.3	85.6	..
Urban	"	70.0	79.0	89.0	91.0	94.3	..
Rural	"	49.0	51.0	89.0	64.3	73.0	..
Access to health care	"	..	50.7	91.0	..	..	..

Population growth rate
(annual average, percent)

☐ Mexico
— Upper-middle-income

GNP per capita growth rate
(annual average, percent)

Development diamond[b]

— Mexico
— Upper-middle-income

a. See the technical notes, p.389.   b. The development diamond, based on four key indicators, shows the average level of development in the country compared with its income group. See the introduction.

Mexico

Indicator	Unit of measure	Latest single year 1970-75	Latest single year 1980-85	Most recent estimate 1987-92	Same region/income group Latin America Caribbean	Same region/income group Upper-middle-income	Next higher income group
Resources and Expenditures							
HUMAN RESOURCES							
Population (mre=1992)	thousands	58,876	74,766	84,967	453,294	477,960	828,221
Age dependency ratio	ratio	1.00	0.80	0.69	0.67	0.64	0.50
Urban	% of pop.	62.8	69.6	73.7	72.9	71.7	78.1
Population growth rate	annual %	3.0	2.0	2.0	1.7	1.6	0.7
Urban	"	4.2	2.9	2.7	2.6	2.5	0.9
Labor force (15-64)	thousands	17,928	26,081	32,463	166,091	181,414	390,033
Agriculture	% of labor force	40	37	..	..	..	..
Industry	"	27	29	..	..	..	..
Female	"	23	27	27	27	29	38
Females per 100 males							
Urban	number	103	..	..	..	..	..
Rural	"	92	..	..	..	..	..
NATURAL RESOURCES							
Area	thou. sq. km	1,958.20	1,958.20	1,958.20	20,507.48	21,836.02	31,709.00
Density	pop. per sq. km	30.1	38.2	42.5	21.7	21.5	24.5
Agricultural land	% of land area	51.5	52.0	52.0	40.2	41.7	42.7
Change in agricultural land	annual %	0.2	0.0	0.0	0.5	0.3	-0.2
Agricultural land under irrigation	%	4.6	5.3	5.2	3.2	9.3	16.1
Forests and woodland	thou. sq. km	512	452	419	..	..	..
Deforestation (net)	annual %	..	..	1.3	..	..	..
INCOME							
Household income							
Share of top 20% of households	% of income	61	56	..	..	..	..
Share of bottom 40% of households	"	10	12	..	..	..	..
Share of bottom 20% of households	"	3	4	..	..	..	..
EXPENDITURE							
Food	% of GDP	29.0	22.0	..	..	..	..
Staples	"	6.8	..	..	..	..	..
Meat, fish, milk, cheese, eggs	"	12.7	..	..	..	..	..
Cereal imports	thou. metric tonnes	3,720	4,780	7,634	25,032	49,174	70,626
Food aid in cereals	"	..	6	69	1,779	282	2
Food production per capita	1987 = 100	93	101	101	104	109	101
Fertilizer consumption	kg/ha	10.9	17.3	15.6	15.5	68.8	162.1
Share of agriculture in GDP	% of GDP	10.8	9.1	8.5	8.9	8.1	2.4
Housing	% of GDP	6.4	5.1	..	..	..	..
Average household size	persons per household	6.0	5.5	..	..	..	..
Urban	"	6.0	..	..	..	..	..
Fixed investment: housing	% of GDP	6.3	4.4	..	..	..	..
Fuel and power	% of GDP	..	..	..	..	..	..
Energy consumption per capita	kg of oil equiv.	869	1,375	1,525	912	1,649	5,101
Households with electricity							
Urban	% of households	..	..	..	..	..	..
Rural	"	..	..	..	..	..	..
Transport and communication	% of GDP	6.0	7.7	..	..	..	..
Fixed investment: transport equipment	"	2.2	3.0	..	..	..	..
Total road length	thou. km	193	224	237	..	..	..
INVESTMENT IN HUMAN CAPITAL							
Health							
Population per physician	persons	1,426	1,184	..	..	..	..
Population per nurse	"	1,373	839	..	..	..	..
Population per hospital bed	"	760	..	801	508	385	144
Oral rehydration therapy (under-5)	% of cases	..	..	66	62	54	..
Education							
Gross enrollment ratio							
Secondary	% of school-age pop.	34	53	55	47	53	92
Female	"	28	52	55	..	..	94
Pupil-teacher ratio: primary	pupils per teacher	45	34	30	25	25	18
Pupil-teacher ratio: secondary	"	18	18	17	..	..	..
Pupils reaching grade 4	% of cohort	59	83	78	..	71	..
Repeater rate: primary	% of total enroll	11	10	9	14	11	..
Illiteracy	% of pop. (age 15+)	26	15	13	15	14	..
Female	% of fem. (age 15+)	..	18	15	17	17	..
Newspaper circulation	per thou. pop.	..	140	138	99	117	..

World Bank International Economics Department, April 1994

Federated States of Micronesia

Indicator	Unit of measure	Latest single year 1970-75	Latest single year 1980-85	Most recent estimate 1987-92	Same region/income group East Asia	Same region/income group Lower-middle-income	Next higher income group
Priority Poverty Indicators							
POVERTY							
Upper poverty line	local curr.	..	..	..	..	..	..
Headcount index	% of pop.	..	..	..	12	..	..
Lower poverty line	local curr.	..	..	..	..	..	..
Headcount index	% of pop.	..	..	..	9	..	..
GNP per capita	US$	..	..	..	760	..	3,870
SHORT TERM INCOME INDICATORS							
Unskilled urban wages	local curr.	..	..	..	..	..	..
Unskilled rural wages	"	..	..	..	..	..	..
Rural terms of trade	"	..	..	..	..	..	..
Consumer price index	1987=100	..	..	..	..	..	..
Lower income	"	..	..	..	..	..	..
Food[a]	"	..	..	..	..	..	..
Urban	"	..	..	..	..	..	..
Rural	"	..	..	..	..	..	..
SOCIAL INDICATORS							
Public expenditure on basic social services	% of GDP	..	..	..	..	..	..
Gross enrollment ratios							
Primary	% school age pop.	..	..	..	121	..	107
Male	"	..	..	..	126	..	..
Female	"	..	..	..	117	..	..
Mortality							
Infant mortality	per thou. live births	..	35.0	36.0	39.0	45.0	40.0
Under 5 mortality	"	..	..	44.3	49.0	59.0	51.0
Immunization							
Measles	% age group	..	..	..	88.4	..	82.0
DPT	"	..	..	..	89.5	..	73.8
Child malnutrition (under-5)	"	..	..	..	24.7	..	..
Life expectancy							
Total	years	..	69	64	68	68	69
Female advantage	"	..	4.5	3.0	3.6	6.4	6.3
Total fertility rate	births per woman	..	..	4.8	2.4	3.1	2.9
Maternal mortality rate	per 100,000 live births	..	..	..	114	..	..
Supplementary Poverty Indicators							
Expenditures on social security	% of total gov't exp.	..	..	..	..	..	..
Social security coverage	% econ. active pop.	..	..	..	..	..	..
Access to safe water: total	% of pop.	..	..	..	72.0	..	85.6
Urban	"	..	..	..	83.4	..	94.3
Rural	"	..	..	..	60.2	..	73.0
Access to health care	"	..	..	..	..	..	..

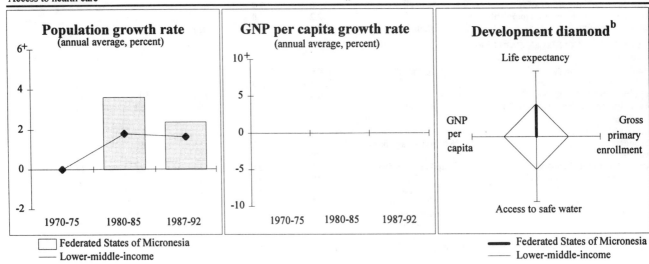

Population growth rate (annual average, percent)

GNP per capita growth rate (annual average, percent)

Development diamond[b]

Life expectancy — GNP per capita — Gross primary enrollment — Access to safe water

☐ Federated States of Micronesia
— Lower-middle-income

▬ Federated States of Micronesia
— Lower-middle-income

a. See the technical notes, p.389.   b. The development diamond, based on four key indicators, shows the average level of development in the country compared with its income group. See the introduction.

Federated States of Micronesia

Indicator	Unit of measure	Latest single year 1970-75	Latest single year 1980-85	Most recent estimate 1987-92	Same region/income group East Asia	Same region/income group Lower-middle-income	Next higher income group
Resources and Expenditures							
HUMAN RESOURCES							
Population (mre=1992)	thousands	..	91	108	1,688,909	942,547	477,960
Age dependency ratio	ratio	..	..	..	0.55	0.66	0.64
Urban	% of pop.	..	..	..	29.4	57.0	71.7
Population growth rate	annual %	..	3.4	2.8	1.4	1.4	1.6
Urban	"	..	..	..	2.9	4.8	2.5
Labor force (15-64)	thousands	..	..	..	928,465	..	181,414
Agriculture	% of labor force	..	..	..	..	..	..
Industry	"	..	..	..	..	..	..
Female	"	..	..	..	41	36	29
Females per 100 males							
Urban	number	..	..	..	..	..	..
Rural	"	..	..	..	..	..	..
NATURAL RESOURCES							
Area	thou. sq. km	..	0.70	0.70	16,367.18	40,697.37	21,836.02
Density	pop. per sq. km	..	..	..	101.8	22.8	21.5
Agricultural land	% of land area	..	..	..	44.5	..	41.7
Change in agricultural land	annual %	..	..	..	0.1	..	0.3
Agricultural land under irrigation	%	..	..	..	14.5	..	9.3
Forests and woodland	thou. sq. km	..	..	..	..	..	..
Deforestation (net)	annual %	..	..	..	..	..	..
INCOME							
Household income							
Share of top 20% of households	% of income	..	..	..	42	..	..
Share of bottom 40% of households	"	..	..	..	18	..	..
Share of bottom 20% of households	"	..	..	..	7	..	..
EXPENDITURE							
Food	% of GDP	..	..	..	..	..	..
Staples	"	..	..	..	..	..	..
Meat, fish, milk, cheese, eggs	"	..	..	..	..	..	..
Cereal imports	thou. metric tonnes	..	..	..	33,591	74,924	49,174
Food aid in cereals	"	..	..	..	581	4,054	282
Food production per capita	1987 = 100	..	..	..	133	..	109
Fertilizer consumption	kg/ha	..	..	..	75.1	..	68.8
Share of agriculture in GDP	% of GDP	..	..	..	21.5	..	8.1
Housing	% of GDP	..	..	..	..	..	..
Average household size	persons per household	..	..	..	..	..	..
Urban	"	..	..	..	..	..	..
Fixed investment: housing	% of GDP	..	..	..	..	..	..
Fuel and power	% of GDP	..	..	..	..	..	..
Energy consumption per capita	kg of oil equiv.	..	..	..	593	1,882	1,649
Households with electricity							
Urban	% of households	..	..	..	..	..	..
Rural	"	..	..	..	..	..	..
Transport and communication	% of GDP	..	..	..	..	..	..
Fixed investment: transport equipment	"	..	..	..	..	..	..
Total road length	thou. km	..	..	..	..	..	..
INVESTMENT IN HUMAN CAPITAL							
Health							
Population per physician	persons	..	..	..	..	..	..
Population per nurse	"	..	..	..	..	..	..
Population per hospital bed	"	..	..	..	553	516	385
Oral rehydration therapy (under-5)	% of cases	..	..	..	51	..	54
Education							
Gross enrollment ratio							
Secondary	% of school-age pop.	..	..	..	53	..	53
Female	"	..	..	..	47	..	..
Pupil-teacher ratio: primary	pupils per teacher	..	..	..	23	26	25
Pupil-teacher ratio: secondary	"	..	..	..	16	..	..
Pupils reaching grade 4	% of cohort	..	..	..	89	..	71
Repeater rate: primary	% of total enroll	..	..	..	6	..	11
Illiteracy	% of pop. (age 15+)	..	..	..	24	..	14
Female	% of fem. (age 15+)	..	..	..	34	..	17
Newspaper circulation	per thou. pop.	..	..	..	..	100	117

World Bank International Economics Department, April 1994

Moldova

Priority Poverty Indicators

Indicator	Unit of measure	Latest single year 1970-75	Latest single year 1980-85	Most recent estimate 1987-92	Same region/income group Europe & Central Asia	Same region/income group Lower-middle-income	Next higher income group
POVERTY							
Upper poverty line	local curr.	..	..	..	..	..	..
Headcount index	% of pop.	..	..	19	..	..	..
Lower poverty line	local curr.	..	..	..	..	..	..
Headcount index	% of pop.	..	..	6	..	..	..
GNP per capita	US$	..	..	1,300	..	..	3,870
SHORT TERM INCOME INDICATORS							
Unskilled urban wages	local curr.	..	..	..	..	..	..
Unskilled rural wages	"	..	..	..	..	..	..
Rural terms of trade	"	..	..	..	..	..	..
Consumer price index	1987=100	..	..	..	..	..	..
Lower income	"	..	..	..	..	..	..
Food[a]	"	..	..	..	..	..	..
Urban	"	..	..	..	..	..	..
Rural	"	..	..	..	..	..	..
SOCIAL INDICATORS							
Public expenditure on basic social services	% of GDP	..	..	8.0	..	..	..
Gross enrollment ratios							
Primary	% school age pop.	..	..	..	..	..	107
Male	"	..	..	..	..	..	..
Female	"	..	..	..	..	..	..
Mortality							
Infant mortality	per thou. live births	..	32.2	23.0	30.0	45.0	40.0
Under 5 mortality	"	..	..	27.5	38.0	59.0	51.0
Immunization							
Measles	% age group	..	..	..	..	..	82.0
DPT	"	..	..	..	..	..	73.8
Child malnutrition (under-5)	"	..	..	..	..	..	..
Life expectancy							
Total	years	..	66	68	70	68	69
Female advantage	"	..	6.3	7.0	8.6	6.4	6.3
Total fertility rate	births per woman	2.5	2.8	2.3	2.2	3.1	2.9
Maternal mortality rate	per 100,000 live births	..	64	34	58	..	..

Supplementary Poverty Indicators

Indicator	Unit of measure	1970-75	1980-85	1987-92	Europe & Central Asia	Lower-middle-income	Next higher income group
Expenditures on social security	% of total gov't exp.	..	..	..	..	..	..
Social security coverage	% econ. active pop.	..	..	..	..	..	..
Access to safe water: total	% of pop.	..	..	..	..	..	85.6
Urban	"	..	..	..	..	..	94.3
Rural	"	..	..	..	..	..	73.0
Access to health care	"	..	..	..	..	..	..

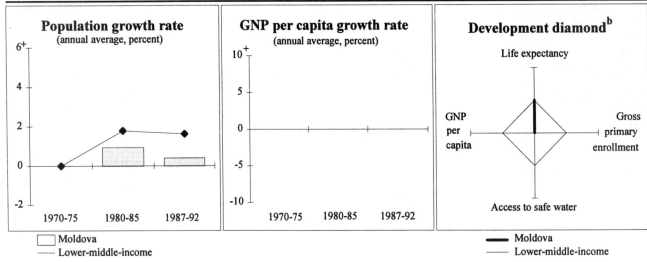

Population growth rate (annual average, percent) — 1970-75, 1980-85, 1987-92. Legend: Moldova, Lower-middle-income.

GNP per capita growth rate (annual average, percent) — 1970-75, 1980-85, 1987-92.

Development diamond[b] — Life expectancy, GNP per capita, Gross primary enrollment, Access to safe water. Legend: Moldova, Lower-middle-income.

a. See the technical notes, p.389.   b. The development diamond, based on four key indicators, shows the average level of development in the country compared with its income group. See the introduction.

Moldova

		Latest single year		Most recent estimate 1987-92	Same region/income group		Next higher income group
Indicator	Unit of measure	1970-75	1980-85		Europe & Central Asia	Lower-middle-income	

Resources and Expenditures

HUMAN RESOURCES

Indicator	Unit of measure	1970-75	1980-85	1987-92	Europe & Central Asia	Lower-middle-income	Next higher income group
Population (mre=1992)	thousands	..	4,192	4,360	495,241	942,547	477,960
Age dependency ratio	ratio	..	..	0.57	0.56	0.66	0.64
Urban	% of pop.	..	..	47.0	63.3	57.0	71.7
Population growth rate	annual %	..	0.9	-0.1	0.5	1.4	1.6
Urban	"	..	..	..	..	4.8	2.5
Labor force (15-64)	thousands	..	2,421	2,429	..	..	181,414
Agriculture	% of labor force	..	..	74	..	..	..
Industry	"	..	..	0	..	..	..
Female	"	..	51	53	46	36	29
Females per 100 males							
Urban	number	..	..	..	..	..	..
Rural	"	..	..	..	..	..	..

NATURAL RESOURCES

Indicator	Unit of measure	1970-75	1980-85	1987-92	Europe & Central Asia	Lower-middle-income	Next higher income group
Area	thou. sq. km	..	..	33.70	24,165.06	40,697.37	21,836.02
Density	pop. per sq. km	..	..	129.5	20.4	22.8	21.5
Agricultural land	% of land area	..	..	..	..	..	41.7
Change in agricultural land	annual %	..	..	..	..	..	0.3
Agricultural land under irrigation	%	..	..	..	..	..	9.3
Forests and woodland	thou. sq. km	..	..	..	..	..	..
Deforestation (net)	annual %	..	..	..	..	..	..

INCOME
Household income

Indicator	Unit of measure	1970-75	1980-85	1987-92	Europe & Central Asia	Lower-middle-income	Next higher income group
Share of top 20% of households	% of income	..	..	..	..	..	..
Share of bottom 40% of households	"	..	..	..	..	..	..
Share of bottom 20% of households	"	..	..	..	..	..	..

EXPENDITURE

Indicator	Unit of measure	1970-75	1980-85	1987-92	Europe & Central Asia	Lower-middle-income	Next higher income group
Food	% of GDP	..	..	19.8	..	..	..
Staples	"	..	..	3.6	..	..	..
Meat, fish, milk, cheese, eggs	"	..	..	8.9	..	..	..
Cereal imports	thou. metric tonnes	..	..	1,350	45,972	74,924	49,174
Food aid in cereals	"	..	..	..	1,639	4,054	282
Food production per capita	1987 = 100	..	..	..	..	..	109
Fertilizer consumption	kg/ha	..	..	..	..	..	68.8
Share of agriculture in GDP	% of GDP	..	28.1	33.5	..	..	8.1
Housing	% of GDP	..	..	4.7	..	..	..
Average household size	persons per household	..	..	3.4	..	..	..
Urban	"	..	..	..	..	..	..
Fixed investment: housing	% of GDP	..	..	4.9	..	..	..
Fuel and power	% of GDP	..	..	1.0	..	..	..
Energy consumption per capita	kg of oil equiv.	..	..	1,600	3,190	1,882	1,649
Households with electricity							
Urban	% of households	..	..	..	..	..	..
Rural	"	..	..	..	..	..	..
Transport and communication	% of GDP	..	..	6.2	..	..	..
Fixed investment: transport equipment	"	..	..	10.3	..	..	..
Total road length	thou. km	..	12	20	..	..	..

INVESTMENT IN HUMAN CAPITAL
Health

Indicator	Unit of measure	1970-75	1980-85	1987-92	Europe & Central Asia	Lower-middle-income	Next higher income group
Population per physician	persons	..	..	249	378	..	..
Population per nurse	"	..	..	..	..	..	..
Population per hospital bed	"	..	..	77	134	516	385
Oral rehydration therapy (under-5)	% of cases	..	..	..	..	..	54

Education
Gross enrollment ratio

Indicator	Unit of measure	1970-75	1980-85	1987-92	Europe & Central Asia	Lower-middle-income	Next higher income group
Secondary	% of school-age pop.	..	..	..	..	..	53
Female	"	..	..	..	..	..	..
Pupil-teacher ratio: primary	pupils per teacher	..	..	..	..	26	25
Pupil-teacher ratio: secondary	"	..	..	..	..	..	..
Pupils reaching grade 4	% of cohort	..	..	..	..	..	71
Repeater rate: primary	% of total enroll	..	..	..	..	..	11
Illiteracy	% of pop. (age 15+)	..	..	..	..	..	14
Female	% of fem. (age 15+)	..	..	..	..	..	17
Newspaper circulation	per thou. pop.	..	..	..	..	100	117

World Bank International Economics Department, April 1994

Mongolia

Indicator	Unit of measure	Latest single year		Most recent estimate	Same region/income group		Next higher income group
		1970-75	1980-85	1987-92	East Asia	Lower-middle-income	

Priority Poverty Indicators

POVERTY

Indicator	Unit of measure	1970-75	1980-85	1987-92	East Asia	Lower-middle-income	Next higher
Upper poverty line	local curr.	..	..	..	..	..	..
Headcount index	% of pop.	..	..	..	12	..	..
Lower poverty line	local curr.	..	..	..	..	..	..
Headcount index	% of pop.	..	..	..	9	..	..
GNP per capita	US$	..	..	..	760	..	3,870
SHORT TERM INCOME INDICATORS							
Unskilled urban wages	local curr.	..	..	..	..	..	..
Unskilled rural wages	"	..	..	..	..	..	..
Rural terms of trade	"	..	..	..	..	..	..
Consumer price index	1987=100	..	..	..	..	..	..
Lower income	"	..	..	..	..	..	..
Food[a]	"	..	..	..	..	..	..
Urban	"	..	..	..	..	..	..
Rural	"	..	..	..	..	..	..
SOCIAL INDICATORS							
Public expenditure on basic social services	% of GDP	..	..	4.1	..	..	..
Gross enrollment ratios							
Primary	% school age pop.	108	103	89	121	..	107
Male	"	111	102	96	126	..	..
Female	"	104	104	100	117	..	..
Mortality							
Infant mortality	per thou. live births	98.0	78.0	60.0	39.0	45.0	40.0
Under 5 mortality	"	..	..	80.9	49.0	59.0	51.0
Immunization							
Measles	% age group	..	18.0	86.0	88.4	..	82.0
DPT	"	..	83.0	84.0	89.5	..	73.8
Child malnutrition (under-5)	"	..	..	..	24.7	..	..
Life expectancy							
Total	years	54	59	64	68	68	69
Female advantage	"	2.5	2.5	2.7	3.6	6.4	6.3
Total fertility rate	births per woman	5.8	5.3	4.6	2.4	3.1	2.9
Maternal mortality rate	per 100,000 live births	..	140	140	114	..	..

Supplementary Poverty Indicators

Indicator	Unit of measure	1970-75	1980-85	1987-92	East Asia	Lower-middle-income	Next higher
Expenditures on social security	% of total gov't exp.	..	..	..	..	..	..
Social security coverage	% econ. active pop.	..	..	..	..	..	..
Access to safe water: total	% of pop.	..	..	66.0	72.0	..	85.6
Urban	"	58.0	..	78.0	83.4	..	94.3
Rural	"	..	..	50.0	60.2	..	73.0
Access to health care	"	..	100.0	100.0	..	..	..

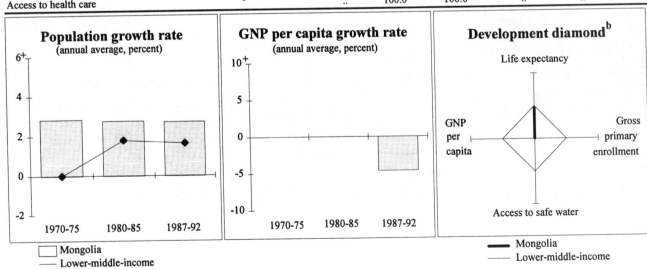

Population growth rate (annual average, percent)

☐ Mongolia
— Lower-middle-income

GNP per capita growth rate (annual average, percent)

Development diamond[b]

Life expectancy — Gross primary enrollment — Access to safe water — GNP per capita

— Mongolia
— Lower-middle-income

a. See the technical notes, p.389.   b. The development diamond, based on four key indicators, shows the average level of development in the country compared with its income group. See the introduction.

Mongolia

Indicator	Unit of measure	Latest single year 1970-75	Latest single year 1980-85	Most recent estimate 1987-92	Same region/income group East Asia	Same region/income group Lower-middle-income	Next higher income group

Resources and Expenditures

HUMAN RESOURCES

Indicator	Unit of measure	1970-75	1980-85	1987-92	East Asia	Lower-middle-income	Next higher income group
Population (mre=1992)	thousands	1,447	1,909	2,311	1,688,909	942,547	477,960
Age dependency ratio	ratio	0.89	0.82	0.79	0.55	0.66	0.64
Urban	% of pop.	48.7	55.0	59.2	29.4	57.0	71.7
Population growth rate	annual %	2.8	2.8	2.7	1.4	1.4	1.6
Urban	"	4.3	3.8	3.7	2.9	4.8	2.5
Labor force (15-64)	thousands	668	894	1,092	928,465	..	181,414
Agriculture	% of labor force	44	40	0	..	..	..
Industry	"	21	21	0	..	..	..
Female	"	45	46	46	41	36	29
Females per 100 males							
Urban	number	..	..	..	..	..	..
Rural	"	..	..	..	..	..	..

NATURAL RESOURCES

Indicator	Unit of measure	1970-75	1980-85	1987-92	East Asia	Lower-middle-income	Next higher income group
Area	thou. sq. km	1,566.50	1,566.50	1,566.50	16,367.18	40,697.37	21,836.02
Density	pop. per sq. km	0.9	1.2	1.4	101.8	22.8	21.5
Agricultural land	% of land area	89.8	79.5	80.4	44.5	..	41.7
Change in agricultural land	annual %	0.0	0.0	0.2	0.1	..	0.3
Agricultural land under irrigation	%	0.0	0.1	0.1	14.5	..	9.3
Forests and woodland	thou. sq. km	152	152	139	..	..	..
Deforestation (net)	annual %	..	..	..	..	..	..

INCOME

Indicator	Unit of measure	1970-75	1980-85	1987-92	East Asia	Lower-middle-income	Next higher income group
Household income							
Share of top 20% of households	% of income	..	..	..	42	..	..
Share of bottom 40% of households	"	..	..	..	18	..	..
Share of bottom 20% of households	"	..	..	..	7	..	..

EXPENDITURE

Indicator	Unit of measure	1970-75	1980-85	1987-92	East Asia	Lower-middle-income	Next higher income group
Food	% of GDP	..	..	37.1	..	..	..
Staples	"	..	..	15.4	..	..	..
Meat, fish, milk, cheese, eggs	"	..	..	14.3	..	..	..
Cereal imports	thou. metric tonnes	56	71	43	33,591	74,924	49,174
Food aid in cereals	"	..	..	5	581	4,054	282
Food production per capita	1987 = 100	122	93	65	133	..	109
Fertilizer consumption	kg/ha	0.0	0.2	0.1	75.1	..	68.8
Share of agriculture in GDP	% of GDP	..	14.0	30.3	21.5	..	8.1
Housing	% of GDP	..	..	13.9	..	..	..
Average household size	persons per household	..	..	..	..	..	..
Urban	"	..	..	..	..	..	..
Fixed investment: housing	% of GDP	..	..	5.4	..	..	..
Fuel and power	% of GDP	..	..	3.8	..	..	..
Energy consumption per capita	kg of oil equiv.	753	1,211	1,082	593	1,882	1,649
Households with electricity							
Urban	% of households	..	..	..	..	..	..
Rural	"	..	..	..	..	..	..
Transport and communication	% of GDP	..	..	2.9	..	..	..
Fixed investment: transport equipment	"	..	..	1.2	..	..	..
Total road length	thou. km	..	..	..	..	..	..

INVESTMENT IN HUMAN CAPITAL

Indicator	Unit of measure	1970-75	1980-85	1987-92	East Asia	Lower-middle-income	Next higher income group
Health							
Population per physician	persons	578	105	369	..	..	..
Population per nurse	"	252	217	..	..	..	..
Population per hospital bed	"	105	90	87	553	516	385
Oral rehydration therapy (under-5)	% of cases	..	..	59	51	..	54
Education							
Gross enrollment ratio							
Secondary	% of school-age pop.	81	90	77	53	..	53
Female	"	84	95	..	47	..	..
Pupil-teacher ratio: primary	pupils per teacher	31	30	25	23	26	25
Pupil-teacher ratio: secondary	"	15	22	18	16	..	..
Pupils reaching grade 4	% of cohort	..	..	..	89	..	71
Repeater rate: primary	% of total enroll	..	1	..	6	..	11
Illiteracy	% of pop. (age 15+)	..	..	..	24	..	14
Female	% of fem. (age 15+)	..	..	..	34	..	17
Newspaper circulation	per thou. pop.	77	95	74	..	100	117

World Bank International Economics Department, April 1994

Morocco

Indicator	Unit of measure	Latest single year 1970-75	Latest single year 1980-85	Most recent estimate 1987-92	Same region/income group Mid-East & North Africa	Same region/income group Lower-middle-income	Next higher income group
Priority Poverty Indicators							
POVERTY							
Upper poverty line	local curr.	..	..	2,568	..	..	..
Headcount index	% of pop.	..	26	13	..	..	..
Lower poverty line	local curr.	..	..	2,070	..	..	..
Headcount index	% of pop.	..	17	7	..	..	..
GNP per capita	US$	500	620	1,030	1,950	..	3,870
SHORT TERM INCOME INDICATORS							
Unskilled urban wages	local curr.	..	..	..	..	..	..
Unskilled rural wages	"	..	..	..	..	..	..
Rural terms of trade	"	..	..	..	..	..	..
Consumer price index	1987=100	35	90	128	..	..	..
Lower income	"	..	..	..	..	..	..
Food[a]	"	..	91	125	..	..	..
Urban	"	..	..	..	..	..	..
Rural	"	..	..	..	..	..	..
SOCIAL INDICATORS							
Public expenditure on basic social services	% of GDP	..	..	..	..	..	..
Gross enrollment ratios							
Primary	% school age pop.	62	77	66	100	..	107
Male	"	78	94	78	107	..	..
Female	"	45	60	54	88	..	..
Mortality							
Infant mortality	per thou. live births	122.0	92.0	57.4	58.0	45.0	40.0
Under 5 mortality	"	..	..	76.8	78.0	59.0	51.0
Immunization							
Measles	% age group	..	..	76.0	81.8	..	82.0
DPT	"	..	44.0	79.0	83.9	..	73.8
Child malnutrition (under-5)	"	..	..	11.8	20.9	..	..
Life expectancy							
Total	years	53	58	63	64	68	69
Female advantage	"	3.1	3.4	3.4	2.4	6.4	6.3
Total fertility rate	births per woman	6.9	5.4	3.8	4.9	3.1	2.9
Maternal mortality rate	per 100,000 live births	..	327	..	..	..	..
Supplementary Poverty Indicators							
Expenditures on social security	% of total gov't exp.	..	..	..	..	..	..
Social security coverage	% econ. active pop.	..	..	..	..	..	..
Access to safe water: total	% of pop.	51.0	58.0	61.0	85.0	..	85.6
Urban	"	92.0	100.0	100.0	97.0	..	94.3
Rural	"	28.0	25.0	25.0	70.1	..	73.0
Access to health care	"	..	93.0	60.0	84.6	..	..

Population growth rate (annual average, percent)

GNP per capita growth rate (annual average, percent)

Development diamond[b]

☐ Morocco
— Lower-middle-income

━ Morocco
— Lower-middle-income

a. See the technical notes, p.389. b. The development diamond, based on four key indicators, shows the average level of development in the country compared with its income group. See the introduction.

Morocco

Indicator	Unit of measure	Latest single year 1970-75	Latest single year 1980-85	Most recent estimate 1987-92	Mid-East & North Africa	Lower-middle-income	Next higher income group
Resources and Expenditures							
HUMAN RESOURCES							
Population (mre=1992)	thousands	17,305	22,061	26,193	252,555	942,547	477,960
Age dependency ratio	ratio	1.03	0.85	0.78	0.87	0.66	0.64
Urban	% of pop.	37.7	43.9	47.0	54.7	57.0	71.7
Population growth rate	annual %	2.3	2.7	2.1	2.8	1.4	1.6
Urban	"	4.0	4.0	3.1	3.8	4.8	2.5
Labor force (15-64)	thousands	4,656	6,676	8,335	69,280	..	181,414
Agriculture	% of labor force	52	46	..	..	..	..
Industry	"	21	25	..	..	..	..
Female	"	16	20	21	15	36	29
Females per 100 males							
Urban	number	108	100	..	..	..	..
Rural	"	104	107	..	..	..	..
NATURAL RESOURCES							
Area	thou. sq. km	446.55	446.55	446.55	10,487.21	40,697.37	21,836.02
Density	pop. per sq. km	38.8	49.4	57.4	23.4	22.8	21.5
Agricultural land	% of land area	60.3	65.7	67.9	30.2	..	41.7
Change in agricultural land	annual %	1.1	0.2	0.3	0.5	..	0.3
Agricultural land under irrigation	%	3.9	4.3	4.2	31.0	..	9.3
Forests and woodland	thou. sq. km	77	79	91	..	..	..
Deforestation (net)	annual %	..	λ	..	..	..	..
INCOME							
Household income							
Share of top 20% of households	% of income	49	39	46			
Share of bottom 40% of households	"	12	23	17	..	..	..
Share of bottom 20% of households	"	4	10	7	..	..	..
EXPENDITURE							
Food	% of GDP	..	30.1	..	..	..	..
Staples	"		9.4				
Meat, fish, milk, cheese, eggs	"	..	8.9	..	..	..	..
Cereal imports	thou. metric tonnes	1,509	2,177	3,095	38,007	74,924	49,174
Food aid in cereals	"	75	518	208	2,484	4,054	282
Food production per capita	1987 = 100	96	108	104	116	..	109
Fertilizer consumption	kg/ha	6.2	10.4	11.1	96.7	..	68.8
Share of agriculture in GDP	% of GDP	17.3	16.6	14.9	13.7	..	8.1
Housing	% of GDP	..	6.7	..	..	..	..
Average household size	persons per household	6.0	5.9	5.7	..	..	..
Urban	"	5.0	5.2	..	..	..	..
Fixed investment: housing	% of GDP	..	4.1	..	..	..	..
Fuel and power	% of GDP	..	1.4	..	..	..	..
Energy consumption per capita	kg of oil equiv.	198	253	278	1,109	1,882	1,649
Households with electricity							
Urban	% of households	..	..	90.0	..	..	..
Rural	"	..	..	13.0	..	..	..
Transport and communication	% of GDP	..	6.3	..	..	..	..
Fixed investment: transport equipment	"	..	1.5	..	..	..	..
Total road length	thou. km	50	58	59	..	..	..
INVESTMENT IN HUMAN CAPITAL							
Health							
Population per physician	persons	13,100	15,580	4,844		..	..
Population per nurse	"	..	920	1,053		..	
Population per hospital bed	"	700	804	809	636	516	385
Oral rehydration therapy (under-5)	% of cases	..	..	13	56	..	54
Education							
Gross enrollment ratio							
Secondary	% of school-age pop.	16	34	28	59	..	53
Female	"	12	27	29	50	..	..
Pupil-teacher ratio: primary	pupils per teacher	42	28	27	27	26	25
Pupil-teacher ratio: secondary	"	24	19	15	21	..	..
Pupils reaching grade 4	% of cohort	85	83	70	..	..	71
Repeater rate: primary	% of total enroll	28	20	15	..	..	11
Illiteracy	% of pop. (age 15+)	79	58	51	45	..	14
Female	% of fem. (age 15+)	..	71	62	58	..	17
Newspaper circulation	per thou. pop.	21	12	13	39	100	117

World Bank International Economics Department, April 1994

Mozambique

Indicator	Unit of measure	Latest single year 1970-75	Latest single year 1980-85	Most recent estimate 1987-92	Same region/income group Sub-Saharan Africa	Same region/income group Low-income	Next higher income group
Priority Poverty Indicators							
POVERTY							
Upper poverty line	local curr.	..	..	..	..	..	..
Headcount index	% of pop.	..	..	..	..	19	..
Lower poverty line	local curr.	..	..	..	..	..	..
Headcount index	% of pop.	..	..	..	..	..	..
GNP per capita	US$	..	190	60	520	390	
SHORT TERM INCOME INDICATORS							
Unskilled urban wages	local curr.	..	..	..	..	..	..
Unskilled rural wages	"	..	..	..	..	..	..
Rural terms of trade	"	..	..	..	..	..	..
Consumer price index	1987=100	..	27	418	..	..	..
Lower income	"	..	..	..	..	..	..
Food[a]	"	..	..	..	..	..	..
Urban	"	..	..	..	..	..	..
Rural	"	..	..	..	..	..	..
SOCIAL INDICATORS							
Public expenditure on basic social services	% of GDP	..	..	13.1	..	..	..
Gross enrollment ratios							
Primary	% school age pop.	47	86	60	66	103	..
Male	"	..	97	69	79	113	..
Female	"	..	75	50	62	96	..
Mortality							
Infant mortality	per thou. live births	143.0	171.2	162.1	99.0	73.0	45.0
Under 5 mortality	"	..	..	276.2	169.0	108.0	59.0
Immunization							
Measles	% age group	..	39.0	23.0	54.0	72.7	..
DPT	"	..	29.0	19.0	54.6	80.6	..
Child malnutrition (under-5)	"	..	..	..	28.4	38.3	..
Life expectancy							
Total	years	35	40	44	52	62	68
Female advantage	"	4.7	5.1	2.4	3.4	2.4	6.4
Total fertility rate	births per woman	6.6	6.3	6.5	6.1	3.4	3.1
Maternal mortality rate	per 100,000 live births	..	300	..	..	..	..
Supplementary Poverty Indicators							
Expenditures on social security	% of total gov't exp.	..	..	..	..	..	..
Social security coverage	% econ. active pop.	..	..	..	..	..	..
Access to safe water: total	% of pop.	..	15.0	24.0	41.1	68.4	..
Urban	"	..	38.0	44.0	77.8	78.9	..
Rural	"	2.0	9.0	17.0	27.3	60.3	..
Access to health care	"	..	40.0	30.0	..	..	..

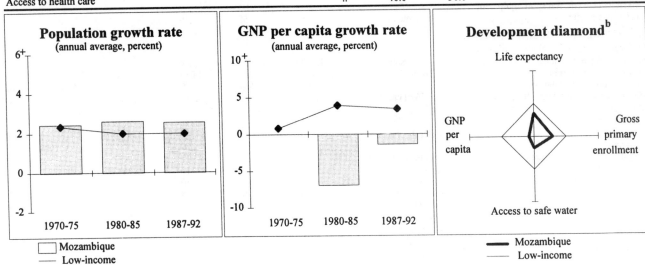

Population growth rate (annual average, percent) — 1970-75, 1980-85, 1987-92 — Mozambique / Low-income

GNP per capita growth rate (annual average, percent) — 1970-75, 1980-85, 1987-92

Development diamond[b] — Life expectancy, GNP per capita, Gross primary enrollment, Access to safe water — Mozambique / Low-income

a. See the technical notes, p.389.   b. The development diamond, based on four key indicators, shows the average level of development in the country compared with its income group. See the introduction.

Mozambique

Indicator	Unit of measure	Latest single year 1970-75	Latest single year 1980-85	Most recent estimate 1987-92	Sub-Saharan Africa	Low-income	Next higher income group
Resources and Expenditures							
HUMAN RESOURCES							
Population (mre=1992)	thousands	10,606	13,791	16,511	546,390	3,194,535	942,547
Age dependency ratio	ratio	0.89	0.88	0.90	0.95	0.67	0.66
Urban	% of pop.	8.6	19.4	29.8	29.5	26.7	57.0
Population growth rate	annual %	2.5	2.6	2.5	2.9	1.8	1.4
Urban	"	9.5	9.3	7.6	5.1	3.4	4.8
Labor force (15-64)	thousands	5,531	7,671	8,791	224,025	1,478,954	..
Agriculture	% of labor force	85	84	..	..	..	..
Industry	"	7	7	..	..	..	..
Female	"	50	49	47	37	33	36
Females per 100 males							
Urban	number	..	83	..	..	..	..
Rural	"	..	119	..	..	..	..
NATURAL RESOURCES							
Area	thou. sq. km	801.59	801.59	801.59	24,274.03	38,401.06	40,697.37
Density	pop. per sq. km	13.2	17.2	20.1	21.9	81.7	22.8
Agricultural land	% of land area	60.0	60.1	60.1	52.7	50.9	..
Change in agricultural land	annual %	0.0	0.0	0.0	0.1	0.0	..
Agricultural land under irrigation	%	0.1	0.2	0.2	0.8	18.2	..
Forests and woodland	thou. sq. km	161	149	141	..	..	..
Deforestation (net)	annual %	..	..	0.8	..	..	..
INCOME							
Household income							
Share of top 20% of households	% of income	..	..	..	..	42	..
Share of bottom 40% of households	"	..	..	..	..	19	..
Share of bottom 20% of households	"	..	..	..	..	8	..
EXPENDITURE							
Food	% of GDP	..	..	29.3	..	..	..
Staples	"	..	..	8.7	..	..	..
Meat, fish, milk, cheese, eggs	"	..	..	10.8	..	..	..
Cereal imports	thou. metric tonnes	191	598	1,164	20,311	46,537	74,924
Food aid in cereals	"	34	379	591	4,303	9,008	4,054
Food production per capita	1987 = 100	116	88	65	90	123	..
Fertilizer consumption	kg/ha	0.1	0.1	0.1	4.2	61.9	..
Share of agriculture in GDP	% of GDP	..	59.8	59.2	18.6	29.6	..
Housing	% of GDP	..	..	8.7	..	..	..
Average household size	persons per household	..	4.3	..	..	..	..
Urban	"	..	..	..	..	..	..
Fixed investment: housing	% of GDP	..	..	3.2	..	..	..
Fuel and power	% of GDP	..	..	4.6	..	..	..
Energy consumption per capita	kg of oil equiv.	74	39	32	258	335	1,882
Households with electricity							
Urban	% of households	..	..	..	..	..	..
Rural	"	..	..	..	..	..	..
Transport and communication	% of GDP	..	..	10.0	..	..	..
Fixed investment: transport equipment	"	..	..	6.4	..	..	..
Total road length	thou. km	39	35	35	..	..	..
INVESTMENT IN HUMAN CAPITAL							
Health							
Population per physician	persons	18,855	49,430	..	..	..	..
Population per nurse	"	4,284	5,761	..	..	..	..
Population per hospital bed	"	850	918	1,280	1,329	1,050	516
Oral rehydration therapy (under-5)	% of cases	..	..	30	36	39	..
Education							
Gross enrollment ratio							
Secondary	% of school-age pop.	5	7	8	18	41	..
Female	"	..	4	5	14	35	..
Pupil-teacher ratio: primary	pupils per teacher	69	62	55	39	37	26
Pupil-teacher ratio: secondary	"	22	40	38	..	19	..
Pupils reaching grade 4	% of cohort	..	..	..	..	..	..
Repeater rate: primary	% of total enroll	28	24	25	..	..	..
Illiteracy	% of pop. (age 15+)	..	72	67	51	39	..
Female	% of fem. (age 15+)	..	84	79	62	52	..
Newspaper circulation	per thou. pop.	7	3	5	14	..	100

World Bank International Economics Department, April 1994

Myanmar

Indicator	Unit of measure	Latest single year 1970-75	Latest single year 1980-85	Most recent estimate 1987-92	Same region/income group East Asia	Same region/income group Low-income	Next higher income group
Priority Poverty Indicators							
POVERTY							
Upper poverty line	local curr.	..	..	..	..	..	..
Headcount index	% of pop.	..	..	..	12	19	..
Lower poverty line	local curr.	..	..	..	..	..	..
Headcount index	% of pop.	..	..	..	9	..	..
GNP per capita	US$	..	..	..	760	390	..
SHORT TERM INCOME INDICATORS							
Unskilled urban wages	local curr.	..	..	..	..	..	..
Unskilled rural wages	"	..	..	..	..	..	..
Rural terms of trade	"	..	..	..	..	..	..
Consumer price index	1987=100	49	73	280	..	..	..
Lower income	"	..	..	..	..	..	..
Food[a]	"	..	74	254	..	..	..
Urban	"	..	..	..	..	..	..
Rural	"	..	..	..	..	..	..
SOCIAL INDICATORS							
Public expenditure on basic social services	% of GDP	..	2.7	..	..	..	
Gross enrollment ratios							
Primary	% school age pop.	83	98	102	121	103	..
Male	"	86	101	107	126	113	..
Female	"	80	96	100	117	96	..
Mortality							
Infant mortality	per thou. live births	115.0	90.0	72.0	39.0	73.0	45.0
Under 5 mortality	"	..	..	99.7	49.0	108.0	59.0
Immunization							
Measles	% age group	..	..	73.0	88.4	72.7	..
DPT	"	..	16.0	69.0	89.5	80.6	..
Child malnutrition (under-5)	"	..	38.1	32.4	24.7	38.3	..
Life expectancy							
Total	years	53	56	60	68	62	68
Female advantage	"	3.1	3.4	3.9	3.6	2.4	6.4
Total fertility rate	births per woman	5.8	4.9	4.2	2.4	3.4	3.1
Maternal mortality rate	per 100,000 live births	..	150	..	114	..	..
Supplementary Poverty Indicators							
Expenditures on social security	% of total gov't exp.	0.2	0.3	0.3	..	..	..
Social security coverage	% econ. active pop.	..	..	..	..	..	..
Access to safe water: total	% of pop.	17.0	27.0	32.5	72.0	68.4	..
Urban	"	31.0	36.0	43.0	83.4	78.9	..
Rural	"	14.0	24.0	29.0	60.2	60.3	..
Access to health care	"	..	48.0	..	..	..	..

Population growth rate (annual average, percent)

GNP per capita growth rate (annual average, percent)

Development diamond[b]

Life expectancy — GNP per capita — Gross primary enrollment — Access to safe water

— Myanmar
— Low-income

a. See the technical notes, p.389.   b. The development diamond, based on four key indicators, shows the average level of development in the country compared with its income group. See the introduction.

242

Myanmar

Indicator	Unit of measure	Latest single year 1970-75	Latest single year 1980-85	Most recent estimate 1987-92	Same region/income group East Asia	Same region/income group Low-income	Next higher income group

Resources and Expenditures

HUMAN RESOURCES

Indicator	Unit of measure	1970-75	1980-85	1987-92	East Asia	Low-income	Next higher income group
Population (mre=1992)	thousands	30,441	37,544	43,718	1,688,909	3,194,535	942,547
Age dependency ratio	ratio	0.80	0.76	0.71	0.55	0.67	0.66
Urban	% of pop.	23.9	24.0	25.4	29.4	26.7	57.0
Population growth rate	annual %	2.2	2.1	2.2	1.4	1.8	1.4
Urban	"	3.2	2.1	3.3	2.9	3.4	4.8
Labor force (15-64)	thousands	13,559	16,699	19,012	928,465	1,478,954	..
Agriculture	% of labor force	56	53	..	..	..	..
Industry	"	17	19	..	..	..	..
Female	"	39	38	37	41	33	36
Females per 100 males							
Urban	number	103	102	..	..	..	..
Rural	"	103	104	..	..	..	..

NATURAL RESOURCES

Indicator	Unit of measure	1970-75	1980-85	1987-92	East Asia	Low-income	Next higher income group
Area	thou. sq. km	676.55	676.55	676.55	16,367.18	38,401.06	40,697.37
Density	pop. per sq. km	45.0	55.5	63.2	101.8	81.7	22.8
Agricultural land	% of land area	15.7	15.9	15.8	44.5	50.9	..
Change in agricultural land	annual %	0.1	0.1	-0.1	0.1	0.0	..
Agricultural land under irrigation	%	9.4	10.4	9.6	14.5	18.2	..
Forests and woodland	thou. sq. km	322	322	324	..	..	..
Deforestation (net)	annual %	..	..	1.3	..	..	..

INCOME

Household income

Indicator	Unit of measure	1970-75	1980-85	1987-92	East Asia	Low-income	Next higher income group
Share of top 20% of households	% of income	40	..	..	42	42	..
Share of bottom 40% of households	"	21	..	..	18	19	..
Share of bottom 20% of households	"	8	..	..	7	8	..

EXPENDITURE

Indicator	Unit of measure	1970-75	1980-85	1987-92	East Asia	Low-income	Next higher income group
Food	% of GDP	..	..	..	..	..	..
Staples	"	..	..	..	..	..	..
Meat, fish, milk, cheese, eggs	"	..	..	..	..	..	..
Cereal imports	thou. metric tonnes	9	7	21	33,591	46,537	74,924
Food aid in cereals	"	9	6	..	581	9,008	4,054
Food production per capita	1987 = 100	87	110	90	133	123	..
Fertilizer consumption	kg/ha	5.3	18.6	6.7	75.1	61.9	..
Share of agriculture in GDP	% of GDP	47.1	48.2	59.4	21.5	29.6	..
Housing	% of GDP	..	..	..	..	..	..
Average household size	persons per household	..	..	..	..	..	..
Urban	"	..	..	..	..	..	..
Fixed investment: housing	% of GDP	..	..	..	..	..	..
Fuel and power	% of GDP	..	..	..	..	..	..
Energy consumption per capita	kg of oil equiv.	47	60	42	593	335	1,882
Households with electricity							
Urban	% of households	..	..	..	..	..	..
Rural	"	..	..	..	..	..	..
Transport and communication	% of GDP	..	..	..	..	..	..
Fixed investment: transport equipment	"	..	..	..	..	..	..
Total road length	thou. km	22	23	..	..	..	..

INVESTMENT IN HUMAN CAPITAL

Health

Indicator	Unit of measure	1970-75	1980-85	1987-92	East Asia	Low-income	Next higher income group
Population per physician	persons	8,819	3,743	12,901	..	..	..
Population per nurse	"	3,057	903	1,241	..	..	..
Population per hospital bed	"	1,176	1,170	1,591	553	1,050	516
Oral rehydration therapy (under-5)	% of cases	..	..	19	51	39	..

Education

Gross enrollment ratio

Indicator	Unit of measure	1970-75	1980-85	1987-92	East Asia	Low-income	Next higher income group
Secondary	% of school-age pop.	21	23	20	53	41	..
Female	"	19	..	23	47	35	..
Pupil-teacher ratio: primary	pupils per teacher	52	40	35	23	37	26
Pupil-teacher ratio: secondary	"	39	21	18	16	19	..
Pupils reaching grade 4	% of cohort	49	..	..	89	..	..
Repeater rate: primary	% of total enroll	20	..	..	6	..	..
Illiteracy	% of pop. (age 15+)	29	22	19	24	39	..
Female	% of fem. (age 15+)	..	31	28	34	52	..
Newspaper circulation	per thou. pop.	10	14	5	..	..	100

World Bank International Economics Department, April 1994

Namibia

Indicator	Unit of measure	Latest single year 1970-75	Latest single year 1980-85	Most recent estimate 1987-92	Same region/income group Sub-Saharan Africa	Same region/income group Lower-middle-income	Next higher income group
Priority Poverty Indicators							
POVERTY							
Upper poverty line	local curr.	..	..	..	..	..	..
Headcount index	% of pop.	..	..	..	..	..	..
Lower poverty line	local curr.	..	..	..	..	..	..
Headcount index	% of pop.	..	..	..	..	..	..
GNP per capita	US$	..	1,070	1,610	520	..	3,870
SHORT TERM INCOME INDICATORS							
Unskilled urban wages	local curr.	..	..	..	..	..	..
Unskilled rural wages	"	..	..	..	..	..	..
Rural terms of trade	"	..	..	..	..	..	..
Consumer price index	1987=100	..	78	192	..	..	..
Lower income	"	..	..	..	..	..	..
Food[a]	"	..	74	..	..	..	..
Urban	"	..	..	..	..	..	..
Rural	"	..	..	..	..	..	..
SOCIAL INDICATORS							
Public expenditure on basic social services	% of GDP	..	..	..	..	..	..
Gross enrollment ratios							
Primary	% school age pop.	..	..	119	66	..	107
Male	"	..	..	112	79	..	..
Female	"	..	..	126	62	..	..
Mortality							
Infant mortality	per thou. live births	113.0	91.0	56.6	99.0	45.0	40.0
Under 5 mortality	"	..	..	85.8	169.0	59.0	51.0
Immunization							
Measles	% age group	..	..	..	54.0	..	82.0
DPT	"	..	..	..	54.6	..	73.8
Child malnutrition (under-5)	"	..	..	..	28.4	..	..
Life expectancy							
Total	years	49	54	59	52	68	69
Female advantage	"	2.5	2.5	2.5	3.4	6.4	6.3
Total fertility rate	births per woman	6.0	6.0	5.4	6.1	3.1	2.9
Maternal mortality rate	per 100,000 live births	..	..	..	..	..	..
Supplementary Poverty Indicators							
Expenditures on social security	% of total gov't exp.	..	..	6.8	..	..	..
Social security coverage	% econ. active pop.	..	..	..	..	..	..
Access to safe water: total	% of pop.	..	..	..	41.1	..	85.6
Urban	"	..	..	..	77.8	..	94.3
Rural	"	..	..	..	27.3	..	73.0
Access to health care	"	..	..	..	..	..	..

Population growth rate (annual average, percent)

□ Namibia
— Lower-middle-income

GNP per capita growth rate (annual average, percent)

Development diamond[b]

— Namibia
— Lower-middle-income

a. See the technical notes, p.389.   b. The development diamond, based on four key indicators, shows the average level of development in the country compared with its income group. See the introduction.

Namibia

Indicator	Unit of measure	Latest single year 1970-75	Latest single year 1980-85	Most recent estimate 1987-92	Same region/income group Sub-Saharan Africa	Same region/income group Lower-middle-income	Next higher income group
Resources and Expenditures							
HUMAN RESOURCES							
Population (mre=1992)	thousands	926	1,235	1,524	546,390	942,547	477,960
Age dependency ratio	ratio	0.89	0.94	0.94	0.95	0.66	0.64
Urban	% of pop.	20.6	25.1	29.0	29.5	57.0	71.7
Population growth rate	annual %	2.7	3.0	2.9	2.9	1.4	1.6
Urban	"	4.7	4.9	5.0	5.1	4.8	2.5
Labor force (15-64)	thousands	389	477	568	224,025	..	181,414
Agriculture	% of labor force	47	43	..	..	..	..
Industry	"	20	22	..	..	..	..
Female	"	24	24	24	37	36	29
Females per 100 males							
Urban	number	..	..	..	..	..	..
Rural	"	..	..	..	..	..	..
NATURAL RESOURCES							
Area	thou. sq. km	824.29	824.29	824.29	24,274.03	40,697.37	21,836.02
Density	pop. per sq. km	1.1	1.5	1.8	21.9	22.8	21.5
Agricultural land	% of land area	47.0	47.0	47.0	52.7	..	41.7
Change in agricultural land	annual %	0.0	0.0	0.0	0.1	..	0.3
Agricultural land under irrigation	%	0.0	0.0	0.0	0.8	..	9.3
Forests and woodland	thou. sq. km	186	183	181	..	..	..
Deforestation (net)	annual %	..	..	0.3	..	..	..
INCOME							
Household income							
Share of top 20% of households	% of income	..	..	..	..	..	..
Share of bottom 40% of households	"	..	..	..	..	..	..
Share of bottom 20% of households	"	..	..	..	..	..	..
EXPENDITURE							
Food	% of GDP	..	..	..	..	..	..
Staples	"	..	..	..	..	..	..
Meat, fish, milk, cheese, eggs	"	..	..	..	..	..	..
Cereal imports	thou. metric tonnes	..	..	188	20,311	74,924	49,174
Food aid in cereals	"	..	..	10	4,303	4,054	282
Food production per capita	1987 = 100	113	71	64	90	..	109
Fertilizer consumption	kg/ha	..	..	..	4.2	..	68.8
Share of agriculture in GDP	% of GDP	..	9.2	9.8	18.6	..	8.1
Housing	% of GDP	..	..	..	..	..	..
Average household size	persons per household	..	..	..	..	..	..
Urban	"	..	..	..	..	..	..
Fixed investment: housing	% of GDP	..	..	..	..	..	..
Fuel and power	% of GDP	..	..	..	..	..	..
Energy consumption per capita	kg of oil equiv.	..	..	..	258	1,882	1,649
Households with electricity							
Urban	% of households	..	..	..	..	..	..
Rural	"	..	..	..	..	..	..
Transport and communication	% of GDP	..	..	..	..	..	..
Fixed investment: transport equipment	"	..	..	..	..	..	..
Total road length	thou. km	..	..	..	..	..	..
INVESTMENT IN HUMAN CAPITAL							
Health							
Population per physician	persons	..	..	4,614	..	..	..
Population per nurse	"	..	..	..	..	..	..
Population per hospital bed	"	..	..	..	1,329	516	385
Oral rehydration therapy (under-5)	% of cases	..	..	..	36	..	54
Education							
Gross enrollment ratio							
Secondary	% of school-age pop.	..	..	41	18	..	53
Female	"	..	..	47	14	..	..
Pupil-teacher ratio: primary	pupils per teacher	..	..	..	39	26	25
Pupil-teacher ratio: secondary	"	..	..	..	..	..	..
Pupils reaching grade 4	% of cohort	..	..	62	..	..	71
Repeater rate: primary	% of total enroll	..	..	..	..	..	11
Illiteracy	% of pop. (age 15+)	..	..	..	51	..	14
Female	% of fem. (age 15+)	..	..	..	62	..	17
Newspaper circulation	per thou. pop.	21	17	153	14	100	117

World Bank International Economics Department, April 1994

Nepal

Indicator	Unit of measure	Latest single year		Most recent estimate 1987-92	Same region/income group		Next higher income group
		1970-75	1980-85		South Asia	Low-income	

Priority Poverty Indicators

POVERTY

Indicator	Unit	1970-75	1980-85	1987-92	South Asia	Low-income	Next
Upper poverty line	local curr.	..	..	..	..		..
Headcount index	% of pop.	..	..	..	28	19	..
Lower poverty line	local curr.	..	..	..	..	..	..
Headcount index	% of pop.	..	..	..	..	..	..
GNP per capita	US$	110	170	170	310	390	..

SHORT TERM INCOME INDICATORS

Indicator	Unit	1970-75	1980-85	1987-92	South Asia	Low-income	Next
Unskilled urban wages	local curr.	..	..	..	..	..	..
Unskilled rural wages	"	..	..	..	..	..	..
Rural terms of trade	"	..	..	..	..	..	..
Consumer price index	1987=100	36	76	174	..	..	..
Lower income	"	..	..	..	..	..	..
Food[a]	"	24	73	151	..	..	..
Urban	"	..	..	..	..	..	..
Rural	"	..	..	..	..	..	..

SOCIAL INDICATORS

Indicator	Unit	1970-75	1980-85	1987-92	South Asia	Low-income	Next
Public expenditure on basic social services	% of GDP	..	3.1	..	..	..	..
Gross enrollment ratios							
Primary	% school age pop.	51	82	82	103	103	..
Male	"	86	110	108	117	113	..
Female	"	16	51	54	88	96	..
Mortality							
Infant mortality	per thou. live births	153.0	139.0	99.0	85.0	73.0	45.0
Under 5 mortality	"	..	..	142.3	116.0	108.0	59.0
Immunization							
Measles	% age group	..	34.0	63.0	56.6	72.7	..
DPT	"	..	32.0	74.0	75.0	80.6	..
Child malnutrition (under-5)	"	29.7	..	69.6	60.9	38.3	..
Life expectancy							
Total	years	43	48	54	60	62	68
Female advantage	"	-1.5	-1.5	-1.0	1.0	2.4	6.4
Total fertility rate	births per woman	6.5	6.3	5.5	4.0	3.4	3.1
Maternal mortality rate	per 100,000 live births	..	..	..	..	..	..

Supplementary Poverty Indicators

Indicator	Unit	1970-75	1980-85	1987-92	South Asia	Low-income	Next
Expenditures on social security	% of total gov't exp.	0.6	0.7	0.0	..	..	..
Social security coverage	% econ. active pop.	..	..	..	..	..	..
Access to safe water: total	% of pop.	8.0	28.0	36.0	71.9	68.4	..
Urban	"	85.0	70.0	66.0	74.2	78.9	..
Rural	"	5.0	25.0	33.0	70.0	60.3	..
Access to health care	"	..	10.0	..	..	..	..

Population growth rate
(annual average, percent)

Nepal
Low-income

GNP per capita growth rate
(annual average, percent)

Development diamond[b]

Life expectancy

GNP per capita

Gross primary enrollment

Access to safe water

Nepal
Low-income

a. See the technical notes, p.389.   b. The development diamond, based on four key indicators, shows the average level of development in the country compared with its income group. See the introduction.

Nepal

Indicator	Unit of measure	Latest single year 1970-75	Latest single year 1980-85	Most recent estimate 1987-92	Same region/income group South Asia	Same region/income group Low-income	Next higher income group
Resources and Expenditures							
HUMAN RESOURCES							
Population (mre=1992)	thousands	12,841	16,682	19,892	1,177,918	3,194,535	942,547
Age dependency ratio	ratio	0.86	0.83	0.84	0.73	0.67	0.66
Urban	% of pop.	5.0	8.5	12.0	25.4	26.7	57.0
Population growth rate	annual %	2.6	2.6	2.5	2.1	1.8	1.4
Urban	"	7.1	7.4	7.3	3.4	3.4	4.8
Labor force (15-64)	thousands	5,588	6,870	8,098	428,847	1,478,954	..
Agriculture	% of labor force	93	93	..	..	..	..
Industry	"	1	1	..	..	..	..
Female	"	35	34	33	22	33	36
Females per 100 males							
Urban	number	79	86	..	..	..	..
Rural	"	101	99	..	..	..	..
NATURAL RESOURCES							
Area	thou. sq. km	140.80	140.80	140.80	5,133.49	38,401.06	40,697.37
Density	pop. per sq. km	91.2	118.5	137.8	224.8	81.7	22.8
Agricultural land	% of land area	30.2	32.6	34.1	58.9	50.9	..
Change in agricultural land	annual %	0.3	1.3	0.1	-0.2	0.0	..
Agricultural land under irrigation	%	5.6	17.1	22.5	29.0	18.2	..
Forests and woodland	thou. sq. km	25	25	25	..	..	..
Deforestation (net)	annual %	..	..	1.1	..	..	..
INCOME							
Household income							
Share of top 20% of households	% of income	..	40	..	41	42	..
Share of bottom 40% of households	"	..	22	..	21	19	..
Share of bottom 20% of households	"	..	9	..	9	8	..
EXPENDITURE							
Food	% of GDP	..	52.0	..	..	..	..
Staples	"	..	..	..	..	..	..
Meat, fish, milk, cheese, eggs	"	..	..	..	..	..	..
Cereal imports	thou. metric tonnes	18	10	15	7,721	46,537	74,924
Food aid in cereals	"	6	9	8	2,558	9,008	4,054
Food production per capita	1987 = 100	111	104	102	116	123	..
Fertilizer consumption	kg/ha	3.0	9.7	15.5	71.5	61.9	..
Share of agriculture in GDP	% of GDP	69.0	53.9	48.7	28.7	29.6	..
Housing	% of GDP	..	12.8	..	..	..	..
Average household size	persons per household	6.0	..	..	..	..	..
Urban	"	..	..	..	..	..	..
Fixed investment: housing	% of GDP	..	..	..	..	..	..
Fuel and power	% of GDP	..	5.7	..	..	..	..
Energy consumption per capita	kg of oil equiv.	9	14	20	209	335	1,882
Households with electricity							
Urban	% of households	..	..	..	..	..	..
Rural	"	..	..	..	..	..	..
Transport and communication	% of GDP	..	1.1	..	..	..	..
Fixed investment: transport equipment	"	..	..	..	..	..	..
Total road length	thou. km	3	6	7	..	..	..
INVESTMENT IN HUMAN CAPITAL							
Health							
Population per physician	persons	51,400	30,221	16,829	2,459	..	..
Population per nurse	"	17,699	4,678	2,755	..	..	..
Population per hospital bed	"	7,100	5,720	4,010	1,652	1,050	516
Oral rehydration therapy (under-5)	% of cases	..	..	14	18	39	..
Education							
Gross enrollment ratio							
Secondary	% of school-age pop.	13	26	30	40	41	..
Female	"	4	12	17	29	35	..
Pupil-teacher ratio: primary	pupils per teacher	29	35	39	59	37	26
Pupil-teacher ratio: secondary	"	21	..	..	23	19	..
Pupils reaching grade 4	% of cohort	..	..	..	..	..	..
Repeater rate: primary	% of total enroll	..	..	21	..	..	..
Illiteracy	% of pop. (age 15+)	81	78	74	54	39	..
Female	% of fem. (age 15+)	..	89	87	68	52	..
Newspaper circulation	per thou. pop.	7	7	8	..	..	100

World Bank International Economics Department, April 1994

Netherlands

Indicator	Unit of measure	Latest single year		Most recent estimate 1987-92	Same region/income group High-income
		1970-75	1980-85		

Priority Poverty Indicators

POVERTY

Indicator	Unit of measure	1970-75	1980-85	1987-92	High-income
Upper poverty line	local curr.	..	..	..	..
Headcount index	% of pop.	..	..	..	..
Lower poverty line	local curr.	..	..	..	..
Headcount index	% of pop.	..	..	..	..
GNP per capita	US$	6,100	9,560	20,480	21,960

SHORT TERM INCOME INDICATORS

Indicator	Unit of measure	1970-75	1980-85	1987-92	High-income
Unskilled urban wages	local curr.	..	..	..	..
Unskilled rural wages	"	..	..	..	..
Rural terms of trade	"	..	..	..	..
Consumer price index	1987=100	61	101	112	..
Lower income	"	..	..	..	..
Food[a]	"	..	102	79	..
Urban	"	..	..	..	..
Rural	"	..	..	..	..

SOCIAL INDICATORS

Indicator	Unit of measure	1970-75	1980-85	1987-92	High-income
Public expenditure on basic social services	% of GDP	..	..	..	..
Gross enrollment ratios					
Primary	% school age pop.	98	114	102	103
Male	"	98	113	100	103
Female	"	99	115	103	103
Mortality					
Infant mortality	per thou. live births	10.6	8.0	6.3	7.0
Under 5 mortality	"	..	..	8.2	10.0
Immunization					
Measles	% age group	..	80.0	94.0	82.4
DPT	"	..	96.0	97.0	90.1
Child malnutrition (under-5)	"	..	..	..	..
Life expectancy					
Total	years	74	76	77	77
Female advantage	"	6.2	6.7	6.3	6.4
Total fertility rate	births per woman	1.7	1.5	1.6	1.7
Maternal mortality rate	per 100,000 live births	..	5	..	..

Supplementary Poverty Indicators

Indicator	Unit of measure	1970-75	1980-85	1987-92	High-income
Expenditures on social security	% of total gov't exp.	34.3	34.9	34.4	..
Social security coverage	% econ. active pop.	..	..	..	..
Access to safe water: total	% of pop.	..	100.0	..	..
Urban	"	..	100.0	..	..
Rural	"	..	99.0	..	..
Access to health care	"	..	100.0	100.0	..

Population growth rate
(annual average, percent)

- Netherlands
- High-income

GNP per capita growth rate
(annual average, percent)

Development diamond[b]

- Netherlands
- High-income

a. See the technical notes, p.389.   b. The development diamond, based on four key indicators, shows the average level of development in the country compared with its income group. See the introduction.

Netherlands

Indicator	Unit of measure	Latest single year		Most recent estimate 1987-92	Same region/income group High-income
		1970-75	1980-85		

Resources and Expenditures

HUMAN RESOURCES

Indicator	Unit of measure	1970-75	1980-85	1987-92	High-income
Population (mre=1992)	thousands	13,666	14,492	15,178	828,221
Age dependency ratio	ratio	0.57	0.45	0.46	0.50
Urban	% of pop.	88.4	88.5	88.7	78.1
Population growth rate	annual %	0.9	0.5	0.7	0.7
Urban	"	1.4	0.5	0.8	0.9
Labor force (15-64)	thousands	5,111	5,861	6,209	390,033
Agriculture	% of labor force	6	6	..	..
Industry	"	35	31	..	..
Female	"	29	31	31	38
Females per 100 males					
Urban	number	100	99	..	..
Rural	"	94	94	..	..

NATURAL RESOURCES

Indicator	Unit of measure	1970-75	1980-85	1987-92	High-income
Area	thou. sq. km	36.95	37.33	37.33	31,709.00
Density	pop. per sq. km	369.9	388.2	403.7	24.5
Agricultural land	% of land area	61.6	59.5	58.7	42.7
Change in agricultural land	annual %	-0.6	0.2	-0.8	-0.2
Agricultural land under irrigation	%	20.7	26.3	28.0	16.1
Forests and woodland	thou. sq. km	3	3	3	..
Deforestation (net)	annual %	..	..	0.0	..

INCOME

Indicator	Unit of measure	1970-75	1980-85	1987-92	High-income
Household income					
Share of top 20% of households	% of income	37	38	..	..
Share of bottom 40% of households	"	22	20	..	..
Share of bottom 20% of households	"	9	7	..	..

EXPENDITURE

Indicator	Unit of measure	1970-75	1980-85	1987-92	High-income
Food	% of GDP	10.6	9.2	..	..
Staples	"	1.8	1.6	..	..
Meat, fish, milk, cheese, eggs	"	5.0	4.0	..	..
Cereal imports	thou. metric tonnes	8,838	5,252	5,052	70,626
Food aid in cereals	"	..	..		2
Food production per capita	1987 = 100	89	104	111	101
Fertilizer consumption	kg/ha	304.9	347.1	265.7	162.1
Share of agriculture in GDP	% of GDP	..	..	3.9	2.4
Housing	% of GDP	7.9	12.1	..	..
Average household size	persons per household	3.2	..	..	..
Urban	"	..	..	..	..
Fixed investment: housing	% of GDP	4.8	3.1	..	..
Fuel and power	% of GDP	2.4	4.0	..	..
Energy consumption per capita	kg of oil equiv.	4,379	4,252	4,560	5,101
Households with electricity					
Urban	% of households	..	..	..	..
Rural	"	..	..	..	..
Transport and communication	% of GDP	6.1	6.6	..	..
Fixed investment: transport equipment	"	2.6	2.9	..	..
Total road length	thou. km	86	110	105	..

INVESTMENT IN HUMAN CAPITAL

Indicator	Unit of measure	1970-75	1980-85	1987-92	High-income
Health					
Population per physician	persons	800	450	412	..
Population per nurse	"	303	168	..	..
Population per hospital bed	"	94	80	170	144
Oral rehydration therapy (under-5)	% of cases	..	..	..	..
Education					
Gross enrollment ratio					
Secondary	% of school-age pop.	88	104	97	92
Female		84	102	96	94
Pupil-teacher ratio: primary	pupils per teacher	28	17	17	18
Pupil-teacher ratio: secondary	"	16	15	..	..
Pupils reaching grade 4	% of cohort	98	96	..	..
Repeater rate: primary	% of total enroll	2	2	..	..
Illiteracy	% of pop. (age 15+)	..	..	†	..
Female	% of fem. (age 15+)	..	..	†	..
Newspaper circulation	per thou. pop.	308	320	311	..

World Bank International Economics Department, April 1994

New Caledonia

| Indicator | Unit of measure | Latest single year | | Most recent estimate 1987-92 | Same region/income group | | Next higher income group |
		1970-75	1980-85		East Asia	Upper-middle-income	
Priority Poverty Indicators							
POVERTY							
Upper poverty line	local curr.	..	..	..	..	..	..
Headcount index	% of pop.	..	..	..	12	..	..
Lower poverty line	local curr.	..	..	..	..	..	..
Headcount index	% of pop.	..	..	..	9	..	..
GNP per capita	US$	..	..	..	760	3,870	21,960
SHORT TERM INCOME INDICATORS							
Unskilled urban wages	local curr.	..	..	..	..	..	..
Unskilled rural wages	"	..	..	..	..	..	..
Rural terms of trade	"	..	..	..	..	..	..
Consumer price index	1987=100	..	98	100	..	..	..
Lower income	"	..	..	..	..	..	..
Food[a]	"	26	102	112	..	..	..
Urban	"	..	..	..	..	..	..
Rural	"	..	..	..	..	..	..
SOCIAL INDICATORS							
Public expenditure on basic social services	% of GDP	..	..	..	..	..	..
Gross enrollment ratios							
Primary	% school age pop.	..	..	..	121	107	103
Male	"	..	..	..	126	..	103
Female	"	..	..	..	117	..	103
Mortality							
Infant mortality	per thou. live births	..	..	17.0	39.0	40.0	7.0
Under 5 mortality	"	..	..	20.5	49.0	51.0	10.0
Immunization							
Measles	% age group	..	15.0	..	88.4	82.0	82.4
DPT	"	..	76.0	..	89.5	73.8	90.1
Child malnutrition (under-5)	"	..	..	..	24.7	..	..
Life expectancy							
Total	years	..	67	70	68	69	77
Female advantage	"	..	3.9	3.0	3.6	6.3	6.4
Total fertility rate	births per woman	4.3	3.6	2.7	2.4	2.9	1.7
Maternal mortality rate	per 100,000 live births	..	..	..	114	..	..
Supplementary Poverty Indicators							
Expenditures on social security	% of total gov't exp.	..	..	..	..	..	..
Social security coverage	% econ. active pop.	..	..	..	..	..	..
Access to safe water: total	% of pop.	..	..	..	72.0	85.6	..
Urban	"	..	..	..	83.4	94.3	..
Rural	"	..	..	..	60.2	73.0	..
Access to health care	"	..	..	..	..	..	..

Population growth rate
(annual average, percent)

New Caledonia
Upper-middle-income

GNP per capita growth rate
(annual average, percent)

Development diamond[b]

Life expectancy

GNP per capita — Gross primary enrollment

Access to safe water

New Caledonia
Upper-middle-income

a. See the technical notes, p.389.   b. The development diamond, based on four key indicators, shows the average level of development in the country compared with its income group. See the introduction.

250

New Caledonia

Indicator	Unit of measure	Latest single year 1970-75	Latest single year 1980-85	Most recent estimate 1987-92	Same region/income group East Asia	Same region/income group Upper-middle-income	Next higher income group
Resources and Expenditures							
HUMAN RESOURCES							
Population (mre=1992)	thousands	132	152	175	1,688,909	477,960	828,221
Age dependency ratio	ratio	..	0.70	0.61	0.55	0.64	0.50
Urban	% of pop.	59.1	75.5	80.5	29.4	71.7	78.1
Population growth rate	annual %	2.3	2.7	2.3	1.4	1.6	0.7
Urban	"	5.7	4.5	3.7	2.9	2.5	0.9
Labor force (15-64)	thousands	..	..	..	928,465	181,414	390,033
Agriculture	% of labor force	..	..	..	..	..	..
Industry	"	..	..	..	..	..	..
Female	"	..	..	..	41	29	38
Females per 100 males							
Urban	number	..	..	..	..	..	..
Rural	"	..	..	..	..	..	..
NATURAL RESOURCES							
Area	thou. sq. km	18.58	18.58	18.58	16,367.18	21,836.02	31,709.00
Density	pop. per sq. km	7.1	8.2	9.2	101.8	21.5	24.5
Agricultural land	% of land area	14.4	16.1	16.5	44.5	41.7	42.7
Change in agricultural land	annual %	0.0	1.0	0.0	0.1	0.3	-0.2
Agricultural land under irrigation	%	..	..	..	14.5	9.3	16.1
Forests and woodland	thou. sq. km	7	7	7	..	..	..
Deforestation (net)	annual %	..	..	..	..	..	..
INCOME							
Household income							
Share of top 20% of households	% of income	..	..	..	42	..	..
Share of bottom 40% of households	"	..	..	..	18	..	..
Share of bottom 20% of households	"	..	..	..	7	..	..
EXPENDITURE							
Food	% of GDP	..	..	..	..	..	..
Staples	"	..	..	..	..	..	..
Meat, fish, milk, cheese, eggs	"	..	..	..	..	..	..
Cereal imports	thou. metric tonnes	17	26	30	33,591	49,174	70,626
Food aid in cereals	"	..	..	..	581	282	2
Food production per capita	1987 = 100	107	108	92	133	109	101
Fertilizer consumption	kg/ha	2.4	1.4	4.0	75.1	68.8	162.1
Share of agriculture in GDP	% of GDP	..	..	..	21.5	8.1	2.4
Housing	% of GDP	..	..	..	..	..	..
Average household size	persons per household	..	..	..	..	..	..
Urban	"	..	..	..	..	..	..
Fixed investment: housing	% of GDP	..	..	..	..	..	..
Fuel and power	% of GDP	..	..	..	..	..	..
Energy consumption per capita	kg of oil equiv.	6,909	3,757	3,377	593	1,649	5,101
Households with electricity							
Urban	% of households	..	..	..	..	..	..
Rural	"	..	..	..	..	..	..
Transport and communication	% of GDP	..	..	..	..	..	..
Fixed investment: transport equipment	"	..	..	..	..	..	..
Total road length	thou. km	5	6	..	..	..	..
INVESTMENT IN HUMAN CAPITAL							
Health							
Population per physician	persons	..	1,526	..	..	..	..
Population per nurse	"	..	414	..	..	..	..
Population per hospital bed	"	..	..	..	553	385	144
Oral rehydration therapy (under-5)	% of cases	..	..	..	51	54	..
Education							
Gross enrollment ratio							
Secondary	% of school-age pop.	..	..	..	53	53	92
Female	"	..	..	..	47	..	94
Pupil-teacher ratio: primary	pupils per teacher	17	20	20	23	25	18
Pupil-teacher ratio: secondary	"	15	14	..	16	..	..
Pupils reaching grade 4	% of cohort	82	88	90	89	71	..
Repeater rate: primary	% of total enroll	10	17	17	6	11	..
Illiteracy	% of pop. (age 15+)	..	..	..	24	14	..
Female	% of fem. (age 15+)	..	..	..	34	17	..
Newspaper circulation	per thou. pop.	136	88	113	..	117	..

World Bank International Economics Department, April 1994

251

New Zealand

Indicator	Unit of measure	Latest single year 1970-75	Latest single year 1980-85	Most recent estimate 1987-92	Same region/income group High-income
Priority Poverty Indicators					
POVERTY					
Upper poverty line	local curr.	..	..	..	..
Headcount index	% of pop.	..	..	..	..
Lower poverty line	local curr.	..	..	..	..
Headcount index	% of pop.	..	..	..	..
GNP per capita	US$	4,620	6,940	12,300	21,960
SHORT TERM INCOME INDICATORS					
Unskilled urban wages	local curr.	..	..	..	..
Unskilled rural wages	"	..	..	..	..
Rural terms of trade	"	..	..	..	..
Consumer price index	1987=100	22	76	124	..
Lower income	"	..	..	..	..
Food[a]	"	14	79	125	..
Urban	"	..	..	..	..
Rural	"	..	..	..	..
SOCIAL INDICATORS					
Public expenditure on basic social services	% of GDP	..	..	..	..
Gross enrollment ratios					
Primary	% school age pop.	106	107	104	103
Male	"	107	108	104	103
Female	"	106	106	103	103
Mortality					
Infant mortality	per thou. live births	15.9	10.8	7.3	7.0
Under 5 mortality	"	..	..	9.3	10.0
Immunization					
Measles	% age group	..	71.0	82.0	82.4
DPT	"	..	72.0	81.0	90.1
Child malnutrition (under-5)	"	..	..	..	..
Life expectancy					
Total	years	72	74	76	77
Female advantage	"	6.1	6.2	6.1	6.4
Total fertility rate	births per woman	2.3	1.9	2.1	1.7
Maternal mortality rate	per 100,000 live births	..	..	..	..
Supplementary Poverty Indicators					
Expenditures on social security	% of total gov't exp.	23.5	29.7	34.0	..
Social security coverage	% econ. active pop.	..	..	..	..
Access to safe water: total	% of pop.	..	..	97.0	..
Urban	"	..	..	100.0	..
Rural	"	..	..	82.0	..
Access to health care	"	..	100.0	..	..

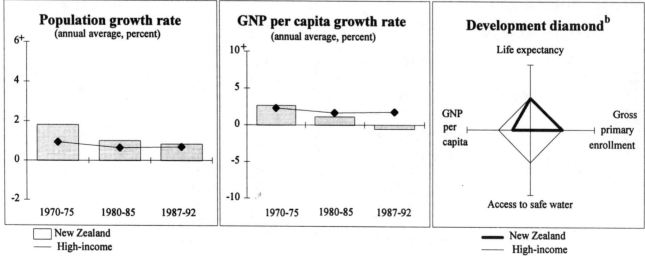

Population growth rate (annual average, percent)

GNP per capita growth rate (annual average, percent)

Development diamond[b]
Life expectancy — GNP per capita — Gross primary enrollment — Access to safe water

— New Zealand
— High-income

a. See the technical notes, p.389.   b. The development diamond, based on four key indicators, shows the average level of development in the country compared with its income group. See the introduction.

New Zealand

Indicator	Unit of measure	Latest single year 1970-75	Latest single year 1980-85	Most recent estimate 1987-92	Same region/income group High-income
Resources and Expenditures					
HUMAN RESOURCES					
Population (mre=1992)	thousands	3,087	3,272	3,443	828,221
Age dependency ratio	ratio	0.63	0.53	0.52	0.50
Urban	% of pop.	82.8	83.7	84.2	78.1
Population growth rate	annual %	2.1	0.6	1.1	0.7
Urban	"	2.5	0.7	1.1	0.9
Labor force (15-64)	thousands	1,245	1,459	1,606	390,033
Agriculture	% of labor force	0	0	..	..
Industry	"	0	0	..	..
Female	"	..	..	..	38
Females per 100 males					
Urban	number	..	102	..	..
Rural	"	..	85	..	..
NATURAL RESOURCES					
Area	thou. sq. km	270.99	270.99	270.99	31,709.00
Density	pop. per sq. km	11.4	12.1	12.6	24.5
Agricultural land	% of land area	52.0	53.7	52.7	42.7
Change in agricultural land	annual %	3.4	-0.6	1.6	-0.2
Agricultural land under irrigation	%	1.1	1.8	2.0	16.1
Forests and woodland	thou. sq. km	71	72	74	..
Deforestation (net)	annual %	..	..	..	..
INCOME					
Household income					
Share of top 20% of households	% of income	41	45	..	..
Share of bottom 40% of households	"	18	16	..	..
Share of bottom 20% of households	"	6	5	..	..
EXPENDITURE					
Food	% of GDP	..	7.8	..	..
Staples	"	..	1.5	..	..
Meat, fish, milk, cheese, eggs	"	..	3.5	..	..
Cereal imports	thou. metric tonnes	188	77	159	70,626
Food aid in cereals	"	..	..	..	2
Food production per capita	1987 = 100	93	112	104	101
Fertilizer consumption	kg/ha	37.0	29.7	27.1	162.1
Share of agriculture in GDP	% of GDP	10.4	8.8	8.6	2.4
Housing	% of GDP	..	9.0	..	..
Average household size	persons per household	3.6	3.0	..	..
Urban	"	..	..	..	..
Fixed investment: housing	% of GDP	6.9	3.6	..	..
Fuel and power	% of GDP	..	1.2	..	..
Energy consumption per capita	kg of oil equiv.	2,743	3,421	4,284	5,101
Households with electricity					
Urban	% of households	..	..	..	..
Rural	"	..	..	..	..
Transport and communication	% of GDP	..	12.3	..	..
Fixed investment: transport equipment	"	5.0	4.6	..	..
Total road length	thou. km	93	93	93	..
INVESTMENT IN HUMAN CAPITAL					
Health					
Population per physician	persons	873	611	..	..
Population per nurse	"	152	145	..	..
Population per hospital bed	"	99	..	149	144
Oral rehydration therapy (under-5)	% of cases	..	..	..	..
Education					
Gross enrollment ratio					
Secondary	% of school-age pop.	81	85	84	92
Female	"	81	87	85	94
Pupil-teacher ratio: primary	pupils per teacher	18	20	19	18
Pupil-teacher ratio: secondary	"	29	19	17	..
Pupils reaching grade 4	% of cohort	..	97	98	..
Repeater rate: primary	% of total enroll	0	3	3	..
Illiteracy	% of pop. (age 15+)	..	..	†	..
Female	% of fem. (age 15+)	..	..	†	..
Newspaper circulation	per thou. pop.	356	317	327	..

World Bank International Economics Department, April 1994

253

Nicaragua

Indicator	Unit of measure	Latest single year 1970-75	Latest single year 1980-85	Most recent estimate 1987-92	Same region/income group Latin America Caribbean	Same region/income group Low-income	Next higher income group
Priority Poverty Indicators							
POVERTY							
Upper poverty line	local curr.	..	..	..	..		..
Headcount index	% of pop.	..	..	..	..	19	..
Lower poverty line	local curr.	..	..	..	..		..
Headcount index	% of pop.	..	..	..	..		..
GNP per capita	US$	620	790	340	2,690	390	..
SHORT TERM INCOME INDICATORS							
Unskilled urban wages	local curr.	..	..	..	..		..
Unskilled rural wages	"	..	..	..	..		..
Rural terms of trade	"	..	..	..	..		..
Consumer price index	1987=100	0	1	1,301,237,000	..		..
Lower income	"	..	..		..		..
Food[a]	"	..	1	2,851	..		..
Urban	"	..	..	..	..		..
Rural	"	..	..	..	..		..
SOCIAL INDICATORS							
Public expenditure on basic social services	% of GDP	..	..	..	..		..
Gross enrollment ratios							
Primary	% school age pop.	82	101	101	106	103	..
Male	"	80	96	98	..	113	..
Female	"	85	107	104	..	96	..
Mortality							
Infant mortality	per thou. live births	100.0	68.0	56.0	44.0	73.0	45.0
Under 5 mortality	"	..	..	71.8	56.0	108.0	59.0
Immunization							
Measles	% age group	..	30.0	54.0	78.9	72.7	..
DPT	"	..	32.0	71.0	73.8	80.6	..
Child malnutrition (under-5)	"	..	22.1	10.5	10.5	38.3	..
Life expectancy							
Total	years	55	59	67	68	62	68
Female advantage	"	3.1	7.2	3.7	5.6	2.4	6.4
Total fertility rate	births per woman	6.8	5.7	4.4	3.0	3.4	3.1
Maternal mortality rate	per 100,000 live births	..	65	300	..	..	..
Supplementary Poverty Indicators							
Expenditures on social security	% of total gov't exp.	..	..	..	..	..	..
Social security coverage	% econ. active pop.	..	..	31.5	..	..	..
Access to safe water: total	% of pop.	56.0	48.0	53.0	80.3	68.4	..
Urban	"	100.0	76.0	76.0	91.0	78.9	..
Rural	"	14.0	11.0	18.0	64.3	60.3	..
Access to health care	"	..	..	..	..	..	..

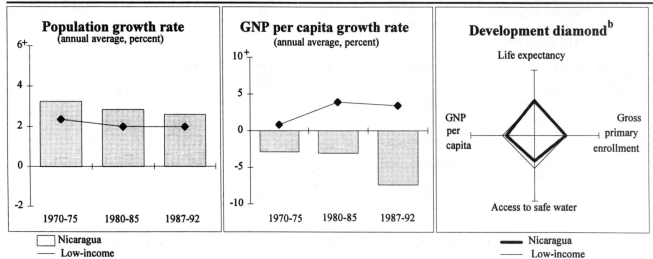

a. See the technical notes, p.389.   b. The development diamond, based on four key indicators, shows the average level of development in the country compared with its income group. See the introduction.

Nicaragua

Indicator	Unit of measure	Latest single year 1970-75	Latest single year 1980-85	Most recent estimate 1987-92	Same region/income group Latin America Caribbean	Low-income	Next higher income group
Resources and Expenditures							
HUMAN RESOURCES							
Population (mre=1992)	thousands	2,426	3,229	3,875	453,294	3,194,535	942,547
Age dependency ratio	ratio	1.01	0.97	0.94	0.67	0.67	0.66
Urban	% of pop.	50.3	56.6	61.0	72.9	26.7	57.0
Population growth rate	annual %	3.1	2.7	2.7	1.7	1.8	1.4
Urban	"	4.4	3.9	3.7	2.6	3.4	4.8
Labor force (15-64)	thousands	722	993	1,308	166,091	1,478,954	..
Agriculture	% of labor force	49	47	..	..	..	..
Industry	"	16	16	..	..	..	..
Female	"	21	23	26	27	33	36
Females per 100 males							
Urban	number	128	128	..	..	..	..
Rural	"	94	91	..	..	..	..
NATURAL RESOURCES							
Area	thou. sq. km	130.00	130.00	130.00	20,507.48	38,401.06	40,697.37
Density	pop. per sq. km	18.7	24.8	29.0	21.7	81.7	22.8
Agricultural land	% of land area	49.1	54.1	56.6	40.2	50.9	..
Change in agricultural land	annual %	0.9	0.8	0.8	0.5	0.0	..
Agricultural land under irrigation	%	1.2	1.3	1.3	3.2	18.2	..
Forests and woodland	thou. sq. km	51	39	33	..	..	..
Deforestation (net)	annual %	..	..	2.0	..	..	..
INCOME							
Household income							
Share of top 20% of households	% of income	65	..	..	..	42	..
Share of bottom 40% of households	"	9	..	..	..	19	..
Share of bottom 20% of households	"	3	..	..	..	8	..
EXPENDITURE							
Food	% of GDP	..	..	..	..	..	..
Staples	"	..	..	..	..	..	..
Meat, fish, milk, cheese, eggs	"	..	..	..	..	..	..
Cereal imports	thou. metric tonnes	58	103	136	25,032	46,537	74,924
Food aid in cereals	"	3	43	128	1,779	9,008	4,054
Food production per capita	1987 = 100	114	70	60	104	123	..
Fertilizer consumption	kg/ha	3.3	9.8	5.2	15.5	61.9	..
Share of agriculture in GDP	% of GDP	22.4	23.7	30.4	8.9	29.6	..
Housing	% of GDP	..	..	..	..	..	..
Average household size	persons per household	..	..	..	..	..	..
Urban	"	..	..	..	..	..	..
Fixed investment: housing	% of GDP	..	..	..	..	..	..
Fuel and power	% of GDP	..	..	..	..	..	..
Energy consumption per capita	kg of oil equiv.	291	271	253	912	335	1,882
Households with electricity							
Urban	% of households	..	..	..	..	..	..
Rural	"	..	..	..	..	..	..
Transport and communication	% of GDP	..	..	..	..	..	..
Fixed investment: transport equipment	"	..	..	..	..	..	..
Total road length	thou. km	18	15	..	..	..	..
INVESTMENT IN HUMAN CAPITAL							
Health							
Population per physician	persons	2,114	1,489	1,492	..	..	..
Population per nurse	"	..	531	..	..	..	..
Population per hospital bed	"	403	394	538	508	1,050	516
Oral rehydration therapy (under-5)	% of cases	..	..	40	62	39	..
Education							
Gross enrollment ratio							
Secondary	% of school-age pop.	24	39	44	47	41	..
Female	"	24	55	46	..	35	..
Pupil-teacher ratio: primary	pupils per teacher	39	33	36	25	37	26
Pupil-teacher ratio: secondary	"	41	30	43	..	19	..
Pupils reaching grade 4	% of cohort	48	63	56	..	..	..
Repeater rate: primary	% of total enroll	14	15	17	14	..	..
Illiteracy	% of pop. (age 15+)	43	13	..	15	39	..
Female	% of fem. (age 15+)	..	..	..	17	52	..
Newspaper circulation	per thou. pop.	38	47	68	99	..	100

World Bank International Economics Department, April 1994

255

Niger

Indicator	Unit of measure	Latest single year 1970-75	Latest single year 1980-85	Most recent estimate 1987-92	Same region/income group Sub-Saharan Africa	Same region/income group Low-income	Next higher income group
Priority Poverty Indicators							
POVERTY							
Upper poverty line	local curr.	..	..	..	..	..	..
Headcount index	% of pop.	..	..	..	..	19	..
Lower poverty line	local curr.	..	..	..	..	..	..
Headcount index	% of pop.	..	..	..	..	..	..
GNP per capita	US$	210	230	280	520	390	..
SHORT TERM INCOME INDICATORS							
Unskilled urban wages	local curr.	..	..	..	..	..	..
Unskilled rural wages	"	..	..	..	..	..	..
Rural terms of trade	"	..	..	..	..	..	..
Consumer price index	1987=100	39	111	84	..	..	..
Lower income	"	..	..	..	..	..	..
Food[a]	"	..	120	81	..	..	..
Urban	"	..	..	..	..	..	..
Rural	"	..	..	..	..	..	..
SOCIAL INDICATORS							
Public expenditure on basic social services	% of GDP	..	..	..	..	..	..
Gross enrollment ratios							
Primary	% school age pop.	20	26	29	66	103	..
Male	"	25	33	37	79	113	..
Female	"	14	18	21	62	96	..
Mortality							
Infant mortality	per thou. live births	166.0	146.0	123.1	99.0	73.0	45.0
Under 5 mortality	"	..	..	207.1	169.0	108.0	59.0
Immunization							
Measles	% age group	..	16.0	24.0	54.0	72.7	..
DPT	"	..	5.0	18.0	54.6	80.6	..
Child malnutrition (under-5)	"	..	49.4	..	28.4	38.3	..
Life expectancy							
Total	years	39	42	46	52	62	68
Female advantage	"	3.1	3.2	4.3	3.4	2.4	6.4
Total fertility rate	births per woman	7.2	7.5	7.4	6.1	3.4	3.1
Maternal mortality rate	per 100,000 live births	..	420	..	..	..	..
Supplementary Poverty Indicators							
Expenditures on social security	% of total gov't exp.	..	..	..	..	..	..
Social security coverage	% econ. active pop.	..	..	..	..	..	..
Access to safe water: total	% of pop.	27.0	46.0	59.0	41.1	68.4	..
Urban	"	36.0	35.0	100.0	77.8	78.9	..
Rural	"	26.0	49.0	52.0	27.3	60.3	..
Access to health care	"	..	48.0	..	..	..	..

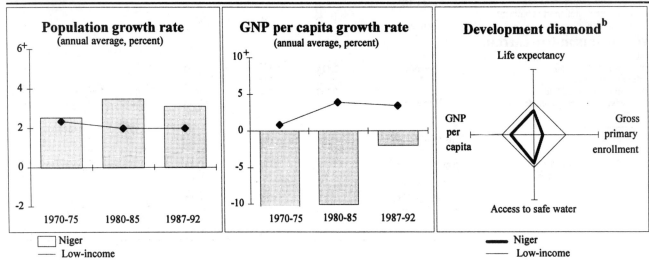

a. See the technical notes, p.389.   b. The development diamond, based on four key indicators, shows the average level of development in the country compared with its income group. See the introduction.

256

Niger

| Indicator | Unit of measure | Latest single year | | Most recent estimate 1987-92 | Same region/income group | | Next higher income group |
		1970-75	1980-85		Sub-Saharan Africa	Low-income	
Resources and Expenditures							
HUMAN RESOURCES							
Population (mre=1992)	thousands	4,704	6,563	8,167	546,390	3,194,535	942,547
Age dependency ratio	ratio	0.96	0.95	1.01	0.95	0.67	0.66
Urban	% of pop.	10.6	16.2	20.9	29.5	26.7	57.0
Population growth rate	annual %	2.8	3.3	3.2	2.9	1.8	1.4
Urban	"	6.9	7.1	6.7	5.1	3.4	4.8
Labor force (15-64)	thousands	2,590	3,203	3,817	224,025	1,478,954	..
Agriculture	% of labor force	93	91	..	..	..	..
Industry	"	1	2	..	..	..	..
Female	"	49	47	46	37	33	36
Females per 100 males							
Urban	number	..	..	..	..	..	..
Rural	"	..	..	..	..	..	..
NATURAL RESOURCES							
Area	thou. sq. km	1,267.00	1,267.00	1,267.00	24,274.03	38,401.06	40,697.37
Density	pop. per sq. km	3.7	5.2	6.2	21.9	81.7	22.8
Agricultural land	% of land area	10.1	9.9	9.9	52.7	50.9	..
Change in agricultural land	annual %	0.0	-1.7	-0.2	0.1	0.0	..
Agricultural land under irrigation	%	0.1	0.2	0.3	0.8	18.2	..
Forests and woodland	thou. sq. km	29	23	19	..	..	..
Deforestation (net)	annual %	..	..	0.0	..	..	..
INCOME							
Household income							
Share of top 20% of households	% of income	..	..	..	..	42	..
Share of bottom 40% of households	"	..	..	..	..	19	..
Share of bottom 20% of households	"	..	..	..	..	8	..
EXPENDITURE							
Food	% of GDP	..	..	..	..	..	..
Staples	"	..	..	..	..	..	..
Meat, fish, milk, cheese, eggs	"	..	..	..	..	..	..
Cereal imports	thou. metric tonnes	17	300	135	20,311	46,537	74,924
Food aid in cereals	"	73	221	46	4,303	9,008	4,054
Food production per capita	1987 = 100	76	62	78	90	123	..
Fertilizer consumption	kg/ha	0.1	0.3	0.0	4.2	61.9	..
Share of agriculture in GDP	% of GDP	50.3	36.8	37.1	18.6	29.6	..
Housing	% of GDP	..	..	..	..	..	..
Average household size	persons per household	..	..	..	..	..	..
Urban	"	..	..	..	..	..	..
Fixed investment: housing	% of GDP	..	..	..	..	..	..
Fuel and power	% of GDP	..	..	..	..	..	..
Energy consumption per capita	kg of oil equiv.	25	42	39	258	335	1,882
Households with electricity							
Urban	% of households	..	..	..	..	..	..
Rural	"	..	..	..	..	..	..
Transport and communication	% of GDP	..	..	..	..	..	..
Fixed investment: transport equipment	"	..	..	..	..	..	..
Total road length	thou. km	7	18	20	..	..	..
INVESTMENT IN HUMAN CAPITAL							
Health							
Population per physician	persons	59,306	39,675	34,845	..	..	..
Population per nurse	"	5,608	458	654	..	..	..
Population per hospital bed	"	1,974	..	..	1,329	1,050	516
Oral rehydration therapy (under-5)	% of cases	..	..	54	36	39	..
Education							
Gross enrollment ratio							
Secondary	% of school-age pop.	2	5	6	18	41	..
Female	"	1	3	4	14	35	..
Pupil-teacher ratio: primary	pupils per teacher	39	37	42	39	37	26
Pupil-teacher ratio: secondary	"	24	26	29	..	19	..
Pupils reaching grade 4	% of cohort	76	83	75	..	..	..
Repeater rate: primary	% of total enroll	13	15	14	..	..	..
Illiteracy	% of pop. (age 15+)	..	79	72	51	39	..
Female	% of fem. (age 15+)	..	89	83	62	52	..
Newspaper circulation	per thou. pop.	0	1	1	14	..	100

World Bank International Economics Department, April 1994

Nigeria

Indicator	Unit of measure	Latest single year 1970-75	Latest single year 1980-85	Most recent estimate 1987-92	Same region/income group Sub-Saharan Africa	Same region/income group Low-income	Next higher income group

Priority Poverty Indicators

POVERTY

Indicator	Unit	1970-75	1980-85	1987-92	Sub-Saharan Africa	Low-income	Next higher
Upper poverty line	local curr.	..	..	..	..	..	..
Headcount index	% of pop.	..	..	..	..	19	..
Lower poverty line	local curr.	..	..	..	..	..	..
Headcount index	% of pop.	..	..	..	..	..	..
GNP per capita	US$	480	990	320	520	390	..

SHORT TERM INCOME INDICATORS

Indicator	Unit	1970-75	1980-85	1987-92	Sub-Saharan Africa	Low-income	Next higher
Unskilled urban wages	local curr.	..	..	..	..	..	..
Unskilled rural wages	"	..	..	..	..	..	..
Rural terms of trade	"	..	..	..	..	..	..
Consumer price index	1987=100	17	85	408	..	..	..
Lower income	"	..	..	..	..	..	..
Food[a]	"	..	92	65	..	..	..
Urban	"	..	..	..	..	..	..
Rural	"	..	..	..	..	..	..

SOCIAL INDICATORS

Indicator	Unit	1970-75	1980-85	1987-92	Sub-Saharan Africa	Low-income	Next higher
Public expenditure on basic social services	% of GDP	..	..	..	..	..	..
Gross enrollment ratios							
Primary	% school age pop.	51	82	71	66	103	..
Male	"	47	91	79	79	113	..
Female	"	27	73	62	62	96	..
Mortality							
Infant mortality	per thou. live births	135.0	95.7	84.0	99.0	73.0	45.0
Under 5 mortality	"	..	..	183.4	169.0	108.0	59.0
Immunization							
Measles	% age group	..	9.0	70.0	54.0	72.7	..
DPT	"	..	9.0	65.0	54.6	80.6	..
Child malnutrition (under-5)	"	23.1	..	35.7	28.4	38.3	..
Life expectancy							
Total	years	42	49	52	52	62	68
Female advantage	"	3.9	3.3	3.4	3.4	2.4	6.4
Total fertility rate	births per woman	6.9	6.9	5.9	6.1	3.4	3.1
Maternal mortality rate	per 100,000 live births	..	1500	800	..	..	..

Supplementary Poverty Indicators

Indicator	Unit	1970-75	1980-85	1987-92	Sub-Saharan Africa	Low-income	Next higher
Expenditures on social security	% of total gov't exp.	..	..	..	..	..	..
Social security coverage	% econ. active pop.	..	..	..	..	..	..
Access to safe water: total	% of pop.	..	45.0	46.0	41.1	68.4	..
Urban	"	..	100.0	100.0	77.8	78.9	..
Rural	"	..	20.0	20.0	27.3	60.3	..
Access to health care	"	..	40.0	..	..	..	..

Population growth rate (annual average, percent)

□ Nigeria
— Low-income

GNP per capita growth rate (annual average, percent)

□ Nigeria
— Low-income

Development diamond[b]

Life expectancy — Gross primary enrollment — Access to safe water — GNP per capita

— Nigeria
— Low-income

a. See the technical notes, p.389. b. The development diamond, based on four key indicators, shows the average level of development in the country compared with its income group. See the introduction.

258

Nigeria

Indicator	Unit of measure	Latest single year 1970-75	Latest single year 1980-85	Most recent estimate 1987-92	Same region/income group Sub-Saharan Africa	Same region/income group Low-income	Next higher income group
Resources and Expenditures							

HUMAN RESOURCES

Indicator	Unit of measure	1970-75	1980-85	1987-92	Sub-Saharan Africa	Low-income	Next higher income group
Population (mre=1992)	thousands	61,241	83,196	101,884	546,390	3,194,535	942,547
Age dependency ratio	ratio	1.00	0.98	0.94	0.95	0.67	0.66
Urban	% of pop.	23.4	31.1	36.8	29.5	26.7	57.0
Population growth rate	annual %	2.9	3.1	2.9	2.9	1.8	1.4
Urban	"	5.8	5.7	5.1	5.1	3.4	4.8
Labor force (15-64)	thousands	27,385	36,568	44,426	224,025	1,478,954	..
Agriculture	% of labor force	70	68	..	..	..	..
Industry	"	11	12	..	..	..	..
Female	"	37	36	34	37	33	36
Females per 100 males							
Urban	number	..	..	..	..	..	..
Rural	"	..	..	..	..	..	..

NATURAL RESOURCES

Indicator	Unit of measure	1970-75	1980-85	1987-92	Sub-Saharan Africa	Low-income	Next higher income group
Area	thou. sq. km	923.77	923.77	923.77	24,274.03	38,401.06	40,697.37
Density	pop. per sq. km	66.3	90.1	107.2	21.9	81.7	22.8
Agricultural land	% of land area	76.9	78.1	79.4	52.7	50.9	..
Change in agricultural land	annual %	0.1	0.3	0.1	0.1	0.0	..
Agricultural land under irrigation	%	1.2	1.2	1.2	0.8	18.2	..
Forests and woodland	thou. sq. km	164	134	116	..	..	..
Deforestation (net)	annual %	..	..	0.7	..	..	..

INCOME
Household income

Indicator	Unit of measure	1970-75	1980-85	1987-92	Sub-Saharan Africa	Low-income	Next higher income group
Share of top 20% of households	% of income	..	..	..	..	42	..
Share of bottom 40% of households	"	..	..	..	..	19	..
Share of bottom 20% of households	"	..	..	..	..	8	..

EXPENDITURE

Indicator	Unit of measure	1970-75	1980-85	1987-92	Sub-Saharan Africa	Low-income	Next higher income group
Food	% of GDP	..	39.6	..	..	..	..
Staples	"	..	15.1	..	..	..	..
Meat, fish, milk, cheese, eggs	"	..	12.3	..	..	..	..
Cereal imports	thou. metric tonnes	447	1,957	1,126	20,311	46,537	74,924
Food aid in cereals	"	7	0	..	4,303	9,008	4,054
Food production per capita	1987 = 100	122	102	125	90	123	..
Fertilizer consumption	kg/ha	0.8	4.1	5.9	4.2	61.9	..
Share of agriculture in GDP	% of GDP	31.2	36.8	35.4	18.6	29.6	..
Housing	% of GDP	..	3.4	..	..	..	..
Average household size	persons per household	..	..	..	..	..	..
Urban	"	4.7	..	..	..	..	..
Fixed investment: housing	% of GDP	2.2	0.6	..	..	..	..
Fuel and power	% of GDP	..	1.1	..	..	..	..
Energy consumption per capita	kg of oil equiv.	72	148	128	258	335	1,882
Households with electricity							
Urban	% of households	..	..	..	..	..	..
Rural	"	..	..	..	..	..	..
Transport and communication	% of GDP	..	2.4	..	..	..	..
Fixed investment: transport equipment	"	2.8	0.7	..	..	..	..
Total road length	thou. km	103	109	113	..	..	..

INVESTMENT IN HUMAN CAPITAL

Health

Indicator	Unit of measure	1970-75	1980-85	1987-92	Sub-Saharan Africa	Low-income	Next higher income group
Population per physician	persons	20,200	5,199	..	..	..	..
Population per nurse	"	4,243	856	..	..	..	..
Population per hospital bed	"	1,799	1,154	599	1,329	1,050	516
Oral rehydration therapy (under-5)	% of cases	..	..	35	36	39	..

Education
Gross enrollment ratio

Indicator	Unit of measure	1970-75	1980-85	1987-92	Sub-Saharan Africa	Low-income	Next higher income group
Secondary	% of school-age pop.	8	29	20	18	41	..
Female	"	3	25	17	14	35	..
Pupil-teacher ratio: primary	pupils per teacher	35	44	39	39	37	26
Pupil-teacher ratio: secondary	"	84	38	..	..	19	..
Pupils reaching grade 4	% of cohort	65	69	80	..	..	..
Repeater rate: primary	% of total enroll	..	..	..	..	..	..
Illiteracy	% of pop. (age 15+)	..	57	49	51	39	..
Female	% of fem. (age 15+)	..	69	61	62	52	..
Newspaper circulation	per thou. pop.	10	6	18	14	..	100

World Bank International Economics Department, April 1994

Norway

Indicator	Unit of measure	Latest single year 1970-75	Latest single year 1980-85	Most recent estimate 1987-92	Same region/income group High-income
Priority Poverty Indicators					
POVERTY					
Upper poverty line	local curr.	..	..	..	..
Headcount index	% of pop.	..	..	..	..
Lower poverty line	local curr.	..	..	..	..
Headcount index	% of pop.	..	..	..	..
GNP per capita	US$	6,600	14,560	25,820	21,960
SHORT TERM INCOME INDICATORS					
Unskilled urban wages	local curr.	..	..	..	..
Unskilled rural wages	"	..	..	..	..
Rural terms of trade	"	..	..	..	..
Consumer price index	1987=100	37	86	123	..
Lower income	"	..	..	..	..
Food[a]	"	24	85	115	..
Urban	"	..	..	..	..
Rural	"	..	..	..	..
SOCIAL INDICATORS					
Public expenditure on basic social services	% of GDP	..	..	..	..
Gross enrollment ratios					
Primary	% school age pop.	101	94	100	103
Male	"	101	94	100	103
Female	"	101	94	100	103
Mortality					
Infant mortality	per thou. live births	11.0	8.5	6.2	7.0
Under 5 mortality	"	..	..	8.1	10.0
Immunization					
Measles	% age group	..	90.0	90.0	82.4
DPT	"	..	85.0	89.0	90.1
Child malnutrition (under-5)	"	..	..	..	..
Life expectancy					
Total	years	74	76	77	77
Female advantage	"	6.2	6.8	6.2	6.4
Total fertility rate	births per woman	2.0	1.7	1.9	1.7
Maternal mortality rate	per 100,000 live births	..	..	..	..
Supplementary Poverty Indicators					
Expenditures on social security	% of total gov't exp.	..	..	..	..
Social security coverage	% econ. active pop.	..	..	..	..
Access to safe water: total	% of pop.	..	..	..	..
Urban	"	..	..	..	..
Rural	"	..	..	..	..
Access to health care	"	..	..	100.0	..

Population growth rate
(annual average, percent)

GNP per capita growth rate
(annual average, percent)

Development diamond[b]

Life expectancy — GNP per capita — Gross primary enrollment — Access to safe water

— Norway
— High-income

a. See the technical notes, p.389.   b. The development diamond, based on four key indicators, shows the average level of development in the country compared with its income group. See the introduction.

Norway

Indicator	Unit of measure	Latest single year 1970-75	Latest single year 1980-85	Most recent estimate 1987-92	Same region/income group High-income
Resources and Expenditures					
HUMAN RESOURCES					
Population (mre=1992)	thousands	4,007	4,153	4,286	828,221
Age dependency ratio	ratio	0.60	0.56	0.55	0.50
Urban	% of pop.	68.2	72.8	75.8	78.1
Population growth rate	annual %	0.6	0.3	0.6	0.7
Urban	"	1.4	1.0	1.1	0.9
Labor force (15-64)	thousands	1,780	2,039	2,159	390,033
Agriculture	% of labor force	10	8	..	..
Industry	"	33	29	..	..
Female	"	35	41	41	38
Females per 100 males					
Urban	number	103	102	..	..
Rural	"	94	94	..	..
NATURAL RESOURCES					
Area	thou. sq. km	323.90	323.90	323.90	31,709.00
Density	pop. per sq. km	12.4	12.8	13.2	24.5
Agricultural land	% of land area	2.9	3.1	3.2	42.7
Change in agricultural land	annual %	-0.3	0.3	0.2	-0.2
Agricultural land under irrigation	%	4.5	9.4	9.9	16.1
Forests and woodland	thou. sq. km	83	83	83	..
Deforestation (net)	annual %	..	..	..	..
INCOME					
Household income					
Share of top 20% of households	% of income	37	..	..	..
Share of bottom 40% of households	"	19	..	..	..
Share of bottom 20% of households	"	6	..	..	..
EXPENDITURE					
Food	% of GDP	..	9.8	..	..
Staples	"	..	1.2	..	..
Meat, fish, milk, cheese, eggs	"	..	5.0	..	..
Cereal imports	thou. metric tonnes	603	227	336	70,626
Food aid in cereals	"	..	..	..	2
Food production per capita	1987 = 100	91	104	100	101
Fertilizer consumption	kg/ha	255.7	248.9	203.5	162.1
Share of agriculture in GDP	% of GDP	4.8	3.0	2.9	2.4
Housing	% of GDP	..	9.1	..	..
Average household size	persons per household	2.9	2.7	..	..
Urban	"	2.8	2.6	..	..
Fixed investment: housing	% of GDP	5.5	3.0	..	..
Fuel and power	% of GDP	..	3.5	..	..
Energy consumption per capita	kg of oil equiv.	3,798	4,910	4,925	5,101
Households with electricity					
Urban	% of households	..	..	..	..
Rural	"	..	..	..	..
Transport and communication	% of GDP	..	9.0	..	..
Fixed investment: transport equipment	"	6.5	4.6	..	..
Total road length	thou. km	78	85	89	..
INVESTMENT IN HUMAN CAPITAL					
Health					
Population per physician	persons	723	411	..	..
Population per nurse	"	157	57	..	..
Population per hospital bed	"	91	67	211	144
Oral rehydration therapy (under-5)	% of cases	..	..	..	..
Education					
Gross enrollment ratio					
Secondary	% of school-age pop.	88	97	103	92
Female	"	88	99	104	94
Pupil-teacher ratio: primary	pupils per teacher	8	7	6	18
Pupil-teacher ratio: secondary	"	12	..	..	..
Pupils reaching grade 4	% of cohort	99	100	100	..
Repeater rate: primary	% of total enroll	0	0	0	..
Illiteracy	% of pop. (age 15+)	..	..	†	..
Female	% of fem. (age 15+)	..	..	†	..
Newspaper circulation	per thou. pop.	414	477	610	..

World Bank International Economics Department, April 1994

Oman

Indicator	Unit of measure	Latest single year 1970-75	Latest single year 1980-85	Most recent estimate 1987-92	Same region/income group Mid-East & North Africa	Same region/income group Upper-middle-income	Next higher income group
Priority Poverty Indicators							
POVERTY							
Upper poverty line	local curr.	..	..	..	..	..	..
Headcount index	% of pop.	..	..	..	..	..	..
Lower poverty line	local curr.	..	..	..	..	..	..
Headcount index	% of pop.	..	..	..	..	..	..
GNP per capita	US$	1,280	7,410	6,480	1,950	3,870	21,960
SHORT TERM INCOME INDICATORS							
Unskilled urban wages	local curr.	..	..	..	..	..	..
Unskilled rural wages	"	..	..	..	..	..	..
Rural terms of trade	"	..	..	..	..	..	..
Consumer price index	1987=100	..	..	..	..	..	..
Lower income	"	..	..	..	..	..	..
Food[a]	"	..	92	103	..	..	..
Urban	"	..	..	..	..	..	..
Rural	"	..	..	..	..	..	..
SOCIAL INDICATORS							
Public expenditure on basic social services	% of GDP	..	..	6.0	..	..	..
Gross enrollment ratios							
Primary	% school age pop.	44	89	100	100	107	103
Male	"	63	97	104	107	..	103
Female	"	24	80	96	88	..	103
Mortality							
Infant mortality	per thou. live births	78.0	35.0	20.0	58.0	40.0	7.0
Under 5 mortality	"	..	..	24.0	78.0	51.0	10.0
Immunization							
Measles	% age group	..	61.0	94.0	81.8	82.0	82.4
DPT	"	..	56.0	96.0	83.9	73.8	90.1
Child malnutrition (under-5)	"	..	..	..	20.9	..	..
Life expectancy							
Total	years	49	63	70	64	69	77
Female advantage	"	2.4	3.0	4.1	2.4	6.3	6.4
Total fertility rate	births per woman	9.3	9.8	7.2	4.9	2.9	1.7
Maternal mortality rate	per 100,000 live births	..	..	..	..	..	..
Supplementary Poverty Indicators							
Expenditures on social security	% of total gov't exp.	..	..	..	..	..	..
Social security coverage	% econ. active pop.	..	..	..	..	..	..
Access to safe water: total	% of pop.	52.0	53.0	64.0	85.0	85.6	..
Urban	"	100.0	90.0	100.0	97.0	94.3	..
Rural	"	48.0	49.0	60.0	70.1	73.0	..
Access to health care	"	..	92.0	..	84.6	..	..

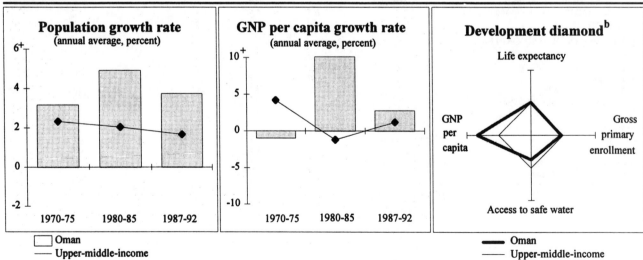

a. See the technical notes, p.389.   b. The development diamond, based on four key indicators, shows the average level of development in the country compared with its income group. See the introduction.

Oman

Indicator	Unit of measure	Latest single year 1970-75	Latest single year 1980-85	Most recent estimate 1987-92	Same region/income group Mid-East & North Africa	Same region/income group Upper-middle-income	Next higher income group
Resources and Expenditures							
HUMAN RESOURCES							
Population (mre=1992)	thousands	766	1,263	1,648	252,555	477,960	828,221
Age dependency ratio	ratio	0.90	0.88	0.98	0.87	0.64	0.50
Urban	% of pop.	6.3	9.2	11.9	54.7	71.7	78.1
Population growth rate	annual %	4.0	4.4	4.0	2.8	1.6	0.7
Urban	"	7.6	7.9	7.8	3.8	2.5	0.9
Labor force (15-64)	thousands	206	361	429	69,280	181,414	390,033
Agriculture	% of labor force	53	50	..	..	..	..
Industry	"	20	22	..	..	..	..
Female	"	7	8	9	15	29	38
Females per 100 males							
Urban	number	..	..	..	..	..	..
Rural	"	..	..	..	..	..	..
NATURAL RESOURCES							
Area	thou. sq. km	212.46	212.46	212.46	10,487.21	21,836.02	31,709.00
Density	pop. per sq. km	3.6	5.9	7.5	23.4	21.5	24.5
Agricultural land	% of land area	4.9	4.9	5.0	30.2	41.7	42.7
Change in agricultural land	annual %	0.1	0.0	0.0	0.5	0.3	-0.2
Agricultural land under irrigation	%	3.3	3.9	5.5	31.0	9.3	16.1
Forests and woodland	thou. sq. km	..	..	..	..	..	..
Deforestation (net)	annual %	..	..	..	..	..	..
INCOME							
Household income							
Share of top 20% of households	% of income	..	..	..	..	..	..
Share of bottom 40% of households	"	..	..	..	..	..	..
Share of bottom 20% of households	"	..	..	..	..	..	..
EXPENDITURE							
Food	% of GDP	..	..	15.8	..	..	..
Staples	"	..	..	3.6	..	..	..
Meat, fish, milk, cheese, eggs	"	..	..	6.4	..	..	..
Cereal imports	thou. metric tonnes	73	202	332	38,007	49,174	70,626
Food aid in cereals	"	..	..	..	2,484	282	2
Food production per capita	1987 = 100	..	..	..	116	109	101
Fertilizer consumption	kg/ha	0.4	2.8	7.7	96.7	68.8	162.1
Share of agriculture in GDP	% of GDP	2.8	2.8	3.7	13.7	8.1	2.4
Housing	% of GDP	..	..	11.1	..	..	..
Average household size	persons per household	..	..	..	..	..	..
Urban	"	..	..	..	..	..	..
Fixed investment: housing	% of GDP	..	..	1.7	..	..	..
Fuel and power	% of GDP	..	..	3.1	..	..	..
Energy consumption per capita	kg of oil equiv.	379	2,551	3,070	1,109	1,649	5,101
Households with electricity							
Urban	% of households	..	..	..	..	..	..
Rural	"	..	..	..	..	..	..
Transport and communication	% of GDP	..	..	3.5	..	..	..
Fixed investment: transport equipment	"	..	..	2.7	..	..	..
Total road length	thou. km	4	22	..	..	..	..
INVESTMENT IN HUMAN CAPITAL							
Health							
Population per physician	persons	8,400	1,728	1,056	..	..	..
Population per nurse	"	3,418	774	395	..	..	..
Population per hospital bed	"	..	558	..	636	385	144
Oral rehydration therapy (under-5)	% of cases	..	..	19	56	54	..
Education							
Gross enrollment ratio							
Secondary	% of school-age pop.	1	33	57	59	53	92
Female	"	0	22	53	50	..	94
Pupil-teacher ratio: primary	pupils per teacher	27	27	27	27	25	18
Pupil-teacher ratio: secondary	"	7	13	17	21	..	..
Pupils reaching grade 4	% of cohort	82	97	99	..	71	..
Repeater rate: primary	% of total enroll	9	12	11	..	11	..
Illiteracy	% of pop. (age 15+)	..	..	..	45	14	..
Female	% of fem. (age 15+)	..	..	..	58	17	..
Newspaper circulation	per thou. pop.	..	..	41	39	117	..

World Bank International Economics Department, April 1994

Pakistan

Indicator	Unit of measure	Latest single year 1970-75	Latest single year 1980-85	Most recent estimate 1987-92	Same region/income group South Asia	Same region/income group Low-income	Next higher income group
Priority Poverty Indicators							
POVERTY							
Upper poverty line	local curr.	..	2,916	..	..	..	..
Headcount index	% of pop.	..	31	..	28	19	..
Lower poverty line	local curr.	..	..	..	..	..	..
Headcount index	% of pop.	..	..	..	..	..	..
GNP per capita	US$	130	370	420	310	390	..
SHORT TERM INCOME INDICATORS							
Unskilled urban wages	local curr.	..	..	..	..	..	..
Unskilled rural wages	"	..	..	192	..	..	..
Rural terms of trade	"	..	..	..	..	..	..
Consumer price index	1987=100	43	92	157	..	..	..
Lower income	"	..	..	..	..	..	..
Food[a]	"	20	92	146	..	..	..
Urban	"	..	..	..	..	..	..
Rural	"	..	..	..	..	..	..
SOCIAL INDICATORS							
Public expenditure on basic social services	% of GDP	..	..	..	..	..	..
Gross enrollment ratios							
Primary	% school age pop.	46	45	46	103	103	..
Male	"	63	57	59	117	113	..
Female	"	28	31	31	88	96	..
Mortality							
Infant mortality	per thou. live births	140.0	120.0	95.0	85.0	73.0	45.0
Under 5 mortality	"	..	..	135.5	116.0	108.0	59.0
Immunization							
Measles	% age group	..	23.0	77.0	56.6	72.7	..
DPT	"	..	30.0	81.0	75.0	80.6	..
Child malnutrition (under-5)	"	..	57.1	40.0	60.9	38.3	..
Life expectancy							
Total	years	49	54	59	60	62	68
Female advantage	"	-2.0	0.0	0.0	1.0	2.4	6.4
Total fertility rate	births per woman	7.0	7.0	5.6	4.0	3.4	3.1
Maternal mortality rate	per 100,000 live births	..	600	270	..	..	..
Supplementary Poverty Indicators							
Expenditures on social security	% of total gov't exp.	0.1	0.3	0.1	..	..	..
Social security coverage	% econ. active pop.	..	..	..	..	..	..
Access to safe water: total	% of pop.	25.0	43.0	56.0	71.9	68.4	..
Urban	"	75.0	83.0	80.0	74.2	78.9	..
Rural	"	5.0	27.0	45.0	70.0	60.3	..
Access to health care	"	..	64.0	85.0	..	..	..

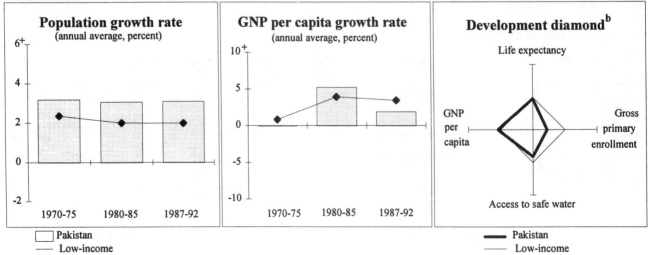

Population growth rate (annual average, percent) — Pakistan / Low-income, for 1970-75, 1980-85, 1987-92

GNP per capita growth rate (annual average, percent) — for 1970-75, 1980-85, 1987-92

Development diamond[b] — Life expectancy, GNP per capita, Gross primary enrollment, Access to safe water — Pakistan / Low-income

a. See the technical notes, p.389.   b. The development diamond, based on four key indicators, shows the average level of development in the country compared with its income group. See the introduction.

Pakistan

Indicator	Unit of measure	Latest single year 1970-75	Latest single year 1980-85	Most recent estimate 1987-92	Same region/income group South Asia	Same region/income group Low-income	Next higher income group
Resources and Expenditures							
HUMAN RESOURCES							
Population (mre=1992)	thousands	71,033	96,180	119,347	1,177,918	3,194,535	942,547
Age dependency ratio	ratio	0.94	0.89	0.89	0.73	0.67	0.66
Urban	% of pop.	26.4	29.8	33.1	25.4	26.7	57.0
Population growth rate	annual %	3.1	3.1	3.0	2.1	1.8	1.4
Urban	"	4.3	4.2	4.6	3.4	3.4	4.8
Labor force (15-64)	thousands	21,950	29,801	35,808	428,847	1,478,954	..
Agriculture	% of labor force	57	55	..	..	..	..
Industry	"	17	16	..	..	..	..
Female	"	10	11	13	22	33	36
Females per 100 males							
Urban	number	79	83	..	..	..	..
Rural	"	89	92	..	..	..	..
NATURAL RESOURCES							
Area	thou. sq. km	796.10	796.10	796.10	5,133.49	38,401.06	40,697.37
Density	pop. per sq. km	89.2	120.8	145.5	224.8	81.7	22.8
Agricultural land	% of land area	32.2	33.2	33.9	58.9	50.9	..
Change in agricultural land	annual %	1.1	1.1	0.2	-0.2	0.0	..
Agricultural land under irrigation	%	54.9	61.5	65.0	29.0	18.2	..
Forests and woodland	thou. sq. km	28	32	35	..	..	..
Deforestation (net)	annual %	..	..	3.1	..	..	..
INCOME							
Household income							
Share of top 20% of households	% of income	42	46	40	41	42	..
Share of bottom 40% of households	"	21	19	21	21	19	..
Share of bottom 20% of households	"	8	8	8	9	8	..
EXPENDITURE							
Food	% of GDP	46.1	28.1	..	..	..	..
Staples	"	16.0	9.3	..	..	..	..
Meat, fish, milk, cheese, eggs	"	14.0	8.4	..	..	..	..
Cereal imports	thou. metric tonnes	1,349	982	2,044	7,721	46,537	74,924
Food aid in cereals	"	584	411	322	2,558	9,008	4,054
Food production per capita	1987 = 100	94	99	111	116	123	..
Fertilizer consumption	kg/ha	22.3	59.0	71.9	71.5	61.9	..
Share of agriculture in GDP	% of GDP	29.9	25.7	24.1	28.7	29.6	..
Housing	% of GDP	9.4	12.4	..	..	..	..
Average household size	persons per household	5.6	6.7	..	..	..	..
Urban	"	5.9	6.7	..	..	..	..
Fixed investment: housing	% of GDP	2.0	1.7	..	..	..	..
Fuel and power	% of GDP	3.8	3.7	..	..	..	..
Energy consumption per capita	kg of oil equiv.	123	177	223	209	335	1,882
Households with electricity							
Urban	% of households	..	71.0	..	..	..	..
Rural	"	..	..	..	..	..	..
Transport and communication	% of GDP	1.6	10.0	..	..	..	..
Fixed investment: transport equipment	"	1.6	1.7	..	..	..	..
Total road length	thou. km	79	126	171	..	..	..
INVESTMENT IN HUMAN CAPITAL							
Health							
Population per physician	persons	4,300	2,931	2,936	2,459	..	..
Population per nurse	"	6,600	5,870	5,042	..	..	..
Population per hospital bed	"	1,900	1,757	1,769	1,652	1,050	516
Oral rehydration therapy (under-5)	% of cases	..	..	34	18	39	..
Education							
Gross enrollment ratio							
Secondary	% of school-age pop.	15	18	21	40	41	..
Female	"	7	10	13	29	35	..
Pupil-teacher ratio: primary	pupils per teacher	40	39	41	59	37	26
Pupil-teacher ratio: secondary	"	18	18	19	23	19	..
Pupils reaching grade 4	% of cohort	57	51	51	..	..	..
Repeater rate: primary	% of total enroll	..	..	..	..	..	..
Illiteracy	% of pop. (age 15+)	79	69	65	54	39	..
Female	% of fem. (age 15+)	..	82	79	68	52	..
Newspaper circulation	per thou. pop.	5	18	16	..	..	100

World Bank International Economics Department, April 1994

Panama

| Indicator | Unit of measure | Latest single year | | Most recent estimate 1987-92 | Same region/income group | | Next higher income group |
		1970-75	1980-85		Latin America Caribbean	Lower-middle-income	
Priority Poverty Indicators							
POVERTY							
Upper poverty line	local curr.	..	..	..	..	..	..
Headcount index	% of pop.	..	..	..	..	..	..
Lower poverty line	local curr.	..	..	..	..	..	..
Headcount index	% of pop.	..	..	..	..	..	..
GNP per capita	US$	1,030	2,380	2,420	2,690	..	3,870
SHORT TERM INCOME INDICATORS							
Unskilled urban wages	local curr.	..	..	..	..	..	..
Unskilled rural wages	"	..	..	..	..	..	..
Rural terms of trade	"	..	..	..	..	..	..
Consumer price index	1987=100	61	99	104	..	..	..
Lower income	"	..	..	..	..	..	..
Food[a]	"	38	97	103	..	..	..
Urban	"	..	..	..	..	..	..
Rural	"	..	..	..	..	..	..
SOCIAL INDICATORS							
Public expenditure on basic social services	% of GDP	..	..	..	..	..	..
Gross enrollment ratios							
Primary	% school age pop.	114	105	106	106	..	107
Male	"	116	107	109	..	..	..
Female	"	111	102	105	..	..	..
Mortality							
Infant mortality	per thou. live births	43.0	26.0	21.0	44.0	45.0	40.0
Under 5 mortality	"	..	..	25.7	56.0	59.0	51.0
Immunization							
Measles	% age group	..	72.0	99.0	78.9	..	82.0
DPT	"	..	70.0	86.0	73.8	..	73.8
Child malnutrition (under-5)	"	..	24.4	15.7	10.5	..	..
Life expectancy							
Total	years	66	71	73	68	68	69
Female advantage	"	2.8	3.7	4.1	5.6	6.4	6.3
Total fertility rate	births per woman	4.9	3.5	2.9	3.0	3.1	2.9
Maternal mortality rate	per 100,000 live births	..	90	60	..	..	..
Supplementary Poverty Indicators							
Expenditures on social security	% of total gov't exp.	9.5	13.4	20.9	..	..	..
Social security coverage	% econ. active pop.	..	..	59.8	..	..	..
Access to safe water: total	% of pop.	77.0	82.0	83.0	80.3	..	85.6
Urban	"	100.0	100.0	100.0	91.0	..	94.3
Rural	"	54.0	63.0	66.0	64.3	..	73.0
Access to health care	"	..	..	82.0	..	..	..

Population growth rate
(annual average, percent)

Panama
Lower-middle-income

GNP per capita growth rate
(annual average, percent)

Development diamond[b]

Life expectancy

GNP per capita — Gross primary enrollment

Access to safe water

Panama
Lower-middle-income

a. See the technical notes, p.389.   b. The development diamond, based on four key indicators, shows the average level of development in the country compared with its income group. See the introduction.

Panama

Indicator	Unit of measure	Latest single year 1970-75	Latest single year 1980-85	Most recent estimate 1987-92	Same region/income group Latin America Caribbean	Same region/income group Lower-middle-income	Next higher income group
Resources and Expenditures							
HUMAN RESOURCES							
Population (mre=1992)	thousands	1,748	2,180	2,515	453,294	942,547	477,960
Age dependency ratio	ratio	0.89	0.72	0.64	0.67	0.66	0.64
Urban	% of pop.	48.7	51.3	53.7	72.9	57.0	71.7
Population growth rate	annual %	2.5	2.1	2.0	1.7	1.4	1.6
Urban	"	2.9	2.8	2.7	2.6	4.8	2.5
Labor force (15-64)	thousands	580	760	921	166,091	..	181,414
Agriculture	% of labor force	37	32	..	..	..	..
Industry	"	18	18	..	..	..	..
Female	"	26	27	28	27	36	29
Females per 100 males							
Urban	number	110	111	..	..	..	..
Rural	"	83	81	..	..	..	..
NATURAL RESOURCES							
Area	thou. sq. km	77.08	77.08	77.08	20,507.48	40,697.37	21,836.02
Density	pop. per sq. km	22.7	28.3	32.0	21.7	22.8	21.5
Agricultural land	% of land area	23.8	27.3	29.3	40.2	..	41.7
Change in agricultural land	annual %	1.2	1.4	0.5	0.5	..	0.3
Agricultural land under irrigation	%	1.3	1.5	1.4	3.2	..	9.3
Forests and woodland	thou. sq. km	43	37	33	..	..	..
Deforestation (net)	annual %	..	..	2.0	..	..	..
INCOME							
Household income							
Share of top 20% of households	% of income	62	..	60	..	..	..
Share of bottom 40% of households	"	7	..	8	..	..	..
Share of bottom 20% of households	"	2	..	2	..	..	..
EXPENDITURE							
Food	% of GDP	..	24.3	..	..	..	..
Staples	"	..	4.5	..	..	..	..
Meat, fish, milk, cheese, eggs	"	..	6.6	..	..	..	..
Cereal imports	thou. metric tonnes	70	125	215	25,032	74,924	49,174
Food aid in cereals	"	3	1	1	1,779	4,054	282
Food production per capita	1987 = 100	104	99	84	104	..	109
Fertilizer consumption	kg/ha	14.1	12.4	11.5	15.5	..	68.8
Share of agriculture in GDP	% of GDP	11.4	10.1	10.9	8.9	..	8.1
Housing	% of GDP	..	6.9	..	..	..	..
Average household size	persons per household	5.0	4.5	..	..	..	..
Urban	"	5.0	4.4	..	..	..	..
Fixed investment: housing	% of GDP	3.8	3.7	..	..	..	..
Fuel and power	% of GDP	..	1.9	..	..	..	..
Energy consumption per capita	kg of oil equiv.	876	495	520	912	1,882	1,649
Households with electricity							
Urban	% of households	..	90.7	..	..	..	..
Rural	"	..	..	..	..	..	..
Transport and communication	% of GDP	..	4.6	..	..	..	..
Fixed investment: transport equipment	"	3.4	2.4	..	..	..	..
Total road length	thou. km	8	10	10	..	..	..
INVESTMENT IN HUMAN CAPITAL							
Health							
Population per physician	persons	1,700	1,000	841	..	..	..
Population per nurse	"	1,564	390	..	..	..	..
Population per hospital bed	"	300	300	..	508	516	385
Oral rehydration therapy (under-5)	% of cases	..	..	55	62	..	54
Education							
Gross enrollment ratio							
Secondary	% of school-age pop.	55	59	60	47	..	53
Female	"	57	63	62	..	..	..
Pupil-teacher ratio: primary	pupils per teacher	27	25	20	25	26	25
Pupil-teacher ratio: secondary	"	26	19	20	..	..	..
Pupils reaching grade 4	% of cohort	85	88	87	..	..	71
Repeater rate: primary	% of total enroll	13	13	10	14	..	11
Illiteracy	% of pop. (age 15+)	22	14	12	15	..	14
Female	% of fem. (age 15+)	..	14	12	17	..	17
Newspaper circulation	per thou. pop.	75	58	70	99	100	117

World Bank International Economics Department, April 1994

Papua New Guinea

Indicator	Unit of measure	Latest single year 1970-75	Latest single year 1980-85	Most recent estimate 1987-92	Same region/income group East Asia	Same region/income group Lower-middle-income	Next higher income group
Priority Poverty Indicators							
POVERTY							
Upper poverty line	local curr.	..	..	..	..	..	..
Headcount index	% of pop.	..	..	..	12	..	..
Lower poverty line	local curr.	..	..	..	..	..	..
Headcount index	% of pop.	..	..	..	9	..	..
GNP per capita	US$	530	750	950	760	..	3,870
SHORT TERM INCOME INDICATORS							
Unskilled urban wages	local curr.	..	..	..	..	..	..
Unskilled rural wages	"	..	..	..	..	..	..
Rural terms of trade	"	..	..	..	..	..	..
Consumer price index	1987=100	47	92	131	..	..	..
Lower income	"	..	..	..	..	..	..
Food[a]	"	..	95	128	..	..	..
Urban	"	..	..	..	..	..	..
Rural	"	..	..	..	..	..	..
SOCIAL INDICATORS							
Public expenditure on basic social services	% of GDP	..	..	..	..	..	..
Gross enrollment ratios							
Primary	% school age pop.	56	60	71	121	..	107
Male	"	68	66	76	126	..	..
Female	"	43	53	65	117	..	..
Mortality							
Infant mortality	per thou. live births	100.0	65.0	54.0	39.0	45.0	40.0
Under 5 mortality	"	..	..	71.4	49.0	59.0	51.0
Immunization							
Measles	% age group	..	27.0	63.0	88.4	..	82.0
DPT	"	..	40.0	64.0	89.5	..	73.8
Child malnutrition (under-5)	"	..	12.8	34.7	24.7	..	..
Life expectancy							
Total	years	48	52	56	68	68	69
Female advantage	"	-0.1	1.5	1.5	3.6	6.4	6.3
Total fertility rate	births per woman	6.1	5.6	4.9	2.4	3.1	2.9
Maternal mortality rate	per 100,000 live births	..	1000	700	114	..	..
Supplementary Poverty Indicators							
Expenditures on social security	% of total gov't exp.	0.1	0.4	0.9	..	..	..
Social security coverage	% econ. active pop.	..	..	..	..	..	..
Access to safe water: total	% of pop.	20.0	26.0	34.0	72.0	..	85.6
Urban	"	30.0	95.0	93.0	83.4	..	94.3
Rural	"	19.0	15.0	23.0	60.2	..	73.0
Access to health care	"	..	93.0	96.0	..	..	..

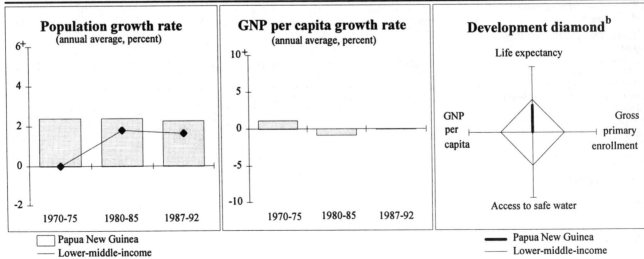

Population growth rate (annual average, percent)

GNP per capita growth rate (annual average, percent)

Development diamond[b]

Life expectancy — GNP per capita — Gross primary enrollment — Access to safe water

1970-75   1980-85   1987-92

☐ Papua New Guinea
— Lower-middle-income

— Papua New Guinea
— Lower-middle-income

a. See the technical notes, p.389.   b. The development diamond, based on four key indicators, shows the average level of development in the country compared with its income group. See the introduction.

Papua New Guinea

Indicator	Unit of measure	Latest single year 1970-75	Latest single year 1980-85	Most recent estimate 1987-92	East Asia	Lower-middle-income	Next higher income group
Resources and Expenditures							
HUMAN RESOURCES							
Population (mre=1992)	thousands	2,729	3,460	4,055	1,688,909	942,547	477,960
Age dependency ratio	ratio	0.82	0.78	0.78	0.55	0.66	0.64
Urban	% of pop.	11.9	14.3	15.8	29.4	57.0	71.7
Population growth rate	annual %	2.4	2.3	2.3	1.4	1.4	1.6
Urban	"	6.0	4.2	4.2	2.9	4.8	2.5
Labor force (15-64)	thousands	1,245	1,458	1,606	928,465	..	181,414
Agriculture	% of labor force	12	11	..	..	..	..
Industry	"	34	33	..	..	..	..
Female	"	32	34	35	41	36	29
Females per 100 males							
Urban	number	..	..	..	..	..	..
Rural	"	..	..	.	..	..	..
NATURAL RESOURCES							
Area	thou. sq. km	462.84	462.84	462.84	16,367.18	40,697.37	21,836.02
Density	pop. per sq. km	5.9	7.5	8.6	101.8	22.8	21.5
Agricultural land	% of land area	1.0	1.0	1.1	44.5	..	41.7
Change in agricultural land	annual %	1.6	1.1	2.5	0.1	..	0.3
Agricultural land under irrigation	%	..	..	..	14.5	..	9.3
Forests and woodland	thou. sq. km	385	383	382	..	..	..
Deforestation (net)	annual %	..	..	0.3	..	..	..
INCOME							
Household income							
Share of top 20% of households	% of income	..	..	..	42	..	..
Share of bottom 40% of households	"	..	..	..	18	..	..
Share of bottom 20% of households	"	..	..	..	7	..	..
EXPENDITURE							
Food	% of GDP	32.5	..	..	..	..	..
Staples	"	..	..	..	..	..	..
Meat, fish, milk, cheese, eggs	"	..	..	..	..	..	..
Cereal imports	thou. metric tonnes	92	172	233	33,591	74,924	49,174
Food aid in cereals	"	..	..	0	581	4,054	282
Food production per capita	1987 = 100	103	105	100	133	..	109
Fertilizer consumption	kg/ha	12.0	18.3	21.8	75.1	..	68.8
Share of agriculture in GDP	% of GDP	29.7	33.8	24.8	21.5	..	8.1
Housing	% of GDP	5.9	..	..	..	..	..
Average household size	persons per household	..	..	..	..	..	..
Urban	"	..	..	..	..	..	..
Fixed investment: housing	% of GDP	..	..	..	..	..	..
Fuel and power	% of GDP	..	..	..	..	..	..
Energy consumption per capita	kg of oil equiv.	204	239	235	593	1,882	1,649
Households with electricity							
Urban	% of households	..	..	..	..	..	..
Rural	"	..	..	..	..	..	..
Transport and communication	% of GDP	4.9	..	..	..	..	..
Fixed investment: transport equipment	"	..	..	..	..	..	..
Total road length	thou. km	18	20	..	..	..	..
INVESTMENT IN HUMAN CAPITAL							
Health							
Population per physician	persons	11,733	6,070	12,874	..	..	..
Population per nurse	"	1,714	878	1,175	..	..	..
Population per hospital bed	"	202	208	299	553	516	385
Oral rehydration therapy (under-5)	% of cases	..	..	46	51	..	54
Education							
Gross enrollment ratio							
Secondary	% of school-age pop.	12	11	12	53	..	53
Female	"	7	8	10	47	..	..
Pupil-teacher ratio: primary	pupils per teacher	32	31	31	23	26	25
Pupil-teacher ratio: secondary	"	23	24	25	16	..	..
Pupils reaching grade 4	% of cohort	87	..	71	89	..	71
Repeater rate: primary	% of total enroll	..	..	0	6	..	11
Illiteracy	% of pop. (age 15+)	68	53	48	24	..	14
Female	% of fem. (age 15+)	..	68	62	34	..	17
Newspaper circulation	per thou. pop.	7	8	13	..	100	117

World Bank International Economics Department, April 1994

Paraguay

Indicator	Unit of measure	Latest single year 1970-75	Latest single year 1980-85	Most recent estimate 1987-92	Same region/income group Latin America Caribbean	Same region/income group Lower-middle-income	Next higher income group
Priority Poverty Indicators							
POVERTY							
Upper poverty line	local curr.	..	..	..	..	..	..
Headcount index	% of pop.	..	..	22	..	..	..
Lower poverty line	local curr.	..	..	..	..	..	..
Headcount index	% of pop.	..	..	4	..	..	..
GNP per capita	US$	550	1,170	1,380	2,690	..	3,870
SHORT TERM INCOME INDICATORS							
Unskilled urban wages	local curr.	..	..	..	..	..	..
Unskilled rural wages	"	..	..	..	..	..	..
Rural terms of trade	"	..	..	..	..	..	..
Consumer price index	1987=100	15	62	306	..	..	..
Lower income	"	..	..	..	..	..	..
Food[a]	"	..	56	262	..	..	..
Urban	"	..	..	..	..	..	..
Rural	"	..	..	..	..	..	..
SOCIAL INDICATORS							
Public expenditure on basic social services	% of GDP	..	..	..	..	..	..
Gross enrollment ratios							
Primary	% school age pop.	102	103	109	106	..	107
Male	"	106	105	111	..	..	..
Female	"	97	100	108	..	..	..
Mortality							
Infant mortality	per thou. live births	55.0	47.1	35.5	44.0	45.0	40.0
Under 5 mortality	"	..	..	43.6	56.0	59.0	51.0
Immunization							
Measles	% age group	..	53.0	74.0	78.9	..	82.0
DPT	"	..	58.0	79.0	73.8	..	73.8
Child malnutrition (under-5)	"	..	32.0	3.7	10.5	..	..
Life expectancy							
Total	years	66	66	67	68	68	69
Female advantage	"	3.9	4.2	4.4	5.6	6.4	6.3
Total fertility rate	births per woman	5.7	4.8	4.6	3.0	3.1	2.9
Maternal mortality rate	per 100,000 live births	..	260	180	..	..	..
Supplementary Poverty Indicators							
Expenditures on social security	% of total gov't exp.	18.4	29.0	11.7	..	..	..
Social security coverage	% econ. active pop.	..	..	..	..	..	..
Access to safe water: total	% of pop.	13.0	26.0	34.0	80.3	..	85.6
Urban	"	25.0	48.0	61.0	91.0	..	94.3
Rural	"	5.0	8.0	9.0	64.3	..	73.0
Access to health care	"	..	..	..	..	..	..

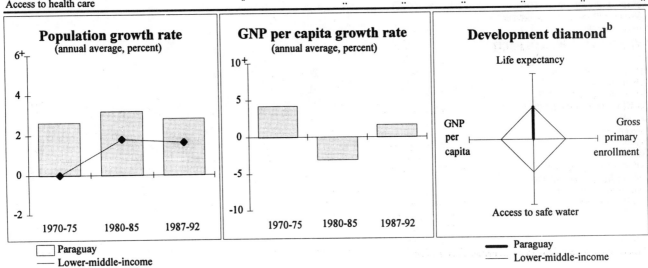

Population growth rate (annual average, percent)

GNP per capita growth rate (annual average, percent)

Development diamond[b]

Life expectancy — GNP per capita — Gross primary enrollment — Access to safe water

Paraguay
Lower-middle-income

a. See the technical notes, p.389.   b. The development diamond, based on four key indicators, shows the average level of development in the country compared with its income group. See the introduction.

Paraguay

World Bank International Economics Department, April 1994

Indicator	Unit of measure	Latest single year		Most recent estimate 1987-92	Same region/income group		Next higher income group
		1970-75	1980-85		Latin America Caribbean	Lower-middle-income	

Resources and Expenditures

HUMAN RESOURCES

Indicator	Unit of measure	1970-75	1980-85	1987-92	Latin America Caribbean	Lower-middle-income	Next higher income group
Population (mre=1992)	thousands	2,682	3,693	4,519	453,294	942,547	477,960
Age dependency ratio	ratio	0.92	0.80	0.80	0.67	0.66	0.64
Urban	% of pop.	39.0	44.4	48.8	72.9	57.0	71.7
Population growth rate	annual %	2.8	3.1	2.7	1.7	1.4	1.6
Urban	"	3.8	4.3	4.1	2.6	4.8	2.5
Labor force (15-64)	thousands	882	1,223	1,494	166,091	..	181,414
Agriculture	% of labor force	51	49	..	..	..	..
Industry	"	20	21	..	..	..	..
Female	"	21	21	21	27	36	29
Females per 100 males							
Urban	number	117	109	..	..	..	..
Rural	"	97	92	..	..	..	..

NATURAL RESOURCES

Indicator	Unit of measure	1970-75	1980-85	1987-92	Latin America Caribbean	Lower-middle-income	Next higher income group
Area	thou. sq. km	406.75	406.75	406.75	20,507.48	40,697.37	21,836.02
Density	pop. per sq. km	6.6	9.1	10.8	21.7	22.8	21.5
Agricultural land	% of land area	40.9	50.3	59.5	40.2	..	41.7
Change in agricultural land	annual %	1.4	2.7	1.4	0.5	..	0.3
Agricultural land under irrigation	%	0.3	0.3	0.3	3.2	..	9.3
Forests and woodland	thou. sq. km	209	178	133	..	..	..
Deforestation (net)	annual %	..	..	2.7	..	..	..

INCOME

Indicator	Unit of measure	1970-75	1980-85	1987-92	Latin America Caribbean	Lower-middle-income	Next higher income group
Household income							
Share of top 20% of households	% of income	..	51	46	..	..	..
Share of bottom 40% of households	"	..	14	16	..	..	..
Share of bottom 20% of households	"	..	5	6	..	..	..

EXPENDITURE

Indicator	Unit of measure	1970-75	1980-85	1987-92	Latin America Caribbean	Lower-middle-income	Next higher income group
Food	% of GDP	..	23.1	..	..	..	..
Staples	"	..	4.5	..	..	..	..
Meat, fish, milk, cheese, eggs	"	..	12.0	..	..	..	..
Cereal imports	thou. metric tonnes	25	85	47	25,032	74,924	49,174
Food aid in cereals	"	10	4	1	1,779	4,054	282
Food production per capita	1987 = 100	84	113	96	104	..	109
Fertilizer consumption	kg/ha	0.1	0.6	0.8	15.5	..	68.8
Share of agriculture in GDP	% of GDP	36.9	28.9	24.5	8.9	..	8.1
Housing	% of GDP	..	15.8	..	..	..	..
Average household size	persons per household	5.4	..	..	..	..	..
Urban	"	5.0	..	..	..	..	..
Fixed investment: housing	% of GDP	..	16.1	..	..	..	..
Fuel and power	% of GDP	..	2.9	..	..	..	..
Energy consumption per capita	kg of oil equiv.	107	174	209	912	1,882	1,649
Households with electricity							
Urban	% of households	..	..	..	..	..	..
Rural	"	..	..	..	..	..	..
Transport and communication	% of GDP	..	7.6	..	..	..	..
Fixed investment: transport equipment	"	4.3	4.4	..	..	..	..
Total road length	thou. km	7	15	15	..	..	..

INVESTMENT IN HUMAN CAPITAL

Indicator	Unit of measure	1970-75	1980-85	1987-92	Latin America Caribbean	Lower-middle-income	Next higher income group
Health							
Population per physician	persons	2,297	1,516	1,250	..	..	..
Population per nurse	"	2,207	882	..	..	..	..
Population per hospital bed	"	599	..	1,087	508	516	385
Oral rehydration therapy (under-5)	% of cases	..	..	42	62	..	54
Education							
Gross enrollment ratio							
Secondary	% of school-age pop.	20	30	30	47	..	53
Female	"	20	30	31	..	..	..
Pupil-teacher ratio: primary	pupils per teacher	29	25	25	25	26	25
Pupil-teacher ratio: secondary	"	11	..	..	..	..	..
Pupils reaching grade 4	% of cohort	70	75	78	..	..	71
Repeater rate: primary	% of total enroll	15	11	9	14	..	11
Illiteracy	% of pop. (age 15+)	20	12	10	15	..	14
Female	% of fem. (age 15+)	..	14	12	17	..	17
Newspaper circulation	per thou. pop.	27	48	39	99	100	117

Peru

Indicator	Unit of measure	Latest single year 1970-75	Latest single year 1980-85	Most recent estimate 1987-92	Same region/income group Latin America Caribbean	Same region/income group Lower-middle-income	Next higher income group
Priority Poverty Indicators							
POVERTY							
Upper poverty line	local curr.	..	..	617	..	..	..
Headcount index	% of pop.	..	..	32	..	..	..
Lower poverty line	local curr.	..	..	315	..	..	..
Headcount index	% of pop.	..	12	22	..	..	..
GNP per capita	US$	1,000	930	950	2,690	..	3,870
SHORT TERM INCOME INDICATORS							
Unskilled urban wages	local curr.	..	..	..	..	..	..
Unskilled rural wages	"	..	..	..	..	..	..
Rural terms of trade	"	..	..	..	..	..	..
Consumer price index	1987=100	0	30	17,989,340	..	..	..
Lower income	"	..	..	..	..	..	..
Food[a]	"	..	33	466	..	..	..
Urban	"	..	..	..	..	..	..
Rural	"	..	..	..	..	..	..
SOCIAL INDICATORS							
Public expenditure on basic social services	% of GDP	..	3.6	2.4	..	..	..
Gross enrollment ratios							
Primary	% school age pop.	113	122	80	106	..	107
Male	"	114	125	..	..	..	..
Female	"	99	120	..	..	..	..
Mortality							
Infant mortality	per thou. live births	96.0	74.0	52.0	44.0	45.0	40.0
Under 5 mortality	"	..	..	68.4	56.0	59.0	51.0
Immunization							
Measles	% age group	..	32.0	81.5	78.9	..	82.0
DPT	"	..	26.0	81.4	73.8	..	73.8
Child malnutrition (under-5)	"	..	13.4	10.8	10.5	..	..
Life expectancy							
Total	years	56	59	65	68	68	69
Female advantage	"	3.4	3.7	3.8	5.6	6.4	6.3
Total fertility rate	births per woman	5.3	4.1	3.3	3.0	3.1	2.9
Maternal mortality rate	per 100,000 live births	..	165	..	..	..	..
Supplementary Poverty Indicators							
Expenditures on social security	% of total gov't exp.	..	..	..	..	..	..
Social security coverage	% econ. active pop.	..	..	39.1	..	..	..
Access to safe water: total	% of pop.	47.0	55.0	58.0	80.3	..	85.6
Urban	"	72.0	73.0	78.0	91.0	..	94.3
Rural	"	15.0	17.0	22.0	64.3	..	73.0
Access to health care	"	..	..	..	..	..	..

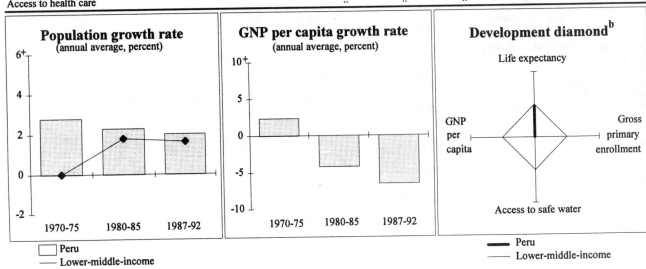

Population growth rate (annual average, percent)

GNP per capita growth rate (annual average, percent)

Development diamond[b]

Life expectancy — GNP per capita — Gross primary enrollment — Access to safe water

Peru / Lower-middle-income

a. See the technical notes, p.389.   b. The development diamond, based on four key indicators, shows the average level of development in the country compared with its income group. See the introduction.

Peru

Indicator	Unit of measure	Latest single year 1970-75	Latest single year 1980-85	Most recent estimate 1987-92	Same region/income group Latin America Caribbean	Same region/income group Lower-middle-income	Next higher income group
Resources and Expenditures							
HUMAN RESOURCES							
Population (mre=1992)	thousands	15,161	19,383	22,370	453,294	942,547	477,960
Age dependency ratio	ratio	0.88	0.77	0.70	0.67	0.66	0.64
Urban	% of pop.	61.5	67.3	70.8	72.9	57.0	71.7
Population growth rate	annual %	2.8	2.2	1.9	1.7	1.4	1.6
Urban	"	4.1	3.0	2.6	2.6	4.8	2.5
Labor force (15-64)	thousands	4,548	6,204	7,563	166,091	..	181,414
Agriculture	% of labor force	43	40	..	..	..	..
Industry	"	18	18	..	..	..	..
Female	"	22	24	24	27	36	29
Females per 100 males							
Urban	number	99	100	..	..	..	..
Rural	"	100	96	..	..	..	..
NATURAL RESOURCES							
Area	thou. sq. km	1,285.22	1,285.22	1,285.22	20,507.48	40,697.37	21,836.02
Density	pop. per sq. km	11.8	15.1	17.1	21.7	22.8	21.5
Agricultural land	% of land area	23.7	24.1	24.1	40.2	..	41.7
Change in agricultural land	annual %	0.0	0.0	0.0	0.5	..	0.3
Agricultural land under irrigation	%	3.7	3.9	4.1	3.2	..	9.3
Forests and woodland	thou. sq. km	722	697	682	..	..	..
Deforestation (net)	annual %	..	..	0.4	..	..	..
INCOME							
Household income							
Share of top 20% of households	% of income	61	..	..	..	..	..
Share of bottom 40% of households	"	7	..	..	..	..	..
Share of bottom 20% of households	"	2	..	..	..	..	..
EXPENDITURE							
Food	% of GDP	..	24.2	..	..	..	..
Staples	"	..	5.8	..	..	..	..
Meat, fish, milk, cheese, eggs	"	..	10.4	..	..	..	..
Cereal imports	thou. metric tonnes	1,182	1,227	2,015	25,032	74,924	49,174
Food aid in cereals	"	37	216	464	1,779	4,054	282
Food production per capita	1987 = 100	117	97	95	104	..	109
Fertilizer consumption	kg/ha	3.4	2.4	2.5	15.5	..	68.8
Share of agriculture in GDP	% of GDP	16.4	10.2	..	8.9	..	8.1
Housing	% of GDP	..	10.4	..	..	..	..
Average household size	persons per household	4.8	..	..	..	..	..
Urban	"	4.9	..	..	..	..	..
Fixed investment: housing	% of GDP	..	5.5	..	..	..	..
Fuel and power	% of GDP	..	2.1	..	..	..	..
Energy consumption per capita	kg of oil equiv.	472	377	330	912	1,882	1,649
Households with electricity							
Urban	% of households	..	17.5	..	..	..	..
Rural	"	..	..	..	..	..	..
Transport and communication	% of GDP	..	7.0	..	..	..	..
Fixed investment: transport equipment	"	3.5	2.2	..	..	..	..
Total road length	thou. km	55	68	70	..	..	..
INVESTMENT IN HUMAN CAPITAL							
Health							
Population per physician	persons	1,900	1,071	939	..	..	..
Population per nurse	"	..	..	..	..	..	..
Population per hospital bed	"	400	590	708	508	516	385
Oral rehydration therapy (under-5)	% of cases	..	..	25	62	..	54
Education							
Gross enrollment ratio							
Secondary	% of school-age pop.	46	63	30	47	..	53
Female	"	41	60	..	..	..	..
Pupil-teacher ratio: primary	pupils per teacher	39	35	28	25	26	25
Pupil-teacher ratio: secondary	"	24	21	21	..	..	..
Pupils reaching grade 4	% of cohort	82	84	..	..	..	71
Repeater rate: primary	% of total enroll	10	14	..	14	..	11
Illiteracy	% of pop. (age 15+)	28	18	15	15	..	14
Female	% of fem. (age 15+)	..	26	21	17	..	17
Newspaper circulation	per thou. pop.	91	83	79	99	100	117

World Bank International Economics Department, April 1994

Philippines

Indicator	Unit of measure	Latest single year 1970-75	Latest single year 1980-85	Most recent estimate 1987-92	Same region/income group East Asia	Same region/income group Lower-middle-income	Next higher income group
Priority Poverty Indicators							
POVERTY							
Upper poverty line	local curr.	..	4,890	6,334	..	..	..
Headcount index	% of pop.	57	65	62	12	..	..
Lower poverty line	local curr.	..	2,520	3,072	..	..	..
Headcount index	% of pop.	35	28	24	9	..	..
GNP per capita	US$	340	540	770	760	..	3,870
SHORT TERM INCOME INDICATORS							
Unskilled urban wages	local curr.	..	..	..	..	..	..
Unskilled rural wages	"	..	..	..	..	..	..
Rural terms of trade	"	..	..	..	..	..	..
Consumer price index	1987=100	21	96	180	..	..	..
Lower income	"	..	..	..	..	..	..
Food[a]	"	9	97	157	..	..	..
Urban	"	..	..	..	..	..	..
Rural	"	..	..	..	..	..	..
SOCIAL INDICATORS							
Public expenditure on basic social services	% of GDP	..	1.5	..	..	..	..
Gross enrollment ratios							
Primary	% school age pop.	107	106	110	121	..	107
Male	"	..	106	113	126	..	..
Female	"	..	107	111	117	..	..
Mortality							
Infant mortality	per thou. live births	64.0	51.0	40.0	39.0	45.0	40.0
Under 5 mortality	"	..	..	50.2	49.0	59.0	51.0
Immunization							
Measles	% age group	..	49.0	85.0	88.4	..	82.0
DPT	"	..	52.0	88.0	89.5	..	73.8
Child malnutrition (under-5)	"	..	32.5	33.5	24.7	..	..
Life expectancy							
Total	years	58	62	65	68	68	69
Female advantage	"	3.0	3.7	3.9	3.6	6.4	6.3
Total fertility rate	births per woman	6.1	4.7	4.1	2.4	3.1	2.9
Maternal mortality rate	per 100,000 live births	..	80	74	114	..	..
Supplementary Poverty Indicators							
Expenditures on social security	% of total gov't exp.	1.5	1.9	1.7	..	..	..
Social security coverage	% econ. active pop.	..	..	..	..	..	..
Access to safe water: total	% of pop.	50.0	52.0	81.0	72.0	..	85.6
Urban	"	67.0	49.0	93.0	83.4	..	94.3
Rural	"	20.0	54.0	72.0	60.2	..	73.0
Access to health care	"	..	..	..	..	..	..

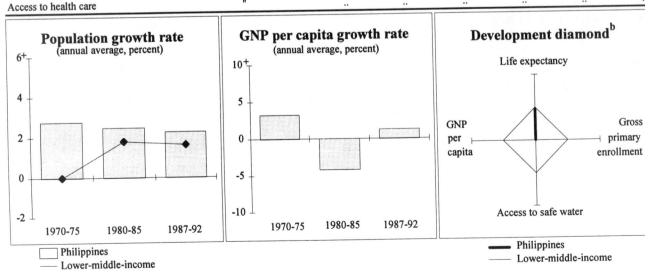

a. See the technical notes, p.389.   b. The development diamond, based on four key indicators, shows the average level of development in the country compared with its income group. See the introduction.

Philippines

Indicator	Unit of measure	Latest single year 1970-75	Latest single year 1980-85	Most recent estimate 1987-92	Same region/income group East Asia	Same region/income group Lower-middle-income	Next higher income group
Resources and Expenditures							
HUMAN RESOURCES							
Population (mre=1992)	thousands	43,103	54,700	64,259	1,688,909	942,547	477,960
Age dependency ratio	ratio	0.83	0.80	0.75	0.55	0.66	0.64
Urban	% of pop.	35.6	40.0	43.9	29.4	57.0	71.7
Population growth rate	annual %	2.6	2.5	2.2	1.4	1.4	1.6
Urban	"	4.0	3.8	3.6	2.9	4.8	2.5
Labor force (15-64)	thousands	15,814	19,874	23,665	928,465	..	181,414
Agriculture	% of labor force	53	52	..	..	..	..
Industry	"	16	16	..	..	..	..
Female	"	33	32	31	41	36	29
Females per 100 males							
Urban	number	108	110	..	..	..	..
Rural	"	96	98	..	..	..	..
NATURAL RESOURCES							
Area	thou. sq. km	300.00	300.00	300.00	16,367.18	40,697.37	21,836.02
Density	pop. per sq. km	143.7	182.3	209.6	101.8	22.8	21.5
Agricultural land	% of land area	27.5	30.4	31.0	44.5	..	41.7
Change in agricultural land	annual %	0.1	0.6	0.2	0.1	..	0.3
Agricultural land under irrigation	%	12.7	15.9	17.1	14.5	..	9.3
Forests and woodland	thou. sq. km	135	114	102	..	..	..
Deforestation (net)	annual %	..	..	3.4	..	..	..
INCOME							
Household income							
Share of top 20% of households	% of income	56	48	48	42	..	..
Share of bottom 40% of households	"	14	15	17	18	..	..
Share of bottom 20% of households	"	5	6	7	7	..	..
EXPENDITURE							
Food	% of GDP	37.5	38.9	..	..	..	..
Staples	"	14.1	16.1	..	..	..	..
Meat, fish, milk, cheese, eggs	"	15.5	15.0	..	..	..	..
Cereal imports	thou. metric tonnes	824	1,524	1,833	33,591	74,924	49,174
Food aid in cereals	"	89	68	78	581	4,054	282
Food production per capita	1987 = 100	94	86	85	133	..	109
Fertilizer consumption	kg/ha	27.7	31.3	47.3	75.1	..	68.8
Share of agriculture in GDP	% of GDP	30.3	24.6	21.7	21.5	..	8.1
Housing	% of GDP	6.2	14.6	..	..	..	..
Average household size	persons per household	5.9	..	..	..	..	..
Urban	"	6.0	..	..	..	..	..
Fixed investment: housing	% of GDP	3.5	2.5	..	..	..	..
Fuel and power	% of GDP	1.6	4.0	..	..	..	..
Energy consumption per capita	kg of oil equiv.	240	264	302	593	1,882	1,649
Households with electricity							
Urban	% of households	..	..	..	..	..	..
Rural	"	..	..	..	..	..	..
Transport and communication	% of GDP	1.5	3.0	..	..	..	..
Fixed investment: transport equipment	"	4.1	0.6	..	..	..	..
Total road length	thou. km	99	157	157	..	..	..
INVESTMENT IN HUMAN CAPITAL							
Health							
Population per physician	persons	9,100	6,566	8,117	..	..	..
Population per nurse	"	2,691	2,684	..	..	..	..
Population per hospital bed	"	600	574	780	553	516	385
Oral rehydration therapy (under-5)	% of cases	..	..	25	51	..	54
Education							
Gross enrollment ratio							
Secondary	% of school-age pop.	54	64	74	53	..	53
Female	"	..	66	75	47	..	..
Pupil-teacher ratio: primary	pupils per teacher	29	31	33	23	26	25
Pupil-teacher ratio: secondary	"	..	32	32	16	..	..
Pupils reaching grade 4	% of cohort	78	77	85	89	..	71
Repeater rate: primary	% of total enroll	..	2	2	6	..	11
Illiteracy	% of pop. (age 15+)	17	12	10	24	..	14
Female	% of fem. (age 15+)	..	13	11	34	..	17
Newspaper circulation	per thou. pop.	16	38	55	..	100	117

World Bank International Economics Department, April 1994

Poland

Indicator	Unit of measure	Latest single year 1970-75	Latest single year 1980-85	Most recent estimate 1987-92	Same region/income group Europe & Central Asia	Same region/income group Lower-middle-income	Next higher income group
Priority Poverty Indicators							
POVERTY							
Upper poverty line	local curr.	..	..	..	..	..	..
Headcount index	% of pop.	..	..	..	..	..	..
Lower poverty line	local curr.	..	..	..	..	..	..
Headcount index	% of pop.	..	..	..	..	..	..
GNP per capita	US$	..	2,100	1,910	..	..	3,870
SHORT TERM INCOME INDICATORS							
Unskilled urban wages	local curr.	..	..	..	..	..	..
Unskilled rural wages	"	..	..	..	..	..	..
Rural terms of trade	"	..	..	..	..	..	..
Consumer price index	1987=100	12	68	9,397	..	..	..
Lower income	"	..	..	..	..	..	..
Food[a]	"	..	70	5,913	..	..	..
Urban	"	..	..	..	..	..	..
Rural	"	..	..	..	..	..	..
SOCIAL INDICATORS							
Public expenditure on basic social services	% of GDP	..	..	..	..	..	..
Gross enrollment ratios							
Primary	% school age pop.	100	101	98	..	..	107
Male	"	102	102	99	..	..	..
Female	"	99	100	97	..	..	..
Mortality							
Infant mortality	per thou. live births	24.8	19.2	14.2	30.0	45.0	40.0
Under 5 mortality	"	..	..	17.3	38.0	59.0	51.0
Immunization							
Measles	% age group	..	94.0	94.0	..	..	82.0
DPT	"	..	96.0	98.0	..	..	73.8
Child malnutrition (under-5)	"	..	..	..	..	..	..
Life expectancy							
Total	years	70	71	70	70	68	69
Female advantage	"	7.1	8.4	9.2	8.6	6.4	6.3
Total fertility rate	births per woman	2.2	2.3	1.9	2.2	3.1	2.9
Maternal mortality rate	per 100,000 live births	..	12	..	58	..	..
Supplementary Poverty Indicators							
Expenditures on social security	% of total gov't exp.	..	..	..	..	..	..
Social security coverage	% econ. active pop.	..	..	..	..	..	..
Access to safe water: total	% of pop.	..	89.0	..	..	..	85.6
Urban	"	75.2	100.0	..	..	..	94.3
Rural	"	12.1	73.0	..	..	..	73.0
Access to health care	"	..	100.0	100.0	..	..	..

Population growth rate
(annual average, percent)

(bar/line chart with years 1970-75, 1980-85, 1987-92; y-axis from -2 to 6+)

Legend: □ Poland — Lower-middle-income

GNP per capita growth rate
(annual average, percent)

(bar chart with years 1970-75, 1980-85, 1987-92; y-axis from -10 to 10+)

Development diamond[b]

(diamond diagram with axes: Life expectancy, Gross primary enrollment, Access to safe water, GNP per capita)

Legend: ▬ Poland — Lower-middle-income

a. See the technical notes, p.389.   b. The development diamond, based on four key indicators, shows the average level of development in the country compared with its income group. See the introduction.

Poland

Indicator	Unit of measure	Latest single year 1970-75	Latest single year 1980-85	Most recent estimate 1987-92	Same region/income group Europe & Central Asia	Same region/income group Lower-middle-income	Next higher income group
Resources and Expenditures							
HUMAN RESOURCES							
Population (mre=1992)	thousands	34,022	37,203	38,365	495,241	942,547	477,960
Age dependency ratio	ratio	0.51	0.54	0.54	0.56	0.66	0.64
Urban	% of pop.	55.4	60.0	62.6	63.3	57.0	71.7
Population growth rate	annual %	1.0	0.8	0.3	0.5	1.4	1.6
Urban	"	2.1	1.4	1.0	..	4.8	2.5
Labor force (15-64)	thousands	18,120	19,221	19,987		..	181,414
Agriculture	% of labor force	34	29	..	..	..	..
Industry	"	37	39	..	..	..	..
Female	"	45	45	46	46	36	29
Females per 100 males							
Urban	number	106	106	..	..	..	..
Rural	"	101	96	..	..	..	..
NATURAL RESOURCES							
Area	thou. sq. km	312.68	312.68	312.68	24,165.06	40,697.37	21,836.02
Density	pop. per sq. km	108.8	119.0	122.3	20.4	22.8	21.5
Agricultural land	% of land area	63.1	62.1	61.6	..	..	41.7
Change in agricultural land	annual %	-0.2	-0.1	-0.2	..	..	0.3
Agricultural land under irrigation	%	1.2	0.5	0.5	..	..	9.3
Forests and woodland	thou. sq. km	86	87	88	..	..	..
Deforestation (net)	annual %	..	..	-0.1	..	..	..
INCOME							
Household income							
Share of top 20% of households	% of income	33	34	36	..	..	..
Share of bottom 40% of households	"	25	25	23	..	..	..
Share of bottom 20% of households	"	10	10	9	..	..	..
EXPENDITURE							
Food	% of GDP	16.5	18.2	..	..	..	..
Staples	"	2.6	2.2	..	..	..	..
Meat, fish, milk, cheese, eggs	"	7.8	8.3	..	..	..	..
Cereal imports	thou. metric tonnes	4,075	2,423	2,282	45,972	74,924	49,174
Food aid in cereals	"	..	68	10	1,639	4,054	282
Food production per capita	1987 = 100	107	106	96	..	..	109
Fertilizer consumption	kg/ha	191.0	180.4	60.5	..	..	68.8
Share of agriculture in GDP	% of GDP	..	14.5	7.3	..	..	8.1
Housing	% of GDP	4.5	4.0	..	..	..	..
Average household size	persons per household	3.3	3.3	..	..	..	..
Urban	"	3.0	3.0	..	..	..	..
Fixed investment: housing	% of GDP	3.6	3.7	..	..	..	..
Fuel and power	% of GDP	1.1	0.9	..	..	..	..
Energy consumption per capita	kg of oil equiv.	2,924	3,399	2,407	3,190	1,882	1,649
Households with electricity							
Urban	% of households	..	..	..	..	..	..
Rural	"	..	..	..	..	..	..
Transport and communication	% of GDP	3.6	5.3	..	..	..	..
Fixed investment: transport equipment	"	4.1	1.4	..	..	..	..
Total road length	thou. km	..	301	361	..	..	..
INVESTMENT IN HUMAN CAPITAL							
Health							
Population per physician	persons	700	487	486	378	..	..
Population per nurse	"	255	187	..	..	..	..
Population per hospital bed	"	131	..	153	134	516	385
Oral rehydration therapy (under-5)	% of cases	..	..	..	..	..	54
Education							
Gross enrollment ratio							
Secondary	% of school-age pop.	73	78	83	..	..	53
Female	"	74	81	86	..	..	..
Pupil-teacher ratio: primary	pupils per teacher	21	18	17	..	26	25
Pupil-teacher ratio: secondary	"	14	16	19	..	..	..
Pupils reaching grade 4	% of cohort	98	98	97	..	..	71
Repeater rate: primary	% of total enroll	3	3	2	..	..	11
Illiteracy	% of pop. (age 15+)	2	..	..	..	..	14
Female	% of fem. (age 15+)	..	..	..	..	..	17
Newspaper circulation	per thou. pop.	248	207	128	..	100	117

World Bank International Economics Department, April 1994

Portugal

Indicator	Unit of measure	Latest single year 1970-75	Latest single year 1980-85	Most recent estimate 1987-92	Same region/income group Europe & Central Asia	Same region/income group Upper-middle-income	Next higher income group
Priority Poverty Indicators							
POVERTY							
Upper poverty line	local curr.	..	..	..	..	..	..
Headcount index	% of pop.	..	..	..	..	..	..
Lower poverty line	local curr.	..	..	..	..	..	..
Headcount index	% of pop.	..	..	..	..	..	..
GNP per capita	US$	1,540	1,980	7,450	..	3,870	21,960
SHORT TERM INCOME INDICATORS							
Unskilled urban wages	local curr.	..	..	..	..	..	..
Unskilled rural wages	"	..	..	..	..	..	..
Rural terms of trade	"	..	..	..	..	..	..
Consumer price index	1987=100	11	82	170	..	..	..
Lower income	"	..	..	..	..	..	..
Food[a]	"	..	84	157	..	..	..
Urban	"	..	..	..	..	..	..
Rural	"	..	..	..	..	..	..
SOCIAL INDICATORS							
Public expenditure on basic social services	% of GDP	..	..	..	..	..	..
Gross enrollment ratios							
Primary	% school age pop.	113	124	122	..	107	103
Male	"	114	127	120	..	..	103
Female	"	111	121	115	..	..	103
Mortality							
Infant mortality	per thou. live births	38.9	17.8	9.3	30.0	40.0	7.0
Under 5 mortality	"	..	..	11.7	38.0	51.0	10.0
Immunization							
Measles	% age group	..	70.0	96.0	..	82.0	82.4
DPT	"	..	72.0	95.0	..	73.8	90.1
Child malnutrition (under-5)	"	..	..	..	..	..	..
Life expectancy							
Total	years	68	72	74	70	69	77
Female advantage	"	6.4	7.0	7.5	8.6	6.3	6.4
Total fertility rate	births per woman	2.5	1.7	1.5	2.2	2.9	1.7
Maternal mortality rate	per 100,000 live births	..	15	..	58	..	..
Supplementary Poverty Indicators							
Expenditures on social security	% of total gov't exp.	..	..	..	..	..	..
Social security coverage	% econ. active pop.	..	..	..	..	..	..
Access to safe water: total	% of pop.	..	58.0	..	..	85.6	..
Urban	"	..	100.0	..	..	94.3	..
Rural	"	..	22.0	..	..	73.0	..
Access to health care	"	..	100.0	100.0	..	..	..

Population growth rate
(annual average, percent)

□ Portugal
— Upper-middle-income

GNP per capita growth rate
(annual average, percent)

Development diamond[b]

Life expectancy

GNP per capita — Gross primary enrollment

Access to safe water

▬ Portugal
— Upper-middle-income

a. See the technical notes, p.389.   b. The development diamond, based on four key indicators, shows the average level of development in the country compared with its income group. See the introduction.

Portugal

Indicator	Unit of measure	Latest single year 1970-75	Latest single year 1980-85	Most recent estimate 1987-92	Same region/income group Europe & Central Asia	Same region/income group Upper-middle-income	Next higher income group
Resources and Expenditures							
HUMAN RESOURCES							
Population (mre=1992)	thousands	9,093	10,157	9,846	495,241	477,960	828,221
Age dependency ratio	ratio	0.61	0.55	0.50	0.56	0.64	0.50
Urban	% of pop.	27.7	31.3	34.7	63.3	71.7	78.1
Population growth rate	annual %	3.8	0.7	-0.1	0.5	1.6	0.7
Urban	"	5.1	1.9	1.6	..	2.5	0.9
Labor force (15-64)	thousands	3,875	4,563	4,820	..	181,414	390,033
Agriculture	% of labor force	28	26	..	..	..	..
Industry	"	35	37	..	..	..	..
Female	"	31	36	37	46	29	38
Females per 100 males							
Urban	number	..	111	..	..	..	..
Rural	"	..	105	..	..	..	..
NATURAL RESOURCES							
Area	thou. sq. km	92.39	92.39	92.39	24,165.06	21,836.02	31,709.00
Density	pop. per sq. km	98.4	109.9	106.6	20.4	21.5	24.5
Agricultural land	% of land area	43.0	43.4	43.6	..	41.7	42.7
Change in agricultural land	annual %	0.1	0.1	0.0	..	0.3	-0.2
Agricultural land under irrigation	%	15.8	15.8	15.7	..	9.3	16.1
Forests and woodland	thou. sq. km	30	30	30	..	..	..
Deforestation (net)	annual %	..	..	-0.3	..	..	..
INCOME							
Household income							
Share of top 20% of households	% of income	56	..	..	..	..	..
Share of bottom 40% of households	"	21	..	..	..	..	..
Share of bottom 20% of households	"	7	..	..	..	..	..
EXPENDITURE							
Food	% of GDP	..	24.1	..	..	..	..
Staples	"	..	6.0	..	..	..	..
Meat, fish, milk, cheese, eggs	"	..	10.8	..	..	..	..
Cereal imports	thou. metric tonnes	1,738	2,225	2,027	45,972	49,174	70,626
Food aid in cereals	"	90	255	..	1,639	282	2
Food production per capita	1987 = 100	123	104	125	..	109	101
Fertilizer consumption	kg/ha	61.9	60.3	62.3	..	68.8	162.1
Share of agriculture in GDP	% of GDP	..	9.4	8.7	..	8.1	2.4
Housing	% of GDP	..	6.1	..	..	..	..
Average household size	persons per household	4.0	..	..	..	..	..
Urban	"	..	..	..	..	..	..
Fixed investment: housing	% of GDP	5.0	3.3	..	..	..	..
Fuel and power	% of GDP	..	2.3	..	..	..	..
Energy consumption per capita	kg of oil equiv.	877	1,124	1,816	3,190	1,649	5,101
Households with electricity							
Urban	% of households	..	..	..	..	..	..
Rural	"	..	..	..	..	..	..
Transport and communication	% of GDP	..	9.0	..	..	..	..
Fixed investment: transport equipment	"	1.8	2.2	..	..	..	..
Total road length	thou. km	47	52	70	..	..	..
INVESTMENT IN HUMAN CAPITAL							
Health							
Population per physician	persons	1,061	412	493	378	..	..
Population per nurse	"	816	..	..	..	..	..
Population per hospital bed	"	193	..	226	134	385	144
Oral rehydration therapy (under-5)	% of cases	..	..	..	..	54	..
Education							
Gross enrollment ratio							
Secondary	% of school-age pop.	53	56	68	..	53	92
Female	"	52	57	74	..	..	94
Pupil-teacher ratio: primary	pupils per teacher	20	17	14	..	25	18
Pupil-teacher ratio: secondary	"	22	14	11	..	..	..
Pupils reaching grade 4	% of cohort	91	..	..	..	71	..
Repeater rate: primary	% of total enroll	11	17	14	..	11	..
Illiteracy	% of pop. (age 15+)	29	18	15	..	14	..
Female	% of fem. (age 15+)	..	23	19	..	17	..
Newspaper circulation	per thou. pop.	67	49	40	..	117	..

World Bank International Economics Department, April 1994

Puerto Rico

Indicator	Unit of measure	Latest single year 1970-75	1980-85	Most recent estimate 1987-92	Same region/income group Latin America Caribbean	Upper-middle-income	Next higher income group
Priority Poverty Indicators							
POVERTY							
Upper poverty line	local curr.	..	..	..	..	..	..
Headcount index	% of pop.	..	..	..	..	..	..
Lower poverty line	local curr.	..	..	..	..	..	..
Headcount index	% of pop.	..	..	..	..	..	..
GNP per capita	US$	2,480	4,460	7,450	2,690	3,870	21,960
SHORT TERM INCOME INDICATORS							
Unskilled urban wages	local curr.	..	..	..	..	..	..
Unskilled rural wages	"	..	..	..	..	..	..
Rural terms of trade	"	..	..	..	..	..	..
Consumer price index	1987=100	..	..	..	..	..	..
Lower income	"	..	..	..	..	..	..
Food[a]	"	36	97	124	..	..	..
Urban	"	..	..	..	..	..	..
Rural	"	..	..	..	..	..	..
SOCIAL INDICATORS							
Public expenditure on basic social services	% of GDP	..	..	..	..	..	..
Gross enrollment ratios							
Primary	% school age pop.	107	94	..	106	107	103
Male	"	..	..	..	..	..	103
Female	"	..	..	..	..	..	103
Mortality							
Infant mortality	per thou. live births	20.8	14.9	13.0	44.0	40.0	7.0
Under 5 mortality	"	..	..	16.0	56.0	51.0	10.0
Immunization							
Measles	% age group	..	..	..	78.9	82.0	82.4
DPT	"	..	..	..	73.8	73.8	90.1
Child malnutrition (under-5)	"	..	..	..	10.5	..	..
Life expectancy							
Total	years	73	74	74	68	69	77
Female advantage	"	7.2	6.8	6.8	5.6	6.3	6.4
Total fertility rate	births per woman	3.0	2.4	2.1	3.0	2.9	1.7
Maternal mortality rate	per 100,000 live births	..	..	21	..	..	..
Supplementary Poverty Indicators							
Expenditures on social security	% of total gov't exp.	..	..	..	..	..	..
Social security coverage	% econ. active pop.	..	..	..	..	..	..
Access to safe water: total	% of pop.	..	..	..	80.3	85.6	..
Urban	"	82.8	..	..	91.0	94.3	..
Rural	"	32.1	..	..	64.3	73.0	..
Access to health care	"	..	..	..	..	..	..

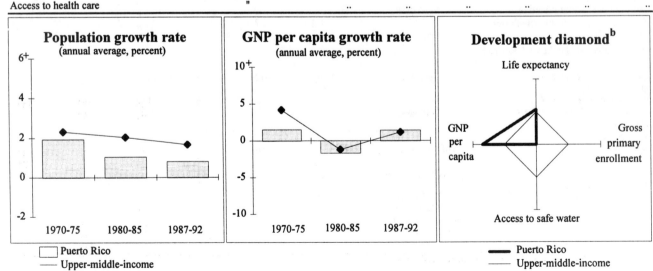

Population growth rate (annual average, percent)
☐ Puerto Rico
— Upper-middle-income

GNP per capita growth rate (annual average, percent)

Development diamond[b]
Life expectancy — Gross primary enrollment — Access to safe water — GNP per capita
— Puerto Rico
— Upper-middle-income

a. See the technical notes, p.389.　b. The development diamond, based on four key indicators, shows the average level of development in the country compared with its income group. See the introduction.

Puerto Rico

Indicator	Unit of measure	Latest single year 1970-75	Latest single year 1980-85	Most recent estimate 1987-92	Same region/income group Latin America Caribbean	Same region/income group Upper-middle-income	Next higher income group
Resources and Expenditures							
HUMAN RESOURCES							
Population (mre=1992)	thousands	2,994	3,377	3,580	453,294	477,960	828,221
Age dependency ratio	ratio	0.66	0.61	0.55	0.67	0.64	0.50
Urban	% of pop.	62.8	70.7	75.0	72.9	71.7	78.1
Population growth rate	annual %	1.9	1.0	0.8	1.7	1.6	0.7
Urban	"	3.3	2.0	1.5	2.6	2.5	0.9
Labor force (15-64)	thousands	928	1,125	1,290	166,091	181,414	390,033
Agriculture	% of labor force	..	..	..	..	..	..
Industry	"	..	..	..	..	..	..
Female	"	..	..	..	27	29	38
Females per 100 males							
Urban	number	111	113	..	..	..	..
Rural	"	103	103	..	..	..	..
NATURAL RESOURCES							
Area	thou. sq. km	8.90	8.90	8.90	20,507.48	21,836.02	31,709.00
Density	pop. per sq. km	336.4	379.4	399.0	21.7	21.5	24.5
Agricultural land	% of land area	55.6	52.0	51.9	40.2	41.7	42.7
Change in agricultural land	annual %	-0.2	-0.7	-0.2	0.5	0.3	-0.2
Agricultural land under irrigation	%	7.9	8.5	8.5	3.2	9.3	16.1
Forests and woodland	thou. sq. km	2	2	2	..	..	..
Deforestation (net)	annual %	..	..	..	..	..	..
INCOME							
Household income							
Share of top 20% of households	% of income	..	..	..	..	..	..
Share of bottom 40% of households	"	..	..	..	..	..	..
Share of bottom 20% of households	"	..	..	..	..	..	..
EXPENDITURE							
Food	% of GDP	..	..	..	..	..	..
Staples	"	..	..	..	..	..	..
Meat, fish, milk, cheese, eggs	"	..	..	..	..	..	..
Cereal imports	thou. metric tonnes	..	..	..	25,032	49,174	70,626
Food aid in cereals	"	..	..	..	1,779	282	2
Food production per capita	1987 = 100	101	83	92	104	109	101
Fertilizer consumption	kg/ha	..	..	..	15.5	68.8	162.1
Share of agriculture in GDP	% of GDP	3.3	1.8	1.4	8.9	8.1	2.4
Housing	% of GDP	..	..	..	..	..	..
Average household size	persons per household	4.2	3.7	..	..	..	..
Urban	"	4.0	..	..	..	..	..
Fixed investment: housing	% of GDP	..	..	..	..	..	..
Fuel and power	% of GDP	..	..	..	..	..	..
Energy consumption per capita	kg of oil equiv.	3,216	1,948	2,018	912	1,649	5,101
Households with electricity							
Urban	% of households	..	..	..	..	..	..
Rural	"	..	..	..	..	..	..
Transport and communication	% of GDP	..	..	..	..	..	..
Fixed investment: transport equipment	"	..	..	..	..	..	..
Total road length	thou. km	..	9	..	..	..	..
INVESTMENT IN HUMAN CAPITAL							
Health							
Population per physician	persons	..	..	..	..	..	..
Population per nurse	"	..	..	..	..	..	..
Population per hospital bed	"	..	..	..	508	385	144
Oral rehydration therapy (under-5)	% of cases	..	..	..	62	54	..
Education							
Gross enrollment ratio							
Secondary	% of school-age pop.	78	74	..	47	53	92
Female	"	..	..	..	..	..	94
Pupil-teacher ratio: primary	pupils per teacher	22	..	..	25	25	18
Pupil-teacher ratio: secondary	"	..	..	..	..	..	..
Pupils reaching grade 4	% of cohort	87	..	..	..	71	..
Repeater rate: primary	% of total enroll	..	..	..	14	11	..
Illiteracy	% of pop. (age 15+)	12	11	..	15	14	..
Female	% of fem. (age 15+)	..	..	..	17	17	..
Newspaper circulation	per thou. pop.	138	167	129	99	117	..

World Bank International Economics Department, April 1994

Qatar

Indicator	Unit of measure	Latest single year 1970-75	Latest single year 1980-85	Most recent estimate 1987-92	Same region/income group High-income
Priority Poverty Indicators					
POVERTY					
Upper poverty line	local curr.	..	..	..	..
Headcount index	% of pop.	..	..	..	..
Lower poverty line	local curr.	..	..	..	..
Headcount index	% of pop.	..	..	..	..
GNP per capita	US$	7,550	19,190	7,450	21,960
SHORT TERM INCOME INDICATORS					
Unskilled urban wages	local curr.	..	..	..	..
Unskilled rural wages	"	..	..	..	..
Rural terms of trade	"	..	..	..	..
Consumer price index	1987=100	..	96	116	..
Lower income	"	..	..	..	..
Food[a]	"	..	98	102	..
Urban	"	..	..	..	..
Rural	"	..	..	..	..
SOCIAL INDICATORS					
Public expenditure on basic social services	% of GDP	..	..	..	..
Gross enrollment ratios					
Primary	% school age pop.	111	122	97	103
Male	"	116	124	103	103
Female	"	107	119	95	103
Mortality					
Infant mortality	per thou. live births	57.0	38.0	26.0	7.0
Under 5 mortality	"	..	..	31.1	10.0
Immunization					
Measles	% age group	..	62.0	73.0	82.4
DPT	"	..	71.0	81.0	90.1
Child malnutrition (under-5)	"	..	..	..	..
Life expectancy					
Total	years	63	68	71	77
Female advantage	"	3.7	4.4	4.9	6.4
Total fertility rate	births per woman	6.8	5.0	4.0	1.7
Maternal mortality rate	per 100,000 live births	..	19	..	..
Supplementary Poverty Indicators					
Expenditures on social security	% of total gov't exp.	..	..	..	..
Social security coverage	% econ. active pop.	..	..	..	..
Access to safe water: total	% of pop.	97.0	..	91.0	..
Urban	"	100.0	..	100.0	..
Rural	"	83.0	..	48.0	..
Access to health care	"	..	95.0	100.0	..

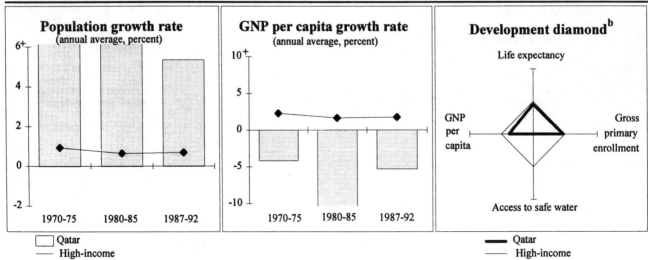

Population growth rate (annual average, percent) — 1970-75, 1980-85, 1987-92 — Qatar / High-income

GNP per capita growth rate (annual average, percent) — 1970-75, 1980-85, 1987-92

Development diamond[b] — Life expectancy, GNP per capita, Gross primary enrollment, Access to safe water — Qatar / High-income

a. See the technical notes, p.389.   b. The development diamond, based on four key indicators, shows the average level of development in the country compared with its income group. See the introduction.

Qatar

Indicator	Unit of measure	Latest single year 1970-75	Latest single year 1980-85	Most recent estimate 1987-92	Same region/income group High-income
Resources and Expenditures					
HUMAN RESOURCES					
Population (mre=1992)	thousands	171	358	508	828,221
Age dependency ratio	ratio	0.55	0.54	0.57	0.50
Urban	% of pop.	82.9	87.9	90.5	78.1
Population growth rate	annual %	6.7	8.8	2.2	0.7
Urban	"	7.4	9.3	2.5	0.9
Labor force (15-64)	thousands	83	146	197	390,033
Agriculture	% of labor force	6	3	..	..
Industry	"	28	28	..	..
Female	"	4	7	8	38
Females per 100 males					
Urban	number	..	..	..	..
Rural	"	..	..	..	..
NATURAL RESOURCES					
Area	thou. sq. km	11.00	11.00	11.00	31,709.00
Density	pop. per sq. km	15.6	32.6	45.2	24.5
Agricultural land	% of land area	4.7	4.9	5.1	42.7
Change in agricultural land	annual %	0.0	0.0	0.0	-0.2
Agricultural land under irrigation	%	..	..	..	16.1
Forests and woodland	thou. sq. km	..	..	..	..
Deforestation (net)	annual %	..	..	..	..
INCOME					
Household income					
Share of top 20% of households	% of income	..	..	..	..
Share of bottom 40% of households	"	..	..	..	..
Share of bottom 20% of households	"	..	..	..	..
EXPENDITURE					
Food	% of GDP	..	..	..	..
Staples	"	..	..	..	..
Meat, fish, milk, cheese, eggs	"	..	..	..	..
Cereal imports	thou. metric tonnes	12	97	151	70,626
Food aid in cereals	"	..	..	..	2
Food production per capita	1987 = 100	..	..	..	101
Fertilizer consumption	kg/ha	3.9	10.7	26.8	162.1
Share of agriculture in GDP	% of GDP	..	..	..	2.4
Housing	% of GDP	..	..	..	..
Average household size	persons per household	..	..	..	..
Urban	"	..	..	..	..
Fixed investment: housing	% of GDP	..	..	..	..
Fuel and power	% of GDP	..	..	..	..
Energy consumption per capita	kg of oil equiv.	2,673	14,218	14,831	5,101
Households with electricity					
Urban	% of households	..	..	..	..
Rural	"	..	..	..	..
Transport and communication	% of GDP	..	..	..	..
Fixed investment: transport equipment	"	..	..	..	..
Total road length	thou. km	..	..	..	..
INVESTMENT IN HUMAN CAPITAL					
Health					
Population per physician	persons	1,947	1,353	667	..
Population per nurse	"	570	483	186	..
Population per hospital bed	"	181	340	..	144
Oral rehydration therapy (under-5)	% of cases	..	..	20	..
Education					
Gross enrollment ratio					
Secondary	% of school-age pop.	52	74	82	92
Female		56	79	83	94
Pupil-teacher ratio: primary	pupils per teacher	19	13	11	18
Pupil-teacher ratio: secondary	"	13	9	8	..
Pupils reaching grade 4	% of cohort	97	99	..	..
Repeater rate: primary	% of total enroll	20	8	6	..
Illiteracy	% of pop. (age 15+)	..	24	..	..
Female	% of fem. (age 15+)	..	28	..	..
Newspaper circulation	per thou. pop.	..	83	165	..

World Bank International Economics Department, April 1994

283

Réunion

Indicator	Unit of measure	Latest single year 1970-75	Latest single year 1980-85	Most recent estimate 1987-92	Same region/income group Sub-Saharan Africa	Same region/income group Upper-middle-income	Next higher income group
Priority Poverty Indicators							
POVERTY							
Upper poverty line	local curr.	..	..	..	..	..	..
Headcount index	% of pop.	..	..	..	..	..	..
Lower poverty line	local curr.	..	..	..	..	..	..
Headcount index	% of pop.	..	..	..	..	..	..
GNP per capita	US$	..	..	..	520	3,870	21,960
SHORT TERM INCOME INDICATORS							
Unskilled urban wages	local curr.	..	..	..	..	..	..
Unskilled rural wages	"	..	..	..	..	..	..
Rural terms of trade	"	..	..	..	..	..	..
Consumer price index	1987=100	39	95	117	..	..	..
Lower income	"	..	..	..	..	..	..
Food[a]	"	..	96	108	..	..	..
Urban	"	..	..	..	..	..	..
Rural	"	..	..	..	..	..	..
SOCIAL INDICATORS							
Public expenditure on basic social services	% of GDP	..	..	..	..	..	..
Gross enrollment ratios							
Primary	% school age pop.	..	..	..	66	107	103
Male	"	..	..	..	79	..	103
Female	"	..	..	..	62	..	103
Mortality							
Infant mortality	per thou. live births	41.0	14.0	7.0	99.0	40.0	7.0
Under 5 mortality	"	..	..	9.0	169.0	51.0	10.0
Immunization							
Measles	% age group	..	..	..	54.0	82.0	82.4
DPT	"	..	..	..	54.6	73.8	90.1
Child malnutrition (under-5)	"	..	..	..	28.4	..	..
Life expectancy							
Total	years	64	70	74	52	69	77
Female advantage	"	7.7	8.5	8.7	3.4	6.3	6.4
Total fertility rate	births per woman	3.9	2.9	2.3	6.1	2.9	1.7
Maternal mortality rate	per 100,000 live births	..	..	..	..	..	..
Supplementary Poverty Indicators							
Expenditures on social security	% of total gov't exp.	..	..	..	..	..	..
Social security coverage	% econ. active pop.	..	..	..	..	..	..
Access to safe water: total	% of pop.	..	..	..	41.1	85.6	..
Urban	"	..	..	..	77.8	94.3	..
Rural	"	..	..	..	27.3	73.0	..
Access to health care	"	..	..	..	..	..	..

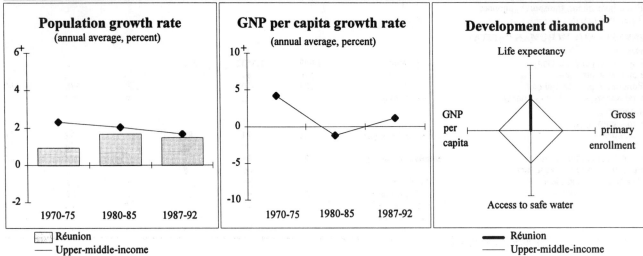

Population growth rate (annual average, percent)

GNP per capita growth rate (annual average, percent)

Development diamond[b]

Life expectancy — GNP per capita — Gross primary enrollment — Access to safe water

Réunion / Upper-middle-income

a. See the technical notes, p.389. b. The development diamond, based on four key indicators, shows the average level of development in the country compared with its income group. See the introduction.

284

Réunion

Indicator	Unit of measure	Latest single year 1970-75	Latest single year 1980-85	Most recent estimate 1987-92	Same region/income group Sub-Saharan Africa	Same region/income group Upper-middle-income	Next higher income group
Resources and Expenditures							
HUMAN RESOURCES							
Population (mre=1992)	thousands	483	550	611	546,390	477,960	828,221
Age dependency ratio	ratio	0.85	0.61	0.57	0.95	0.64	0.50
Urban	% of pop.	49.1	59.5	65.5	29.5	71.7	78.1
Population growth rate	annual %	0.6	1.7	1.5	2.9	1.6	0.7
Urban	"	2.9	3.3	2.7	5.1	2.5	0.9
Labor force (15-64)	thousands	152	209	248	224,025	181,414	390,033
Agriculture	% of labor force	28	18	..	..	..	..
Industry	"	19	17	..	..	..	..
Female	"	27	33	34	37	29	38
Females per 100 males							
Urban	number	..	..	..	..	..	..
Rural	"	..	..	..	..	..	..
NATURAL RESOURCES							
Area	thou. sq. km	2.51	2.51	2.51	24,274.03	21,836.02	31,709.00
Density	pop. per sq. km	192.4	219.1	239.8	21.9	21.5	24.5
Agricultural land	% of land area	22.4	26.0	25.6	52.7	41.7	42.7
Change in agricultural land	annual %	0.0	0.0	0.0	0.1	0.3	-0.2
Agricultural land under irrigation	%	8.9	7.7	9.4	0.8	9.3	16.1
Forests and woodland	thou. sq. km	1	1	1	..	..	..
Deforestation (net)	annual %	..	..	..	..	..	..
INCOME							
Household income							
Share of top 20% of households	% of income	..	..	..	..	..	..
Share of bottom 40% of households	"	..	..	..	..	..	..
Share of bottom 20% of households	"	..	..	..	..	..	..
EXPENDITURE							
Food	% of GDP	..	..	..	..	..	..
Staples	"	..	..	..	..	..	..
Meat, fish, milk, cheese, eggs	"	..	..	..	..	..	..
Cereal imports	thou. metric tonnes	94	139	221	20,311	49,174	70,626
Food aid in cereals	"	..	..	..	4,303	282	2
Food production per capita	1987 = 100	87	86	94	90	109	101
Fertilizer consumption	kg/ha	233.3	219.6	218.8	4.2	68.8	162.1
Share of agriculture in GDP	% of GDP	..	..	..	18.6	8.1	2.4
Housing	% of GDP	..	..	..	..	..	..
Average household size	persons per household	..	..	..	..	..	..
Urban	"	..	..	..	..	..	..
Fixed investment: housing	% of GDP	..	..	..	..	..	..
Fuel and power	% of GDP	..	..	..	..	..	..
Energy consumption per capita	kg of oil equiv.	350	722	689	258	1,649	5,101
Households with electricity							
Urban	% of households	..	..	..	..	..	..
Rural	"	..	..	..	..	..	..
Transport and communication	% of GDP	..	..	..	..	..	..
Fixed investment: transport equipment	"	..	..	..	..	..	..
Total road length	thou. km	..	..	..	..	..	..
INVESTMENT IN HUMAN CAPITAL							
Health							
Population per physician	persons	2,665	1,447	..	..	..	..
Population per nurse	"	260	..	..	..	..	..
Population per hospital bed	"	121	..	..	1,329	385	144
Oral rehydration therapy (under-5)	% of cases	..	..	..	36	54	..
Education							
Gross enrollment ratio							
Secondary	% of school-age pop.	..	..	..	18	53	92
Female	"	..	..	..	14	..	94
Pupil-teacher ratio: primary	pupils per teacher	26	19	..	39	25	18
Pupil-teacher ratio: secondary	"	22	16	..	..	..	..
Pupils reaching grade 4	% of cohort	..	91	..	..	71	..
Repeater rate: primary	% of total enroll	22	16	..	..	11	..
Illiteracy	% of pop. (age 15+)	..	21	..	51	14	..
Female	% of fem. (age 15+)	..	..	..	62	17	..
Newspaper circulation	per thou. pop.	56	97	110	14	117	..

World Bank International Economics Department, April 1994

Romania

Indicator	Unit of measure	Latest single year 1970-75	Latest single year 1980-85	Most recent estimate 1987-92	Same region/income group Europe & Central Asia	Same region/income group Lower-middle-income	Next higher income group
Priority Poverty Indicators							
POVERTY							
Upper poverty line	local curr.	..	..	..	..	..	..
Headcount index	% of pop.	..	..	..	..	..	..
Lower poverty line	local curr.	..	..	..	..	..	..
Headcount index	% of pop.	..	..	..	..	..	..
GNP per capita	US$	..	..	1,130	..	..	3,870
SHORT TERM INCOME INDICATORS							
Unskilled urban wages	local curr.	..	..	..	..	..	..
Unskilled rural wages	"	..	..	..	..	..	..
Rural terms of trade	"	..	..	..	..	..	..
Consumer price index	1987=100	..	..	..	..	..	..
Lower income	"	..	..	..	..	..	..
Food[a]	"	..	99	190	..	..	..
Urban	"	..	..	..	..	..	..
Rural	"	..	..	..	..	..	..
SOCIAL INDICATORS							
Public expenditure on basic social services	% of GDP	..	..	..	..	..	..
Gross enrollment ratios							
Primary	% school age pop.	107	98	90	..	..	107
Male	"	108	98	90	..	..	..
Female	"	107	98	90	..	..	..
Mortality							
Infant mortality	per thou. live births	34.6	25.6	23.3	30.0	45.0	40.0
Under 5 mortality	"	..	..	27.9	38.0	59.0	51.0
Immunization							
Measles	% age group	..	88.0	92.0	..	..	82.0
DPT	"	..	95.0	97.0	..	..	73.8
Child malnutrition (under-5)	"	..	..	..	..	..	..
Life expectancy							
Total	years	69	70	70	70	68	69
Female advantage	"	4.5	6.0	6.0	8.6	6.4	6.3
Total fertility rate	births per woman	2.6	2.3	1.5	2.2	3.1	2.9
Maternal mortality rate	per 100,000 live births	..	180	..	58	..	..
Supplementary Poverty Indicators							
Expenditures on social security	% of total gov't exp.	..	16.6	25.1	..	..	..
Social security coverage	% econ. active pop.	..	..	..	..	..	..
Access to safe water: total	% of pop.	..	..	..	..	..	85.6
Urban	"	..	..	..	..	..	94.3
Rural	"	..	..	..	..	..	73.0
Access to health care	"	..	100.0	..	..	..	..

Population growth rate
(annual average, percent)

- Romania
- Lower-middle-income

GNP per capita growth rate
(annual average, percent)

Development diamond[b]

- Romania
- Lower-middle-income

a. See the technical notes, p.389.   b. The development diamond, based on four key indicators, shows the average level of development in the country compared with its income group. See the introduction.

286

Romania

Indicator	Unit of measure	Latest single year 1970-75	Latest single year 1980-85	Most recent estimate 1987-92	Same region/income group Europe & Central Asia	Same region/income group Lower-middle-income	Next higher income group
Resources and Expenditures							
HUMAN RESOURCES							
Population (mre=1992)	thousands	21,245	22,725	22,748	495,241	942,547	477,960
Age dependency ratio	ratio	0.53	0.52	0.52	0.56	0.66	0.64
Urban	% of pop.	46.2	51.4	54.7	63.3	57.0	71.7
Population growth rate	annual %	1.0	0.4	-1.0	0.5	1.4	1.6
Urban	"	3.0	1.3	-0.1	..	4.8	2.5
Labor force (15-64)	thousands	11,107	11,418	11,998			181,414
Agriculture	% of labor force	40	31	..	..	..	..
Industry	"	37	43	..	..	..	..
Female	"	45	46	47	46	36	29
Females per 100 males							
Urban	number	100	..	..	..	..	..
Rural	"	105	..	..	..	..	..
NATURAL RESOURCES							
Area	thou. sq. km	237.50	237.50	237.50	24,165.06	40,697.37	21,836.02
Density	pop. per sq. km	89.5	95.7	96.7	20.4	22.8	21.5
Agricultural land	% of land area	64.9	65.2	64.2	..	..	41.7
Change in agricultural land	annual %	0.1	0.2	0.2	..	..	0.3
Agricultural land under irrigation	%	9.9	19.7	21.6	..	..	9.3
Forests and woodland	thou. sq. km	65	66	67	..	..	..
Deforestation (net)	annual %	..	..	0.0	..	..	..
INCOME							
Household income							
Share of top 20% of households	% of income	..	..	..	..	..	..
Share of bottom 40% of households	"	..	..	..	..	..	..
Share of bottom 20% of households	"	..	..	..	..	..	..
EXPENDITURE							
Food	% of GDP	19.1	..	..	..	..	..
Staples	"	4.1	..	..	..	..	..
Meat, fish, milk, cheese, eggs	"	9.1	..	..	..	..	..
Cereal imports	thou. metric tonnes	1,228	331	1,779	45,972	74,924	49,174
Food aid in cereals	"	123	..	375	1,639	4,054	282
Food production per capita	1987 = 100	68	102	66	..	..	109
Fertilizer consumption	kg/ha	80.1	91.5	31.2	..	..	68.8
Share of agriculture in GDP	% of GDP	14.6	14.0	18.9	..	..	8.1
Housing	% of GDP	3.7	..	..	..	..	..
Average household size	persons per household	..	..	..	..	..	..
Urban	"	..	..	..	..	..	..
Fixed investment: housing	% of GDP	..	3.6	..	..	..	..
Fuel and power	% of GDP	1.4	..	..	..	..	..
Energy consumption per capita	kg of oil equiv.	2,351	2,779	1,958	3,190	1,882	1,649
Households with electricity							
Urban	% of households	..	..	..	..	..	..
Rural	"	..	..	..	..	..	..
Transport and communication	% of GDP	3.6	..	..	..	..	..
Fixed investment: transport equipment	"	2.8	..	..	..	..	..
Total road length	thou. km	..	73	73	..	..	..
INVESTMENT IN HUMAN CAPITAL							
Health							
Population per physician	persons	844	567	559	378	..	..
Population per nurse	"	430	277	..	..	..	..
Population per hospital bed	"	120	114	113	134	516	385
Oral rehydration therapy (under-5)	% of cases	..	..	..	..	..	54
Education							
Gross enrollment ratio							
Secondary	% of school-age pop.	65	75	80	..	..	53
Female	"	66	76	80	..	..	..
Pupil-teacher ratio: primary	pupils per teacher	20	21	17	..	26	25
Pupil-teacher ratio: secondary	"	17	14	15	..	..	..
Pupils reaching grade 4	% of cohort	90	..	..	..	..	71
Repeater rate: primary	% of total enroll	..	..	2	..	..	11
Illiteracy	% of pop. (age 15+)	..	..	..	..	..	14
Female	% of fem. (age 15+)	..	..	..	..	..	17
Newspaper circulation	per thou. pop.	129	187	..	..	100	117

World Bank International Economics Department, April 1994

Russian Federation

Indicator	Unit of measure	Latest single year 1970-75	Latest single year 1980-85	Most recent estimate 1987-92	Same region/income group Europe & Central Asia	Same region/income group Lower-middle-income	Next higher income group
Priority Poverty Indicators							
POVERTY							
Upper poverty line	local curr.	..	..	..	..	..	..
Headcount index	% of pop.	..	..	11	..	..	..
Lower poverty line	local curr.	..	..	..	..	..	..
Headcount index	% of pop.	..	..	3	..	..	..
GNP per capita	US$	..	..	2,510	..	..	3,870
SHORT TERM INCOME INDICATORS							
Unskilled urban wages	local curr.	..	..	..	..	..	..
Unskilled rural wages	"	..	..	..	..	..	..
Rural terms of trade	"	..	..	..	..	..	..
Consumer price index	1987=100	..	..	..	..	..	..
Lower income	"	..	..	..	..	..	..
Food[a]	"	..	..	..	..	..	..
Urban	"	..	..	..	..	..	..
Rural	"	..	..	..	..	..	..
SOCIAL INDICATORS							
Public expenditure on basic social services	% of GDP	..	..	5.4	..	..	..
Gross enrollment ratios							
Primary	% school age pop.	..	..	..	..	..	107
Male	"	..	..	..	..	..	..
Female	"	..	..	..	..	..	..
Mortality							
Infant mortality	per thou. live births	..	25.4	20.0	30.0	45.0	40.0
Under 5 mortality	"	..	..	24.0	38.0	59.0	51.0
Immunization							
Measles	% age group	..	..	..	..	..	82.0
DPT	"	..	..	..	..	..	73.8
Child malnutrition (under-5)	"	..	..	..	..	..	..
Life expectancy							
Total	years	..	69	69	70	68	69
Female advantage	"	..	10.2	10.5	8.6	6.4	6.3
Total fertility rate	births per woman	2.0	2.1	1.7	2.2	3.1	2.9
Maternal mortality rate	per 100,000 live births	..	68	49	58	..	..
Supplementary Poverty Indicators							
Expenditures on social security	% of total gov't exp.	..	..	..	..	..	..
Social security coverage	% econ. active pop.	..	..	..	..	..	..
Access to safe water: total	% of pop.	..	..	..	..	..	85.6
Urban	"	..	..	..	..	..	94.3
Rural	"	..	..	..	..	..	73.0
Access to health care	"	..	..	..	..	..	..

Population growth rate (annual average, percent)

Legend: Russian Federation — Lower-middle-income
(1970-75, 1980-85, 1987-92)

GNP per capita growth rate (annual average, percent)
(1970-75, 1980-85, 1987-92)

Development diamond[b]

Life expectancy — GNP per capita — Gross primary enrollment — Access to safe water

Legend: Russian Federation — Lower-middle-income

a. See the technical notes, p.389.   b. The development diamond, based on four key indicators, shows the average level of development in the country compared with its income group. See the introduction.

Russian Federation

Indicator	Unit of measure	Latest single year 1970-75	Latest single year 1980-85	Most recent estimate 1987-92	Same region/income group Europe & Central Asia	Same region/income group Lower-middle-income	Next higher income group
Resources and Expenditures							
HUMAN RESOURCES							
Population (mre=1992)	thousands	134,200	143,858	148,986	495,241	942,547	477,960
Age dependency ratio	ratio	..	..	0.51	0.56	0.66	0.64
Urban	% of pop.	..	..	74.0	63.3	57.0	71.7
Population growth rate	annual %	..	0.8	0.2	0.5	1.4	1.6
Urban	"	..	..	..	..	4.8	2.5
Labor force (15-64)	thousands	..	..	78,682			181,414
Agriculture	% of labor force	..	..	..	..	..	..
Industry	"	..	..	..	..	..	..
Female	"	..	..	52	46	36	29
Females per 100 males							
Urban	number	..	..	..	..	..	..
Rural	"	..	..	..	..	..	..
NATURAL RESOURCES							
Area	thou. sq. km	..	..	17,075.41	24,165.06	40,697.37	21,836.02
Density	pop. per sq. km	..	..	8.7	20.4	22.8	21.5
Agricultural land	% of land area	..	..	..	..	..	41.7
Change in agricultural land	annual %	..	..	..	..	..	0.3
Agricultural land under irrigation	%	..	..	..	..	..	9.3
Forests and woodland	thou. sq. km	..	..	..	..	..	..
Deforestation (net)	annual %	..	..	..	..	..	..
INCOME							
Household income							
Share of top 20% of households	% of income	..	..	..	..	..	..
Share of bottom 40% of households	"	..	..	..	..	..	..
Share of bottom 20% of households	"	..	..	..	..	..	..
EXPENDITURE							
Food	% of GDP	..	..	13.3	..	..	..
Staples	"	..	..	2.4	..	..	..
Meat, fish, milk, cheese, eggs	"	..	..	6.0	..	..	..
Cereal imports	thou. metric tonnes	..	..	25,600	45,972	74,924	49,174
Food aid in cereals	"	..	..	13	1,639	4,054	282
Food production per capita	1987 = 100	..	..	..	..	..	109
Fertilizer consumption	kg/ha	..	..	..	..	..	68.8
Share of agriculture in GDP	% of GDP	..	11.6	12.5	..	..	8.1
Housing	% of GDP	..	..	3.1	..	..	..
Average household size	persons per household	..	..	3.2	..	..	..
Urban	"	..	..	..	..	..	..
Fixed investment: housing	% of GDP	..	..	5.7	..	..	..
Fuel and power	% of GDP	..	..	0.7	..	..	..
Energy consumption per capita	kg of oil equiv.	..	..	5,665	3,190	1,882	1,649
Households with electricity							
Urban	% of households	..	..	..	..	..	..
Rural	"	..	..	..	..	..	..
Transport and communication	% of GDP	..	..	4.2	..	..	..
Fixed investment: transport equipment	"	..	..	11.9	..	..	..
Total road length	thou. km	..	694	850	..	..	..
INVESTMENT IN HUMAN CAPITAL							
Health							
Population per physician	persons	..	..	214	378	..	..
Population per nurse	"	..	..	..	..	..	..
Population per hospital bed	"	..	..	73	134	516	385
Oral rehydration therapy (under-5)	% of cases	..	..	..	..	..	54
Education							
Gross enrollment ratio							
Secondary	% of school-age pop.	..	..	..	..	..	53
Female	"	..	..	..	..	..	..
Pupil-teacher ratio: primary	pupils per teacher	..	..	..	..	26	25
Pupil-teacher ratio: secondary	"	..	..	..	..	..	..
Pupils reaching grade 4	% of cohort	..	..	..	..	..	71
Repeater rate: primary	% of total enroll	..	..	..	..	..	11
Illiteracy	% of pop. (age 15+)	..	..	..	..	..	14
Female	% of fem. (age 15+)	..	..	..	..	..	17
Newspaper circulation	per thou. pop.	..	..	..	..	100	117

World Bank International Economics Department, April 1994

Rwanda

Indicator	Unit of measure	Latest single year		Most recent estimate 1987-92	Same region/income group		Next higher income group
		1970-75	1980-85		Sub-Saharan Africa	Low-income	
Priority Poverty Indicators							
POVERTY							
Upper poverty line	local curr.	4,276	13,810	17,999	..	..	..
Headcount index	% of pop.	..	40	54	..	19	..
Lower poverty line	local curr.	3,450	11,142	14,522	..	..	..
Headcount index	% of pop.	..	20	..	..	..	..
GNP per capita	US$	90	280	250	520	390	..
SHORT TERM INCOME INDICATORS							
Unskilled urban wages	local curr.	..	..	..	..	..	..
Unskilled rural wages	"	..	..	..	..	..	..
Rural terms of trade	"	..	..	..	..	..	.. (
Consumer price index	1987=100	41	97	142	..	..	..
Lower income	"	..	..	..	..	..	..
Food[a]	"	..	102	133	..	..	..
Urban	"	33	88	137	..	..	..
Rural	"	..	..	..	..	..	..
SOCIAL INDICATORS							
Public expenditure on basic social services	% of GDP	..	3.3	4.1	..	..	..
Gross enrollment ratios							
Primary	% school age pop.	56	63	71	66	103	..
Male	"	61	64	72	79	113	..
Female	"	51	61	70	62	96	..
Mortality							
Infant mortality	per thou. live births	142.0	124.0	117.0	99.0	73.0	45.0
Under 5 mortality	"	..	..	195.9	169.0	108.0	59.0
Immunization							
Measles	% age group	..	52.0	89.0	54.0	72.7	..
DPT	"	..	50.0	89.0	54.6	80.6	..
Child malnutrition (under-5)	"	..	..	30.0	28.4	38.3	..
Life expectancy							
Total	years	45	46	46	52	62	68
Female advantage	"	3.2	3.4	2.9	3.4	2.4	6.4
Total fertility rate	births per woman	7.9	8.5	6.2	6.1	3.4	3.1
Maternal mortality rate	per 100,000 live births	..	210	300	..	..	..
Supplementary Poverty Indicators							
Expenditures on social security	% of total gov't exp.	..	..	..	..	..	..
Social security coverage	% econ. active pop.	..	..	..	..	..	..
Access to safe water: total	% of pop.	67.0	49.0	64.0	41.1	68.4	..
Urban	"	81.0	79.0	66.0	77.8	78.9	..
Rural	"	66.0	48.0	64.0	27.3	60.3	..
Access to health care	"	..	100.0	60.0	..	..	..

Population growth rate
(annual average, percent)

GNP per capita growth rate
(annual average, percent)

Development diamond[b]

Rwanda
Low-income

a. See the technical notes, p.389.   b. The development diamond, based on four key indicators, shows the average level of development in the country compared with its income group. See the introduction.

Rwanda

| Indicator | Unit of measure | Latest single year | | Most recent estimate 1987-92 | Same region/income group | | Next higher income group |
		1970-75	1980-85		Sub-Saharan Africa	Low-income	
Resources and Expenditures							
HUMAN RESOURCES							
Population (mre=1992)	thousands	4,384	5,960	7,320	546,390	3,194,535	942,547
Age dependency ratio	ratio	1.03	1.06	1.02	0.95	0.67	0.66
Urban	% of pop.	4.0	5.2	5.8	29.5	26.7	57.0
Population growth rate	annual %	3.4	3.0	2.5	2.9	1.8	1.4
Urban	"	7.5	4.9	4.2	5.1	3.4	4.8
Labor force (15-64)	thousands	2,274	3,063	3,736	224,025	1,478,954	..
Agriculture	% of labor force	93	93	..	..	..	..
Industry	"	3	3	..	..	..	..
Female	"	50	49	47	37	33	36
Females per 100 males							
Urban	number	94	..	..	..	..	..
Rural	"	114	..	..	..	..	..
NATURAL RESOURCES							
Area	thou. sq. km	26.34	26.34	26.34	24,274.03	38,401.06	40,697.37
Density	pop. per sq. km	166.4	226.3	271.1	21.9	81.7	22.8
Agricultural land	% of land area	61.1	65.9	65.6	52.7	50.9	..
Change in agricultural land	annual %	-0.1	0.1	0.1	0.1	0.0	..
Agricultural land under irrigation	%	0.3	0.3	0.3	0.8	18.2	..
Forests and woodland	thou. sq. km	6	6	6	..	..	..
Deforestation (net)	annual %	..	..	0.0	..	..	..
INCOME							
Household income							
Share of top 20% of households	% of income	..	39	..	..	42	..
Share of bottom 40% of households	"	..	23	..	..	19	..
Share of bottom 20% of households	"	..	10	..	..	8	..
EXPENDITURE							
Food	% of GDP	..	24.4	..	..	..	..
Staples	"	..	8.6	..	..	..	..
Meat, fish, milk, cheese, eggs	"	..	8.6	..	..	..	..
Cereal imports	thou. metric tonnes	17	33	14	20,311	46,537	74,924
Food aid in cereals	"	19	35	11	4,303	9,008	4,054
Food production per capita	1987 = 100	95	106	80	90	123	..
Fertilizer consumption	kg/ha	0.2	0.9	1.0	4.2	61.9	..
Share of agriculture in GDP	% of GDP	49.2	41.8	40.6	18.6	29.6	..
Housing	% of GDP	..	12.8	..	..	..	..
Average household size	persons per household	..	..	..	..	..	..
Urban	"	..	..	..	..	..	..
Fixed investment: housing	% of GDP	..	3.1	..	..	..	..
Fuel and power	% of GDP	..	5.2	..	..	..	..
Energy consumption per capita	kg of oil equiv.	22	45	28	258	335	1,882
Households with electricity							
Urban	% of households	..	..	..	..	..	..
Rural	"	..	..	..	..	..	..
Transport and communication	% of GDP	..	7.5	..	..	..	..
Fixed investment: transport equipment	"	..	3.1	..	..	..	..
Total road length	thou. km	6	12	13	..	..	..
INVESTMENT IN HUMAN CAPITAL							
Health							
Population per physician	persons	59,956	36,564	40,609	..	..	..
Population per nurse	"	5,607	3,627	2,331	..	..	..
Population per hospital bed	"	805	675	605	1,329	1,050	516
Oral rehydration therapy (under-5)	% of cases	..	..	24	36	39	..
Education							
Gross enrollment ratio							
Secondary	% of school-age pop.	2	6	8	18	41	..
Female	"	1	5	7	14	35	..
Pupil-teacher ratio: primary	pupils per teacher	50	56	58	39	37	26
Pupil-teacher ratio: secondary	"	13	..	..	..	19	..
Pupils reaching grade 4	% of cohort	69	78	74	..	..	..
Repeater rate: primary	% of total enroll	21	12	11	..	..	..
Illiteracy	% of pop. (age 15+)	..	55	50	51	39	..
Female	% of fem. (age 15+)	..	68	63	62	52	..
Newspaper circulation	per thou. pop.	..	0	0	14	..	100

World Bank International Economics Department, April 1994

St. Kitts and Nevis

Indicator	Unit of measure	Latest single year		Most recent estimate 1987-92	Same region/income group		Next higher income group
		1970-75	1980-85		Latin America Caribbean	Upper-middle-income	

Priority Poverty Indicators

Indicator	Unit of measure	1970-75	1980-85	1987-92	Latin America Caribbean	Upper-middle-income	Next higher income group
POVERTY							
Upper poverty line	local curr.	..	..	..	..	..	..
Headcount index	% of pop.	..	..	..	..	..	..
Lower poverty line	local curr.	..	..	..	..	..	..
Headcount index	% of pop.	..	..	..	..	..	..
GNP per capita	US$	..	1,770	3,990	2,690	3,870	21,960
SHORT TERM INCOME INDICATORS							
Unskilled urban wages	local curr.	..	..	..	..	..	..
Unskilled rural wages	"	..	..	..	..	..	..
Rural terms of trade	"	..	..	..	..	..	..
Consumer price index	1987=100	..	99	118	..	..	..
Lower income	"	..	..	..	..	..	..
Food[a]	"	..	99	114	..	..	..
Urban	"	..	..	..	..	..	..
Rural	"	..	..	..	..	..	..
SOCIAL INDICATORS							
Public expenditure on basic social services	% of GDP	..	..	..	..	..	..
Gross enrollment ratios							
Primary	% school age pop.	..	..	98	106	107	103
Male	"	..	..	..	..	..	103
Female	"	..	..	..	..	..	103
Mortality							
Infant mortality	per thou. live births	..	45.0	34.0	44.0	40.0	7.0
Under 5 mortality	"	..	..	41.7	56.0	51.0	10.0
Immunization							
Measles	% age group	..	85.0	99.0	78.9	82.0	82.4
DPT	"	..	97.0	99.0	73.8	73.8	90.1
Child malnutrition (under-5)	"	..	..	..	10.5	..	..
Life expectancy							
Total	years	..	64	68	68	69	77
Female advantage	"	..	4.0	4.0	5.6	6.3	6.4
Total fertility rate	births per woman	3.5	3.3	2.6	3.0	2.9	1.7
Maternal mortality rate	per 100,000 live births	..	..	..	..	..	..

Supplementary Poverty Indicators

Indicator	Unit of measure	1970-75	1980-85	1987-92	Latin America Caribbean	Upper-middle-income	Next higher income group
Expenditures on social security	% of total gov't exp.	..	..	..	..	..	..
Social security coverage	% econ. active pop.	..	..	..	..	..	..
Access to safe water: total	% of pop.	..	..	..	80.3	85.6	..
Urban	"	..	..	..	91.0	94.3	..
Rural	"	..	..	..	64.3	73.0	..
Access to health care	"	..	99.0	100.0	..	..	..

Population growth rate
(annual average, percent)

- ☐ St. Kitts and Nevis
- — Upper-middle-income

GNP per capita growth rate
(annual average, percent)

Development diamond[b]

- ▬ St. Kitts and Nevis
- — Upper-middle-income

a. See the technical notes, p.389.   b. The development diamond, based on four key indicators, shows the average level of development in the country compared with its income group. See the introduction.

St. Kitts and Nevis

Indicator	Unit of measure	Latest single year 1970-75	Latest single year 1980-85	Most recent estimate 1987-92	Same region/income group Latin America Caribbean	Same region/income group Upper-middle-income	Next higher income group
Resources and Expenditures							
HUMAN RESOURCES							
Population (mre=1992)	thousands	44	43	42	453,294	477,960	828,221
Age dependency ratio	ratio	..	0.87	0.77	0.67	0.64	0.50
Urban	% of pop.	37.7	45.0	50.4	72.9	71.7	78.1
Population growth rate	annual %	-0.5	-2.1	-0.5	1.7	1.6	0.7
Urban	"	1.4	-0.5	1.0	2.6	2.5	0.9
Labor force (15-64)	thousands	..	..	..	166,091	181,414	390,033
Agriculture	% of labor force	..	..	..	..	..	..
Industry	"	..	..	..	..	..	..
Female	"	..	..	..	27	29	38
Females per 100 males							
Urban	number	..	..	..	..	..	..
Rural	"	..	..	..	..	..	..
NATURAL RESOURCES							
Area	thou. sq. km	0.36	0.36	0.36	20,507.48	21,836.02	31,709.00
Density	pop. per sq. km	121.1	118.7	116.1	21.7	21.5	24.5
Agricultural land	% of land area	41.7	41.7	41.7	40.2	41.7	42.7
Change in agricultural land	annual %	0.0	0.0	0.0	0.5	0.3	-0.2
Agricultural land under irrigation	%	..	..	..	3.2	9.3	16.1
Forests and woodland	thou. sq. km	0	0	0	..	..	..
Deforestation (net)	annual %	..	..	..	..	..	..
INCOME							
Household income							
Share of top 20% of households	% of income	..	..	..	..	..	..
Share of bottom 40% of households	"	..	..	..	..	..	..
Share of bottom 20% of households	"	..	..	..	..	..	..
EXPENDITURE							
Food	% of GDP	..	..	..	..	..	..
Staples	"	..	..	..	..	..	..
Meat, fish, milk, cheese, eggs	"	..	..	..	..	..	..
Cereal imports	thou. metric tonnes	4	5	6	25,032	49,174	70,626
Food aid in cereals	"	0	0	5	1,779	282	2
Food production per capita	1987 = 100	..	..	..	104	109	101
Fertilizer consumption	kg/ha	180.0	186.7	73.3	15.5	68.8	162.1
Share of agriculture in GDP	% of GDP	..	7.8	5.3	8.9	8.1	2.4
Housing	% of GDP	..	..	..	..	..	..
Average household size	persons per household	..	..	..	..	..	..
Urban	"	..	..	..	..	..	..
Fixed investment: housing	% of GDP	..	..	..	..	..	..
Fuel and power	% of GDP	..	..	..	..	..	..
Energy consumption per capita	kg of oil equiv.	0	398	481	912	1,649	5,101
Households with electricity							
Urban	% of households	..	..	..	..	..	..
Rural	"	..	..	..	..	..	..
Transport and communication	% of GDP	..	..	..	..	..	..
Fixed investment: transport equipment	"	..	..	..	..	..	..
Total road length	thou. km	..	..	..	..	..	..
INVESTMENT IN HUMAN CAPITAL							
Health							
Population per physician	persons	3,207	2,183	..	..	..	..
Population per nurse	"	271	128	..	..	..	..
Population per hospital bed	"	168	117	..	508	385	144
Oral rehydration therapy (under-5)	% of cases	..	..	5	62	54	..
Education							
Gross enrollment ratio							
Secondary	% of school-age pop.	..	..	103	47	53	92
Female	"	..	..	..	..	..	94
Pupil-teacher ratio: primary	pupils per teacher	..	22	21	25	25	18
Pupil-teacher ratio: secondary	"	..	15	15	..	..	..
Pupils reaching grade 4	% of cohort	..	..	..	..	71	..
Repeater rate: primary	% of total enroll	..	..	..	14	11	..
Illiteracy	% of pop. (age 15+)	2	..	..	15	14	..
Female	% of fem. (age 15+)	..	..	..	17	17	..
Newspaper circulation	per thou. pop.	34	165	..	99	117	..

World Bank International Economics Department, April 1994

St. Lucia

Indicator	Unit of measure	Latest single year 1970-75	Latest single year 1980-85	Most recent estimate 1987-92	Same region/income group Latin America Caribbean	Same region/income group Upper-middle-income	Next higher income group
Priority Poverty Indicators							
POVERTY							
Upper poverty line	local curr.	..	..	..	..	..	..
Headcount index	% of pop.	..	..	..	..	..	..
Lower poverty line	local curr.	..	..	..	..	..	..
Headcount index	% of pop.	..	..	..	..	..	..
GNP per capita	US$	..	..	2,920	2,690	3,870	21,960
SHORT TERM INCOME INDICATORS							
Unskilled urban wages	local curr.	..	..	..	..	..	..
Unskilled rural wages	"	..	..	..	..	..	..
Rural terms of trade	"	..	..	..	..	..	..
Consumer price index	1987=100	42	91	122	..	..	..
Lower income	"	..	..	..	..	..	..
Food[a]	"	..	87	116	..	..	..
Urban	"	..	..	..	..	..	..
Rural	"	..	..	..	..	..	..
SOCIAL INDICATORS							
Public expenditure on basic social services	% of GDP	..	..	..	..	..	..
Gross enrollment ratios							
Primary	% school age pop.	..	..	..	106	107	103
Male	"	..	..	..	..	..	103
Female	"	..	..	..	..	..	103
Mortality							
Infant mortality	per thou. live births	..	25.0	18.5	44.0	40.0	7.0
Under 5 mortality	"	..	..	22.6	56.0	51.0	10.0
Immunization							
Measles	% age group	..	60.0	82.0	78.9	82.0	82.4
DPT	"	..	83.0	89.0	73.8	73.8	90.1
Child malnutrition (under-5)	"	..	..	..	10.5	..	..
Life expectancy							
Total	years	62	69	70	68	69	77
Female advantage	"	3.6	4.0	4.0	5.6	6.3	6.4
Total fertility rate	births per woman	5.5	4.0	3.2	3.0	2.9	1.7
Maternal mortality rate	per 100,000 live births	..	..	..	..	..	..
Supplementary Poverty Indicators							
Expenditures on social security	% of total gov't exp.	..	..	..	..	..	..
Social security coverage	% econ. active pop.	..	..	..	..	..	..
Access to safe water: total	% of pop.	..	..	..	80.3	85.6	..
Urban	"	..	..	..	91.0	94.3	..
Rural	"	..	..	..	64.3	73.0	..
Access to health care	"	..	100.0	100.0	..	..	..

Population growth rate
(annual average, percent)

□ St. Lucia
— Upper-middle-income

GNP per capita growth rate
(annual average, percent)

Development diamond[b]

Life expectancy

GNP per capita — Gross primary enrollment

Access to safe water

— St. Lucia
— Upper-middle-income

a. See the technical notes, p.389.   b. The development diamond, based on four key indicators, shows the average level of development in the country compared with its income group. See the introduction.

St. Lucia

Indicator	Unit of measure	Latest single year 1970-75	Latest single year 1980-85	Most recent estimate 1987-92	Same region/income group Latin America Caribbean	Same region/income group Upper-middle-income	Next higher income group
Resources and Expenditures							
HUMAN RESOURCES							
Population (mre=1992)	thousands	112	137	155	453,294	477,960	828,221
Age dependency ratio	ratio	..	1.11	0.81	0.67	0.64	0.50
Urban	% of pop.	41.0	42.7	44.9	72.9	71.7	78.1
Population growth rate	annual %	2.0	2.0	1.6	1.7	1.6	0.7
Urban	"	2.4	2.4	2.5	2.6	2.5	0.9
Labor force (15-64)	thousands	..	..	..	166,091	181,414	390,033
Agriculture	% of labor force	..	..	..	..	..	..
Industry	"	..	..	..	..	..	..
Female	"	..	..	..	27	29	38
Females per 100 males							
Urban	number	..	..	..	..	..	..
Rural	"	..	..	..	..	..	..
NATURAL RESOURCES							
Area	thou. sq. km	0.62	0.62	0.62	20,507.48	21,836.02	31,709.00
Density	pop. per sq. km	180.5	220.7	246.3	21.7	21.5	24.5
Agricultural land	% of land area	32.8	32.8	34.4	40.2	41.7	42.7
Change in agricultural land	annual %	0.0	0.0	0.0	0.5	0.3	-0.2
Agricultural land under irrigation	%	5.0	5.0	4.8	3.2	9.3	16.1
Forests and woodland	thou. sq. km	0	0	0	..	..	..
Deforestation (net)	annual %	..	..	..	..	..	..
INCOME							
Household income							
Share of top 20% of households	% of income	..	..	..	..	..	..
Share of bottom 40% of households	"	..	..	..	..	..	..
Share of bottom 20% of households	"	..	..	..	..	..	..
EXPENDITURE							
Food	% of GDP	..	28.2	..	..	..	..
Staples	"	..	5.9	..	..	..	..
Meat, fish, milk, cheese, eggs	"	..	11.7	..	..	..	..
Cereal imports	thou. metric tonnes	8	15	19	25,032	49,174	70,626
Food aid in cereals	"	0	0	8	1,779	282	2
Food production per capita	1987 = 100	99	115	115	104	109	101
Fertilizer consumption	kg/ha	205.0	93.9	309.5	15.5	68.8	162.1
Share of agriculture in GDP	% of GDP	..	13.3	11.8	8.9	8.1	2.4
Housing	% of GDP	..	11.5	..	..	..	..
Average household size	persons per household	4.6	..	..	..	..	..
Urban	"	..	..	..	..	..	..
Fixed investment: housing	% of GDP	..	3.3	..	..	..	..
Fuel and power	% of GDP	..	3.5	..	..	..	..
Energy consumption per capita	kg of oil equiv.	223	329	335	912	1,649	5,101
Households with electricity							
Urban	% of households	..	..	..	..	..	..
Rural	"	..	..	..	..	..	..
Transport and communication	% of GDP	..	3.9	..	..	..	..
Fixed investment: transport equipment	"	..	6.3	..	..	..	..
Total road length	thou. km	..	..	..	..	..	..
INVESTMENT IN HUMAN CAPITAL							
Health							
Population per physician	persons	5,316	3,831	..	..	..	..
Population per nurse	"	697	..	..	..	..	..
Population per hospital bed	"	197	..	..	508	385	144
Oral rehydration therapy (under-5)	% of cases	..	..	75	62	54	..
Education							
Gross enrollment ratio							
Secondary	% of school-age pop.	..	..	..	47	53	92
Female	"	..	..	..	..	..	94
Pupil-teacher ratio: primary	pupils per teacher	31	30	28	25	25	18
Pupil-teacher ratio: secondary	"	18	19	18	..	..	..
Pupils reaching grade 4	% of cohort	..	..	97	..	71	..
Repeater rate: primary	% of total enroll	..	7	..	14	11	..
Illiteracy	% of pop. (age 15+)	18	..	..	15	14	..
Female	% of fem. (age 15+)	..	..	..	17	17	..
Newspaper circulation	per thou. pop.	40	30	..	99	117	..

World Bank International Economics Department, April 1994

St. Vincent

Indicator	Unit of measure	Latest single year 1970-75	Latest single year 1980-85	Most recent estimate 1987-92	Same region/income group Latin America Caribbean	Same region/income group Lower-middle-income	Next higher income group
Priority Poverty Indicators							
POVERTY							
Upper poverty line	local curr.	..	..	..	..	..	..
Headcount index	% of pop.	..	..	..	..	..	..
Lower poverty line	local curr.	..	..	..	..	..	..
Headcount index	% of pop.	..	..	..	..	..	..
GNP per capita	US$	350	1,080	1,990	2,690	..	3,870
SHORT TERM INCOME INDICATORS							
Unskilled urban wages	local curr.	..	..	..	..	..	..
Unskilled rural wages	"	..	..	..	..	..	..
Rural terms of trade	"	..	..	..	..	..	..
Consumer price index	1987=100	40	96	121	..	..	..
Lower income	"	..	..	..	..	..	..
Food[a]	"	..	..	118	..	..	..
Urban	"	..	..	..	..	..	..
Rural	"	..	..	..	..	..	..
SOCIAL INDICATORS							
Public expenditure on basic social services	% of GDP	..	..	10.4	..	..	..
Gross enrollment ratios							
Primary	% school age pop.	..	..	..	106	..	107
Male	"	..	..	..	..	..	..
Female	"	..	..	..	..	..	..
Mortality							
Infant mortality	per thou. live births	..	26.5	20.1	44.0	45.0	40.0
Under 5 mortality	"	..	..	24.7	56.0	59.0	51.0
Immunization							
Measles	% age group	..	92.0	96.0	78.9	..	82.0
DPT	"	..	86.0	98.0	73.8	..	73.8
Child malnutrition (under-5)	"	..	..	..	10.5	..	..
Life expectancy							
Total	years	63	68	71	68	68	69
Female advantage	"	2.7	4.6	6.1	5.6	6.4	6.3
Total fertility rate	births per woman	5.0	3.3	2.5	3.0	3.1	2.9
Maternal mortality rate	per 100,000 live births	..	..	..	..	..	..
Supplementary Poverty Indicators							
Expenditures on social security	% of total gov't exp.	..	1.5	0.0	..	..	..
Social security coverage	% econ. active pop.	..	..	..	..	..	..
Access to safe water: total	% of pop.	..	..	..	80.3	..	85.6
Urban	"	..	..	..	91.0	..	94.3
Rural	"	..	..	..	64.3	..	73.0
Access to health care	"	..	80.0	80.0	..	..	..

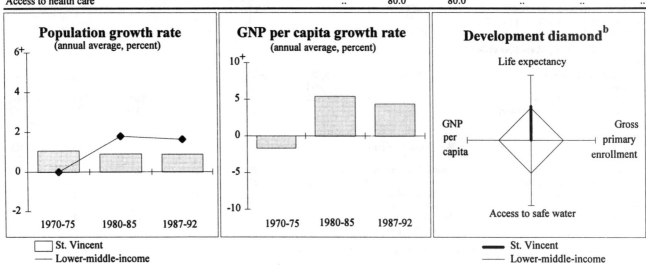

Population growth rate (annual average, percent)

1970-75, 1980-85, 1987-92

☐ St. Vincent
— Lower-middle-income

GNP per capita growth rate (annual average, percent)

1970-75, 1980-85, 1987-92

Development diamond[b]

Life expectancy
GNP per capita — Gross primary enrollment
Access to safe water

— St. Vincent
— Lower-middle-income

a. See the technical notes, p.389.   b. The development diamond, based on four key indicators, shows the average level of development in the country compared with its income group. See the introduction.

St. Vincent

Indicator	Unit of measure	Latest single year 1970-75	Latest single year 1980-85	Most recent estimate 1987-92	Same region/income group Latin America Caribbean	Same region/income group Lower-middle-income	Next higher income group
Resources and Expenditures							
HUMAN RESOURCES							
Population (mre=1992)	thousands	93	102	109	453,294	942,547	477,960
Age dependency ratio	ratio	..	0.75	0.69	0.67	0.66	0.64
Urban	% of pop.	16.3	18.9	21.1	72.9	57.0	71.7
Population growth rate	annual %	1.1	0.9	0.8	1.7	1.4	1.6
Urban	"	2.6	2.3	2.6	2.6	4.8	2.5
Labor force (15-64)	thousands	..	..	..	166,091	..	181,414
Agriculture	% of labor force	..	..	..	..	..	..
Industry	"	..	..	..	..	..	..
Female	"	..	..	..	27	36	29
Females per 100 males							
Urban	number	..	..	..	..	..	..
Rural	"	..	..	..	..	..	..
NATURAL RESOURCES							
Area	thou. sq. km	0.39	0.39	0.39	20,507.48	40,697.37	21,836.02
Density	pop. per sq. km	238.0	262.3	276.9	21.7	22.8	21.5
Agricultural land	% of land area	25.6	30.8	33.3	40.2	..	41.7
Change in agricultural land	annual %	0.0	0.0	0.0	0.5	..	0.3
Agricultural land under irrigation	%	10.0	8.3	7.7	3.2	..	9.3
Forests and woodland	thou. sq. km	0	0	0	..	..	..
Deforestation (net)	annual %	..			..	..	..
INCOME							
Household income							
Share of top 20% of households	% of income	..	..	..	..	..	..
Share of bottom 40% of households	"	..	..	..	..	..	..
Share of bottom 20% of households	"	..	..	..	..	..	..
EXPENDITURE							
Food	% of GDP	..	..	39.7	..	..	..
Staples	"	..	..	8.3	..	..	..
Meat, fish, milk, cheese, eggs	"	..	..	16.4	..	..	..
Cereal imports	thou. metric tonnes	8	33	41	25,032	74,924	49,174
Food aid in cereals	"	..	0	7	1,779	4,054	282
Food production per capita	1987 = 100	91	145	142	104	..	109
Fertilizer consumption	kg/ha	400.0	341.7	176.9	15.5	..	68.8
Share of agriculture in GDP	% of GDP	..	16.3	15.0	8.9	..	8.1
Housing	% of GDP	..	..	12.1	..	..	..
Average household size	persons per household	..	..	..	..	..	..
Urban	"	..	..	..	..	..	..
Fixed investment: housing	% of GDP	..	..	3.4	..	..	..
Fuel and power	% of GDP	..	..	4.2	..	..	..
Energy consumption per capita	kg of oil equiv.	151	176	202	912	1,882	1,649
Households with electricity							
Urban	% of households	..	..	..	..	..	..
Rural	"	..	..	..	..	..	..
Transport and communication	% of GDP	..	..	2.5	..	..	..
Fixed investment: transport equipment	"	..	..	6.4	..	..	..
Total road length	thou. km	..	..	..	..	..	..
INVESTMENT IN HUMAN CAPITAL							
Health							
Population per physician	persons	5,500	3,756	..	..	..	..
Population per nurse	"	642	..	..	..	..	..
Population per hospital bed	"	200	..	..	508	516	385
Oral rehydration therapy (under-5)	% of cases	..	..	98	62	..	54
Education							
Gross enrollment ratio							
Secondary	% of school-age pop.	..	..	..	47	..	53
Female	"	..	..	..	..	..	..
Pupil-teacher ratio: primary	pupils per teacher	18	19	20	25	26	25
Pupil-teacher ratio: secondary	"	22	18	27	..	..	..
Pupils reaching grade 4	% of cohort	..	..	..	..	..	71
Repeater rate: primary	% of total enroll	..	..	..	14	..	11
Illiteracy	% of pop. (age 15+)	4	..	..	15	..	14
Female	% of fem. (age 15+)	..	..	..	17	..	17
Newspaper circulation	per thou. pop.	..	..	..	99	100	117

World Bank International Economics Department, April 1994

São Tomé and Principe

Indicator	Unit of measure	Latest single year 1970-75	Latest single year 1980-85	Most recent estimate 1987-92	Same region/income group Sub-Saharan Africa	Same region/income group Low-income	Next higher income group
Priority Poverty Indicators							
POVERTY							
Upper poverty line	local curr.	..	..	..	..	..	..
Headcount index	% of pop.	..	..	..	..	19	..
Lower poverty line	local curr.	..	..	..	..	..	..
Headcount index	% of pop.	..	..	..	..	..	..
GNP per capita	US$	440	340	360	520	390	..
SHORT TERM INCOME INDICATORS							
Unskilled urban wages	local curr.	..	..	..	..	..	..
Unskilled rural wages	"	..	..	..	..	..	..
Rural terms of trade	"	..	..	..	..	..	..
Consumer price index	1987=100	..	..	..	..	..	..
Lower income	"	..	..	..	..	..	..
Food[a]	"	..	..	..	..	..	..
Urban	"	..	..	..	..	..	..
Rural	"	..	..	..	..	..	..
SOCIAL INDICATORS							
Public expenditure on basic social services	% of GDP	..	..	23.1	..	..	..
Gross enrollment ratios							
Primary	% school age pop.	..	..	138	66	103	..
Male	"	..	..	..	79	113	..
Female	"	..	..	..	62	96	..
Mortality							
Infant mortality	per thou. live births	89.0	80.4	65.4	99.0	73.0	45.0
Under 5 mortality	"	..	..	85.0	169.0	108.0	59.0
Immunization							
Measles	% age group	..	35.0	57.0	54.0	72.7	..
DPT	"	..	42.0	77.0	54.6	80.6	..
Child malnutrition (under-5)	"	..	..	..	28.4	38.3	..
Life expectancy							
Total	years	..	63	68	52	62	68
Female advantage	"	..	3.8	5.5	3.4	2.4	6.4
Total fertility rate	births per woman	..	5.3	5.0	6.1	3.4	3.1
Maternal mortality rate	per 100,000 live births	..	..	..	..	..	..
Supplementary Poverty Indicators							
Expenditures on social security	% of total gov't exp.	..	..	..	..	..	..
Social security coverage	% econ. active pop.	..	..	..	..	..	..
Access to safe water: total	% of pop.	..	42.0	..	41.1	68.4	..
Urban	"	..	33.0	..	77.8	78.9	..
Rural	"	..	45.0	..	27.3	60.3	..
Access to health care	"	..	..	88.0	..	..	..

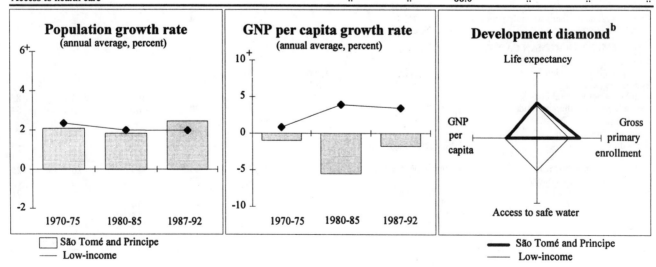

Population growth rate (annual average, percent)

□ São Tomé and Principe
— Low-income

GNP per capita growth rate (annual average, percent)

Development diamond[b]

Life expectancy

GNP per capita — Gross primary enrollment

Access to safe water

— São Tomé and Principe
— Low-income

a. See the technical notes, p.389.   b. The development diamond, based on four key indicators, shows the average level of development in the country compared with its income group. See the introduction.

298

São Tomé and Principe

Indicator	Unit of measure	Latest single year 1970-75	Latest single year 1980-85	Most recent estimate 1987-92	Same region/income group Sub-Saharan Africa	Same region/income group Low-income	Next higher income group
Resources and Expenditures							
HUMAN RESOURCES							
Population (mre=1992)	thousands	81	103	121	546,390	3,194,535	942,547
Age dependency ratio	ratio	..	0.87	0.86	0.95	0.67	0.66
Urban	% of pop.	27.9	37.6	44.1	29.5	26.7	57.0
Population growth rate	annual %	2.5	2.0	2.5	2.9	1.8	1.4
Urban	"	5.8	7.1	4.5	5.1	3.4	4.8
Labor force (15-64)	thousands	..	..	..	224,025	1,478,954	..
Agriculture	% of labor force	..	..	..	..	..	..
Industry	"	..	..	..	..	..	..
Female	"	..	..	..	37	33	36
Females per 100 males							
Urban	number	..	..	..	..	..	..
Rural	"	..	..	..	..	..	..
NATURAL RESOURCES							
Area	thou. sq. km	0.96	0.96	0.96	24,274.03	38,401.06	40,697.37
Density	pop. per sq. km	84.4	107.3	122.9	21.9	81.7	22.8
Agricultural land	% of land area	38.5	39.6	39.6	52.7	50.9	..
Change in agricultural land	annual %	0.0	2.7	0.0	0.1	0.0	..
Agricultural land under irrigation	%	..	..	..	0.8	18.2	..
Forests and woodland	thou. sq. km	..	..	..	..	..	..
Deforestation (net)	annual %	..	..	..	..	..	..
INCOME							
Household income							
Share of top 20% of households	% of income	..	..	..	..	42	..
Share of bottom 40% of households	"	..	..	..	..	19	..
Share of bottom 20% of households	"	..	..	..	..	8	..
EXPENDITURE							
Food	% of GDP	..	..	43.3	..	..	..
Staples	"	..	..	9.3	..	..	..
Meat, fish, milk, cheese, eggs	"	..	..	21.6	..	..	..
Cereal imports	thou. metric tonnes	4	10	9	20,311	46,537	74,924
Food aid in cereals	"		10	1	4,303	9,008	4,054
Food production per capita	1987 = 100	120	75	58	90	123	..
Fertilizer consumption	kg/ha	..	..	..	4.2	61.9	..
Share of agriculture in GDP	% of GDP	..	..	28.9	18.6	29.6	..
Housing	% of GDP	..	..	12.8	..	..	..
Average household size	persons per household	..	3.8	..	..	..	..
Urban	"	..	..	..	..	..	..
Fixed investment: housing	% of GDP	..	..	0.6	..	..	..
Fuel and power	% of GDP	..	..	5.2	..	..	..
Energy consumption per capita	kg of oil equiv.	74	126	190	258	335	1,882
Households with electricity							
Urban	% of households	..	..	..	..	..	..
Rural	"	..	..	..	..	..	..
Transport and communication	% of GDP	..	..	6.3	..	..	..
Fixed investment: transport equipment	"	..	..	2.8	..	..	..
Total road length	thou. km	..	..	..	..	..	..
INVESTMENT IN HUMAN CAPITAL							
Health							
Population per physician	persons	4,294	1,941	1,885	..	..	..
Population per nurse	"	1,116	280	190	..	..	..
Population per hospital bed	"	37	..	..	1,329	1,050	516
Oral rehydration therapy (under-5)	% of cases	..	..	46	36	39	..
Education							
Gross enrollment ratio							
Secondary	% of school-age pop.	..	..	..	18	41	..
Female	"	..	..	..	14	35	..
Pupil-teacher ratio: primary	pupils per teacher	34	31	35	39	37	26
Pupil-teacher ratio: secondary	"	13	21	23	..	19	..
Pupils reaching grade 4	% of cohort	..	82	..	..	..	..
Repeater rate: primary	% of total enroll	..	21	29	..	..	..
Illiteracy	% of pop. (age 15+)	..	43	33	51	39	..
Female	% of fem. (age 15+)	..	..	..	62	52	..
Newspaper circulation	per thou. pop.	..	..	..	14	..	100

World Bank International Economics Department, April 1994

Saudi Arabia

Indicator	Unit of measure	Latest single year 1970-75	Latest single year 1980-85	Most recent estimate 1987-92	Same region/income group Mid-East & North Africa	Same region/income group Upper-middle-income	Next higher income group
Priority Poverty Indicators							
POVERTY							
Upper poverty line	local curr.	..	..	..	..	..	..
Headcount index	% of pop.	..	..	..	..	..	..
Lower poverty line	local curr.	..	..	..	..	..	..
Headcount index	% of pop.	..	..	..	..	..	..
GNP per capita	US$	3,280	8,700	7,510	1,950	3,870	21,960
SHORT TERM INCOME INDICATORS							
Unskilled urban wages	local curr.	..	..	..	..	..	..
Unskilled rural wages	"	..	..	..	..	..	..
Rural terms of trade	"	..	..	..	..	..	..
Consumer price index	1987=100	69	105	109	..	..	..
Lower income	"	..	..	..	..	..	..
Food[a]	"	..	103	112	..	..	..
Urban	"	..	..	..	..	..	..
Rural	"	..	..	..	..	..	..
SOCIAL INDICATORS							
Public expenditure on basic social services	% of GDP	..	..	1.6	..	..	..
Gross enrollment ratios							
Primary	% school age pop.	58	69	77	100	107	103
Male	"	72	77	82	107	..	103
Female	"	43	61	72	88	..	103
Mortality							
Infant mortality	per thou. live births	105.0	58.0	28.0	58.0	40.0	7.0
Under 5 mortality	"	..	..	33.6	78.0	51.0	10.0
Immunization							
Measles	% age group	..	46.0	90.0	81.8	82.0	82.4
DPT	"	..	50.0	94.0	83.9	73.8	90.1
Child malnutrition (under-5)	"	..	..	..	20.9	..	..
Life expectancy							
Total	years	54	63	69	64	69	77
Female advantage	"	3.1	2.7	2.5	2.4	6.3	6.4
Total fertility rate	births per woman	7.3	7.3	6.4	4.9	2.9	1.7
Maternal mortality rate	per 100,000 live births	..	52	..	..	..	..
Supplementary Poverty Indicators							
Expenditures on social security	% of total gov't exp.	..	..	..	..	..	..
Social security coverage	% econ. active pop.	..	..	..	..	..	..
Access to safe water: total	% of pop.	64.0	93.0	95.0	85.0	85.6	..
Urban	"	97.0	100.0	100.0	97.0	94.3	..
Rural	"	56.0	68.0	74.0	70.1	73.0	..
Access to health care	"	..	90.0	93.0	84.6	..	..

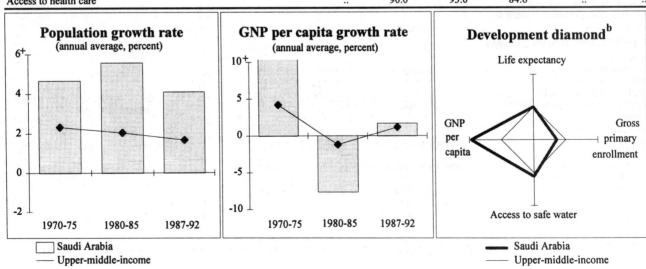

a. See the technical notes, p.389. b. The development diamond, based on four key indicators, shows the average level of development in the country compared with its income group. See the introduction.

Saudi Arabia

Indicator	Unit of measure	Latest single year 1970-75	Latest single year 1980-85	Most recent estimate 1987-92	Same region/income group Mid-East & North Africa	Same region/income group Upper-middle-income	Next higher income group
Resources and Expenditures							
HUMAN RESOURCES							
Population (mre=1992)	thousands	7,251	12,379	16,831	252,555	477,960	828,221
Age dependency ratio	ratio	0.90	0.90	0.93	0.87	0.64	0.50
Urban	% of pop.	58.7	73.0	78.5	54.7	71.7	78.1
Population growth rate	annual %	4.9	5.3	3.2	2.8	1.6	0.7
Urban	"	8.4	7.0	3.9	3.8	2.5	0.9
Labor force (15-64)	thousands	2,042	3,405	4,383	69,280	181,414	390,033
Agriculture	% of labor force	56	48	..	..	..	..
Industry	"	13	14	..	..	..	..
Female	"	6	7	8	15	29	38
Females per 100 males							
Urban	number	..	..	..	..	..	..
Rural	"	..	..	..	..	..	..
NATURAL RESOURCES							
Area	thou. sq. km	2,149.69	2,149.69	2,149.69	10,487.21	21,836.02	31,709.00
Density	pop. per sq. km	3.4	5.8	7.6	23.4	21.5	24.5
Agricultural land	% of land area	40.3	40.6	40.7	30.2	41.7	42.7
Change in agricultural land	annual %	0.1	0.1	0.0	0.5	0.3	-0.2
Agricultural land under irrigation	%	0.5	0.8	1.1	31.0	9.3	16.1
Forests and woodland	thou. sq. km	16	12	12	..	..	..
Deforestation (net)	annual %	..	..	..	..	..	..
INCOME							
Household income							
Share of top 20% of households	% of income	..	..	..	..	..	..
Share of bottom 40% of households	"	..	..	..	..	..	..
Share of bottom 20% of households	"	..	..	..	..	..	..
EXPENDITURE							
Food	% of GDP	..	..	13.9	..	..	..
Staples	"	..	..	3.6	..	..	..
Meat, fish, milk, cheese, eggs	"	..	..	6.1	..	..	..
Cereal imports	thou. metric tonnes	523	6,971	6,846	38,007	49,174	70,626
Food aid in cereals	"	..	..	..	2,484	282	2
Food production per capita	1987 = 100	190	112	231	116	109	101
Fertilizer consumption	kg/ha	0.1	3.9	5.8	96.7	68.8	162.1
Share of agriculture in GDP	% of GDP	1.0	4.4	6.3	13.7	8.1	2.4
Housing	% of GDP	..	..	13.1	..	..	..
Average household size	persons per household	..	..	..	..	..	..
Urban	"	..	..	..	..	..	..
Fixed investment: housing	% of GDP	..	..	11.2	..	..	..
Fuel and power	% of GDP	..	..	1.3	..	..	..
Energy consumption per capita	kg of oil equiv.	1,446	5,112	4,463	1,109	1,649	5,101
Households with electricity							
Urban	% of households	..	..	..	..	..	..
Rural	"	..	..	..	..	..	..
Transport and communication	% of GDP	..	..	7.0	..	..	..
Fixed investment: transport equipment	"	..	..	2.9	..	..	..
Total road length	thou. km	26	69	..	..	..	..
INVESTMENT IN HUMAN CAPITAL							
Health							
Population per physician	persons	7,461	1,819	698	..	..	..
Population per nurse	"	2,070	738	451	..	..	..
Population per hospital bed	"	846	686	401	636	385	144
Oral rehydration therapy (under-5)	% of cases	..	..	45	56	54	..
Education							
Gross enrollment ratio							
Secondary	% of school-age pop.	22	42	46	59	53	92
Female	"	15	33	41	50	..	94
Pupil-teacher ratio: primary	pupils per teacher	20	16	16	27	25	18
Pupil-teacher ratio: secondary	"	15	14	13	21	..	..
Pupils reaching grade 4	% of cohort	92	93	..	..	71	..
Repeater rate: primary	% of total enroll	15	12	10	..	11	..
Illiteracy	% of pop. (age 15+)	..	42	38	45	14	..
Female	% of fem. (age 15+)	..	58	52	58	17	..
Newspaper circulation	per thou. pop.	14	..	38	39	117	..

World Bank International Economics Department, April 1994

Senegal

Indicator	Unit of measure	Latest single year 1970-75	Latest single year 1980-85	Most recent estimate 1987-92	Same region/income group Sub-Saharan Africa	Same region/income group Lower-middle-income	Next higher income group
Priority Poverty Indicators							
POVERTY							
Upper poverty line	local curr.	..	..	..	..	..	..
Headcount index	% of pop.	..	..	..	..	..	..
Lower poverty line	local curr.	..	..	..	..	..	..
Headcount index	% of pop.	..	..	..	..	..	..
GNP per capita	US$	350	380	780	520	..	3,870
SHORT TERM INCOME INDICATORS							
Unskilled urban wages	local curr.	..	..	..	..	..	..
Unskilled rural wages	"	..	..	..	..	..	..
Rural terms of trade	"	..	..	..	..	..	..
Consumer price index	1987=100	40	98	97	..	..	..
Lower income	"	..	..	..	..	..	..
Food[a]	"	21	102	98	..	..	..
Urban	"	..	..	..	..	..	..
Rural	"	..	..	..	..	..	..
SOCIAL INDICATORS							
Public expenditure on basic social services	% of GDP	..	..	..	..	..	..
Gross enrollment ratios							
Primary	% school age pop.	41	56	59	66	..	107
Male	"	48	67	70	79	..	..
Female	"	34	46	49	62	..	..
Mortality							
Infant mortality	per thou. live births	122.0	97.0	68.0	99.0	45.0	40.0
Under 5 mortality	"	..	..	105.8	169.0	59.0	51.0
Immunization							
Measles	% age group	..	40.0	59.0	54.0	..	82.0
DPT	"	..	54.0	60.0	54.6	..	73.8
Child malnutrition (under-5)	"	..	..	17.5	28.4	..	..
Life expectancy							
Total	years	43	45	49	52	68	69
Female advantage	"	2.0	3.3	2.0	3.4	6.4	6.3
Total fertility rate	births per woman	6.5	6.7	5.9	6.1	3.1	2.9
Maternal mortality rate	per 100,000 live births	..	530	..	..	..	..
Supplementary Poverty Indicators							
Expenditures on social security	% of total gov't exp.	..	..	..	..	..	..
Social security coverage	% econ. active pop.	..	..	..	..	..	..
Access to safe water: total	% of pop.	..	55.0	..	41.1	..	85.6
Urban	"	56.0	79.0	..	77.8	..	94.3
Rural	"	..	38.0	..	27.3	..	73.0
Access to health care	"	..	..	40.0	..	..	..

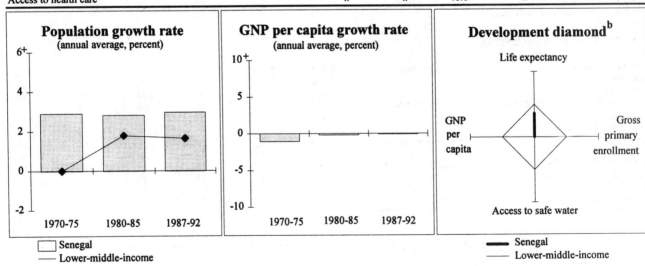

Population growth rate (annual average, percent)

□ Senegal
— Lower-middle-income

GNP per capita growth rate (annual average, percent)

Development diamond[b]

Life expectancy

GNP per capita — Gross primary enrollment

Access to safe water

▬ Senegal
— Lower-middle-income

a. See the technical notes, p.389.   b. The development diamond, based on four key indicators, shows the average level of development in the country compared with its income group. See the introduction.

Senegal

Indicator	Unit of measure	Latest single year 1970-75	Latest single year 1980-85	Most recent estimate 1987-92	Same region/income group Sub-Saharan Africa	Same region/income group Lower-middle-income	Next higher income group
Resources and Expenditures							
HUMAN RESOURCES							
Population (mre=1992)	thousands	4,806	6,375	7,841	546,390	942,547	477,960
Age dependency ratio	ratio	0.88	0.97	0.98	0.95	0.66	0.64
Urban	% of pop.	34.2	37.9	40.8	29.5	57.0	71.7
Population growth rate	annual %	2.9	2.9	2.8	2.9	1.4	1.6
Urban	"	3.4	4.0	4.0	5.1	4.8	2.5
Labor force (15-64)	thousands	2,245	2,897	3,329	224,025	..	181,414
Agriculture	% of labor force	82	81	..	..	..	..
Industry	"	6	6	..	..	..	..
Female	"	41	40	39	37	36	29
Females per 100 males							
Urban	number	..	..	..	..	..	..
Rural	"	..	..	..	..	..	..
NATURAL RESOURCES							
Area	thou. sq. km	196.72	196.72	196.72	24,274.03	40,697.37	21,836.02
Density	pop. per sq. km	24.4	32.4	38.8	21.9	22.8	21.5
Agricultural land	% of land area	28.3	28.3	28.3	52.7	..	41.7
Change in agricultural land	annual %	0.0	0.0	0.0	0.1	..	0.3
Agricultural land under irrigation	%	2.9	3.2	3.3	0.8	..	9.3
Forests and woodland	thou. sq. km	113	108	105	..	..	..
Deforestation (net)	annual %	..	..	0.8	..	..	..
INCOME							
Household income							
Share of top 20% of households	% of income	..	..	59	..	..	..
Share of bottom 40% of households	"	..	..	11	..	..	..
Share of bottom 20% of households	"	..	..	4	..	..	..
EXPENDITURE							
Food	% of GDP	..	42.4	..	..	..	..
Staples	"	..	13.0	..	..	..	..
Meat, fish, milk, cheese, eggs	"	..	14.3	..	..	..	..
Cereal imports	thou. metric tonnes	220	557	585	20,311	74,924	49,174
Food aid in cereals	"	27	131	51	4,303	4,054	282
Food production per capita	1987 = 100	192	100	81	90	..	109
Fertilizer consumption	kg/ha	8.7	3.8	2.8	4.2	..	68.8
Share of agriculture in GDP	% of GDP	30.2	18.8	19.4	18.6	..	8.1
Housing	% of GDP	..	9.8	..	..	..	..
Average household size	persons per household	7.6	..	..	..	..	..
Urban	"	..	..	..	..	..	..
Fixed investment: housing	% of GDP	..	3.9	..	..	..	..
Fuel and power	% of GDP	..	3.6	..	..	..	..
Energy consumption per capita	kg of oil equiv.	138	141	111	258	1,882	1,649
Households with electricity							
Urban	% of households	..	..	..	..	..	..
Rural	"	..	..	..	..	..	..
Transport and communication	% of GDP	..	4.7	..	..	..	..
Fixed investment: transport equipment	"	..	1.3	..	..	..	..
Total road length	thou. km	14	14	15	..	..	..
INVESTMENT IN HUMAN CAPITAL							
Health							
Population per physician	persons	16,278	13,038	17,646	..	..	..
Population per nurse	"	1,675	2,024	..	..	..	..
Population per hospital bed	"	775	..	1,385	1,329	516	385
Oral rehydration therapy (under-5)	% of cases	..	..	27	36	..	54
Education							
Gross enrollment ratio							
Secondary	% of school-age pop.	10	14	16	18	..	53
Female	"	6	9	11	14	..	..
Pupil-teacher ratio: primary	pupils per teacher	41	46	58	39	26	25
Pupil-teacher ratio: secondary	"	29	35	35	..	..	..
Pupils reaching grade 4	% of cohort	..	90	92	..	..	71
Repeater rate: primary	% of total enroll	18	16	16	..	..	11
Illiteracy	% of pop. (age 15+)	..	68	62	51	..	14
Female	% of fem. (age 15+)	..	81	75	62	..	17
Newspaper circulation	per thou. pop.	5	7	7	14	100	117

World Bank International Economics Department, April 1994

Seychelles

Indicator	Unit of measure	Latest single year 1970-75	Latest single year 1980-85	Most recent estimate 1987-92	Same region/income group Sub-Saharan Africa	Same region/income group Upper-middle-income	Next higher income group
Priority Poverty Indicators							
POVERTY							
Upper poverty line	local curr.	..	..	..	..	..	..
Headcount index	% of pop.	..	..	..	..	..	..
Lower poverty line	local curr.	..	..	..	..	..	..
Headcount index	% of pop.	..	..	..	..	..	..
GNP per capita	US$	800	2,580	5,460	520	3,870	21,960
SHORT TERM INCOME INDICATORS							
Unskilled urban wages	local curr.	..	..	..	..	..	..
Unskilled rural wages	"	..	..	484	..	..	..
Rural terms of trade	"	..	..	..	..	..	..
Consumer price index	1987=100	42	97	113	..	..	..
Lower income	"	..	..	..	..	..	..
Food[a]	"	..	96	111	..	..	..
Urban	"	..	..	..	..	..	..
Rural	"	..	..	..	..	..	..
SOCIAL INDICATORS							
Public expenditure on basic social services	% of GDP	..	..	10.1	..	..	..
Gross enrollment ratios							
Primary	% school age pop.	..	..	..	66	107	103
Male	"	..	..	..	79	..	103
Female	"	..	..	..	62	..	103
Mortality							
Infant mortality	per thou. live births	..	19.3	16.2	99.0	40.0	7.0
Under 5 mortality	"	..	..	20.0	169.0	51.0	10.0
Immunization							
Measles	% age group	..	90.0	89.0	54.0	82.0	82.4
DPT	"	..	86.0	97.0	54.6	73.8	90.1
Child malnutrition (under-5)	"	..	..	5.7	28.4	..	..
Life expectancy							
Total	years	..	69	71	52	69	77
Female advantage	"	..	5.5	7.3	3.4	6.3	6.4
Total fertility rate	births per woman	..	3.5	2.7	6.1	2.9	1.7
Maternal mortality rate	per 100,000 live births	..	..	..	..	..	..
Supplementary Poverty Indicators							
Expenditures on social security	% of total gov't exp.	..	..	..	..	..	..
Social security coverage	% econ. active pop.	..	..	..	..	..	..
Access to safe water: total	% of pop.	..	97.0	99.0	41.1	85.6	..
Urban	"	..	100.0	100.0	77.8	94.3	..
Rural	"	..	95.0	98.0	27.3	73.0	..
Access to health care	"	..	99.0	99.0	..	..	..

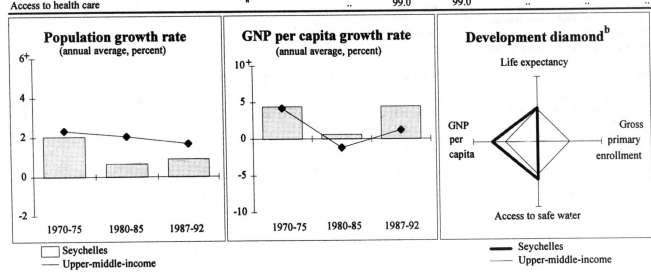

Population growth rate
(annual average, percent)

GNP per capita growth rate
(annual average, percent)

Development diamond[b]

Life expectancy — GNP per capita — Gross primary enrollment — Access to safe water

□ Seychelles
— Upper-middle-income

—— Seychelles
— Upper-middle-income

a. See the technical notes, p.389.   b. The development diamond, based on four key indicators, shows the average level of development in the country compared with its income group. See the introduction.

Seychelles

Indicator	Unit of measure	Latest single year 1970-75	Latest single year 1980-85	Most recent estimate 1987-92	Same region/income group Sub-Saharan Africa	Same region/income group Upper-middle-income	Next higher income group

Resources and Expenditures

HUMAN RESOURCES

Indicator	Unit of measure	1970-75	1980-85	1987-92	Sub-Saharan Africa	Upper-middle-income	Next higher income group
Population (mre=1992)	thousands	59	65	69	546,390	477,960	828,221
Age dependency ratio	ratio	..	0.76	0.69	0.95	0.64	0.50
Urban	% of pop.	33.2	51.8	61.6	29.5	71.7	78.1
Population growth rate	annual %	1.7	0.6	0.9	2.9	1.6	0.7
Urban	"	6.1	4.2	2.8	5.1	2.5	0.9
Labor force (15-64)	thousands	..	..	..	224,025	181,414	390,033
Agriculture	% of labor force	..	..	..	..	..	..
Industry	"	..	..	..	..	..	..
Female	"	..	..	..	37	29	38
Females per 100 males							
Urban	number	..	..	..	..	..	..
Rural	"	..	..	..	..	..	..

NATURAL RESOURCES

Indicator	Unit of measure	1970-75	1980-85	1987-92	Sub-Saharan Africa	Upper-middle-income	Next higher income group
Area	thou. sq. km	0.28	0.28	0.28	24,274.03	21,836.02	31,709.00
Density	pop. per sq. km	210.7	232.9	245.0	21.9	21.5	24.5
Agricultural land	% of land area	18.5	22.2	25.9	52.7	41.7	42.7
Change in agricultural land	annual %	0.0	0.0	16.7	0.1	0.3	-0.2
Agricultural land under irrigation	%	..	..	..	0.8	9.3	16.1
Forests and woodland	thou. sq. km	0	0	0	..	..	..
Deforestation (net)	annual %	..	..	..	..	..	..

INCOME

Indicator	Unit of measure	1970-75	1980-85	1987-92	Sub-Saharan Africa	Upper-middle-income	Next higher income group
Household income							
Share of top 20% of households	% of income	..	..	..	..	..	..
Share of bottom 40% of households	"	..	..	..	..	..	..
Share of bottom 20% of households	"	..	..	..	..	..	..

EXPENDITURE

Indicator	Unit of measure	1970-75	1980-85	1987-92	Sub-Saharan Africa	Upper-middle-income	Next higher income group
Food	% of GDP	..	..	21.3	..	..	..
Staples	"	..	..	2.8	..	..	..
Meat, fish, milk, cheese, eggs	"	..	..	13.5	..	..	..
Cereal imports	thou. metric tonnes	6	7	14	20,311	49,174	70,626
Food aid in cereals	"	0	1	0	4,303	282	2
Food production per capita	1987 = 100	..	..	..	90	109	101
Fertilizer consumption	kg/ha	..	66.3	..	4.2	68.8	162.1
Share of agriculture in GDP	% of GDP	..	5.8	5.1	18.6	8.1	2.4
Housing	% of GDP	..	..	11.6	..	..	..
Average household size	persons per household	4.7	..	..	..	..	..
Urban	"	4.7	..	..	..	..	..
Fixed investment: housing	% of GDP	..	..	4.6	..	..	..
Fuel and power	% of GDP	..	..	1.9	..	..	..
Energy consumption per capita	kg of oil equiv.	644	1,580	4,581	258	1,649	5,101
Households with electricity							
Urban	% of households	..	..	..	..	..	..
Rural	"	..	..	..	..	..	..
Transport and communication	% of GDP	..	..	4.8	..	..	..
Fixed investment: transport equipment	"	..	..	1.7	..	..	..
Total road length	thou. km	..	..	..	..	..	..

INVESTMENT IN HUMAN CAPITAL

Health

Indicator	Unit of measure	1970-75	1980-85	1987-92	Sub-Saharan Africa	Upper-middle-income	Next higher income group
Population per physician	persons	4,400	2,173	..	..	..	..
Population per nurse	"	671	..	..	..	..	..
Population per hospital bed	"	200	201	..	1,329	385	144
Oral rehydration therapy (under-5)	% of cases	..	..	88	36	54	..

Education

Gross enrollment ratio

Indicator	Unit of measure	1970-75	1980-85	1987-92	Sub-Saharan Africa	Upper-middle-income	Next higher income group
Secondary	% of school-age pop.	..	..	..	18	53	92
Female	"	..	..	..	14	..	94
Pupil-teacher ratio: primary	pupils per teacher	24	22	19	39	25	18
Pupil-teacher ratio: secondary	"	24	13	18	..	..	..
Pupils reaching grade 4	% of cohort	93	98	97	..	71	..
Repeater rate: primary	% of total enroll	1	0	0	..	11	..
Illiteracy	% of pop. (age 15+)	42	..	..	51	14	..
Female	% of fem. (age 15+)	..	..	..	62	17	..
Newspaper circulation	per thou. pop.	59	59	44	14	117	..

World Bank International Economics Department, April 1994

305

Sierra Leone

Indicator	Unit of measure	Latest single year 1970-75	Latest single year 1980-85	Most recent estimate 1987-92	Same region/income group Sub-Saharan Africa	Same region/income group Low-income	Next higher income group
Priority Poverty Indicators							
POVERTY							
Upper poverty line	local curr.	..	..	..	..	..	..
Headcount index	% of pop.	..	..	..	..	19	..
Lower poverty line	local curr.	..	..	..	..	..	..
Headcount index	% of pop.	..	..	..	..	..	..
GNP per capita	US$	220	340	160	520	390	..
SHORT TERM INCOME INDICATORS							
Unskilled urban wages	local curr.	..	..	..	..	..	..
Unskilled rural wages	"	..	..	..	..	..	..
Rural terms of trade	"	..	..	..	..	..	..
Consumer price index	1987=100	1	20	1,512	..	..	..
Lower income	"	..	..		..	..	..
Food[a]	"	..	20	475	..	..	..
Urban	"	..	..	..	..	..	..
Rural	"	..	..	..	..	..	..
SOCIAL INDICATORS							
Public expenditure on basic social services	% of GDP	..	2.4	3.6	..	..	..
Gross enrollment ratios							
Primary	% school age pop.	39	61	48	66	103	..
Male	"	47	73	56	79	113	..
Female	"	30	50	39	62	96	..
Mortality							
Infant mortality	per thou. live births	193.0	167.0	142.9	99.0	73.0	45.0
Under 5 mortality	"	..	..	241.3	169.0	108.0	59.0
Immunization							
Measles	% age group	..	23.0	74.0	54.0	72.7	..
DPT	"	..	29.0	75.0	54.6	80.6	..
Child malnutrition (under-5)	"	..	27.0	23.2	28.4	38.3	..
Life expectancy							
Total	years	35	39	43	52	62	68
Female advantage	"	3.0	3.1	3.2	3.4	2.4	6.4
Total fertility rate	births per woman	6.5	6.5	6.5	6.1	3.4	3.1
Maternal mortality rate	per 100,000 live births	..	450	..	..	..	..
Supplementary Poverty Indicators							
Expenditures on social security	% of total gov't exp.	..	1.5	1.9	..	..	..
Social security coverage	% econ. active pop.	..	..	..	..	..	..
Access to safe water: total	% of pop.	12.0	26.0	42.0	41.1	68.4	..
Urban	"	75.0	68.0	83.0	77.8	78.9	..
Rural	"	1.0	7.0	22.0	27.3	60.3	..
Access to health care	"	..	36.2	..	..	..	..

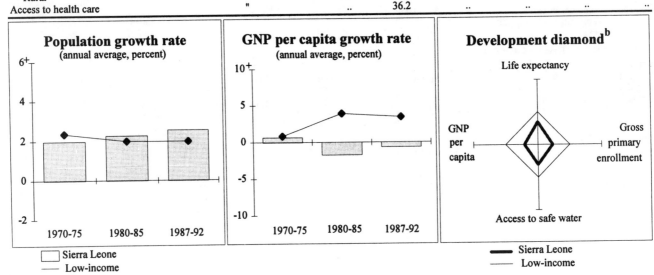

a. See the technical notes, p.389.   b. The development diamond, based on four key indicators, shows the average level of development in the country compared with its income group. See the introduction.

Sierra Leone

Indicator	Unit of measure	Latest single year 1970-75	Latest single year 1980-85	Most recent estimate 1987-92	Same region/income group Sub-Saharan Africa	Same region/income group Low-income	Next higher income group
Resources and Expenditures							
HUMAN RESOURCES							
Population (mre=1992)	thousands	2,931	3,654	4,354	546,390	3,194,535	942,547
Age dependency ratio	ratio	0.84	0.83	0.89	0.95	0.67	0.66
Urban	% of pop.	21.1	28.3	33.8	29.5	26.7	57.0
Population growth rate	annual %	2.0	2.4	2.6	2.9	1.8	1.4
Urban	"	4.9	5.1	5.0	5.1	3.4	4.8
Labor force (15-64)	thousands	1,216	1,352	1,481	224,025	1,478,954	..
Agriculture	% of labor force	73	70	..	..	..	..
Industry	"	13	14	..	..	..	..
Female	"	35	34	32	37	33	36
Females per 100 males							
Urban	number	..	..	..	..	..	..
Rural	"	..	..	..	..	..	..
NATURAL RESOURCES							
Area	thou. sq. km	71.74	71.74	71.74	24,274.03	38,401.06	40,697.37
Density	pop. per sq. km	40.9	50.9	59.1	21.9	81.7	22.8
Agricultural land	% of land area	38.5	39.4	39.7	52.7	50.9	..
Change in agricultural land	annual %	0.2	0.2	0.0	0.1	0.0	..
Agricultural land under irrigation	%	0.5	1.0	1.2	0.8	18.2	..
Forests and woodland	thou. sq. km	21	21	21	..	..	..
Deforestation (net)	annual %	..	..	0.5	..	..	..
INCOME							
Household income							
Share of top 20% of households	% of income	53	..	..	..	42	..
Share of bottom 40% of households	"	15	..	..	..	19	..
Share of bottom 20% of households	"	6	..	..	..	8	..
EXPENDITURE							
Food	% of GDP	..	47.7	..	..	..	..
Staples	"	..	18.4	..	..	..	..
Meat, fish, milk, cheese, eggs	"	..	19.1	..	..	..	..
Cereal imports	thou. metric tonnes	26	119	133	20,311	46,537	74,924
Food aid in cereals	"	10	21	45	4,303	9,008	4,054
Food production per capita	1987 = 100	113	94	85	90	123	..
Fertilizer consumption	kg/ha	1.1	1.3	0.2	4.2	61.9	..
Share of agriculture in GDP	% of GDP	32.5	43.3	35.0	18.6	29.6	..
Housing	% of GDP	..	12.7	..	..	..	..
Average household size	persons per household	7.0	..	..	..	..	..
Urban	"	6.0	..	..	..	..	..
Fixed investment: housing	% of GDP	..	1.0	..	..	..	..
Fuel and power	% of GDP	..	4.9	..	..	..	..
Energy consumption per capita	kg of oil equiv.	77	79	73	258	335	1,882
Households with electricity							
Urban	% of households	..	..	..	..	..	..
Rural	"	..	..	..	..	..	..
Transport and communication	% of GDP	..	10.3	..	..	..	..
Fixed investment: transport equipment	"	2.0	1.0	..	..	..	..
Total road length	thou. km	7	8	9	..	..	..
INVESTMENT IN HUMAN CAPITAL							
Health							
Population per physician	persons	18,544	13,622	..	..	..	..
Population per nurse	"	2,807	1,089	..	..	..	..
Population per hospital bed	"	1,103	830	..	1,329	1,050	516
Oral rehydration therapy (under-5)	% of cases	..	..	60	36	39	..
Education							
Gross enrollment ratio							
Secondary	% of school-age pop.	11	19	16	18	41	..
Female	"	7	12	12	14	35	..
Pupil-teacher ratio: primary	pupils per teacher	32	39	34	39	37	26
Pupil-teacher ratio: secondary	"	20	33	18	..	19	..
Pupils reaching grade 4	% of cohort	..	..	..	..	..	..
Repeater rate: primary	% of total enroll	..	15	..	..	..	..
Illiteracy	% of pop. (age 15+)	..	87	79	51	39	..
Female	% of fem. (age 15+)	..	94	89	62	52	..
Newspaper circulation	per thou. pop.	10	3	2	14	..	100

World Bank International Economics Department, April 1994

Singapore

Indicator	Unit of measure	Latest single year		Most recent estimate 1987-92	Same region/income group High-income
		1970-75	1980-85		

Priority Poverty Indicators

POVERTY					
Upper poverty line	local curr.	..	..	..	..
Headcount index	% of pop.	..	..	..	..
Lower poverty line	local curr.	..	..	..	..
Headcount index	% of pop.	..	..	..	..
GNP per capita	US$	2,820	7,880	15,730	21,960
SHORT TERM INCOME INDICATORS					
Unskilled urban wages	local curr.	..	..	..	..
Unskilled rural wages	"	..	..	..	
Rural terms of trade	"	..	..	..	
Consumer price index	1987=100	72	101	114	
Lower income	"	..	..	..	..
Food[a]	"	..	102	105	..
Urban	"	..	..	..	..
Rural	"	..	..	..	..
SOCIAL INDICATORS					
Public expenditure on basic social services	% of GDP	..	10.0	..	..
Gross enrollment ratios					
Primary	% school age pop.	110	115	108	103
Male	"	113	117	110	103
Female	"	107	113	107	103
Mortality					
Infant mortality	per thou. live births	13.9	9.3	5.0	7.0
Under 5 mortality	"	..	..	6.7	10.0
Immunization					
Measles	% age group	..	75.0	92.0	82.4
DPT	"	..	78.0	91.0	90.1
Child malnutrition (under-5)	"	14.4	..	..	..
Life expectancy					
Total	years	69	72	75	77
Female advantage	"	5.0	5.4	5.6	6.4
Total fertility rate	births per woman	2.1	1.7	1.8	1.7
Maternal mortality rate	per 100,000 live births	..	11	10	..

Supplementary Poverty Indicators

Expenditures on social security	% of total gov't exp.	1.7	1.5	1.9	..
Social security coverage	% econ. active pop.	..	..	..	..
Access to safe water: total	% of pop.	100.0	100.0	100.0	..
Urban	"	100.0	100.0	100.0	..
Rural	"	..	..	..	..
Access to health care	"	..	100.0	100.0	..

Population growth rate
(annual average, percent)

Singapore
High-income

GNP per capita growth rate
(annual average, percent)

Development diamond[b]

Life expectancy

GNP per capita — Gross primary enrollment

Access to safe water

Singapore
High-income

a. See the technical notes, p.389. b. The development diamond, based on four key indicators, shows the average level of development in the country compared with its income group. See the introduction.

Singapore

Indicator	Unit of measure	Latest single year 1970-75	Latest single year 1980-85	Most recent estimate 1987-92	Same region/income group High-income
Resources and Expenditures					
HUMAN RESOURCES					
Population (mre=1992)	thousands	2,037	2,483	2,818	828,221
Age dependency ratio	ratio	0.59	0.42	0.43	0.50
Urban	% of pop.	100.0	100.0	100.0	78.1
Population growth rate	annual %	1.8	1.6	2.0	0.7
Urban	"	1.8	1.6	2.0	0.9
Labor force (15-64)	thousands	909	1,226	1,316	390,033
Agriculture	% of labor force	3	2	..	..
Industry	"	34	38	..	..
Female	"	31	33	32	38
Females per 100 males					
Urban	number	..	..	..	..
Rural	"	..	..	..	..
NATURAL RESOURCES					
Area	thou. sq. km	0.62	0.62	0.62	31,709.00
Density	pop. per sq. km	3285.5	4004.8	4456.5	24.5
Agricultural land	% of land area	13.1	8.2	1.6	42.7
Change in agricultural land	annual %	-11.1	-16.7	0.0	-0.2
Agricultural land under irrigation	%	..	..	..	16.1
Forests and woodland	thou. sq. km	0	0	0	..
Deforestation (net)	annual %	..	..	..	..
INCOME					
Household income					
Share of top 20% of households	% of income	..	49	..	..
Share of bottom 40% of households	"	..	15	..	..
Share of bottom 20% of households	"	..	5	..	..
EXPENDITURE					
Food	% of GDP	15.6	9.8	..	..
Staples	"	..	..	..	..
Meat, fish, milk, cheese, eggs	"	..	..	..	..
Cereal imports	thou. metric tonnes	727	907	784	70,626
Food aid in cereals	"	0	..	..	2
Food production per capita	1987 = 100	111	96	52	101
Fertilizer consumption	kg/ha	375.0	1040.0	5600.0	162.1
Share of agriculture in GDP	% of GDP	1.9	0.8	0.2	2.4
Housing	% of GDP	6.8	5.6	..	..
Average household size	persons per household	5.4	4.7	..	..
Urban	"	..	..	..	..
Fixed investment: housing	% of GDP	7.8	13.5	..	..
Fuel and power	% of GDP	..	..	..	..
Energy consumption per capita	kg of oil equiv.	2,041	3,157	4,399	5,101
Households with electricity					
Urban	% of households	..	..	..	..
Rural	"	..	..	..	..
Transport and communication	% of GDP	7.5	6.9	..	..
Fixed investment: transport equipment	"	5.4	4.9	..	..
Total road length	thou. km	2	3	3	..
INVESTMENT IN HUMAN CAPITAL					
Health					
Population per physician	persons	1,350	1,046	822	..
Population per nurse	"	254	321	..	..
Population per hospital bed	"	270	235	275	144
Oral rehydyration therapy (under-5)	% of cases	..	..	..	..
Education					
Gross enrollment ratio					
Secondary	% of school-age pop.	52	62	70	92
Female	"	52	64	71	94
Pupil-teacher ratio: primary	pupils per teacher	30	27	26	18
Pupil-teacher ratio: secondary	"	24	22	20	..
Pupils reaching grade 4	% of cohort	99	100	100	..
Repeater rate: primary	% of total enroll	8	1	..	..
Illiteracy	% of pop. (age 15+)	31	14	..	..
Female	% of fem. (age 15+)	..	21	..	..
Newspaper circulation	per thou. pop.	210	286	282	..

World Bank International Economics Department, April 1994

Slovak Republic

Indicator	Unit of measure	Latest single year 1970-75	Latest single year 1980-85	Most recent estimate 1987-92	Same region/income group Europe & Central Asia	Same region/income group Lower-middle-income	Next higher income group
Priority Poverty Indicators							
POVERTY							
Upper poverty line	local curr.	..	..	..	..	..	..
Headcount index	% of pop.	..	..	..	..	..	..
Lower poverty line	local curr.	..	..	..	..	..	..
Headcount index	% of pop.	..	..	..	..	..	..
GNP per capita	US$	..	..	1,930	..	..	3,870
SHORT TERM INCOME INDICATORS							
Unskilled urban wages	local curr.	..	..	..	..	..	..
Unskilled rural wages	"	..	..	..	..	..	..
Rural terms of trade	"	..	..	..	..	..	..
Consumer price index	1987=100	..	..	..	..	..	..
Lower income	"	..	..	..	..	..	..
Food[a]	"	..	..	..	..	..	..
Urban	"	..	..	..	..	..	..
Rural	"	..	..	..	..	..	..
SOCIAL INDICATORS							
Public expenditure on basic social services	% of GDP	..	..	..	..	..	..
Gross enrollment ratios							
Primary	% school age pop.	..	..	..	..	..	107
Male	"	..	..	..	..	..	..
Female	"	..	..	..	..	..	..
Mortality							
Infant mortality	per thou. live births	24.6	16.3	12.6	30.0	45.0	40.0
Under 5 mortality	"	..	..	15.5	38.0	59.0	51.0
Immunization							
Measles	% age group	..	..	..	..	..	82.0
DPT	"	..	..	..	..	..	73.8
Child malnutrition (under-5)	"	..	..	..	..	..	..
Life expectancy							
Total	years	70	71	71	70	68	69
Female advantage	"	7.0	7.8	8.3	8.6	6.4	6.3
Total fertility rate	births per woman	2.6	..	2.0	2.2	3.1	2.9
Maternal mortality rate	per 100,000 live births	..	..	..	58	..	..
Supplementary Poverty Indicators							
Expenditures on social security	% of total gov't exp.	..	..	..	..	..	..
Social security coverage	% econ. active pop.	..	..	..	..	..	..
Access to safe water: total	% of pop.	..	..	..	..	..	85.6
Urban	"	..	..	..	..	..	94.3
Rural	"	..	..	..	..	..	73.0
Access to health care	"	..	..	..	..	..	..

Population growth rate (annual average, percent)

Slovak Republic
Lower-middle-income

GNP per capita growth rate (annual average, percent)

Development diamond[b]

Life expectancy
GNP per capita
Gross primary enrollment
Access to safe water

Slovak Republic
Lower-middle-income

a. See the technical notes, p.389.   b. The development diamond, based on four key indicators, shows the average level of development in the country compared with its income group. See the introduction.

Slovak Republic

Indicator	Unit of measure	Latest single year 1970-75	Latest single year 1980-85	Most recent estimate 1987-92	Europe & Central Asia	Lower-middle-income	Next higher income group
Resources and Expenditures							
HUMAN RESOURCES							
Population (mre=1992)	thousands	4,742	5,162	5,299	495,241	942,547	477,960
Age dependency ratio	ratio	..	..	..	0.56	0.66	0.64
Urban	% of pop.	..	..	..	63.3	57.0	71.7
Population growth rate	annual %	0.9	0.6	0.4	0.5	1.4	1.6
Urban	"	..	..	..	..	4.8	2.5
Labor force (15-64)	thousands	..	..	..	..	..	181,414
Agriculture	% of labor force	..	..	..	..	..	..
Industry	"	..	..	..	..	..	..
Female	"	..	..	..	46	36	29
Females per 100 males							
Urban	number	..	..	..	..	..	..
Rural	"	..	..	..	..	..	..
NATURAL RESOURCES							
Area	thou. sq. km	49.04	49.04	49.04	24,165.06	40,697.37	21,836.02
Density	pop. per sq. km	..	..	..	20.4	22.8	21.5
Agricultural land	% of land area	..	..	..	..	..	41.7
Change in agricultural land	annual %	..	..	..	..	..	0.3
Agricultural land under irrigation	%	..	..	..	..	..	9.3
Forests and woodland	thou. sq. km	..	..	..	..	..	..
Deforestation (net)	annual %	..	..	..	..	..	..
INCOME							
Household income							
Share of top 20% of households	% of income	..	..	..	..	..	..
Share of bottom 40% of households	"	..	..	..	..	..	..
Share of bottom 20% of households	"	..	..	..	..	..	..
EXPENDITURE							
Food	% of GDP	..	..	..	..	..	..
Staples	"	..	..	..	..	..	..
Meat, fish, milk, cheese, eggs	"	..	..	..	..	..	..
Cereal imports	thou. metric tonnes	..	..	50	45,972	74,924	49,174
Food aid in cereals	"	..	..	..	1,639	4,054	282
Food production per capita	1987 = 100	..	..	..	..	..	109
Fertilizer consumption	kg/ha	..	..	..	..	..	68.8
Share of agriculture in GDP	% of GDP	..	..	..	..	..	8.1
Housing	% of GDP	..	..	..	..	..	..
Average household size	persons per household	..	..	..	..	..	..
Urban	"	..	..	..	..	..	..
Fixed investment: housing	% of GDP	..	..	..	..	..	..
Fuel and power	% of GDP	..	..	..	..	..	..
Energy consumption per capita	kg of oil equiv.	..	..	..	3,190	1,882	1,649
Households with electricity							
Urban	% of households	..	..	..	..	..	..
Rural	"	..	..	..	..	..	..
Transport and communication	% of GDP	..	..	..	..	..	..
Fixed investment: transport equipment	"	..	..	..	..	..	..
Total road length	thou. km	..	..	..	..	..	..
INVESTMENT IN HUMAN CAPITAL							
Health							
Population per physician	persons	..	..	..	378	..	..
Population per nurse	"	..	..	..	..	..	..
Population per hospital bed	"	..	..	..	134	516	385
Oral rehydration therapy (under-5)	% of cases	..	..	..	..	..	54
Education							
Gross enrollment ratio							
Secondary	% of school-age pop.	..	..	..	..	..	53
Female	"	..	..	..	..	..	..
Pupil-teacher ratio: primary	pupils per teacher	..	..	..	..	26	25
Pupil-teacher ratio: secondary	"	..	..	..	..	..	..
Pupils reaching grade 4	% of cohort	..	..	..	..	..	71
Repeater rate: primary	% of total enroll	..	..	..	..	..	11
Illiteracy	% of pop. (age 15+)	..	..	..	..	..	14
Female	% of fem. (age 15+)	..	..	..	..	..	17
Newspaper circulation	per thou. pop.	..	..	..	..	100	117

World Bank International Economics Department, April 1994

Slovenia

Indicator	Unit of measure	Latest single year 1970-75	Latest single year 1980-85	Most recent estimate 1987-92	Same region/income group Europe & Central Asia	Same region/income group Upper-middle-income	Next higher income group
Priority Poverty Indicators							
POVERTY							
Upper poverty line	local curr.	..	..	..	..	..	..
Headcount index	% of pop.	..	..	..	..	..	..
Lower poverty line	local curr.	..	..	..	..	..	..
Headcount index	% of pop.	..	..	..	..	..	..
GNP per capita	US$	..	..	..	..	3,870	21,960
SHORT TERM INCOME INDICATORS							
Unskilled urban wages	local curr.	..	..	..	..	..	..
Unskilled rural wages	"	..	..	..	..	..	..
Rural terms of trade	"	..	..	..	..	..	..
Consumer price index	1987=100	..	..	..	..	..	..
Lower income	"	..	..	..	..	..	..
Food[a]	"	..	..	..	..	..	..
Urban	"	..	..	..	..	..	..
Rural	"	..	..	..	..	..	..
SOCIAL INDICATORS							
Public expenditure on basic social services	% of GDP	..	..	..	..	..	..
Gross enrollment ratios							
Primary	% school age pop.	..	..	..	..	107	103
Male	"	..	..	..	..	..	103
Female	"	..	..	..	..	..	103
Mortality							
Infant mortality	per thou. live births	..	15.0	8.4	30.0	40.0	7.0
Under 5 mortality	"	..	..	10.6	38.0	51.0	10.0
Immunization							
Measles	% age group	..	..	..	..	82.0	82.4
DPT	"	..	..	..	..	73.8	90.1
Child malnutrition (under-5)	"	..	..	..	..	..	..
Life expectancy							
Total	years	..	70	73	70	69	77
Female advantage	"	..	8.4	7.9	8.6	6.3	6.4
Total fertility rate	births per woman	..	..	1.5	2.2	2.9	1.7
Maternal mortality rate	per 100,000 live births	..	..	..	58	..	..
Supplementary Poverty Indicators							
Expenditures on social security	% of total gov't exp.	..	..	..	..	..	..
Social security coverage	% econ. active pop.	..	..	..	..	..	..
Access to safe water: total	% of pop.	..	..	..	..	85.6	..
Urban	"	..	..	..	..	94.3	..
Rural	"	..	..	..	..	73.0	..
Access to health care	"	..	..	..	..	..	..

Population growth rate
(annual average, percent)

□ Slovenia
— Upper-middle-income

GNP per capita growth rate
(annual average, percent)

Development diamond[b]

Life expectancy

GNP per capita

Gross primary enrollment

Access to safe water

— Slovenia
— Upper-middle-income

a. See the technical notes, p.389.   b. The development diamond, based on four key indicators, shows the average level of development in the country compared with its income group. See the introduction.

312

Slovenia

Indicator	Unit of measure	Latest single year 1970-75	Latest single year 1980-85	Most recent estimate 1987-92	Same region/income group Europe & Central Asia	Same region/income group Upper-middle-income	Next higher income group
Resources and Expenditures							
HUMAN RESOURCES							
Population (mre=1992)	thousands	1,775	1,925	1,999	495,241	477,960	828,221
Age dependency ratio	ratio	..	..	0.47	0.56	0.64	0.50
Urban	% of pop.	..	..	..	63.3	71.7	78.1
Population growth rate	annual %	0.9	0.2	-0.2	0.5	1.6	0.7
Urban	"	..	..	..	..	2.5	0.9
Labor force (15-64)	thousands	..	..	..	..	181,414	390,033
Agriculture	% of labor force	..	..	..	..	..	..
Industry	"	..	..	..	..	..	..
Female	"	..	..	..	46	29	38
Females per 100 males							
Urban	number	..	..	..	..	..	..
Rural	"	..	..	..	..	..	..
NATURAL RESOURCES							
Area	thou. sq. km	..	..	20.25	24,165.06	21,836.02	31,709.00
Density	pop. per sq. km	..	..	98.9	20.4	21.5	24.5
Agricultural land	% of land area	..	..	..	..	41.7	42.7
Change in agricultural land	annual %	..	..	..	..	0.3	-0.2
Agricultural land under irrigation	%	..	..	..	..	9.3	16.1
Forests and woodland	thou. sq. km	..	..	..	..	..	..
Deforestation (net)	annual %	..	..	..	..	..	..
INCOME							
Household income							
Share of top 20% of households	% of income	..	..	..	..	..	..
Share of bottom 40% of households	"	..	..	..	..	..	..
Share of bottom 20% of households	"	..	..	..	..	..	..
EXPENDITURE							
Food	% of GDP	..	..	..	..	..	..
Staples	"	..	..	..	..	..	..
Meat, fish, milk, cheese, eggs	"	..	..	..	..	..	..
Cereal imports	thou. metric tonnes	..	..	..	45,972	49,174	70,626
Food aid in cereals	"	..	..	..	1,639	282	2
Food production per capita	1987 = 100	..	..	..	..	109	101
Fertilizer consumption	kg/ha	..	..	..	..	68.8	162.1
Share of agriculture in GDP	% of GDP	..	..	4.7	..	8.1	2.4
Housing	% of GDP	..	..	..	..	..	..
Average household size	persons per household	..	..	..	..	..	..
Urban	"	..	..	..	..	..	..
Fixed investment: housing	% of GDP	..	..	..	..	..	..
Fuel and power	% of GDP	..	..	..	..	..	..
Energy consumption per capita	kg of oil equiv.	..	..	..	3,190	1,649	5,101
Households with electricity							
Urban	% of households	..	..	..	..	..	..
Rural	"	..	..	..	..	..	..
Transport and communication	% of GDP	..	..	..	..	..	..
Fixed investment: transport equipment	"	..	..	..	..	..	..
Total road length	thou. km	..	..	..	..	..	..
INVESTMENT IN HUMAN CAPITAL							
Health							
Population per physician	persons	..	..	..	378	..	..
Population per nurse	"	..	..	..	..	..	..
Population per hospital bed	"	..	..	..	134	385	144
Oral rehydration therapy (under-5)	% of cases	..	..	..	..	54	..
Education							
Gross enrollment ratio							
Secondary	% of school-age pop.	..	..	20	..	53	92
Female	"	..	..	..	..	..	94
Pupil-teacher ratio: primary	pupils per teacher	..	..	..	..	25	18
Pupil-teacher ratio: secondary	"	..	..	..	..	..	..
Pupils reaching grade 4	% of cohort	..	..	..	..	71	..
Repeater rate: primary	% of total enroll	..	..	..	..	11	..
Illiteracy	% of pop. (age 15+)	..	..	..	..	14	..
Female	% of fem. (age 15+)	..	..	..	..	17	..
Newspaper circulation	per thou. pop.	..	..	152	..	117	..

World Bank International Economics Department, April 1994

Solomon Islands

Indicator	Unit of measure	Latest single year 1970-75	Latest single year 1980-85	Most recent estimate 1987-92	Same region/income group East Asia	Same region/income group Lower-middle-income	Next higher income group
Priority Poverty Indicators							
POVERTY							
Upper poverty line	local curr.	..	..	..	..	..	..
Headcount index	% of pop.	..	..	..	12	..	..
Lower poverty line	local curr.	..	..	..	..	..	..
Headcount index	% of pop.	..	..	..	9	..	..
GNP per capita	US$	290	530	710	760	..	3,870
SHORT TERM INCOME INDICATORS							
Unskilled urban wages	local curr.	..	..	..	..	..	..
Unskilled rural wages	"	..	..	..	..	..	..
Rural terms of trade	"	..	..	..	..	..	..
Consumer price index	1987=100	32	79	186	..	..	..
Lower income	"	..	..	..	..	..	..
Food[a]	"	..	83	180	..	..	..
Urban	"	..	..	..	..	..	..
Rural	"	..	..	..	..	..	..
SOCIAL INDICATORS							
Public expenditure on basic social services	% of GDP	..	..	..	..	..	..
Gross enrollment ratios							
Primary	% school age pop.	..	..	..	121	..	107
Male	"	..	..	..	126	..	..
Female	"	..	..	..	117	..	..
Mortality							
Infant mortality	per thou. live births	24.6	16.3	12.6	39.0	45.0	40.0
Under 5 mortality	"	..	..	15.5	49.0	59.0	51.0
Immunization							
Measles	% age group	..	..	92.0	88.4	..	82.0
DPT	"	..	38.0	67.0	89.5	..	73.8
Child malnutrition (under-5)	"	20.3	..	..	24.7	..	..
Life expectancy							
Total	years	70	71	71	68	68	69
Female advantage	"	7.0	7.8	8.3	3.6	6.4	6.3
Total fertility rate	births per woman	2.6	6.4	2.0	2.4	3.1	2.9
Maternal mortality rate	per 100,000 live births	..	..	..	114	..	..
Supplementary Poverty Indicators							
Expenditures on social security	% of total gov't exp.	..	..	0.6	..	..	..
Social security coverage	% econ. active pop.	..	..	..	..	..	..
Access to safe water: total	% of pop.	..	..	69.0	72.0	..	85.6
Urban	"	..	..	82.0	83.4	..	94.3
Rural	"	..	..	68.0	60.2	..	73.0
Access to health care	"	..	58.2	80.0	..	..	..

Population growth rate
(annual average, percent)

[Bar chart showing Solomon Islands (bars) and Lower-middle-income (line) for periods 1970-75, 1980-85, 1987-92. Y-axis from -2 to 6+]

□ Solomon Islands
— Lower-middle-income

GNP per capita growth rate
(annual average, percent)

[Bar chart showing values for periods 1970-75, 1980-85, 1987-92. Y-axis from -10 to 10+]

Development diamond[b]

[Development diamond chart with axes: Life expectancy (top), Gross primary enrollment (right), Access to safe water (bottom), GNP per capita (left)]

━ Solomon Islands
— Lower-middle-income

a. See the technical notes, p.389.   b. The development diamond, based on four key indicators, shows the average level of development in the country compared with its income group. See the introduction.

314

Solomon Islands

Indicator	Unit of measure	Latest single year 1970-75	Latest single year 1980-85	Most recent estimate 1987-92	Same region/income group East Asia	Same region/income group Lower-middle-income	Next higher income group
Resources and Expenditures							
HUMAN RESOURCES							
Population (mre=1992)	thousands	194	274	335	1,688,909	942,547	477,960
Age dependency ratio	ratio	..	1.05	0.92	0.55	0.66	0.64
Urban	% of pop.	9.1	9.7	10.6	29.4	57.0	71.7
Population growth rate	annual %	3.7	3.0	3.0	1.4	1.4	1.6
Urban	"	4.1	4.0	4.6	2.9	4.8	2.5
Labor force (15-64)	thousands	..	..	..	928,465	..	181,414
Agriculture	% of labor force	..	..	..	..	..	..
Industry	"	..	..	..	..	..	..
Female	"	..	..	..	41	36	29
Females per 100 males							
Urban	number	48	..	..	..	..	..
Rural	"	96	..	..	..	..	..
NATURAL RESOURCES							
Area	thou. sq. km	28.90	28.90	28.90	16,367.18	40,697.37	21,836.02
Density	pop. per sq. km	6.7	9.5	11.3	101.8	22.8	21.5
Agricultural land	% of land area	3.2	3.4	3.4	44.5	..	41.7
Change in agricultural land	annual %	0.0	1.1	0.0	0.1	..	0.3
Agricultural land under irrigation	%	..	..	..	14.5	..	9.3
Forests and woodland	thou. sq. km	26	26	26	..	..	..
Deforestation (net)	annual %	..	..	..	..	..	..
INCOME							
Household income							
Share of top 20% of households	% of income	..	..	..	42	..	..
Share of bottom 40% of households	"	..	..	..	18	..	..
Share of bottom 20% of households	"	..	..	..	7	..	..
EXPENDITURE							
Food	% of GDP	..	..	..	..	..	..
Staples	"	..	..	..	..	..	..
Meat, fish, milk, cheese, eggs	"	..	..	..	..	..	..
Cereal imports	thou. metric tonnes	6	15	19	33,591	74,924	49,174
Food aid in cereals	"	1	..	1	581	4,054	282
Food production per capita	1987 = 100	89	93	79	133	..	109
Fertilizer consumption	kg/ha	..	..	..	75.1	..	68.8
Share of agriculture in GDP	% of GDP	..	..	..	21.5	..	8.1
Housing	% of GDP	..	..	..	..	..	..
Average household size	persons per household	5.4	..	..	..	..	..
Urban	"	5.4	..	..	..	..	..
Fixed investment: housing	% of GDP	..	..	..	..	..	..
Fuel and power	% of GDP	..	..	..	..	..	..
Energy consumption per capita	kg of oil equiv.	918	182	170	593	1,882	1,649
Households with electricity							
Urban	% of households	..	..	..	..	..	..
Rural	"	..	..	..	..	..	..
Transport and communication	% of GDP	..	..	..	..	..	..
Fixed investment: transport equipment	"	..	..	..	..	..	..
Total road length	thou. km	..	..	..	..	..	..
INVESTMENT IN HUMAN CAPITAL							
Health							
Population per physician	persons	4,970	..	6,532	..	..	..
Population per nurse	"	679	..	..	..	..	..
Population per hospital bed	"	139	179	..	553	516	385
Oral rehydration therapy (under-5)	% of cases	..	..	77	51	..	54
Education							
Gross enrollment ratio							
Secondary	% of school-age pop.	..	..	..	53	..	53
Female	"	..	..	..	47	..	..
Pupil-teacher ratio: primary	pupils per teacher	26	26	21	23	26	25
Pupil-teacher ratio: secondary	"	18	19	17	16	..	..
Pupils reaching grade 4	% of cohort	80	86	..	89	..	71
Repeater rate: primary	% of total enroll	5	4	..	6	..	11
Illiteracy	% of pop. (age 15+)	..	..	..	24	..	14
Female	% of fem. (age 15+)	..	..	..	34	..	17
Newspaper circulation	per thou. pop.	..	..	..	..	100	117

World Bank International Economics Department, April 1994

Somalia

Indicator	Unit of measure	Latest single year 1970-75	Latest single year 1980-85	Most recent estimate 1987-92	Same region/income group Sub-Saharan Africa	Same region/income group Low-income	Next higher income group
Priority Poverty Indicators							
POVERTY							
Upper poverty line	local curr.	..	..	..	..	..	..
Headcount index	% of pop.	..	..	..	..	19	..
Lower poverty line	local curr.	..	..	..	..	..	..
Headcount index	% of pop.	..	..	..	..	..	..
GNP per capita	US$	140	120	120	520	390	..
SHORT TERM INCOME INDICATORS							
Unskilled urban wages	local curr.	..	..	..	..	..	..
Unskilled rural wages	"	..	..	..	..	..	..
Rural terms of trade	"	..	..	..	..	..	..
Consumer price index	1987=100	3	57	182	..	..	..
Lower income	"	..	..	..	..	..	..
Food[a]	"	..	62	..	..	..	..
Urban	"	..	..	..	..	..	..
Rural	"	..	..	..	..	..	..
SOCIAL INDICATORS							
Public expenditure on basic social services	% of GDP	..	..	..	..	..	..
Gross enrollment ratios							
Primary	% school age pop.	59	15	..	66	103	..
Male	"	76	20	..	79	113	..
Female	"	42	10	..	62	96	..
Mortality							
Infant mortality	per thou. live births	155.0	143.0	132.0	99.0	73.0	45.0
Under 5 mortality	"	..	..	195.7	169.0	108.0	59.0
Immunization							
Measles	% age group	..	34.0	30.0	54.0	72.7	..
DPT	"	..	22.0	18.0	54.6	80.6	..
Child malnutrition (under-5)	"	23.0	..	..	28.4	38.3	..
Life expectancy							
Total	years	41	45	49	52	62	68
Female advantage	"	3.2	3.3	3.4	3.4	2.4	6.4
Total fertility rate	births per woman	6.7	6.8	6.8	6.1	3.4	3.1
Maternal mortality rate	per 100,000 live births	..	1100	..	..	..	..
Supplementary Poverty Indicators							
Expenditures on social security	% of total gov't exp.	..	..	..	..	..	..
Social security coverage	% econ. active pop.	..	..	..	..	..	..
Access to safe water: total	% of pop.	15.0	31.0	56.0	41.1	68.4	..
Urban	"	17.0	58.0	58.0	77.8	78.9	..
Rural	"	14.0	22.0	55.0	27.3	60.3	..
Access to health care	"	..	20.0	..	..	..	..

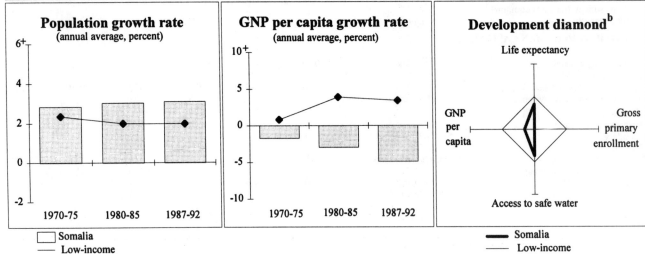

Population growth rate (annual average, percent) — Somalia, Low-income

GNP per capita growth rate (annual average, percent) — Somalia, Low-income

Development diamond[b] — Life expectancy, GNP per capita, Gross primary enrollment, Access to safe water — Somalia, Low-income

a. See the technical notes, p.389. b. The development diamond, based on four key indicators, shows the average level of development in the country compared with its income group. See the introduction.

Somalia

Indicator	Unit of measure	Latest single year 1970-75	Latest single year 1980-85	Most recent estimate 1987-92	Same region/income group Sub-Saharan Africa	Same region/income group Low-income	Next higher income group
Resources and Expenditures							
HUMAN RESOURCES							
Population (mre=1992)	thousands	4,967	6,686	8,301	546,390	3,194,535	942,547
Age dependency ratio	ratio	0.90	0.94	0.97	0.95	0.67	0.66
Urban	% of pop.	21.3	23.2	24.8	29.5	26.7	57.0
Population growth rate	annual %	2.9	3.1	3.1	2.9	1.8	1.4
Urban	"	3.7	4.0	4.3	5.1	3.4	4.8
Labor force (15-64)	thousands	1,516	1,999	2,219	224,025	1,478,954	..
Agriculture	% of labor force	77	76	..	..	..	..
Industry	"	8	8	..	..	..	..
Female	"	41	40	38	37	33	36
Females per 100 males							
Urban	number	..	..	..	..	..	..
Rural	"	..	..	..	..	..	..
NATURAL RESOURCES							
Area	thou. sq. km	637.66	637.66	637.66	24,274.03	38,401.06	40,697.37
Density	pop. per sq. km	7.8	10.5	12.6	21.9	81.7	22.8
Agricultural land	% of land area	70.1	70.2	70.2	52.7	50.9	..
Change in agricultural land	annual %	0.0	0.0	0.0	0.1	0.0	..
Agricultural land under irrigation	%	0.2	0.3	0.3	0.8	18.2	..
Forests and woodland	thou. sq. km	92	91	91	..	..	..
Deforestation (net)	annual %	..	..	0.0	..	..	..
INCOME							
Household income							
Share of top 20% of households	% of income	..	..	..	..	42	..
Share of bottom 40% of households	"	..	..	..	..	19	..
Share of bottom 20% of households	"	..	..	..	..	8	..
EXPENDITURE							
Food	% of GDP	..	38.9	..	..	..	..
Staples	"	..	12.1	..	..	..	..
Meat, fish, milk, cheese, eggs	"	..	10.1	..	..	..	..
Cereal imports	thou. metric tonnes	169	180	296	20,311	46,537	74,924
Food aid in cereals	"	111	248	114	4,303	9,008	4,054
Food production per capita	1987 = 100	103	94	30	90	123	..
Fertilizer consumption	kg/ha	0.1	0.1	0.1	4.2	61.9	..
Share of agriculture in GDP	% of GDP	48.7	63.6	62.7	18.6	29.6	..
Housing	% of GDP	..	11.9	..	..	..	..
Average household size	persons per household	..	..	..	..	..	..
Urban	"	..	..	..	..	..	..
Fixed investment: housing	% of GDP	..	2.3	..	..	..	..
Fuel and power	% of GDP	..	3.1	..	..	..	..
Energy consumption per capita	kg of oil equiv.	36	67	7	258	335	1,882
Households with electricity							
Urban	% of households	..	..	..	..	..	..
Rural	"	..	..	..	..	..	..
Transport and communication	% of GDP	..	1.7	..	..	..	..
Fixed investment: transport equipment	"	..	4.6	..	..	..	..
Total road length	thou. km	17	21	22	..	..	..
INVESTMENT IN HUMAN CAPITAL							
Health							
Population per physician	persons	31,625	13,450	..	..	..	..
Population per nurse	"	..	1,898	..	..	..	..
Population per hospital bed	"	845	..	1,333	1,329	1,050	516
Oral rehydration therapy (under-5)	% of cases	..	..	78	36	39	..
Education							
Gross enrollment ratio							
Secondary	% of school-age pop.	6	10	..	18	41	..
Female	"	3	7	..	14	35	..
Pupil-teacher ratio: primary	pupils per teacher	57	19	..	39	37	26
Pupil-teacher ratio: secondary	"	23	19	..	..	19	..
Pupils reaching grade 4	% of cohort	50	63	..	..	..	..
Repeater rate: primary	% of total enroll	..	..	..	..	..	..
Illiteracy	% of pop. (age 15+)	..	83	76	51	39	..
Female	% of fem. (age 15+)	..	91	86	62	52	..
Newspaper circulation	per thou. pop.	1	..	1	14	..	100

World Bank International Economics Department, April 1994

South Africa

Indicator	Unit of measure	Latest single year 1970-75	Latest single year 1980-85	Most recent estimate 1987-92	Same region/income group Sub-Saharan Africa	Same region/income group Upper-middle-income	Next higher income group
Priority Poverty Indicators							
POVERTY							
Upper poverty line	local curr.	..	..	..	..	..	..
Headcount index	% of pop.	..	..	..	..	..	..
Lower poverty line	local curr.	..	..	..	..	..	..
Headcount index	% of pop.	..	..	..	..	..	..
GNP per capita	US$	1,460	2,010	2,670	520	3,870	21,960
SHORT TERM INCOME INDICATORS							
Unskilled urban wages	local curr.	..	..	..	..	..	..
Unskilled rural wages	"	..	..	..	..	..	..
Rural terms of trade	"	..	..	..	..	..	..
Consumer price index	1987=100	22	73	194	..	..	..
Lower income	"	..	..	..	..	..	..
Food[a]	"	11	68	..	..	..	..
Urban	"	..	..	..	..	..	..
Rural	"	..	..	..	..	..	..
SOCIAL INDICATORS							
Public expenditure on basic social services	% of GDP	..	2.2	3.0	..	..	..
Gross enrollment ratios							
Primary	% school age pop.	105	..	..	66	107	103
Male	"	105	..	..	79	..	103
Female	"	105	..	..	62	..	103
Mortality							
Infant mortality	per thou. live births	76.0	63.0	53.0	99.0	40.0	7.0
Under 5 mortality	"	..	..	69.8	169.0	51.0	10.0
Immunization							
Measles	% age group	..	..	63.0	54.0	82.0	82.4
DPT	"	..	..	67.0	54.6	73.8	90.1
Child malnutrition (under-5)	"	..	43.0	..	28.4	..	..
Life expectancy							
Total	years	54	58	63	52	69	77
Female advantage	"	6.0	6.0	5.9	3.4	6.3	6.4
Total fertility rate	births per woman	5.5	4.8	4.1	6.1	2.9	1.7
Maternal mortality rate	per 100,000 live births	..	84	..	..	..	..
Supplementary Poverty Indicators							
Expenditures on social security	% of total gov't exp.	..	..	..	..	..	..
Social security coverage	% econ. active pop.	..	..	..	..	..	..
Access to safe water: total	% of pop.	..	..	..	41.1	85.6	..
Urban	"	..	..	..	77.8	94.3	..
Rural	"	..	..	..	27.3	73.0	..
Access to health care	"	..	..	..	..	..	..

Population growth rate
(annual average, percent)

☐ South Africa
— Upper-middle-income

GNP per capita growth rate
(annual average, percent)

Development diamond[b]

— South Africa
— Upper-middle-income

a. See the technical notes, p.389.   b. The development diamond, based on four key indicators, shows the average level of development in the country compared with its income group. See the introduction.

318

South Africa

Indicator	Unit of measure	Latest single year 1970-75	Latest single year 1980-85	Most recent estimate 1987-92	Same region/income group Sub-Saharan Africa	Same region/income group Upper-middle-income	Next higher income group
Resources and Expenditures							
HUMAN RESOURCES							
Population (mre=1992)	thousands	25,842	33,597	39,766	546,390	477,960	828,221
Age dependency ratio	ratio	0.78	0.72	0.73	0.95	0.64	0.50
Urban	% of pop.	48.0	48.3	49.8	29.5	71.7	78.1
Population growth rate	annual %	2.8	2.5	2.3	2.9	1.6	0.7
Urban	"	2.9	2.6	3.0	5.1	2.5	0.9
Labor force (15-64)	thousands	8,854	10,831	13,151	224,025	181,414	390,033
Agriculture	% of labor force	25	16	..	..	..	..
Industry	"	32	35	..	..	..	..
Female	"	34	35	36	37	29	38
Females per 100 males							
Urban	number	80	100	..	..	..	..
Rural	"	138	112	..	..	..	..
NATURAL RESOURCES							
Area	thou. sq. km	1,221.04	1,221.04	1,221.04	24,274.03	21,836.02	31,709.00
Density	pop. per sq. km	21.2	27.5	31.8	21.9	21.5	24.5
Agricultural land	% of land area	77.9	77.4	77.4	52.7	41.7	42.7
Change in agricultural land	annual %	-0.2	0.0	0.0	0.1	0.3	-0.2
Agricultural land under irrigation	%	1.1	1.2	1.2	0.8	9.3	16.1
Forests and woodland	thou. sq. km	42	45	45	..	..	..
Deforestation (net)	annual %	..	..	..	..	..	..
INCOME							
Household income							
Share of top 20% of households	% of income	..	..	..	..	..	..
Share of bottom 40% of households	"	..	..	..	..	..	..
Share of bottom 20% of households	"	..	..	..	..	..	..
EXPENDITURE							
Food	% of GDP	13.2	14.1	12.4	..	..	..
Staples	"	..	..	2.3	..	..	..
Meat, fish, milk, cheese, eggs	"	..	..	5.9	..	..	..
Cereal imports	thou. metric tonnes	96	765	4,855	20,311	49,174	70,626
Food aid in cereals	"	..	..	..	4,303	282	2
Food production per capita	1987 = 100	97	84	63	90	109	101
Fertilizer consumption	kg/ha	8.1	9.3	8.1	4.2	68.8	162.1
Share of agriculture in GDP	% of GDP	8.0	5.3	3.6	18.6	8.1	2.4
Housing	% of GDP	5.8	6.8	13.1	..	..	..
Average household size	persons per household	..	..	..	..	..	..
Urban	"	..	..	..	..	..	..
Fixed investment: housing	% of GDP	3.6	2.9	2.3	..	..	..
Fuel and power	% of GDP	..	..	1.4	..	..	..
Energy consumption per capita	kg of oil equiv.	..	..	..	258	1,649	5,101
Households with electricity							
Urban	% of households	..	..	..	..	..	..
Rural	"	..	..	..	..	..	..
Transport and communication	% of GDP	8.7	9.2	8.8	..	..	..
Fixed investment: transport equipment	"	3.3	2.3	11.5	..	..	..
Total road length	thou. km	185	184	184	..	..	..
INVESTMENT IN HUMAN CAPITAL							
Health							
Population per physician	persons	1,940	..	1,750	..	..	..
Population per nurse	"	297	..	..	..	..	..
Population per hospital bed	"	..	..	..	1,329	385	144
Oral rehydration therapy (under-5)	% of cases	..	..	..	36	54	..
Education							
Gross enrollment ratio							
Secondary	% of school-age pop.	20	..	..	18	53	92
Female	"	19	..	..	14	..	94
Pupil-teacher ratio: primary	pupils per teacher	33	24	..	39	25	18
Pupil-teacher ratio: secondary	"	..	..	..	..	..	..
Pupils reaching grade 4	% of cohort	..	..	..	..	71	..
Repeater rate: primary	% of total enroll	..	..	..	..	11	..
Illiteracy	% of pop. (age 15+)	..	..	..	51	14	..
Female	% of fem. (age 15+)	..	..	..	62	17	..
Newspaper circulation	per thou. pop.	69	40	35	14	117	..

World Bank International Economics Department, April 1994

Spain

Indicator	Unit of measure	Latest single year 1970-75	Latest single year 1980-85	Most recent estimate 1987-92	Same region/income group High-income
Priority Poverty Indicators					
POVERTY					
Upper poverty line	local curr.	..	..	..	..
Headcount index	% of pop.	..	..	..	..
Lower poverty line	local curr.	..	..	..	..
Headcount index	% of pop.	..	..	..	..
GNP per capita	US$	2,750	4,370	13,970	21,960
SHORT TERM INCOME INDICATORS					
Unskilled urban wages	local curr.	..	..	..	..
Unskilled rural wages	"	..	..	..	..
Rural terms of trade	"	..	..	..	..
Consumer price index	1987=100	21	87	134	..
Lower income	"	..	..	..	..
Food[a]	"	13	86	121	..
Urban	"	..	..	..	..
Rural	"	..	..	..	..
SOCIAL INDICATORS					
Public expenditure on basic social services	% of GDP	..	..	..	..
Gross enrollment ratios					
Primary	% school age pop.	111	113	109	103
Male	"	111	113	109	103
Female	"	111	112	108	103
Mortality					
Infant mortality	per thou. live births	18.9	8.9	7.9	7.0
Under 5 mortality	"	..	..	10.1	10.0
Immunization					
Measles	% age group	..	79.0	84.0	82.4
DPT	"	..	79.0	73.0	90.1
Child malnutrition (under-5)	"	..	..	..	..
Life expectancy					
Total	years	73	76	77	77
Female advantage	"	5.8	5.4	7.2	6.4
Total fertility rate	births per woman	2.8	1.6	1.2	1.7
Maternal mortality rate	per 100,000 live births	..	10	..	..
Supplementary Poverty Indicators					
Expenditures on social security	% of total gov't exp.	50.5	38.6	36.4	..
Social security coverage	% econ. active pop.	..	..	..	..
Access to safe water: total	% of pop.	..	98.0	..	..
Urban	"	..	100.0	..	..
Rural	"	..	81.0	..	..
Access to health care	"	..	95.0	..	..

Population growth rate
(annual average, percent)

1970-75 1980-85 1987-92

☐ Spain
— High-income

GNP per capita growth rate
(annual average, percent)

1970-75 1980-85 1987-92

Development diamond[b]

Life expectancy
GNP per capita — Gross primary enrollment
Access to safe water

—— Spain
— High-income

a. See the technical notes, p.389.   b. The development diamond, based on four key indicators, shows the average level of development in the country compared with its income group. See the introduction.

320

Spain

Indicator	Unit of measure	Latest single year		Most recent estimate 1987-92	Same region/income group
		1970-75	1980-85		High-income
Resources and Expenditures					

HUMAN RESOURCES

Indicator	Unit of measure	1970-75	1980-85	1987-92	High-income
Population (mre=1992)	thousands	35,515	38,574	39,085	828,221
Age dependency ratio	ratio	0.60	0.54	0.49	0.50
Urban	% of pop.	69.6	75.8	79.3	78.1
Population growth rate	annual %	1.0	0.6	0.2	0.7
Urban	"	2.1	1.4	0.7	0.9
Labor force (15-64)	thousands	12,369	13,725	14,719	390,033
Agriculture	% of labor force	21	17	..	..
Industry	"	37	37	..	..
Female	"	22	24	25	38
Females per 100 males					
Urban	number	108	..	..	..
Rural	"	97	..	..	..

NATURAL RESOURCES

Indicator	Unit of measure	1970-75	1980-85	1987-92	High-income
Area	thou. sq. km	504.78	504.78	504.78	31,709.00
Density	pop. per sq. km	70.4	76.4	77.3	24.5
Agricultural land	% of land area	63.9	61.5	60.9	42.7
Change in agricultural land	annual %	-0.5	0.3	-0.3	-0.2
Agricultural land under irrigation	%	8.8	10.5	11.2	16.1
Forests and woodland	thou. sq. km	149	156	159	..
Deforestation (net)	annual %	..	..	0.0	..

INCOME
Household income

Indicator	Unit of measure	1970-75	1980-85	1987-92	High-income
Share of top 20% of households	% of income	44	40	..	..
Share of bottom 40% of households	"	17	19	..	..
Share of bottom 20% of households	"	6	7	..	..

EXPENDITURE

Indicator	Unit of measure	1970-75	1980-85	1987-92	High-income
Food	% of GDP	21.9	17.3	..	..
Staples	"	2.7	2.5	..	..
Meat, fish, milk, cheese, eggs	"	12.1	9.7	..	..
Cereal imports	thou. metric tonnes	4,760	4,139	3,783	70,626
Food aid in cereals	"	..	..	..	2
Food production per capita	1987 = 100	92	107	111	101
Fertilizer consumption	kg/ha	43.9	56.5	61.9	162.1
Share of agriculture in GDP	% of GDP	..	5.9	4.0	2.4
Housing	% of GDP	9.1	11.0	..	..
Average household size	persons per household	3.8	3.5	..	..
Urban	"	..	..	..	..
Fixed investment: housing	% of GDP	6.1	3.2	..	..
Fuel and power	% of GDP	2.0	2.0	..	..
Energy consumption per capita	kg of oil equiv.	..	..	..	5,101
Households with electricity					
Urban	% of households	..	..	..	..
Rural	"	..	..	..	..
Transport and communication	% of GDP	7.2	9.6	..	..
Fixed investment: transport equipment	"	2.1	1.9	..	..
Total road length	thou. km	216	319	324	..

INVESTMENT IN HUMAN CAPITAL

Health

Indicator	Unit of measure	1970-75	1980-85	1987-92	High-income
Population per physician	persons	745	316	278	..
Population per nurse	"	..	259	..	..
Population per hospital bed	"	192	..	209	144
Oral rehydration therapy (under-5)	% of cases	..	..	..	..

Education
Gross enrollment ratio

Indicator	Unit of measure	1970-75	1980-85	1987-92	High-income
Secondary	% of school-age pop.	73	99	108	92
Female	"	71	104	113	94
Pupil-teacher ratio: primary	pupils per teacher	21	25	21	18
Pupil-teacher ratio: secondary	"	22	21	19	..
Pupils reaching grade 4	% of cohort	95	96	97	..
Repeater rate: primary	% of total enroll	..	5	3	..
Illiteracy	% of pop. (age 15+)	8	6	5	..
Female	% of fem. (age 15+)	..	8	7	..
Newspaper circulation	per thou. pop.	98	77	82	..

World Bank International Economics Department, April 1994

Sri Lanka

Indicator	Unit of measure	Latest single year 1970-75	Latest single year 1980-85	Most recent estimate 1987-92	Same region/income group South Asia	Same region/income group Low-income	Next higher income group
Priority Poverty Indicators							
POVERTY							
Upper poverty line	local curr.	..	..	..	..	..	..
Headcount index	% of pop.	..	..	..	28	19	..
Lower poverty line	local curr.	..	..	..	..	..	..
Headcount index	% of pop.	..	..	..	..	..	..
GNP per capita	US$	290	390	540	310	390	..
SHORT TERM INCOME INDICATORS							
Unskilled urban wages	local curr.	..	..	..	..	..	..
Unskilled rural wages	"	..	..	..	..	..	..
Rural terms of trade	"	..	..	..	..	..	..
Consumer price index	1987=100	30	86	193	..	..	..
Lower income	"	..	..	..	..	..	..
Food[a]	"	20	86	175	..	..	..
Urban	"	..	..	..	..	..	..
Rural	"	..	..	..	..	..	..
SOCIAL INDICATORS							
Public expenditure on basic social services	% of GDP	..	..	..	..	..	..
Gross enrollment ratios							
Primary	% school age pop.	77	103	108	103	103	..
Male	"	81	104	110	117	113	..
Female	"	74	101	106	88	96	..
Mortality							
Infant mortality	per thou. live births	48.0	30.0	17.6	85.0	73.0	45.0
Under 5 mortality	"	..	..	21.6	116.0	108.0	59.0
Immunization							
Measles	% age group	..	18.0	79.0	56.6	72.7	..
DPT	"	..	64.0	86.0	75.0	80.6	..
Child malnutrition (under-5)	"	..	47.5	36.6	60.9	38.3	..
Life expectancy							
Total	years	65	69	72	60	62	68
Female advantage	"	2.0	4.0	4.3	1.0	2.4	6.4
Total fertility rate	births per woman	4.0	3.3	2.5	4.0	3.4	3.1
Maternal mortality rate	per 100,000 live births	..	90	80	..	..	..
Supplementary Poverty Indicators							
Expenditures on social security	% of total gov't exp.	..	..	..	..	..	..
Social security coverage	% econ. active pop.	..	..	..	..	..	..
Access to safe water: total	% of pop.	19.0	40.0	60.0	71.9	68.4	..
Urban	"	36.0	82.0	80.0	74.2	78.9	..
Rural	"	13.0	29.0	55.0	70.0	60.3	..
Access to health care	"	..	90.0	90.0	..	..	..

Population growth rate
(annual average, percent)

□ Sri Lanka
— Low-income

GNP per capita growth rate
(annual average, percent)

Development diamond[b]

—— Sri Lanka
— Low-income

a. See the technical notes, p.389.   b. The development diamond, based on four key indicators, shows the average level of development in the country compared with its income group. See the introduction.

322

Sri Lanka

Indicator	Unit of measure	Latest single year		Most recent estimate 1987-92	Same region/income group		Next higher income group
		1970-75	1980-85		South Asia	Low-income	
Resources and Expenditures							

Indicator	Unit of measure	1970-75	1980-85	1987-92	South Asia	Low-income	Next higher income group
HUMAN RESOURCES							
Population (mre=1992)	thousands	13,496	15,837	17,405	1,177,918	3,194,535	942,547
Age dependency ratio	ratio	0.77	0.63	0.59	0.73	0.67	0.66
Urban	% of pop.	22.0	21.1	21.8	25.4	26.7	57.0
Population growth rate	annual %	1.6	1.5	0.9	2.1	1.8	1.4
Urban	"	1.7	1.0	1.8	3.4	3.4	4.8
Labor force (15-64)	thousands	4,773	5,920	6,574	428,847	1,478,954	..
Agriculture	% of labor force	54	53	..	..	..	..
Industry	"	14	14	..	..	..	..
Female	"	26	27	27	22	33	36
Females per 100 males							
Urban	number	83	88	..	..	..	..
Rural	"	97	99	..	..	..	..
NATURAL RESOURCES							
Area	thou. sq. km	65.61	65.61	65.61	5,133.49	38,401.06	40,697.37
Density	pop. per sq. km	205.7	241.4	262.9	224.8	81.7	22.8
Agricultural land	% of land area	36.4	35.8	36.2	58.9	50.9	..
Change in agricultural land	annual %	-0.3	0.2	0.1	-0.2	0.0	..
Agricultural land under irrigation	%	20.4	25.2	22.6	29.0	18.2	..
Forests and woodland	thou. sq. km	18	17	21	..	..	..
Deforestation (net)	annual %	..	..	1.6	..	..	..
INCOME							
Household income							
Share of top 20% of households	% of income	43	..	39	41	42	..
Share of bottom 40% of households	"	19	..	22	21	19	..
Share of bottom 20% of households	"	7	..	9	9	8	..
EXPENDITURE							
Food	% of GDP	52.2	34.0	..	..	..	..
Staples	"	30.5	13.9	..	..	..	..
Meat, fish, milk, cheese, eggs	"	5.7	6.1	..	..	..	..
Cereal imports	thou. metric tonnes	1,164	911	1,055	7,721	46,537	74,924
Food aid in cereals	"	271	276	442	2,558	9,008	4,054
Food production per capita	1987 = 100	88	102	80	116	123	..
Fertilizer consumption	kg/ha	30.8	84.4	75.7	71.5	61.9	..
Share of agriculture in GDP	% of GDP	29.3	24.9	23.6	28.7	29.6	..
Housing	% of GDP	4.3	4.3	..	..	..	..
Average household size	persons per household	6.0	4.9	..	..	..	..
Urban	"	6.0	..	..	..	..	..
Fixed investment: housing	% of GDP	2.2	6.1	..	..	..	..
Fuel and power	% of GDP	1.7	2.3	..	..	..	..
Energy consumption per capita	kg of oil equiv.	78	89	101	209	335	1,882
Households with electricity							
Urban	% of households	..	45.9	..	..	..	..
Rural	"	..	..	..	..	..	..
Transport and communication	% of GDP	5.3	12.1	..	..	..	..
Fixed investment: transport equipment	"	1.5	3.4	..	..	..	..
Total road length	thou. km	26	25	26	..	..	..
INVESTMENT IN HUMAN CAPITAL							
Health							
Population per physician	persons	5,900	5,516	..	2,459	..	..
Population per nurse	"	1,280	1,288	..	..	..	..
Population per hospital bed	"	300	340	365	1,652	1,050	516
Oral rehydration therapy (under-5)	% of cases	..	..	76	18	39	..
Education							
Gross enrollment ratio							
Secondary	% of school-age pop.	48	63	74	40	41	..
Female	"	49	66	77	29	35	..
Pupil-teacher ratio: primary	pupils per teacher	14	16	12	59	37	26
Pupil-teacher ratio: secondary	"	..	..	..	23	19	..
Pupils reaching grade 4	% of cohort	83	98	98	..	..	..
Repeater rate: primary	% of total enroll	16	8	8	..	..	..
Illiteracy	% of pop. (age 15+)	22	13	12	54	39	..
Female	% of fem. (age 15+)	..	19	17	68	52	..
Newspaper circulation	per thou. pop.	41	106	32	..	..	100

World Bank International Economics Department, April 1994

Sudan

Indicator	Unit of measure	Latest single year 1970-75	Latest single year 1980-85	Most recent estimate 1987-92	Same region/income group Sub-Saharan Africa	Same region/income group Low-income	Next higher income group
Priority Poverty Indicators							
POVERTY							
Upper poverty line	local curr.	..	..	..	..	..	..
Headcount index	% of pop.	..	..	..	..	19	..
Lower poverty line	local curr.	..	..	..	..	..	..
Headcount index	% of pop.	..	..	..	..	..	..
GNP per capita	US$	250	370	..	520	390	..
SHORT TERM INCOME INDICATORS							
Unskilled urban wages	local curr.	..	..	..	..	..	..
Unskilled rural wages	"	..	..	..	..	..	..
Rural terms of trade	"	..	..	..	..	..	..
Consumer price index	1987=100	7	67	2,207	..	..	..
Lower income	"	..	..	..	..	..	..
Food[a]	"	..	62	118	..	..	..
Urban	"	..	..	..	..	..	..
Rural	"	..	..	..	..	..	..
SOCIAL INDICATORS							
Public expenditure on basic social services	% of GDP	..	..	..	..	..	..
Gross enrollment ratios							
Primary	% school age pop.	47	50	50	66	103	..
Male	"	59	58	56	79	113	..
Female	"	34	41	43	62	96	..
Mortality							
Infant mortality	per thou. live births	145.0	118.0	98.7	99.0	73.0	45.0
Under 5 mortality	"	..	..	161.6	169.0	108.0	59.0
Immunization							
Measles	% age group	..	6.0	58.0	54.0	72.7	..
DPT	"	..	8.0	63.0	54.6	80.6	..
Child malnutrition (under-5)	"	..	55.2	..	28.4	38.3	..
Life expectancy							
Total	years	43	48	52	52	62	68
Female advantage	"	2.5	2.4	2.4	3.4	2.4	6.4
Total fertility rate	births per woman	6.7	6.6	6.1	6.1	3.4	3.1
Maternal mortality rate	per 100,000 live births	..	655	..	..	..	..
Supplementary Poverty Indicators							
Expenditures on social security	% of total gov't exp.	0.9	2.2	..	..	..	..
Social security coverage	% econ. active pop.	..	..	..	..	..	..
Access to safe water: total	% of pop.	50.0	..	..	41.1	68.4	..
Urban	"	96.0	..	..	77.8	78.9	..
Rural	"	43.0	..	..	27.3	60.3	..
Access to health care	"	..	70.0	70.0	..	..	..

Population growth rate (annual average, percent)

□ Sudan
— Low-income

GNP per capita growth rate (annual average, percent)

Development diamond[b]

Life expectancy / GNP per capita / Gross primary enrollment / Access to safe water

— Sudan
— Low-income

a. See the technical notes, p.389.　b. The development diamond, based on four key indicators, shows the average level of development in the country compared with its income group. See the introduction.

Sudan

Indicator	Unit of measure	Latest single year 1970-75	Latest single year 1980-85	Most recent estimate 1987-92	Same region/income group Sub-Saharan Africa	Same region/income group Low-income	Next higher income group

Resources and Expenditures

HUMAN RESOURCES

Indicator	Unit	1970-75	1980-85	1987-92	Sub-Saharan Africa	Low-income	Next higher
Population (mre=1992)	thousands	16,550	21,931	26,524	546,390	3,194,535	942,547
Age dependency ratio	ratio	0.89	0.92	0.92	0.95	0.67	0.66
Urban	% of pop.	18.9	21.0	23.3	29.5	26.7	57.0
Population growth rate	annual %	2.9	2.7	2.7	2.9	1.8	1.4
Urban	"	5.6	3.7	4.5	5.1	3.4	4.8
Labor force (15-64)	thousands	5,328	6,991	8,613	224,025	1,478,954	..
Agriculture	% of labor force	74	71	..	..	..	..
Industry	"	7	7	..	..	..	..
Female	"	20	21	22	37	33	36
Females per 100 males							
Urban	number	82	77	..	..	..	..
Rural	"	112	108	..	..	..	..

NATURAL RESOURCES

Indicator	Unit	1970-75	1980-85	1987-92	Sub-Saharan Africa	Low-income	Next higher
Area	thou. sq. km	2,505.81	2,505.81	2,505.81	24,274.03	38,401.06	40,697.37
Density	pop. per sq. km	6.6	8.8	10.3	21.9	81.7	22.8
Agricultural land	% of land area	46.4	47.4	51.7	52.7	50.9	..
Change in agricultural land	annual %	0.1	1.9	0.0	0.1	0.0	..
Agricultural land under irrigation	%	1.5	1.6	1.6	0.8	18.2	..
Forests and woodland	thou. sq. km	493	463	445	..	..	..
Deforestation (net)	annual %	..	..	1.1	..	..	..

INCOME

Indicator	Unit	1970-75	1980-85	1987-92	Sub-Saharan Africa	Low-income	Next higher
Household income							
Share of top 20% of households	% of income	..	..	..	..	42	..
Share of bottom 40% of households	"	..	..	..	..	19	..
Share of bottom 20% of households	"	..	..	..	..	8	..

EXPENDITURE

Indicator	Unit	1970-75	1980-85	1987-92	Sub-Saharan Africa	Low-income	Next higher
Food	% of GDP	..	56.1	..	..	..	..
Staples	"	..	..	..	..	..	..
Meat, fish, milk, cheese, eggs	"	..	..	..	..	..	..
Cereal imports	thou. metric tonnes	124	1,561	654	20,311	46,537	74,924
Food aid in cereals	"	46	815	481	4,303	9,008	4,054
Food production per capita	1987 = 100	101	85	90	90	123	..
Fertilizer consumption	kg/ha	0.9	0.8	0.8	4.2	61.9	..
Share of agriculture in GDP	% of GDP	38.4	27.4	32.1	18.6	29.6	..
Housing	% of GDP	..	13.0	..	..	..	..
Average household size	persons per household	5.1	..	..	..	..	..
Urban	"	5.7	..	..	..	..	..
Fixed investment: housing	% of GDP	..	1.8	..	..	..	..
Fuel and power	% of GDP	..	4.0	..	..	..	..
Energy consumption per capita	kg of oil equiv.	57	64	69	258	335	1,882
Households with electricity							
Urban	% of households	..	..	..	..	..	..
Rural	"	..	..	..	..	..	..
Transport and communication	% of GDP	..	2.2	..	..	..	..
Fixed investment: transport equipment	"	..	2.2	..	..	..	..
Total road length	thou. km	15	10	10	..	..	..

INVESTMENT IN HUMAN CAPITAL

Health

Indicator	Unit	1970-75	1980-85	1987-92	Sub-Saharan Africa	Low-income	Next higher
Population per physician	persons	14,500	10,190	..	..	..	..
Population per nurse	"	989	1,258	..	..	..	..
Population per hospital bed	"	1,000	1,136	959	1,329	1,050	516
Oral rehydration therapy (under-5)	% of cases	..	..	37	36	39	..

Education

Gross enrollment ratio

Indicator	Unit	1970-75	1980-85	1987-92	Sub-Saharan Africa	Low-income	Next higher
Secondary	% of school-age pop.	14	20	22	18	41	..
Female	"	8	17	20	14	35	..
Pupil-teacher ratio: primary	pupils per teacher	37	35	34	39	37	26
Pupil-teacher ratio: secondary	"	22	25	23	..	19	..
Pupils reaching grade 4	% of cohort	..	81	..	..	..	..
Repeater rate: primary	% of total enroll	3	0	..	..	..	..
Illiteracy	% of pop. (age 15+)	..	76	73	51	39	..
Female	% of fem. (age 15+)	..	90	88	62	52	..
Newspaper circulation	per thou. pop.	9	5	24	14	..	100

World Bank International Economics Department, April 1994

Suriname

Indicator	Unit of measure	Latest single year 1970-75	Latest single year 1980-85	Most recent estimate 1987-92	Same region/income group Latin America Caribbean	Same region/income group Upper-middle-income	Next higher income group
Priority Poverty Indicators							
POVERTY							
Upper poverty line	local curr.	..	..	..	..	..	..
Headcount index	% of pop.	..	..	..	..	..	..
Lower poverty line	local curr.	..	..	..	..	..	..
Headcount index	% of pop.	..	..	..	..	..	..
GNP per capita	US$	1,340	2,420	4,280	2,690	3,870	21,960
SHORT TERM INCOME INDICATORS							
Unskilled urban wages	local curr.	..	..	..	..	..	..
Unskilled rural wages	"	..	..	..	..	..	..
Rural terms of trade	"	..	..	..	..	..	..
Consumer price index	1987=100	23	55	238	..	..	..
Lower income	"	..	..	..	..	..	..
Food[a]	"	14	44	164	..	..	..
Urban	"	..	..	..	..	..	..
Rural	"	..	..	..	..	..	..
SOCIAL INDICATORS							
Public expenditure on basic social services	% of GDP	..	..	..	..	..	..
Gross enrollment ratios							
Primary	% school age pop.	108	136	127	106	107	103
Male	"	111	139	129	..	..	103
Female	"	105	133	125	..	..	103
Mortality							
Infant mortality	per thou. live births	52.0	45.0	36.5	44.0	40.0	7.0
Under 5 mortality	"	..	..	45.0	56.0	51.0	10.0
Immunization							
Measles	% age group	..	..	65.0	78.9	82.0	82.4
DPT	"	..	80.0	83.0	73.8	73.8	90.1
Child malnutrition (under-5)	"	..	..	..	10.5	..	..
Life expectancy							
Total	years	64	65	69	68	69	77
Female advantage	"	4.0	3.9	5.8	5.6	6.3	6.4
Total fertility rate	births per woman	5.3	4.1	2.8	3.0	2.9	1.7
Maternal mortality rate	per 100,000 live births	..	82	..	..	..	..
Supplementary Poverty Indicators							
Expenditures on social security	% of total gov't exp.	5.6	8.5	..	..	..	..
Social security coverage	% econ. active pop.	..	..	..	..	..	..
Access to safe water: total	% of pop.	..	98.0	..	80.3	85.6	..
Urban	"	..	100.0	..	91.0	94.3	..
Rural	"	..	94.0	..	64.3	73.0	..
Access to health care	"	..	100.0	91.0	..	..	..

Population growth rate
(annual average, percent)

GNP per capita growth rate
(annual average, percent)

Development diamond[b]

Suriname
Upper-middle-income

a. See the technical notes, p.389.   b. The development diamond, based on four key indicators, shows the average level of development in the country compared with its income group. See the introduction.

Suriname

Indicator	Unit of measure	Latest single year 1970-75	Latest single year 1980-85	Most recent estimate 1987-92	Same region/income group Latin America Caribbean	Same region/income group Upper-middle-income	Next higher income group
Resources and Expenditures							
HUMAN RESOURCES							
Population (mre=1992)	thousands	365	398	404	453,294	477,960	828,221
Age dependency ratio	ratio	1.06	0.67	0.67	0.67	0.64	0.50
Urban	% of pop.	44.8	45.7	48.7	72.9	71.7	78.1
Population growth rate	annual %	-4.5	2.8	0.0	1.7	1.6	0.7
Urban	"	-5.0	3.2	1.2	2.6	2.5	0.9
Labor force (15-64)	thousands	96	117	143	166,091	181,414	390,033
Agriculture	% of labor force	22	20	..	..	..	..
Industry	"	20	20	..	..	..	..
Female	"	26	29	30	27	29	38
Females per 100 males							
Urban	number	..	..	..	..	..	..
Rural	"	..	..	..	..	..	..
NATURAL RESOURCES							
Area	thou. sq. km	163.27	163.27	163.27	20,507.48	21,836.02	31,709.00
Density	pop. per sq. km	2.2	2.4	2.5	21.7	21.5	24.5
Agricultural land	% of land area	0.4	0.5	0.6	40.2	41.7	42.7
Change in agricultural land	annual %	1.8	5.2	1.1	0.5	0.3	-0.2
Agricultural land under irrigation	%	56.9	67.9	66.3	3.2	9.3	16.1
Forests and woodland	thou. sq. km	149	149	149			
Deforestation (net)	annual %	..		0.1	..	..	..
INCOME							
Household income							
Share of top 20% of households	% of income	..	..	..	..	..	..
Share of bottom 40% of households	"	..	..	..	..	..	..
Share of bottom 20% of households	"	..	..	..	..	..	..
EXPENDITURE							
Food	% of GDP	..	27.8	..	..	..	..
Staples	"	..	6.3	..	..	..	..
Meat, fish, milk, cheese, eggs	"	..	10.6	..	..	..	..
Cereal imports	thou. metric tonnes	42	48	54	25,032	49,174	70,626
Food aid in cereals	"	1	..	..	1,779	282	2
Food production per capita	1987 = 100	74	111	83	104	109	101
Fertilizer consumption	kg/ha	48.3	143.9	11.2	15.5	68.8	162.1
Share of agriculture in GDP	% of GDP	6.3	8.4	10.3	8.9	8.1	2.4
Housing	% of GDP	..	6.1	..	..	..	..
Average household size	persons per household	..	..	..	..	..	..
Urban	"	..	..	..	..	..	..
Fixed investment: housing	% of GDP	..	5.3	..	..	..	..
Fuel and power	% of GDP	..	2.0	..	..	..	..
Energy consumption per capita	kg of oil equiv.	2,461	1,586	1,903	912	1,649	5,101
Households with electricity							
Urban	% of households	..	..	..	..	..	..
Rural	"	..	..	..	..	..	..
Transport and communication	% of GDP	..	4.9	..	..	..	..
Fixed investment: transport equipment	"	..	1.6	..	..	..	..
Total road length	thou. km	3	9	9	..	..	..
INVESTMENT IN HUMAN CAPITAL							
Health							
Population per physician	persons	2,150	1,264	..	..	..	..
Population per nurse	"	709	276	..	..	..	..
Population per hospital bed	"	176	112	..	508	385	144
Oral rehydration therapy (under-5)	% of cases	..	..	47	62	54	..
Education							
Gross enrollment ratio							
Secondary	% of school-age pop.	46	51	54	47	53	92
Female	"	51	..	58	..	..	94
Pupil-teacher ratio: primary	pupils per teacher	31	25	23	25	25	18
Pupil-teacher ratio: secondary	"	23	18	21	..	..	..
Pupils reaching grade 4	% of cohort	..	92	..	..	71	..
Repeater rate: primary	% of total enroll	24	22	..	14	11	..
Illiteracy	% of pop. (age 15+)	..	7	5	15	14	..
Female	% of fem. (age 15+)	..	8	5	17	17	..
Newspaper circulation	per thou. pop.	91	78	99	99	117	..

World Bank International Economics Department, April 1994

Swaziland

Indicator	Unit of measure	Latest single year 1970-75	Latest single year 1980-85	Most recent estimate 1987-92	Same region/income group Sub-Saharan Africa	Same region/income group Lower-middle-income	Next higher income group
Priority Poverty Indicators							
POVERTY							
Upper poverty line	local curr.	..	..	..	..	..	..
Headcount index	% of pop.	..	..	..	..	..	..
Lower poverty line	local curr.	..	..	..	..	..	..
Headcount index	% of pop.	..	..	..	..	..	..
GNP per capita	US$	590	810	1,090	520	..	3,870
SHORT TERM INCOME INDICATORS							
Unskilled urban wages	local curr.	..	..	..	..	..	..
Unskilled rural wages	"	..	..	..	..	..	..
Rural terms of trade	"	..	..	..	..	..	..
Consumer price index	1987=100	20	78	162	..	..	..
Lower income	"	..	..	..	..	..	..
Food[a]	"	13	78	113	..	..	..
Urban	"	..	..	..	..	..	..
Rural	"	..	..	..	..	..	..
SOCIAL INDICATORS							
Public expenditure on basic social services	% of GDP	..	..	..	..	..	..
Gross enrollment ratios							
Primary	% school age pop.	99	107	111	66	..	107
Male	"	100	108	111	79	..	..
Female	"	97	106	111	62	..	..
Mortality							
Infant mortality	per thou. live births	144.0	129.0	108.2	99.0	45.0	40.0
Under 5 mortality	"	..	..	162.3	169.0	59.0	51.0
Immunization							
Measles	% age group	..	49.0	..	54.0	..	82.0
DPT	"	..	61.0	..	54.6	..	73.8
Child malnutrition (under-5)	"	..	9.7	9.7	28.4	..	..
Life expectancy							
Total	years	47	53	57	52	68	69
Female advantage	"	4.5	3.6	3.5	3.4	6.4	6.3
Total fertility rate	births per woman	6.5	6.5	6.6	6.1	3.1	2.9
Maternal mortality rate	per 100,000 live births	..	..	129	..	..	..
Supplementary Poverty Indicators							
Expenditures on social security	% of total gov't exp.	..	..	..	..	..	..
Social security coverage	% econ. active pop.	..	..	..	..	..	..
Access to safe water: total	% of pop.	..	21.0	30.0	41.1	..	85.6
Urban	"	..	..	100.0	77.8	..	94.3
Rural	"	..	7.0	7.0	27.3	..	73.0
Access to health care	"	..	66.0	..	..	..	..

Population growth rate (annual average, percent)

□ Swaziland
— Lower-middle-income

GNP per capita growth rate (annual average, percent)

Development diamond[b]

Life expectancy
GNP per capita — Gross primary enrollment
Access to safe water

— Swaziland
— Lower-middle-income

a. See the technical notes, p.389.   b. The development diamond, based on four key indicators, shows the average level of development in the country compared with its income group. See the introduction.

Swaziland

Indicator	Unit of measure	Latest single year 1970-75	Latest single year 1980-85	Most recent estimate 1987-92	Same region/income group Sub-Saharan Africa	Same region/income group Lower-middle-income	Next higher income group
		Resources and Expenditures					
HUMAN RESOURCES							
Population (mre=1992)	thousands	482	659	858	546,390	942,547	477,960
Age dependency ratio	ratio	0.94	1.04	1.05	0.95	0.66	0.64
Urban	% of pop.	14.0	21.8	28.3	29.5	57.0	71.7
Population growth rate	annual %	3.0	3.4	3.7	2.9	1.4	1.6
Urban	"	9.3	7.1	7.1	5.1	4.8	2.5
Labor force (15-64)	thousands	220	273	323	224,025	..	181,414
Agriculture	% of labor force	77	74	..	..	..	..
Industry	"	8	9	..	..	..	..
Female	"	42	40	38	37	36	29
Females per 100 males							
Urban	number	..	..	..	..	..	..
Rural	"	..	..	..	..	..	..
NATURAL RESOURCES							
Area	thou. sq. km	17.36	17.36	17.36	24,274.03	40,697.37	21,836.02
Density	pop. per sq. km	27.8	38.0	47.6	21.9	22.8	21.5
Agricultural land	% of land area	76.3	74.7	81.1	52.7	..	41.7
Change in agricultural land	annual %	-11.4	1.2	0.4	0.1	..	0.3
Agricultural land under irrigation	%	4.3	4.8	4.6	0.8	..	9.3
Forests and woodland	thou. sq. km	1	1	1	..	..	..
Deforestation (net)	annual %	..	..	..	..	..	..
INCOME							
Household income							
Share of top 20% of households	% of income	..	..	..	..	..	..
Share of bottom 40% of households	"	..	..	..	..	..	..
Share of bottom 20% of households	"	..	..	..	..	..	..
EXPENDITURE							
Food	% of GDP	..	26.4	..	..	..	..
Staples	"	..	8.9	..	..	..	..
Meat, fish, milk, cheese, eggs	"	..	9.2	..	..	..	..
Cereal imports	thou. metric tonnes	15	31	85	20,311	74,924	49,174
Food aid in cereals	"	1	1	5	4,303	4,054	282
Food production per capita	1987 = 100	99	96	81	90	..	109
Fertilizer consumption	kg/ha	7.2	6.9	8.3	4.2	..	68.8
Share of agriculture in GDP	% of GDP	25.1	17.0	9.5	18.6	..	8.1
Housing	% of GDP	..	4.0	..	..	..	..
Average household size	persons per household	..	..	..	..	..	..
Urban	"	..	..	..	..	..	..
Fixed investment: housing	% of GDP	..	3.3	..	..	..	..
Fuel and power	% of GDP	..	1.9	..	..	..	..
Energy consumption per capita	kg of oil equiv.	284	310	265	258	1,882	1,649
Households with electricity							
Urban	% of households	..	..	..	..	..	..
Rural	"	..	..	..	..	..	..
Transport and communication	% of GDP	..	9.9	..	..	..	..
Fixed investment: transport equipment	"	..	2.8	..	..	..	..
Total road length	thou. km	2	3	3	..	..	..
INVESTMENT IN HUMAN CAPITAL							
Health							
Population per physician	persons	8,058	18,697	9,488	..	..	..
Population per nurse	"	529	1,046	232	..	..	..
Population per hospital bed	"	296	..	..	1,329	516	385
Oral rehydration therapy (under-5)	% of cases	..	..	85	36	..	54
Education							
Gross enrollment ratio							
Secondary	% of school-age pop.	32	42	48	18	..	53
Female	"	29	41	47	14	..	..
Pupil-teacher ratio: primary	pupils per teacher	38	34	32	39	26	25
Pupil-teacher ratio: secondary	"	22	19	18	..	..	..
Pupils reaching grade 4	% of cohort	83	85	86	..	..	71
Repeater rate: primary	% of total enroll	10	14	15	..	..	11
Illiteracy	% of pop. (age 15+)	..	32	..	51	..	14
Female	% of fem. (age 15+)	..	34	..	62	..	17
Newspaper circulation	per thou. pop.	10	14	13	14	100	117

World Bank International Economics Department, April 1994

Sweden

Indicator	Unit of measure	Latest single year 1970-75	Latest single year 1980-85	Most recent estimate 1987-92	Same region/income group High-income

Priority Poverty Indicators

POVERTY

Indicator	Unit of measure	1970-75	1980-85	1987-92	High-income
Upper poverty line	local curr.	..	..	..	..
Headcount index	% of pop.	..	..	..	..
Lower poverty line	local curr.	..	..	..	..
Headcount index	% of pop.	..	..	..	..
GNP per capita	US$	8,330	12,040	27,010	21,960

SHORT TERM INCOME INDICATORS

Unskilled urban wages	local curr.	..	..	..	..
Unskilled rural wages	"	..	..	..	..
Rural terms of trade	"	..	..	..	..
Consumer price index	1987=100	36	92	139	
Lower income	"	..	..	..	
Food[a]	"	21	90	125	
Urban	"	..	..	..	..
Rural	"	..	..	..	..

SOCIAL INDICATORS

Public expenditure on basic social services	% of GDP	..	..	..	..
Gross enrollment ratios					
Primary	% school age pop.	101	98	100	103
Male	"	101	97	100	103
Female	"	102	99	100	103
Mortality					
Infant mortality	per thou. live births	8.6	6.8	5.3	7.0
Under 5 mortality	"	..	..	7.0	10.0
Immunization					
Measles	% age group	..	92.0	95.0	82.4
DPT	"	..	99.0	99.0	90.1
Child malnutrition (under-5)	"	..	..	..	..
Life expectancy					
Total	years	75	76	78	77
Female advantage	"	5.4	5.9	6.0	6.4
Total fertility rate	births per woman	1.8	1.7	2.1	1.7
Maternal mortality rate	per 100,000 live births	..	4	..	..

Supplementary Poverty Indicators

Expenditures on social security	% of total gov't exp.	35.9	38.7	48.1	..
Social security coverage	% econ. active pop.	..	..	..	..
Access to safe water: total	% of pop.	..	..	..	..
Urban	"	..	..	..	..
Rural	"	..	..	..	..
Access to health care	"	..	100.0	100.0	..

Population growth rate
(annual average, percent)

GNP per capita growth rate
(annual average, percent)

Development diamond[b]

- Sweden
- High-income

a. See the technical notes, p.389.   b. The development diamond, based on four key indicators, shows the average level of development in the country compared with its income group. See the introduction.

Sweden

Indicator	Unit of measure	Latest single year 1970-75	Latest single year 1980-85	Most recent estimate 1987-92	Same region/income group High-income

Resources and Expenditures

HUMAN RESOURCES

Population (mre=1992)	thousands	8,193	8,350	8,678	828,221
Age dependency ratio	ratio	0.55	0.55	0.55	0.50
Urban	% of pop.	82.7	83.4	84.3	78.1
Population growth rate	annual %	0.4	0.2	0.5	0.7
Urban	"	0.8	0.2	0.7	0.9
Labor force (15-64)	thousands	3,923	4,237	4,346	390,033
Agriculture	% of labor force	7	6	..	..
Industry	"	37	33	..	..
Female	"	40	44	45	38
Females per 100 males					
Urban	number	100	100	..	..
Rural	"	85	86	..	..

NATURAL RESOURCES

Area	thou. sq. km	449.96	449.96	449.96	31,709.00
Density	pop. per sq. km	18.2	18.6	19.2	24.5
Agricultural land	% of land area	9.1	8.5	8.1	42.7
Change in agricultural land	annual %	-0.2	-3.2	-1.7	-0.2
Agricultural land under irrigation	%	1.2	2.8	3.5	16.1
Forests and woodland	thou. sq. km	278	280	280	..
Deforestation (net)	annual %	..	..	..	..

INCOME

Household income

Share of top 20% of households	% of income	37	37	..	..
Share of bottom 40% of households	"	20	21	..	..
Share of bottom 20% of households	"	7	8	..	..

EXPENDITURE

Food	% of GDP	..	9.6	..	..
Staples	"	..	1.7	..	..
Meat, fish, milk, cheese, eggs	"	..	4.3	..	..
Cereal imports	thou. metric tonnes	110	111	167	70,626
Food aid in cereals	"	..	..	..	2
Food production per capita	1987 = 100	92	108	81	101
Fertilizer consumption	kg/ha	140.9	120.1	79.2	162.1
Share of agriculture in GDP	% of GDP	..	3.3	2.2	2.4
Housing	% of GDP	..	13.9	..	..
Average household size	persons per household	2.4	2.3	..	..
Urban	"	2.4	2.3	..	..
Fixed investment: housing	% of GDP	4.0	3.6	..	..
Fuel and power	% of GDP	..	3.2	..	..
Energy consumption per capita	kg of oil equiv.	4,821	5,702	5,395	5,101
Households with electricity					
Urban	% of households	..	..	..	..
Rural	"	..	..	..	..
Transport and communication	% of GDP	..	8.2	..	..
Fixed investment: transport equipment	"	1.7	1.9	..	..
Total road length	thou. km	125	136	134	..

INVESTMENT IN HUMAN CAPITAL

Health

Population per physician	persons	735	387	367	..
Population per nurse	"	145	95	..	..
Population per hospital bed	"	67	68	161	144
Oral rehydration therapy (under-5)	% of cases	..	..	..	..

Education

Gross enrollment ratio

Secondary	% of school-age pop.	78	86	91	92
Female	"	82	91	93	94
Pupil-teacher ratio: primary	pupils per teacher	20	..	6	18
Pupil-teacher ratio: secondary	"	10	..	..	..
Pupils reaching grade 4	% of cohort	99	99	..	..
Repeater rate: primary	% of total enroll	0	0	0	..
Illiteracy	% of pop. (age 15+)	..	..	†	..
Female	% of fem. (age 15+)	..	..	†	..
Newspaper circulation	per thou. pop.	539	522	526	..

World Bank International Economics Department, April 1994

Switzerland

Indicator	Unit of measure	Latest single year		Most recent estimate 1987-92	Same region/income group High-income
		1970-75	1980-85		

Priority Poverty Indicators

POVERTY

Indicator	Unit of measure	1970-75	1980-85	1987-92	High-income
Upper poverty line	local curr.	..	..	..	..
Headcount index	% of pop.	..	..	..	..
Lower poverty line	local curr.	..	..	..	..
Headcount index	% of pop.	..	..	..	..
GNP per capita	US$	7,940	16,340	36,080	21,960
SHORT TERM INCOME INDICATORS					
Unskilled urban wages	local curr.	..	..	..	..
Unskilled rural wages	"	..	..	..	..
Rural terms of trade	"	..	..	..	..
Consumer price index	1987=100	71	98	122	
Lower income	"	..	..	..	..
Food[a]	"	47	98	115	..
Urban	"	..	..	..	..
Rural	"	..	..	..	..
SOCIAL INDICATORS					
Public expenditure on basic social services	% of GDP	..	..	..	..
Gross enrollment ratios					
Primary	% school age pop.	..	..	103	103
Male	"	..	..	103	103
Female	"	..	..	104	103
Mortality					
Infant mortality	per thou. live births	10.7	6.9	6.0	7.0
Under 5 mortality	"	..	..	7.8	10.0
Immunization					
Measles	% age group	..	..	90.0	82.4
DPT	"	..	..	90.0	90.1
Child malnutrition (under-5)	"	..	..	..	..
Life expectancy					
Total	years	74	76	78	77
Female advantage	"	6.2	6.7	7.4	6.4
Total fertility rate	births per woman	1.6	1.5	1.7	1.7
Maternal mortality rate	per 100,000 live births	..	5		..

Supplementary Poverty Indicators

Indicator	Unit of measure	1970-75	1980-85	1987-92	High-income
Expenditures on social security	% of total gov't exp.	48.1	49.9	..	..
Social security coverage	% econ. active pop.	..	..	..	..
Access to safe water: total	% of pop.	..	..	..	..
Urban	"	..	100.0	..	..
Rural	"	..	..	..	..
Access to health care	"	..	100.0	100.0	..

Population growth rate
(annual average, percent)

Switzerland
High-income

GNP per capita growth rate
(annual average, percent)

Development diamond[b]

Life expectancy

GNP per capita — Gross primary enrollment

Access to safe water

Switzerland
High-income

a. See the technical notes, p.389.   b. The development diamond, based on four key indicators, shows the average level of development in the country compared with its income group. See the introduction.

Switzerland

Indicator	Unit of measure	Latest single year		Most recent estimate 1987-92	Same region/income group
		1970-75	1980-85		High-income

Resources and Expenditures

HUMAN RESOURCES

Indicator	Unit of measure	1970-75	1980-85	1987-92	High-income
Population (mre=1992)	thousands	6,405	6,470	6,905	828,221
Age dependency ratio	ratio	0.54	0.46	0.48	0.50
Urban	% of pop.	55.7	59.2	62.5	78.1
Population growth rate	annual %	-0.6	0.4	1.2	0.7
Urban	"	-0.2	1.2	2.0	0.9
Labor force (15-64)	thousands	3,026	3,173	3,204	390,033
Agriculture	% of labor force	7	6	..	..
Industry	"	44	39	..	..
Female	"	35	37	36	38
Females per 100 males					
Urban	number	103	104	..	..
Rural	"	94	94	..	..

NATURAL RESOURCES

Indicator	Unit of measure	1970-75	1980-85	1987-92	High-income
Area	thou. sq. km	41.29	41.29	41.29	31,709.00
Density	pop. per sq. km	155.1	156.7	165.2	24.5
Agricultural land	% of land area	50.8	50.8	50.8	42.7
Change in agricultural land	annual %	0.0	0.0	0.0	-0.2
Agricultural land under irrigation	%	1.2	1.2	1.2	16.1
Forests and woodland	thou. sq. km	11	11	11	..
Deforestation (net)	annual %	..	..	-0.9	..

INCOME

Indicator	Unit of measure	1970-75	1980-85	1987-92	High-income
Household income					
Share of top 20% of households	% of income	..	45	..	..
Share of bottom 40% of households	"	..	17	..	..
Share of bottom 20% of households	"	..	5	..	..

EXPENDITURE

Indicator	Unit of measure	1970-75	1980-85	1987-92	High-income
Food	% of GDP	12.9	12.7	..	..
Staples	"	..	..	..	..
Meat, fish, milk, cheese, eggs	"	..	..	..	..
Cereal imports	thou. metric tonnes	1,439	926	454	70,626
Food aid in cereals	"	..	..	..	2
Food production per capita	1987 = 100	91	102	100	101
Fertilizer consumption	kg/ha	71.0	88.9	81.6	162.1
Share of agriculture in GDP	% of GDP	..	3.6	..	2.4
Housing	% of GDP	11.6	12.4	..	..
Average household size	persons per household	2.9	2.5	..	..
Urban	"	2.7	2.3	..	..
Fixed investment: housing	% of GDP	..	..	..	..
Fuel and power	% of GDP	3.5	4.2	..	..
Energy consumption per capita	kg of oil equiv.	2,803	3,569	3,694	5,101
Households with electricity					
Urban	% of households	..	..	..	..
Rural	"	..	..	..	..
Transport and communication	% of GDP	6.5	6.9	..	..
Fixed investment: transport equipment	"	..	..	..	..
Total road length	thou. km	62	71	71	..

INVESTMENT IN HUMAN CAPITAL

Indicator	Unit of measure	1970-75	1980-85	1987-92	High-income
Health					
Population per physician	persons	705	696	627	..
Population per nurse	"	..	129	..	..
Population per hospital bed	"	90	..	93	144
Oral rehydration therapy (under-5)	% of cases	..	..	..	..
Education					
Gross enrollment ratio					
Secondary	% of school-age pop.	..	..	91	92
Female	"	..	..	88	94
Pupil-teacher ratio: primary	pupils per teacher	..	..	..	18
Pupil-teacher ratio: secondary	"	..	..	..	..
Pupils reaching grade 4	% of cohort	93	99	..	..
Repeater rate: primary	% of total enroll	..	2	2	..
Illiteracy	% of pop. (age 15+)	..	..	†	..
Female	% of fem. (age 15+)	..	..	†	..
Newspaper circulation	per thou. pop.	402	383	456	..

World Bank International Economics Department, April 1994

333

Syrian Arab Republic

Indicator	Unit of measure	Latest single year 1970-75	Latest single year 1980-85	Most recent estimate 1987-92	Same region/income group Mid-East & North Africa	Same region/income group Lower-middle-income	Next higher income group
Priority Poverty Indicators							
POVERTY							
Upper poverty line	local curr.	..	..	..	..	..	..
Headcount index	% of pop.	..	..	..	..	..	..
Lower poverty line	local curr.	..	..	..	..	..	..
Headcount index	% of pop.	..	..	..	..	..	..
GNP per capita	US$	860	1,750	1,170	1,950	..	3,870
SHORT TERM INCOME INDICATORS							
Unskilled urban wages	local curr.	..	..	..	..	..	..
Unskilled rural wages	"	..	..	..	..	..	..
Rural terms of trade	"	..	..	..	..	..	..
Consumer price index	1987=100	15	46	193	..	..	..
Lower income	"	..	..	..	..	..	..
Food[a]	"	8	43	196	..	..	..
Urban	"	..	..	..	..	..	..
Rural	"	..	..	..	..	..	..
SOCIAL INDICATORS							
Public expenditure on basic social services	% of GDP	..	..	..	..	..	..
Gross enrollment ratios							
Primary	% school age pop.	96	107	109	100	..	107
Male	"	112	116	115	107	..	..
Female	"	78	101	103	88	..	..
Mortality							
Infant mortality	per thou. live births	88.0	49.0	36.0	58.0	45.0	40.0
Under 5 mortality	"	..	..	44.4	78.0	59.0	51.0
Immunization							
Measles	% age group	..	30.0	84.0	81.8	..	82.0
DPT	"	..	26.0	89.0	83.9	..	73.8
Child malnutrition (under-5)	"	..	25.0	..	20.9	..	..
Life expectancy							
Total	years	57	63	67	64	68	69
Female advantage	"	3.3	3.6	4.0	2.4	6.4	6.3
Total fertility rate	births per woman	7.7	7.4	6.2	4.9	3.1	2.9
Maternal mortality rate	per 100,000 live births	..	280	143	..	..	..
Supplementary Poverty Indicators							
Expenditures on social security	% of total gov't exp.	4.9	7.9	1.6	..	..	..
Social security coverage	% econ. active pop.	..	..	..	..	..	..
Access to safe water: total	% of pop.	71.0	..	79.0	85.0	..	85.6
Urban	"	98.0	..	91.0	97.0	..	94.3
Rural	"	50.0	..	68.0	70.1	..	73.0
Access to health care	"	..	80.0	83.0	84.6	..	..

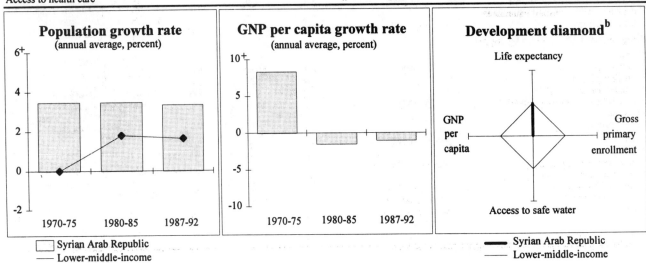

Population growth rate (annual average, percent)

GNP per capita growth rate (annual average, percent)

Development diamond[b]

Life expectancy — GNP per capita — Gross primary enrollment — Access to safe water

☐ Syrian Arab Republic
— Lower-middle-income

▬ Syrian Arab Republic
— Lower-middle-income

a. See the technical notes, p.389. b. The development diamond, based on four key indicators, shows the average level of development in the country compared with its income group. See the introduction.

Syrian Arab Republic

Indicator	Unit of measure	Latest single year 1970-75	Latest single year 1980-85	Most recent estimate 1987-92	Same region/income group Mid-East & North Africa	Same region/income group Lower-middle-income	Next higher income group
Resources and Expenditures							
HUMAN RESOURCES							
Population (mre=1992)	thousands	7,438	10,348	12,958	252,555	942,547	477,960
Age dependency ratio	ratio	1.09	1.04	1.04	0.87	0.66	0.64
Urban	% of pop.	45.1	48.4	51.1	54.7	57.0	71.7
Population growth rate	annual %	3.3	3.5	3.4	2.8	1.4	1.6
Urban	"	4.0	4.2	4.2	3.8	4.8	2.5
Labor force (15-64)	thousands	1,850	2,596	3,372	69,280	..	181,414
Agriculture	% of labor force	41	32	..	..	..	..
Industry	"	26	32	..	..	..	..
Female	"	13	16	18	15	36	29
Females per 100 males							
Urban	number	93	92	92	..	..	..
Rural	"	103	105	106	..	..	..
NATURAL RESOURCES							
Area	thou. sq. km	185.18	185.18	185.18	10,487.21	40,697.37	21,836.02
Density	pop. per sq. km	40.2	55.9	67.7	23.4	22.8	21.5
Agricultural land	% of land area	76.6	75.8	72.7	30.2	..	41.7
Change in agricultural land	annual %	-2.8	-0.2	-0.9	0.5	..	0.3
Agricultural land under irrigation	%	3.7	4.7	5.2	31.0	..	9.3
Forests and woodland	thou. sq. km	4	5	7	..	..	..
Deforestation (net)	annual %	..	..	..	..	..	..
INCOME							
Household income							
Share of top 20% of households	% of income	..	..	..	..	..	..
Share of bottom 40% of households	"	..	..	..	..	..	..
Share of bottom 20% of households	"	..	..	..	..	..	..
EXPENDITURE							
Food	% of GDP	31.8	..	..	..	..	..
Staples	"	5.3	..	..	..	..	..
Meat, fish, milk, cheese, eggs	"	8.0	..	..	..	..	..
Cereal imports	thou. metric tonnes	345	1,025	1,440	38,007	74,924	49,174
Food aid in cereals	"	47	32	13	2,484	4,054	282
Food production per capita	1987 = 100	79	90	83	116	..	109
Fertilizer consumption	kg/ha	5.1	16.4	23.1	96.7	..	68.8
Share of agriculture in GDP	% of GDP	18.0	21.0	29.8	13.7	..	8.1
Housing	% of GDP	8.1	..	..	..	..	..
Average household size	persons per household	6.0	6.2	..	..	..	..
Urban	"	6.0	5.9	..	..	..	..
Fixed investment: housing	% of GDP	4.3	6.2	..	..	..	..
Fuel and power	% of GDP	3.3	..	..	..	..	..
Energy consumption per capita	kg of oil equiv.	495	812	823	1,109	1,882	1,649
Households with electricity							
Urban	% of households	..	..	..	..	..	..
Rural	"	..	..	..	..	..	..
Transport and communication	% of GDP	2.5	..	..	..	..	..
Fixed investment: transport equipment	"	5.0	1.6	..	..	..	..
Total road length	thou. km	15	29	31	..	..	..
INVESTMENT IN HUMAN CAPITAL							
Health							
Population per physician	persons	3,900	2,160	1,159	..	..	..
Population per nurse	"	1,795	1,421	874	..	..	..
Population per hospital bed	"	1,000	873	920	636	516	385
Oral rehydration therapy (under-5)	% of cases	..	..	89	56	..	54
Education							
Gross enrollment ratio							
Secondary	% of school-age pop.	43	60	50	59	..	53
Female	"	28	49	43	50	..	..
Pupil-teacher ratio: primary	pupils per teacher	34	26	25	27	26	25
Pupil-teacher ratio: secondary	"	20	18	18	21	..	..
Pupils reaching grade 4	% of cohort	91	96	92	..	..	..
Repeater rate: primary	% of total enroll	10	7	7	..	..	71
Illiteracy	% of pop. (age 15+)	60	41	36	45	..	11
Female	% of fem. (age 15+)	..	57	49	58	..	14
Newspaper circulation	per thou. pop.	9	7	23	39	100	117

World Bank International Economics Department, April 1994

Tajikistan

Indicator	Unit of measure	Latest single year 1970-75	Latest single year 1980-85	Most recent estimate 1987-92	Same region/income group Europe & Central Asia	Same region/income group Low-income	Next higher income group
Priority Poverty Indicators							
POVERTY							
Upper poverty line	local curr.	..	..	..	..	..	..
Headcount index	% of pop.	..	..	68	..	19	..
Lower poverty line	local curr.	..	..	..	..	..	..
Headcount index	% of pop.	..	..	23	..	..	..
GNP per capita	US$	..	..	490	..	390	..
SHORT TERM INCOME INDICATORS							
Unskilled urban wages	local curr.	..	..	..	..	..	..
Unskilled rural wages	"	..	..	..	..	..	..
Rural terms of trade	"	..	..	..	..	..	..
Consumer price index	1987=100	..	..	..	..	..	..
Lower income	"	..	..	..	..	..	..
Food[a]	"	..	..	..	..	..	..
Urban	"	..	..	..	..	..	..
Rural	"	..	..	..	..	..	..
SOCIAL INDICATORS							
Public expenditure on basic social services	% of GDP	..	..	8.0	..	..	..
Gross enrollment ratios							
Primary	% school age pop.	..	..	..	..	103	..
Male	"	..	..	..	..	113	..
Female	"	..	..	..	..	96	..
Mortality							
Infant mortality	per thou. live births	..	72.0	49.0	30.0	73.0	45.0
Under 5 mortality	"	..	..	63.7	38.0	108.0	59.0
Immunization							
Measles	% age group	..	..	..	..	72.7	..
DPT	"	..	..	..	..	80.6	..
Child malnutrition (under-5)	"	..	..	..	..	38.3	..
Life expectancy							
Total	years	..	69	69	70	62	68
Female advantage	"	..	4.6	5.1	8.6	2.4	6.4
Total fertility rate	births per woman	6.3	5.6	5.1	2.2	3.4	3.1
Maternal mortality rate	per 100,000 live births	..	94	39	58	..	..
Supplementary Poverty Indicators							
Expenditures on social security	% of total gov't exp.	..	..	..	..	..	..
Social security coverage	% econ. active pop.	..	..	..	..	..	..
Access to safe water: total	% of pop.	..	..	..	..	68.4	..
Urban	"	..	..	..	..	78.9	..
Rural	"	..	..	..	..	60.3	..
Access to health care	"	..	..	..	..	..	..

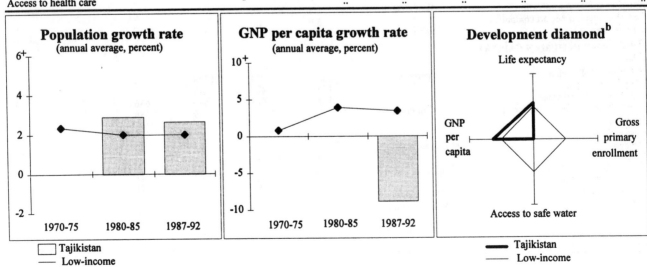

a. See the technical notes, p.389.   b. The development diamond, based on four key indicators, shows the average level of development in the country compared with its income group. See the introduction.

Tajikistan

Indicator	Unit of measure	Latest single year 1970-75	Latest single year 1980-85	Most recent estimate 1987-92	Same region/income group Europe & Central Asia	Same region/income group Low-income	Next higher income group
Resources and Expenditures							
HUMAN RESOURCES							
Population (mre=1992)	thousands	..	4,580	5,552	495,241	3,194,535	942,547
Age dependency ratio	ratio	..	..	0.97	0.56	0.67	0.66
Urban	% of pop.	..	..	32.0	63.3	26.7	57.0
Population growth rate	annual %	..	2.9	2.1	0.5	1.8	1.4
Urban	"	..	..	..	..	3.4	4.8
Labor force (15-64)	thousands	..	2,169	2,468	..	1,478,954	..
Agriculture	% of labor force	..	..	..	..	..	..
Industry	"	..	..	..	..	..	..
Female	"	..	..	35	46	33	36
Females per 100 males							
Urban	number	..	..	..	..	..	..
Rural	"	..	..	..	..	..	..
NATURAL RESOURCES							
Area	thou. sq. km	..	..	143.10	24,165.06	38,401.06	40,697.37
Density	pop. per sq. km	..	..	38.0	20.4	81.7	22.8
Agricultural land	% of land area	..	..	..	..	50.9	..
Change in agricultural land	annual %	..	..	..	..	0.0	..
Agricultural land under irrigation	%	..	..	..	..	18.2	..
Forests and woodland	thou. sq. km	..	..	..	..	..	..
Deforestation (net)	annual %	..	..	..	..	..	..
INCOME							
Household income							
Share of top 20% of households	% of income	..	..	..	..	42	..
Share of bottom 40% of households	"	..	..	..	..	19	..
Share of bottom 20% of households	"	..	..	..	..	8	..
EXPENDITURE							
Food	% of GDP	..	..	19.8	..	..	..
Staples	"	..	..	3.6	..	..	..
Meat, fish, milk, cheese, eggs	"	..	..	8.9	..	..	..
Cereal imports	thou. metric tonnes	..	..	550	45,972	46,537	74,924
Food aid in cereals	"	..	..	..	1,639	9,008	4,054
Food production per capita	1987 = 100	..	..	..	..	123	..
Fertilizer consumption	kg/ha	..	..	..	..	61.9	..
Share of agriculture in GDP	% of GDP	..	28.4	33.2	..	29.6	..
Housing	% of GDP	..	..	4.7	..	..	..
Average household size	persons per household	..	..	6.1	..	..	..
Urban	"	..	..	..	..	..	..
Fixed investment: housing	% of GDP	..	..	4.9	..	..	..
Fuel and power	% of GDP	..	..	1.0	..	..	..
Energy consumption per capita	kg of oil equiv.	..	..	..	3,190	335	1,882
Households with electricity							
Urban	% of households	..	..	..	..	..	..
Rural	"	..	..	..	..	..	..
Transport and communication	% of GDP	..	..	6.2	..	..	..
Fixed investment: transport equipment	"	..	..	10.3	..	..	..
Total road length	thou. km	..	17	30	..	..	..
INVESTMENT IN HUMAN CAPITAL							
Health							
Population per physician	persons	..	..	353	378	..	..
Population per nurse	"	..	..	..	..	..	..
Population per hospital bed	"	..	..	96	134	1,050	516
Oral rehydration therapy (under-5)	% of cases	..	..	..	..	39	..
Education							
Gross enrollment ratio							
Secondary	% of school-age pop.	..	..	..	..	41	..
Female	"	..	..	..	..	35	..
Pupil-teacher ratio: primary	pupils per teacher	..	..	..	..	37	26
Pupil-teacher ratio: secondary	"	..	..	..	..	19	..
Pupils reaching grade 4	% of cohort	..	..	..	..	..	..
Repeater rate: primary	% of total enroll	..	..	..	..	..	..
Illiteracy	% of pop. (age 15+)	..	..	..	..	39	..
Female	% of fem. (age 15+)	..	..	..	..	52	..
Newspaper circulation	per thou. pop.	..	..	..	..	..	100

World Bank International Economics Department, April 1994

337

Tanzania

Indicator	Unit of measure	Latest single year		Most recent estimate 1987-92	Same region/income group		Next higher income group
		1970-75	1980-85		Sub-Saharan Africa	Low-income	

Priority Poverty Indicators

Indicator	Unit of measure	1970-75	1980-85	1987-92	Sub-Saharan Africa	Low-income	Next higher
POVERTY							
Upper poverty line	local curr.	..	..	..	..	..	..
Headcount index	% of pop.	..	..	..	..	19	..
Lower poverty line	local curr.	..	..	..	..	..	..
Headcount index	% of pop.	..	..	..	..	..	..
GNP per capita	US$	170	290	110	520	390	..
SHORT TERM INCOME INDICATORS							
Unskilled urban wages	local curr.	..	..	..	..	..	..
Unskilled rural wages	"	..	..	..	..	..	..
Rural terms of trade	"	..	..	..	..	..	..
Consumer price index	1987=100	8	58	295	..	..	..
Lower income	"	..	..	..	..	..	..
Food[a]	"	..	57	..	..	..	..
Urban	"	..	..	..	..	..	..
Rural	"	..	..	..	..	..	..
SOCIAL INDICATORS							
Public expenditure on basic social services	% of GDP	..	..	..	..	..	..
Gross enrollment ratios							
Primary	% school age pop.	53	72	69	66	103	..
Male	"	62	73	70	79	113	..
Female	"	44	71	68	62	96	..
Mortality							
Infant mortality	per thou. live births	130.0	119.2	91.6	99.0	73.0	45.0
Under 5 mortality	"	..	..	148.4	169.0	108.0	59.0
Immunization							
Measles	% age group	..	66.0	75.0	54.0	72.7	..
DPT	"	..	67.0	79.0	54.6	80.6	..
Child malnutrition (under-5)	"	..	20.0	25.2	28.4	38.3	..
Life expectancy							
Total	years	46	51	51	52	62	68
Female advantage	"	3.2	3.5	3.0	3.4	2.4	6.4
Total fertility rate	births per woman	6.3	7.0	6.3	6.1	3.4	3.1
Maternal mortality rate	per 100,000 live births	..	370	..	..	..	..

Supplementary Poverty Indicators

Indicator	Unit of measure	1970-75	1980-85	1987-92	Sub-Saharan Africa	Low-income	Next higher
Expenditures on social security	% of total gov't exp.	..	0.5	..	..	..	..
Social security coverage	% econ. active pop.	..	..	..	..	..	..
Access to safe water: total	% of pop.	39.0	49.0	52.0	41.1	68.4	..
Urban	"	88.0	90.0	75.0	77.8	78.9	..
Rural	"	36.0	42.0	46.0	27.3	60.3	..
Access to health care	"	..	73.0	..	..	..	..

Population growth rate
(annual average, percent)

Tanzania
Low-income

GNP per capita growth rate
(annual average, percent)

Development diamond[b]

Life expectancy

GNP per capita — Gross primary enrollment

Access to safe water

Tanzania
Low-income

a. See the technical notes, p.389.   b. The development diamond, based on four key indicators, shows the average level of development in the country compared with its income group. See the introduction.

Tanzania

Indicator	Unit of measure	Latest single year 1970-75	Latest single year 1980-85	Most recent estimate 1987-92	Same region/income group Sub-Saharan Africa	Same region/income group Low-income	Next higher income group
Resources and Expenditures							
HUMAN RESOURCES							
Population (mre=1992)	thousands	15,379	21,161	25,946	546,390	3,194,535	942,547
Age dependency ratio	ratio	1.01	0.99	0.99	0.95	0.67	0.66
Urban	% of pop.	10.1	17.6	22.2	29.5	26.7	57.0
Population growth rate	annual %	2.8	3.0	3.0	2.9	1.8	1.4
Urban	"	9.8	6.3	6.3	5.1	3.4	4.8
Labor force (15-64)	thousands	8,226	10,913	13,404	224,025	1,478,954	..
Agriculture	% of labor force	88	86	..	..	..	..
Industry	"	4	5	..	..	..	..
Female	"	50	49	47	37	33	36
Females per 100 males							
Urban	number	..	..	..	..	..	..
Rural	"	..	..	..	..	..	..
NATURAL RESOURCES							
Area	thou. sq. km	945.09	945.09	945.09	24,274.03	38,401.06	40,697.37
Density	pop. per sq. km	16.3	22.4	26.7	21.9	81.7	22.8
Agricultural land	% of land area	43.2	43.3	43.3	52.7	50.9	..
Change in agricultural land	annual %	0.0	0.0	0.0	0.1	0.0	..
Agricultural land under irrigation	%	0.1	0.3	0.4	0.8	18.2	..
Forests and woodland	thou. sq. km	427	415	408	..	..	..
Deforestation (net)	annual %	..	..	1.2	..	..	..
INCOME							
Household income							
Share of top 20% of households	% of income	50	..	63	..	42	..
Share of bottom 40% of households	"	16	..	8	..	19	..
Share of bottom 20% of households	"	6	..	2	..	8	..
EXPENDITURE							
Food	% of GDP	..	55.0	..	..	..	..
Staples	"	..	27.4	..	..	..	..
Meat, fish, milk, cheese, eggs	"	..	9.4	..	..	..	..
Cereal imports	thou. metric tonnes	461	412	252	20,311	46,537	74,924
Food aid in cereals	"	148	125	15	4,303	9,008	4,054
Food production per capita	1987 = 100	100	102	81	90	123	..
Fertilizer consumption	kg/ha	0.8	1.0	1.4	4.2	61.9	..
Share of agriculture in GDP	% of GDP	36.9	50.8	53.1	18.6	29.6	..
Housing	% of GDP	..	6.9	..	..	..	..
Average household size	persons per household	..	..	..	..	..	..
Urban	"	..	..	..	..	..	..
Fixed investment: housing	% of GDP	2.1	1.7	..	..	..	..
Fuel and power	% of GDP	..	2.2	..	..	..	..
Energy consumption per capita	kg of oil equiv.	52	35	30	258	335	1,882
Households with electricity							
Urban	% of households	..	..	..	..	..	..
Rural	"	..	..	..	..	..	..
Transport and communication	% of GDP	..	1.8	..	..	..	..
Fixed investment: transport equipment	"	3.7	2.5	..	..	..	..
Total road length	thou. km	40	82	83	..	..	..
INVESTMENT IN HUMAN CAPITAL							
Health							
Population per physician	persons	21,802	27,446	24,973	..	..	..
Population per nurse	"	3,312	7,772	5,485	..	..	..
Population per hospital bed	"	..	747	938	1,329	1,050	516
Oral rehydration therapy (under-5)	% of cases	..	..	83	36	39	..
Education							
Gross enrollment ratio							
Secondary	% of school-age pop.	3	3	5	18	41	..
Female	"	2	2	4	14	35	..
Pupil-teacher ratio: primary	pupils per teacher	54	34	36	39	37	26
Pupil-teacher ratio: secondary	"	20	19	19	..	19	..
Pupils reaching grade 4	% of cohort	91	89	89	..	..	..
Repeater rate: primary	% of total enroll	0	1	5	..	..	..
Illiteracy	% of pop. (age 15+)	..	..	..	51	39	..
Female	% of fem. (age 15+)	..	..	..	62	52	..
Newspaper circulation	per thou. pop.	5	10	8	14	..	100

World Bank International Economics Department, April 1994

Thailand

Indicator	Unit of measure	Latest single year 1970-75	Latest single year 1980-85	Most recent estimate 1987-92	Same region/income group East Asia	Same region/income group Lower-middle-income	Next higher income group
Priority Poverty Indicators							
POVERTY							
Upper poverty line	local curr.	..	..	..	..	..	..
Headcount index	% of pop.	30	23	22	12	..	..
Lower poverty line	local curr.	..	..	..	..	..	..
Headcount index	% of pop.	..	..	..	9	..	..
GNP per capita	US$	360	810	1,840	760	..	3,870
SHORT TERM INCOME INDICATORS							
Unskilled urban wages	local curr.	..	..	..	..	..	..
Unskilled rural wages	"	..	..	..	..	..	..
Rural terms of trade	"	..	..	..	..	..	..
Consumer price index	1987=100	47	96	128	..	..	..
Lower income	"	..	..	..	..	..	..
Food[a]	"	31	98	134	..	..	..
Urban	"	..	..	..	..	..	..
Rural	"	..	..	..	..	..	..
SOCIAL INDICATORS							
Public expenditure on basic social services	% of GDP	..	4.6	..	..	..	..
Gross enrollment ratios							
Primary	% school age pop.	83	96	113	121	..	107
Male	"	87	100	92	126	..	..
Female	"	80	97	88	117	..	..
Mortality							
Infant mortality	per thou. live births	55.0	44.0	26.0	39.0	45.0	40.0
Under 5 mortality	"	..	..	31.1	49.0	59.0	51.0
Immunization							
Measles	% age group	..	22.0	60.0	88.4	..	82.0
DPT	"	..	47.0	69.0	89.5	..	73.8
Child malnutrition (under-5)	"	..	..	13.0	24.7	..	..
Life expectancy							
Total	years	60	64	69	68	68	69
Female advantage	"	3.9	4.6	5.1	3.6	6.4	6.3
Total fertility rate	births per woman	5.0	3.5	2.2	2.4	3.1	2.9
Maternal mortality rate	per 100,000 live births	..	270	37	114	..	..
Supplementary Poverty Indicators							
Expenditures on social security	% of total gov't exp.	4.0	2.9	3.5	..	..	..
Social security coverage	% econ. active pop.	..	..	..	..	..	..
Access to safe water: total	% of pop.	25.0	56.0	72.0	72.0	..	85.6
Urban	"	69.0	..	85.0	83.4	..	94.3
Rural	"	16.0	66.0	..	60.2	..	73.0
Access to health care	"	..	30.0	93.0	..	..	..

Population growth rate
(annual average, percent)

□ Thailand
— Lower-middle-income

GNP per capita growth rate
(annual average, percent)

Development diamond[b]

— Thailand
— Lower-middle-income

a. See the technical notes, p.389.   b. The development diamond, based on four key indicators, shows the average level of development in the country compared with its income group. See the introduction.

340

Thailand

Indicator	Unit of measure	Latest single year 1970-75	Latest single year 1980-85	Most recent estimate 1987-92	Same region/income group East Asia	Same region/income group Lower-middle-income	Next higher income group
Resources and Expenditures							
HUMAN RESOURCES							
Population (mre=1992)	thousands	41,359	51,683	57,992	1,688,909	942,547	477,960
Age dependency ratio	ratio	0.92	0.67	0.58	0.55	0.66	0.64
Urban	% of pop.	15.1	19.5	23.5	29.4	57.0	71.7
Population growth rate	annual %	2.7	1.9	1.5	1.4	1.4	1.6
Urban	"	5.1	4.4	4.2	2.9	4.8	2.5
Labor force (15-64)	thousands	20,491	26,657	30,571	928,465	..	181,414
Agriculture	% of labor force	75	71	..	..	..	..
Industry	"	8	10	..	..	..	..
Female	"	47	46	44	41	36	29
Females per 100 males							
Urban	number	103	106	..	..	..	..
Rural	"	102	102	..	..	..	..
NATURAL RESOURCES							
Area	thou. sq. km	513.12	513.12	513.12	16,367.18	40,697.37	21,836.02
Density	pop. per sq. km	80.6	100.7	111.4	101.8	22.8	21.5
Agricultural land	% of land area	33.7	40.3	47.0	44.5	..	41.7
Change in agricultural land	annual %	2.0	2.6	0.5	0.1	..	0.3
Agricultural land under irrigation	%	14.1	18.6	18.3	14.5	..	9.3
Forests and woodland	thou. sq. km	185	149	140	..	..	..
Deforestation (net)	annual %	..	..	3.4	..	..	..
INCOME							
Household income							
Share of top 20% of households	% of income	50	..	51	42	..	..
Share of bottom 40% of households	"	15	..	16	18	..	..
Share of bottom 20% of households	"	6	..	6	7	..	..
EXPENDITURE							
Food	% of GDP	31.4	19.2	..	..	..	..
Staples	"	9.7	4.6	..	..	..	..
Meat, fish, milk, cheese, eggs	"	10.7	8.3	..	..	..	..
Cereal imports	thou. metric tonnes	62	174	992	33,591	74,924	49,174
Food aid in cereals	"	2	4	75	581	4,054	282
Food production per capita	1987 = 100	89	110	104	133	..	109
Fertilizer consumption	kg/ha	10.5	21.1	35.3	75.1	..	68.8
Share of agriculture in GDP	% of GDP	26.9	16.8	11.9	21.5	..	8.1
Housing	% of GDP	4.2	4.6	..	..	..	..
Average household size	persons per household	5.8	5.2	..	..	..	..
Urban	"	5.8	4.9	..	..	..	..
Fixed investment: housing	% of GDP	2.6	3.6	..	..	..	..
Fuel and power	% of GDP	2.1	2.1	..	..	..	..
Energy consumption per capita	kg of oil equiv.	203	300	614	593	1,882	1,649
Households with electricity							
Urban	% of households	..	..	..	..	..	..
Rural	"	..	..	..	..	..	..
Transport and communication	% of GDP	5.0	8.5	..	..	..	..
Fixed investment: transport equipment	"	4.3	1.9	..	..	..	..
Total road length	thou. km	57	76	72	..	..	..
INVESTMENT IN HUMAN CAPITAL							
Health							
Population per physician	persons	8,394	5,975	4,497	..	..	..
Population per nurse	"	1,171	1,845	928	..	..	..
Population per hospital bed	"	899	651	620	553	516	385
Oral rehydration therapy (under-5)	% of cases	..	..	43	51	..	54
Education							
Gross enrollment ratio							
Secondary	% of school-age pop.	26	30	33	53	..	53
Female	"	23	28	32	47	..	..
Pupil-teacher ratio: primary	pupils per teacher	28	19	18	23	26	25
Pupil-teacher ratio: secondary	"	32	18	18	16	..	..
Pupils reaching grade 4	% of cohort	79	84	85	89	..	71
Repeater rate: primary	% of total enroll	10	8	3	6	..	11
Illiteracy	% of pop. (age 15+)	21	9	7	24	..	14
Female	% of fem. (age 15+)	..	13	10	34	..	17
Newspaper circulation	per thou. pop.	22	52	71	..	100	117

World Bank International Economics Department, April 1994

341

Togo

Indicator	Unit of measure	Latest single year 1970-75	Latest single year 1980-85	Most recent estimate 1987-92	Same region/income group Sub-Saharan Africa	Same region/income group Low-income	Next higher income group
Priority Poverty Indicators							
POVERTY							
Upper poverty line	local curr.	..	..	..	..	..	..
Headcount index	% of pop.	..	..	..	..	19	..
Lower poverty line	local curr.	..	..	..	..	..	..
Headcount index	% of pop.	..	..	..	..	..	..
GNP per capita	US$	250	250	390	520	390	..
SHORT TERM INCOME INDICATORS							
Unskilled urban wages	local curr.	..	..	..	..	..	..
Unskilled rural wages	"	..	..	..	..	..	..
Rural terms of trade	"	..	..	..	..	..	..
Consumer price index	1987=100	42	96	100	..	..	..
Lower income	"	..	..	..	..	..	..
Food[a]	"	27	97	92	..	..	..
Urban	"	..	..	..	..	..	..
Rural	"	..	..	..	..	..	..
SOCIAL INDICATORS							
Public expenditure on basic social services	% of GDP	..	..	5.5	..	..	..
Gross enrollment ratios							
Primary	% school age pop.	99	93	111	66	103	..
Male	"	130	114	134	79	113	..
Female	"	68	71	87	62	96	..
Mortality							
Infant mortality	per thou. live births	129.0	105.0	85.0	99.0	73.0	45.0
Under 5 mortality	"	..	..	136.4	169.0	108.0	59.0
Immunization							
Measles	% age group	..	..	61.0	54.0	72.7	..
DPT	"	..	9.0	73.0	54.6	80.6	..
Child malnutrition (under-5)	"	..	12.2	24.4	28.4	38.3	..
Life expectancy							
Total	years	45	50	55	52	62	68
Female advantage	"	3.2	3.4	3.6	3.4	2.4	6.4
Total fertility rate	births per woman	6.5	6.8	6.5	6.1	3.4	3.1
Maternal mortality rate	per 100,000 live births	..	476	..	..	..	..
Supplementary Poverty Indicators							
Expenditures on social security	% of total gov't exp.	..	5.2	6.5	..	..	..
Social security coverage	% econ. active pop.	..	..	..	..	..	..
Access to safe water: total	% of pop.	16.0	26.7	71.0	41.1	68.4	..
Urban	"	49.0	100.0	100.0	77.8	78.9	..
Rural	"	10.0	41.0	61.0	27.3	60.3	..
Access to health care	"	..	..	..	..	..	..

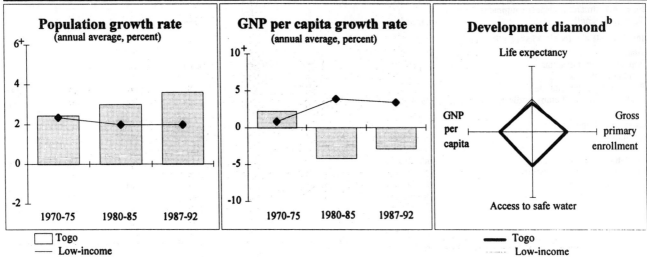

a. See the technical notes, p.389.   b. The development diamond, based on four key indicators, shows the average level of development in the country compared with its income group. See the introduction.

342

Togo

Indicator	Unit of measure	Latest single year 1970-75	Latest single year 1980-85	Most recent estimate 1987-92	Same region/income group Sub-Saharan Africa	Same region/income group Low-income	Next higher income group
Resources and Expenditures							
HUMAN RESOURCES							
Population (mre=1992)	thousands	2,282	3,038	3,900	546,390	3,194,535	942,547
Age dependency ratio	ratio	0.89	1.00	1.05	0.95	0.67	0.66
Urban	% of pop.	16.3	26.5	29.4	29.5	26.7	57.0
Population growth rate	annual %	2.4	3.1	3.4	2.9	1.8	1.4
Urban	"	6.5	5.8	5.0	5.1	3.4	4.8
Labor force (15-64)	thousands	998	1,244	1,469	224,025	1,478,954	..
Agriculture	% of labor force	75	73	..	..	..	..
Industry	"	9	10	..	..	..	..
Female	"	39	37	36	37	33	36
Females per 100 males							
Urban	number	..	..	..	..	..	..
Rural	"	..	..	..	..	..	..
NATURAL RESOURCES							
Area	thou. sq. km	56.79	56.79	56.79	24,274.03	38,401.06	40,697.37
Density	pop. per sq. km	40.2	53.5	66.4	21.9	81.7	22.8
Agricultural land	% of land area	44.1	44.8	45.2	52.7	50.9	..
Change in agricultural land	annual %	0.2	0.2	0.0	0.1	0.0	..
Agricultural land under irrigation	%	0.3	0.3	0.3	0.8	18.2	..
Forests and woodland	thou. sq. km	18	17	16	..	..	..
Deforestation (net)	annual %	..	..	1.3	..	..	..
INCOME							
Household income							
Share of top 20% of households	% of income	..	..	..	..	42	..
Share of bottom 40% of households	"	..	..	..	..	19	..
Share of bottom 20% of households	"	..	..	..	..	8	..
EXPENDITURE							
Food	% of GDP	..	..	33.7	..	..	..
Staples	"	..	..	11.8	..	..	..
Meat, fish, milk, cheese, eggs	"	..	..	11.9	..	..	..
Cereal imports	thou. metric tonnes	2	57	124	20,311	46,537	74,924
Food aid in cereals	"	11	23	5	4,303	9,008	4,054
Food production per capita	1987 = 100	107	90	84	90	123	..
Fertilizer consumption	kg/ha	1.0	4.0	2.4	4.2	61.9	..
Share of agriculture in GDP	% of GDP	26.6	33.7	36.0	18.6	29.6	..
Housing	% of GDP	..	..	8.5	..	..	..
Average household size	persons per household	6.0	..	..	..	..	..
Urban	"	..	..	..	..	..	..
Fixed investment: housing	% of GDP	..	..	5.0	..	..	..
Fuel and power	% of GDP	..	..	3.5	..	..	..
Energy consumption per capita	kg of oil equiv.	60	49	46	258	335	1,882
Households with electricity							
Urban	% of households	..	..	..	..	..	..
Rural	"	..	..	..	..	..	..
Transport and communication	% of GDP	..	..	2.5	..	..	..
Fixed investment: transport equipment	"	..	..	5.0	..	..	..
Total road length	thou. km	7	7	8	..	..	..
INVESTMENT IN HUMAN CAPITAL							
Health							
Population per physician	persons	28,900	8,742	..	..	..	..
Population per nurse	"	1,591	1,241	..	..	..	..
Population per hospital bed	"	700	..	686	1,329	1,050	516
Oral rehydration therapy (under-5)	% of cases	..	..	33	36	39	..
Education							
Gross enrollment ratio							
Secondary	% of school-age pop.	19	21	23	18	41	..
Female	"	9	10	12	14	35	..
Pupil-teacher ratio: primary	pupils per teacher	60	46	59	39	37	26
Pupil-teacher ratio: secondary	"	44	23	28	..	19	..
Pupils reaching grade 4	% of cohort	84	73	57	..	..	..
Repeater rate: primary	% of total enroll	29	35	37	..	..	..
Illiteracy	% of pop. (age 15+)	84	62	57	51	39	..
Female	% of fem. (age 15+)	..	75	69	62	52	..
Newspaper circulation	per thou. pop.	3	5	3	14	..	100

World Bank International Economics Department, April 1994

Tonga

Indicator	Unit of measure	Latest single year 1970-75	Latest single year 1980-85	Most recent estimate 1987-92	Same region/income group East Asia	Same region/income group Lower-middle-income	Next higher income group
Priority Poverty Indicators							
POVERTY							
Upper poverty line	local curr.	..	..	..	..	..	..
Headcount index	% of pop.	..	..	..	12	..	..
Lower poverty line	local curr.	..	..	..	..	..	..
Headcount index	% of pop.	..	..	..	9	..	..
GNP per capita	US$	..	750	1,480	760	..	3,870
SHORT TERM INCOME INDICATORS							
Unskilled urban wages	local curr.	..	..	..	..	..	..
Unskilled rural wages	"	..	..	..	..	..	..
Rural terms of trade	"	..	..	..	..	..	..
Consumer price index	1987=100	27	79	150	..	..	..
Lower income	"	..	..	..	..	..	..
Food[a]	"	14	77	124	..	..	..
Urban	"	..	..	..	..	..	..
Rural	"	..	..	..	..	..	..
SOCIAL INDICATORS							
Public expenditure on basic social services	% of GDP	..	..	..	..	..	..
Gross enrollment ratios							
Primary	% school age pop.	..	..	..	121	..	107
Male	"	..	..	..	126	..	..
Female	"	..	..	..	117	..	..
Mortality							
Infant mortality	per thou. live births	..	43.0	21.0	39.0	45.0	40.0
Under 5 mortality	"	..	..	25.2	49.0	59.0	51.0
Immunization							
Measles	% age group	..	81.0	81.0	88.4	..	82.0
DPT	"	..	92.0	92.0	89.5	..	73.8
Child malnutrition (under-5)	"	..	..	..	24.7	..	..
Life expectancy							
Total	years	..	62	68	68	68	69
Female advantage	"	..	3.0	3.9	3.6	6.4	6.3
Total fertility rate	births per woman	..	4.7	3.6	2.4	3.1	2.9
Maternal mortality rate	per 100,000 live births	..	..	..	114	..	..
Supplementary Poverty Indicators							
Expenditures on social security	% of total gov't exp.	..	1.2	0.8	..	..	..
Social security coverage	% econ. active pop.	..	..	..	..	..	..
Access to safe water: total	% of pop.	83.0	99.0	96.0	72.0	..	85.6
Urban	"	100.0	100.0	98.0	83.4	..	94.3
Rural	"	71.0	99.0	92.0	60.2	..	73.0
Access to health care	"	..	80.0	100.0	..	..	..

Population growth rate
(annual average, percent)

GNP per capita growth rate
(annual average, percent)

Development diamond[b]

□ Tonga
— Lower-middle-income

━ Tonga
— Lower-middle-income

a. See the technical notes, p.389.   b. The development diamond, based on four key indicators, shows the average level of development in the country compared with its income group. See the introduction.

Tonga

World Bank International Economics Department, April 1994

Indicator	Unit of measure	Latest single year 1970-75	Latest single year 1980-85	Most recent estimate 1987-92	Same region/income group East Asia	Same region/income group Lower-middle-income	Next higher income group
Resources and Expenditures							
HUMAN RESOURCES							
Population (mre=1992)	thousands	90	95	92	1,688,909	942,547	477,960
Age dependency ratio	ratio	..	0.78	0.72	0.55	0.66	0.64
Urban	% of pop.	20.5	19.7	20.5	29.4	57.0	71.7
Population growth rate	annual %	1.1	0.0	1.1	1.4	1.4	1.6
Urban	"	0.2	0.0	0.8	2.9	4.8	2.5
Labor force (15-64)	thousands	..	40	..	928,465	..	181,414
Agriculture	% of labor force	..	0	..	..	..	..
Industry	"	..	0	..	..	..	..
Female	"	..	..	..	41	36	29
Females per 100 males							
Urban	number	..	..	..	..	..	..
Rural	"	..	..	..	..	..	..
NATURAL RESOURCES							
Area	thou. sq. km	0.75	0.75	0.75	16,367.18	40,697.37	21,836.02
Density	pop. per sq. km	120.0	126.7	121.3	101.8	22.8	21.5
Agricultural land	% of land area	69.4	72.2	72.2	44.5	..	41.7
Change in agricultural land	annual %	-3.9	0.0	0.0	0.1	..	0.3
Agricultural land under irrigation	%	..	..	..	14.5	..	9.3
Forests and woodland	thou. sq. km	0	0	0	..	..	..
Deforestation (net)	annual %	..	..	..	..	..	..
INCOME							
Household income							
Share of top 20% of households	% of income	..	..	..	42	..	..
Share of bottom 40% of households	"	..	..	..	18	..	..
Share of bottom 20% of households	"	..	..	..	7	..	..
EXPENDITURE							
Food	% of GDP	..	..	..	..	..	..
Staples	"	..	..	..	..	..	..
Meat, fish, milk, cheese, eggs	"	..	..	..	..	..	..
Cereal imports	thou. metric tonnes	6	6	8	33,591	74,924	49,174
Food aid in cereals	"	1	0	..	581	4,054	282
Food production per capita	1987 = 100	113	79	67	133	..	109
Fertilizer consumption	kg/ha	..	1.9	..	75.1	..	68.8
Share of agriculture in GDP	% of GDP	42.4	35.7	..	21.5	..	8.1
Housing	% of GDP	..	..	..	..	..	..
Average household size	persons per household	..	..	..	..	..	..
Urban	"	..	..	..	..	..	..
Fixed investment: housing	% of GDP	..	..	..	..	..	..
Fuel and power	% of GDP	..	..	..	..	..	..
Energy consumption per capita	kg of oil equiv.	122	158	196	593	1,882	1,649
Households with electricity							
Urban	% of households	..	..	..	..	..	..
Rural	"	..	..	..	..	..	..
Transport and communication	% of GDP	..	..	..	..	..	..
Fixed investment: transport equipment	"	..	..	..	..	..	..
Total road length	thou. km	..	..	..	..	..	..
INVESTMENT IN HUMAN CAPITAL							
Health							
Population per physician	persons	3,909	1,667	1,936	..	..	..
Population per nurse	"	..	546	..	..	..	..
Population per hospital bed	"	386	284	..	553	516	385
Oral rehydration therapy (under-5)	% of cases	..	..	25	51	..	54
Education							
Gross enrollment ratio							
Secondary	% of school-age pop.	..	..	..	53	..	53
Female	"	..	..	..	47	..	..
Pupil-teacher ratio: primary	pupils per teacher	28	23	23	23	26	25
Pupil-teacher ratio: secondary	"	22	19	18	16	..	..
Pupils reaching grade 4	% of cohort	..	97	..	89	..	71
Repeater rate: primary	% of total enroll	..	8	4	6	..	11
Illiteracy	% of pop. (age 15+)	..	..	..	24	..	14
Female	% of fem. (age 15+)	..	..	..	34	..	17
Newspaper circulation	per thou. pop.	..	..	77	..	100	117

345

Trinidad and Tobago

Indicator	Unit of measure	Latest single year 1970-75	Latest single year 1980-85	Most recent estimate 1987-92	Same region/income group Latin America Caribbean	Same region/income group Upper-middle-income	Next higher income group
Priority Poverty Indicators							
POVERTY							
Upper poverty line	local curr.	..	..	..	..	..	..
Headcount index	% of pop.	..	..	..	..	..	..
Lower poverty line	local curr.	..	..	..	..	..	..
Headcount index	% of pop.	..	..	..	..	..	..
GNP per capita	US$	1,720	7,120	3,940	2,690	3,870	21,960
SHORT TERM INCOME INDICATORS							
Unskilled urban wages	local curr.	..	..	..	..	..	..
Unskilled rural wages	"	..	..	..	..	..	..
Rural terms of trade	"	..	..	..	..	..	..
Consumer price index	1987=100	25	84	147	..	..	..
Lower income	"	..	..	..	..	..	..
Food[a]	"	11	76	172	..	..	..
Urban	"	..	..	..	..	..	..
Rural	"	..	..	..	..	..	..
SOCIAL INDICATORS							
Public expenditure on basic social services	% of GDP	..	..	..	..	..	..
Gross enrollment ratios							
Primary	% school age pop.	99	96	96	106	107	103
Male	"	97	95	96	..	..	103
Female	"	100	97	96	..	..	103
Mortality							
Infant mortality	per thou. live births	50.0	31.0	15.0	44.0	40.0	7.0
Under 5 mortality	"	..	..	18.2	56.0	51.0	10.0
Immunization							
Measles	% age group	..	10.0	70.0	78.9	82.0	82.4
DPT	"	..	65.0	82.0	73.8	73.8	90.1
Child malnutrition (under-5)	"	..	..	5.9	10.5	..	..
Life expectancy							
Total	years	66	69	71	68	69	77
Female advantage	"	4.7	5.0	5.0	5.6	6.3	6.4
Total fertility rate	births per woman	3.5	3.3	2.8	3.0	2.9	1.7
Maternal mortality rate	per 100,000 live births	..	81	89	..	..	..
Supplementary Poverty Indicators							
Expenditures on social security	% of total gov't exp.	..	..	..	..	..	..
Social security coverage	% econ. active pop.	..	..	..	..	..	..
Access to safe water: total	% of pop.	93.0	98.0	96.0	80.3	85.6	..
Urban	"	79.0	100.0	100.0	91.0	94.3	..
Rural	"	100.0	95.0	87.0	64.3	73.0	..
Access to health care	"	..	..	99.0	..	..	..

Population growth rate
(annual average, percent)

☐ Trinidad and Tobago
— Upper-middle-income

GNP per capita growth rate
(annual average, percent)

Development diamond[b]

— Trinidad and Tobago
— Upper-middle-income

a. See the technical notes, p.389.   b. The development diamond, based on four key indicators, shows the average level of development in the country compared with its income group. See the introduction.

346

Trinidad and Tobago

Indicator	Unit of measure	Latest single year 1970-75	Latest single year 1980-85	Most recent estimate 1987-92	Same region/income group Latin America Caribbean	Same region/income group Upper-middle-income	Next higher income group
Resources and Expenditures							
HUMAN RESOURCES							
Population (mre=1992)	thousands	1,012	1,160	1,268	453,294	477,960	828,221
Age dependency ratio	ratio	0.71	0.65	0.65	0.67	0.64	0.50
Urban	% of pop.	63.0	63.6	65.5	72.9	71.7	78.1
Population growth rate	annual %	0.9	1.4	1.2	1.7	1.6	0.7
Urban	"	0.9	1.6	1.7	2.6	2.5	0.9
Labor force (15-64)	thousands	364	450	522	166,091	181,414	390,033
Agriculture	% of labor force	14	10	..	..	..	..
Industry	"	37	39	..	..	..	..
Female	"	28	30	30	27	29	38
Females per 100 males							
Urban	number	..	..	..	..	..	..
Rural	"	..	..	..	..	..	..
NATURAL RESOURCES							
Area	thou. sq. km	5.13	5.13	5.13	20,507.48	21,836.02	31,709.00
Density	pop. per sq. km	197.3	226.1	244.3	21.7	21.5	24.5
Agricultural land	% of land area	24.6	25.2	25.5	40.2	41.7	42.7
Change in agricultural land	annual %	0.0	0.0	0.0	0.5	0.3	-0.2
Agricultural land under irrigation	%	14.3	17.1	16.8	3.2	9.3	16.1
Forests and woodland	thou. sq. km	2	2	2	..	..	..
Deforestation (net)	annual %	..	..	0.0	..	..	..
INCOME							
Household income							
Share of top 20% of households	% of income	50	..	..	..	..	..
Share of bottom 40% of households	"	13	..	..	..	..	..
Share of bottom 20% of households	"	4	..	..	..	..	..
EXPENDITURE							
Food	% of GDP	..	12.2	..	..	..	..
Staples	"	..	2.0	..	..	..	..
Meat, fish, milk, cheese, eggs	"	..	5.3	..	..	..	..
Cereal imports	thou. metric tonnes	218	196	246	25,032	49,174	70,626
Food aid in cereals	"	0	..	..	1,779	282	2
Food production per capita	1987 = 100	138	88	95	104	109	101
Fertilizer consumption	kg/ha	55.7	55.0	67.2	15.5	68.8	162.1
Share of agriculture in GDP	% of GDP	3.3	3.0	2.9	8.9	8.1	2.4
Housing	% of GDP	..	11.6	..	..	..	..
Average household size	persons per household	5.0	4.5	..	..	..	..
Urban	"	..	..	..	..	..	..
Fixed investment: housing	% of GDP	8.7	4.1	..	..	..	..
Fuel and power	% of GDP	..	0.7	..	..	..	..
Energy consumption per capita	kg of oil equiv.	2,303	4,488	4,910	912	1,649	5,101
Households with electricity							
Urban	% of households	..	91.6	..	..	..	..
Rural	"	..	..	..	..	..	..
Transport and communication	% of GDP	..	7.7	..	..	..	..
Fixed investment: transport equipment	"	1.1	1.9	..	..	..	..
Total road length	thou. km	7	5	..	..	..	..
INVESTMENT IN HUMAN CAPITAL							
Health							
Population per physician	persons	2,207	943	..	..	..	..
Population per nurse	"	201	253	..	..	..	..
Population per hospital bed	"	201	..	..	508	385	144
Oral rehydration therapy (under-5)	% of cases	..	..	70	62	54	..
Education							
Gross enrollment ratio							
Secondary	% of school-age pop.	48	80	81	47	53	92
Female	"	51	79	82	..	..	94
Pupil-teacher ratio: primary	pupils per teacher	31	22	26	25	25	18
Pupil-teacher ratio: secondary	"	39	19	20	..	..	..
Pupils reaching grade 4	% of cohort	74	95	95	..	71	..
Repeater rate: primary	% of total enroll	..	5	4	14	11	..
Illiteracy	% of pop. (age 15+)	8	4	..	15	14	..
Female	% of fem. (age 15+)	..	5	..	17	17	..
Newspaper circulation	per thou. pop.	99	148	77	99	117	..

World Bank International Economics Department, April 1994

Tunisia

Indicator	Unit of measure	Latest single year 1970-75	Latest single year 1980-85	Most recent estimate 1987-92	Same region/income group Mid-East & North Africa	Same region/income group Lower-middle-income	Next higher income group
Priority Poverty Indicators							
POVERTY							
Upper poverty line	local curr.	87	190	278	..	..	..
Headcount index	% of pop.	27	8	7	..	..	..
Lower poverty line	local curr.	43	95	139	..	..	..
Headcount index	% of pop.	18	7	6	..	..	..
GNP per capita	US$	710	1,180	1,720	1,950		3,870
SHORT TERM INCOME INDICATORS							
Unskilled urban wages	local curr.	..	..	..	..	..	..
Unskilled rural wages	"	..	..	..	..	..	..
Rural terms of trade	"	..	..	..	..	..	..
Consumer price index	1987=100	40	88	139	..	..	..
Lower income	"	..	..	..	..	..	..
Food[a]	"	..	89	136	..	..	..
Urban	"	..	..	..	..	..	..
Rural	"	..	..	..	..	..	..
SOCIAL INDICATORS							
Public expenditure on basic social services	% of GDP	..	..	6.4	..	..	..
Gross enrollment ratios							
Primary	% school age pop.	97	116	117	100	..	107
Male	"	116	126	123	107	..	..
Female	"	78	106	110	88	..	..
Mortality							
Infant mortality	per thou. live births	110.0	62.0	48.0	58.0	45.0	40.0
Under 5 mortality	"	..	..	57.0	78.0	59.0	51.0
Immunization							
Measles	% age group	..	65.0	80.0	81.8	..	82.0
DPT	"	..	70.0	90.0	83.9	..	73.8
Child malnutrition (under-5)	"	21.4	..	7.8	20.9	..	..
Life expectancy							
Total	years	56	63	68	64	68	69
Female advantage	"	1.0	1.0	1.8	2.4	6.4	6.3
Total fertility rate	births per woman	6.2	4.9	3.8	4.9	3.1	2.9
Maternal mortality rate	per 100,000 live births		1000	127	..	..	..
Supplementary Poverty Indicators							
Expenditures on social security	% of total gov't exp.	15.3	9.4	12.2	..	..	..
Social security coverage	% econ. active pop.	..	..	..	..	..	..
Access to safe water: total	% of pop.	49.0	68.0	..	85.0	..	85.6
Urban	"	93.0	100.0	..	97.0	..	94.3
Rural	"	17.0	31.0	..	70.1	..	73.0
Access to health care	"	..	91.0	90.0	84.6	..	..

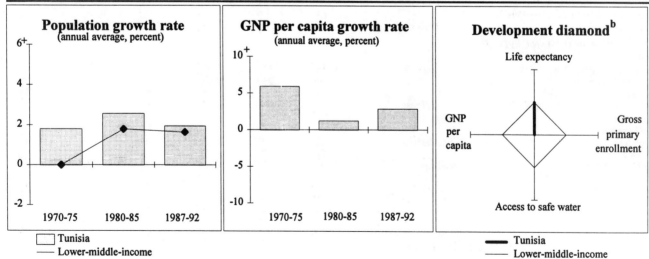

Population growth rate (annual average, percent)

GNP per capita growth rate (annual average, percent)

Development diamond[b]

Life expectancy — GNP per capita — Gross primary enrollment — Access to safe water

— Tunisia
— Lower-middle-income

a. See the technical notes, p.389.   b. The development diamond, based on four key indicators, shows the average level of development in the country compared with its income group. See the introduction.

Tunisia

Indicator	Unit of measure	Latest single year 1970-75	Latest single year 1980-85	Most recent estimate 1987-92	Same region/income group Mid-East & North Africa	Same region/income group Lower-middle-income	Next higher income group

Resources and Expenditures

HUMAN RESOURCES

Indicator	Unit	1970-75	1980-85	1987-92	Mid-East & North Africa	Lower-middle-income	Next higher income group
Population (mre=1992)	thousands	5,611	7,261	8,418	252,555	942,547	477,960
Age dependency ratio	ratio	0.90	0.77	0.71	0.87	0.66	0.64
Urban	% of pop.	47.6	53.1	57.2	54.7	57.0	71.7
Population growth rate	annual %	2.1	2.4	2.2	2.8	1.4	1.6
Urban	"	3.8	3.5	3.2	3.8	4.8	2.5
Labor force (15-64)	thousands	1,608	2,224	2,748	69,280	..	181,414
Agriculture	% of labor force	38	35	..	..	..	..
Industry	"	31	36	..	..	..	..
Female	"	16	23	25	15	36	29
Females per 100 males							
Urban	number	101	98	..	..	..	..
Rural	"	99	101	..	..	..	..

NATURAL RESOURCES

Indicator	Unit	1970-75	1980-85	1987-92	Mid-East & North Africa	Lower-middle-income	Next higher income group
Area	thou. sq. km	163.61	163.61	163.61	10,487.21	40,697.37	21,836.02
Density	pop. per sq. km	34.3	44.4	50.4	23.4	22.8	21.5
Agricultural land	% of land area	52.7	53.4	59.3	30.2	..	41.7
Change in agricultural land	annual %	1.1	-0.6	12.2	0.5	..	0.3
Agricultural land under irrigation	%	1.5	2.5	2.5	31.0	..	9.3
Forests and woodland	thou. sq. km	5	6	7	..	..	..
Deforestation (net)	annual %	..	..	..	..	..	..

INCOME

Indicator	Unit	1970-75	1980-85	1987-92	Mid-East & North Africa	Lower-middle-income	Next higher income group
Household income							
Share of top 20% of households	% of income	42	..	46	..	..	..
Share of bottom 40% of households	"	15	..	16	..	..	..
Share of bottom 20% of households	"	6	..	6	..	..	..

EXPENDITURE

Indicator	Unit	1970-75	1980-85	1987-92	Mid-East & North Africa	Lower-middle-income	Next higher income group
Food	% of GDP	..	26.5	..	..	..	..
Staples	"	..	4.9	..	..	..	..
Meat, fish, milk, cheese, eggs	"	..	9.6	..	..	..	..
Cereal imports	thou. metric tonnes	337	732	1,015	38,007	74,924	49,174
Food aid in cereals	"	59	192	79	2,484	4,054	282
Food production per capita	1987 = 100	130	116	114	116	..	109
Fertilizer consumption	kg/ha	6.4	11.3	10.8	96.7	..	68.8
Share of agriculture in GDP	% of GDP	18.5	15.2	15.6	13.7	..	8.1
Housing	% of GDP	..	9.4	..	..	..	..
Average household size	persons per household	5.5	..	..	..	..	..
Urban	"	5.5	..	..	..	..	..
Fixed investment: housing	% of GDP	..	5.1	..	..	..	..
Fuel and power	% of GDP	..	2.7	..	..	..	..
Energy consumption per capita	kg of oil equiv.	330	516	567	1,109	1,882	1,649
Households with electricity							
Urban	% of households	..	..	..	..	..	..
Rural	"	..	..	..	..	..	..
Transport and communication	% of GDP	..	5.1	..	..	..	..
Fixed investment: transport equipment	"	..	3.1	..	..	..	..
Total road length	thou. km	18	26	29	..	..	..

INVESTMENT IN HUMAN CAPITAL

Indicator	Unit	1970-75	1980-85	1987-92	Mid-East & North Africa	Lower-middle-income	Next higher income group
Health							
Population per physician	persons	5,900	3,643	1,530	..	..	..
Population per nurse	"	938	956	300	..	..	..
Population per hospital bed	"	400	470	516	636	516	385
Oral rehydration therapy (under-5)	% of cases	..	..	63	56	..	54
Education							
Gross enrollment ratio							
Secondary	% of school-age pop.	21	39	46	59	..	53
Female	"	15	32	42	50	..	..
Pupil-teacher ratio: primary	pupils per teacher	40	32	26	27	26	25
Pupil-teacher ratio: secondary	"	..	..	..	21	..	..
Pupils reaching grade 4	% of cohort	88	93	75	..	..	71
Repeater rate: primary	% of total enroll	19	20	20	..	..	11
Illiteracy	% of pop. (age 15+)	62	42	35	45	..	14
Female	% of fem. (age 15+)	..	53	44	58	..	17
Newspaper circulation	per thou. pop.	34	38	37	39	100	117

World Bank International Economics Department, April 1994

Turkey

Indicator	Unit of measure	Latest single year 1970-75	Latest single year 1980-85	Most recent estimate 1987-92	Same region/income group Europe & Central Asia	Same region/income group Lower-middle-income	Next higher income group
Priority Poverty Indicators							
POVERTY							
Upper poverty line	local curr.	..	..	..	..	..	..
Headcount index	% of pop.	..	..	..	..	..	..
Lower poverty line	local curr.	..	..	..	..	..	..
Headcount index	% of pop.	..	..	..	..	..	..
GNP per capita	US$	830	1,080	1,980	..	..	3,870
SHORT TERM INCOME INDICATORS							
Unskilled urban wages	local curr.	..	..	..	..	..	..
Unskilled rural wages	"	..	..	..	..	..	..
Rural terms of trade	"	..	..	..	..	..	..
Consumer price index	1987=100	1	54	1,283	..	..	..
Lower income	"		..		..	..	..
Food[a]	"	..	279	852	..	..	..
Urban	"	..	..	..	..	..	..
Rural	"	..	..	..	..	..	..
SOCIAL INDICATORS							
Public expenditure on basic social services	% of GDP	..	..	..	..	..	..
Gross enrollment ratios							
Primary	% school age pop.	108	113	110	..	..	107
Male	"	124	117	115	..	..	..
Female	"	94	110	110	..	..	..
Mortality							
Infant mortality	per thou. live births	140.0	83.0	54.0	30.0	45.0	40.0
Under 5 mortality	"	..	..	68.9	38.0	59.0	51.0
Immunization							
Measles	% age group	..	45.0	66.0	..	..	82.0
DPT	"	..	64.0	72.0	..	..	73.8
Child malnutrition (under-5)	"	..	..	..	..	..	..
Life expectancy							
Total	years	58	63	67	70	68	69
Female advantage	"	4.1	4.7	5.1	8.6	6.4	6.3
Total fertility rate	births per woman	4.7	4.1	3.4	2.2	3.1	2.9
Maternal mortality rate	per 100,000 live births	..	207	146	58	..	..
Supplementary Poverty Indicators							
Expenditures on social security	% of total gov't exp.	1.3	0.5	0.8	..	..	..
Social security coverage	% econ. active pop.	..	..	..	..	..	..
Access to safe water: total	% of pop.	68.0	..	92.0	..	..	85.6
Urban	"	74.0	..	..	..	..	94.3
Rural	"	64.0	..	..	..	..	73.0
Access to health care	"	..	..	100.0	..	..	..

Population growth rate (annual average, percent)

☐ Turkey
— Lower-middle-income

GNP per capita growth rate (annual average, percent)

Development diamond[b]

— Turkey
— Lower-middle-income

a. See the technical notes, p.389.   b. The development diamond, based on four key indicators, shows the average level of development in the country compared with its income group. See the introduction.

Turkey

Indicator	Unit of measure	Latest single year 1970-75	Latest single year 1980-85	Most recent estimate 1987-92	Same region/income group Europe & Central Asia	Same region/income group Lower-middle-income	Next higher income group
Resources and Expenditures							
HUMAN RESOURCES							
Population (mre=1992)	thousands	40,078	50,306	58,544	495,241	942,547	477,960
Age dependency ratio	ratio	0.81	0.68	0.65	0.56	0.66	0.64
Urban	% of pop.	41.6	52.5	64.1	63.3	57.0	71.7
Population growth rate	annual %	2.3	2.4	2.1	0.5	1.4	1.6
Urban	"	3.9	5.8	4.6	..	4.8	2.5
Labor force (15-64)	thousands	17,640	21,385	24,687	..	..	181,414
Agriculture	% of labor force	65	58	..	..	..	..
Industry	"	14	17	..	..	..	..
Female	"	37	34	34	46	36	29
Females per 100 males							
Urban	number	..	88	..	..	..	..
Rural	"	..	106	..	..	..	..
NATURAL RESOURCES							
Area	thou. sq. km	779.45	779.45	779.45	24,165.06	40,697.37	21,836.02
Density	pop. per sq. km	51.4	64.5	73.6	20.4	22.8	21.5
Agricultural land	% of land area	49.3	47.3	47.0	..	..	41.7
Change in agricultural land	annual %	-1.0	0.1	0.0	..	..	0.3
Agricultural land under irrigation	%	5.2	6.1	6.6	..	..	9.3
Forests and woodland	thou. sq. km	202	202	202	..	..	..
Deforestation (net)	annual %	..	..	0.0	..	..	..
INCOME							
Household income							
Share of top 20% of households	% of income	55	..	50	..	..	..
Share of bottom 40% of households	"	11	..	15	..	..	..
Share of bottom 20% of households	"	4	..	5	..	..	..
EXPENDITURE							
Food	% of GDP	..	29.5	..	..	..	..
Staples	"	..	6.3	..	..	..	..
Meat, fish, milk, cheese, eggs	"	..	10.6	..	..	..	..
Cereal imports	thou. metric tonnes	560	1,082	605	45,972	74,924	49,174
Food aid in cereals	"	16	0	13	1,639	4,054	282
Food production per capita	1987 = 100	96	96	93	..	..	109
Fertilizer consumption	kg/ha	23.5	39.2	48.8	..	..	68.8
Share of agriculture in GDP	% of GDP	26.2	17.4	12.9	..	..	8.1
Housing	% of GDP	..	9.2	..	..	..	..
Average household size	persons per household	5.8	..	..	..	..	..
Urban	"	6.6	..	..	..	..	..
Fixed investment: housing	% of GDP	2.6	0.6	..	..	..	..
Fuel and power	% of GDP	..	4.9	..	..	..	..
Energy consumption per capita	kg of oil equiv.	668	776	948	3,190	1,882	1,649
Households with electricity							
Urban	% of households	..	..	..	..	..	..
Rural	"	..	..	..	..	..	..
Transport and communication	% of GDP	..	3.5	..	..	..	..
Fixed investment: transport equipment	"	..	2.8	..	..	..	..
Total road length	thou. km	52	59	59	..	..	..
INVESTMENT IN HUMAN CAPITAL							
Health							
Population per physician	persons	2,200	1,391	1,033	378	..	..
Population per nurse	"	1,005	1,030	1,167	..	..	..
Population per hospital bed	"	500	488	505	134	516	385
Oral rehydration therapy (under-5)	% of cases	..	..	26	..	..	54
Education							
Gross enrollment ratio							
Secondary	% of school-age pop.	29	42	51	..	..	53
Female	"	19	30	40	..	..	..
Pupil-teacher ratio: primary	pupils per teacher	32	31	29	..	26	25
Pupil-teacher ratio: secondary	"	31	24	26	..	..	..
Pupils reaching grade 4	% of cohort	80	..	92	..	..	71
Repeater rate: primary	% of total enroll	..	8	7	..	..	11
Illiteracy	% of pop. (age 15+)	40	24	19	..	..	14
Female	% of fem. (age 15+)	..	36	29	..	..	17
Newspaper circulation	per thou. pop.	37	..	71	..	100	117

World Bank International Economics Department, April 1994

Turkmenistan

Indicator	Unit of measure	Latest single year 1970-75	1980-85	Most recent estimate 1987-92	Same region/income group Europe & Central Asia	Lower-middle-income	Next higher income group
Priority Poverty Indicators							
POVERTY							
Upper poverty line	local curr.	..	..	..	..	..	..
Headcount index	% of pop.	..	..	49	..	..	..
Lower poverty line	local curr.	..	..	..	..	..	..
Headcount index	% of pop.	..	..	22	..	..	..
GNP per capita	US$	..	..	1,230		..	3,870
SHORT TERM INCOME INDICATORS							
Unskilled urban wages	local curr.	..	..	..	..	..	..
Unskilled rural wages	"	..	..	..	..	..	..
Rural terms of trade	"	..	..	..	..	..	..
Consumer price index	1987=100	..	..	..	..	..	..
Lower income	"	..	..	..	..	..	..
Food[a]	"	..	..	..	..	..	..
Urban	"	..	..	..	..	..	..
Rural	"	..	..	..	..	..	..
SOCIAL INDICATORS							
Public expenditure on basic social services	% of GDP	..	..	8.0	..	..	..
Gross enrollment ratios							
Primary	% school age pop.	..	..	..	..	..	107
Male	"	..	..	..	..	..	..
Female	"	..	..	..	..	..	..
Mortality							
Infant mortality	per thou. live births	..	61.2	54.0	30.0	45.0	40.0
Under 5 mortality	"	..	..	71.4	38.0	59.0	51.0
Immunization							
Measles	% age group	..	..	..	..	..	82.0
DPT	"	..	..	..	..	..	73.8
Child malnutrition (under-5)	"	..	..	..	..	..	..
Life expectancy							
Total	years	..	65	66	70	68	69
Female advantage	"	..	6.4	6.8	8.6	6.4	6.3
Total fertility rate	births per woman	5.7	4.7	4.2	2.2	3.1	2.9
Maternal mortality rate	per 100,000 live births	..	41	55	58	..	..
Supplementary Poverty Indicators							
Expenditures on social security	% of total gov't exp.	..	..	..	..	..	..
Social security coverage	% econ. active pop.	..	..	..	..	..	..
Access to safe water: total	% of pop.	..	..	..	..	..	85.6
Urban	"	..	..	..	..	..	94.3
Rural	"	..	..	..	..	..	73.0
Access to health care	"	..	..	..	..	..	..

Population growth rate
(annual average, percent)

Turkmenistan
Lower-middle-income

GNP per capita growth rate
(annual average, percent)

Development diamond[b]

Life expectancy — GNP per capita — Gross primary enrollment — Access to safe water

Turkmenistan
Lower-middle-income

a. See the technical notes, p.389. b. The development diamond, based on four key indicators, shows the average level of development in the country compared with its income group. See the introduction.

352

Turkmenistan

Indicator	Unit of measure	Latest single year 1970-75	Latest single year 1980-85	Most recent estimate 1987-92	Same region/income group Europe & Central Asia	Same region/income group Lower-middle-income	Next higher income group

Resources and Expenditures

HUMAN RESOURCES

Indicator	Unit of measure	1970-75	1980-85	1987-92	Europe & Central Asia	Lower-middle-income	Next higher income group
Population (mre=1992)	thousands	..	3,230	3,857	495,241	942,547	477,960
Age dependency ratio	ratio	..	..	0.83	0.56	0.66	0.64
Urban	% of pop.	..	..	45.0	63.3	57.0	71.7
Population growth rate	annual %	..	2.4	2.5	0.5	1.4	1.6
Urban	"	..	..	..	..	4.8	2.5
Labor force (15-64)	thousands	..	1,604	1,870	..	..	181,414
Agriculture	% of labor force	..	..	..	..	..	..
Industry	"	..	..	..	..	..	..
Female	"	..	..	42	46	36	29
Females per 100 males							
Urban	number	..	..	..	..	..	..
Rural	"	..	..	..	..	..	..

NATURAL RESOURCES

Indicator	Unit of measure	1970-75	1980-85	1987-92	Europe & Central Asia	Lower-middle-income	Next higher income group
Area	thou. sq. km	..	..	488.10	24,165.06	40,697.37	21,836.02
Density	pop. per sq. km	..	..	7.7	20.4	22.8	21.5
Agricultural land	% of land area	..	..	..	..	..	41.7
Change in agricultural land	annual %	..	..	..	..	..	0.3
Agricultural land under irrigation	%	..	..	..	..	..	9.3
Forests and woodland	thou. sq. km	..	..	..	..	..	..
Deforestation (net)	annual %	..	..	..	..	..	..

INCOME
Household income

Indicator	Unit of measure	1970-75	1980-85	1987-92	Europe & Central Asia	Lower-middle-income	Next higher income group
Share of top 20% of households	% of income	..	..	..	..	..	..
Share of bottom 40% of households	"	..	..	..	..	..	..
Share of bottom 20% of households	"	..	..	..	..	..	..

EXPENDITURE

Indicator	Unit of measure	1970-75	1980-85	1987-92	Europe & Central Asia	Lower-middle-income	Next higher income group
Food	% of GDP	..	..	19.8	..	..	..
Staples	"	..	..	3.6	..	..	..
Meat, fish, milk, cheese, eggs	"	..	..	8.9	..	..	..
Cereal imports	thou. metric tonnes	..	..	..	45,972	74,924	49,174
Food aid in cereals	"	..	..	..	1,639	4,054	282
Food production per capita	1987 = 100	..	..	..	..	..	109
Fertilizer consumption	kg/ha	..	..	..	..	..	68.8
Share of agriculture in GDP	% of GDP	..	29.2	33.2	..	..	8.1
Housing	% of GDP	..	..	4.7	..	..	..
Average household size	persons per household	..	..	5.6	..	..	..
Urban	"	..	..	..	..	..	..
Fixed investment: housing	% of GDP	..	..	4.9	..	..	..
Fuel and power	% of GDP	..	..	1.0	..	..	..
Energy consumption per capita	kg of oil equiv.	..	..	..	3,190	1,882	1,649
Households with electricity							
Urban	% of households	..	..	..	..	..	..
Rural	"	..	..	..	..	..	..
Transport and communication	% of GDP	..	..	6.2	..	..	..
Fixed investment: transport equipment	"	..	..	10.3	..	..	..
Total road length	thou. km	..	16	21	..	..	..

INVESTMENT IN HUMAN CAPITAL

Health

Indicator	Unit of measure	1970-75	1980-85	1987-92	Europe & Central Asia	Lower-middle-income	Next higher income group
Population per physician	persons	..	..	287	378	..	..
Population per nurse	"	..	..	..	..	..	..
Population per hospital bed	"	..	..	92	134	516	385
Oral rehydration therapy (under-5)	% of cases	..	..	..	..	..	54

Education

Gross enrollment ratio

Indicator	Unit of measure	1970-75	1980-85	1987-92	Europe & Central Asia	Lower-middle-income	Next higher income group
Secondary	% of school-age pop.	..	..	..	..	..	53
Female	"	..	..	..	..	..	..
Pupil-teacher ratio: primary	pupils per teacher	..	..	..	..	26	25
Pupil-teacher ratio: secondary	"	..	..	..	..	..	..
Pupils reaching grade 4	% of cohort	..	..	..	..	..	71
Repeater rate: primary	% of total enroll	..	..	..	..	..	11
Illiteracy	% of pop. (age 15+)	..	..	..	..	..	14
Female	% of fem. (age 15+)	..	..	..	..	..	17
Newspaper circulation	per thou. pop.	..	..	..	..	100	117

World Bank International Economics Department, April 1994

Uganda

Indicator	Unit of measure	Latest single year 1970-75	Latest single year 1980-85	Most recent estimate 1987-92	Same region/income group Sub-Saharan Africa	Same region/income group Low-income	Next higher income group

Priority Poverty Indicators

POVERTY

Indicator	Unit of measure	1970-75	1980-85	1987-92	Sub-Saharan Africa	Low-income	Next higher income group
Upper poverty line	local curr.	..	..	6,000	..	..	..
Headcount index	% of pop.	..	..	55	..	19	..
Lower poverty line	local curr.	..	..	3,000	..	..	..
Headcount index	% of pop.	..	..	19	..	..	..
GNP per capita	US$	..	170	170	520	390	..
SHORT TERM INCOME INDICATORS							
Unskilled urban wages	local curr.	..	..	..	..	..	..
Unskilled rural wages	"	..	..	..	..	..	..
Rural terms of trade	"	..	..	..	..	..	..
Consumer price index	1987=100	..	13	1,242	..	..	..
Lower income	"	..	..	..	..	..	..
Food[a]	"	..	15	297	..	..	..
Urban	"	..	..	..	..	..	..
Rural	"	..	..	..	..	..	..
SOCIAL INDICATORS							
Public expenditure on basic social services	% of GDP	..	..	5.5	..	..	..
Gross enrollment ratios							
Primary	% school age pop.	44	70	71	66	103	..
Male	"	53	66	..	79	113	..
Female	"	35	49	63	62	96	..
Mortality							
Infant mortality	per thou. live births	104.4	115.5	122.0	99.0	73.0	45.0
Under 5 mortality	"	..	..	205.2	169.0	108.0	59.0
Immunization							
Measles	% age group	..	17.0	74.0	54.0	72.7	..
DPT	"	..	14.0	77.0	54.6	80.6	..
Child malnutrition (under-5)	"	..	..	23.3	28.4	38.3	..
Life expectancy							
Total	years	51	48	43	52	62	68
Female advantage	"	1.6	1.6	1.5	3.4	2.4	6.4
Total fertility rate	births per woman	7.1	7.3	7.1	6.1	3.4	3.1
Maternal mortality rate	per 100,000 live births	..	300	550	..	..	..

Supplementary Poverty Indicators

Indicator	Unit of measure	1970-75	1980-85	1987-92	Sub-Saharan Africa	Low-income	Next higher income group
Expenditures on social security	% of total gov't exp.	0.0	1.6	..	..	..	..
Social security coverage	% econ. active pop.	..	..	..	..	..	..
Access to safe water: total	% of pop.	22.0	21.0	..	41.1	68.4	..
Urban	"	88.0	37.0	..	77.8	78.9	..
Rural	"	17.0	18.0	..	27.3	60.3	..
Access to health care	"	..	42.0	70.0	..	..	..

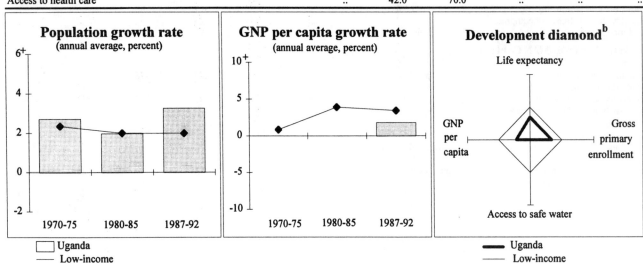

Population growth rate (annual average, percent)

GNP per capita growth rate (annual average, percent)

Development diamond[b]

Life expectancy — GNP per capita — Gross primary enrollment — Access to safe water

Uganda
Low-income

a. See the technical notes, p.389.   b. The development diamond, based on four key indicators, shows the average level of development in the country compared with its income group. See the introduction.

Uganda

Indicator	Unit of measure	Latest single year 1970-75	Latest single year 1980-85	Most recent estimate 1987-92	Same region/income group Sub-Saharan Africa	Same region/income group Low-income	Next higher income group
Resources and Expenditures							
HUMAN RESOURCES							
Population (mre=1992)	thousands	11,228	14,134	17,459	546,390	3,194,535	942,547
Age dependency ratio	ratio	1.00	1.09	1.05	0.95	0.67	0.66
Urban	% of pop.	8.3	9.9	11.7	29.5	26.7	57.0
Population growth rate	annual %	2.6	2.0	3.3	2.9	1.8	1.4
Urban	"	3.3	4.2	5.7	5.1	3.4	4.8
Labor force (15-64)	thousands	5,331	7,054	8,641	224,025	1,478,954	..
Agriculture	% of labor force	88	86	..	..	..	..
Industry	"	4	4	..	..	..	..
Female	"	43	42	41	37	33	36
Females per 100 males							
Urban	number	..	..	..	..	..	..
Rural	"	..	..	..	..	..	..
NATURAL RESOURCES							
Area	thou. sq. km	235.88	235.88	235.88	24,274.03	38,401.06	40,697.37
Density	pop. per sq. km	47.6	59.9	71.6	21.9	81.7	22.8
Agricultural land	% of land area	36.1	42.1	42.9	52.7	50.9	..
Change in agricultural land	annual %	2.0	1.2	0.5	0.1	0.0	..
Agricultural land under irrigation	%	0.1	0.1	0.1	0.8	18.2	..
Forests and woodland	thou. sq. km	63	58	55			
Deforestation (net)	annual %	..	..	1.1	..	..	
INCOME							
Household income							
Share of top 20% of households	% of income	47	..	42	..	42	..
Share of bottom 40% of households	"	17	..	21	..	19	..
Share of bottom 20% of households	"	6	..	9	..	8	..
EXPENDITURE							
Food	% of GDP	..	..	46.8	..	..	..
Staples	"	..	..	25.4	..	..	..
Meat, fish, milk, cheese, eggs	"	..	..	11.0	..	..	..
Cereal imports	thou. metric tonnes	6	16	22	20,311	46,537	74,924
Food aid in cereals	"	0	31	25	4,303	9,008	4,054
Food production per capita	1987 = 100	140	99	103	90	123	..
Fertilizer consumption	kg/ha	0.2	0.0	0.2	4.2	61.9	..
Share of agriculture in GDP	% of GDP	66.6	56.9	54.1	18.6	29.6	..
Housing	% of GDP	..	..	12.0	..	..	..
Average household size	persons per household	4.8	..	5.4	..	..	..
Urban	"	..	..	..	..	..	..
Fixed investment: housing	% of GDP	..	..	2.6	..	..	..
Fuel and power	% of GDP	..	..	1.7	..	..	..
Energy consumption per capita	kg of oil equiv.	43	25	24	258	335	1,882
Households with electricity							
Urban	% of households	..	..	..	..	..	..
Rural	"	..	..	..	..	..	..
Transport and communication	% of GDP	..	..	4.3	..	..	..
Fixed investment: transport equipment	"	..	..	2.6	..	..	..
Total road length	thou. km	26	28	29	..	..	..
INVESTMENT IN HUMAN CAPITAL							
Health							
Population per physician	persons	9,302	22,679	..	..	..	..
Population per nurse	"	..	2,049	..	..	..	..
Population per hospital bed	"	607	661	1,248	1,329	1,050	516
Oral rehydration therapy (under-5)	% of cases	..	..	30	36	39	..
Education							
Gross enrollment ratio							
Secondary	% of school-age pop.	4	10	13	18	41	..
Female	"	2	5	35	14	35	..
Pupil-teacher ratio: primary	pupils per teacher	34	34	35	39	37	26
Pupil-teacher ratio: secondary	"	23	23	18	..	19	..
Pupils reaching grade 4	% of cohort	..	..	..	..	..	..
Repeater rate: primary	% of total enroll	10	10	..	..	..	..
Illiteracy	% of pop. (age 15+)	..	57	46	51	39	..
Female	% of fem. (age 15+)	..	71	55	62	52	..
Newspaper circulation	per thou. pop.	7	2	2	14	..	100

World Bank International Economics Department, April 1994

Ukraine

Indicator	Unit of measure	Latest single year 1970-75	Latest single year 1980-85	Most recent estimate 1987-92	Same region/income group Europe & Central Asia	Same region/income group Lower-middle-income	Next higher income group
Priority Poverty Indicators							
POVERTY							
Upper poverty line	local curr.	..	..	..	..	..	..
Headcount index	% of pop.	..	..	11	..	..	..
Lower poverty line	local curr.	..	..	..	..	..	..
Headcount index	% of pop.	..	..	3	..	..	..
GNP per capita	US$	..	..	1,820	..	..	3,870
SHORT TERM INCOME INDICATORS							
Unskilled urban wages	local curr.	..	..	..	..	..	..
Unskilled rural wages	"	..	..	..	..	..	..
Rural terms of trade	"	..	..	..	..	..	..
Consumer price index	1987=100	..	..	..	..	..	..
Lower income	"	..	..	..	..	..	..
Food[a]	"	..	91	101	..	..	..
Urban	"	..	..	..	..	..	..
Rural	"	..	..	..	..	..	..
SOCIAL INDICATORS							
Public expenditure on basic social services	% of GDP	..	..	8.0	..	..	..
Gross enrollment ratios							
Primary	% school age pop.	..	..	..	..	..	107
Male	"	..	..	..	..	..	..
Female	"	..	..	..	..	..	..
Mortality							
Infant mortality	per thou. live births	19.2	20.0	17.5	30.0	45.0	40.0
Under 5 mortality	"	..	..	21.1	38.0	59.0	51.0
Immunization							
Measles	% age group	..	..	..	..	..	82.0
DPT	"	..	..	..	..	..	73.8
Child malnutrition (under-5)	"	..	..	..	..	..	..
Life expectancy							
Total	years	70	70	70	70	68	69
Female advantage	"	7.0	8.5	9.5	8.6	6.4	6.3
Total fertility rate	births per woman	2.0	2.1	1.8	2.2	3.1	2.9
Maternal mortality rate	per 100,000 live births	..	45	33	58	..	..
Supplementary Poverty Indicators							
Expenditures on social security	% of total gov't exp.	..	..	..	..	..	..
Social security coverage	% econ. active pop.	..	..	..	..	..	..
Access to safe water: total	% of pop.	..	..	..	..	..	85.6
Urban	"	..	..	..	..	..	94.3
Rural	"	..	..	..	..	..	73.0
Access to health care	"	..	100.0	100.0	..	..	..

Population growth rate
(annual average, percent)

  □ Ukraine
  — Lower-middle-income

GNP per capita growth rate
(annual average, percent)

Development diamond[b]

  — Ukraine
  — Lower-middle-income

a. See the technical notes, p.389. b. The development diamond, based on four key indicators, shows the average level of development in the country compared with its income group. See the introduction.

Ukraine

Indicator	Unit of measure	Latest single year 1970-75	Latest single year 1980-85	Most recent estimate 1987-92	Same region/income group Europe & Central Asia	Same region/income group Lower-middle-income	Next higher income group
Resources and Expenditures							
HUMAN RESOURCES							
Population (mre=1992)	thousands	..	50,917	52,126	495,241	942,547	477,960
Age dependency ratio	ratio	..	..	0.55	0.56	0.66	0.64
Urban	% of pop.	..	66.4	66.9	63.3	57.0	71.7
Population growth rate	annual %	..	0.3	0.2	0.5	1.4	1.6
Urban	"	..	1.4	16.2	..	4.8	2.5
Labor force (15-64)	thousands	..	..	..	..	..	181,414
Agriculture	% of labor force	..	..	..	..	..	..
Industry	"	..	..	..	..	..	..
Female	"	..	..	..	46	36	29
Females per 100 males							
Urban	number	..	..	..	..	..	..
Rural	"	..	..	..	..	..	..
NATURAL RESOURCES							
Area	thou. sq. km	..	..	603.70	24,165.06	40,697.37	21,836.02
Density	pop. per sq. km	..	..	86.2	20.4	22.8	21.5
Agricultural land	% of land area	..	..	..	..	..	41.7
Change in agricultural land	annual %	..	..	..	..	..	0.3
Agricultural land under irrigation	%	..	..	..	..	..	9.3
Forests and woodland	thou. sq. km	..	..	..	..	..	..
Deforestation (net)	annual %	..	..	-0.2	..	..	..
INCOME							
Household income							
Share of top 20% of households	% of income	..	..	..	..	..	..
Share of bottom 40% of households	"	..	..	..	..	..	..
Share of bottom 20% of households	"	..	..	..	..	..	..
EXPENDITURE							
Food	% of GDP	..	..	19.8	..	..	..
Staples	"	..	..	3.6	..	..	..
Meat, fish, milk, cheese, eggs	"	..	..	8.9	..	..	..
Cereal imports	thou. metric tonnes	..	..	2,700	45,972	74,924	49,174
Food aid in cereals	"	..	..	..	1,639	4,054	282
Food production per capita	1987 = 100	..	..	..	..	..	109
Fertilizer consumption	kg/ha	..	..	..	..	..	68.8
Share of agriculture in GDP	% of GDP	..	19.3	23.4	..	..	8.1
Housing	% of GDP	..	..	4.7	..	..	..
Average household size	persons per household	..	..	3.2	..	..	..
Urban	"	..	..	..	..	..	..
Fixed investment: housing	% of GDP	..	..	4.9	..	..	..
Fuel and power	% of GDP	..	..	1.0	..	..	..
Energy consumption per capita	kg of oil equiv.	..	..	3,885	3,190	1,882	1,649
Households with electricity							
Urban	% of households	..	..	..	..	..	..
Rural	"	..	..	..	..	..	..
Transport and communication	% of GDP	..	..	6.2	..	..	..
Fixed investment: transport equipment	"	..	..	10.3	..	..	..
Total road length	thou. km	..	210	259	..	..	..
INVESTMENT IN HUMAN CAPITAL							
Health							
Population per physician	persons	..	..	232	378	..	..
Population per nurse	"	..	..	..	..	..	..
Population per hospital bed	"	..	..	7	134	516	385
Oral rehydration therapy (under-5)	% of cases	..	..	..	..	..	54
Education							
Gross enrollment ratio							
Secondary	% of school-age pop.	..	..	..	..	..	53
Female	"	..	..	..	..	..	..
Pupil-teacher ratio: primary	pupils per teacher	13	9	8	..	26	25
Pupil-teacher ratio: secondary	"	..	..	..	..	..	..
Pupils reaching grade 4	% of cohort	99	89	..	..	..	71
Repeater rate: primary	% of total enroll	..	..	..	..	..	11
Illiteracy	% of pop. (age 15+)	..	..	..	..	..	14
Female	% of fem. (age 15+)	..	..	..	..	..	17
Newspaper circulation	per thou. pop.	..	..	251	..	100	117

World Bank International Economics Department, April 1994

357

United Arab Emirates

Indicator	Unit of measure	Latest single year		Most recent estimate 1987-92	Same region/income group High-income
		1970-75	1980-85		

Priority Poverty Indicators

POVERTY

Upper poverty line	local curr.	..	..	..	..
Headcount index	% of pop.	..	..	..	..
Lower poverty line	local curr.	..	..	..	..
Headcount index	% of pop.	..	..	..	..
GNP per capita	US$	13,240	21,620	22,020	21,960

SHORT TERM INCOME INDICATORS

Unskilled urban wages	local curr.	..	..	..	..
Unskilled rural wages	"	..	..	..	..
Rural terms of trade	"	..	..	..	..
Consumer price index	1987=100	..	..	..	..
Lower income	"	..	..	..	..
Food[a]	"	..	..	..	..
Urban	"	..	..	..	..
Rural	"	..	..	..	..

SOCIAL INDICATORS

Public expenditure on basic social services	% of GDP	..	..	..	..
Gross enrollment ratios					
Primary	% school age pop.	101	93	115	103
Male	"	104	94	117	103
Female	"	97	93	114	103
Mortality					
Infant mortality	per thou. live births	88.0	29.0	20.0	7.0
Under 5 mortality	"	..	..	24.4	10.0
Immunization					
Measles	% age group	..	49.0	66.0	82.4
DPT	"	..	58.0	81.0	90.1
Child malnutrition (under-5)	"	..	..	..	..
Life expectancy					
Total	years	63	69	72	77
Female advantage	"	3.7	4.3	4.3	6.4
Total fertility rate	births per woman	6.4	5.2	4.5	1.7
Maternal mortality rate	per 100,000 live births	..	..	..	..

Supplementary Poverty Indicators

Expenditures on social security	% of total gov't exp.	..	..	..	..
Social security coverage	% econ. active pop.	..	..	..	..
Access to safe water: total	% of pop.	..	..	100.0	..
Urban	"	..	77.0	100.0	..
Rural	"	..	65.0	100.0	..
Access to health care	"	..	96.0	100.0	..

Population growth rate
(annual average, percent)

United Arab Emirates
High-income

GNP per capita growth rate
(annual average, percent)

Development diamond[b]

Life expectancy

GNP per capita — Gross primary enrollment

Access to safe water

United Arab Emirates
High-income

a. See the technical notes, p.389.   b. The development diamond, based on four key indicators, shows the average level of development in the country compared with its income group. See the introduction.

United Arab Emirates

Indicator	Unit of measure	Latest single year 1970-75	Latest single year 1980-85	Most recent estimate 1987-92	Same region/income group High-income
		Resources and Expenditures			
HUMAN RESOURCES					
Population (mre=1992)	thousands	505	1,349	1,683	828,221
Age dependency ratio	ratio	0.43	0.47	0.49	0.50
Urban	% of pop.	65.4	76.9	82.2	78.1
Population growth rate	annual %	18.0	3.1	2.7	0.7
Urban	"	20.5	4.5	3.4	0.9
Labor force (15-64)	thousands	267	683	816	390,033
Agriculture	% of labor force	9	5	..	..
Industry	"	37	38	..	..
Female	"	4	6	7	38
Females per 100 males					
Urban	number	29	..	..	..
Rural	"	40	..	..	..
NATURAL RESOURCES					
Area	thou. sq. km	83.60	83.60	83.60	31,709.00
Density	pop. per sq. km	6.0	16.1	19.6	24.5
Agricultural land	% of land area	2.6	2.8	2.9	42.7
Change in agricultural land	annual %	0.5	1.3	0.0	-0.2
Agricultural land under irrigation	%	2.3	2.1	2.1	16.1
Forests and woodland	thou. sq. km	0	0	0	..
Deforestation (net)	annual %	..	..	..	..
INCOME					
Household income					
Share of top 20% of households	% of income	..	..	..	..
Share of bottom 40% of households	"	..	..	..	..
Share of bottom 20% of households	"	..	..	..	..
EXPENDITURE					
Food	% of GDP	..	..	..	..
Staples	"	..	..	..	..
Meat, fish, milk, cheese, eggs	"	..	..	..	..
Cereal imports	thou. metric tonnes	168	420	524	70,626
Food aid in cereals	"	..	..	..	2
Food production per capita	1987 = 100	..	..	..	101
Fertilizer consumption	kg/ha	4.2	16.0	73.1	162.1
Share of agriculture in GDP	% of GDP	0.8	1.5	2.1	2.4
Housing	% of GDP	..	..	..<	..
Average household size	persons per household	..	..	..	..
Urban	"	..	..	..	..
Fixed investment: housing	% of GDP	..	..	..	..
Fuel and power	% of GDP	..	..	..	..
Energy consumption per capita	kg of oil equiv.	3,915	11,231	14,631	5,101
Households with electricity					
Urban	% of households	..	..	..	..
Rural	"	..	..	..	..
Transport and communication	% of GDP	..	..	..	..
Fixed investment: transport equipment	"	..	..	..	..
Total road length	thou. km	..	..	..	..
INVESTMENT IN HUMAN CAPITAL					
Health					
Population per physician	persons	1,100	1,023	1,041	..
Population per nurse	"	..	393	549	..
Population per hospital bed	"	..	346	..	144
Oral rehydration therapy (under-5)	% of cases	..	..	81	..
Education					
Gross enrollment ratio					
Secondary	% of school-age pop.	33	59	69	92
Female	"	29	63	73	94
Pupil-teacher ratio: primary	pupils per teacher	16	25	18	18
Pupil-teacher ratio: secondary	"	9	14	..	..
Pupils reaching grade 4	% of cohort	95	92	94	..
Repeater rate: primary	% of total enroll	14	6	4	..
Illiteracy	% of pop. (age 15+)	47	..	..	..
Female	% of fem. (age 15+)	..	..	..	..
Newspaper circulation	per thou. pop.	4	52	157	..

World Bank International Economics Department, April 1994

United Kingdom

Indicator	Unit of measure	Latest single year		Most recent estimate 1987-92	Same region/income group
		1970-75	1980-85		High-income

Priority Poverty Indicators

POVERTY

Indicator	Unit of measure	1970-75	1980-85	1987-92	High-income
Upper poverty line	local curr.	..	..	..	..
Headcount index	% of pop.	..	..	..	..
Lower poverty line	local curr.	..	..	..	..
Headcount index	% of pop.	..	..	..	..
GNP per capita	US$	3,900	8,520	17,790	21,960

SHORT TERM INCOME INDICATORS

Indicator	Unit of measure	1970-75	1980-85	1987-92	High-income
Unskilled urban wages	local curr.	..	..	..	..
Unskilled rural wages	"	..	..	..	..
Rural terms of trade	"	..	..	..	..
Consumer price index	1987=100	34	93	136	
Lower income	"	..	..	..	..
Food[a]	"	18	94	124	..
Urban	"	..	..	..	..
Rural	"	..	..	..	..

SOCIAL INDICATORS

Indicator	Unit of measure	1970-75	1980-85	1987-92	High-income
Public expenditure on basic social services	% of GDP	..	..	..	..
Gross enrollment ratios					
Primary	% school age pop.	105	104	104	103
Male	"	105	104	104	103
Female	"	106	105	105	103
Mortality					
Infant mortality	per thou. live births	16.0	9.3	7.0	7.0
Under 5 mortality	"	..	..	9.0	10.0
Immunization					
Measles	% age group	..	60.0	89.0	82.4
DPT	"	..	44.0	85.0	90.1
Child malnutrition (under-5)	"	..	..	..	..
Life expectancy					
Total	years	72	74	76	77
Female advantage	"	6.3	6.2	5.6	6.4
Total fertility rate	births per woman	1.8	1.8	1.8	1.7
Maternal mortality rate	per 100,000 live births	..	7	..	..

Supplementary Poverty Indicators

Indicator	Unit of measure	1970-75	1980-85	1987-92	High-income
Expenditures on social security	% of total gov't exp.	..	..	..	..
Social security coverage	% econ. active pop.	..	..	..	..
Access to safe water: total	% of pop.	..	100.0	..	..
Urban	"	..	100.0	..	..
Rural	"	..	100.0	..	..
Access to health care	"	..	100.0	100.0	..

Population growth rate
(annual average, percent)

☐ United Kingdom
— High-income

GNP per capita growth rate
(annual average, percent)

Development diamond[b]

Life expectancy — GNP per capita — Gross primary enrollment — Access to safe water

— United Kingdom
— High-income

a. See the technical notes, p.389.   b. The development diamond, based on four key indicators, shows the average level of development in the country compared with its income group. See the introduction.

360

United Kingdom

Indicator	Unit of measure	Latest single year 1970-75	Latest single year 1980-85	Most recent estimate 1987-92	Same region/income group High-income
Resources and Expenditures					
HUMAN RESOURCES					
Population (mre=1992)	thousands	56,226	56,618	57,848	828,221
Age dependency ratio	ratio	0.59	0.52	0.54	0.50
Urban	% of pop.	88.7	88.8	89.3	78.1
Population growth rate	annual %	0.0	0.3	0.3	0.7
Urban	"	0.0	0.3	0.4	0.9
Labor force (15-64)	thousands	25,991	27,432	27,803	390,033
Agriculture	% of labor force	3	3	..	..
Industry	"	42	38	..	..
Female	"	37	39	39	38
Females per 100 males					
Urban	number	..	..	..	..
Rural	"	..	..	..	..
NATURAL RESOURCES					
Area	thou. sq. km	244.88	244.88	244.88	31,709.00
Density	pop. per sq. km	229.6	231.2	235.4	24.5
Agricultural land	% of land area	76.8	75.2	73.6	42.7
Change in agricultural land	annual %	-0.3	-0.2	-0.3	-0.2
Agricultural land under irrigation	%	0.5	0.8	0.9	16.1
Forests and woodland	thou. sq. km	20	23	24	..
Deforestation (net)	annual %	..	..	-1.3	..
INCOME					
Household income					
Share of top 20% of households	% of income	..	..	..	..
Share of bottom 40% of households	"	..	..	..	..
Share of bottom 20% of households	"	..	..	..	..
EXPENDITURE					
Food	% of GDP	11.2	8.5	..	..
Staples	"	2.1	1.6	..	..
Meat, fish, milk, cheese, eggs	"	5.3	3.9	..	..
Cereal imports	thou. metric tonnes	7,853	3,521	3,559	70,626
Food aid in cereals	"	..	..	..	2
Food production per capita	1987 = 100	88	108	108	101
Fertilizer consumption	kg/ha	97.9	138.9	117.7	162.1
Share of agriculture in GDP	% of GDP	2.4	1.7	1.5	2.4
Housing	% of GDP	11.8	12.5	..	..
Average household size	persons per household	2.9	2.8	..	..
Urban	"	..	..	..	..
Fixed investment: housing	% of GDP	4.1	3.5	..	..
Fuel and power	% of GDP	2.8	3.2	..	..
Energy consumption per capita	kg of oil equiv.	3,591	3,586	3,743	5,101
Households with electricity					
Urban	% of households	..	..	..	..
Rural	"	..	..	..	..
Transport and communication	% of GDP	8.1	10.1	..	..
Fixed investment: transport equipment	"	2.8	2.6	..	..
Total road length	thou. km	346	347	357	..
INVESTMENT IN HUMAN CAPITAL					
Health					
Population per physician	persons	809	611	..	..
Population per nurse	"	243	120	..	..
Population per hospital bed	"	105	107	160	144
Oral rehydyration therapy (under-5)	% of cases	..	..	..	..
Education					
Gross enrollment ratio					
Secondary	% of school-age pop.	83	84	86	92
Female	"	83	86	88	94
Pupil-teacher ratio: primary	pupils per teacher	20	18	20	18
Pupil-teacher ratio: secondary	"	16	14	13	..
Pupils reaching grade 4	% of cohort	..	..	..	..
Repeater rate: primary	% of total enroll	..	..	..	..
Illiteracy	% of pop. (age 15+)	..	..	†	..
Female	% of fem. (age 15+)	..	..	†	..
Newspaper circulation	per thou. pop.	386	416	394	..

World Bank International Economics Department, April 1994

United States

Indicator	Unit of measure	Latest single year 1970-75	Latest single year 1980-85	Most recent estimate 1987-92	Same region/income group High-income
Priority Poverty Indicators					
POVERTY					
Upper poverty line	local curr.	..	..	..	..
Headcount index	% of pop.	..	..	..	..
Lower poverty line	local curr.	..	..	..	..
Headcount index	% of pop.	..	..	..	..
GNP per capita	US$	7,390	16,910	23,240	21,960
SHORT TERM INCOME INDICATORS					
Unskilled urban wages	local curr.	..	..	..	..
Unskilled rural wages	"	..	..	..	..
Rural terms of trade	"	..	..	..	..
Consumer price index	1987=100	47	95	123	
Lower income	"	..	..	..	..
Food[a]	"	35	93	122	..
Urban	"	..	..	..	..
Rural	"	..	..	..	..
SOCIAL INDICATORS					
Public expenditure on basic social services	% of GDP	..	..	..	..
Gross enrollment ratios					
Primary	% school age pop.	99	99	104	103
Male	"	..	99	104	103
Female	"	..	100	104	103
Mortality					
Infant mortality	per thou. live births	16.1	10.5	8.6	7.0
Under 5 mortality	"	..	..	10.8	10.0
Immunization					
Measles	% age group	..	96.0	98.0	82.4
DPT	"	..	37.0	97.0	90.1
Child malnutrition (under-5)	"	..	..	..	..
Life expectancy					
Total	years	73	75	77	77
Female advantage	"	7.8	7.2	6.6	6.4
Total fertility rate	births per woman	1.8	1.8	2.1	1.7
Maternal mortality rate	per 100,000 live births	..	9	..	..
Supplementary Poverty Indicators					
Expenditures on social security	% of total gov't exp.	30.6	24.1	20.6	..
Social security coverage	% econ. active pop.	..	..	..	..
Access to safe water: total	% of pop.	..	..	..	..
Urban	"	..	..	..	..
Rural	"	..	..	..	..
Access to health care	"	..	100.0	..	..

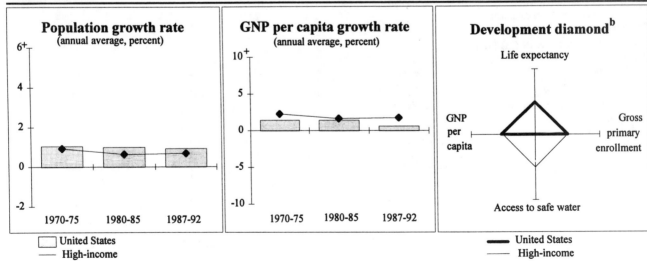

Population growth rate (annual average, percent)

GNP per capita growth rate (annual average, percent)

Development diamond[b]

☐ United States
— High-income

— United States
— High-income

a. See the technical notes, p.389.   b. The development diamond, based on four key indicators, shows the average level of development in the country compared with its income group. See the introduction.

United States

<table>
<tr><td rowspan="3">Indicator</td><td rowspan="3">Unit of
measure</td><td colspan="2">Latest single year</td><td rowspan="3">Most
recent
estimate
1987-92</td><td colspan="1">Same region/income group</td></tr>
<tr><td>1970-75</td><td>1980-85</td><td>High-
income</td></tr>
<tr></tr>
<tr><td colspan="6">Resources and Expenditures</td></tr>
<tr><td colspan="6">HUMAN RESOURCES</td></tr>
<tr><td>Population (mre=1992)</td><td>thousands</td><td>215,973</td><td>239,279</td><td>255,414</td><td>828,221</td></tr>
<tr><td>Age dependency ratio</td><td>ratio</td><td>0.55</td><td>0.51</td><td>0.53</td><td>0.50</td></tr>
<tr><td>Urban</td><td>% of pop.</td><td>73.7</td><td>74.5</td><td>75.6</td><td>78.1</td></tr>
<tr><td>Population growth rate</td><td>annual %</td><td>1.0</td><td>1.0</td><td>1.1</td><td>0.7</td></tr>
<tr><td>Urban</td><td>"</td><td>1.0</td><td>1.2</td><td>1.3</td><td>0.9</td></tr>
<tr><td>Labor force (15-64)</td><td>thousands</td><td>97,852</td><td>116,800</td><td>123,883</td><td>390,033</td></tr>
<tr><td>Agriculture</td><td>% of labor force</td><td>4</td><td>3</td><td>..</td><td>..</td></tr>
<tr><td>Industry</td><td>"</td><td>32</td><td>31</td><td>..</td><td>..</td></tr>
<tr><td>Female</td><td>"</td><td>39</td><td>42</td><td>41</td><td>38</td></tr>
<tr><td>Females per 100 males</td><td></td><td></td><td></td><td></td><td></td></tr>
<tr><td>Urban</td><td>number</td><td>107</td><td>105</td><td>..</td><td>..</td></tr>
<tr><td>Rural</td><td>"</td><td>101</td><td>99</td><td>..</td><td>..</td></tr>
<tr><td colspan="6">NATURAL RESOURCES</td></tr>
<tr><td>Area</td><td>thou. sq. km</td><td>9,372.61</td><td>9,372.61</td><td>9,372.61</td><td>31,709.00</td></tr>
<tr><td>Density</td><td>pop. per sq. km</td><td>23.0</td><td>25.5</td><td>27.0</td><td>24.5</td></tr>
<tr><td>Agricultural land</td><td>% of land area</td><td>47.1</td><td>47.1</td><td>46.6</td><td>42.7</td></tr>
<tr><td>Change in agricultural land</td><td>annual %</td><td>0.0</td><td>0.0</td><td>0.0</td><td>-0.2</td></tr>
<tr><td>Agricultural land under irrigation</td><td>%</td><td>3.9</td><td>4.6</td><td>4.4</td><td>16.1</td></tr>
<tr><td>Forests and woodland</td><td>thou. sq. km</td><td>3,000</td><td>2,904</td><td>2,868</td><td>..</td></tr>
<tr><td>Deforestation (net)</td><td>annual %</td><td>..</td><td>..</td><td>0.1</td><td>..</td></tr>
<tr><td colspan="6">INCOME</td></tr>
<tr><td>Household income</td><td></td><td></td><td></td><td></td><td></td></tr>
<tr><td>Share of top 20% of households</td><td>% of income</td><td>43</td><td>42</td><td>..</td><td>..</td></tr>
<tr><td>Share of bottom 40% of households</td><td>"</td><td>15</td><td>16</td><td>..</td><td>..</td></tr>
<tr><td>Share of bottom 20% of households</td><td>"</td><td>5</td><td>5</td><td>..</td><td>..</td></tr>
<tr><td colspan="6">EXPENDITURE</td></tr>
<tr><td>Food</td><td>% of GDP</td><td>9.2</td><td>6.8</td><td>..</td><td>..</td></tr>
<tr><td>Staples</td><td>"</td><td>1.4</td><td>1.2</td><td>..</td><td>..</td></tr>
<tr><td>Meat, fish, milk, cheese, eggs</td><td>"</td><td>3.8</td><td>3.2</td><td>..</td><td>..</td></tr>
<tr><td>Cereal imports</td><td>thou. metric tonnes</td><td>401</td><td>1,001</td><td>3,718</td><td>70,626</td></tr>
<tr><td>Food aid in cereals</td><td>"</td><td>..</td><td>..</td><td>..</td><td>2</td></tr>
<tr><td>Food production per capita</td><td>1987 = 100</td><td>93</td><td>103</td><td>103</td><td>101</td></tr>
<tr><td>Fertilizer consumption</td><td>kg/ha</td><td>44.0</td><td>41.3</td><td>43.9</td><td>162.1</td></tr>
<tr><td>Share of agriculture in GDP</td><td>% of GDP</td><td>3.3</td><td>2.1</td><td>2.0</td><td>2.4</td></tr>
<tr><td>Housing</td><td>% of GDP</td><td>12.6</td><td>12.7</td><td>..</td><td>..</td></tr>
<tr><td>Average household size</td><td>persons per household</td><td>3.1</td><td>2.7</td><td>..</td><td>..</td></tr>
<tr><td>Urban</td><td>"</td><td>3.1</td><td>..</td><td>..</td><td>..</td></tr>
<tr><td>Fixed investment: housing</td><td>% of GDP</td><td>3.3</td><td>4.1</td><td>..</td><td>..</td></tr>
<tr><td>Fuel and power</td><td>% of GDP</td><td>2.6</td><td>2.6</td><td>..</td><td>..</td></tr>
<tr><td>Energy consumption per capita</td><td>kg of oil equiv.</td><td>7,625</td><td>7,405</td><td>7,662</td><td>5,101</td></tr>
<tr><td>Households with electricity</td><td></td><td></td><td></td><td></td><td></td></tr>
<tr><td>Urban</td><td>% of households</td><td>..</td><td>..</td><td>..</td><td>..</td></tr>
<tr><td>Rural</td><td>"</td><td>..</td><td>..</td><td>..</td><td>..</td></tr>
<tr><td>Transport and communication</td><td>% of GDP</td><td>9.6</td><td>10.0</td><td>..</td><td>..</td></tr>
<tr><td>Fixed investment: transport equipment</td><td>"</td><td>1.7</td><td>2.3</td><td>..</td><td>..</td></tr>
<tr><td>Total road length</td><td>thou. km</td><td>6,206</td><td>6,242</td><td>6,243</td><td>..</td></tr>
<tr><td colspan="6">INVESTMENT IN HUMAN CAPITAL</td></tr>
<tr><td colspan="6">Health</td></tr>
<tr><td>Population per physician</td><td>persons</td><td>634</td><td>473</td><td>421</td><td>..</td></tr>
<tr><td>Population per nurse</td><td>"</td><td>158</td><td>74</td><td>..</td><td>..</td></tr>
<tr><td>Population per hospital bed</td><td>"</td><td>127</td><td>171</td><td>194</td><td>144</td></tr>
<tr><td>Oral rehydration therapy (under-5)</td><td>% of cases</td><td>..</td><td>..</td><td>..</td><td>..</td></tr>
<tr><td colspan="6">Education</td></tr>
<tr><td>Gross enrollment ratio</td><td></td><td></td><td></td><td></td><td></td></tr>
<tr><td>Secondary</td><td>% of school-age pop.</td><td>..</td><td>97</td><td>90</td><td>92</td></tr>
<tr><td>Female</td><td>"</td><td>..</td><td>97</td><td>90</td><td>94</td></tr>
<tr><td>Pupil-teacher ratio: primary</td><td>pupils per teacher</td><td>23</td><td>20</td><td>..</td><td>18</td></tr>
<tr><td>Pupil-teacher ratio: secondary</td><td>"</td><td>..</td><td>13</td><td>..</td><td>..</td></tr>
<tr><td>Pupils reaching grade 4</td><td>% of cohort</td><td>95</td><td>93</td><td>..</td><td>..</td></tr>
<tr><td>Repeater rate: primary</td><td>% of total enroll</td><td>..</td><td>..</td><td>..</td><td>..</td></tr>
<tr><td>Illiteracy</td><td>% of pop. (age 15+)</td><td>..</td><td>..</td><td>†</td><td>..</td></tr>
<tr><td>Female</td><td>% of fem. (age 15+)</td><td>..</td><td>..</td><td>†</td><td>..</td></tr>
<tr><td>Newspaper circulation</td><td>per thou. pop.</td><td>283</td><td>263</td><td>249</td><td>..</td></tr>
</table>

World Bank International Economics Department, April 1994

363

Uruguay

Indicator	Unit of measure	Latest single year 1970-75	Latest single year 1980-85	Most recent estimate 1987-92	Same region/income group Latin America Caribbean	Same region/income group Upper-middle-income	Next higher income group
Priority Poverty Indicators							
POVERTY							
Upper poverty line	local curr.	..	..	..	..	..	..
Headcount index	% of pop.	..	..	..	..	..	..
Lower poverty line	local curr.	..	..	..	..	..	..
Headcount index	% of pop.	..	..	..	..	..	..
GNP per capita	US$	1,300	1,550	3,340	2,690	3,870	21,960
SHORT TERM INCOME INDICATORS							
Unskilled urban wages	local curr.	..	..	..	..	..	..
Unskilled rural wages	"	..	..	..	..	..	..
Rural terms of trade	"	..	..	..	..	..	..
Consumer price index	1987=100	1	35	2,116	..	..	..
Lower income	"	..	..	..	..	..	..
Food[a]	"	..	33	1,166	..	..	..
Urban	"	..	..	..	..	..	..
Rural	"	..	..	..	..	..	..
SOCIAL INDICATORS							
Public expenditure on basic social services	% of GDP	..	..	..	..	..	..
Gross enrollment ratios							
Primary	% school age pop.	107	107	110	106	107	103
Male	"	107	107	109	..	..	103
Female	"	106	106	107	..	..	103
Mortality							
Infant mortality	per thou. live births	46.0	33.0	20.0	44.0	40.0	7.0
Under 5 mortality	"	..	..	24.0	56.0	51.0	10.0
Immunization							
Measles	% age group	..	17.0	82.0	78.9	82.0	82.4
DPT	"	..	57.0	88.0	73.8	73.8	90.1
Child malnutrition (under-5)	"	..	..	7.4	10.5	..	..
Life expectancy							
Total	years	69	71	72	68	69	77
Female advantage	"	6.6	6.5	6.4	5.6	6.3	6.4
Total fertility rate	births per woman	3.0	2.6	2.3	3.0	2.9	1.7
Maternal mortality rate	per 100,000 live births	..	56	36	..	..	..
Supplementary Poverty Indicators							
Expenditures on social security	% of total gov't exp.	43.9	42.0	50.2	..	..	..
Social security coverage	% econ. active pop.	..	..	73.0	..	..	..
Access to safe water: total	% of pop.	98.0	..	84.0	80.3	85.6	..
Urban	"	100.0	..	95.0	91.0	94.3	..
Rural	"	87.0	..	100.0	64.3	73.0	..
Access to health care	"	..	..	..	..	..	..

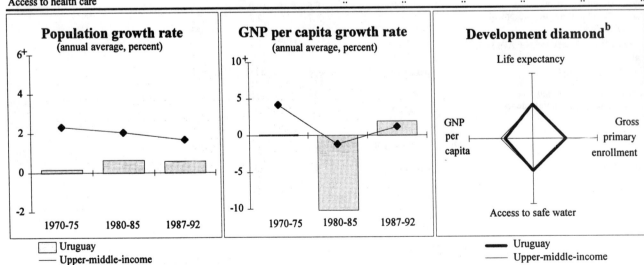

Population growth rate
(annual average, percent)

GNP per capita growth rate
(annual average, percent)

Development diamond[b]

Life expectancy

GNP per capita — Gross primary enrollment

Access to safe water

□ Uruguay
— Upper-middle-income

━━ Uruguay
— Upper-middle-income

a. See the technical notes, p.389. b. The development diamond, based on four key indicators, shows the average level of development in the country compared with its income group. See the introduction.

364

Uruguay

Indicator	Unit of measure	Latest single year 1970-75	Latest single year 1980-85	Most recent estimate 1987-92	Same region/income group Latin America Caribbean	Same region/income group Upper-middle-income	Next higher income group
Resources and Expenditures							
HUMAN RESOURCES							
Population (mre=1992)	thousands	2,829	3,008	3,130	453,294	477,960	828,221
Age dependency ratio	ratio	0.60	0.61	0.59	0.67	0.64	0.50
Urban	% of pop.	83.1	87.2	89.5	72.9	71.7	78.1
Population growth rate	annual %	0.3	0.6	0.6	1.7	1.6	0.7
Urban	"	0.5	1.1	0.9	2.6	2.5	0.9
Labor force (15-64)	thousands	1,106	1,171	1,240	166,091	181,414	390,033
Agriculture	% of labor force	17	16	..	..	..	..
Industry	"	29	29	..	..	..	..
Female	"	28	30	31	27	29	38
Females per 100 males							
Urban	number	112	..	..	..	..	..
Rural	"	70	..	..	..	..	..
NATURAL RESOURCES							
Area	thou. sq. km	177.41	177.41	177.41	20,507.48	21,836.02	31,709.00
Density	pop. per sq. km	16.0	17.0	17.5	21.7	21.5	24.5
Agricultural land	% of land area	86.2	85.2	84.8	40.2	41.7	42.7
Change in agricultural land	annual %	0.0	-0.2	0.0	0.5	0.3	-0.2
Agricultural land under irrigation	%	0.4	0.7	0.9	3.2	9.3	16.1
Forests and woodland	thou. sq. km	6	7	7	..	..	..
Deforestation (net)	annual %	..	..	..	..	..	..
INCOME							
Household income							
Share of top 20% of households	% of income	..	46	48	..	..	..
Share of bottom 40% of households	"	..	16	15	..	..	..
Share of bottom 20% of households	"	..	6	6	..	..	..
EXPENDITURE							
Food	% of GDP	25.6	24.4	..	..	..	..
Staples	"	5.5	5.3	..	..	..	..
Meat, fish, milk, cheese, eggs	"	10.4	9.9	..	..	..	..
Cereal imports	thou. metric tonnes	4	30	311	25,032	49,174	70,626
Food aid in cereals	"	6	7	20	1,779	282	2
Food production per capita	1987 = 100	103	102	119	104	109	101
Fertilizer consumption	kg/ha	3.2	4.0	5.3	15.5	68.8	162.1
Share of agriculture in GDP	% of GDP	15.2	13.6	10.8	8.9	8.1	2.4
Housing	% of GDP	8.8	8.4	..	..	..	..
Average household size	persons per household	3.4	..	..	..	..	..
Urban	"	3.4	..	..	..	..	..
Fixed investment: housing	% of GDP	3.1	5.2	..	..	..	..
Fuel and power	% of GDP	3.4	3.1	..	..	..	..
Energy consumption per capita	kg of oil equiv.	736	505	642	912	1,649	5,101
Households with electricity							
Urban	% of households	..	..	..	..	..	..
Rural	"	..	..	..	..	..	..
Transport and communication	% of GDP	7.8	6.8	..	..	..	..
Fixed investment: transport equipment	"	1.0	1.0	..	..	..	..
Total road length	thou. km	25	52	53	..	..	..
INVESTMENT IN HUMAN CAPITAL							
Health							
Population per physician	persons	900	513	..	..	..	..
Population per nurse	"	..	..	..	..	..	..
Population per hospital bed	"	200	308	221	508	385	144
Oral rehydration therapy (under-5)	% of cases	..	..	96	62	54	..
Education							
Gross enrollment ratio							
Secondary	% of school-age pop.	60	72	84	47	53	92
Female	"	64	62	..	..	..	94
Pupil-teacher ratio: primary	pupils per teacher	24	25	22	25	25	18
Pupil-teacher ratio: secondary	"	..	..	..	..	..	..
Pupils reaching grade 4	% of cohort	96	96	97	..	71	..
Repeater rate: primary	% of total enroll	14	11	9	14	11	..
Illiteracy	% of pop. (age 15+)	6	5	4	15	14	..
Female	% of fem. (age 15+)	..	5	4	17	17	..
Newspaper circulation	per thou. pop.	225	182	233	99	117	..

World Bank International Economics Department, April 1994

Uzbekistan

Priority Poverty Indicators

Indicator	Unit of measure	Latest single year 1970-75	Latest single year 1980-85	Most recent estimate 1987-92	Same region/income group Europe & Central Asia	Same region/income group Lower-middle-income	Next higher income group
POVERTY							
Upper poverty line	local curr.	..	..	..	..	..	..
Headcount index	% of pop.	..	..	57	..	..	..
Lower poverty line	local curr.	..	..	..	..	..	..
Headcount index	% of pop.	..	..	34	..	..	..
GNP per capita	US$	..	..	850	..	..	3,870
SHORT TERM INCOME INDICATORS							
Unskilled urban wages	local curr.	..	..	..	..	..	..
Unskilled rural wages	"	..	..	..	..	..	..
Rural terms of trade	"	..	..	..	..	..	..
Consumer price index	1987=100	..	..	..	..	..	..
Lower income	"	..	..	..	..	..	..
Food[a]	"	..	..	..	..	..	..
Urban	"	..	..	..	..	..	..
Rural	"	..	..	..	..	..	..
SOCIAL INDICATORS							
Public expenditure on basic social services	% of GDP	..	..	8.0	..	..	..
Gross enrollment ratios							
Primary	% school age pop.	..	..	..	..	..	107
Male	"	..	..	..	..	..	..
Female	"	..	..	..	..	..	..
Mortality							
Infant mortality	per thou. live births	..	55.0	42.0	30.0	45.0	40.0
Under 5 mortality	"	..	..	53.1	38.0	59.0	51.0
Immunization							
Measles	% age group	..	..	..	..	..	82.0
DPT	"	..	..	..	..	..	73.8
Child malnutrition (under-5)	"	..	..	..	..	..	..
Life expectancy							
Total	years	..	68	69	70	68	69
Female advantage	"	..	5.9	6.3	8.6	6.4	6.3
Total fertility rate	births per woman	5.7	4.7	4.1	2.2	3.1	2.9
Maternal mortality rate	per 100,000 live births	..	46	43	58	..	..

Supplementary Poverty Indicators

Indicator	Unit of measure	1970-75	1980-85	1987-92	Europe & Central Asia	Lower-middle-income	Next higher income group
Expenditures on social security	% of total gov't exp.	..	..	..	..	..	..
Social security coverage	% econ. active pop.	..	..	..	..	..	..
Access to safe water: total	% of pop.	..	..	..	..	..	85.6
Urban	"	..	..	..	..	..	94.3
Rural	"	..	..	..	..	..	73.0
Access to health care	"	..	..	..	..	..	..

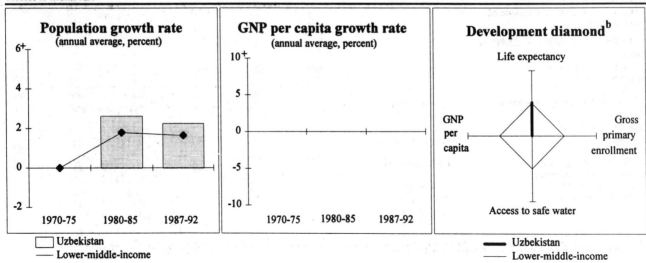

Population growth rate (annual average, percent)

GNP per capita growth rate (annual average, percent)

Development diamond[b]
Life expectancy / GNP per capita / Gross primary enrollment / Access to safe water

☐ Uzbekistan
— Lower-middle-income

▬ Uzbekistan
— Lower-middle-income

a. See the technical notes, p.389.   b. The development diamond, based on four key indicators, shows the average level of development in the country compared with its income group. See the introduction.

366

Uzbekistan

Indicator	Unit of measure	Latest single year 1970-75	Latest single year 1980-85	Most recent estimate 1987-92	Same region/income group Europe & Central Asia	Same region/income group Lower-middle-income	Next higher income group
Resources and Expenditures							
HUMAN RESOURCES							
Population (mre=1992)	thousands	..	18,174	21,458	495,241	942,547	477,960
Age dependency ratio	ratio	..	..	0.85	0.56	0.66	0.64
Urban	% of pop.	..	..	41.0	63.3	57.0	71.7
Population growth rate	annual %	..	2.7	2.4	0.5	1.4	1.6
Urban	"	..	..	..	..	4.8	2.5
Labor force (15-64)	thousands	..	..	..	..	..	..
Agriculture	% of labor force	..	..	..	..	..	181,414
Industry	"	..	..	..	..	..	..
Female	"	..	..	..	..	..	..
Females per 100 males		..	..	..	46	36	29
Urban	number	..	..	..	..	..	..
Rural	"	..	..	..	..	..	..
NATURAL RESOURCES							
Area	thou. sq. km	..	..	447.40	24,165.06	40,697.37	21,836.02
Density	pop. per sq. km	..	..	46.8	20.4	22.8	21.5
Agricultural land	% of land area	..	..	..	..	..	41.7
Change in agricultural land	annual %	..	..	..	..	..	0.3
Agricultural land under irrigation	%	..	..	..	..	..	9.3
Forests and woodland	thou. sq. km	..	..	..	..	..	..
Deforestation (net)	annual %	..	..	..	..	..	..
INCOME							
Household income							
Share of top 20% of households	% of income	..	..	..	..	..	..
Share of bottom 40% of households	"	..	..	..	..	..	..
Share of bottom 20% of households	"	..	..	..	..	..	..
EXPENDITURE							
Food	% of GDP	..	..	19.8	..	..	..
Staples	"	..	..	3.6	..	..	..
Meat, fish, milk, cheese, eggs	"	..	..	8.9	..	..	..
Cereal imports	thou. metric tonnes	..	..	2,600	45,972	74,924	49,174
Food aid in cereals	"	..	..	..	1,639	4,054	282
Food production per capita	1987 = 100	..	..	..	..	..	109
Fertilizer consumption	kg/ha	..	..	..	..	..	68.8
Share of agriculture in GDP	% of GDP	..	28.0	33.1	..	..	8.1
Housing	% of GDP	..	..	4.7	..	..	..
Average household size	persons per household	..	..	5.5	..	..	..
Urban	"	..	..	..	..	..	..
Fixed investment: housing	% of GDP	..	..	4.9	..	..	..
Fuel and power	% of GDP	..	..	1.0	..	..	..
Energy consumption per capita	kg of oil equiv.	..	..	..	3,190	1,882	1,649
Households with electricity							
Urban	% of households	..	..	..	..	..	..
Rural	"	..	..	..	..	..	..
Transport and communication	% of GDP	..	..	6.2	..	..	..
Fixed investment: transport equipment	"	..	..	10.3	..	..	..
Total road length	thou. km	..	63	71	..	..	..
INVESTMENT IN HUMAN CAPITAL							
Health							
Population per physician	persons	..	..	285	378	..	..
Population per nurse	"	..	..	..	..	..	..
Population per hospital bed	"	..	..	83	134	516	385
Oral rehydration therapy (under-5)	% of cases	..	..	..	..	..	54
Education							
Gross enrollment ratio							
Secondary	% of school-age pop.	..	..	..	..	..	53
Female	"	..	..	..	..	..	..
Pupil-teacher ratio: primary	pupils per teacher	..	..	..	..	26	25
Pupil-teacher ratio: secondary	"	..	..	..	..	..	..
Pupils reaching grade 4	% of cohort	..	..	..	..	..	71
Repeater rate: primary	% of total enroll	..	..	..	..	..	11
Illiteracy	% of pop. (age 15+)	..	..	..	..	..	14
Female	% of fem. (age 15+)	..	..	..	..	..	17
Newspaper circulation	per thou. pop.	..	..	..	..	100	117

World Bank International Economics Department, April 1994

Vanuatu

Indicator	Unit of measure	Latest single year 1970-75	Latest single year 1980-85	Most recent estimate 1987-92	Same region/income group East Asia	Same region/income group Lower-middle-income	Next higher income group
Priority Poverty Indicators							
POVERTY							
Upper poverty line	local curr.	..	..	..	..	..	..
Headcount index	% of pop.	..	..	..	12	..	..
Lower poverty line	local curr.	..	..	..	..	..	..
Headcount index	% of pop.	..	..	..	9	..	..
GNP per capita	US$	..	980	1,210	760	..	3,870
SHORT TERM INCOME INDICATORS							
Unskilled urban wages	local curr.	..	..	..	..	..	..
Unskilled rural wages	"	..	..	..	..	..	..
Rural terms of trade	"	..	..	..	..	..	..
Consumer price index	1987=100	..	82	136	..	..	..
Lower income	"	..	..	..	..	..	..
Food[a]	"	..	78	123	..	..	..
Urban	"	..	..	..	..	..	..
Rural	"	..	..	..	..	..	..
SOCIAL INDICATORS							
Public expenditure on basic social services	% of GDP	..	..	..	..	..	..
Gross enrollment ratios							
Primary	% school age pop.	..	..	..	121	..	107
Male	"	..	..	..	126	..	..
Female	"	..	..	..	117	..	..
Mortality							
Infant mortality	per thou. live births	..	94.0	45.0	39.0	45.0	40.0
Under 5 mortality	"	..	..	57.6	49.0	59.0	51.0
Immunization							
Measles	% age group	..	25.0	46.0	88.4	..	82.0
DPT	"	..	28.0	61.0	89.5	..	73.8
Child malnutrition (under-5)	"	..	19.7	..	24.7	..	..
Life expectancy							
Total	years	..	55	63	68	68	69
Female advantage	"	..	-2.5	2.5	3.6	6.4	6.3
Total fertility rate	births per woman	..	6.2	5.3	2.4	3.1	2.9
Maternal mortality rate	per 100,000 live births	..	..	..	114	..	..
Supplementary Poverty Indicators							
Expenditures on social security	% of total gov't exp.	..	1.1	0.0	..	..	..
Social security coverage	% econ. active pop.	..	..	..	..	..	..
Access to safe water: total	% of pop.	..	61.0	71.0	72.0	..	85.6
Urban	"	..	95.0	100.0	83.4	..	94.3
Rural	"	..	54.0	64.0	60.2	..	73.0
Access to health care	"	..	80.0	..	..	..	..

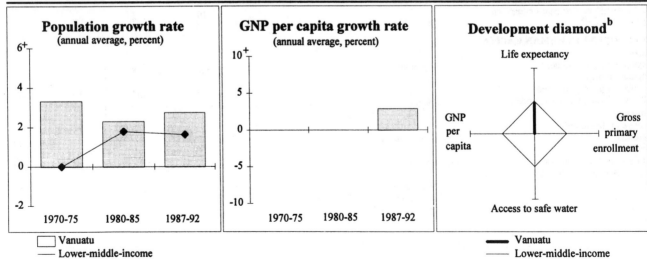

Population growth rate (annual average, percent)

GNP per capita growth rate (annual average, percent)

Development diamond[b]
Life expectancy / GNP per capita / Gross primary enrollment / Access to safe water

Vanuatu
Lower-middle-income

a. See the technical notes, p.389.   b. The development diamond, based on four key indicators, shows the average level of development in the country compared with its income group. See the introduction.

Vanuatu

Indicator	Unit of measure	Latest single year 1970-75	1980-85	Most recent estimate 1987-92	East Asia	Lower-middle-income	Next higher income group
Resources and Expenditures							
HUMAN RESOURCES							
Population (mre=1992)	thousands	98	129	156	1,688,909	942,547	477,960
Age dependency ratio	ratio	..	0.93	0.88	0.55	0.66	0.64
Urban	% of pop.	16.9	19.1	20.3	29.4	57.0	71.7
Population growth rate	annual %	3.1	1.6	2.6	1.4	1.4	1.6
Urban	"	7.2	2.9	4.6	2.9	4.8	2.5
Labor force (15-64)	thousands	..	..	..	928,465	..	181,414
Agriculture	% of labor force	..	..	..	..	..	..
Industry	"	..	..	..	..	..	..
Female	"	..	..	..	41	36	29
Females per 100 males							
Urban	number	..	..	..	..	..	..
Rural	"	..	..	..	..	..	..
NATURAL RESOURCES							
Area	thou. sq. km	12.19	12.19	12.19	16,367.18	40,697.37	21,836.02
Density	pop. per sq. km	8.0	10.6	12.5	101.8	22.8	21.5
Agricultural land	% of land area	10.3	14.0	13.9	44.5	..	41.7
Change in agricultural land	annual %	5.0	0.0	0.0	0.1	..	0.3
Agricultural land under irrigation	%	..	..	..	14.5	..	9.3
Forests and woodland	thou. sq. km	9	9	9	..	..	..
Deforestation (net)	annual %	..	..	..	..	..	..
INCOME							
Household income							
Share of top 20% of households	% of income	..	..	..	42	..	..
Share of bottom 40% of households	"	..	..	..	18	..	..
Share of bottom 20% of households	"	..	..	..	7	..	..
EXPENDITURE							
Food	% of GDP	..	..	..	..	..	..
Staples	"	..	..	..	..	..	..
Meat, fish, milk, cheese, eggs	"	..	..	..	..	..	..
Cereal imports	thou. metric tonnes	6	11	11	33,591	74,924	49,174
Food aid in cereals	"	..	..	0	581	4,054	282
Food production per capita	1987 = 100	89	92	83	133	..	109
Fertilizer consumption	kg/ha	..	..	..	75.1	..	68.8
Share of agriculture in GDP	% of GDP	..	29.5	20.0	21.5	..	8.1
Housing	% of GDP	..	..	..	..	..	..
Average household size	persons per household	..	..	..	..	..	..
Urban	"	..	..	..	..	..	..
Fixed investment: housing	% of GDP	..	..	..	..	..	..
Fuel and power	% of GDP	..	..	..	..	..	..
Energy consumption per capita	kg of oil equiv.	367	302	288	593	1,882	1,649
Households with electricity							
Urban	% of households	..	..	..	..	..	..
Rural	"	..	..	..	..	..	..
Transport and communication	% of GDP	..	..	..	..	..	..
Fixed investment: transport equipment	"	..	..	..	..	..	..
Total road length	thou. km	..	..	..	..	..	..
INVESTMENT IN HUMAN CAPITAL							
Health							
Population per physician	persons	3,320	5,318	7,944	..	..	..
Population per nurse	"	279	461	..	..	..	..
Population per hospital bed	"	93	162	..	553	516	385
Oral rehydration therapy (under-5)	% of cases	..	..	66	51	..	54
Education							
Gross enrollment ratio							
Secondary	% of school-age pop.	..	..	..	53	..	53
Female	"	..	..	..	47	..	..
Pupil-teacher ratio: primary	pupils per teacher	24	24	29	23	26	25
Pupil-teacher ratio: secondary	"	15	15	18	16	..	..
Pupils reaching grade 4	% of cohort	83	85	..	89	..	71
Repeater rate: primary	% of total enroll	..	..	..	6	..	11
Illiteracy	% of pop. (age 15+)	..	..	..	24	..	14
Female	% of fem. (age 15+)	..	..	..	34	..	17
Newspaper circulation	per thou. pop.	..	..	..	..	100	117

World Bank International Economics Department, April 1994

Venezuela

Indicator	Unit of measure	Latest single year 1970-75	Latest single year 1980-85	Most recent estimate 1987-92	Same region/income group Latin America Caribbean	Same region/income group Upper-middle-income	Next higher income group
Priority Poverty Indicators							
POVERTY							
Upper poverty line	local curr.	..	..	..	..	..	..
Headcount index	% of pop.	..	24	31	..	..	..
Lower poverty line	local curr.	..	..	..	..	..	..
Headcount index	% of pop.	..	11	22	..	..	..
GNP per capita	US$	2,370	3,910	2,910	2,690	3,870	21,960
SHORT TERM INCOME INDICATORS							
Unskilled urban wages	local curr.	..	..	..	..	..	..
Unskilled rural wages	"	..	..	..	..	..	..
Rural terms of trade	"	..	..	..	..	..	..
Consumer price index	1987=100	24	70	593	..	..	..
Lower income	"	..	..	..	..	..	..
Food[a]	"	10	59	466	..	..	..
Urban	"	..	..	..	..	..	..
Rural	"	..	..	..	..	..	..
SOCIAL INDICATORS							
Public expenditure on basic social services	% of GDP	..	7.8	9.6	..	..	..
Gross enrollment ratios							
Primary	% school age pop.	97	108	99	106	107	103
Male	"	97	109	98	..	..	103
Female	"	97	108	100	..	..	103
Mortality							
Infant mortality	per thou. live births	49.0	39.0	33.0	44.0	40.0	7.0
Under 5 mortality	"	..	..	39.2	56.0	51.0	10.0
Immunization							
Measles	% age group	..	25.0	54.0	78.9	82.0	82.4
DPT	"	..	27.0	54.0	73.8	73.8	90.1
Child malnutrition (under-5)	"	..	5.0	5.9	10.5	..	..
Life expectancy							
Total	years	66	69	70	68	69	77
Female advantage	"	5.6	6.1	6.2	5.6	6.3	6.4
Total fertility rate	births per woman	5.0	3.9	3.6	3.0	2.9	1.7
Maternal mortality rate	per 100,000 live births	..	65	200	..	..	..
Supplementary Poverty Indicators							
Expenditures on social security	% of total gov't exp.	..	5.7	8.3	..	..	..
Social security coverage	% econ. active pop.	..	..	54.3	..	..	..
Access to safe water: total	% of pop.	75.0	80.0	89.0	80.3	85.6	..
Urban	"	92.0	80.0	89.0	91.0	94.3	..
Rural	"	38.0	80.0	89.0	64.3	73.0	..
Access to health care	"	..	..	..	..	..	..

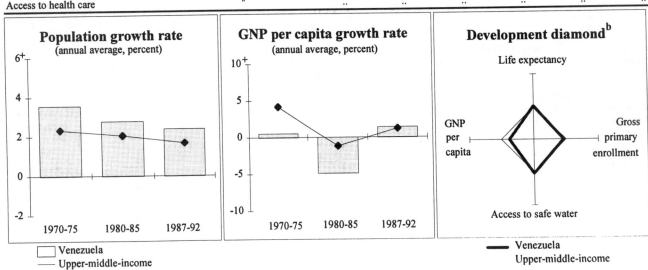

Population growth rate (annual average, percent)

GNP per capita growth rate (annual average, percent)

Development diamond[b]

Life expectancy — GNP per capita — Gross primary enrollment — Access to safe water

— Venezuela
Upper-middle-income

a. See the technical notes, p.389.   b. The development diamond, based on four key indicators, shows the average level of development in the country compared with its income group. See the introduction.

Venezuela

Indicator	Unit of measure	Latest single year 1970-75	Latest single year 1980-85	Most recent estimate 1987-92	Same region/income group Latin America Caribbean	Same region/income group Upper-middle-income	Next higher income group
Resources and Expenditures							
HUMAN RESOURCES							
Population (mre=1992)	thousands	12,665	17,077	20,249	453,294	477,960	828,221
Age dependency ratio	ratio	0.87	0.75	0.71	0.67	0.64	0.50
Urban	% of pop.	77.8	87.3	91.5	72.9	71.7	78.1
Population growth rate	annual %	3.7	2.7	2.3	1.7	1.6	0.7
Urban	"	5.1	3.6	2.8	2.6	2.5	0.9
Labor force (15-64)	thousands	3,909	5,871	7,293	166,091	181,414	390,033
Agriculture	% of labor force	21	16	..	..	..	..
Industry	"	27	28	..	..	..	..
Female	"	23	27	28	27	29	38
Females per 100 males							
Urban	number	..	103	103	..	..	..
Rural	"	..	87	86	..	..	..
NATURAL RESOURCES							
Area	thou. sq. km	912.05	912.05	912.05	20,507.48	21,836.02	31,709.00
Density	pop. per sq. km	13.9	18.7	21.7	21.7	21.5	24.5
Agricultural land	% of land area	23.1	24.1	24.6	40.2	41.7	42.7
Change in agricultural land	annual %	0.3	0.3	0.3	0.5	0.3	-0.2
Agricultural land under irrigation	%	0.4	0.8	0.9	3.2	9.3	16.1
Forests and woodland	thou. sq. km	345	316	299	..	..	..
Deforestation (net)	annual %	..	..	1.2	..	..	..
INCOME							
Household income							
Share of top 20% of households	% of income	54	..	50	..	..	..
Share of bottom 40% of households	"	10	..	14	..	..	..
Share of bottom 20% of households	"	3	..	5	..	..	..
EXPENDITURE							
Food	% of GDP	19.2	26.0	..	..	..	..
Staples	"	..	4.3	..	..	..	..
Meat, fish, milk, cheese, eggs	"	..	4.9	..	..	..	..
Cereal imports	thou. metric tonnes	1,299	2,795	1,468	25,032	49,174	70,626
Food aid in cereals	"	..	..	..	1,779	282	2
Food production per capita	1987 = 100	101	97	97	104	109	101
Fertilizer consumption	kg/ha	6.9	22.5	18.0	15.5	68.8	162.1
Share of agriculture in GDP	% of GDP	5.0	5.8	5.5	8.7	8.1	2.4
Housing	% of GDP	4.0	5.2	..	..	..	..
Average household size	persons per household	6.0	5.4	..	..	..	..
Urban	"	..	5.4	..	..	..	..
Fixed investment: housing	% of GDP	5.9	1.9	..	..	..	..
Fuel and power	% of GDP	..	..	..	..	..	..
Energy consumption per capita	kg of oil equiv.	2,238	2,172	2,296	912	1,649	5,101
Households with electricity							
Urban	% of households	..	..	..	..	..	..
Rural	"	..	..	..	..	..	..
Transport and communication	% of GDP	6.1	6.7	..	..	..	..
Fixed investment: transport equipment	"	3.1	2.8	..	..	..	..
Total road length	thou. km	62	63	78	..	..	..
INVESTMENT IN HUMAN CAPITAL							
Health							
Population per physician	persons	1,100	833	633	..	..	..
Population per nurse	"	443	313	329	..	..	..
Population per hospital bed	"	3,000	370	385	508	385	144
Oral rehydration therapy (under-5)	% of cases	..	..	80	62	54	..
Education							
Gross enrolment ratio							
Secondary	% of school-age pop.	43	45	34	47	53	92
Female	"	45	50	40	..	..	94
Pupil-teacher ratio: primary	pupils per teacher	30	33	23	25	25	18
Pupil-teacher ratio: secondary	"	20	..	..	..	..	..
Pupils reaching grade 4	% of cohort	72	83	79	..	71	..
Repeater rate: primary	% of total enroll	3	7	8	14	11	..
Illiteracy	% of pop. (age 15+)	24	14	7	15	14	..
Female	% of fem. (age 15+)	..	12	14	17	17	..
Newspaper circulation	per thou. pop.	84	165	145	99	117	..

World Bank International Economics Department, April 1994

Viet Nam

Indicator	Unit of measure	Latest single year 1970-75	Latest single year 1980-85	Most recent estimate 1987-92	Same region/income group East Asia	Same region/income group Low-income	Next higher income group
Priority Poverty Indicators							
POVERTY							
Upper poverty line	local curr.	..	..	..	..	..	..
Headcount index	% of pop.	..	..	..	12	19	..
Lower poverty line	local curr.	..	..	..	..	..	..
Headcount index	% of pop.	..	..	..	9	..	..
GNP per capita	US$	..	..	..	760	390	..
SHORT TERM INCOME INDICATORS							
Unskilled urban wages	local curr.	..	..	..	..	..	..
Unskilled rural wages	"	..	..	..	..	..	..
Rural terms of trade	"	..	..	..	..	..	..
Consumer price index	1987=100	..	..	..	..	..	..
Lower income	"	..	..	..	..	..	..
Food[a]	"	..	61	..	..	..	..
Urban	"	..	..	..	..	..	..
Rural	"	..	..	..	..	..	..
SOCIAL INDICATORS							
Public expenditure on basic social services	% of GDP	..	..	8.0	..	..	..
Gross enrollment ratios							
Primary	% school age pop.	119	102	103	121	103	..
Male	"	125	105	101	126	113	..
Female	"	114	99	103	117	96	..
Mortality							
Infant mortality	per thou. live births	90.0	52.9	36.0	39.0	73.0	45.0
Under 5 mortality	"	..	..	44.4	49.0	108.0	59.0
Immunization							
Measles	% age group	..	19.0	85.0	88.4	72.7	..
DPT	"	..	42.0	83.0	89.5	80.6	..
Child malnutrition (under-5)	"	..	52.0	41.9	24.7	38.3	..
Life expectancy							
Total	years	58	64	67	68	62	68
Female advantage	"	3.5	3.8	4.5	3.6	2.4	6.4
Total fertility rate	births per woman	5.9	4.6	3.7	2.4	3.4	3.1
Maternal mortality rate	per 100,000 live births	..	110	105	114	..	..
Supplementary Poverty Indicators							
Expenditures on social security	% of total gov't exp.	..	..	..	..	..	..
Social security coverage	% econ. active pop.	..	..	..	..	..	..
Access to safe water: total	% of pop.	..	46.0	50.0	72.0	68.4	..
Urban	"	..	70.0	70.0	83.4	78.9	..
Rural	"	..	39.0	33.0	60.2	60.3	..
Access to health care	"	..	75.0	97.0	..	..	..

Population growth rate (annual average, percent)

□ Viet Nam
— Low-income

GNP per capita growth rate (annual average, percent)

Development diamond[b]

Life expectancy / GNP per capita / Gross primary enrollment / Access to safe water

— Viet Nam
— Low-income

a. See the technical notes, p.389.   b. The development diamond, based on four key indicators, shows the average level of development in the country compared with its income group. See the introduction.

372

Viet Nam

Indicator	Unit of measure	Latest single year 1970-75	Latest single year 1980-85	Most recent estimate 1987-92	Same region/income group East Asia	Same region/income group Low-income	Next higher income group
HUMAN RESOURCES							
Population (mre=1992)	thousands	48,030	58,868	69,306	1,688,909	3,194,535	942,547
Age dependency ratio	ratio	0.91	0.82	0.77	0.55	0.67	0.66
Urban	% of pop.	18.8	19.6	20.3	29.4	26.7	57.0
Population growth rate	annual %	2.3	2.0	2.2	1.4	1.8	1.4
Urban	"	2.9	2.4	3.1	2.9	3.4	4.8
Labor force (15-64)	thousands	22,316	28,755	34,824	928,465	1,478,954	..
Agriculture	% of labor force	72	67	..	..	..	..
Industry	"	9	12	..	..	..	..
Female	"	48	47	47	41	33	36
Females per 100 males							
Urban	number	..	..	..	..	..	..
Rural	"	..	..	..	..	..	..
NATURAL RESOURCES							
Area	thou. sq. km	331.69	331.69	331.69	16,367.18	38,401.06	40,697.37
Density	pop. per sq. km	144.8	177.5	204.3	101.8	81.7	22.8
Agricultural land	% of land area	20.0	20.7	20.7	44.5	50.9	..
Change in agricultural land	annual %	0.1	-2.3	0.0	0.1	0.0	..
Agricultural land under irrigation	%	15.4	26.2	27.5	14.5	18.2	..
Forests and woodland	thou. sq. km	136	96	93	..	..	..
Deforestation (net)	annual %	..	..	1.6	..	..	..
INCOME							
Household income							
Share of top 20% of households	% of income	..	..	..	42	42	..
Share of bottom 40% of households	"	..	..	..	18	19	..
Share of bottom 20% of households	"	..	..	..	7	8	..
EXPENDITURE							
Food	% of GDP	..	..	19.8	..	..	..
Staples	"	..	..	3.6	..	..	..
Meat, fish, milk, cheese, eggs	"	..	..	8.9	..	..	..
Cereal imports	thou. metric tonnes	1,050	426	583	33,591	46,537	74,924
Food aid in cereals	"	64	21	96	581	9,008	4,054
Food production per capita	1987 = 100	88	116	135	133	123	..
Fertilizer consumption	kg/ha	50.7	57.1	110.5	75.1	61.9	..
Share of agriculture in GDP	% of GDP	..	..	34.5	21.5	29.6	..
Housing	% of GDP	..	..	4.7	..	..	..
Average household size	persons per household	..	..	..	..	..	..
Urban	"	..	..	..	..	..	..
Fixed investment: housing	% of GDP	..	..	4.9	..	..	..
Fuel and power	% of GDP	..	..	1.0	..	..	..
Energy consumption per capita	kg of oil equiv.	125	95	88	593	335	1,882
Households with electricity							
Urban	% of households	..	..	..	..	..	..
Rural	"	..	..	..	..	..	..
Transport and communication	% of GDP	..	..	6.2	..	..	..
Fixed investment: transport equipment	"	..	..	10.3	..	..	..
Total road length	thou. km	..	..	..	..	..	..
INVESTMENT IN HUMAN CAPITAL							
Health							
Population per physician	persons	..	4,048	2,284	..	..	..
Population per nurse	"	4,304	1,241	399	..	..	..
Population per hospital bed	"	..	271	261	553	1,050	516
Oral rehydration therapy (under-5)	% of cases	..	..	53	51	39	..
Education							
Gross enrollment ratio							
Secondary	% of school-age pop.	46	42	33	53	41	..
Female	"	45	40	..	47	35	..
Pupil-teacher ratio: primary	pupils per teacher	36	34	35	23	37	26
Pupil-teacher ratio: secondary	"	27	23	18	16	19	..
Pupils reaching grade 4	% of cohort	..	63	64	89	..	..
Repeater rate: primary	% of total enroll	..	..	..	6	..	..
Illiteracy	% of pop. (age 15+)	..	16	12	24	39	..
Female	% of fem. (age 15+)	..	20	16	34	52	..
Newspaper circulation	per thou. pop.	..	9	9	..	..	100

World Bank International Economics Department, April 1994

Western Samoa

Indicator	Unit of measure	Latest single year 1970-75	Latest single year 1980-85	Most recent estimate 1987-92	Same region/income group East Asia	Same region/income group Lower-middle-income	Next higher income group
Priority Poverty Indicators							
POVERTY							
Upper poverty line	local curr.	..	..	..	..	..	..
Headcount index	% of pop.	..	..	..	12	..	..
Lower poverty line	local curr.	..	..	..	..	..	..
Headcount index	% of pop.	..	..	..	9	..	..
GNP per capita	US$	..	630	940	760	..	3,870
SHORT TERM INCOME INDICATORS							
Unskilled urban wages	local curr.	..	..	..	..	..	..
Unskilled rural wages	"	..	..	..	..	..	..
Rural terms of trade	"	..	..	..	..	..	..
Consumer price index	1987=100	25	90	143	..	..	..
Lower income	"	..	..	..	..	..	..
Food[a]	"	..	91	..	..	..	..
Urban	"	..	..	..	..	..	..
Rural	"	..	..	..	..	..	..
SOCIAL INDICATORS							
Public expenditure on basic social services	% of GDP	..	..	2.8	..	..	..
Gross enrollment ratios							
Primary	% school age pop.	..	..	..	121	..	107
Male	"	..	..	..	126	..	
Female	"	..	..	..	117	..	
Mortality							
Infant mortality	per thou. live births	..	..	25.0	39.0	45.0	40.0
Under 5 mortality	"	..	..	29.9	49.0	59.0	51.0
Immunization							
Measles	% age group	..	78.0	..	88.4	..	82.0
DPT	"	..	84.0	..	89.5	..	73.8
Child malnutrition (under-5)	"	..	..	..	24.7	..	..
Life expectancy							
Total	years	..	63	65	68	68	69
Female advantage	"	..	2.0	3.0	3.6	6.4	6.3
Total fertility rate	births per woman	5.9	5.5	4.5	2.4	3.1	2.9
Maternal mortality rate	per 100,000 live births	..	..	..	114	..	..
Supplementary Poverty Indicators							
Expenditures on social security	% of total gov't exp.	..	..	..	..	..	..
Social security coverage	% econ. active pop.	..	..	..	..	..	..
Access to safe water: total	% of pop.	43.0	69.0	82.0	72.0	..	85.6
Urban	"	86.0	75.0	100.0	83.4	..	94.3
Rural	"	..	67.0	77.0	60.2	..	73.0
Access to health care	"	..	100.0	..	..	..	..

Population growth rate
(annual average, percent)

GNP per capita growth rate
(annual average, percent)

Development diamond[b]

Life expectancy — GNP per capita — Gross primary enrollment — Access to safe water

Western Samoa
Lower-middle-income

a. See the technical notes, p.389.   b. The development diamond, based on four key indicators, shows the average level of development in the country compared with its income group. See the introduction.

Western Samoa

Indicator	Unit of measure	Latest single year 1970-75	Latest single year 1980-85	Most recent estimate 1987-92	Same region/income group East Asia	Same region/income group Lower-middle-income	Next higher income group
Resources and Expenditures							
HUMAN RESOURCES							
Population (mre=1992)	thousands	151	157	162	1,688,909	942,547	477,960
Age dependency ratio	ratio	..	0.81	0.78	0.55	0.66	0.64
Urban	% of pop.	21.0	21.8	22.9	29.4	57.0	71.7
Population growth rate	annual %	0.7	0.0	0.6	1.4	1.4	1.6
Urban	"	1.3	0.4	1.6	2.9	4.8	2.5
Labor force (15-64)	thousands	..	..	..	928,465	..	181,414
Agriculture	% of labor force	..	..	..	..	..	..
Industry	"	..	..	..	..	..	..
Female	"	..	..	..	41	36	29
Females per 100 males							
Urban	number	99	..	..	..	..	..
Rural	"	93	..	..	..	..	..
NATURAL RESOURCES							
Area	thou. sq. km	2.84	2.84	2.84	16,367.18	40,697.37	21,836.02
Density	pop. per sq. km	53.2	55.3	56.7	101.8	22.8	21.5
Agricultural land	% of land area	42.1	43.5	43.5	44.5	..	41.7
Change in agricultural land	annual %	0.0	0.0	0.0	0.1	..	0.3
Agricultural land under irrigation	%	..	..	..	14.5	..	9.3
Forests and woodland	thou. sq. km	1	1	1	..	..	..
Deforestation (net)	annual %	..	..	..	..	..	..
INCOME							
Household income							
Share of top 20% of households	% of income	..	..	..	42	..	..
Share of bottom 40% of households	"	..	..	..	18	..	..
Share of bottom 20% of households	"	..	..	..	7	..	..
EXPENDITURE							
Food	% of GDP	..	..	59.4	..	..	..
Staples	"	..	..	20.9	..	..	..
Meat, fish, milk, cheese, eggs	"	..	..	12.4	..	..	..
Cereal imports	thou. metric tonnes	12	14	12	33,591	74,924	49,174
Food aid in cereals	"	..	0	2	581	4,054	282
Food production per capita	1987 = 100	90	102	75	133	..	109
Fertilizer consumption	kg/ha	0.1	3.7	..	75.1	..	68.8
Share of agriculture in GDP	% of GDP	..	45.6	30.2	21.5	..	8.1
Housing	% of GDP	..	..	6.5	..	..	..
Average household size	persons per household	5.8	..	..	..	..	..
Urban	"	6.5	..	..	..	..	..
Fixed investment: housing	% of GDP	..	..	4.5	..	..	..
Fuel and power	% of GDP	..	..	2.1	..	..	..
Energy consumption per capita	kg of oil equiv.	..	..	432	593	1,882	1,649
Households with electricity							
Urban	% of households	..	..	..	..	..	..
Rural	"	..	..	..	..	..	..
Transport and communication	% of GDP	..	..	9.1	..	..	..
Fixed investment: transport equipment	"	..	..	3.7	..	..	..
Total road length	thou. km	..	..	..	..	..	..
INVESTMENT IN HUMAN CAPITAL							
Health							
Population per physician	persons	2,860	2,476	4,818	..	..	..
Population per nurse	"	634	406	..	..	..	..
Population per hospital bed	"	220	229	..	553	516	385
Oral rehydration therapy (under-5)	% of cases	..	..	7	51	..	54
Education							
Gross enrollment ratio							
Secondary	% of school-age pop.	..	..	..	53	..	53
Female	"	..	..	..	47	..	..
Pupil-teacher ratio: primary	pupils per teacher	27	21	..	23	26	25
Pupil-teacher ratio: secondary	"	43	39	..	16	..	..
Pupils reaching grade 4	% of cohort	..	98	..	89	..	71
Repeater rate: primary	% of total enroll	..	..	..	6	..	11
Illiteracy	% of pop. (age 15+)	2	..	..	24	..	14
Female	% of fem. (age 15+)	..	..	..	34	..	17
Newspaper circulation	per thou. pop.	..	..	..	..	100	117

World Bank International Economics Department, April 1994

Republic of Yemen

Indicator	Unit of measure	Latest single year 1970-75	1980-85	Most recent estimate 1987-92	Same region/income group Mid-East & North Africa	Low-income	Next higher income group
Priority Poverty Indicators							
POVERTY							
Upper poverty line	local curr.	..	..	..	..	..	..
Headcount index	% of pop.	..	..	..	..	19	..
Lower poverty line	local curr.	..	..	..	..	..	..
Headcount index	% of pop.	..	..	..	..	..	..
GNP per capita	US$	..	..	520	1,950	390	
SHORT TERM INCOME INDICATORS							
Unskilled urban wages	local curr.	..	..	..	..	..	..
Unskilled rural wages	"	..	..	..	..	..	..
Rural terms of trade	"	..	..	..	..	..	..
Consumer price index	1987=100	..	..	..	..	..	..
Lower income	"	..	..	..	..	..	..
Food[a]	"	..	96	..	..	..	..
Urban	"	..	..	..	..	..	..
Rural	"	..	..	..	..	..	..
SOCIAL INDICATORS							
Public expenditure on basic social services	% of GDP	..	..	..	..	..	..
Gross enrollment ratios							
Primary	% school age pop.	41	..	76	100	103	..
Male	"	63	..	112	107	113	..
Female	"	17	..	37	88	96	..
Mortality							
Infant mortality	per thou. live births	168.0	135.0	106.0	58.0	73.0	45.0
Under 5 mortality	"	..	..	153.3	78.0	108.0	59.0
Immunization							
Measles	% age group	..	..	57.0	81.8	72.7	..
DPT	"	..	..	62.0	83.9	80.6	..
Child malnutrition (under-5)	"	..	..	30.0	20.9	38.3	..
Life expectancy							
Total	years	43	48	53	64	62	68
Female advantage	"	0.5	0.7	0.7	2.4	2.4	6.4
Total fertility rate	births per woman	7.8	7.7	7.6	4.9	3.4	3.1
Maternal mortality rate	per 100,000 live births	..	330	..	..	..	..
Supplementary Poverty Indicators							
Expenditures on social security	% of total gov't exp.	..	..	..	..	..	..
Social security coverage	% econ. active pop.	..	..	..	..	..	..
Access to safe water: total	% of pop.	..	..	..	85.0	68.4	..
Urban	"	..	..	..	97.0	78.9	..
Rural	"	..	..	..	70.1	60.3	..
Access to health care	"	..	36.0	40.0	84.6	..	..

Population growth rate
(annual average, percent)

- Republic of Yemen
- Low-income

GNP per capita growth rate
(annual average, percent)

Development diamond[b]

Life expectancy / GNP per capita / Gross primary enrollment / Access to safe water

- Republic of Yemen
- Low-income

a. See the technical notes, p.389.   b. The development diamond, based on four key indicators, shows the average level of development in the country compared with its income group. See the introduction.

Republic of Yemen

Indicator	Unit of measure	Latest single year 1970-75	Latest single year 1980-85	Most recent estimate 1987-92	Mid-East & North Africa	Low-income	Next higher income group
Resources and Expenditures							
HUMAN RESOURCES							
Population (mre=1992)	thousands	6,991	9,670	12,999	252,555	3,194,535	942,547
Age dependency ratio	ratio	..	1.02	1.08	0.87	0.67	0.66
Urban	% of pop.	16.4	24.4	30.8	54.7	26.7	57.0
Population growth rate	annual %	2.5	3.0	3.6	2.8	1.8	1.4
Urban	"	6.4	6.5	6.7	3.8	3.4	4.8
Labor force (15-64)	thousands	1,764	2,235	2,790	69,280	1,478,954	..
Agriculture	% of labor force	66	62	..	..	..	..
Industry	"	10	11	..	..	..	..
Female	"	10	13	14	15	33	36
Females per 100 males							
Urban	number	..	..	..	..	..	..
Rural	"	..	..	..	..	..	..
NATURAL RESOURCES							
Area	thou. sq. km	5,280.00	5,280.00	5,280.00	10,487.21	38,401.06	40,697.37
Density	pop. per sq. km	1.3	1.8	2.1	23.4	81.7	22.8
Agricultural land	% of land area	33.2	33.2	33.2	30.2	50.9	..
Change in agricultural land	annual %	0.1	0.0	0.0	0.5	0.0	..
Agricultural land under irrigation	%	..	..	..	31.0	18.2	..
Forests and woodland	thou. sq. km	325	315	310	..	..	..
Deforestation (net)	annual %	..	..	..	..	..	..
INCOME							
Household income							
Share of top 20% of households	% of income	..	..	..	..	42	..
Share of bottom 40% of households	"	..	..	..	..	19	..
Share of bottom 20% of households	"	..	..	..	..	8	..
EXPENDITURE							
Food	% of GDP	..	..	..	..	..	..
Staples	"	..	..	..	..	..	..
Meat, fish, milk, cheese, eggs	"	..	..	..	..	..	..
Cereal imports	thou. metric tonnes	295	1,182	2,185	38,007	46,537	74,924
Food aid in cereals	"	..	..	59	2,484	9,008	4,054
Food production per capita	1987 = 100	..	..	..	116	123	..
Fertilizer consumption	kg/ha	..	..	..	96.7	61.9	..
Share of agriculture in GDP	% of GDP	..	23.0	19.6	13.7	29.6	..
Housing	% of GDP	..	..	..	..	..	..
Average household size	persons per household	..	..	..	..	..	..
Urban	"	..	..	..	..	..	..
Fixed investment: housing	% of GDP	..	..	..	..	..	..
Fuel and power	% of GDP	..	..	..	..	..	..
Energy consumption per capita	kg of oil equiv.	111	226	241	1,109	335	1,882
Households with electricity							
Urban	% of households	..	..	..	..	..	..
Rural	"	..	..	..	..	..	..
Transport and communication	% of GDP	..	..	..	..	..	..
Fixed investment: transport equipment	"	..	..	..	..	..	..
Total road length	thou. km	4	37	37	..	..	..
INVESTMENT IN HUMAN CAPITAL							
Health							
Population per physician	persons	34,791	5,603	..	..	..	..
Population per nurse	"	..	1,939	..	..	..	..
Population per hospital bed	"	1,155	..	1,136	636	1,050	516
Oral rehydration therapy (under-5)	% of cases	..	..	6	56	39	..
Education							
Gross enrollment ratio							
Secondary	% of school-age pop.	8	..	31	59	41	..
Female	"	1	..	..	50	35	..
Pupil-teacher ratio: primary	pupils per teacher	39	54	37	27	37	26
Pupil-teacher ratio: secondary	"	22	21	33	21	19	..
Pupils reaching grade 4	% of cohort	..	..	..	..	..	..
Repeater rate: primary	% of total enroll	..	19	..	..	..	..
Illiteracy	% of pop. (age 15+)	..	68	62	45	39	..
Female	% of fem. (age 15+)	..	80	74	58	52	..
Newspaper circulation	per thou. pop.	..	..	..	39	..	100

World Bank International Economics Department, April 1994

Federal Republic of Yugoslavia

Indicator	Unit of measure	Latest single year 1970-75	Latest single year 1980-85	Most recent estimate 1987-92	Same region/income group Europe & Central Asia	Same region/income group Lower-middle-income	Next higher income group
Priority Poverty Indicators							
POVERTY							
Upper poverty line	local curr.	..	..	..	..	..	..
Headcount index	% of pop.	..	..	..	..	..	..
Lower poverty line	local curr.	..	..	..	..	..	..
Headcount index	% of pop.	..	..	..	..	..	..
GNP per capita	US$	..	..	..	..	..	3,870
SHORT TERM INCOME INDICATORS							
Unskilled urban wages	local curr.	..	..	..	..	..	..
Unskilled rural wages	"	..	..	..	..	..	..
Rural terms of trade	"	..	..	..	..	..	..
Consumer price index	1987=100	..	..	..	..	..	..
Lower income	"	..	..	..	..	..	..
Food[a]	"	..	..	..	..	..	..
Urban	"	..	..	..	..	..	..
Rural	"	..	..	..	..	..	..
SOCIAL INDICATORS							
Public expenditure on basic social services	% of GDP	..	..	..	..	..	..
Gross enrollment ratios							
Primary	% school age pop.	..	..	..	..	..	107
Male	"	..	..	..	..	..	..
Female	"	..	..	..	..	..	..
Mortality							
Infant mortality	per thou. live births	..	..	28.0	30.0	45.0	40.0
Under 5 mortality	"	..	..	33.6	38.0	59.0	51.0
Immunization							
Measles	% age group	..	..	75.0	..	..	82.0
DPT	"	..	..	79.0	..	..	73.8
Child malnutrition (under-5)	"	..	..	..	..	..	..
Life expectancy							
Total	years	..	..	72	70	68	69
Female advantage	"	..	..	5.5	8.6	6.4	6.3
Total fertility rate	births per woman	..	..	2.1	2.2	3.1	2.9
Maternal mortality rate	per 100,000 live births	..	..	..	58	..	..
Supplementary Poverty Indicators							
Expenditures on social security	% of total gov't exp.	..	..	..	..	..	..
Social security coverage	% econ. active pop.	..	..	..	..	..	..
Access to safe water: total	% of pop.	..	..	..	..	..	85.6
Urban	"	..	..	..	..	..	94.3
Rural	"	..	..	..	..	..	73.0
Access to health care	"	..	..	100.0	..	..	..

Population growth rate
(annual average, percent)

GNP per capita growth rate
(annual average, percent)

Development diamond[b]

Life expectancy — GNP per capita — Gross primary enrollment — Access to safe water

□ Federal Republic of Yugoslavia
— Lower-middle-income

━━ Federal Republic of Yugoslavia
— Lower-middle-income

a. See the technical notes, p.389.   b. The development diamond, based on four key indicators, shows the average level of development in the country compared with its income group. See the introduction.

378

Federal Republic of Yugoslavia

Indicator	Unit of measure	Latest single year 1970-75	Latest single year 1980-85	Most recent estimate 1987-92	Same region/income group Europe & Central Asia	Same region/income group Lower-middle-income	Next higher income group
Resources and Expenditures							
HUMAN RESOURCES							
Population (mre=1992)	thousands	..	10,009	10,597	495,241	942,547	477,960
Age dependency ratio	ratio	..	0.48	0.46	0.56	0.66	0.64
Urban	% of pop.	..	..	..	63.3	57.0	71.7
Population growth rate	annual %	..	..	0.8	0.5	1.4	1.6
Urban	"	..	..	..	..	4.8	2.5
Labor force (15-64)	thousands	..	..	..	..	..	181,414
Agriculture	% of labor force	..	..	..	..	..	..
Industry	"	..	..	..	..	..	..
Female	"	..	..	..	46	36	29
Females per 100 males							
Urban	number	..	..	..	..	..	..
Rural	"	..	..	..	..	..	..
NATURAL RESOURCES							
Area	thou. sq. km	..	..	25.33	24,165.06	40,697.37	21,836.02
Density	pop. per sq. km	..	..	418.4	20.4	22.8	21.5
Agricultural land	% of land area	..	..	..	..	..	41.7
Change in agricultural land	annual %	..	..	..	..	..	0.3
Agricultural land under irrigation	%	..	..	..	..	..	9.3
Forests and woodland	thou. sq. km	..	..	..	..	..	..
Deforestation (net)	annual %	..	..	..	..	..	
INCOME							
Household income							
Share of top 20% of households	% of income	..	..	..	..	..	..
Share of bottom 40% of households	"	..	..	..	..	..	..
Share of bottom 20% of households	"	..	..	..	..	..	..
EXPENDITURE							
Food	% of GDP	..	..	..	..	..	..
Staples	"	..	..	..	..	..	..
Meat, fish, milk, cheese, eggs	"	..	..	..	..	..	..
Cereal imports	thou. metric tonnes	..	..	..	45,972	74,924	49,174
Food aid in cereals	"	..	..	..	1,639	4,054	282
Food production per capita	1987 = 100	..	..	..	..	..	109
Fertilizer consumption	kg/ha	..	..	..	..	..	68.8
Share of agriculture in GDP	% of GDP	..	..	..	..	..	8.1
Housing	% of GDP	..	..	..	..	..	..
Average household size	persons per household	..	..	..	..	..	..
Urban	"	..	..	..	..	..	..
Fixed investment: housing	% of GDP	..	..	..	..	..	..
Fuel and power	% of GDP	..	..	..	..	..	..
Energy consumption per capita	kg of oil equiv.	..	..	..	3,190	1,882	1,649
Households with electricity							
Urban	% of households	..	..	..	..	..	..
Rural	"	..	..	..	..	..	..
Transport and communication	% of GDP	..	..	..	..	..	..
Fixed investment: transport equipment	"	..	..	..	..	..	..
Total road length	thou. km	..	..	..	..	..	..
INVESTMENT IN HUMAN CAPITAL							
Health							
Population per physician	persons	..	..	..	378	..	..
Population per nurse	"	..	..	..	..	..	..
Population per hospital bed	"	..	..	..	134	516	385
Oral rehydration therapy (under-5)	% of cases	..	..	..	..	..	54
Education							
Gross enrollment ratio							
Secondary	% of school-age pop.	..	..	..	..	..	53
Female	"	..	..	..	..	..	..
Pupil-teacher ratio: primary	pupils per teacher	..	..	..	..	26	25
Pupil-teacher ratio: secondary	"	..	..	..	..	..	..
Pupils reaching grade 4	% of cohort	..	..	..	..	..	71
Repeater rate: primary	% of total enroll	..	..	..	..	..	11
Illiteracy	% of pop. (age 15+)	..	..	..	..	..	14
Female	% of fem. (age 15+)	..	..	..	..	..	17
Newspaper circulation	per thou. pop.	..	..	..	..	100	117

World Bank International Economics Department, April 1994

Zaire

Indicator	Unit of measure	Latest single year 1970-75	Latest single year 1980-85	Most recent estimate 1987-92	Same region/income group Sub-Saharan Africa	Same region/income group Low-income	Next higher income group
Priority Poverty Indicators							
POVERTY							
Upper poverty line	local curr.	..	..	..	..	..	..
Headcount index	% of pop.	..	..	..	..	19	..
Lower poverty line	local curr.	..	..	..	..	..	..
Headcount index	% of pop.	..	..	..	..	..	..
GNP per capita	US$	410	250	230	520	390	..
SHORT TERM INCOME INDICATORS							
Unskilled urban wages	local curr.	..	..	..	..	..	..
Unskilled rural wages	"	..	..	..	..	..	..
Rural terms of trade	"	..	..	..	..	..	..
Consumer price index	1987=100	0	36	644,621	..	..	..
Lower income	"	..	..	..	..	..	..
Food[a]	"	..	..	..	..	..	..
Urban	"	..	..	33,892	..	..	..
Rural	"	..	..	..	..	..	..
SOCIAL INDICATORS							
Public expenditure on basic social services	% of GDP	..	1.0	4.0	..	..	..
Gross enrollment ratios							
Primary	% school age pop.	88	89	76	66	103	..
Male	"	104	107	87	79	113	..
Female	"	72	71	64	62	96	..
Mortality							
Infant mortality	per thou. live births	125.0	111.0	90.9	99.0	73.0	45.0
Under 5 mortality	"	..	..	147.1	169.0	108.0	59.0
Immunization							
Measles	% age group	..	41.0	31.0	54.0	72.7	..
DPT	"	..	37.0	32.0	54.6	80.6	..
Child malnutrition (under-5)	"	28.8	20.0	28.8	28.4	38.3	..
Life expectancy							
Total	years	46	49	52	52	62	68
Female advantage	"	3.2	3.4	3.2	3.4	2.4	6.4
Total fertility rate	births per woman	6.1	6.3	6.2	6.1	3.4	3.1
Maternal mortality rate	per 100,000 live births	..	500	600	..	..	..
Supplementary Poverty Indicators							
Expenditures on social security	% of total gov't exp.	..	..	..	..	..	..
Social security coverage	% econ. active pop.	..	..	..	..	..	..
Access to safe water: total	% of pop.	19.0	33.0	34.0	41.1	68.4	..
Urban	"	38.0	52.0	59.0	77.8	78.9	..
Rural	"	12.0	21.0	17.0	27.3	60.3	..
Access to health care	"	..	33.0	50.0	..	..	..

Population growth rate (annual average, percent)

□ Zaire
— Low-income

GNP per capita growth rate (annual average, percent)

Development diamond[b]

— Zaire
— Low-income

a. See the technical notes, p.389. b. The development diamond, based on four key indicators, shows the average level of development in the country compared with its income group. See the introduction.

Zaire

Indicator	Unit of measure	Latest single year 1970-75	Latest single year 1980-85	Most recent estimate 1987-92	Same region/income group Sub-Saharan Africa	Same region/income group Low-income	Next higher income group
Resources and Expenditures							
HUMAN RESOURCES							
Population (mre=1992)	thousands	23,251	31,667	39,787	546,390	3,194,535	942,547
Age dependency ratio	ratio	0.90	0.95	0.98	0.95	0.67	0.66
Urban	% of pop.	29.5	27.9	28.5	29.5	26.7	57.0
Population growth rate	annual %	2.8	3.3	3.1	2.9	1.8	1.4
Urban	"	2.3	2.7	3.8	5.1	3.4	4.8
Labor force (15-64)	thousands	9,503	11,666	13,788	224,025	1,478,954	..
Agriculture	% of labor force	75	72	..	..	..	..
Industry	"	12	13	..	..	..	..
Female	"	40	37	35	37	33	36
Females per 100 males							
Urban	number	..	93	..	..	..	..
Rural	"	..	113	..	..	..	..
NATURAL RESOURCES							
Area	thou. sq. km	2,345.41	2,345.41	2,345.41	24,274.03	38,401.06	40,697.37
Density	pop. per sq. km	9.9	13.5	16.5	21.9	81.7	22.8
Agricultural land	% of land area	9.9	10.1	10.1	52.7	50.9	..
Change in agricultural land	annual %	0.0	0.2	0.1	0.1	0.0	..
Agricultural land under irrigation	%	..	0.0	0.1	0.8	18.2	..
Forests and woodland	thou. sq. km	1,793	1,760	1,740	..	..	..
Deforestation (net)	annual %	..	..	0.6	..	..	..
INCOME							
Household income							
Share of top 20% of households	% of income	..	..	..	..	42	..
Share of bottom 40% of households	"	..	..	..	..	19	..
Share of bottom 20% of households	"	..	..	..	..	8	..
EXPENDITURE							
Food	% of GDP	..	..	48.1	..	..	..
Staples	"	..	4.5	24.0	..	..	..
Meat, fish, milk, cheese, eggs	"	..	7.3	8.2	..	..	..
Cereal imports	thou. metric tonnes	302	320	219	20,311	46,537	74,924
Food aid in cereals	"	1	138	121	4,303	9,008	4,054
Food production per capita	1987 = 100	108	99	90	90	123	..
Fertilizer consumption	kg/ha	0.5	0.3	0.4	4.2	61.9	..
Share of agriculture in GDP	% of GDP	16.5	29.9	30.2	18.6	29.6	..
Housing	% of GDP	..	3.4	9.9	..	..	..
Average household size	persons per household	..	..	..	..	..	..
Urban	"	6.0	..	..	..	..	..
Fixed investment: housing	% of GDP	..	2.2	1.8	..	..	..
Fuel and power	% of GDP	..	1.9	3.2	..	..	..
Energy consumption per capita	kg of oil equiv.	58	50	48	258	335	1,882
Households with electricity							
Urban	% of households	..	..	..	..	..	..
Rural	"	..	..	..	..	..	..
Transport and communication	% of GDP	..	1.7	4.5	..	..	..
Fixed investment: transport equipment	"	..	1.8	2.6	..	..	..
Total road length	thou. km	145	145	146	..	..	..
INVESTMENT IN HUMAN CAPITAL							
Health							
Population per physician	persons	28,131	..	13,546	..	..	..
Population per nurse	"	6,708	..	1,881	..	..	..
Population per hospital bed	"	311	..	701	1,329	1,050	515
Oral rehydration therapy (under-5)	% of cases	..	..	45	36	39	..
Education							
Gross enrollment ratio							
Secondary	% of school-age pop.	16	23	24	18	41	..
Female	"	8	14	15	14	35	..
Pupil-teacher ratio: primary	pupils per teacher	41	42	..	39	37	26
Pupil-teacher ratio: secondary	"	..	..	..	..	19	..
Pupils reaching grade 4	% of cohort	62	63	56	..	..	..
Repeater rate: primary	% of total enroll	21	19	21	..	..	..
Illiteracy	% of pop. (age 15+)	..	34	28	51	39	..
Female	% of fem. (age 15+)	..	47	39	62	52	..
Newspaper circulation	per thou. pop.	3	1	..	14	..	100

World Bank International Economics Department, April 1994

Zambia

Indicator	Unit of measure	Latest single year 1970-75	Latest single year 1980-85	Most recent estimate 1987-92	Same region/income group Sub-Saharan Africa	Same region/income group Low-income	Next higher income group
Priority Poverty Indicators							
POVERTY							
Upper poverty line	local curr.	..	..	1,380	..	..	..
Headcount index	% of pop.	..	..	64	..	19	..
Lower poverty line	local curr.	..	..	962	..	..	..
Headcount index	% of pop.	..	..	54	..	..	..
GNP per capita	US$	560	350	450	520	390	..
SHORT TERM INCOME INDICATORS							
Unskilled urban wages	local curr.	..	..	..	..	..	..
Unskilled rural wages	"	..	..	..	..	..	..
Rural terms of trade	"	..	..	..	..	..	..
Consumer price index	1987=100	9	46	4,415	..	..	..
Lower income	"	..	..	..	..	..	..
Food[a]	"	6	46	1,469	..	..	..
Urban	"	..	..	..	..	..	..
Rural	"	..	..	..	..	..	..
SOCIAL INDICATORS							
Public expenditure on basic social services	% of GDP	..	..	3.4	..	..	..
Gross enrollment ratios							
Primary	% school age pop.	97	99	92	66	103	..
Male	"	105	105	101	79	113	..
Female	"	88	93	92	62	96	..
Mortality							
Infant mortality	per thou. live births	100.0	89.0	107.0	99.0	73.0	45.0
Under 5 mortality	"	..	..	177.5	169.0	108.0	59.0
Immunization							
Measles	% age group	..	55.0	76.0	54.0	72.7	..
DPT	"	..	47.0	79.0	54.6	80.6	..
Child malnutrition (under-5)	"	24.1	24.7	23.0	28.4	38.3	..
Life expectancy							
Total	years	47	51	48	52	62	68
Female advantage	"	3.3	3.4	3.3	3.4	2.4	6.4
Total fertility rate	births per woman	6.7	7.2	6.5	6.1	3.4	3.1
Maternal mortality rate	per 100,000 live births	..	151	..	..	..	..
Supplementary Poverty Indicators							
Expenditures on social security	% of total gov't exp.	..	1.3	1.5	..	..	..
Social security coverage	% econ. active pop.	..	..	..	..	..	..
Access to safe water: total	% of pop.	42.0	58.0	59.0	41.1	68.4	..
Urban	"	86.0	76.0	76.0	77.8	78.9	..
Rural	"	16.0	41.0	43.0	27.3	60.3	..
Access to health care	"	..	70.0	75.0	..	..	..

Population growth rate
(annual average, percent)

Zambia
Low-income

GNP per capita growth rate
(annual average, percent)

Development diamond[b]

Life expectancy

GNP per capita — Gross primary enrollment

Access to safe water

Zambia
Low-income

a. See the technical notes, p.389.   b. The development diamond, based on four key indicators, shows the average level of development in the country compared with its income group. See the introduction.

Zambia

Indicator	Unit of measure	Latest single year 1970-75	Latest single year 1980-85	Most recent estimate 1987-92	Same region/income group Sub-Saharan Africa	Same region/income group Low-income	Next higher income group
Resources and Expenditures							
HUMAN RESOURCES							
Population (mre=1992)	thousands	4,841	6,680	8,272	546,390	3,194,535	942,547
Age dependency ratio	ratio	0.97	1.04	1.05	0.95	0.67	0.66
Urban	% of pop.	34.8	40.9	42.4	29.5	26.7	57.0
Population growth rate	annual %	2.9	3.2	3.0	2.9	1.8	1.4
Urban	"	5.6	3.7	3.6	5.1	3.4	4.8
Labor force (15-64)	thousands	1,665	2,242	2,844	224,025	1,478,954	..
Agriculture	% of labor force	75	73	..	..	..	..
Industry	"	9	10	..	..	..	..
Female	"	28	28	30	37	33	36
Females per 100 males							
Urban	number	87	93	..	..	..	..
Rural	"	123	124	..	..	..	..
NATURAL RESOURCES							
Area	thou. sq. km	752.61	752.61	752.61	24,274.03	38,401.06	40,697.37
Density	pop. per sq. km	6.4	8.9	10.7	21.9	81.7	22.8
Agricultural land	% of land area	47.1	47.3	47.4	52.7	50.9	..
Change in agricultural land	annual %	0.0	0.1	0.0	0.1	0.0	..
Agricultural land under irrigation	%	0.1	0.1	0.1	0.8	18.2	..
Forests and woodland	thou. sq. km	299	292	288	..	..	..
Deforestation (net)	annual %	..	..	1.1	..	..	..
INCOME							
Household income							
Share of top 20% of households	% of income	63	..	50	..	42	..
Share of bottom 40% of households	"	10	..	15	..	19	..
Share of bottom 20% of households	"	4	..	6	..	8	..
EXPENDITURE							
Food	% of GDP	22.7	25.8	..	..	..	..
Staples	"	5.9	5.5	..	..	..	..
Meat, fish, milk, cheese, eggs	"	10.0	12.8	..	..	..	..
Cereal imports	thou. metric tonnes	164	201	651	20,311	46,537	74,924
Food aid in cereals	"	5	116	330	4,303	9,008	4,054
Food production per capita	1987 = 100	141	95	73	90	123	..
Fertilizer consumption	kg/ha	1.5	2.3	1.8	4.2	61.9	..
Share of agriculture in GDP	% of GDP	13.1	13.1	15.7	18.6	29.6	..
Housing	% of GDP	5.8	7.6	..	..	..	..
Average household size	persons per household	4.0	..	..	..	..	..
Urban	"	..	..	..	..	..	..
Fixed investment: housing	% of GDP	4.8	0.3	..	..	..	..
Fuel and power	% of GDP	1.9	3.1	..	..	..	..
Energy consumption per capita	kg of oil equiv.	383	237	158	258	335	1,882
Households with electricity							
Urban	% of households	..	..	..	..	..	..
Rural	"	..	..	..	..	..	..
Transport and communication	% of GDP	3.9	3.8	..	..	..	..
Fixed investment: transport equipment	"	6.0	1.7	..	..	..	..
Total road length	thou. km	36	37	39	..	..	..
INVESTMENT IN HUMAN CAPITAL							
Health							
Population per physician	persons	13,486	7,076	10,917	..	..	..
Population per nurse	"	1,698	743	583	..	..	..
Population per hospital bed	"	300	284	..	1,329	1,050	516
Oral rehydration therapy (under-5)	% of cases	..	..	89	36	39	..
Education							
Gross enrollment ratio							
Secondary	% of school-age pop.	15	18	20	18	41	..
Female	"	10	13	14	14	35	..
Pupil-teacher ratio: primary	pupils per teacher	48	49	44	39	37	26
Pupil-teacher ratio: secondary	"	23	23	28	..	19	..
Pupils reaching grade 4	% of cohort	96	100	..	..	..	..
Repeater rate: primary	% of total enroll	2	2	..	..	..	..
Illiteracy	% of pop. (age 15+)	..	33	27	51	39	..
Female	% of fem. (age 15+)	..	41	35	62	52	..
Newspaper circulation	per thou. pop.	22	18	13	14	..	100

World Bank International Economics Department, April 1994

Zimbabwe

| Indicator | Unit of measure | Latest single year | | Most recent estimate 1987-92 | Same region/income group | | Next higher income group |
		1970-75	1980-85		Sub-Saharan Africa	Low-income	
Priority Poverty Indicators							
POVERTY							
Upper poverty line	local curr.	..	..	516	..	..	..
Headcount index	% of pop.	..	..	37	..	19	..
Lower poverty line	local curr.	..	..	296	..	..	..
Headcount index	% of pop.	..	..	13	..	..	..
GNP per capita	US$	550	640	570	520	390	..
SHORT TERM INCOME INDICATORS							
Unskilled urban wages	local curr.	..	..	..	..	..	..
Unskilled rural wages	"	..	..	..	..	..	..
Rural terms of trade	"	..	..	..	..	..	..
Consumer price index	1987=100	24	78	249	..	..	..
Lower income	"	..	..	..	..	..	..
Food[a]	"	..	77	184	..	..	..
Urban	"	..	..	..	..	.	..
Rural	"	..	..	..	..	..	..
SOCIAL INDICATORS							
Public expenditure on basic social services	% of GDP	..	..	..	..	..	..
Gross enrollment ratios							
Primary	% school age pop.	73	135	117	66	103	..
Male	"	79	140	120	79	113	..
Female	"	67	131	118	62	96	..
Mortality							
Infant mortality	per thou. live births	93.0	80.0	46.5	99.0	73.0	45.0
Under 5 mortality	"	..	..	59.6	169.0	108.0	59.0
Immunization							
Measles	% age group	..	78.0	87.0	54.0	72.7	..
DPT	"	..	72.0	89.0	54.6	80.6	..
Child malnutrition (under-5)	"	..	20.7	10.0	28.4	38.3	..
Life expectancy							
Total	years	52	56	60	52	62	68
Female advantage	"	3.5	3.6	3.0	3.4	2.4	6.4
Total fertility rate	births per woman	7.5	6.6	4.6	6.1	3.4	3.1
Maternal mortality rate	per 100,000 live births	..	145	80	..	..	..
Supplementary Poverty Indicators							
Expenditures on social security	% of total gov't exp.	..	2.9	2.5	..	..	..
Social security coverage	% econ. active pop.	..	..	..	..	..	..
Access to safe water: total	% of pop.	..	..	36.0	41.1	68.4	..
Urban	"	..	..	..	77.8	78.9	..
Rural	"	..	..	14.0	27.3	60.3	..
Access to health care	"	..	71.0	..	..	..	..

Population growth rate
(annual average, percent)

GNP per capita growth rate
(annual average, percent)

Development diamond[b]

Life expectancy

GNP per capita — Gross primary enrollment

Access to safe water

— Zimbabwe
— Low-income

a. See the technical notes, p.389.   b. The development diamond, based on four key indicators, shows the average level of development in the country compared with its income group. See the introduction.

Zimbabwe

Indicator	Unit of measure	Latest single year 1970-75	Latest single year 1980-85	Most recent estimate 1987-92	Same region/income group Sub-Saharan Africa	Same region/income group Low-income	Next higher income group

Resources and Expenditures

HUMAN RESOURCES

Indicator	Unit of measure	1970-75	1980-85	1987-92	Sub-Saharan Africa	Low-income	Next higher income group
Population (mre=1992)	thousands	6,065	8,319	10,364	546,390	3,194,535	942,547
Age dependency ratio	ratio	1.07	0.99	0.91	0.95	0.67	0.66
Urban	% of pop.	19.6	25.2	29.9	29.5	26.7	57.0
Population growth rate	annual %	2.8	3.4	3.3	2.9	1.8	1.4
Urban	"	5.6	5.7	5.7	5.1	3.4	4.8
Labor force (15-64)	thousands	2,575	3,410	4,172	224,025	1,478,954	..
Agriculture	% of labor force	75	73	..	..	..	..
Industry	"	10	10	..	..	..	..
Female	"	37	36	34	37	33	36
Females per 100 males							
Urban	number	..	79	..	..	..	..
Rural	"	..	122	..	..	..	..

NATURAL RESOURCES

Indicator	Unit of measure	1970-75	1980-85	1987-92	Sub-Saharan Africa	Low-income	Next higher income group
Area	thou. sq. km	390.58	390.58	390.58	24,274.03	38,401.06	40,697.37
Density	pop. per sq. km	15.5	21.3	25.7	21.9	81.7	22.8
Agricultural land	% of land area	19.1	19.6	19.8	52.7	50.9	..
Change in agricultural land	annual %	0.0	0.7	0.0	0.1	0.0	..
Agricultural land under irrigation	%	1.0	2.5	2.9	0.8	18.2	..
Forests and woodland	thou. sq. km	203	195	191	..	..	..
Deforestation (net)	annual %	..	..	0.7	..	..	..

INCOME

Indicator	Unit of measure	1970-75	1980-85	1987-92	Sub-Saharan Africa	Low-income	Next higher income group
Household income							
Share of top 20% of households	% of income	..	..	62	..	42	..
Share of bottom 40% of households	"	..	..	11	..	19	..
Share of bottom 20% of households	"	..	..	4	..	8	..

EXPENDITURE

Indicator	Unit of measure	1970-75	1980-85	1987-92	Sub-Saharan Africa	Low-income	Next higher income group
Food	% of GDP	..	25.6	..	..	..	..
Staples	"	..	5.8	..	..	..	..
Meat, fish, milk, cheese, eggs	"	..	12.0	..	..	..	..
Cereal imports	thou. metric tonnes	57	153	1,493	20,311	46,537	74,924
Food aid in cereals	"	..	131	116	4,303	9,008	4,054
Food production per capita	1987 = 100	116	109	44	90	123	..
Fertilizer consumption	kg/ha	20.0	22.4	19.4	4.2	61.9	..
Share of agriculture in GDP	% of GDP	16.2	18.0	19.6	18.6	29.6	..
Housing	% of GDP	..	8.0	..	..	..	..
Average household size	persons per household	..	..	..	..	..	..
Urban	"	..	..	..	..	..	..
Fixed investment: housing	% of GDP	..	0.8	..	..	..	..
Fuel and power	% of GDP	..	3.2	..	..	..	..
Energy consumption per capita	kg of oil equiv.	441	391	450	258	335	1,882
Households with electricity							
Urban	% of households	..	..	..	..	..	..
Rural	"	..	..	..	..	..	..
Transport and communication	% of GDP	..	3.9	..	..	..	..
Fixed investment: transport equipment	"	..	2.0	..	..	..	..
Total road length	thou. km	81	78	78	..	..	..

INVESTMENT IN HUMAN CAPITAL

Health

Indicator	Unit of measure	1970-75	1980-85	1987-92	Sub-Saharan Africa	Low-income	Next higher income group
Population per physician	persons	6,300	5,942	7,110	..	..	..
Population per nurse	"	645	990	988	..	..	..
Population per hospital bed	"	300	693	1,959	1,329	1,050	516
Oral rehydration therapy (under-5)	% of cases	..	..	77	36	39	..

Education

Indicator	Unit of measure	1970-75	1980-85	1987-92	Sub-Saharan Africa	Low-income	Next higher income group
Gross enrollment ratio							
Secondary	% of school-age pop.	9	42	48	18	41	..
Female	"	7	33	42	14	35	..
Pupil-teacher ratio: primary	pupils per teacher	41	40	39	39	37	26
Pupil-teacher ratio: secondary	"	18	28	27	..	19	..
Pupils reaching grade 4	% of cohort	80	85	77	..	..	..
Repeater rate: primary	% of total enroll	..	1	..	..	..	..
Illiteracy	% of pop. (age 15+)	..	38	33	51	39	..
Female	% of fem. (age 15+)	..	45	40	62	52	..
Newspaper circulation	per thou. pop.	19	24	21	14	..	100

World Bank International Economics Department, April 1994

Table 1a. Basic indicators for other economies

		Population (thousands) mid-1992	Area (thousands of square kilometers)	GNP per capita (US$) 1992	Life expectancy at birth (years) 1992	Adult illiteracy (percent)	
						Female 1990	Total 1990
1	American Samoa	39	0.20	a	..	..	..
2	Andorra	61	0.45	a	..	..	..
3	Aruba	67	0.19	a	..	..	..
4	Channel Islands	144	0.20	b	77	..	..
5	Eritrea c	..	117.60	d	..	..	..
6	Faeroe Islands	48	1.40	b	..	..	..
7	Gibraltar	32	0.01	a	..	..	..
8	Greenland	58	341.70	b	..	..	..
9	Guam	139	0.55	a	72	..	..
10	Isle of Man	71	0.57	a	..	..	..
11	Mayotte	79	0.37	a	..	..	..
12	Netherlands Antilles	194	0.80	a	77	..	..
13	Northern Mariana Islands	47	0.48	e	..	..	..
14	San Marino	23	0.06	b	..	..	..
15	Virgin Islands (U.S.)	99	0.34	b	75	..	..

a. GNP per capita estimated to be upper-middle income. b. GNP per capita estimated to be high-income. c. Data for Eritrea, not yet disaggregated, are included in Ethiopia. d. GNP per capita estimated to be low-income. e. GNP per capita estimated to be lower-middle income.

Technical Notes

Sources and Methods

By drawing on data already reviewed by specialized international agencies dealing with education (UNESCO), health (WHO), and other social concerns, the World Bank starts with the most consistent and reliable series. These agencies generally collect statistics directly from the countries concerned; the countries endeavor to apply standard U.N. procedures, definitions, and classifications while using their special country knowledge to fit the data. But the specialized international agencies rarely have the resources to collect information universally each year: the available series are incomplete and sometimes inaccurate. The coordination processes involved and the delays in getting responses mean that series tend to be less current in the specialized international agencies than in national agencies. Standard sources for this volume may therefore be supplemented by estimates from member governments and figures obtained directly from countries. Another useful source is information published or provided by bilateral organizations which have field staff and resident missions in many countries, such as the U.S. Agency for International Development and similar entities in Europe. Finally, the World Bank's own files provide additonal data processed by country economists and resident missions in the course of regular contacts with member governments.

Social Indicators of Development provides a much fuller explanation of these sources and methods and, where appropriate, goes beyond conventional definitions to clarify some common misunderstandings.

Social change is measured at the level of the individual, the household, and the community, as well as the nation as a whole. The numéraire is chosen for its appropriateness and relevance to policy issues. Thus income is measured for both individuals and households; population change is measured for urban areas and the country as a whole. The position of women and the impact of development on them is specifically identified wherever possible.

Data Reliability

Despite considerable effort to standardize the data, statistical methods, coverage, practices, and definitions differ widely and the usual warnings about using the figures carefully still apply. In addition, the statistical systems in many developing economies are still weak, and this affects the availability and reliability of data. Moreover, cross-country and cross-time comparisons always involve complex technical problems, which cannot be fully and unequivocally resolved. The data are drawn from sources thought to be most authoritative, but many of them are subject to considerable margins of error. Readers are urged to take these limitations into account in interpreting the indicators, particularly when making comparisons across countries and economies.

Most country data are drawn from regular administrative files, although some come from special surveys or periodic census inquiries. In the case of survey and census data, figures for intermediate years have to be interpolated or otherwise estimated from the base reference statistics. Likewise, because not all data are updated, some figures—especially those relating to current periods—may be extrapolated. Several indicators are derived from models based on assumptions about behavior and prevailing conditions. Issues related to the reliability of demographic indicators are reviewed in the U.N.'s *World Population Trends and Policies*. Regular reports on sources of basic population data are given in the U.N.'s *Population and Vital Statistics Report*. The table of most recent "actual" demographic estimates, in the technical notes, was prepared by referring to these sources in *World Population Projections, 1994-95 Edition (forthcoming)*.

Inevitably, a few series report numbers on the borderline of acceptable quality and reliability. Although World Bank staff try to delete clearly misleading numbers, borderline figures are usually included to give the benefit of the doubt to the compiler and to provide a more general perspective. They must be viewed in the context of the other information in the tables used to describe a country's situation.

The bibliography lists major sources for basic statistical series and social indicators. Data from these sources as well as those of the World Bank are reviewed in the World Bank's Socio-Economic Data Division, which checks for consistency, combines reports from various sources, and creates "derived" indicators—such as school persistence rates—using information provided by other agencies.

An important aim of *Social Indicators of Development* is to promote greater international comparability and consistency in social statistics, but sometimes this is achieved at the cost of precision.

Group Aggregates

Special problems arise in estimating group measures consistently whether by income level or geographical region—over time and across topics. For a given group, data availability varies across indicators, especially among low-income countries, so estimation procedures are used to fill the gaps and weights are applied as necessary, using a suitable common numéraire. The methods used to compute group measures are broadly the same as those used in other statistical publications issued by the World Bank, as described in the technical notes to the World Development Indicators (WDI) in the *World Development Report*.

The same technique is applied to regional groupings in this volume's table on Social and Economic Conditions and to the comparator groups on country pages. The benchmarking procedure underlying group measures requires that two-third of the data be available and that some weight be assigned to each economy within the group. Uncurrent reporters (and those not providing ample history) are then assumed to behave like the sample of the group that does provide estimates. For an economy reporting inadequate data in every year, World Bank staff must choose some arbitrary 1987 base value within a broad range of plausible estimates. Readers should keep in mind that the purpose is to maintain an appropriate relationship across topics, despite myriad country data issues and that nothing meaningful can be deduced about behavior at the country level by working back from group indicators. In addition, the weighting process may result in discrepancies between summed subgroup figures and overall totals.

Measures for the next higher income group are also given, where possible. This is not meant to imply a linear path of development but simply to illustrate differences between countries at various income levels. High-income economies are compared to their own income group only. The regional groups are defined by the World Bank and are not standard geographic categories. They are shown here to suggest another form of comparative analysis. See Appendix A for tables listing country classification.

Most indicators are weighted by population; some indicators use indicator specific weights for group totals. Data refer to calendar years unless otherwise noted (although demographic indicators refer to midyear).

Explanation of Terms

POVERTY

Poverty lines: Country-specific and not comparable across countries; the upper poverty line is the cutoff for the poor; the lower poverty line is the cutoff for the very poor.
Headcount index: Proportion of the population in each of the above categories.
GNP per capita: Estimates are for 1992 at current market prices in U.S. dollars, calculated by the conversion method used for the *World Bank Atlas*.

SHORT-TERM INCOME INDICATORS

Unskilled urban wages: Weekly wages of casual labourers without other income sources.
Unskilled rural wages: Weekly wages of casual farm la-

bourers without any land, or without enough land to meet their subsistence needs.

Rural terms of trade: Wholesale prices of foodgrain divided by wholesale prices for manufactured goods.

Consumer price index: Prices of goods and services used for private consumption of households. The CPI for lower income comprises the price index based on the poor's consumption basket.

Food price index: The index (including the urban/rural data separately where available) are from the U.N. Statistical Division. Since the overall CPI is more up-to-date than the food price index, the data presented may represent different years and therefore may not be comparable.

SOCIAL INDICATORS

Public expenditure on basic social services: Percentage share of primary education and health expenditure in GDP, based on national account estimates. For countries covered by ICP, computed from the SNA defined details of GDP, collected for ICP Phase III (1975), Phase IV (1980) and Phase V (1985).

Primary enrollment ratios: Gross enrollment of all ages at the primary level as a percentage of school-age children as defined by each country. Although many countries consider primary school-age to be 6-11 years, others use different age groups. Gross enrollment may be reported in excess of 100 percent if some pupils are younger or older than the country's standard range of primary school age.

Infant mortality rate: Number of deaths of infants under one year of age per 1,000 live births in a given year. The data are a combination of observed values and interpolated and projected estimates. A few countries, such as the economies of the former Soviet Union, employ an atypical definition of live births, which reduces the reported infant mortality rates relative to the standard (World Health Organization) definition.

Under-5 mortality rate: Shows the probability of a newborn baby dying before reaching age 5.

Immunization: Measures (as a percentage of the age group) the full vaccination coverage of children under one year of age for two of the target diseases of the Expanded Programmed of Immunization – measles and DPT (diphtheria, pertussis and tetanus). Coverage rates are supplied by member states. Note that for some countries the ages at which children are vaccinated may differ from the recommended ages. This is particularly true of European countries.

Child malnutrition: Percentage of children under five years with deficiency or excess of nutrients that interferes with the children's health and genetic potential for growth. Methods of assessment vary, but the most commonly used are less than 80 percent of the standard weight for age, less than minus two standard deviations from the 50th percentile

of the weight for age reference population, or the Gomez scale of malnutrition. *Note* that for a few countries the figures are for children 3 or 4 years and younger.

Life expectancy at birth: Number of years a newborn infant would live if prevailing patterns of mortality at the time of its birth were to stay the same throughout its life. As in *infant mortality rate*, the data are a combination of vital registration based information and interpolated and projected estimates.

Total fertility rate: Average number of children who would be born alive to a woman during her lifetime, if she were to bear children at each age in accordance with prevailing age-specific fertility rates. As in *infant mortality rate*, the data are a combination of observed values and interpolated and projected estimates.

Maternal mortality: The number of female deaths that occur during childbirth per 100,000 live births. Because deaths during childbirth are defined more widely in some countries to include abortion complications of pregnancy or the period after childbirth, and because many pregnant women die from lack of suitable health care, maternal mortality is difficult to measure consistently and reliably across countries.

Expenditures on social security: Compensation for loss of income to the sick and temporarily disabled, payments to the elderly, the permanently disabled, and the unemployed; family, maternity, and child allowances; and the cost of welfare services, such as care of the aged, the disabled, and children, as percentage of total government expenditures.

Social security coverage: Percentage of the "economically active" population covered by social security.

Access to safe water: Percentage of the population with reasonable access to safe water supply (includes treated surface waters or untreated but uncontaminated water such as that from springs, sanitary wells, and protected boreholes). In an urban area this may be a public fountain or standpost located not more than 200 meters away. In rural areas it implies that members of the household do not have to spend a disproportionate part of the day fetching water. The definition of safe water has changed over time.

Access to health care: Percentage of the population that can reach local health services by the usual means of transportation in no more than one hour. Note that facilities tend to be concentrated in urban areas. Some separate figures for rural areas show a much lower level of coverage and access.

HUMAN RESOURCES

Population (U.N. and World Bank)

Population: World Bank estimates for 1992, based, in most cases, on a de facto definition. Note that refugees not permanently settled in the country of asylum are generally considered to be part of the population of their country of origin.

Age dependency ratio: Ratio of the population defined as dependent (under 15 and over 64 years) to the working-age population (15-64).

Population growth rate: Annual average growth rate (1970-75, 1980-85, and 1991-92) calculated from mid-year total and urban populations.

Labor force (ILO)

Total labor force: The "economically active" population; a restrictive concept that includes the armed forces and the unemployed, but excludes homemakers and other unpaid caregivers.

Agriculture: Labor force in farming, forestry, hunting and fishing as a percentage of total labor force.

Industry: Labor force in mining, manufacturing, construction, and electricity, water, and gas as a percentage of total labor force.

Female: Female labor force as a percentage of total labor force. Labor force numbers in several developing countries reflect a significant underestimate of female participation rates.

Females per 100 males (15-64): Ratio of females to males in the total population. The significant differences between the urban and rural gender ratios reflect migration patterns.

NATURAL RESOURCES (FAO)

Area: Total surface area in square kilometers, comprising land area and all inland waters.

Density: Population per square kilometer of total surface area.

Agricultural land: Estimate of area used for crops, pastures, market and kitchen gardens, or lying fallow, as a percentage of total land area (excluding area under inland water and rivers).

Change in agricultural land: Annual rate of change in agricultural land.

Agricultural land under irrigation: Areas provided with water (including land flooded by river water) for crop production or pasture improvement, whether these areas are irrigated several times or only once during the year stated. For some African countries, data on irrigation have been revised recently on the basis of new studies.

Forests and woodland: Land under natural or planted stands of trees, whether productive or not, including land from which forests have been cleared but that will be reforested in the foreseeable future.

Deforestation rate (net): Annual rate of change of forests and woodland area. A positive sign indicates an increase in the forested area.

INCOME

Total household income: Income (both in cash and kind)

accruing to percentile groups of household ranked by total households income. In some cases statistics obtained from other agencies are revised by World Bank staff.

EXPENDITURE

Food (UN, FAO, World Bank)

Food (as percentage of GDP): Percentage share of food in total household consumption expenditure, computed from the SNA defined details of GDP, collected for ICP Phase III (1975), Phase IV(1980) and Phase V(1985). For countries not covered by ICP, less detailed national accounts estimates are included, where available.

Staples: Bread, cereals, potatoes and tubers: a major subitem of food relating to the consumption of carbohydrates.

Meat, fish, milk, cheese, eggs: A protein measure but excluding beans, nuts, and other high protein-content food product.

Cereal imports: Measured in grain equivalents and defined as comprising all cereals in the Standard International Trade Classification, revision 2, groups 041-046. Cereal imports are based on calendar-year data.

Food aid in cereals: Wheat and flour, bulgur, coarse grains, and the cereal component of blended foods; based on data for crop years reported by donor countries and international organizations, including the International Wheat Council and the World Food Programme. Food aid information by donors may not correspond to actual receipts by beneficiaries during a given period because of delays in transportation or recording, or because it is sometimes not reported to the FAO or other relevant international organizations.

Food production per capita: The average annual quantity of food produced per capita in 1989-92 in relation to that produced in 1979-81. Food is defined as comprising nuts, pulses, fruit, cereals, vegetables, sugarcane, sugar beets, starchy roots, edible oils, livestock, and livestock products. Quantities of food produced are measured net of animal feed, seeds for agriculture, and food lost in processing.(The data are weighted by value and not calorie content which gives rise to different perspective depending on the relative share of low-value high-calorie carbohydrates versus high-value lower-calorie livestock products).

Fertilizer consumption: Total consumption of nitrogenous, phosphatic and potash fertilizers divided by the area of agricultural land.

Share of Agriculture in GDP: Forestry, hunting, fishing, and agriculture; in developing countries with high level of subsistence farming, much of agricultural production is either not exchanged, or not exchanged for money. This increases the difficulty of measuring the contribution of agriculture to GDP and reduces the reliability and comparability of such numbers.

Housing

Housing (as a percentage of GDP): Percentage, computed as in *food* and reflecting actual and imputed household expenditure outlays, such as actual and imputed rents and repair and maintenance charges, as well as fuel and power for heating, lighting, cooking, and so forth.

Average household size: A group of individuals who share living quarters and main meals.

Fixed investment: housing: Percentage is computed as in *food*. Includes all outlays, public and private, on residential buildings, plus net changes in the level of inventory which in this context relates primarily to work in progress. (A major renovation or reconstruction would be included as capital formation).

Fuel and power

Fuel and power (as percentage of GDP): Percentage is computed as in *food*. Includes electricity, gas, liquid and other fuels, and ice.

Energy consumption per capita: Annual consumption of commercial primary energy (coal, lignite, petroleum, natural gas, and hydro, nuclear, and geothermal electricity) in kilograms of oil equivalent per capita.

Household with electricity: Conventional dwellings with electricity in living quarters, as a percentage of all dwellings.

Transportation and communication

Transportation and communication (as percentage of GDP): Percentage is computed as in *food*. Includes the purchase of motor cars.

Fixed investment: transport equipment: Computed as in *food*. Includes all outlay, public and private, on transport equipment, plus net changes in level of inventory.

Total road length: Includes main paved and unpaved roads as well as unclassified lower standard roads.

INVESTMENT IN HUMAN CAPITAL

Health (WHO)

Population per physician: Physicians includes the total number of registered practitioners in the country. Note that the definition of recognized medical practitioners differs among countries.

Population per nurse: Nursing persons include auxiliary nurses and paraprofessional personnel such as traditional birth attendants. Inclusion of auxiliary and paraprofessional personnel provides a more realistic estimate of available nursing/health care overall.

Population per hospital bed: Number of hospital beds available in public and private, general and specialized hospital, and rehabilitation centers. Hospitals are establishments permanently staffed by at least one physician.

Oral rehydration therapy use: Percentage of diarrhea episodes in children under 5 years of age treated with oral rehydration salts or a physiologically appropriate household solution.

Education (UNESCO)

Secondary school enrollment: Computed in the same manner as the primary school ratio; the age group again varies but is usually 12-17.

Pupil-teacher ratio: Number of pupils enrolled in school divided by the total number of teachers. In the case of secondary education, the ratio refers to pupils and teachers in general education only.

Pupils reaching grade 4: Percentage of children starting primary school and continuing until grade 4, based on enrollment records. The data are affected by repeaters.

Repeater rate primary: Children in primary school who repeat a grade as a percentage of all enrolled children.

Illiteracy rate: Defined here as the proportion of the population 15 years of age and older who cannot, with understanding, both read and write a short simple statement on everyday life. This is only one of three widely accepted definitions and its application is subject to significant qualifiers in a number of countries. The data for the most recent estimates are from the illiteracy estimates and projections prepared in 1989 by UNESCO. More recent information and a modified model have been used, therefore the data for 1990 are not strictly consistent with those published in previous years.

Newspaper circulation: Average circulation of a "daily, general interest newspaper," defined as a news periodical published at least four times a week.

Demographic Parameters: Latest Years Studied

The dates given below refer to the most recent censuses, national demographic surveys, and vital registration-based estimates underlying each country's demographic indicators. This information is included to show the currentness of the sources of demographic indicators, which can be a reflection of the overall quality of a country's indicators. Beyond these years, demographic estimates may be generated by projection models, extrapolation routines, and other methods. Other demographics indicators, such as life expectancies, birth and death rates, and under-5 mortality rates, are usually derived from the same sources. Explanations of how World Bank estimates and projections, reported in *Social Indicators of Development* country pages, are derived from the sources, as well as more information on the sources, are given in *World Population Projections, 1994-95 Edition (forthcoming)*.

Country	Census	Infant mortality	Total fertility	Contraceptive prevalence
Afghanistan	1979	1979	1979	1972-73
Albania	1989	1991	1991	
Algeria	1987	1992	1992	1987
Angola	1970		1984	1977
Argentina	1991	1990	1990	1977
Armenia	1989	1991	1991	
Australia	1991	1992	1992	1986
Austria	1991	1992	1992	1981-82
Azerbaijan	1989	1991	1991	
Bahrain	1991	1989	1989	1988
Bangladesh	1991	1991	1991	1991
Barbados	1990	1992	1992	1987
Belarus	1989	1991	1991	
Belgium	1991	1992	1992	1982-83
Benin	1992	1981-82	1981-82	1981-82
Bhutan	1969		1984	
Bolivia	1992	1989	1989	1989
Bosnia and Herzegovina	1991	1989	1989	
Botswana	1991	1988	1988	1988
Brazil	1991	1986	1986	1986
Bulgaria	1992	1992	1992	1976
Burkina Faso	1985	1976	1992	1993
Burundi	1990	1987	1987	1987
Cambodia	1962		1982	
Cameroon	1987	1991	1991	1991
Canada	1991	1992	1991	1984
Cape Verde	1990	1985	1988	
Central African Rep.	1988	1975	1959	
Chad	1993	1964	1964	1977
Chile	1992	1991	1991	1978

392

Country	Census	Infant Mortality	Total Fertility	Contraceptive Prevalence
China	1990	1990	1992	1992
Colombia	1985	1990	1990	1990
Comoros	1991	1976	1980	
Congo	1984	1974	1974	
Costa Rica	1984	1991	1991	1986
Côte d'Ivoire	1988	1979	1988	1980-81
Croatia	1991	1989	1989	
Cuba	1981	1992	1992	1987
Cyprus	1976	1991	1991	
Czech Republic	1991	1991	1991	1993
Denmark	1981	1992	1992	1975
Djibouti	1991		1989	
Dominican Republic	1981	1991	1991	1991
Ecuador	1990	1989	1989	1989
Egypt	1986	1988	1992	1992
El Salvador	1992	1988	1988	1993
Equatorial Guinea	1983			
Eritrea	1984			
Estonia	1989	1991	1991	
Ethiopia	1984		1988	1990
Fiji	1986	1987	1990	1978
Finland	1990	1991	1992	1977
France	1990	1992	1992	1988
Gabon	1980	1960-61	1960-61	
Gambia, The	1993	1970	1975	1977
Georgia	1989	1991	1991	
Germany	1991	1992	1992	1985
Ghana	1984	1988	1988	1988
Greece	1991	1992	1992	
Guadeloupe	1982	1986	1986	1976
Guatemala	1981	1987	1987	1987
Guinea	1983	1954-55	1954-55	1977
Guinea-Bissau	1979		1950	1977
Guyana	1980	1982	1981	1975
Haiti	1982	1987	1987	1989
Honduras	1988	1987-88	1987-88	1991
Hong Kong	1991	1992	1992	1987
Hungary	1990	1992	1992	1986
Iceland	1970	1992	1992	
India	1991	1992	1992	1993
Indonesia	1990	1991	1991	1991
Iran, Islamic Rep.	1991	1991	1991	1978
Iraq	1987	1974-75	1974-75	1974
Ireland	1991	1991	1992	1990
Israel	1983	1992	1991	
Italy	1991	1992	1992	1979
Jamaica	1991	1989	1990	1989
Japan	1990	1992	1992	1988
Jordan	1979	1990-91	1990-91	1990-91
Kazakhstan	1989	1991	1991	
Kenya	1989	1989	1993	1993
Kyrgyz Republic	1989	1991	1991	
Korea, Dem. Rep.	1944			
Korea, Rep.	1990	1992	1991	1988
Kuwait	1985	1989	1987	1987
Lao PDR	1985	1988	1988	
Latvia	1989	1990	1990	
Lebanon	1970	1971	1971	1971
Lesotho	1986	1991	1991	1991
Liberia	1984	1986	1986	1986
Libya	1984	1969	1988	
Lithuania	1989	1991	1991	
Luxembourg	1991	1992	1992	
Macedonia, F.Y.R.	1991	1991	1989	
Madagascar	1974-75	1992	1992	1992
Malawi	1987	1992	1992	1992
Malaysia	1991	1991	1984	1988
Mali	1987	1987	1987	1992
Malta	1985	1991	1990	
Martinique	1990	1990	1990	
Mauritania	1988	1975	1987-88	1981
Mauritius	1990	1992	1992	1991
Mexico	1990	1987	1987	1987
Moldova	1989	1991	1991	
Mongolia	1989	1989		
Morocco	1982	1992	1992	1992
Mozambique	1980	1980	1980	
Myanmar	1983	1983	1983	1980

Country	Census	Infant Mortality	Total Fertility	Contraceptive Prevalence
Namibia	1991	1992	1992	1992
Nepal	1991	1987	1987	1986
Netherlands	1971	1992	1992	1988
New Zealand	1991	1991	1991	1976
Nicaragua	1971	1985	1985	1985
Niger	1988	1992	1992	1992
Nigeria	1991	1990	1990	1990
Norway	1990	1991	1992	1979
Oman		1989	1989	1989
Pakistan	1981	1990-91	1990-91	1990-91
Panama	1990	1985-87	1990	1984
Papua New Guinea	1990	1980	1980	1980
Paraguay	1992	1990	1990	1990
Peru	1981	1991-92	1991-92	1991-92
Philippines	1990		1988	1993
Poland	1988	1991	1992	1977
Portugal	1991	1992	1992	1979-80
Qatar	1986	1987	1987	1987
Réunion	1990	1990	1990	
Romania	1992	1990	1991	1978
Russian Federation	1989	1992	1992	
Rwanda	1991	1983	1992	1992
Saudi Arabia	1992	1990	1990	
Senegal	1988	1992-93	1992-93	1992
Sierra Leone	1985	1971	1975	1982
Singapore	1990	1991	1991	1982
Slovak Republic	1991	1991	1991	
Slovenia	1991	1990	1990	
Somalia	1987	1980	1980	
South Africa	1991	1980	1981	1980
Spain	1991	1992	1992	1985
Sri Lanka	1981	1988	1989	1987
Sudan	1983	1989-90	1989-90	1989-90
Suriname	1980			
Swaziland	1986	1972	1980	
Sweden	1990	1992	1992	1981
Switzerland	1990	1991	1991	1980
Syrian Arab Rep.	1981	1990	1981	1978
Tajikistan	1989	1991	1991	
Tanzania	1988	1971-92	1991-92	1991-92
Thailand	1990	1989	1987	1987
Togo	1981	1988	1988	1988
Trinidad & Tobago	1990	1989	1989	1987
Tunisia	1984	1988	1990	1988
Turkey	1990	1988	1988	1988
Turkmenistan	1989	1991	1991	
Uganda	1991	1991	1991	1988-89
Ukraine	1989	1991	1991	
United Arab Emirates	1985	1987	1987	
United Kingdom	1991	1992	1992	1983
United States	1990	1992	1992	1988
Uruguay	1985	1990	1990	
Uzbekistan	1989	1991	1991	
Venezuela	1990	1989	1990	1977
Viet Nam	1989	1989	1989	1988
Yemen, Rep.	1986/88	1991-92	1991-92	1991-92
Yugoslavia, Fed. Rep.	1991	1991	1990	1976
Zaire	1984	1984	1984	1977
Zambia	1990	1992	1992	1992
Zimbabwe	1992	1988-89	1988-89	1988-89

Data Notes

The notes on infant mortality and total fertility rates, presented below and included in the diskette version, are for 1992. Publication of these Data Notes is the first step toward a more comprehensive exercise of amplifying the sources and processes and of arriving at more recent estimates from sometimes dated sources.

AFGHANISTAN
IMR and TFR
UN *World Population Prospects 1992 revision*

ALBANIA
IMR and TFR
Population and Vital Statistics Report (PVSR)

ALGERIA
IMR
National Statistical Office, Algeria, 1993
TFR
Algeria Maternal and Child Health Survey 1992

ANGOLA
IMR and TFR
Bank assessment

ANTIGUA AND BARBUDA
IMR and TFR
PVSR

ARGENTINA
IMR and TFR
UN *World Population Prospects 1992 revision*

ARMENIA
IMR
PVSR and Institute Nationale d'Etude Démographique (INED) 1993
TFR
USSR census and Council of Europe 1993

AUSTRALIA
IMR and TFR
PVSR

AUSTRIA
IMR
PVSR and Eurostat 1993
TFR
Eurostat 1993

AZERBAIJAN
IMR and TFR
Council of Europe 1993

BAHAMAS
IMR and TFR
PVSR

BAHRAIN
IMR
Central Statistical Organization, Bahrain
TFR
Bahrain Child Health Survey 1989

BANGLADESH
IMR
Sample Registration System 1991
TFR
Bangladesh Fertility Survey 1988 and Contraceptive Prevalence Survey 1991

BARBADOS
IMR
UN *World Population Prospects 1992 revision*
TFR
PVSR

BELARUS
IMR
USSR census 1989 and INED 1992
TFR
USSR census 1989 and INED 1993

BELGIUM
IMR
Eurostat 1990-93 and PVSR
TFR
Eurostat 1993 and PVSR

BELIZE
IMR
Bank assessment
TFR
Bank estimate, based on USBOC 1989 and 1991 census at 4.6=TFR.

BENIN
IMR and TFR
World Fertility Survey 1982

BHUTAN
IMR and TFR
UN *World Population Prospects 1992 revision*

BOLIVIA
IMR and TFR
Demographic and Health Survey 1989

BOSNIA AND HERZEGOVINA
IMR and TFR
Statistical Office, Belgrade 1988 and INED 1992

BOTSWANA
IMR and TFR
Demographic and Health Survey 1988

BRAZIL
IMR and TFR
UN *World Population Prospects 1992 revision*

BRUNEI
IMR
PVSR
TFR
UN *World Population Prospects 1992 revision*

BULGARIA
IMR and TFR
PVSR and INED 1993

BURKINA FASO
IMR
Bank assessment
TFR
Demographic and Health Survey 1992

BURUNDI
IMR and TFR
UN *World Population Prospects 1992 revision*

CAMBODIA
IMR and TFR
UN *World Population Prospects 1992 revision*

CAMEROON
IMR and TFR
Demographic and Health Survey 1991

CANADA
IMR and TFR
INED 1992 and 1993

CAPE VERDE
IMR
UN *World Population Prospects 1992 revision*
TFR
Survey 1988

CENTRAL AFRICAN REPUBLIC
IMR
UN *World Population Prospects 1992 revision*
TFR
Bank assessment

CHAD
IMR and TFR
UN *World Population Prospects 1992 revision*

CHILE
IMR and TFR
UN *World Population Prospects 1992 revision*

CHINA
IMR
Children Survey 1992
TFR
State Statistical Bureau, Bejing, 1990-92

COLOMBIA
IMR and TFR
Demographic and Health Survey 1990

COMOROS
IMR
UN *World Population Prospects 1992 revision*
TFR
Bank assessment

CONGO
IMR
Census 1984
TFR
Bank assessment

COSTA RICA
IMR and TFR
UN *World Population Prospects 1992 revision*

COTE D'IVOIRE
IMR
UN *World Population Prospects 1992 revision*
TFR
Census 1988

CROATIA
IMR
Statistical Office, Belgrade, 1988 and INED 1992
TFR
Central Bureau of Statistics 1992, and INED 1992

CUBA
IMR and TFR
PVSR

CYPRUS
IMR and TFR
PVSR

CZECH REPUBLIC
IMR
Czech Statistical Office, Prague, 1993
TFR
Federal Statistical Office, Prague, 1990-92

DENMARK
IMR and TFR
Eurostat 1993

DJIBOUTI
IMR
UN *World Population Prospects 1992 revision*
TFR
Intercensal Demographic Survey 1989

DOMINICA
IMR and TFR
PVSR

DOMINICAN REPUBLIC
IMR and TFR
Demographic and Health Survey 1991

ECUADOR
IMR
Demographic and Maternal Health Survey 1989
TFR
Family Planning and Child Survival Survey 1989

EGYPT, ARAB REPUBLIC
IMR
UN *World Population Prospects 1992 revision*
TFR
Demographic and Health Survey 1992

EL SALVADOR
IMR and TFR
Family Health Survey 1988 and 1993

EQUATORIAL GUINEA
IMR
UN *World Population Prospects 1992 revision*
TFR
Bank assessment

ESTONIA
IMR
INED 1993
TFR
Council of Europe 1993

ETHIOPIA
IMR
UN *World Population Prospects 1992 revision*
TFR
Family and Fertility Survey 1990

FIJI
IMR and TFR
UN *World Population Prospects 1992 revision*

FINLAND
IMR and TFR
INED 1993

FRANCE
IMR
Eurostat 1989-93
TFR
Eurostat 1992-93

FRENCH POLYNESIA
IMR and TFR
PVSR

GABON
IMR
UN *World Population Prospects 1992 revision*
TFR
Bank assessment

GAMBIA, THE
IMR
UN *World Population Prospects 1992 revision*
TFR
Bank assessment

GEORGIA
IMR and TFR
Council of Europe 1993

GERMANY
IMR and TFR
Eurostat 1993 and INED 1993

GHANA
IMR
UN *World Population Prospects 1992 revision*
TFR
Demographic and Health Survey 1988

GREECE
IMR and TFR
Eurostat 1993 and INED 1993

GRENADA
IMR
Bank assessment
TFR
Ministry of Finance, Grenadines, 1980-85

GUADELOUPE
IMR and TFR
UN *World Population Prospects 1992 revision*

GUATEMALA
IMR and TFR
Demographic and Health Survey 1987

GUINEA
IMR and TFR
Bank assessment

GUINEA-BISSAU
IMR
UN *World Population Prospects 1992 revision*
TFR
Bank assessment

GUYANA
IMR
UN *World Population Prospects 1992 revision*
TFR
Statistical Office, Guyana

HAITI
IMR and TFR
UN *World Population Prospects 1992 revision*

HONDURAS
IMR and TFR
Health and Fertility Survey 1991-92

HONG KONG
IMR
Census and Statistics Department, Hong Kong, 1992
TFR
Census 1991

HUNGARY
IMR and TFR
INED 1992-93

ICELAND
IMR
PVSR and INED 1993
TFR
INED 1993

INDIA
IMR and TFR
Sample Registration System, 1992

INDONESIA
IMR
Census 1990 and Demographic and Health Survey 1991
TFR
Demographic and Health Survey 1991

IRAN, ISLAMIC REP.
IMR
Census 1986 and KAP Survey 1992
TFR
KAP Survey 1992

IRAQ
IMR and TFR
UN *World Population Prospects 1992 revision*

IRELAND
IMR
Eurostat 1991-93, INED 1993, and PVSR
TFR
Eurostat 1991-92

ISRAEL
IMR and TFR
UN *World Population Prospects 1992 revision*

ITALY
IMR
Eurostat 1990-93 and INED 1993
TFR
Eurostat 1989-92

JAMAICA
IMR
UN *World Population Prospects 1992 revision*
TFR
PVSR

JAPAN
IMR
Ministry of Health, Tokyo, 1993
TFR
Ministry of Health and Welfare, Tokyo, 1993

JORDAN
IMR and TFR
Demographic and Health Survey 1990

KAZAKHSTAN
IMR
PVSR
TFR
Council of Europe 1993

KENYA
IMR
UN *World Population Prospects 1992 revision* and Demographic and Health Survey 1988
TFR
Demographic and Health Survey 1993

KIRIBATI
IMR
Statistics Office, Kiribati, 1993
TFR
Statistics Office, Kiribati, 1990

KOREA, REPUBLIC
IMR
National Statistical Office, Rep. of Korea, 1992
TFR
PVSR

KOREA, DEM. REP.
IMR and TFR
UN *World Population Prospects 1992 revision*

KUWAIT
IMR
Child Health Survey 1989
TFR
UN *World Population Prospects 1992 revision*

KYRGYZ REPUBLIC
IMR
PVSR
TFR
Council of Europe 1993

LAO PDR
IMR and TFR
UN *World Population Prospects 1992 revision*

LATVIA
IMR
PVSR
TFR
USSR census 1989 and INED 1992

LEBANON
IMR and TFR
UN *World Population Prospects 1992 revision*

LESOTHO
IMR and TFR
Demographic and Health Survey 1991

LIBERIA
IMR
Bank assessment
TFR
Demographic and Health Survey 1986

LIBYA
IMR and TFR
UN *World Population Prospects 1992 revision*

LITHUANIA
IMR
Statistical Department, Lithuania, 1992
TFR
Council of Europe 1993

LUXEMBOURG
IMR
Eurostat 1990-93 and INED 1992-93
TFR
Eurostat 1989-93 and INED 1992-93

MACAO
IMR and TFR
Statistical Office, Macao, 1992

MACEDONIA, FYR
IMR
Statistical Office of Macedonia, 1993
TFR
Statistical Office, Belgrade, 1988 and INED 1992

MADAGASCAR
IMR and TFR
Demographic and Health Survey 1992

MALAWI
IMR and TFR
Demographic and Health Survey 1992

MALAYSIA
IMR and TFR
Department of Statistics, Malaysia, 1993

MALDIVES
IMR
Census 1990
TFR
PVSR

MALI
IMR and TFR
Demographic and Health Survey 1987

MALTA
IMR and TFR
PVSR and INED 1993

MARTINIQUE
IMR and TFR
UN *World Population Prospects 1992 revision*

MAURITANIA
IMR
UN *World Population Prospects 1992 revision*
TFR
Census 1988

MAURITIUS
IMR and TFR
UN *World Population Prospects 1992 revision*

MEXICO
IMR
UN *World Population Prospects 1992 revision*
TFR
Demographic and Health Survey 1987

MICRONESIA, FED. STS.
IMR and TFR
Bank assessment

MOLDOVA
IMR
USSR Census 1989, and INED 1992
TFR
Council of Europe 1993

MONGOLIA
IMR and TFR
UN *World Population Prospects 1992 revision*

MOROCCO
IMR and TFR
Demographic and Health Survey 1992

MOZAMBIQUE
IMR
National Statistical Department 1990
TFR
Bank assessment

MYANMAR
IMR
Census 1983
TFR
UN *World Population Prospects 1992 revision*

NAMIBIA
IMR and TFR
Demographic and Health Survey 1992

NEPAL
IMR
UN *World Population Prospects 1992 revision*
TFR
Fertility Survey 1992 (?)

NETHERLANDS
IMR
Eurostat 1989-93 and INED 1993
TFR
Eurostat 1991-93 and INED 1993

NETHERLANDS ANTILLES
IMR and TFR
PVSR

NEW CALEDONIA
IMR and TFR
Statistical Office, New Caledonia, 1993

NEW ZEALAND
IMR and TFR
Department of Statistics, New Zealand, 1993

NICARAGUA
IMR and TFR
Demographic and Health Survey 1992-93

NIGER
IMR
Demographic and Health Survey 1992
TFR
Census 1988 and Demographic and Health Survey 1992

NIGERIA
IMR and TFR
Demographic and Health Survey 1990

NORWAY
IMR and TFR
INED 1993

OMAN
IMR and TFR
Child Health Survey 1989

PAKISTAN
IMR and TFR
Integrated Household Survey 1991 and Demographic and
  Health Survey 1991-92

PANAMA
IMR and TFR
UN *World Population Prospects 1992 revision*

PAPUA NEW GUINEA
IMR and TFR
UN *World Population Prospects 1992 revision*

PARAGUAY
IMR and TFR
Demographic and Health Survey 1990

PERU
IMR and TFR
Demographic and Health Survey 1991-92

PHILIPPINES
IMR
UN *World Population Prospects 1992 revision*
TFR
Demographic and Health Survey 1993

POLAND
IMR and TFR
INED 1993

PORTUGAL
IMR
Eurostat 1989-93 and INED 1993
TFR
Eurostat 1991-93 and INED 1992-93

PUERTO RICO
IMR and TFR
PVSR

QATAR
IMR and TFR
Child Health Survey 1987

REUNION
IMR and TFR
UN *World Population Prospects 1992 revision*

ROMANIA
IMR and TFR
Statistics Office, Romania, 1990 and INED 1991

RUSSIAN FEDERATION
IMR
USSR Census 1989 and INED 1992
TFR
INED 1993

RWANDA
IMR
UN *World Population Prospects 1992 revision*
TFR
Demographic and Health Survey 1992

ST. KITTS AND NEVIS
IMR
Planning Unit, St. Kitts and Nevis, (?)
TFR
PVSR

ST. LUCIA
IMR and TFR
PVSR

ST. VINCENT AND THE GRENADINES
IMR and TFR
PVSR

SAO TOME AND PRINCIPE
IMR
PVSR
TFR
Bank assessement

SAUDI ARABIA
IMR and TFR
Child Health Survey 1990

SENEGAL
IMR and TFR
Demographic and Health Survey 1992-93

SEYCHELLES
IMR
Statistical Division, Seychelles, 1990
TFR
PVSR

SIERRA LEONE
IMR and TFR
UN *World Population Prospects 1992 revision*

SINGAPORE
IMR and TFR
Department of Statistics, Singapore, 1992

SLOVAK REPUBLIC
IMR and TFR
Federal Statistical Office, Prague, 1990-92

SLOVENIA
IMR and TFR
Council of Europe 1993

SOLOMON ISLANDS
IMR and TFR
Bank assessment

SOMALIA
IMR and TFR
Bank assessment

SOUTH AFRICA
IMR and TFR
UN1992 revision

SPAIN
IMR
Eurostat 1993 and INED 1993
TFR
Eurostat 1992-93

SRI LANKA
IMR
Demographic and Health Survey 1987
TFR
Demographic and Health Survey 1987 and PVSR

SUDAN
IMR and TFR
UN *World Population 1992 revision*

SURINAME
IMR
Bank assessment
TFR
Central Bureau of Civil Affairs, Surinam and PVSR

SWAZILAND
IMR and TFR
Bank assessment

SWEDEN
IMR and TFR
INED 1992-93

SWITZERLAND
IMR
INED 1993 and Eurostat 1993
TFR
INED 1993

SYRIAN ARAB REP.
IMR
Child Mortality Survey 1990
TFR
UN *World Population Prospects 1992 revision*

TAJIKISTAN
IMR
PVSR
TFR
Council of Europe 1993

TANZANIA
IMR and TFR
Demographic and Health Survey 1991-92

THAILAND
IMR and TFR
Demographic and Health Survey 1987

TOGO
IMR
UN *World Population Prospects 1992 revision*
TFR
Demographic and Health Survey 1988

TONGA
IMR and TFR
Statistics Department, Tonga, 1991

TRINIDAD AND TOBAGO
IMR and TFR
Demographic and Health Survey 1987

TUNISIA
IMR and TFR
Demographic and Health Survey 1988

TURKEY
IMR and TFR
Statistical Institute, Turkey, 1993

TURKMENISTAN
IMR
PVSR
TFR
Council of Europe 1993

UGANDA
IMR
Census 1991
TFR
Census 1991 and Demographic and Health Survey 1988-89

UKRAINE
IMR and TFR
PVSR and INED 1992

UNITED ARAB EMIRATES
IMR
Child Health Survey 1987
TFR
UN *World Population Prospects 1992 revision*

UNITED KINGDOM
IMR and TFR
Eurostat 1993 and INED 1993

UNITED STATES
IMR
INED 1993
TFR
PVSR

URUGUAY
IMR
UN *World Population Prospects 1992 revision*
TFR
Census 1985

UZBEKISTAN
IMR
PVSR
TFR
Council of Europe 1993

VANUATU
IMR and TFR
Census 1989

VENEZUELA
IMR
UN *World Population Prospects 1992 revision*
TFR
Statistical Office, Venezuela, 1991

VIET NAM
IMR
Census 1989
TFR
Census 1989 and Survey 1990

WESTERN SAMOA
IMR
Department of Statistics, Western Samoa, 1991
TFR
Census 1991

YEMEN, REP.
IMR
UN *World Population Prospects 1992 revision*
TFR
Demographic and Health Survey 1992

YUGOSLAVIA, FED. REP.
IMR and TFR
Statistical Office, Belgrade, 1988 and INED 1992

ZAIRE
IMR and TFR
Census 1984

ZAMBIA
IMR and TFR
Demographic and Health Survey 1992

ZIMBABWE
IMR and TFR
Demographic and Health Survey 1988

Selected References

Many of the statistics assembled in this volume come from special agencies that have used questionnaires and surveys to collect country data. In some cases, particularly for population and related statistics, Bank staff revise these statistics with more recent information they have obtained from the country. Statistics are also generated through the work programs of sectoral divisions or through special studies undertaken by Bank staff, such as the information on poverty lines. This volume includes only a portion of the social indicators available from source agencies. Additional data and other indicators can be obtained from the organizations listed below and from their recent publications.

Poverty

U.S.S.R. Goskomstat. 1992. *National Economy of the USSR in 1991*, Moscow.

World Bank. 1992. *China: Strategies for Reducing Poverty in the 1990s*. World Bank Country Study. Washington, D.C.

Living Standard Measurement Surveys.

World Bank data.

Human Resources

Bos, Eduard, My T. Vu, Ernest Massiah, and Rodolfo A. Bulatao. 1994. *World Population Projections, 1994-1995 Edition (forthcoming)*. Baltimore, Md. John Hopkins University Press.

Coale, A.J., and P. Demeny (with B. Vaughn). 1983. *Regional Model Life Tables and Stable Populations*. 2nd ed. New York. Academic Press.

Council of Europe. 1993. *Recent Demographic Developments in Europe and North America, 1992*. Council of Europe Press.

Eurostat. 1993. *Demographic Statistics*. Luxembourg. Statististical Office of the European Community.

Institute for Resource Development/Westinghouse. 1987. *Child Survival: Risks and the Road to Health*. Columbia, Md.

International Labour Office. 1984. *Yearbook of Labour Statistics*. Geneva.

___. 1986. *Labour Force Estimates and Projections, 1950-2000*. Geneva.

United Nations Department of International Economic and Social Affairs. Various years. *Population and Vital Statistics Report*. New York.

___. 1988. *Mortality of Children under Age 5: Projections 1950-2025*. New York.

___. 1988. *World Population Trends and Policies: 1987 Monitoring Report*, New York.

___. 1991. *The World Urbanization Prospects, 1992 Revision*. U.N. Department of Economics and Social Information and Policy Analysis. New York. 1993.

___. *The World Population Prospects 1992 Revision*. U.N. Department of Economics and Social Information and Policy Analysis. New York. 1993.

U.N. Statistical Office. 1989. *Demographic Yearbook* data.

United States Bureau of Census. 1984. *Women of the World*. USAID. Office of Women in Development. Washington, D.C.

___. Various years. *World Population - Recent Estimates for the Countries and Regions of the World*. Washington, D.C. U.S. Government Printing Office.

U.S.S.R. Goskomstat. 1990. *Demographic Yearbook of the USSR*, Moscow.

World Health Organization. 1991. *Maternal Mortality - a Global Factbook*, Geneva.

McGreevey, William. 1990. *Social Security in Latin America: Issues and Options for the World Bank*, World Bank Discussion Papers no. 110. Washington, D.C.

ILO data.

Natural Resources and the Environment

World Health Organization. 1976. *World Health Statistics Report*, Volume 29. Geneva.

___. 1987. The *International Drinking Water Supply and Sanitation Decade (as at December 1985)*. Geneva.

___. 1990. *The International Drinking Water Supply and Sanitation Decade* (as at December 1988). Geneva.

World Resources Institute, International Institute for Environmental Development, United Nations Environmental Programme. 1988. *World Resources, 1988/89 and 1992/93*. New York. Basic Books, Inc.

Food and Agriculture Organization data.

WHO data.

Income

Carlson, Beverly A., and Tessa M. Wardlaw. *A Global, Regional and Country Assessment of Child Malnutrition*. Staff Working Paper No. 7. New York. UNICEF.

U.N. Administrative Committee on Coordination — Subcomittee on Nutrition. 1993. *Second Report on the World Nutrition Situation*. 1993. Geneva.

U.N. Department of International Economic and Social Affairs. Various years. *Monthly Bulletin of Statistics*. New York.

World Bank. 1992. *World Bank Atlas 1992*. Washington, D.C.

World Bank data.

Expenditure

FAO. 1983. *Food Aid in Figures*. (December). Rome.

International Road Federation. 1991. *World Road Statistics 1960-1990*. Washington, DC.

Kravis, Irving, Alan Heston, and Robert Summers. 1982. *World Product and Income: International Comparisons of Real Gross Product*. United Nations and World Bank, Baltimore.

Organization for Economic Cooperation and Development. Department of Economics and Statistics. 1987. *Purchasing Power Parities and Real Expenditures, 1985*. Paris.

U.N. Commission of the European Communities. 1987. *World Comparisons of Purchasing Power and Real Product for 1980*. Phase IV. New York.

U.N. Department of International Economic and Social Affairs. 1983. *Compendium of Human Settlement Statistics*. New York.

___. Various years. *Statistical Yearbook*. New York.

UNICEF. 1987. *Statistics on Children in UNICEF Assisted Countries*. New York.

___. 1989. *The State of the World's Children*. Oxford: Oxford University Press.

World Bank. 1988. *Road Deterioration in Developing Countries: Causes and Remedies*. Policy Study. Washington, D.C.

United Nations national accounts data.

Government Finance Statistics (GFS), 1992. IMF, Washington, D.C.

Investment in Human Capital

Ross, John, and others. 1993. *Family Planning and Population: A Compendium of International Statistics*. New York: The Population Council.

UNESCO. 1989. *Compendium of Statistics on Illiteracy*. Paris.

___. Various years. *Statistical Yearbook*. Paris.

World Health Organization. 1986. *World Health Statistics Annual*. Geneva.

___. Programme for Control of Diarrhoeal Diseases. *Sixth Programme Report, 1986-87*. Geneva.

___. Programme for Control of Diarrhoeal Diseases. Various years. *Interim Programme Report*. Geneva.

___. Various years. Expanded Programme on Immunization. *Information System: Summary for the WHO*. Geneva.

UNESCO data.

Classification of Economies

Table 1 Classification of economies by income and region, 1993-94

Income group	Subgroup	Sub-Saharan Africa		Asia		Europe and Central Asia		Middle East and North Africa		Americas
		East and Southern Africa	West Africa	East Asia and Pacific	South Asia	Eastern Europe and Central Asia	Rest of Europe	Middle East	North Africa	
Low-income		Burundi Comoros Eritrea Ethiopia Kenya Lesotho Madagascar Malawi Mozambique Rwanda Somalia Sudan Tanzania Uganda Zaire Zambia Zimbabwe	Benin Burkina Faso Central African Republic Chad Equatorial Guinea Gambia, The Ghana Guinea Guinea-Bissau Liberia Mali Mauritania Niger Nigeria São Tomé and Principe Sierra Leone Togo	Cambodia China Indonesia Lao PDR Myanmar Viet Nam	Afghanistan Bangladesh Bhutan India Maldives Nepal Pakistan Sri Lanka	Tajikistan		Yemen, Rep.	Egypt, Arab Rep.	Guyana Haiti Honduras Nicaragua
Middle-income	Lower	Angola Djibouti Namibia Swaziland	Cameroon Cape Verde Congo Côte d'Ivoire Senegal	Fiji Kiribati Korea, Dem. Rep. Marshall Islands Micronesia, Fed. Sts. Mongolia N. Mariana Is. Papua New Guinea Philippines Solomon Islands Thailand Tonga Vanuatu Western Samoa		Albania Armenia Azerbaijan Bosnia and Herzegovina Bulgaria Croatia Czech Republic Georgia Kazakhstan Kyrgyz Republic Latvia Lithuania Macedonia FYR[a] Moldova Poland Romania Russian Federation Slovak Republic Turkmenistan Ukraine Uzbekistan Yugoslavia, Fed. Rep.	Turkey	Iran, Islamic Rep. Iraq Jordan Lebanon Syrian Arab Rep.	Algeria Morocco Tunisia	Belize Bolivia Chile Colombia Costa Rica Cuba Dominica Dominican Republic Ecuador El Salvador Grenada Guatemala Jamaica Panama Paraguay Peru St. Vincent and the Grenadines
	Upper	Botswana Mauritius Mayotte Reunion Seychelles South Africa	Gabon	American Samoa Guam Korea, Rep. Macao Malaysia New Caledonia		Belarus Estonia Hungary Slovenia	Gibraltar Greece Isle of Man Malta Portugal	Bahrain Oman Saudi Arabia	Libya	Antigua and Barbuda Argentina Aruba Barbados Brazil French Guiana Guadeloupe Martinique Mexico Netherlands Antilles Puerto Rico St. Kitts and Nevis St. Lucia Suriname Trinidad and Tobago Uruguay Venezuela
Subtotal:	169	27	23	26	8	27	6	9	5	38

406

Table 1 (continued)

Income group	Subgroup	Sub-Saharan Africa — East and Southern Africa	West Africa	Asia — East Asia and Pacific	South Asia	Europe and Central Asia — Eastern Europe and Central Asia	Rest of Europe	Middle East and North Africa — Middle East	North Africa	Americas
High-income	OECD countries			Australia Japan New Zealand			Austria Belgium Denmark Finland France Germany Iceland Ireland Italy Luxembourg Netherlands Norway Spain Sweden Switzerland United Kingdom			Canada United States
	Non OECD countries			Brunei French Polynesia Hong Kong Singapore OAE[b]			Andorra Channel Islands Cyprus Faeroe Islands Greenland San Marino	Israel Kuwait Qatar United Arab Emirates		Bahamas, The Bermuda Virgin Islands (US)
Total: 208		27	23	34	8	27	28	13	5	43

a. Former Yugoslav Republic of Macedonia.
b. Other Asian economies—Taiwan, China.

Definitions of groups

These tables classify all World Bank member economies, and all other economies with populations of more than 30,000.

Income group: Economies are divided according to 1992 GNP per capita, calculated using the *World Bank Atlas* method. The groups are: low-income, $675 or less; lower-middle-income, $676–2,695; upper-middle-income, $2,696–$8,355; and high-income, $8,356 or more.

The estimates for the republics of the former Soviet Union are preliminary and their classification will be kept under review.

Table 2 Classification of economies by major export category and indebtedness, 1993–94

	Low- and middle-income						Not classified by indebtedness	High-income	
	Low-income			Middle-income					
Group	Severely indebted	Moderately indebted	Less indebted	Severely indebted	Moderately indebted	Less indebted		OECD	nonOECD
Exporters of manu-factures			China	Bulgaria Poland	Hungary Russian Federation	Armenia Belarus Estonia Georgia Korea, Dem. Rep. Korea, Rep. Kyrgyz Republic Latvia Lebanon Lithuania Macao Moldova Romania Ukraine Uzbekistan		Canada Finland Germany Ireland Italy Japan Sweden Switzerland	Hong Kong Israel Singapore OAE[a]
Exporters of nonfuel primary products	Afghanistan Burundi Equatorial Guinea Ethiopia Ghana Guinea-Bissau Guyana Honduras Liberia Madagascar Mali Mauritania Myanmar Nicaragua Niger Rwanda São Tomé and Principe Somalia Sudan Tanzania Uganda Viet Nam Zaire Zambia	Guinea Malawi Togo Zimbabwe	Chad	Albania Argentina Bolivia Côte d'Ivoire Cuba Peru	Chile Guatemala Papua New Guinea	American Samoa Botswana Mongolia Namibia Paraguay Solomon Islands St. Vincent and the Grenadines Suriname Swaziland	French Guiana Guadeloupe Reunion	Iceland New Zealand	Faeroe Islands Greenland
Exporters of fuels (mainly oil)	Nigeria			Algeria Angola Congo Iraq	Gabon Venezuela	Bahrain Iran, Islamic Rep. Libya Oman Saudi Arabia Trinidad and Tobago Turkmenistan			Brunei Qatar United Arab Emirates
Exporters of services	Cambodia Egypt, Arab Rep.	Gambia, The Maldives Nepal Yemen, Rep.	Benin Bhutan Burkina Faso Haiti Lesotho	Jamaica Jordan Panama	Dominican Republic Greece	Antigua and Barbuda Aruba Barbados Belize Cape Verde Djibouti El Salvador Fiji Grenada Kiribati Malta Netherlands Antilles Seychelles St. Kitts and Nevis St. Lucia Tonga Vanuatu Western Samoa	Martinique	United Kingdom	Bahamas, The Bermuda Cyprus French Polynesia

Table 2 *(continued)*

| | Low- and middle-income | | | | | | | High-income | |
| | Low-income | | | Middle-income | | | Not classified by indebtedness | | |
Group	Severely indebted	Moderately indebted	Less indebted	Severely indebted	Moderately indebted	Less indebted		OECD	nonOECD
*Diversified exporters*b	Central African Republic Kenya Lao PDR Mozambique Sierra Leone	Bangladesh Comoros India Indonesia Pakistan	Sri Lanka Tajikistan	Brazil Cameroon Ecuador Mexico Morocco Syrian Arab Rep.	Colombia Costa Rica Philippines Senegal Tunisia Turkey Uruguay	Azerbaijan Dominica Kazakhstan Malaysia Mauritius Portugal South Africa Thailand	Yugoslavia Fed. Rep.	Australia Austria Belgium Denmark France Luxembourg Netherlands Norway Spain United States	Kuwait
Not classified by export category					Gibraltar		Bosnia and Herzegovina Croatia Czech Republic Eritrea Guam Isle of Man Macedonia FYRa Marshall Islands Mayotte Micronesia, Fed. Sts. New Caledonia N. Mariana Is. Puerto Rico Slovak Republic Slovenia		Andorra Channel Islands San Marino Virgin Islands (US)
Total:208	32	13	9	21	17	57	20	21	18

a. Other Asian economies—Taiwan, China.
b. Economies in which no single export category accounts for more than 50 percent of total exports.
c. Former Yugoslav Republic of Macedonia.

Definitions of groups

These tables classify all World Bank member economies, plus all other economies with populations of more than 30,000.

Major export category: Major exports are those that account for 50 percent or more of total exports of goods and services from one category, in the period 1987–91. The categories are: nonfuel primary (SITC 0,1,2, 4, plus 68), fuels (SITC 3), manufactures (SITC 5 to 9, less 68), and services (factor and nonfactor service receipts plus workers' remittances). If no single category accounts for 50 percent or more of total exports, the economy is classified as *diversified*.

Indebtedness: Standard World Bank definitions of severe and moderate indebtedness, averaged over three years (1990–92) are used to classify economies in this table. Severely indebted means either of the two key ratios is above critical levels: present value of debt service to GNP (80 percent) and present value of debt service to exports (220 percent). Moderately indebted means either of the two key ratios exceeds 60 percent of, but does not reach, the critical levels. For economies that do not report detailed debt statistics to the World Bank Debtor Reporting System, present-value calculation is not possible. Instead the following methodology is used to classify the non-DRS economies. Severely indebted means three of four key ratios (averaged over 1990–92) are above critical levels: debt to GNP (50 percent); debt to exports (275 percent), debt service to exports (30 percent); and interest to exports (20 percent). Moderately indebted means three of four key ratios exceed 60 percent of, but do not reach, the critical levels. All other classified low- and middle-income economies are listed as less-indebted.

Distributors of World Bank Publications

ARGENTINA
Carlos Hirsch, SRL
Galeria Guemes
Florida 165, 4th Floor-Ofc. 453/465
1333 Buenos Aires

AUSTRALIA, PAPUA NEW GUINEA,
FIJI, SOLOMON ISLANDS,
VANUATU, AND WESTERN SAMOA
D.A. Information Services
648 Whitehorse Road
Mitcham 3132
Victoria

AUSTRIA
Gerold and Co.
Graben 31
A-1011 Wien

BANGLADESH
Micro Industries Development
  Assistance Society (MIDAS)
House 5, Road 16
Dhanmondi R/Area
Dhaka 1209

  Branch offices:
  Pine View, 1st Floor
  100 Agrabad Commercial Area
  Chittagong 4100

BELGIUM
Jean De Lannoy
Av. du Roi 202
1060 Brussels

CANADA
Le Diffuseur
151A Boul. de Mortagne
Boucherville, Québec
J4B 5E6

Renouf Publishing Co.
1294 Algoma Road
Ottawa, Ontario
K1B 3W8

CHILE
Invertec IGT S.A.
Av. Santa Maria 6400
Edificio INTEC, Of. 201
Santiago

CHINA
China Financial & Economic
  Publishing House
8, Da Fo Si Dong Jie
Beijing

COLOMBIA
Infoenlace Ltda.
Apartado Aereo 34270
Bogota D.E.

COTE D'IVOIRE
Centre d'Edition et de Diffusion
  Africaines (CEDA)
04 B.P. 541
Abidjan 04 Plateau

CYPRUS
Center of Applied Research
Cyprus College
6, Diogenes Street, Engomi
P.O. Box 2006
Nicosia

DENMARK
SamfundsLitteratur
Rosenoerns Allé 11
DK-1970 Frederiksberg C

DOMINICAN REPUBLIC
Editora Taller, C. por A.
Restauración e Isabel la Católica 309
Apartado de Correos 2190 Z-1
Santo Domingo

EGYPT, ARAB REPUBLIC OF
Al Ahram
Al Galaa Street
Cairo

The Middle East Observer
41, Sherif Street
Cairo

FINLAND
Akateeminen Kirjakauppa
P.O. Box 128
SF-00101 Helsinki 10

FRANCE
World Bank Publications
66, avenue d'Iéna
75116 Paris

GERMANY
UNO-Verlag
Poppelsdorfer Allee 55
53115 Bonn

HONG KONG, MACAO
Asia 2000 Ltd.
46-48 Wyndham Street
Winning Centre
7th Floor
Central Hong Kong

HUNGARY
Foundation for Market Economy
Dombovari Ut 17-19
H-1117 Budapest

INDIA
Allied Publishers Private Ltd.
751 Mount Road
Madras - 600 002

  Branch offices:
  15 J.N. Heredia Marg
  Ballard Estate
  Bombay - 400 038

  13/14 Asaf Ali Road
  New Delhi - 110 002

  17 Chittaranjan Avenue
  Calcutta - 700 072

  Jayadeva Hostel Building
  5th Main Road, Gandhinagar
  Bangalore - 560 009

  3-5-1129 Kachiguda
    Cross Road
  Hyderabad - 500 027

  Prarthana Flats, 2nd Floor
  Near Thakore Baug, Navrangpura
  Ahmedabad - 380 009

  Patiala House
  16-A Ashok Marg
  Lucknow - 226 001

  Central Bazaar Road
  60 Bajaj Nagar
  Nagpur 440 010

INDONESIA
Pt. Indira Limited
Jalan Borobudur 20
P.O. Box 181
Jakarta 10320

IRAN
Kowkab Publishers
P.O. Box 19575-511
Tehran

IRELAND
Government Supplies Agency
4-5 Harcourt Road
Dublin 2

ISRAEL
Yozmot Literature Ltd.
P.O. Box 56055
Tel Aviv 61560

ITALY
Licosa Commissionaria Sansoni SPA
Via Duca Di Calabria, 1/1
Casella Postale 552
50125 Firenze

JAPAN
Eastern Book Service
Hongo 3-Chome, Bunkyo-ku 113
Tokyo

KENYA
Africa Book Service (E.A.) Ltd.
Quaran House, Mfangano Street
P.O. Box 45245
Nairobi

KOREA, REPUBLIC OF
Pan Korea Book Corporation
P.O. Box 101, Kwangwhamun
Seoul

Korean Stock Book Centre
P.O. Box 34
Yeoeido
Seoul

MALAYSIA
University of Malaya Cooperative
  Bookshop, Limited
P.O. Box 1127, Jalan Pantai Baru
59700 Kuala Lumpur

MEXICO
INFOTEC
Apartado Postal 22-860
14060 Tlalpan, Mexico D.F.

NETHERLANDS
De Lindeboom/InOr-Publikaties
P.O. Box 202
7480 AE Haaksbergen

NEW ZEALAND
EBSCO NZ Ltd.
Private Mail Bag 99914
New Market
Auckland

NIGERIA
University Press Limited
Three Crowns Building Jericho
Private Mail Bag 5095
Ibadan

NORWAY
Narvesen Information Center
Book Department
P.O. Box 6125 Etterstad
N-0602 Oslo 6

PAKISTAN
Mirza Book Agency
65, Shahrah-e-Quaid-e-Azam
P.O. Box No. 729
Lahore 54000

PERU
Editorial Desarrollo SA
Apartado 3824
Lima 1

PHILIPPINES
International Book Center
Suite 1703, Cityland 10
Condominium Tower 1
Ayala Avenue, H.V. dela
  Costa Extension
Makati, Metro Manila

POLAND
International Publishing Service
Ul. Piekna 31/37
00-677 Warzawa

For subscription orders:
IPS Journals
Ul. Okrezna 3
02-916 Warszawa

PORTUGAL
Livraria Portugal
Rua Do Carmo 70-74
1200 Lisbon

SAUDI ARABIA, QATAR
Jarir Book Store
P.O. Box 3196
Riyadh 11471

SINGAPORE, TAIWAN,
MYANMAR, BRUNEI
Gower Asia Pacific Pte Ltd.
Golden Wheel Building
41, Kallang Pudding, #04-03
Singapore 1334

SOUTH AFRICA, BOTSWANA
For single titles:
Oxford University Press
  Southern Africa
P.O. Box 1141
Cape Town 8000

For subscription orders:
International Subscription Service
P.O. Box 41095
Craighall
Johannesburg 2024

SPAIN
Mundi-Prensa Libros, S.A.
Castello 37
28001 Madrid

Librería Internacional AEDOS
Consell de Cent, 391
08009 Barcelona

SRI LANKA AND THE MALDIVES
Lake House Bookshop
P.O. Box 244
100, Sir Chittampalam A.
  Gardiner Mawatha
Colombo 2

SWEDEN
For single titles:
Fritzes Fackboksforetaget
Regeringsgatan 12, Box 16356
S-103 27 Stockholm

For subscription orders:
Wennergren-Williams AB
P. O. Box 1305
S-171 25 Solna

SWITZERLAND
For single titles:
Librairie Payot
Case postale 3212
CH 1002 Lausanne

For subscription orders:
Librairie Payot
Service des Abonnements
Case postale 3312
CH 1002 Lausanne

THAILAND
Central Department Store
306 Silom Road
Bangkok

TRINIDAD & TOBAGO, ANTIGUA
BARBUDA, BARBADOS,
DOMINICA, GRENADA, GUYANA,
JAMAICA, MONTSERRAT, ST.
KITTS & NEVIS, ST. LUCIA,
ST. VINCENT & GRENADINES
Systematics Studies Unit
#9 Watts Street
Curepe
Trinidad, West Indies

UNITED KINGDOM
Microinfo Ltd.
P.O. Box 3
Alton, Hampshire GU34 2PG
England